# Identifying, Treating, and Preventing Childhood Trauma in Rural Communities

Marion Baker
*Center of Hope Arizona, USA*

Jacqueline Ford
*Center of Hope Arizona, USA & Walden University, USA*

Brittany Canfield
*Center of Hope Arizona, USA & Fielding Graduate University, USA*

Traci Grabb
*Arizona's Children Association, USA & Center of Hope Arizona, USA*

A volume in the Advances in Psychology, Mental Health, and Behavioral Studies (APMHBS) Book Series

Information Science REFERENCE
An Imprint of IGI Global

Published in the United States of America by
Information Science Reference (an imprint of IGI Global)
701 E. Chocolate Avenue
Hershey PA, USA 17033
Tel: 717-533-8845
Fax: 717-533-8661
E-mail: cust@igi-global.com
Web site: http://www.igi-global.com



Library of Congress Cataloging-in-Publication Data

Names: Baker, Marion A., editor.
Title: Identifying, treating, and preventing childhood trauma in rural communities / Marion Baker, Jacqueline Ford, Brittany Canfield, and Tracie Grabb, editors.
Description: Hershey, PA : Information Science Reference, [2016] | Includes bibliographical references and index.
Identifiers: LCCN 2016003154| ISBN 9781522502289 (hardcover) | ISBN 9781522502296 (ebook)
Subjects: LCSH: Rural children--Mental health--United States. | Child mental health services--United States. | Psychic trauma in children--United States. | Child welfare--United States.
Classification: LCC RJ501.A2 I34 2016 | DDC 362.20830973--dc23 LC record available at http://lccn.loc.gov/2016003154

This book is published in the IGI Global book series Advances in Psychology, Mental Health, and Behavioral Studies (APMHBS) (ISSN: pending; eISSN: pending)

British Cataloguing in Publication Data
A Cataloguing in Publication record for this book is available from the British Library.

# Advances in Psychology, Mental Health, and Behavioral Studies (APMHBS) Book Series

Bryan Christiansen
*PryMarke, LLC, USA*

ISSN: pending
EISSN: pending

Mission

The complexity of the human mind has puzzled researchers and physicians for centuries. While widely studied, the brain still remains largely misunderstood.

The **Advances in Psychology, Mental Health, and Behavioral Studies (APMHBS)** book series presents comprehensive research publications focusing on topics relating to the human psyche, cognition, psychiatric care, mental and developmental disorders, as well as human behavior and interaction. Featuring diverse and innovative research, publications within APMHBS are ideally designed for use by mental health professionals, academicians, researchers, and upper-level students.

Coverage

- Treatment & Care
- Human Interaction
- Human Behavior
- Cognition
- Emotional Health
- Mental Health & Disorders
- Trauma & Stress
- Personality Disorders
- Socialization
- Psychiatry

IGI Global is currently accepting manuscripts for publication within this series. To submit a proposal for a volume in this series, please contact our Acquisition Editors at Acquisitions@igi-global.com or visit: http://www.igi-global.com/publish/.

The Advances in Psychology, Mental Health, and Behavioral Studies (APMHBS) Book Series (ISSN pending) is published by IGI Global, 701 E. Chocolate Avenue, Hershey, PA 17033-1240, USA, www.igi-global.com. This series is composed of titles available for purchase individually; each title is edited to be contextually exclusive from any other title within the series. For pricing and ordering information please visit http://www.igi-global.com/book-series/advances-psychology-mental-health-behavioral/110200. Postmaster: Send all address changes to above address. 

## Titles in this Series

*For a list of additional titles in this series, please visit: www.igi-global.com*

*Handbook of Research on Diagnosing, Treating, and Managing Intellectual Disabilities*
Rejani Thudalikunnil Gopalan (Gujarat Forensic Sciences University, India)
Information Science Reference • copyright 2016 • 496pp • H/C (ISBN: 9781522500896) • US $210.00 (our price)

*Neuroeconomics and the Decision-Making Process*
Bryan Christiansen (PryMarke LLC, USA) and Ewa Lechman (Gdansk University of Technology, Poland)
Business Science Reference • copyright 2016 • 354pp • H/C (ISBN: 9781466699892) • US $195.00 (our price)

*Integrating Technology in Positive Psychology Practice*
Daniela Villani (Università Cattolica del Sacro Cuore, Italy) Pietro Cipresso (Università Cattolica del Sacro Cuore, Italy & I.R.C.C.S. Istituto Auxologico Italiano, Italy) Andrea Gaggioli (Università Cattolica del Sacro Cuore, Italy & I.R.C.C.S. Istituto Auxologico Italiano, Italy) and Giuseppe Riva (Università Cattolica del Sacro Cuore, Italy & I.R.C.C.S. Istituto Auxologico Italiano, Italy)
Information Science Reference • copyright 2016 • 447pp • H/C (ISBN: 9781466699861) • US $185.00 (our price)

*Global Perspectives on Youth Gang Behavior, Violence, and Weapons Use*
Simon Harding (Middlesex University, UK) and Marek Palasinski (Liverpool John Moores University, UK)
Information Science Reference • copyright 2016 • 425pp • H/C (ISBN: 9781466699380) • US $185.00 (our price)

*Exploring the Collective Unconscious in the Age of Digital Media*
Stephen Brock Schafer (Digipen Institute of Technology, USA)
Information Science Reference • copyright 2016 • 316pp • H/C (ISBN: 9781466698918) • US $175.00 (our price)

*Psychosocial Studies of the Individual's Changing Perspectives in Alzheimer's Disease*
Cordula Dick-Muehlke (University of California, Irvine, USA) Ruobing Li (University of California, Irvine, USA) and Myron Orleans (California State University, Fullerton, USA)
Medical Information Science Reference • copyright 2015 • 434pp • H/C (ISBN: 9781466684782) • US $225.00 (our price)

*Psychological and Social Implications Surrounding Internet and Gaming Addiction*
Jonathan Bishop (Centre for Research into Online Communities and E-Learning Systems, Swansea, UK)
Information Science Reference • copyright 2015 • 335pp • H/C (ISBN: 9781466685956) • US $195.00 (our price)

IGI GLOBAL
DISSEMINATOR OF KNOWLEDGE
www.igi-global.com

701 E. Chocolate Ave., Hershey, PA 17033
Order online at www.igi-global.com or call 717-533-8845 x100
To place a standing order for titles released in this series, contact: cust@igi-global.com
Mon-Fri 8:00 am - 5:00 pm (est) or fax 24 hours a day 717-533-8661

# Table of Contents

# Detailed Table of Contents



This chapter reviews the psycho-social aspects of trauma and related disorders. A wealth of information has accumulated over the decades of research on the trauma and related disorders. However, some aspects of trauma are still debatable globally such as definition of trauma, diversity in expression and response across individuals and cultures. Exposure to trauma can lead to troubling memories, psycho-physical arousal and avoidance of the event, has been a central theme in literature. Until researchers have realized the complexity of trauma transcends the relatively narrow definition of trauma. Cultural diversity in trauma and related disorders have brought into notice the multi-dimensional nature of trauma which is the focus of this chapter.



For more than half a century, child maltreatment prevention programs have been implemented in communities across America with hopes of stopping the abuse and neglect of children. To broaden the understanding of maltreatment in rural families, risk markers and protective factors are discussed with specific attention to contextual stressors and resources available in rural communities. Furthermore, primary maltreatment prevention initiatives directed at improving parenting practices and increasing public awareness of child maltreatment are reviewed. Also discussed are empirically supported secondary and tertiary maltreatment prevention programs that are commonly used to intervene with families at risk for interfacing with child welfare and protection agencies, or in instances of substantiated maltreatment. Preventing ill-treatment of children in rural communities requires ingenuity, community engagement and leadership, and governmental funding to best serve children and their families.

Substance abuse is a difficult situation for anyone to deal with, but the problem is compacted when children are involved. Parents who are substance abusers may knowingly or unknowingly be causing a number of problems for their child. Substance abuse in a parent can lead to child abuse and neglect. A child can develop anxiety; this can include overachievement, constant need to please others, fear of harm coming to the family, and concern about getting home on time. Children can experience depression including symptoms like fatigue, listlessness, and no interest in pleasurable activities. For a child with a parent who abuses drugs or alcohol, there is a strong likelihood they will experience psychosomatic illness and complaining often about not feeling well. The child may also show behaviours evident of regression, including thumb-sucking, enuresis and infantile behaviour. Phobias can occur, which sometimes are about attending school. Some additional effects on a child can include low self-esteem and social isolation. These can encompass difficulty making decisions, self put downs, reluctance to try new activities, keeping to one's self, no friends and avoiding peer contact. This chapter aims to describe and increase awareness of the harmful effects of parental substance abuse on children. Therefore, the trends in substance abuse are being discussed to give the reader an understanding of the widespread and complex social phenomenon and the ones most affected; the children.



Domestic Violence is a societal issue that affects all members of a family where it occurs; children are especially vulnerable even when violence isn't directed towards them. Exposure to family violence has been shown to impact all the developmental stages of childhood; the consequences this exposure to trauma can have lifelong effects. As a result many programs attempt to provide children services to assist with increasing resiliency as well as mitigating the effects caused by exposure to violence. Rural communities face specific barriers unique to their areas – this chapter will explore the impact Domestic Violence has on people living in these underserved regions. While there is limited research on the impact of domestic violence on children living in rural communities this chapter will summarize some of the risks faced by families as well as discuss considerations with assessment and treatment.



The focus of this chapter will be to discuss the treatment of child sexual abuse in a rural setting. Children in rural communities who have experienced such traumas are entitled to the same access and quality of services available in urban centres. Although the rates of trauma are similar in urban and rural settings, rural centres often lack adequate mental health services for children and families. Each year in the United States approximately 22% of children between the ages of two and seventeen experience trauma. As we know, the impacts of trauma on the developing brain are significant, as are the negative outcomes on affective, behavioral and cognitive functioning. Mental health service providers face unique challenges in terms of practicing in rural or remote communities. Multiple barriers exist to practice in these communities, including lack of resources, lack of specialist knowledge, and the training and supervision of professionals, to name a few.

School violence gained increased attention after highly publicized school shootings occurred in a variety of different school districts across the United States. Some of these school shootings occurred in nonurban communities, suggesting that such violence can occur in all areas, even those originally thought to be immune to such violence. As a result of these incidences, more research was conducted on school violence in nonurban communities and it quickly became clear that children and adolescents from rural school districts were often exposed to school violence at similar levels as those children and adolescents from urban areas. The aim of this chapter was to review research concerning school violence among children and adolescents in rural school districts, and to make recommendations for policy and school violence reduction programs as well as future research.



Guided by the lens of psychodynamic theory, Ford investigated the challenges faced by adoptive families of traumatized children. Fifteen families were randomly selected to participate in this study from a group of 30 parents who adopted traumatized children in Arizona. Thematic categories were drawn and summarized. Textual descriptions evolved from the thematic groups acknowledging their experiences and how these lived experiences guided their decision to adopt a traumatized child. Verification techniques, data mining, journaling, clustering, brainstorming, and peer reviews were used to ensure the quality of data. Emergent themes emphasized the need for adoption-focused training specific to traumatized children. Ford's study revealed that these adoptive families desired to be equipped with specialized therapeutic training before and after their adoptions.



Childhood exposure to trauma is prevalent and has been shown to contribute to both immediate and long-term psychological distress and functional impairment. Most mental health professionals will encounter trauma-related issues in their work, regardless of their specialty or the context in which they work, however, in rural communities it may be difficult for mental health practitioners to seek specialty training in working with survivors of trauma. The aim of this chapter is to provide practitioners with basic knowledge about the effects of trauma on children and adolescents, clinical skills and available measures designed to appropriately assess exposure to trauma and subsequent trauma-related symptoms, and ethical and cultural considerations required when assessing trauma in children and adolescents in rural communities.

Isolation is often a key factor and contributor to childhood trauma in rural communities. Not only does it potentially mean that there are less "eyes" on a family but it also means less supports and positive connections for a family. It means less ways out of the maze of childhood trauma and poverty. This chapter will explore how to build community in rural areas so that families feel connected and supported. It will give tools and tips for engaging traditional and non-traditional partners to create a web of support for families. It will call upon research and scientifically proven tactics for community engagement as well as more grass roots efforts that work in rural communities. In addition the article will give real life examples from some of the most rural areas in the state of Maine of how communities have come together to support children and ensure better screening, intervention and treatment.



Religion appears to shape the daily lives of most children in America; the influence of religion often serves as a template for making decisions, establishing relationships, comprehending the world, and finding meaning in confusing and/or traumatic situations that children may encounter. To ignore the role of religion and spirituality in behavioral and mental health treatment is to dismiss a central domain of child and adolescent development as well as a potential path to healing. In this chapter, we discuss the role of spirituality and religion in children in rural communities and how they can be integrated into counseling and therapy as a path to healing.



In this chapter, the authors discuss eight types of trauma that Latino children are likely to encounter by residing in rural or geographically-isolated communities. The authors contend that there exist more "rural-specific" types of childhood trauma that Latino children are at-risk for when compared to "urban-specific" types of trauma. For example, Latino children who reside in rural communities are more likely to traumatized by parental deportation, migrating from one town to another because parents follow the harvest, language brokering or translating for their parents, experiencing or witnessing farming accidents, relocating from the city to the country, isolation from extended family, pesticide poisoning of the child or a family member, and living in labor camps or substandard housing. It is important to note that Latino children, like children from other cultural, racial, and ethnic backgrounds, can experience all types of trauma irrespective of whether they reside in urban or rural settings.

Internationally, burns stemming from Juvenile Fire Setting and Bomb Making (JFSB) represent a major healthcare problem as signaled by traumatic deaths and injuries sustained by youth involved in these unfortunate incidents. While JFSB incidents may occur with greater frequency in non-rural locales, emerging evidence shows that the clinical forensic issues secondary to these burn cases can be surprisingly more complex in rural settings. The treatment challenges that rural areas have are fueled by a limited availability of mental health emergency resources. Further compounding it, the treatment professionals accessible to families often have insufficient experience or qualifications for competently managing the traumatic issues presented by combined JFSB/Burn Survivor (BS-JFSB) cases. This chapter aims to demonstrate how trauma-focused approaches can be integrated into existing clinical forensic practices in rural settings. The treatment requires altering how the concerns presented by these BS-JFSB children are addressed within a risk assessment paradigm.



This chapter details the experiences author had while attempting to obtain medical and psychological help for her children while living in a rural area. This chapter, per the author's request, addresses childhood trauma and barriers that need to be broken down so that emotional healing can begin. This submission is personal, and real occurrences. Rural areas generally have less resources available and because rural areas are sometimes remote, financial resources may not be available for a parent or caregiver to travel to obtain the needed help. Rural towns are normally condensed. This means that there is less privacy, and more ways for perpetrators to work a system of abuse within the schools, community, and churches in order to continue "getting to" the victim-- the child, or in this submission, child and parent. Healing from trauma can only begin when the barriers are recognized, broken down, and eliminated.



Research has been increasingly clear regarding the critical importance of the first years of life, especially the first three years, on personality development and the ability to adapt and adjust throughout life. Children with histories of traumas such as abuse, neglect, drug exposure, inconsistent caregiving, or violence during these critical early years can have profound disruptions in their development, including severe behavioral and emotional problems. The parents who adopt a child with a history of trauma are vulnerable to developing their own vicarious, or secondary trauma. This chapter explores this contagion of trauma within adoptive families, following the story of one such affected family. Treatment has focused on the needs of the traumatized child individually and through behaviorally-based parenting interventions. The individual clinical needs of the attachment figures, the parents, have not received the attention they deserve. These needs are as critical as addressing the child's trauma in order to allow for creation of a secure attachment with the child.

# Preface

## OVERVIEW OF SUBJECT MATTER

Childhood trauma has been a social issue throughout history. Research in this area is vast and continues to serve toward the greater understanding of this issue, the impact it has on the lifespan, and barriers to treatment. Rural community mental health is a topic with growing interest and exposure as rural or remote areas have been subjected to further marginalization, misunderstanding, and the recipient of inadequate care when care is provided or available. As child maltreatment in rural families shows trends of mirroring child maltreatment seen in urban families (Mattingly & Walsh, 2010), there is grave need to promote adequate education, services and support. In *Identifying, Treating, and Preventing Childhood Trauma in Rural Communities,* the editors aim to address key components of childhood trauma with an emphasis on the impact within rural communities. Special issues will also be addressed to capture additional challenges, risks and prevalence of childhood trauma in rural communities. Lastly, a personal account of a mother's experience with childhood trauma in a rural setting will be highlighted, followed by a book review on trauma and attachment.

## DESCRIPTION OF TOPIC IN THE WORLD TODAY

### Rural Communities

Rural communities include populations that are not classified as urban areas and are located outside the urban parameters of those living in areas, which contain a population of 2,500 or more (US Bureau of the Census, 2015). In 2010, the United States Census reported 59,492,267 individuals living in rural areas, comprising 19.3% of the total population (US Bureau of the Census, 2015). Areas lacking supportive services are at higher risk of impediments, including successful outcomes. Chronic shortages in mental health services continue to stimulate problems rendering services in rural communities (Gale & Coburn, 2003). While mental health services have shifted toward the primary care sector (Gale & Coburn, 2003), such as seen in the integration of the medicalized model, primary care subdivisions are recognized as being the catalyst for providing mental health services in rural communities (National Advisory Committee, 2004). Though rural health clinics are becoming more accessible, there is evidence for fewer mental health clinics employing psychologists (12%) or clinical social workers (7%) (Gale & Coburn, 2003).

## Childhood Trauma

The National Center for PTSD does not have record of a population-based epidemiological sample regarding the prevalence of PTSD among children (Gradus, 2015). While there is limited research on the lifetime prevalence of PTSD among children, there are many risk factors involved in the etiology of PTSD: young children, child abuse or other adverse childhood factors, trauma severity, low socio-economic status, and lack of social support (Brewin, Andrews, & Valentine, 2000; Cited in Brewin, 2005). Additional cited risk factors include: increased risk for females; minority status groups; lack of education; life stress; psychiatric history; and family psychiatric history (Brewin, Andrews, & Valentine, 2000; Cited in Brewin, 2005). Although risk factors offer important insights as to the etiology of trauma and those affected, they can often be skewed, isolated in generalizability, and exclusionary. PTSD can go undiagnosed in stigmatized and highly marginalized populations and populations lacking adequate and accessible mental healthcare.

## TARGET AUDIENCE

The purpose of *Identifying, Treating, and Preventing Childhood Trauma in Rural Communities* is to increase awareness of the challenges of providing treatment for childhood trauma in remote or rural communities. As there are barriers to treatment in this population, such as language, culture, and lack of sources, this publication serves to increase awareness of these barriers to treatment, educate various professional communities (i.e. clinical, research, academic, medical), and with the hope to eventually decrease the barriers to providing treatment for children who have experienced trauma. This publication is intended for mental health clinicians, researchers, educators, social services, and medical providers. Potential uses include: new research on barriers to treatment and how to overcome them; the importance of advocating and providing services to this population; the implications of the lack of services to this population; understanding the needs of this population as a resource for community service providers; diagnostic implications for mental health clinicians, social services, and medical providers; and possibility function as a catalyst for future research and development in this area.

## DESCRIPTION AND IMPORTANCE OF CHAPTERS

The chapters in *Identifying, Treating, and Preventing Childhood Trauma in Rural Communities* address a spectrum of topics and issues currently relevant to childhood trauma in rural communities. In Chapter 1, War provides an overview of the psychosocial aspects of trauma and related disorders. Discussion of trauma and related disorders diagnostic criteria covers the universalization of PTSD and the biomedical and social models. War addresses PTSD and related disorders from a psychological, social, moral and political framework, while also highlighting the importance of cross-cultural intervention. Chapter 2 covers the expansive topic of childhood maltreatment and prevention in rural communities. Authors Alabi and Barnes address childhood maltreatment risk markers, protective factors, and prevention models within the context of maltreatment in rural communities. Both community-based models of prevention and empirically supported prevention programs are focal points of Chapter 2.

Dandona emphasizes the impact of parental substance abuse on children in Chapter 3. The author aims to describe the harmful effects of parental substance abuse, current trends, and advocates for increased awareness in order to understand this complex social phenomenon. In Chapter 4, family violence is examined within rural communities with a focus on the widespread nature of domestic violence impacting all levels of society. Adi discusses rural considerations for treatment, the impact of intimate partner violence, and challenges over the lifespan. In addition, Adi incorporates topics of law enforcement, transportation, poverty, and other barriers within the context of family violence within rural communities.

Chapter 5 places focus on treating child sexual abuse in rural communities. Kenyon-George provides an overview of child sexual abuse, treatment challenges, and discussion on rural service providers. Rural treatment models within rural communities are featured within rural treatment sites providing care for children with histories of sexual abuse. Wright uncovers the implications behind the nature of school violence, prevalence, and consequences within rural districts in Chapter 6. Wright examines school violence within a social context and provides an overview of the unique challenges faced within rural communities.

Based on a doctoral dissertation, Ford examines the challenges of child trauma on adoptive families and the impact on families' social and emotional systems in Chapter 7. Ford utilizes psychodynamic theory to qualitatively investigate challenges faced among adoptive families of traumatized children. Additional topics include failed adoption, well-informed decision-making, and wrongful adoption. In Chapter 8, authors Alexander and Harrelson provide a thorough overview on assessment of childhood trauma in rural settings. Alexander and Harrelson discuss important considerations when assessing trauma in rural communities, clinical interviewing, assessment measures, cultural factors, and ethical considerations.

Hoffman Frances elaborates on the role of community engagement and collaboration in Chapter 9. Issues of isolation, poverty, historical trauma, resilience, and tele-health are addressed. In Chapter 10, authors Barnes and Alabi examine the role of spirituality in the path to healing for children impacted by trauma in rural communities. Barnes and Alabi discuss the role religion and spirituality play on rural childhood trauma treatment, counseling, psychological practice, and professional issues. Velasquez and Juarez provide a thorough examination of the prevalence of childhood trauma in rural Latino communities in Chapter 11. The authors draw attention to the comparative risks when examining "rural-specific" and "urban-specific" forms of trauma.

In Chapter 12, authors Johnson, Jacobs, Grace, Klas, and Murillo address the clinical forensic issues of child trauma. Specifically, the authors emphasize culturally responsive risk assessment and treatment parameters within the context of juvenile fire setting and bomb making, as part of the book's special issues. Chapter 13 provides a personal account of a mother's experience with childhood trauma in a rural setting. As part of the book's special issues, Salcido uncovers the barriers within rural communities and personal insight into the matter of childhood trauma within this context. Lastly, Dumesnil explores attachment through the book review of *Love Lessons* in Chapter 14, the last contribution to the book's special issues.

## CONCLUSION

As knowledge and awareness increases on the role mental health plays on rural communities, we are challenged by the task of bridging the gap of literature within rural communities as it pertains to childhood trauma. Though research on childhood trauma is vast, the issue persists. There are multiple factors that are involved in the incidence of childhood trauma including: lack of resources, faults in the system ensuring safety, misdiagnosis, underreporting, foster care and adoption, domestic violence, parental substance abuse, generational trauma and maltreatment, and cultural barriers. This book serves to address these factors involved in childhood trauma and how these factors interact with childhood trauma and rural communities. Additional issues will be discussed such as assessment, treatment modalities, and spirituality.

## REFERENCES

Brewin, C. R. (2005). Risk factor effect sizes in PTSD: What this means for intervention. *Journal of Trauma & Dissociation*, *6*(2), 123–130. doi:10.1300/J229v06n02_11 PMID:16150674

Brewin, C. R., Andrews, B., & Valentine, J. D. (2000). Meta-analysis of risk factors for posttraumatic stress disorder in trauma-exposed adults. *Journal of Consulting and Clinical Psychology*, *68*(5), 748–766. doi:10.1037/0022-006X.68.5.748 PMID:11068961

Gale, J. A., & Coburn, A. F. (2003). *The characteristics and roles of rural health clinics in the United States: A chartbook*. Portland, ME: University of Southern Maine.

Gradus, J. L. (2015). Epidemiology of PTSD. *National Center for PTSD*. Retrieved from http://www.ptsd.va.gov/professional/PTSD-overview/epidemiological-facts-ptsd.asp

Mattingly, M. J., & Walsh, W. A. (2010). Rural families with a child abuse report are more likely headed by a single parent and endure economic and family stress. Carsey Institute, 10.

United States Bureau of the Census. (2010). *2010 census urban and rural classification and urban area criteria*. Retrieved from http://www.census.gov

# Acknowledgment

First and foremost, we would like to acknowledge the children and families with whom we have had the privilege of being witness to their stories and serving. We would like to extend appreciation to the incredible authors of this book, their contributions and collaboration on this project.

# Chapter 1
# Psychosocial Aspects of Trauma and Related Disorders

**Firdous War**
*IIT Kanpur, India*

## ABSTRACT

*This chapter reviews the psycho-social aspects of trauma and related disorders. A wealth of information has accumulated over the decades of research on the trauma and related disorders. However, some aspects of trauma are still debatable globally such as definition of trauma, diversity in expression and response across individuals and cultures. Exposure to trauma can lead to troubling memories, psycho-physical arousal and avoidance of the event, has been a central theme in literature. Until researchers have realized the complexity of trauma transcends the relatively narrow definition of trauma. Cultural diversity in trauma and related disorders have brought into notice the multi-dimensional nature of trauma which is the focus of this chapter.*

## INTRODUCTION

The debate and concern over the existence of Post-traumatic stress disorder (PTSD) started soon, after its inception in the diagnostic manual of American psychiatric association in 1980's (Breslau, 2004; Summerfield, 1995; Young, 2004). While mostly research directly or indirectly accepts its existence as a disorder. However, studies question the universalization and conceptualization of post traumatic disorder using biomedical model of trauma without considering the socio-political context (Bracken, Giller & Summerfield, 1995; Kleinman, 1988; Summerfield, 1999; Miro Jakovljević, et al., 2012; Van Ommeren, Saxena & Saraceno, 2005). There have been concerns and debates regarding understanding of trauma in the current scenario from its operationalization to intervention but the major ones can be summarized as follows (Bracken, Giller & Summerfield, 1995; Breslau, 2004 Kleinman, 1988; Summerfield, 1999; Miro Jakovljević, et al., 2012; Van Ommeren, Saxena & Saraceno, 2005).

DOI: 10.4018/978-1-5225-0228-9.ch001

1. Universalization of Post-traumatic stress disorder.
2. Biomedical model and social model of understanding Post-traumatic stress disorder.
3. Psychological, social, moral and political aspects of trauma.
4. Appropriateness of a trauma based intervention cross-culturally.

## 1. UNIVERSALIZATION OF POST-TRAUMATIC STRESS DISORDER

Traumatology has two meanings, depends on the definition of trauma. In medicine, it refers to the study of wounds and injuries caused by accidents or violence to a person. In psychology, it refers to the development and application of psychological services for people who have experienced extreme events. The focus of this chapter is the psychological aspects of trauma. The universalization of Post-traumatic stress disorder (PTSD) diagnosis remains controversial from decades due to many psycho-socio-political reasons (Bracken, Giller & Summerfield, 1995; Kleinman, 1988; Summerfield, 1999; Miro Jakovljević, et al., 2012; Van Ommeren, Saxena & Saraceno, 2005). Symptoms suggestive of Post-traumatic stress disorder (PTSD) have been noted following any significant catastrophe over the centuries in the research literature (Young, 1995, 2004). However the actual terms Post-traumatic stress disorder (PTSD) did not appear until 1980 (Young, 2004). In the 19$^{th}$ century, an attempt was made to categorize psychological disorders, in which the term "fright neurosis" was used to capture anxiety symptoms following any significant accident and injury (Kraepelin, 1896). Exposure to overwhelming terror can lead to troubling memories, arousal, and avoidance but with a varied manifestation and underlying dynamics. With time, various diagnostic systems came into existence which are used in different parts of the world. Among these diagnostic systems, Diagnostic and Statistical Manual of Mental Disorders (DSM) by American Psychiatric Association and the International Classification of Disorders (ICD) by World Health Organisation are widely used. The latest version of diagnostic manual of American Psychiatric Association has some changes in diagnostic criteria of trauma and other psychiatric disorders. The World Health Organisation is going to revise it manual in its next edition of ICD-10.

There is a little difference in the way DSM and ICD has conceptualized trauma. DSM- IV-TR has defined trauma as a personal experience of an event or events that involved actual or threatened death or serious injury, or a threat to the physical integrity of self or others (DSM-IV-TR, 2000). In its latest version, DSM-5, also maintains its emphasis on 'physical' aspect of trauma but has included indirect exposure and cultural specific interview schedule as well (DSM-5, 2013). However, ICD-10 conceptualises a traumatic event or situation as one that is "exceptionally threatening or catastrophic" and one that "is likely to cause pervasive distress in almost anyone" (WHO, 1992). Importantly, ICD-10 requires a person to be present at the scene of the trauma to qualify as a trauma survivor (WHO, 1992). Apart from defining a traumatic event, both the manuals have also mentioned about its manifestation and impact on socio-occupational functioning of an individual, which is important for reaching a diagnosis. Below is the diagnostic criteria given in these manuals. It is quite evident that both the diagnostic manuals are similar with minor differences.

## 1.1 DSM and ICD Diagnostic Criteria of PTSD

DSM-IV Criteria for Post-traumatic stress disorder (PTSD) (APA, 2000: 463-438).

1. The person has been exposed to a traumatic event in which both of the following have been present:
    a. The person experienced, witnessed, or was confronted with an event or events that involved actual or threatened death or serious injury, or a threat to the physical integrity of self or others.
    b. The person's response involved intense fear, helplessness, or horror. Note: In children, this may be expressed instead by disorganized or agitated behavior.
2. The traumatic event is persistently re-experienced in one (or more) of the following ways:
    a. Recurrent and intrusive distressing recollections of the event, including images, thoughts, or perceptions. (Note: In young children, repetitive play may occur in which themes or aspects of the trauma are expressed.)
    b. Recurrent distressing dreams of the event. (Note: In children, there may be frightening dreams without recognizable content.)
    c. Acting or feeling as if the traumatic event were recurring (includes a sense of reliving the experience, illusions, hallucinations, and dissociative flashback episodes, including those that occur upon awakening or when intoxicated).Note: In young children, trauma-specific re-enactment may occur.
    d. Intense psychological distress at exposure to internal or external cues that symbolize or resemble an aspect of the traumatic event.
    e. Physiological reactivity on exposure to internal or external cues that symbolize or resemble an aspect of the traumatic event.
3. Persistent avoidance of stimuli associated with the trauma and numbing of general responsiveness (not present before the trauma), as indicated by three (or more) of the following:
    a. Efforts to avoid thoughts, feelings, or conversations associated with the trauma.
    b. Efforts to avoid activities, places, or people that arouse recollections of the trauma.
    c. Inability to recall an important aspect of the trauma.
    d. Markedly diminished interest or participation in significant activities.
    e. Feeling of detachment or estrangement from others.
    f. Restricted range of affect (e.g., unable to have loving feelings).
    g. Sense of a foreshortened future (e.g., does not expect to have a career, marriage, children, or a normal life span).
4. Persistent symptoms of increased arousal (not present before the trauma), as indicated by two (or more) of the following:
    a. Difficulty falling or staying asleep.
    b. Irritability or outbursts of anger.
    c. Difficulty concentrating.
    d. Hyper-vigilance
    e. Exaggerated startle response.
5. Duration of the disturbance (symptoms in Criteria B, C, and D) is more than one month.
6. The disturbance causes clinically significant distress or impairment in social, occupational, or other important areas of functioning.

**Specify If:** If duration of symptoms is less than 3 months
**Chronic:** If duration of symptoms is 3 months or more (Acute).
**Specify If:** If onset of symptoms is at least 6 months after the stressor (with Delayed Onset).

ICD-10 diagnosis criteria of Post-traumatic stress disorder (PTSD) (WHO, 1992: 145-149).

1. Exposure to a stressful event or situation (either short or long lasting) of exceptionally threatening or catastrophic nature, which is likely to cause pervasive distress in almost anyone.
2. Persistent remembering or "reliving" the stressor by intrusive flash backs, vivid memories, recurring dreams, or by experiencing distress when exposed to circumstances resembling or associated with the stressor.
3. Actual or preferred avoidance of circumstances resembling or associated with the stressor (not present before exposure to the stressor).
4. Either (a) or (b):
    a. Inability to recall, either partially or completely, some important aspects of the period of exposure to the stressor.
    b. Persistent symptoms of increased psychological sensitivity and arousal (not present before exposure to the stressor) shown by any two of the following:
        i. Difficulty in falling or staying asleep.
        ii. Irritability or outbursts of anger.
        iii. Difficulty in concentrating.
        iv. Hyper-vigilance
        v. Exaggerated startle response.
    c. Criteria B, C and D all occurred within six months of the stressful event, or the end of a period of stress. (For some purposes, onset delayed more than six months may be included but this should be clearly specified separately).

Both DSM-IV and ICD-10 diagnostic criteria's exclude non-physical trauma such as harassment, abandonment, or existential trauma associated with sexual abuse. Exclusion of ongoing trauma such as racism, cross-generation transmission of severe poverty or relative deprivation, torture, and genocide that threaten the collective identity of the person (Cassiman, 2005; Kira et al., 2008). Post-traumatic stress disorder (PTSD) is more conceptualized in terms of the biological fight or flight response and psychologically incomplete processing of trauma. However, it is not the case across individuals and cultures. Many studies have reported Post-traumatic stress disorder (PTSD) such as symptoms following exposure to stressors that do not meet the diagnostic criteria for trauma and/or PTSD as described in the ICD and the DSM (Mol et al., 2005). It is important that the stressor qualifies the criteria for trauma described in both the manuals to receive the diagnosis of Post-traumatic stress disorder (PTSD). For example, in one survey, 89.6% adults of South-eastern Michigan were trauma survivors by DSM-IV criteria (Breslau & Kessler, 2001). Dentists have reported Post-traumatic stress disorder (PTSD) like symptoms in dental patients following wisdom tooth extraction (de Jongh et al., 2008), and in people whose stressors include giving birth to a healthy baby after a routine delivery (Olde et al., 2006), and exposure to rude jokes (McDonald, 2003).

## 1.2 Universalization of Trauma

Post-traumatic stress disorder (PTSD) has its origin rooted in experiences of US veteran of the Vietnam War (Young, 1995). However the concept expanded dramatically to other traumatic experiences from road accidents to childhood abuse. Since the acceptance of the PTSD diagnosis in the formal psychiatric nomenclature, epidemiological studies made the existence of PTSD and other related disorders felt across cultures into global health arena regardless of the background culture, current situation, and subjective meaning of survivors (Bracken, Giller & Summerfield, 1995; Breslau 2004; Kleinman, 1988; Summerfield, 1999; Kleinman & Good 1995). Although PTSD and other related disorders are possible outcome of exposure to a traumatic events, psychiatrists and social scientists believe that reifying every experience as a disorder increases the danger of ignoring the psycho-socio-political context, which makes it meaningful (Bracken, Giller & Summerfield, 1995; Kleinman, 1988; Summerfield, 1999; Miro Jakovljević, et al., 2012; Van Ommeren, Saxena & Saraceno, 2005). For example in Japan, an epidemiological report after *Hanshin-Awaji (Kobe)* earthquake, entitled "The invisible human crisis," predicted the emergence of thousands of cases of psychiatric disorders in the short-term future and a need to intervene (Mollica, et al., 1995). However, Post-traumatic Stress Disorder (PTSD) has been rarely diagnosed prior to the event despite of having an extensive mental health care system outside the United States and Europe. Establishing Post-traumatic stress disorder (PTSD) as a disorder in the midst of a humanitarian disaster requires a concerted and sophisticated campaign. Findings from other studies which have been published, including surveys of Post-traumatic stress disorder (PTSD) among people displaced by the eruption of Mount Pinatubo in the Philippines, and people effected by political violence in Mozambique, Bhutan, Cambodia, Bosnia, and Gaza (Fawzi et al., 1997; Howard et al., 1999; Jones et al., 1997; Jong et al., 2001; Reeler & Immerman, 1994; Thulesius & Hakansson, 1999; Van Ommerren et al., 2001). This demonstrates how epidemiological surveys can become instruments for Post-traumatic stress disorder (PTSD) activism in the global arena without considering the context or understanding trauma. The work of Van Ommerren et al., (2001) in Nepal refugee camps highlights amalgamation of science and politics. Researchers set out to look for Post-traumatic stress disorder (PTSD) caused by torture inflicted by the Bhutanese soldiers and police. Standard diagnostic interview tools were used. They compared Post-traumatic stress disorder (PTSD) morbidity between refugees who were tortured with non-tortured refugees group. In this survey, tortured refugees had five times increased chances of having Post-traumatic stress disorder (PTSD) than non-torture refugees group. Overall, tortured refugees were 1.6 times more vulnerable for psychiatric disorders than the non-tortured ones. This research extends Post-traumatic stress disorder (PTSD) and other psychiatric disorders into a new local setting which not only make it visible locally but also attributes traumatic event to other psychiatric disorders without looking into the political dimension. This is what Kleinman (1988) termed as category fallacy and a major critique of typical epidemiological research. Kleinman (1988) defined category fallacy as the reification of a nosological category developed for a particular cultural group that is then applied to members of another culture for whom it lacks coherence and its validity has not been established. There is need of multidisciplinary studies to tapper all these issues.

De Jong (2004) does acknowledge the concern of cultural diversity and highlights how care had been taken to incorporate those dimensions during the study to avoid category fallacy and not apparent secondary gains which makes Post-traumatic stress disorder (PTSD) as diagnosis more valid. He also questions the social theories of trauma and how much a natural disaster is social. He further adds that social is always mediated by the personal and the biological aspects. He even talks about cross cultural presence of different mental disorders for example Algerians, Cambodians, Afghanis, Ethiopians, Tibetans, or Sri Lankans and is not limited to the western hemisphere. He feels there is a need to rethink social causation of mental disorders and a need to broad the horizon to presence of other mental health disorders than Post-traumatic stress disorder (PTSD). He quotes works of Flaherty, Manson, Weiss, Kirmayer, Kleinman, Good, Del Vecchio Good, Marsella, Westermeyer, Weine, Patel, Bolton, Otto, and Hinton in the field of cultural psychiatry and psychology supports his study. He highlights the need of cross cultural inventory which could tap local expressions behaviors like traumatic stress reactions employing combination of qualitative and quantitative methods (De Jong & Van Ommeren, 2002). This would result into universal biological end of a continuum, and large a variety of culturally induced phenomena at the socio-psychological end of the continuum.

## 2. BIOMEDICAL MODEL AND SOCIAL MODEL OF UNDERSTANDING POST-TRAUMATIC STRESS DISORDER

Most of the mental disorders were initially thought to be caused by experiences a person had in his past or present. However with the advancement in technology, particularly in the field of drugs. The scenario drastically changed from psychosocial to biomedical causation because of many reasons like pharmacy companies & fast effect etc. However there is not a single theory which can explain a mental disorder totally on the basis of biology even today.

In addition to lack of biological theory explaining Post-traumatic stress disorder (PTSD) or differences in response to traumatic events, sociocultural factors are also an important and determining factor. The cultural context acts as a filter and provides meanings to individual experiences and interpretations. Although we can prove biological basis of almost all the psychological illnesses, but biological bases, are also strongly influenced by the cultural filter and therefore should be considered sociobiological phenomena as well than mere biological process (Sack, Seeley, & Clarke, 1997). This stand true for most of the psychiatric disorders especially trauma related such as Post-traumatic stress disorder (PTSD) (Mezzich et al., 1999). Conducting cross cultural research is on psychiatric disorder are quite difficult and prevalence rate of Post-traumatic stress disorder (PTSD) varies widely across cultures. De Jong et al., (2001) reported prevalence of Post-traumatic stress disorder (PTSD) as 37.4% in Algeria, 28.4% in Cambodia, 15.8% in Ethiopia, and 17.8% in Gaza. Other studies on immigrating Asians into United States, prevalence rate vary from 3-85%. Collective cultures as that of Cambodian have a collective view of self than individual reactions, therefore, the individually oriented DSM definitions fall short to be reliably applied to their culture. The author here does not wish to imply that biological process do not play any role but more of trying to emphasize that culture plays a vital role in an individual life as well. Culture has an immense impact on an individual. An individual's pattern of thought, feeling, values, morals and action, usually called as the psyche, the self, mind, mentalities, or ways of being is grounded in his social world (Lewis-Fernandez & Kleinman, 1994; Spencer-Oatey, 2012). These patterns and culture share a mutual relationship and can be analysed and understood together (Adams & Markus, 2004; Kashima, 2000).

As we see that human behavior and thinking pattern varies from person to person so do their response pattern during different events (Kleinman, 1988). Even we can see difference in identical twins whose genetic composition is hundred per cent same, which emphasis role of culture. What makes an individual unique is his culture which is also because of lot of inter-cultural as well as intra cultural diversity leads to different individual's response to same kind or different kinds of problems (Lewis-Fernandez & Kleinman, 1994). Some cultures are more collectivistic, while, others are individualistic. And we see people think and behave accordingly. In Western thought individual plays a vital role, shaping and defining political, socio-cultural, value and morality discourses. Social relationships are often seen as arising from consent and contract between autonomous individual. Individualistic cultures are oriented around the self, independent instead of identifying with a group mentality. They see each other as only loosely linked, and value personal goals above that of the group (Rothwell, 2011). While the collectivistic cultures especially Asian, are totally opposite, were emphasis is not on independence of every human. For example in Chinese/ Taiwan culture role of intimate relationship and close interpersonal relation are more important than individual thought, fantasies, desire, emotion, and personal problem. Family and other close interpersonal relations become a person's paramount interest. In African-American and Latin cultures, family plays an important role for strong reliance and social support. They are hyper vigilant to perceived threats and this expression in turn could can be mistaken as a Post-traumatic symptoms. Similar is true for Mexican-Amercian cultures were shared belief system and culturally specific meaning about self, body and health particularly illness are given importance. Our perception, cognitions, emotions and values play an important role in shaping our interaction with our surroundings. Expression of any psychopathology such as depression is not just a liner relationship between mind and body but the symptoms also represent social, cultural, political, interpersonal communication, loss of social network factors (Kleinman, 1988). Psychopathology is understood in terms of person relationship with his/her surrounding rather than individual factor. Self is understood depending on social context. According to Summerfield (1999) certain culture place of high value on stoicism (indifference to pleasure/pain) and active forgetting as seen in psychological response to war and atrocity. In an epidemiological study of 824 asylum seeker from Kosovo in Great Britain, vast majority did not complain about psychological symptoms. The main complain of their concern with work, family, and school (Summerfield, 2002). Illness seen in individualistic cultures may be different than in collectivistic and healing process varies accordingly (Kleinman, 1988).

So it is clear now that culture play important role in modifying the response of an individual be it trauma or other life event. Many cultures such as Muslim culture believes strongly in fate or accept role of divine intervention. That is because of the belief system which Islam propagates, which leads to its acceptance but same event may be seen as due to lack of resources or coping skills in other cultures. This questions the effectiveness of Therapeutic techniques developed in western cultures or which emphasize the need to verbalization of the problem as means to resolve it which may not be appropriate in other cultures.

Breslau (2001, 2004) focuses on social aspects of Post-traumatic stress disorder (PTSD) which varies from individual to individual qualitatively so does the response to it. He raises the question why only a portion of a population manifests Post-traumatic stress disorder (PTSD) symptoms, when exposed to some traumatic event. However De Jong is more in favour of biological model with cultural variation. He supports his claim by quoting studies on Post-traumatic stress disorder (PTSD) which claim neurological basis of the disorder (Bremner, 2002; Young, 1995). He even highlights presence of Post-traumatic stress disorder (PTSD) across cultures.

## 3. PSYCHOLOGICAL, SOCIAL, MORAL, AND POLITICAL ASPECTS OF TRAUMA

The clinical significance of PTSD has been side-lined, and the other reasons become more important, like how individual suffering is highly linked to the political reasons, the social justice system, the cause of humanitarian agencies, and the work of "philanthropists". When we speak in terms of what a person gets out it, "a refugee status", a means for compensation, and insurance, or the label of victimhood, which in itself becomes the hallmark of a person's existence.

The disorder becomes lens to look at people's pain rather 'scientifically'. The focus goes from the spotlight on the person per se to coming up with a diagnostic psychiatric category aimed at scientifically proving a point, or imposing their own cultural ad profession frames. Further, there is this assumption that people who are unable to identify and report these symptoms know less. The question here is that are we using the lens for our own advantage or using a lens that benefits the people concerned Power dynamics come in the form of an `expert' and the expertise at the centre of things, and the war victim relegated to the role of consumer patient. Summerfield (1999) emphasizes that the focus is on service provision, and authorship and knowledge is centred on the service provider, leaving no scope for the sufferer to voice his concerns. The tag of victimhood has its own disadvantages, for it may bring along a chain of socio-political implications with it. It is important to consider whether this may have the effect increasing an individual's sense of him or herself as passive victim rather than active survivor. Imposing therapy, rather than empowering resources should be the main motto. Somasundaram (1996) found `large numbers with PTSD' amongst survivors of aerial bombing in Sri Lanka. He concedes that none of the subjects considered themselves psychiatrically ill, and just saw their symptoms as an inevitable part of the war, and their concerns were mainly socio-economic. However, he dismissed all these as lack of awareness in the victims.

The critique of the keys concepts in PTSD doesn't mean that it is of no use. The increasing concern about "human pain", and the quick and easy flow of information, has led to perhaps more help assisted programs. Many international organizations do their best in doing a lot in disaster inflicted areas. The role of humanitarian agencies cannot be just nullified. The focus here is to reconsider some the assumptions around this model of help and assistance, to make it more encompassing. Short term interventions has been the focus of many organizations, which can in long term be very detrimental to the well-being of the sufferer. Expertise in terms of skills is required, because the concern here is not just "providing help", rather empowering them. The approach should be interdisciplinary in the sense that a lot of factors should be taken into account before coming to a conclusion. Demarcation of boundaries between personal, social and cultural, or even economic and political may not help here. Rather there is a need to look from above and focus on the rehabilitation of the masses, giving due respect to their needs and culture. The need is to rethink and reformulate the concept of a disaster; in terms of not the generalized notions what it does to people, but what the concerned persons think of it, in reference to their own selves.

Trauma does not occur in vacuum nor do humans exist in vacuum. Breslau (2004) highlights how science and politics gets mixture in trauma research. He points toward the work of Van Ommerren et al., (2001) in Nepal, were about 90,000 people have lived since fleeing Bhutan in the early 1990s. They were ethnically Nepalese and religiously Hindu minority in Bhutan migrated to Bhutan for work. Due to discrimination and political repression there, many fled into India and Nepal and the camps have been at the center of an international dispute between Nepal and Bhutan for more than a decade (Joseph, 1999). Researchers tried to look at the nature of trauma inflicted, was a cause of Post-traumatic stress disorder (PTSD) and other mental health problems in this group without trying to understand the Post-traumatic stress disorder (PTSD) in large socio-political context. The diagnosis of Post-traumatic stress disorder (PTSD) connects not only individual with symptoms but whole societies with powerful narratives of cultural advancement, political legitimacy, and social justice. The clinical concept provides a moral paradigm that identifies victims and perpetrators. While torture is a traumatic experience, in this case these experiences have special clinical meaning parallels pre-existing political discourse. In this political context, Post-traumatic stress disorder (PTSD) plays a symbolic role. Some case vignettes from Bracken, Giller and Summerfield (1995), may make it bit clear.

Case 1: 28 year women witness of her husband killed, and she was not able bury body, 6 month latter she return that place but her husband body could not be trace. Latter after 5 years she develops nightmare and shame. In this case we see women has lost her husband and she is not able to perform certain cultural rituals for her husband dead body, although she had developed Post-traumatic stress disorder (PTSD) symptoms but her cause of distress is she is not able to perform certain cultural meaningful ritual for her husband. It was this aspect of her loss that seemed to cause her most distress. What is more important here is subjective meaning rather than individual symptoms.

Case 2: 25 year women were sexually assault several times by soldier. After 4 year she develop venereal disease, foul vaginal discharge, consulted many doctor and taken various treatment, she believe that she become infertile (battered self). Here in Uganda culture rape is considered as loss of fertility, and women fertility is given great importance and sexual assault has been considered failure of conceiving again. Women are presenting their conflict and uncertainty about conceiving in the form of somatoform. So we can clearly see the role of culture in describing traumatic experiences.

Case 3: A 40 year old Ugandan prominent politician in the past was arrested. He was held for seven days. During this time he was beaten and humiliated while being interrogated. After his release he was referred to see one of us by a friend who assumed that he would be in need of some form of psychiatric help. When interviewed, however, he denied any great distress. He told us that he was a Christian but that prior to his imprisonment his faith had not meant a great deal to him. While he was in detention he felt a strong identification with the figure of Jesus Christ who had also suffered torture and humiliation. He found that his own suffering and his identification with Christ brought him closer to his religion and since his ordeal the quality of his spiritual life was intensified. He indicated that because of this the overall effect of his experience had been positive for him. Here again individual meaning which is derived from culture plays an important role in trauma.

These cases highlight a need for alternative paradigm to understand trauma not just by biological factors but my sociopolitical factors as well. Bracken, Giller and Summerfield (1995) conceptualized trauma in terms holistically in terms of social, political and cultural factors. Social include, family circumstance, social network, socio-economic position, employment status, gender, class and ethnic. Political include, individual engagement and culture include, linguistic position, spiritual, and religious involvement.

## 4. APPROPRIATENESS OF A TRAUMA BASED INTERVENTION CROSS-CULTURALLY

Recent research has questioned the use of intervention cross culturally. The critics point out towards medicalization of normal distress and possible harm of assuming universalization of western models of illness and healing are valid cross culturally. The authors have criticized trauma focused interventions like psychological debriefing and benzodiazepine medication in poor countries. Have little evidence of effectiveness if any and there indiscriminate use can have harmful effects.

It is important to understand why it is important to study culture and what implications it has in clinical practice, mental health training programmes? Culture in it broadest sense is cultivated behaviour which includes set of norms, meanings, and values used by a member of a society to construct their unique meaning or view of the world and their identity. It includes traditions, language, rituals, values, customs, moral values, beliefs, taboos and status of an individual. It becomes important in mental health and illness because mental health is a subjective and social process. Substantial number of studies from anthropology, sociology and cross-cultural research have clearly demonstrated a very strong ground in favour of culture specific care. Culture colours every facets of any individual's illness expression (Helman, 2007). In psychiatry, verbal expression and behavior is a key for diagnosis and differentiating normal from abnormal behavior. The social and cultural context becomes important here because the identification of abnormal behavior is basically a social judgement that may be the reason why there is a wide variation in the prevalence of many psychiatric disorders across region and cultures.

Following a disaster in resource poor countries, clinician often come to promote Post-traumatic stress disorder (PTSD) and trauma focused interventions without taking into account the pre-existing human and community resources, social interventions and care for people with premorbid mental health. Exposure to trauma severely disrupts social structures and on-going formal and informal care system. A range of strategies seems to have wide support from experts is that they are tailored to the local context, needs and resources. Summerfield (2005), mentions his visit to Palestine territories and counselling was offered to help them do deal with their problems. Most of the Palestinian do not, as counselling is not a culturally familiar activity. He criticizes that most of these programs are funded under the umbrella term "psychosocial." He talks about difference between psychological and social dimension. He urges psychologist for looking outside body in way we live and consider meaning of things than inside. He emphasizes focus on restoration of social life after trauma. International organizations working in the poor countries have criticized use of bio psychiatric approach in the name of psychosocial approach. Separation of psychosocial and biological intervention does seem a viable option and my further divide the care system which is already fragmented.

A 19 year old ex-soldier was interviewed in a village medical clinic. He complained of headaches and feeling generally unwell. When interviewed he also spoke about nightmares in which he would see friends of his who had been killed in the war and also some of the people he had killed himself. He was very disturbed by these nightmares and believed that he was being visited by dead spirits. He told us that he had joined the army after his father was killed by a rebel group. He was only 16 years old when he had joined. He left his mother and two sisters behind in the home village. He had spent many months engaged in the wartime fighting and was nearly killed on at least two occasions himself. He was discharged from the army on medical grounds. When this happened he returned to his home village. Although his ankle healed well and he was able to walk he still felt ill. He found it difficult to settle back into civilian life and became preoccupied with his nightmares. He was seen by our team on a number of occasions and he also attended a traditional healer in his village who diagnosed that he was being persecuted by harmful spirits (mayembe). He prescribed the sacrifice of chicken and certain rituals to be carried out by the patient and his family. The patient felt relieved when these had been performed and also felt closer to his family (Bracken, Giller & Summerfield, 1995).

Interventions based on western culture actively encourage traumatised refugees to talk openly about their distress and trauma which may be in conflict with their cultural norms. Some cultures do not allow expression of emotions openly and is consider as weakness. Containing emotion is considered as a sign of maturity (Kirmayer & Young, 1998). So not talking about distress, murder, and rape does not necessarily mean that the person is using defensive strategies as per psychodynamic school of thought. Anthropology literature on burial rituals and bereavement in variety of cultural contexts shows a diversity in beliefs and rituals about death and rebirth. How the manner of death influences rebirth, contact between deceased and living, and rituals about after death (Brison 1995; Brison & Leavitt 1995). Anthropological studies have shown the state of remorse and longing many a times continues even after death and how different ways are used to overcome it which may be culturally appropriate (Hollan 1995; Robben 2004). Among Cambodians, bereavement means a tendency to live in the past, to be visited by supernatural forces from the past, to feel guilt, to be distressed, and a yearning to complete obligations to the dead (Eisenbruch, 1990). So bereavement in these cases resides in the comfort of religious belief and participation in religious rituals rather than use of western intervention such as medication or cognitive behavioural therapy.

Many international organisations do their best in dealing with disaster inflicted areas. The role of humanitarian agencies cannot be just nullified. The focus here is to reconsider some the assumptions around this model of help and assistance, to make it more encompassing. Short term interventions has been the focus of many organisations, which can in long term be very detrimental to the wellbeing of the sufferer. Expertise in terms of skills is required, because the concern here is not just providing help, rather empowering them. The approach should be interdisciplinary in the sense that a lot of factors should be taken into account before coming to a conclusion. Demarcation of boundaries between personal, social and cultural, or even economic and political may not help here. Rather there is a need to look from above and focus on the rehabilitation of the masses, giving due respect to their needs and culture. The need is to rethink and reformulate the concept of a disaster; in terms of not the generalised notions what it does to people, but what the concerned persons think of it, in reference to their own selves, The possible way to incorporate the cultural and socio-political context is to involve the community services, social structures available and traditional healer in healing process.

## CONCLUSION

Post-traumatic stress disorder (PTSD) is most debilitating conditions. Human response to trauma is one of the most important issues in modern psychiatry. Traumatic events and ways how individuals and group of people deal with them, plays a crucial role in the development psychopathology. Post-traumatic stress disorder (PTSD) is a complex and multi-dimensional, so it is improbable that not only biological perspective will be sufficient to provide a comprehensive understanding and treatment of this disorder but many other significant factors such as psycho-socio-political also play a vital role in the understanding the disorder. Research have highlighted that psychological trauma has intimate connection with cultural, social, historical and political conditions, and the ways that people approach trauma. There is need of paradigm shift to understand the psychopathology and a need to develop new perspectives and refine old ones for better understanding of trauma across cultures.

## REFERENCES

Adams, G., & Markus, H. R. (2004). Toward a conception of culture suitable for a social psychology of culture. In M. Schaller & C. S. Crandall (Eds.), *The psychological foundations of culture* (pp. 335–360). Hillsdale, NJ: Erlbaum.

American Psychiatric Association. (2000). Diagnostic and Statistical Manual of Mental Disorders-text revision (DSM-TR-IV). Washington, DC: APA.

Bracken, P. J., Giller, J. E., & Summerfield, D. (1995). Psychological responses to war and atrocity: The limitations of current concepts. *Social Science & Medicine*, *40*(8), 1073–1082. doi:10.1016/0277-9536(94)00181-R PMID:7597460

Bremner, J. D. (2002). *Does stress damage the brain? Understanding trauma related disorders from a mind-body perspective*. New York: W.W. Norton.

Breslau, J. (2000). Globalizing Disaster Trauma: Science, Culture and Psychiatry after the Kobe Earthquake. *Ethos (Berkeley, Calif.)*, *28*(2), 174–197. doi:10.1525/eth.2000.28.2.174

Breslau, J. (2004). Cultures of Trauma: Anthropological Views of Post-traumatic Stress Disorders in International Health. *Culture, Medicine and Psychiatry*, *28*(2), 113–126. doi:10.1023/B:MEDI.0000034421.07612.c8 PMID:15470944

Breslau, N., & Kessler, R. C. (2001). The stressor criterion in DSMIV Post-traumatic stress disorder. *Biological Psychiatry*, *50*, 699–704. doi:10.1016/S0006-3223(01)01167-2 PMID:11704077

Brison, K. J. (1995). You Will Never Forget: Narrative, Bereavement, and Worldview among Kwanga Women. *Ethos (Berkeley, Calif.)*, *23*(4), 474–488. doi:10.1525/eth.1995.23.4.02a00060

Brison, K. J., & Leavitt, S. C. (1995). Coping with Bereavement: Long-Term Persectives on Grief and Mourning. *Ethos (Berkeley, Calif.)*, *23*(4), 395–400. doi:10.1525/eth.1995.23.4.02a00010

Cardena. (2001). Psychiatric Disorders Among Tortured Bhutanese Refugees in Nepal. *Archives of General Psychiatry*, *58*(5), 475–482.

Cassiman, S. A. (2005). Toward more inclusive poverty knowledge: Traumatological contributions to the poverty discourse. The Social Policy Journal, and. *Cutting Edge of Social Policy Research*, *4*, 93–106.

De Jong, J. T. V. M. (2004). Public Mental Health and Culture: Disasters as a Challenge to Western Mental Health Care Models, the Self, and PTSD. In J. P. Wilson & B. Drozdek (Eds.), *Broken Spirits: The Treatment of Asylum Seekers and Refugees with PTSD* (pp. 157–176). New York: Brunner/Routledge.

De Jong, J. T. V. M., & Van Ommeren, M. H. (2002). Toward A Culture-informed Epidemiology: Combining Qualitative and Quantitative Research in Transcultural Contexts. *Transcultural Psychiatry*, *39*(4), 422–433. doi:10.1177/136346150203900402

De Jongh, A., Olff, M., van Hoolwerff, H., Aartman, I. H., Broekman, B., Lindauer, R., & Boer, F. (2008). Anxiety and Post-traumatic stress symptoms following wisdom tooth removal. *Behaviour Research and Therapy*, *46*(12), 1305–1310. doi:10.1016/j.brat.2008.09.004 PMID:18954863

Eisenbruch, M. (1990). The cultural bereavement interview: A new clinical and research approach with refugees. *The Psychiatric Clinics of North America*, *13*, 715–735. PMID:2281015

Fawzi, M. C., Pham, T., Lin, L., Nguyen, T. V., Ngo, D., Murphy, E., & Mollica, R. (1997). The Validity of Post-traumatic Stress Disorder Among Vietnamese Refugees. *Journal of Traumatic Stress*, *10*(1), 101–108. doi:10.1002/jts.2490100109 PMID:9018680

Helman, C. G. (2007). *Culture, Health, and Illness* (5th ed.). London: Hodder Arnold.

Hollan, D. (1995). To the Afterworld and Back: Mourning and Dreams of the Dead among the Toraja. *Ethos (Berkeley, Calif.)*, *23*(4), 424–436. doi:10.1525/eth.1995.23.4.02a00030

Howard, W. T., Loberiza, R. F., Pfohl, B. M., Thorne, P. S., Magpantay, R. L., & Woolson, R. F. (1999). Initial Results, Reliability, and Validity of a Mental Health Survey of Mount Pinatubo Disaster Victims. *The Journal of Nervous and Mental Disease*, *187*(11), 661–672. doi:10.1097/00005053-199911000-00003 PMID:10579594

Jakovljević, M., Brajković, L., Jakšić, N., Lončar, M., Aukst-Margetić, B., & Lasić, D. (2012). Post-raumatic stress disorders (PTSD) from different perspectives: A transdisciplinary integrative approach. *Psychiatria Danubina*, *24*(3), 246–255. PMID:23013627

Jones, M. C., Dauphinais, P., Sack, W., & Somervell, P. (1997). Trauma-Related Symptomatology Among American Indian Adolescents. *Journal of Traumatic Stress*, *10*(2), 163–173. doi:10.1002/jts.2490100202 PMID:9136086

Joseph, C. M. (1999). *Ethnic Conflict in Bhutan*. New Delhi: Nirala Publications.

Kashima, Y. (2000). Conceptions of culture and person for psychology. *Journal of Cross-Cultural Psychology*, *31*(1), 14–32. doi:10.1177/0022022100031001003

Khaled, W. (2001). Lifetime Events and Post-traumatic Stress Disorder in Four Postconflict Settings. *Journal of the American Medical Association*, *286*(5), 555–562. doi:10.1001/jama.286.5.555 PMID:11476657

Kira, I. A., Lewandowski, L., Templin, T. N., Ramaswamy, V., Chiodo, L. M., Ozkan, B., & Mohanesh, J. (2008b). *Measuring cumulative trauma dose, types, and profiles using a development-based taxonomy of traumas: The long version*. American Psychological Association.

Kirmayer, L., & Young, A. (1998). Culture and somatization: Clinical, epidemiological and ethnographic perspectives. *Psychosomatic Medicine*, *60*(4), 420–429. doi:10.1097/00006842-199807000-00006 PMID:9710287

Kleinman, A. (1988a). *The illness narratives: Suffering, healing and human condition*. New York: Basic Books.

Kleinman, A. (1988b). *Rethinking psychiatry: From cultural category to personal experience*. New York: The Free Press.

Lewis-Fernandez, R., & Kleinman, A. (1994). Culture, personality, and psychopathology. *Journal of Abnormal Psychology*, *103*(1), 67–71. doi:10.1037/0021-843X.103.1.67 PMID:8040483

McDonald, J. J. Jr. (2003). Post-traumatic stress dishonesty. *Employee Relations Law Journal*, *28*, 93–111.

Mezzich, J. E., Kirmayer, L. J., Kleinman, A., Fabrega, H. Jr, Parron, D. L., Good, B. J., & Manson, S. M. et al. (1999). The place of culture in DSM-IV. *The Journal of Nervous and Mental Disease*, *187*(8), 457–464. doi:10.1097/00005053-199908000-00001 PMID:10463062

Mol, S. S. L., Arntz, A., Metsemakers, J., Dinant, G. J., Vilters-Van Montfort, P. A., & Knottnerus, J. A. (2005). Symptoms of Post-traumatic stress disorder after nontraumatic events. *The British Journal of Psychiatry*, *186*, 494–499. doi:10.1192/bjp.186.6.494 PMID:15928360

Mollica, R. F., Kikuchi, Y., Lavelle, J., & Allden, K. (1995). *The Invisible Human Crisis: Mental Health Recommendations for the Care of Persons Evacuated and Displaced by the Hanshin-Awaji (Kobe) Earthquake*. Boston: Harvard Program in Refugee Trauma.

Olde, E., van der Hart, O., Kleber, R., & van Son, M. (2006). Post-traumatic stress disorder following childbirth. *Clinical Psychology Review*, *26*(1), 1–16. doi:10.1016/j.cpr.2005.07.002 PMID:16176853

Reeler, A. P., & Immerman, R. (1994). A Preliminary Investigation Into Psychological Disorders Among Mozambican Refugees: Prevalence and Clinical Features. *The Central African Journal of Medicine*, *40*(11), 309–315. PMID:7859272

Robben, A. C. G. M. (2004). *Death, Mourning, and Burial: A Cross-Cultural Reader*. Malden, MA: Blackwell Pub.

Rothwell, J. D. (2010). In the Company of Others, An Introduction to Communication. New York: Oxford University Press.

Sack, W. H., Seeley, J. R., & Clarke, G. N. (1997). Does PTSD transcend cultural barriers? A Study from the Khmer Adolescent Refugee Project. *Journal of the American Academy of Child and Adolescent Psychiatry*, *36*(1), 49–54. doi:10.1097/00004583-199701000-00017 PMID:9000781

Somasundaram, D. J. (1996). Post-traumatic responses to aerial bombing population. *Social Science & Medicine*, *42*(11), 1465–1471. doi:10.1016/0277-9536(95)00249-9 PMID:8771629

Spencer-Oatey, H. (2012). *What is culture? A compilation of quotations*. Retrieved from https://www2.warwick.ac.uk/fac/soc/al/globalpad/openhouse/interculturalskills/global_pad_-_what_is_culture.pdf

Summerfield, D. (1995). Addressing human response to war and atrocity. In *Beyond Trauma* (pp. 17–29). New York: Plenum. doi:10.1007/978-1-4757-9421-2_2

Summerfield, D. (1999). A critique of seven assumptions behind psychological trauma programmes in war-affected areas. *Social Science & Medicine*, *48*(10), 1449–1462. doi:10.1016/S0277-9536(98)00450-X PMID:10369444

Summerfield, D. (2005). Cross-cultural perspective on the medicalization of human suffering. In Post-traumatic Stress Disorder – Issues and Controversies, (pp. 233-245). John Wiley & Sons.

Thulesius, H., & Hakansson, A. (1999). Screening for Post-traumatic Stress Disorder Symptoms Among Bosnian Refugees. *Journal of Traumatic Stress*, *12*(1), 167–174. doi:10.1023/A:1024758718971 PMID:10027150

Van Ommeren, M., Saxena, S., & Saraceno, B. (2005). Mental and social health during and after acute emergencies: Emerging consensus? *Bulletin of the World Health Organization*, *83*(1). PMID:15682252

World Health Organization. (1992). *The ICD-10 Classification of Mental and Behavioural*. Geneva: Disorders.

Young, A. (1995). *The harmony of illusions: inventing Post-traumatic stress disorder*. Princeton, NJ: Princeton University Press.

Young, A. (2004). When Traumatic Memory Was a Problem: On the Historical Antecedents of PTSD. In G. M. Rosen (Ed.), *Post-traumatic Stress Disorder – Issues and Controversies*. West Sussex, UK: John Wiley and Sons.

# Chapter 2
# Child Maltreatment Prevention in Rural Communities

**Tosin O. Alabi**
*Fielding Graduate University, USA*

**Sandra D. Barnes**
*Fielding Graduate University, USA*

## ABSTRACT

*For more than half a century, child maltreatment prevention programs have been implemented in communities across America with hopes of stopping the abuse and neglect of children. To broaden the understanding of maltreatment in rural families, risk markers and protective factors are discussed with specific attention to contextual stressors and resources available in rural communities. Furthermore, primary maltreatment prevention initiatives directed at improving parenting practices and increasing public awareness of child maltreatment are reviewed. Also discussed are empirically supported secondary and tertiary maltreatment prevention programs that are commonly used to intervene with families at risk for interfacing with child welfare and protection agencies, or in instances of substantiated maltreatment. Preventing ill-treatment of children in rural communities requires ingenuity, community engagement and leadership, and governmental funding to best serve children and their families.*

## INTRODUCTION

An estimated 65 million people live in rural or remote areas where "few people live across a large geographic area" (Sedlak et al, 2010; The Housing Assistance Council, n.d, p.14) of the United States. Children make up 23% of America's rural population (The Housing Assistance Council, n.d). According to the Carsey Institute, 28% of the reported cases of maltreatment in rural areas were for physical abuse, 14% for sexual abuse, 47% for neglect, 12% for other abuse (e.g., abandonment, emotional, and moral/legal maltreatment), and 26% were categorized under multiple abuses (Mattingly & Walsh, 2010). The reality is that children typically experience more than one form of maltreatment (Belsky, 1993; Chaffin, Silovsky, Funderburk et al., 2004)

DOI: 10.4018/978-1-5225-0228-9.ch002

Of the known cases of abuse and neglect, national surveys reveal a steady decline in the recurrence of ill-treatment of children. For instance, the Fourth National Incidence Study of Child Abuse and Neglect (NIS-4) showed a 36% reduction in ill treatment of children between 1996 and 2006 (Sedlak, Mettenburg, Basena et al., 2010), and the Carsey Institute reported a 52% reduction for confirmed physical and sexual abuse cases between 1990 and 2007 (Mattingly & Walsh, 2010). Even though these findings are promising, the numbers do not account for unreported child victimization and known cases of abuse that are not addressed because they do not meet the definition of child maltreatment per regional/state definitions (Fallon, Trocme, Fluke, et al., 2010). For this reason, there is a significant need for prevention and intervention strategies that reach vulnerable children who are not accounted for in the child welfare and protection system.

## BACKGROUND

### Defining Maltreatment and Prevention

As a society, we have made gains in detecting maltreatment and transforming social standards and expectations of what is considered appropriate and inappropriate treatment of children (Finkelhor & Jones, 2006). Some authors (Paxson & Haskin, 2009; Prinz et al., 2009) have examined the effectiveness of maltreatment deterrence in America and concluded that current strategies for averting the ill-treatment of children are inconsistent from region to region. At issue is the fact that the regionalized definition of abuse and neglect determine which children and families receive much-needed preventive services. Also, state-by-state comparisons of child maltreatment are unlikely because of the wide range of legal classifications of maltreatment across the nation (Fallon et al., 2010; Paxson & Haskins, 2009).

Without a universal or a collective classification system of maltreatment, the true extent of child maltreatment cannot be ascertained (Fallon et al., 2010; Paxson & Haskins, 2009). More importantly, regionalized definitions of maltreatment not only limit victim identification, but set a cap on which children get access to essential social and mental services (Paxson & Haskins, 2009). The present system, in which child protective services (CPS) agents act as gatekeepers to preventive services, encourages the practice of monitoring for accumulated risks until arbitrary thresholds are met before CPS responds. Regionalized definitions of maltreatment are relevant to determining who can access preventive services (Paxson & Haskins, 2009; Petersen, et al., 2013), but it is unclear if regional constructions of maltreatment inform how preventive strategies are developed and implemented.

Maltreatment prevention is segmented into primary, secondary, and tertiary levels. Primary prevention is focused on averting negative events and conditions in the general population through education, health promotion, and home visits (Paxson & Haskins, 2009; Schorr & Marchand, 2007). Secondary prevention is aimed at meeting individual and family needs by screening people for risk factors and linking those deemed at risk for maltreatment to services and supports to avert adverse outcomes (Paxson & Haskins, 2009; Schorr & Marchand, 2007). Tertiary maltreatment prevention is intended to keep children from further harm and to alleviate difficulties resulting from damaging abusive and neglectful experiences (Paxson & Haskins, 2009; Schorr & Marchand, 2007).

At present, maltreatment prevention focuses mainly on intervening with confirmed cases of maltreatment and persons at imminent risk for maltreatment; therefore, secondary and tertiary prevention methods are major avenues for keeping ill-treated children safe from continued suffering (Cowart-Osborne et al., 2014; Prinz et al., 2009). Overreliance on secondary and tertiary maltreatment prevention fails to undercut child abuse and neglect before it starts and may not be an effective way of maximizing limited human and financial resources. Also, retaining the current detect-and-intervene model of prevention puts children living in underserved and disadvantaged situations at high risk for harm.

The status quo cannot be maintained because secondary and tertiary services are scarce in rural and geographically remote areas. As such, it would be helpful to invest in and employ primary maltreatment prevention models that help families receive early support or intervention. To this aim, strategies such as integrating prevention into medical model of care delivery may be a culturally acceptable way of reaching families early, before maltreatment starts or risks accumulate. Recognizing that the current approaches to maltreatment prevention are skewed toward adverse events is important to shift how lay persons, community professionals, and society think about protecting children from ill-treatment.

## Maltreatment Risk Markers and Protective Factors

The home should be a safe and nurturing environment for children. However, most incidents of maltreatment occur in interactions with trusted caregivers (Sedlak et al, 2010). This violation of trust within the parent-child or caregiver-child relationship is believed to impact the child's ability to be empathic and form close bonds with others (Belsky, 1993; Center for the Study of Social Policy, 2003). Victimized rural children are likely residing in chronically stressed homes with parents who have limited access to support that can help mitigate stressors. (Mattingly & Walsh, 2010; Sedlak et al, 2010). The literature suggests that maltreated children live with caregivers who have poor problem-solving and parenting skills, and inadequate psychological resources to manage stressors (Edwards & Lutzek, 2008; Finkelhor & Jones, 2006).

Social isolation is a common maltreatment risk factor that delays early detection of parents who may need extra support to better manage the demands of parenting. Infants and toddlers living in under-resourced families and socially isolated families are believed to be at increased risk for undetected maltreatment (Sedlak et al, 2010; Mattingly & Walsh, 2010). In such circumstances, it has been suggested that enrollment in early childhood programs can help connect both parent and child with their community (Center for the Study of Social Policy, 2003). Early childhood programs can provide warm and supportive environments to stimulate the child's cognitive, psychological, and social development (Center for the Study of Social Policy, 2003). Parental connection to a community program can help parents learn better ways to interact with their children and possibly improve the parent-child relationship.

Research consistently demonstrates that being economically disadvantaged is associated with all the risk markers for child maltreatment (Sedlak et al, 2010). That said, Belksy (1993) warned against examining child maltreatment from a lens of single risk markers and, similarly, Mackenzie, Kotch, and Lee (2011) encouraged moving from specific causal models of maltreatment. These authors suggest that computing total adversity risk provides a better sense of families who are at risk for maltreatment (Mackenzie, Kotch, & Lee, 2011). Many variables converge to further the likelihood of maltreatment, but not all parents challenged by adverse circumstances harm their children (Mackenzie et al., 2011).

Maltreatment does not occur solely in single-parent or economically disadvantaged households, but is a byproduct of multiple proximal and distal factors. Proximal factors include parent and family characteristics (e.g., household structure, economic status, emotional functioning); distal factors are conditions in the local community that are influenced by higher level variables, such as government policies and societal values. It could be said that neglectful parents who are unable to meet a child's basic needs may likely have individual (e.g., unemployment, single-parent status) and environmental variables (e.g., unavailable or inadequate social services) come together to foster conditions that put children at increased risk for ill-treatment (Mackenzie et al., 2011). Mackenzie (2011) and associates recommend adopting an ecological model of maltreatment that captures the complex interactions between child, parent, and environment.

To examine the predictive value of the total-risk approach, Mackenzie, Kotch, and Lee (2011) tracked a group of women from pregnancy onward for a decade and found that women with higher adversity risk were more likely to have negative perceptions of their pregnancies. Also, women in the high-risk group had difficulty attending to the physical and emotional needs of their children. In addition, women in the high-risk group perceived their children to be more temperamental than other children (Mackenzie, Kotch, & Lee, 2011). Researchers posit that parents who have difficulty managing emotional reactions to situational stress may be more prone to misreading their children's behaviors and, in turn, responding to their children with harmful words and actions (Finkelhor & Jones, 2006; Mackenzie, Kotch, & Lee, 2011), although a study of poor African-American single mothers demonstrated that optimism was a psychological buffer for abusive and neglectful parenting (Taylor, Larsen-Rife, Conger, et al., 2010). The findings of the aforementioned studies reflect the importance of parental psychological resources in moderating ecological risks toward or away from child maltreatment (Belsky, 1993; Center for the Study of Social Policy, 2003).

Not all parents with high levels of adversity end up maltreating their children, but this is not to suggest that resilient parents are immune from the negative effects of chronic stress (Taylor, Larsen-Rife, Conger et al., 2010). Literature reveals that resilient parents are more adept at redefining their circumstances and usually have more psychological resources available to moderate stress (Center for the Study of Social Policy, 2003; Taylor, Larsen-Rife, Conger, et al., 2010). The Center for Study on Social Policy (2003) pinpointed parent, child, and contextual factors that insulate children from maltreatment. The first factor is parental resilience, which is evidenced as psychological resources available to a parent to endure tough times.

The Center for the Study of Social Policy (2003) indicated that personal belief systems and communication skills help parents manage life stress. Other protective factors include positive engagement within social networks, knowledge of parenting and child development, access to supports to meet basic needs, and healthy social and emotional functioning (Center for the Study of Social Policy, 2003).

Taken together, economic stability appears to be a major component of strengthening rural families and protecting children from harm. Therefore, policy makers have a clear role to play in funding initiatives that encourage the financial security and viability of rural families (Taylor, Larsen-Rife, Conger, et al., 2010). Beyond helping families meet basic needs for food and shelter, social agencies can help empower rural parents through vocational training, childcare resources, household and financial management skills, and improving parental community engagement (Center for the Study of Social Policy, 2003). Because the pathway to maltreatment is multilayered (Belsky, 1993), a multipronged preventive approach is necessary to moderate the complex interactions amongst multiple risk markers of maltreatment.

## Context of Maltreatment in Rural Communities

At the heart of this chapter is the question of how to stop maltreatment before it starts or effective ways to reduce risks and promote protective factors in rural communities. First, it is important to note that the picture of child abuse and neglect is similar in rural or metropolitan areas of America (Mattingly &

Walsh, 2010). According to the Carsey Institute, incidence rates of child abuse and neglect in rural areas are comparable to frequencies observed in urban populations (Mattingly & Walsh, 2010). Consistently, neglectful parenting (followed by physical abuse) is the most common reason rural and urban parents are reported to child protective services (Mattingly & Walsh, 2010).

Regardless of geographical location, rural or urban, American families at highest risk for child maltreatment appear to be socially isolated and economically disadvantaged. Forty percent of maltreated rural children live in poverty, a risk marker that is strongly correlated with other known risk markers for abuse and neglect (Number, 2014; Sedlak et al, 2010). In addition, these families may be dealing with alcohol and drug abuse, mental health problems, and intimate partner violence (Mattingly & Walsh, 2010; Sedlack et al., 2010). Also, victimized children in rural areas are far more likely to live in single-family households that are burdened with chronic stressors, such as difficulty paying for basic necessities, unemployment, and conflictual family relationships (Mattingly & Walsh, 2010, p.4). Addressing promoters of maltreatment is cost intensive, and not all families have access to community and mental health services (Petersen, Joseph & Feit, 2013; Mattingly & Walsh, 2010). In some instances, families are reluctant to seek help because of the stigma associated with seeking social and mental health services.

Rural populations have distinctive strengths and problems that demand careful deliberation in developing maltreatment prevention programs that best fit rural families and communities. Although the rates of abuse and neglect are similar across communities, urban or rural, the contextual stressors in rural settings differ from those in urban areas (Mattingly & Walsh, 2010). For instance, as the country moves out of the Great Recession, rural children and families continue to deal with population decline and worsening economic growth that lags behind metropolitan areas (Number, 2014).

A prevailing picture of people living in rural America is one of hard-working and upstanding farmers and working-class people of European descent (Burton et al., 2013; Silovsky, Bard, Chaffin, et al., 2011). A more accurate narrative, highlighted in a recent review by Burton (2013) and colleagues, is of the changing racial/ethnic makeup of rural communities, which is linked to the arrival of poor urban minorities and Hispanic/Latino immigrants. At the same time, rural populations are aging while younger rural residents are moving into urban areas to escape impoverished conditions (Burton et al. 2013). It is believed that by improving social and economic conditions in rural communities, contextual stressors that could increase parental distress and contribute to negative parent-child interactions (or the neglect of a child's basic needs) can be reduced (Belsky, 1993; Burton et al. 2013; Sedlak et al, 2010).

Taken together, poverty is a notable problem in rural communities (Burton, Lichter, Baker & Eason, 2013; Mattingly & Walsh, 2010; Taylor, Larsen-Rife, Conger et al., 2010) that cannot be ignored in the design and implementation of prevention programs. Presently, the social conditions in rural communities are being shaped by dwindling economic opportunities that threaten family structure and stability, health and human services infrastructure, community development and integration, and education (Burton, Lichter, Baker & Eason, 2013). At the same time, rural communities have a culture of self-reliance and strong ties to their community and religious institutions that can be protective, and sometimes problematic, when people are faced with life challenges (Silovsky et al., 2011).

## Maltreatment Prevention Models

Parenting is critical to the health and development of the growing child and has far reaching consequences over the life course. Most parents enter into the parent-child relationship with minimal knowledge and skills, typically parenting as they were parented (Sanders, 1999). With adequate education and support, most parents become better experienced at attending to their children's needs while managing the demands of parenthood. However, some parents engage in coercive parenting behaviors that include harsh physical punishments, critical speech, and neglectful care. Unlike physically abusive parents, neglectful parents tend have limited interactions with their children. These parenting practices have been linked to emotional and behavioral problems in children (Cowart-Osborne et al., 2014; Eisenstadt et al., 1993; Petersen et al., 2013)

A core component of maltreatment intervention programs focuses on teaching parenting skills and decreasing parental distress through individual and group-based services that take place in the home, community, or clinical settings. Ordinarily, parenting education and support seem to be adequate methods for integrating isolated parents into communities and changing parenting behaviors; however, research shows that support groups are mainly effective at reducing parental distress (Cowart-Osborne et al., 2014). Improvements in parental distress is unlikely to repair the fractured parent-child relationship without direct intervention that fosters parental understanding of a child's behavior and needs; and acquisition of a repertoire strategies for engaging with their children (Chaffin et al., 2004; Petersen et al., 2013).

The accepted approach to addressing the problems of parents and children is through an ecological approach that targets individual needs (e.g., parent, child), relational problems (e.g., parent-child interaction, marital discord), and environmental factors (Schorr & Marchand, 2007). The National Academy of Sciences Committee on Child Maltreatment Research, Policy, and Practice acknowledged that preventing child maltreatment requires an intensive level of services to deal with the host of child, parent, and family problems linked to maltreatment (Petersen et al., 2013). Conversely, research shows that targeting one problem at a time, rather than delivering a multitude of interventions concurrently, is most effective at reducing negative outcomes (Chaffin et al., 2004; Peterson et al., 2013).

Numerous prevention services exist that include community-wide parent education and support groups, anger-management programs, and home-based services. For all services, empirical evidence supporting program effectiveness and the efficacy of preventive services in stopping future physical abuse or neglect is mixed (Chaffin et al., 2004). Models of child maltreatment prevention have primarily focused on modifying parent behaviors and interactions that increase the risk for physical abuse and neglect, instead of directly addressing risk markers (Cowart-Osborne et al., 2014; Peterson et al., 2013). A review of the literature shows that reduction in parental maltreatment behaviors and improved parent-child relationships are likely to enhance child safety and wellbeing (Peterson et al., 2013). Although behavioral programs are known to be efficacious in reducing physically abusive parenting behaviors in controlled settings, there is some question about similar gains in real-world settings (Chaffin et al, 2004).

Generally, preventive programs educate caregivers and the community about healthy caregiving and interactions with children, However, little is known about what models of education and support are used within maltreatment prevention programs, including what models are effective and for whom (Belsky, 1993; Peacock et al., 2013). Empirically based preventive programs have shown benefits for up to a year. Little is known about the long-term benefits of the programs (Belsky, 1993; Peacock et al., 2013). One such program is a behavioral parenting program that emphasized direct observation and coaching, role-playing activities, and corrective feedback to increase adaptive parenting skills (Chaffin et al., 2004).

## Community-Based Model of Prevention

Most maltreatment literature is focused on predicting risk and identifying deficits of families; however rural families and communities have strengths that aided generations in enduring persistent economic and social adversity (Burton et al., 2013). Giving rural families a voice in identifying what supports and services are needed in their communities may likely increase buy-in and commitment to improving parenting ecological context (Sanders, 1999). In that vein, Counts et al. (2010) assert that a strength-based conceptualization and marketing of maltreatment prevention services is needed to decrease the stigma of seeking support. Also, community leaders and faith organizations can act as partners in coordinating and promoting preventive services in a culturally meaningful way.

The Rural Healthy People 2020 report articulated the need for community-wide prevention models oriented towards problem-solving (Bolin & Bellamy, n.d.). An applicable maltreatment prevention model, formulated by Schorr and Marchand (2007), suggests that maltreatment prevention efforts should be guided by "local wisdom" in identifying problem areas; formulating and implementing solutions; and measuring outcomes to inform decision making and actions. A community-based model of prevention requires an integration of services, which requires careful community planning and partnerships.

Schorr and Marchand (2007) identified six maltreatment-prevention objectives: 1) Nurture, engage, and ensure the safety of children and youth; 2) Keep families strong and connected; 3) Identify and connect families to services and supports; 4) Families address substance abuse and mental illness; 5) Caring and responsive communities, and. 6) Targeted services and supports for at-risk populations. The authors noted Objectives 1, 2, and 5 of the community-based conceptual model are fitting for primary prevention programming; Objectives 3 and 6 are secondary prevention strategies; and Objective 4 is considered a tertiary prevention (Schorr & Marchand, 2007). In sum, an overriding theme of Schorr and Marchand's (2007) proposed model is a sense of shared community responsibility in identifying and solving problems that could be a framework for maltreatment prevention in rural and remote areas.

## EMPIRICALLY SUPPORTED PREVENTION PROGRAMS

Empirically-based prevention services are not accessible in all communities, and, when available, the quality of the service varies, leaving many children and families with inadequate or no services (Petersen et al., 2013). All the same, improving access to empirically supported preventive services is a societal priority that is supported by government-funded projects. For instance, the federal government allocated $1.5 billion for empirically supported home-visitation programs for at risk pregnant women and infants (Child Welfare Information Gateway, 2011). Starting in the early 1990s, home-visitation programs were put in place to better serve high-risk pregnant women and postpartum maternal-child care with the intent of improving health outcomes (Peacock et al, 2013; Sivosky et al., 2011) Over time, home-visitation programs were expanded to reach low-income and socially isolated populations, and this slowly became an accepted way of preventing maltreatment (Paxson & Haskins, 2009; Peacock et al, 2013). Home visitation programs focus on parent education and skills development to reduce the likelihood of ill treatment of children (Edwards & Lutzker, 2008; Paxson & Haskins, 2009).

Despite continued federal government funding and the increasing use of home-visitation programs, there is limited empirical support that home-visitation programs, originally designed for intervening with high-risk pregnant women, reduce maltreatment (Child Welfare Information Gateway, 2011; Silvosky et al., 2011). Peacock and colleagues (2013) commented that home visitation programs that solely focus on parenting skills and supports are unlikely to counteract the everyday realities of being economically under-resourced. Ideally, home visitation programs may be a targeted way of improving access to social supports and connecting families to additional help such as nutrition and income and childcare assistance. Also, home visitation program provide social service- and mental health-providers direct access to families while eliminating barriers (e.g., lack of transportation) to services. It should be noted that the success of home visitation programs depend the willingness and comfortability with having service providers come into their homes.

## Parent Child Interaction Therapy

Parent Child Interaction Therapy (PCIT) is an empirically supported intervention that is framed within social learning theory and aimed at reducing physically abusive parenting behaviors and negative parent-child relations (Chaffin et al., 2004). It is a dyadic intervention model designed to improve the quality of the parent-child relationship and the ability of parents to solve problems and better manage their children's behavior (Eisenstadt, Eyberg, Bodiford-McNeil, Newcomb, & Funderburk, 1993). Within the program, parents practice consistent and attuned attention, positive affect, and non-critical communication with their children. The PCIT program is cognitively demanding and requires parents to learn and practice skills within the session and complete homework assignments.

Although the PCIT was created for children between the ages of 2.5 and 7 years, it has been successfully adapted and implemented in school-age children (Chaffin et al., 2004). A 2004 study involving physically abusive biological/step-parents and their school-age children compared the efficacy of the PCIT-only group to a community support group and an Enhanced PCIT group that received additional services (e.g., individual and family therapy, home-visitation, substance abuse, domestic violence treatment, and pharmacotherapy) (Chaffin et al., 2004, p. 504). For the PCIT only and Enhanced PCIT groups, parents were required to successfully complete six sessions of motivation enhancement orientation before starting the 12–14 session PCIT program with their children (Chaffin et al., 2004). While parents were in the community support group, children partook in social skills programs while their parents received support and education. Post treatment, parents in all groups reported decreased stress, more adaptive parenting beliefs, and better understanding of their children's behaviors. However, the PCIT-only group demonstrated better parent-child interactions and had lower rates of post-treatment contact with child protective services.

The finding suggests that parents in the PCIT-only group may have benefited from focusing on changing abusive parenting behaviors, a risk marker that is more strongly linked with physical abuse recurrence (Cowart-Osborne et al., 2014). It is likely that intervening directly in improving the parent-child relationship helps parents begin the process of reconnecting with their children, which sets the groundwork for successful application of parenting skills (Eisenstadt et al., 1993). Other empirical investigations of the PCIT model reveal gains in changing harsh parental discipline and limit setting, which was associated with reduction in disruptive, aggressive, and oppositional behaviors in preschool-age children (Eisenstadt et al. 1993; Schuhmann, Foote, Eyberg, Boggs & Algina; 1998). Of significance is the potential implication of PCIT for improving the quality parent-child interaction and reducing negative parental practices that are known facilitators of future conduct problems, criminal activity, and socio-emotional difficulties (Cowart-Osborne et al., 2014; Schuhmann et al., 1998).

## SafeCare

The SafeCare program is a modified version of Project 12-Ways, a state-funded parenting program for rural families involved with the Illinois child protective service agency (Edwards & Lutzker, 2008). Although Project 12-Ways was developed and tested on rural populations, the feasibility of the program for rural communities is limited because the program required people to travel into the city to receive intensive services. The majority of participants in the Project 12-Ways program were from lower socioeconomic families with single mothers as head of household. Project 12-Ways involved initial skills assessment and potential engagement in 12 services that include "assertiveness and self-control, alcohol treatment, training behavior management, parent-infant/parent-child interaction training, employment search, money management, leisure time counseling, health and nutrition, social support, and relationship counseling" (Edwards & Lutzker, 2008, p. 39). The aforementioned services were geared towards individual needs and all participants may not have needed all available services.

The SafeCare program, designed on the eco-behavioral framework, addresses parent skills and characteristics, poor parent-child interactions, environmental risks to physical health (e.g., unclean home, poor self-care), culture, and larger community factors (Edwards & Lutzker, 2008). SafeCare is a skills-based program that educates parents about how to improve identified deficit areas. Research findings suggest that a Safe-Care home-based program showed promise for increasing participation of high-risk rural families in using prevention services (Silvosky et al., 2011). Silvosky et al. attributed high levels of family engagement with the program to the motivational interviewing component of the program. Furthermore, these authors noted that motivation to change was a key component to the success of interventions with high-risk families (Silvosky et al., 2011). The program has been delivered in-person in clinics, through home visits by case managers, and by using telephone and online formats (Edwards & Lutzker, 2008).

## Triple P

The Triple P program is a five-staged primary prevention program for parents raising infants through school-age children. The goal of the program is to advance positive-parenting skills and healthy child development (Sanders, 1999). The program was designed to be flexible to match community needs and resources. The initial stage of the Triple P program provides community-wide parenting education through in-person consultation, self-directed learning through print and video materials, group classes, and media campaigns. The initial phase is aimed at providing parents healthy strategies for dealing with growth-related concerns and behaviors (Sanders, 1999). The community-wide approach is meant to change parenting attitudes, beliefs, expectations, and practices at a population level with the intent of creating an environment that recognizes the difficulties of parenting and increases awareness of community-based supports to ease parental stress (Sanders, 1999).

The remaining four stages involve targeted interventions for parents who are experiencing difficulty managing mild-to-severe problems related to sleep and eating problems, learning and mood difficulties, and temper tantrums (Sanders, 1999). As with the first stage of the Triple P intervention, the modalities of service delivery (e.g., positive parenting training, family therapy) vary depending on need and the severity of the problem (Sanders, 1999). By and large, the Triple P program relies heavily on frontline medical caregivers who consult with and educate parents through mediums such as support groups and audio-visuals (Sanders, 1999). Portions of the program are self-initiated and more fitting for families who have adequate personal resources to seek out external supports (Sanders, 1999). For instance, Wilson and associates (2012) noted that many Triple P studies relied on self-referral participants who are economically advantaged and are less likely to interface with child welfare agencies.

Numerous randomized clinical trials have demonstrated the positive impact of Triple P intervention on child behavior problems, but two German studies have shown negative treatment outcomes (Wilson et al., 2012). An independent examination of Triple P studies (Wilson et al., 2012) asked the following questions: What population does the intervention works for? What are the long-term benefits? How effective are population-wide interventions? Using the Preferred Items for Systematic Reviews and Meta-analyses guidelines, Wilson (2012) and associates articulated that the interventions based on level 4 and 5 groups demonstrated immediate improvement in child behaviors based on maternal reports. However, child outcome reports completed by fathers and independent observers typically demonstrated no significant change in maternal behavior. For that reason, Wilson (2012) and associates postulated that maternal reports may be associated with increased optimism. Additionally, these authors concluded that mothers may have a better sense of the extent of problems in comparison to fathers, and independent observers are more apt to notice shifts in behaviors. A handful of studies examined the effectiveness of Triple P level 1 intervention (i.e., a community-wide program) and there was no evidence of changes in child behavior.

A chief criticism of prevention programs, such as SafeCare and PCIT, are geared towards addressing physical abusive and neglectful parenting. SafeCare has been shown to be most effective with neglectful parents (Edwards & Lutzker, 2008), whereas PCIT is believed to reduce consequences of physical abuse (Cowart-Osborne et al., 2014; Schuhmann et al., 1998). Some researchers (Chaffin et al., 2004) suggest that these interventions indirectly lessen the consequences of other forms of abuse. Further scientific investigation is needed in rural areas for determining the true benefit and feasibility of empirically supported programs for children and families living in rural areas (Sivosky et al., 2011).

Prevention programs reviewed for this chapter were designed for parents of children from infancy through school-age. Additionally, the programs did not sufficiently address the complexity of intervening with a parent who has multiple children of different ages and developmental needs. Of all programs reviewed, the SafeCare program seemed to have the most comprehensive services to reduce the risk of further victimization of children, whereas the Triple P program was the only program to provide opportunities for changing societal thinking about seeking parenting help before harm occurs. It is not clear if primary prevention has immediate effects on parenting attitudes and skills. Also, the question remains whether parents who receive early (e.g., infancy and preschool age) preventive maltreatment education and support continue to demonstrate positive parenting behaviors as their children become school-age and adolescents. Finally, none of the prevention programs adequately discussed how to reach those socially isolated parents who are not seeking information or live in underserved communities.

## SOLUTIONS AND RECOMMENDATIONS

Many of the programs mentioned in this chapter demand a network of community professionals that includes primary care medical providers, case managers, and mental health practitioners. Research shows that, with adequate training and supervision, clinicians are able to master skills and better comply with treatment protocol (Chaffin et al., 2004). Challenges to adapting empirically supported programs for rural areas include insufficient trained professionals who can deploy preventive services.

Rural and remote areas have limited access to community professional services, which in turn impedes access to direct services. To maintain fidelity, empirical programs demand that clinicians receive ongoing training and supervision; a professional resource that may not be available to rural professionals.

To better serve children and families residing in remote areas, preventive professionals need to be supported with continued training and consultation within a regional and national network of professionals (Sanders, 1999). Rising above this human resource challenge requires some creativity in delivering services at a distance via tele-health mediums. Professional networks may likely enhance clinical practice, and decrease the disconnect between research and clinical practice, and may also provide needed support for beginning-level providers. A discussion of the opportunities and concerns related to this format of service delivery is well beyond this chapter, but its importance to child maltreatment prevention in rural America should not be overlooked.

Other issues, such as lack of transportation and child care, may keep parents from participating in prevention programs, which can be remedied with complementary on-site child and sibling care service and transportation support. Also, motivating families to sign-up for and stay with prevention programs could be challenging if families are not mandated to complete the program or are under considerable stress; therefore, motivational enhancement sessions, like that used in the SafeCare program, may be valuable to increasing peoples willingness to participate in maltreatment prevention programs (Silvosky et al., 2011). Also, participation in prevention interventions may be delayed cultural beliefs about help-seeking and associated stigma (Sanders, Baker & Turner, 2012). Community and religious leaders are critical allies for giving the programs credibility and increasing community acceptance. Making prevention programs accessible to all members of a community demands an interdisciplinary approach that provides multiple service delivery channels that include telephone consults, groups, and home visitation (Prinz et al., 2009; Sanders, 2008).

## CONCLUSION

This chapter covered child maltreatment prevention in rural or remote areas of America. Much child-maltreatment literature and research was geared towards urban communities and was later modified for rural communities. Without argument, maltreatment programs designed for rural people and communities are long overdue. Translating the current understanding of risk makers and protective factors into primary prevention programs has perhaps been curtailed by overreliance on a surveillance system and lack of funding for building up the economic, social, and technological infrastructure of rural areas (Burton et al. 2013; Fallon et al., 2010; Paxson & Haskins, 2009).

Maltreatment detection has been muddled with prevention and intervention, and the unintended outcome is that resources are mostly directed at children and families with accumulated risks. It could be argued that finite public resources are better used for preventing escalation of cumulative risk makers and increasing early access to preventive services. Indeed, maltreatment prevention is complex, and there is no one particular answer to the problem, but it is important that we reconsider the reliance on legal determination for preventive services. Societal acceptance of a detection and intervention system, at some level, reflects inadequate appreciation of the value of community-based approaches to changing parenting practices and for promoting social and economic conditions that safeguard the youngest members of our communities.

Empirically supported prevention and intervention programs seem promising for promoting healthy parenting and parent-child relationships, and encouraging positive parenting. However, the fact remains that many randomized controlled maltreatment prevention studies have not been widely disseminated nor adapted to families living in geographically restricted areas. Alternatives to traditional face-to-face service delivery modalities have been developed and evaluated. However, there is concern that less-motivated and resourced individuals may not benefit from the services. Electronic-based services using the telephone and Internet, and satellite tele-health centers integrated into medical care, may be the answer to increasing access to services in rural and remote regions of America. Policy makers and community leaders are pivotal for providing funding to improve infrastructure and economies of geographically remote communities to better the lives of children and families.

## REFERENCES

Begle, A. M., Dumas, J. E., & Hanson, R. F. (2010). Predicting child abuse potential: An empirical investigation of two theoretical frameworks. *Journal of Clinical Child and Adolescent Psychology: The Official Journal for the Society of Clinical Child and Adolescent Psychology, 39*(2), 208–219. doi:10.1080/15374410903532650

Bolin, J. N., & Bellamy, G. (n.d.). *Rural healthy people 2020*. Retrieved from http://sph.tamhsc.edu/srhrc/docs/rhp2020.pdf

Burton, L. M., Lichter, D. T., Baker, R. S., & Eason, J. M. (2013). Inequality, family processes, and health in the "new" rural America. *The American Behavioral Scientist*.

Center for the Study of Social Policy. (2003). *Protective factors literature review: Early care and education programs and the prevention of child abuse and neglect*. Retrieved from http://www.cssp.org/reform/strengthening-families/resources/body/LiteratureReview.pdf

Chaffin, M., Silovsky, J. F., Funderburk, B., Valle, L. A., Brestan, E. V., Balachova, T., & Bonner, B. L. (2004). Parent-child interaction therapy with physically abusive parents: Efficacy for reducing future abuse reports. *Journal of Consulting and Clinical Psychology*, *72*(3), 500–510. doi:10.1037/0022-006X.72.3.500 PMID:15279533

Child Welfare Information Gateway. (2011). *Child Maltreatment Prevention: Past, Present and Future*. Retrieved from https://www.childwelfare.gov/pubPDFs/ cm_prevention.pdf

Child Welfare Information Gateway. (n.d.). *What is prevention and why is it important?* Retrieved from https://www.childwelfare.gov/topics/preventing/overview/whatiscap/?hasBeenRedirected=1#one

Counts, J. M., Buffington, E. S., Chang Rios, K., Rasmussen, H. N., & Preacher, K. J. (2010). The development and validation of the protective factors survey: A self-report measure of protective factors against child maltreatment. *Child Abuse & Neglect*, *34*(10), 762–772. doi:10.1016/j.chiabu.2010.03.003 PMID:20851466

Cowart-Osborne, M., Jackson, M., Chege, E., Baker, E., Whitaker, D., & Self-Brown, S. (2014). Technology-based innovations in child maltreatment prevention programs: Examples from SafeCare®. *Social Sciences*, *3*(3), 427–440. doi:10.3390/socsci3030427 PMID:25606347

Cullen, J. P., Ownbey, J. B., & Ownbey, M. A. (2010). The effects of the Healthy Families America Home Visitation Program on parenting attitudes and practices and child social and emotional competence. *Child & Adolescent Social Work Journal*, *27*(5), 335–354. doi:10.1007/s10560-010-0206-9

Damashek, A., Doughty, D., Ware, L., & Silovsky, J. (2011). Predictors of client engagement and attrition in home-based child maltreatment prevention services. *Child Maltreatment*, *16*(1), 9–20. doi:10.1177/1077559510388507 PMID:21148600

Edwards, A., & Lutzker, J. R. (2008). Iterations of the SafeCare model: An evidence-based child maltreatment prevention program. *Behavior Modification*, *32*(5), 736–756. doi:10.1177/0145445508317137 PMID:18441332

Eisenstadt, T. H., Eyberg, S., McNeil, C. B., Newcomb, K., & Funderburk, B. (1993). Parent-child interaction therapy with behavior problem children: Relative effectiveness of two stages and overall treatment outcome. *Journal of Clinical Child Psychology*, *22*(1), 42–51. doi:10.1207/s15374424jccp2201_4

Fallon, B., Trocmé, N., Fluke, J., MacLaurin, B., Tonmyr, L., & Yuan, Y. Y. (2010). Methodological challenges in measuring child maltreatment. *Child Abuse & Neglect*, *34*(1), 70–79. doi:10.1016/j.chiabu.2009.08.008 PMID:20053453

Finkelhor, D., & Jones, L. (2006). Why have child maltreatment and child victimization declined? *The Journal of Social Issues*, *62*(4), 685–716. doi:10.1111/j.1540-4560.2006.00483.x

MacKenzie, M. J., Kotch, J. B., & Lee, L. C. (2011). Toward a cumulative ecological risk model for the etiology of child maltreatment. *Children and Youth Services Review*, *33*(9), 1638–1647. doi:10.1016/j.childyouth.2011.04.018 PMID:24817777

Mattingly, M. J., & Walsh, W. A. (2010). *Rural families with a child abuse report are more likely headed by a single parent and endure economic and family stress (10)*. Durham, NH: Carsey Institute.

Number, E.B. (2014). Rural America at a Glance: 2013 Edition. *USDA-ERS Economic Brief*, (26).

Petersen, A., Joseph, J., & Feit, M. (Eds.). (2014). *New directions in child abuse and neglect research*. Washington, DC: National Academies Press.

Pullmann, M. D., VanHooser, S., Hoffman, C., & Heflinger, C. A. (2010). Barriers to and supports of family participation in a rural system of care for children with serious emotional problems. *Community Mental Health Journal*, *46*(3), 211–220. doi:10.1007/s10597-009-9208-5 PMID:19551506

Ronald, J. P., Matthew, R. S., Cheri, J. S., Daniel, J. W., & John, R. L. (2009). Population-based prevention of child maltreatment: The U.S. Triple P system population trial. *Prevention Science*, *10*(1), 1–12. doi:10.1007/s11121-009-0123-3 PMID:19160053

Sanders, M. R. (1999). Triple P-Positive Parenting Program: Towards an empirically validated multilevel parenting and family support strategy for the prevention of behavior and emotional problems in children. *Clinical Child and Family Psychology Review*, *2*(2), 71–90. doi:10.1023/A:1021843613840 PMID:11225933

Sanders, M. R. (2008). Triple P-Positive Parenting Program as a public health approach to strengthening parenting. *Journal of Family Psychology*, *22*(4), 506–517. doi:10.1037/0893-3200.22.3.506 PMID:18729665

Sanders, M. R., Baker, S., & Turner, K. M. (2012). A randomized controlled trial evaluating the efficacy of Triple P Online with parents of children with early-onset conduct problems. *Behaviour Research and Therapy*, *50*(11), 675–684. doi:10.1016/j.brat.2012.07.004 PMID:22982082

Schorr, L. B., & Marchand, V. (2007). *Pathway to the Prevention of Child Abuse and Neglect*. Retrieved from http://www.childsworld.ca.gov/res/pdf/Pathway.pdf

Schuhmann, E. M., Foote, R. C., Eyberg, S. M., Boggs, S. R., & Algina, J. (1998). Efficacy of parent-child interaction therapy: Interim report of a randomized trial with short-term maintenance. *Journal of Clinical Child Psychology*, *27*(1), 34–45. doi:10.1207/s15374424jccp2701_4 PMID:9561935

Sedlak, A. J., Mettenburg, J., Basena, M., Petta, I., McPherson, K., Greene, A., & Li, S. (2010). *Fourth National Incidence Study of Child Abuse and Neglect (NIS–4): Report to Congress, Executive Summary*. Washington, DC: U.S. Department of Health and Human Services, Administration for Children and Families.

Silovsky, J. F., Bard, D., Chaffin, M., Hecht, D., Burris, L., Owora, A., & Lutzker, J. (2011). Prevention of child maltreatment in high-risk rural families: A randomized clinical trial with child welfare outcomes. *Children and Youth Services Review*, *33*(8), 1435–1444. doi:10.1016/j.childyouth.2011.04.023

Taylor, Z. E., Larsen-Rife, D., Conger, R. D., Widaman, K. F., & Cutrona, C. E. (2010). Life stress, maternal optimism, and adolescent competence in single mother, African American families. *Journal of Family Psychology*, *24*(4), 468–477. doi:10.1037/a0019870 PMID:20731493

The Housing Assistance Council. (n.d.). *Social, Economic, and Housing Conditions in Rural America*. Retrieved from http://www.ruralhome.org/storage/documents/ts2010/ts-report/ts10_rural_people.pdf

Whitaker, D. J., Ryan, K. A., Wild, R. C., Self-Brown, S., Lutzker, J. R., Shanley, J. R., … Hodges, A. E. (2012). Initial implementation indicators from a statewide rollout of SafeCare within a child welfare system. *Child Maltreatment, 17*(1), 96-101. doi:55951143072210.1177/1077

Wilson, P., Rush, R., Hussey, S., Puckering, C., Sim, F., Allely, C. S., & Gillberg, C. et al. (2012). How evidence-based is an 'evidence-based parenting program'? A PRISMA systematic review and meta-analysis of Triple P. *BMC Medicine*, *10*(1), 130. doi:10.1186/1741-7015-10-130 PMID:23121760

# Chapter 3
# The Impact of Parental Substance Abuse on Children

**Anu Dandona**
*Amity University, India*

## ABSTRACT

*Substance abuse is a difficult situation for anyone to deal with, but the problem is compacted when children are involved. Parents who are substance abusers may knowingly or unknowingly be causing a number of problems for their child. Substance abuse in a parent can lead to child abuse and neglect. A child can develop anxiety; this can include overachievement, constant need to please others, fear of harm coming to the family, and concern about getting home on time. Children can experience depression including symptoms like fatigue, listlessness, and no interest in pleasurable activities. For a child with a parent who abuses drugs or alcohol, there is a strong likelihood they will experience psychosomatic illness and complaining often about not feeling well. The child may also show behaviours evident of regression, including thumb-sucking, enuresis and infantile behaviour. Phobias can occur, which sometimes are about attending school. Some additional effects on a child can include low self-esteem and social isolation. These can encompass difficulty making decisions, self put downs, reluctance to try new activities, keeping to one's self, no friends and avoiding peer contact. This chapter aims to describe and increase awareness of the harmful effects of parental substance abuse on children. Therefore, the trends in substance abuse are being discussed to give the reader an understanding of the widespread and complex social phenomenon and the ones most affected; the children.*

## INTRODUCTION

Parenting is a complex endeavour, particularly if it is to be carried out in a manner that enriches psychosocial outcomes for children. The substance abuse of a parent has a long lasting effect on all young children. There are a number of substances that can become a problem in people's lives, including marijuana, alcohol, stimulants, depressants, narcotics, hallucinogens and inhalants (Substance Abuse Training Tri-Town Head Start, 2007).

DOI: 10.4018/978-1-5225-0228-9.ch003

Children who have parents who abuse alcohol or other substances are often the forgotten victims. Substance abuse often results to unpredictable behaviour, lack of appropriate care and no structure to a home life are often. It can be scary, painful and lead to many problems in the future for a child. If family members are addicted to drugs or alcohol, children can be exposed to violence, abuse, neglect, financial problems and even malnourishment.

An adult struggle to control their behaviour, mood and even actions when he/she is addicted to alcohol or other substance. For a child, this can be very confusing to have a parent going through unpredictable mood swings, depression and even times of abandonment for the sake of being high or being drunk. Sometimes children do not understand why their parent would be behaving this way and they may blame themselves for the mood swings. This can have a disturbing effect on a child as they develop.

When a child becomes older, they begin to distance themselves from friends because they think that people will judge them on their parent behavior. Often they will not invite school friends over, avoid going to events where a parent is invited, they even lie to friends about a family member being sick or absent. A child does not talk to anyone about their substance abusing parent for fear of people's reactions because their family is a guilty secret for them.

Children does not like to talk about what is happening in their family, but living with an adult who is abusing alcohol or other substance can affect a child's behavior. The child might:

- Be mean to others,
- Be quiet or keep to themselves,
- Act like a parent and try to take care of everyone,
- Get in trouble at school or have falling grades,
- Have nightmares or other sleeping problems,
- Not be able to focus or finish tasks,
- Miss many days of school or daycare,
- Believe the problems in the family are their fault,
- Worry about what will happen next,
- Hurt themselves or others,
- Feel helpless,
- Feel scared,
- Be sad, angry or cry a lot,
- Feel bad about themselves.

Parents who abuse drugs often have children who are at increased risk of abusing drugs because the drug use is viewed as a normal activity by them or because they might think they need to turn to substances to deal with emotional or social problems.

## Neglect

Although parents who are addicted to drugs might make an effort to provide a stable home for their children, the financial cost of drug use could prevent them from providing adequate food, housing and clothing for their children. Furthermore, when a parent is under the influence of drugs, he might be unable to respond to the child's emotional and physical needs adequately. This can lead to poor parent-child bonds. In turn, these poor bonds might lead to behavioral problems in school and other social settings.

### Increased Substance Abuse Risk

When children grow up in homes with parents who abuse drugs, they are at a higher risk of becoming addicts themselves, according to the National Center on Addictions and Substance Abuse. This increased risk of substance abuse comes from the environmental stress associated with living with a parent who is an addict. For example, adolescents might use alcohol or other drugs to alleviate the anxiety of an unstable home environment or absentee parent. Additionally, drug addiction has a genetic component, which means that some children of addict parents are born predisposed to drug and alcohol addiction.

### Unstable Family Systems

When one of the parent is addicted to drugs, the other one might struggle to maintain routine and structure. In particular, in addict families, children might be asked to assume adult roles such as cleaning, cooking and caring for younger siblings when the drug addicted parent is under the influence of substances. Furthermore, the effects of drugs can lead to inconsistent parenting. For example, a parent who is addicted to drugs might have difficulty maintaining a regular system of rules and consequences for breaking those rules. This can lead to behavioural difficulties.

### Separation from Parents

In families with severe substance abuse issues, child protection agencies might remove the children from the addict parents and place them in foster care or the care of a stable relative. This can cause significant trauma for the child, even if he/she was at risk while in the care of her parents. Furthermore, even if the state does not remove the child from the home voluntarily, the substance-abusing parent might be arrested or incarcerated, which further strains the parent-child relationship and makes bonding difficult.

## CHILD MALTREATMENT

Substance abuse in families is a common, yet, underestimated form of child maltreatment and domestic violence. At its worst, children are exposed to abuse, abandonment and neglect that have a direct impact on their physical and mental health. (Ministry of Social Affairs and Health 2009: 19 – 20.) However, it cannot be assumed that all children in substance abusing families are suffering harm from misuse but it does expose tens of thousands of children to the maltreatment. (Peltoniemi 2003: 167.) WHO (2006: 9) has defined child maltreatment in the following way in the Guide of Preventing Child Maltreatment:

*All forms of physical and/or emotional ill-treatment, sexual abuse, neglect or negligent treatment or commercial or other exploitation, resulting in actual or potential harm to the child's health, survival, development or dignity in the context of a relationship of responsibility, trust or power (WHO 2006: 9).*

Child maltreatment consists of physical abuse, sexual abuse, emotional and psychological abuse (Turunen 2004: 187). Maltreating parents fail to promote their child's ability to overcome developmental tasks of childhood which may lead to a failure in further developmental phases. These childhood developmental tasks include forming of a secure attachment, the development of functioning interpersonal relationships and emotions as well as the development of autonomy. When the attachment relationship between the parent and the child is secure, it provides the child trust, comfort and promotes the emotional development as well as environmental exploration. Nevertheless, the majority of maltreating parents fail to function accordingly and therefore, the attachment relationship develops insecurely. (Egeland, Bosquet & Levy Chung, 2002: 221 – 222.) Hence, the parents are unable to fulfil their children's needs but expect the children to respond to their emotions. (Egeland et al., 2002: 224.) An intoxicated parent does not have the resources to nurture the child as the substance abuse and its consequences take the parent's energy and time. Children may suffer from hunger, lack of sleep and may need to take care of the household tasks in addition to their own homework. (Itäpuisto, 2008: 55.)

### Emotional Maltreatment of a Child

Emotional maltreatment is disregarding the child's emotional needs which can be either unintentional or intentional e.g. due to the substance abuse (Kalland, 2005: 208). Emotional maltreatment is often a part of all maltreatment but it can also occur solely. Vulnerable issues such as violence and substance abuse in a family are a form of emotional maltreatment (Söderholm, 2004: 10 - 11). According to Itäpuisto (2008: 33) the observation of emotions is essential as they have a direct influence on the well-being and health of the child. The negative impacts can be summed up into three main feelings; fear, hate and shame that are surrounded by other negative feelings such as insecurity and anxiety. These feelings are more than just feelings but can develop into illnesses and cause psychosomatic symptoms. (Itäpuisto, 2008: 34 – 36.) The immediate effects of emotional maltreatment are such that the child can adjust to them. Hence, the character of the child, the developmental phase, the quality of maltreatment and protective factors such as a secure attachment relationship between the child and parent influences the effects and recovery of the maltreatment. (Turunen, 2004: 189.) A secure attachment at least with the other parent is sufficient in order for the child to develop normally, whereas insecurely attached child is at risk of not being able to recuperate from the maltreatment (Turunen, 2004: 192). Moreover, a child living in a family of substance abuse is being traumatised that causes emotional numbness by obliterating the emotional reactions of the traumatising experiences. (Kujasalo & Nykänen 2005: 64 – 65).

## ATTACHMENT THEORY

The attachment theory is a theory of normal development but initially aspired to explain disturbed functioning of individuals who have suffered traumatising experiences (Bowlby 1980 as cited in Crittenden & Ainsworth, 1989: 435). Nowadays, the behaviour of maltreated children and maltreating parents has been explained through the attachment theory as the attachment relationships affect the individual's functioning throughout life even if the attachment types change. (Bowlby 1980 as cited in Crittenden & Ainsworth, 1989: 445.)

Attachment relationships are essential for the child's development throughout his/her life. Especially, the early attachment relationship with the primary care giver should provide protection for a child which may be in danger when the child is living with maltreating parents, in this study with substance abusing parents. A secure attachment relationship enables the child to function better in other life aspects as well. However, the children of maltreating families are argued to form an insecure attachment with the parents (Crittenden & Ainsworth, 1989: 445- 446.), but it does not completely void the chance of forming secure attachment in the future. (Sinkkonen & Kalland, 2005: 9).

The basis for all developmental stages should be built during infancy (Holmberg, 2003: 26). According to Bowlby (1969 as cited in Crittenden & Ainsworth, 1989: 435), the feeling of security in infancy is formed through proximity to the parent. As the child's language skills develop and therefore the effectiveness of communication increases, it is easier for the child to comprehend the parent's perspective since they are able to negotiate and establish an agreement. This increases the child's sense of security as mutual trust and understanding has been reached. However, if the parent is unable to interact sufficiently with the child, the mutual understanding and trust stay undeveloped and the attachment relationship becomes insecure. (Crittenden & Ainsworth, 1989: 435.)

The attachment relationship develops throughout life and the tolerance of maintaining without actual physical proximity increases as well. For infants, the sense of security enhances the autonomy. (Crittenden & Ainsworth, 1989: 436.) Nevertheless, Bowlby (1969: 207) states that most children and adults do experience the feelings of loneliness and anxiousness when separated from their close ones for longer periods of time and need their support during periods of distress. Bowlby (1969: 207) argues as well that attachment, primarily to the parent and in adult life towards the partner, builds the basic security for all individuals. The attachment behaviour towards the parent continues from childhood into adulthood, and the attachment between the mother and daughter is shown to form a significant part of their social life. (Bowlby, 1969: 207.)

The attachment relationship forms the basis of emotional self-regulation. The securely attached children's emotions have been accepted and shared with the primary caregiver that builds the basis for emotional expression. The insecurely attached children may be exposed to emotional disturbances as they adopt dysfunctional ways of handling stressful situations which then expose them to psychosomatic symptoms (Niemi, 2008: 251) as they are unable to express their emotions verbally (Niemi, 2008: 248). Insecurely attached children have not experienced proximity, separation and reunification with the parent securely. Proximity may have been experienced as frightening behaviour from the substance abusing parent's part, separation may have been experienced as an abandonment and reunion may have felt uncertain e.g. if the child has woken up alone. (Kalland, 2005: 204.) The child may connect feelings of helplessness to fear of abandonment and has not learned to trust adults. The home environment has been insecure and the child may seek to control separation by causing them himself/herself. As the child's needs are not met, he/she often begins to foster the substance abusing parent. (Kalland, 2005: 206.)

To conclude, Bowlby (1969: 209) states that no other behaviour is associated with such strong feelings than attachment behaviour. The child feels secure as long as the primary attachment figure is present or he/she knows where the attachment figure is to be found. The feelings of anxiety and sorrow rise, which transfers into anger when the child is facing the threat of losing the attachment figure. (Bowlby, 1969: 209.)

## Disturbances in Attachment

It is a complex task to explain disturbances and disorders in attachment since children change and develop constantly. Children may not be able to explain their experiences themselves but their experiences can be examined through various documents. Yet, the observers' records include their subjective views of the situation and they may not know the children well or may know them in certain context which affects the recording. When defining attachment disturbances or disorders, it is essential to differentiate and know when the symptoms represent attachments disturbances and disorders rather than other disorders. (Zeanah Jr. & Boris 2000: 353 - 354.)

Zeanah Jr. and Boris (2000: 364) have described that the children with attachment disturbances have shown to experience the following behavioural symptoms:

- Indiscriminate sociability with strangers,
- Lack of emotional responsiveness,
- Aggressiveness and self-endangering behaviour,
- Inhibition of exploration and excessive clinging,
- Excessive vigilance and anxiousness,
- Role reversal.

According to Zeanah Jr. and Boris (2000: 359), the attachment disorder of no discriminated attachment figure includes indiscriminate sociability and emotional withdrawal. This signifies that the child has no primary attachment figure. Indiscriminate sociability suggests that children seek proximity and comfort from unfamiliar adults instead of the attachment figure. These children also express lack of differentiation among adults and have no emotional responsiveness towards the primary caregiver. Furthermore, children at the age of 2 – 4 years express no stranger anxiety when around unfamiliar adults which is typical at this stage of age. Children with emotional withdrawal have problems with self-regulation and are avoidant. Their attachment behaviour, such as comfort seeking and showing affection towards familiar adults and relatives, is disturbed. These children show stereotypical symptoms such as head banging and body swinging (Kalland, 2005: 206). Maltreated children have especially been stated to show this disturbance. (Zeanah Jr. & Boris, 2000: 359.)

Zeanah Jr. and Boris (2000: 364) state additionally that maltreated children show attachment disorders of secure base distortions. These include; self-endangering, clinging and inhibited exploration, vigilance and hypercompliance and role reversal. This disorder defines that these children are insecurely attached to their caregiver and seek safety from unfamiliar adults. Aggressiveness and self-endangering attachment behaviour normally appears among young children. This attachment behaviour is relationship specific, which entails that the child does not seek to maintain or return to proximity with the parent. Besides this, the child puts themselves into danger and acts provocatively within the presence of the parent and may behave aggressively towards himself/herself or towards the parent. Disorder or disturbance with self-endangerment is claimed to appear when young children seek attention and protection from a parent who is undependable or unavailable. (Zeanah Jr. & Boris, 2000: 361.)

When young children seek to constantly maintain proximity to their parents and are not willing to explore surroundings in an age-expected manner, they can be considered as having an attachment disorder or disturbance with clinging or inhibited exploration. This disturbance commonly occurs when the child is in an unfamiliar environment with the parent or in the presence of an unfamiliar adult with their parent. (Zeanah Jr. & Boris, 2000: 361.) Disorder or disturbance with excessive vigilance and hypercompliance implies that the child is constantly vigilant and attempts to fulfil the attachment figure's requests. The emotional responses of the child are extremely powerful in comparison the situation (Zeanah Jr & Boris, 2000: 362.) involving e.g. strong outbursts, threats, kicking and screaming (Crittenden, 1999 as cited in Kalland, 2005: 212). The last distortion of the secure base concerns role reversal. The child is taking responsibility of the caregiver who is not providing protection and support for the child. This disorder is only recognised when the child is old enough to show clear anxiety of the well-being of the caregiver. (Zeanah Jr & Boris, 2000: 363.)

The child's behaviours and symptoms should be sought to comprehend the child's way to express his/her experiences. Through understanding the child's early childhood, the interpretation of the feelings and symptoms is possible. (Kalland, 2005: 233.) The attachment theory gives grounds for this study in comprehending the child's experiences in a substance abusing family and explains where and why the disturbances and negative feelings emerge. The findings of Itäpuisto and Fragile Childhood- surveys may be seen as deriving from the attachment theory, more specifically from the definition of insecure attachment and its disturbances, as well. Four significant emotions arise from each; aggression, insecurity, anxiety and restlessness, in addition of having to witnessing domestic violence. However, significant information may be excluded from the documentation as the child may not remember or the documents lack information (Kalland, 2005: 233).

## INTERVENTIONS WITH A REASONABLE CHANCE OF SUPPORTING CHANGE

According to the National Institute of Drug Abuse, drug addiction is a complex but treatable brain disease. It is characterized by compulsive drug craving, seeking, and use that persist even in the face of severe adverse consequences. For many people, drug addiction becomes chronic, with relapses possible even after long periods of abstinence. As a chronic, recurring illness, addiction may require repeated treatments to increase the intervals between relapses and diminish their intensity, until abstinence is achieved. Through treatment tailored to individual needs, people with drug addiction can recover and lead productive lives.

The ultimate goal of drug addiction treatment is to enable an individual to achieve lasting abstinence, but the immediate goals are to reduce drug abuse, improve the patient's ability to function, and minimize the medical and social complications of drug abuse and addiction.

Scientific research since the mid-1970s shows that treatment works. Research from the Substance Abuse and Mental Health Services Administration suggests that treatment can cut drug abuse in half, reduce criminal activity up to 80 percent, and reduce arrests up to 64 percent. Recovery from drug addiction is a long-term process and frequently requires multiple episodes of treatment. Studies show that treatment does not have to be voluntary to be effective.

Based on research, key principles have been identified that should form the basis of any effective treatment program:

- No single treatment is appropriate for all individuals.
- Treatment needs to be available when the individual is willing to enter.
- Medical management of withdrawal syndrome is only the first stage of addiction treatment and by itself does little to change long-term drug use.
- Remaining in treatment for an adequate period of time is critical for treatment effectiveness. The recommended treatment period is three months (90 days). In practice, this is often achieved by enrolling in consecutive treatment modalities (e.g., intensive outpatient followed by regular outpatient).
- Counseling and other behavioral therapies are critical components of virtually all effective treatments for addiction.
- For certain types of disorders, medications are an important element of treatment, especially when combined with counseling and other behavioral therapies.

- As is the case with other chronic, relapsing diseases, recovery from drug addiction can be a long-term process and typically requires multiple episodes of treatment, including "booster" sessions and other forms of continuing care.
- Effective treatment attends to multiple needs of the individual, not just his or her drug addiction.
- Addicted or drug-abusing individuals with coexisting mental disorders (dual diagnosis) should have both disorders treated in an integrated way.

## Effective Treatment Approaches

Medication and behavioral therapy, alone or in combination, are aspects of an overall therapeutic process that often begins with detoxification, followed by treatment and relapse prevention. Easing withdrawal symptoms can be important in the initiation of treatment; preventing relapse is necessary for maintaining its effects. Sometimes, as with other chronic conditions, episodes of relapse may require a return to prior treatment components.

Medications can be used to help with different aspects of the treatment process:

- **Withdrawal:** Medications offer help in suppressing withdrawal symptoms during detoxification. However, medically assisted withdrawal is not in itself "treatment"—it is only the first step in the treatment process. Patients who go through medically assisted withdrawal but do not receive any further treatment show drug abuse patterns similar to those who were never treated.
- **Treatment:** Medications can be used to help re-establish normal brain function and to prevent relapse and diminish cravings throughout the treatment process. Currently, there are medications for opioid (heroin, morphine) and tobacco (nicotine) addiction, and are developing others for treating stimulant (cocaine, methamphetamine) and cannabis (marijuana) addiction. Methadone and buprenorphine are effective medications for the treatment of opiate addiction. Acting on the same targets in the brain as heroin and morphine, these medications block the drug's effects, suppress withdrawal symptoms, and relieve craving for the drug. This helps patients to disengage from drug-seeking and related criminal behavior and be more receptive to behavioral treatments.
- **Behavioral Treatments:** Help patients engage in the treatment process, modify their attitudes and behaviors related to drug abuse, and increase healthy life skills. Behavioral treatments can also enhance the effectiveness of medications and help people stay in treatment longer.
- **Outpatient Behavioral Treatment:** Encompasses a wide variety of programs for patients who visit a clinic at regular intervals. Most of the programs involve individual or group drug counseling. Some programs also offer other forms of behavioral treatment such as:
    - **Cognitive Behavioral Therapy:** Which seeks to help patients recognize, avoid, and cope with the situations in which they are most likely to abuse drugs.
    - **Multidimensional Family Therapy:** Which addresses a range of influences on the drug abuse patterns of adolescents and is designed for them and their families.
    - **Motivational Interviewing:** Which capitalizes on the readiness of individuals to change their behavior and enter treatment.
    - **Motivational Incentives (Contingency Management):** Which uses positive reinforcement to encourage abstinence from drugs.

*Residential treatment programs* can also be very effective, especially for those with more severe problems. For example, therapeutic communities (TCs) are highly structured programs in which patients remain at a residence, typically for 6 to 12 months. Patients in TCs may include those with relatively long histories of drug addiction, involvement in serious criminal activities, and seriously impaired social functioning. TCs are now also being designed to accommodate the needs of women who are pregnant or have children. The focus of the TC is on the re-socialization of the patient to a drug-free, crime-free lifestyle.

Family and friends influence the decisions of persons with substance abuse problems to get help, complete treatment, and maintain sobriety. A study of people who had recently entered outpatient substance abuse treatment or Alcoholics Anonymous found that the groups who sought help had more encouragement to seek help and less encouragement to drink from family and friends (George & Tucker, 1996).

Men are more likely to get support for treatment and recovery than are women; women are more likely to receive opposition to treatment from family, spouses, paramours, and friends than are men (Beckman & Amaro, 1984; Kane-Cavaiola & Rullo-Cooney, 1991; Reed, 1987).

In Gregoire and Schultz's study of 167 child welfare clients referred for substance abuse assessment, thirty-five (21.0%) clients were described as having significant others who supported the substance abuse assessment and treatment; 132 (79.0%) did not have the support of significant others. Further analysis of the non-supportive significant others revealed that 61 (36.5%) of the 167 clients had neutral significant others, and 71 (42.5%) had opposing significant others.

Significant others' support was positively associated with assessment completion (27.8% v. 5.8%) and treatment completion (33.3% v. 17.0%). Sobriety was also associated with significant others' support (43.6% v. 11.6). Significant others' support emerged as having a strong relationship with treatment and custody outcomes. Gender differences existed, with females less likely to receive support than males. Concurrently, females were also more likely than were males to have substance-abusing spouses or paramours, which may in part account for this lack of support. These women were also younger and had lower incomes, increasing their vulnerability to remaining with these non-supportive men.

Strategies that appear to hold promise require shifting the focus from the substance abusing parent to the total family context, including significant others (Magura & Lauder, 1996), and the provision of ongoing support services for clients and their families in recovery. According to Finkelstein (1994), the role of significant others must be recognized if substance abuse interventions are to be successful and recovery is to be maintained. Caseworkers should assess the needs and roles of significant others before any intervention is done with addicted persons. More than half of the substance abusing clients in Gregoire's and Schultz's study were involved with someone who had drug and alcohol problems. Significant others are not likely to provide support for someone else's recovery until they have committed to their own recovery.

Given the obstacles to recovery and the power of addiction, clients and their significant others need multiple sources of support. In the early stages of recovery, child welfare caseworkers, substance abuse professional and paraprofessional treatment personnel, and other recovering people who are part of aftercare programs and 12-step groups are in key positions to provide support. Caseworkers can increase the likelihood of recovery for addicted persons and their families by making referrals to inpatient and outpatient treatment programs that provide family counselling (Rotunda & O'Farrell, 1997).

To assist clients with ongoing recovery, workers can strengthen existing support systems and link clients with new ones. Single parents or those with oppositional partners especially benefit from formal programs. Parenting classes and groups, particularly those designed for persons in recovery, offer support as well as education. Often, faith-based organizations can address both the spiritual and social needs of clients in a safe environment. Former substance-abusing clients who have successfully integrated into the community are able to serve child welfare families as paraprofessionals, offering hope and modeling recovery.

## Family-Centered Substance Abuse Treatment Programs

Families in which one or both primary caregivers is chemically dependent typically face challenges in a number of domains, including economic, legal, and medical. Mothers report concerns about their children's health, behavior, and education, as well as the need for child care in order to participate in substance abuse treatment. Research shows that programs that address multiple family needs report higher success rates in terms of length of stay and achievement of abstinence. Offering benefits to the children of participants may work in three ways: removing barriers to participation (i.e., lack of child care), helping parents face their guilt about the effects of their substance abuse on their children by linking the parent's participation to child benefits, and improving the family's overall health and well-being. (Schottenfeld, R. et al., in Besharov, D. ed. When Drug Addicts Have Children, CWLA (1994))

# SOLUTIONS AND RECOMMENDATIONS

Parental substance abuse continues to be a serious issue in the child welfare system. Maltreated children of substance abusing parents often remain in the child welfare system longer and experience poorer outcomes. The inability of residential programs to accommodate children can result in an additional barrier. Some agencies have developed innovative approaches for addressing child maltreatment and substance abuse, but many have not. Given the prevalence of substance use disorders among the child welfare population, several approaches should be initiated in every country to address this issue:

## Focus on Early Identification of At-Risk Families in Substance Abuse Programs

Such preventive efforts can reduce the number of maltreated children and help families obtain needed services (U.S. Department of Health and Human Services, 1999).

- *Improve communication between the child welfare system and the substance abuse treatment system.* Communication, understanding, and active collaboration between service systems are vital to ensuring that child welfare-involved parents in need of substance abuse treatment are accurately identified and receive appropriate treatment in a timely manner (Child Welfare League of America, 2001; U.S. Department of Health and Human Services, 1999).
- *Close the gap between treatment need and available treatment slots.* Even with strong working relationships among systems, more treatment slots, particularly in the more intensive levels of care and providing gender-specific comprehensive services, need to be developed to meet the need for all parents. Creative financing and resource development need to be priorities for administrators and policymakers (U.S. Department of Health and Human Services, 1999).

## CONCLUSION

Children of all ages suffer when a parent abuses alcohol or drugs. Even if the parent is always home physically, their children experienced a psychological or emotional absence when they abused drugs or alcohol. They may have neglected or abused their children, or allowed them to be neglected or abused by someone else. Typically, children of all ages experience confusion, fear, worry, sadness, and anger—but children show and express their feelings differently.

Children who were neglected or abused might not have learned basic things like how to brush their teeth properly, how to take groom themselves, table manners, and how to make and keep friends. They might have learned to hoard food or other items if there was not enough to eat, or if their things were taken away in order for a parent to get drugs or alcohol. Older children might have learned to take care of themselves, and their younger siblings. They might be used to playing the role of the caregiver and not be ready to give up that role now that their parent is in recovery.

These children and teens may distrust authority figures because they have learned from experience to expect disappointment from parents. Others have an excessive need to be in control in order to balance out the chaos in their lives. Or they may constantly need approval, to reassure themselves that they have value. Some become aggressive.

Interventions must be directed toward substance abuse/child maltreatment. Interventions must take place at multiple levels: with the substance abusing parent, with their children, and with the context in which they exist. Substance abuse treatment programs must recognize the special problems faced by chemically dependent parents who cannot turn away from their other responsibilities to focus all their energies on getting clean and sober as the traditional substance abuse treatment model requires. These programs must begin to address the multiple factors in the lives of parents which make sobriety difficult to sustain, particularly their struggles with parenting their children and with their own childhood trauma. And, parenting programs must recognize that training in the skills of child management is not enough. They must pay attention to the substance abusing parent's difficulties in interpersonal functioning, their lack of social skills, and their diminished social network, as well as their relationships with their children. Parenting programs aimed at enhancing attachment behaviors in parents of new borns show great promise for maltreating parents who lack sensitivity and responsiveness to their infants (van Ijzendoorn, Juffer, &Duyvensteyn, 1995).

## REFERENCES

Beckman, L. J., & Amaro, H. (1984). Patterns of women's use of alcohol treatment agencies. In S. C. Wilsnack & L. J. Beckman (Eds.), *Alcohol problems in women* (pp. 319–348). New York: Guilford Press.

Besharov, D. J. (Ed.). (1994). *When drug addicts have children: Reorienting child welfare's response*. Washington, DC: CWLA.

Bowlby, J. (1969). Attachment and Loss: Vol. I. *Attachment*. London: The Hogarth Press.

Child Welfare League of America. (2001). *Alcohol, other drugs, & child welfare*. Washington, DC: Author. Retrieved from www.cwla.org/programs/bhd/aodbrochure.pdf

Crittenden, P. M., & Ainsworth, M. D. S. (1989). Child maltreatment and attachment theory. In D. Cicchetti & V. Carlson (Eds.), *Child Maltreatment: Theory and research on the causes and consequences of child abuse and neglect*. Cambridge, UK: University of Cambrindge. doi:10.1017/CBO9780511665707.015

Egeland, B., Bosquet, M., & Levy Chung, A. (2002). Continuities and Discontinuities in the Intergenerational Tranmission of Child Maltreatment: Implications for Breaking the Cycle of Abuse. In K. Browne et al. (Eds.), *Early Prediction and Prevention of Child Abuse: A Handbook*. John Wiley & Sons Ltd.

Finkelstein, N. (1994). Treatment issues for alcohol- and drug-dependent pregnant and parenting women. *Health & Social Work, 19*(1), 7–15. PMID:8168782

George, A. A., & Tucker, J. A. (1996). Help-seeking for alcohol-related problems: Social contexts surrounding entry into alcoholism treatment or Alcoholics Anonymous. *Journal of Studies on Alcohol, 57*(4), 449–457. doi:10.15288/jsa.1996.57.449 PMID:8776687

Gregoire, K. A., & Schultz, D. J. (2001). Substance-abusing child welfare parents: Treatment and child placement outcomes. *Child Welfare, 80*(4), 433–452. PMID:11480487

Holmberg, T. (2003). *Lapsetjavanhempienpäihdeongelma: opasvanhemmille, lastensuojelunammattilaisillejamuillelastenkanssatyöskenteleville. Saarijärvi*. Saarijärven Offset.

Itäpuisto, M. (2008). *Pullonpohjimmaiset: lapsi, perhejaalkoholi*. Helsinki: Kirjapaja.

Kalland, M. (2005). Kiintymissuhdeteoriankliininenmerkitys: soveltaminenerityistilanteissa. In J. Sinkkonen & M. Kalland (Eds.), *Varhaisetihmissuhteetjaniidenhäiriintyminen*. Vantaa: Werner SöderströmOy.

Kane-Cavaiola, C., & Rullo-Cooney, D. (1991). Addicted women: Their families' effect on treatment outcome. *Journal of Chemical Dependency Treatment, 4*(1), 111–119. doi:10.1300/J034v04n01_08

Kujasalo, A., & Nykänen, H. (2005). *Viininviemää – Nainenalkoholinansassa. Hämeenlinna*. KaristoOy.

Magura, S., & Laudet, A. B. (1996). Parental substance abuse and child maltreatment: Review and implications for intervention. *Children and Youth Services Review, 18*(3), 193–220. doi:10.1016/0190-7409(96)00001-1

Ministry of Social Affairs and Health. (2009). Raskaanaolevienpäihdeongelmaistennaistenhoidonvarmistaminen – työryhmänraportti. *Sosiaali-jaterveysministeriönselvityksiä, 4*.

Niemi, P. M. (2008). Psykosomatiikka. In S. Kähkönen, I. Karila, & N. Holmberg (Eds.), *Kognitiivinenpsykoterapia. Hämeenlinna: KaristoOy:nkirjapaino*.

Peltoniemi, T. (2003) Päihdeperheidenlapsetauttamisjärjestelmissä. In K. Utslahti & T. Peltoniemi (Eds.), Pikkuaikuisia- KirjoituskilpailunkertomuksiajatutkimustietoaLasinenLapsuushankkeesta. Jyväskylä: GummerusKirjapainoOy.

Reed, B. G. (1987). Developing women-sensitive drug dependence treatment services: Why so difficult? *Journal of Psychoactive Drugs, 19*(2), 151–16. doi:10.1080/02791072.1987.10472399 PMID:3612383

Rotunda, R. J., & O'Farrell, T. J. (1997). Marital and family therapy of alcohol use disorders: Bridging the gap between research and practice. *Professional Psychology, Research and Practice, 28*(3), 246–4. doi:10.1037/0735-7028.28.3.246

Sinkkonen, J., & Kalland, M. (2005). Johdanto: Ihminentarvitseetoistenläheisyyttäjaturvaa. In J. Sinkkonen & M. Kalland (Eds.), *VarhaisetIhmissuhteetjaniidenhäiriintyminen*. Vantaa: Werner SöderströmOsakeyhtiö.

Söderholm, A. (2004). Johdanto. In A. Söderholm et al. (Eds.), *Lapsenkaltoinkohtelu. Keuruu: OtavanKirjapainoOy*.

Substance Abuse Training. (2007, October 19). *Tri-Town Head Start*.

Turunen, M.-M. (2004). Lapsenkaltoinkohtelunpsyykkisistäseurauksista. In *Lapsenkaltoinkohtelu. Keuruu: OtavanKirjapainoOy*.

U.S. Department of Health and Human Services. (1999). *Blending perspectives and building common ground: A report to Congress on substance abuse and child protection*. Washington, DC: U.S. Government Printing Office.

World Health Organization and International Society for Prevention of Child Abuse and Neglect. (2006). *Preventing Child Maltreatment: a guide to taking action and generating evidence*. Geneva: WHO.

Zeanah, C. H., Jr., & Boris, N. W. (2000) Disturbance and Disorders of Attachment in Early Childhood. In C. H. Jr. Zeanah (Ed.), Handbook of Infant Mental Health. New York: The Guilford Press.

# Chapter 4
# Does Location Matter?
## The Impact of Family Violence in Rural Areas

**Samar Adi**
*COPE Community Services, USA*

## ABSTRACT

*Domestic Violence is a societal issue that affects all members of a family where it occurs; children are especially vulnerable even when violence isn't directed towards them. Exposure to family violence has been shown to impact all the developmental stages of childhood; the consequences this exposure to trauma can have lifelong effects. As a result many programs attempt to provide children services to assist with increasing resiliency as well as mitigating the effects caused by exposure to violence. Rural communities face specific barriers unique to their areas – this chapter will explore the impact Domestic Violence has on people living in these underserved regions. While there is limited research on the impact of domestic violence on children living in rural communities this chapter will summarize some of the risks faced by families as well as discuss considerations with assessment and treatment.*

## INTRODUCTION

Domestic violence (DV) is often seen as a family problem rather than a societal issue. Even with decades of research on the negative consequences and impact it has on childhood development and individuals, in general, there is a denial of the extent to which it exists. There is a culture of secrecy and shame surrounding it, which leads to many incidents of abuse being never reported. Due to DV's long-term health consequences and its potential lethality on those who are being abused—especially the children, who are the most vulnerable—DV can be considered a major public health problem that impacts all levels of society. As a societal problem, DV occurs in both rural and urban areas, and it is impacted by a variety of factors as to its extent within either area. In dealing with DV, rural areas that are considered geographically isolated face different kinds of challenges as compared to those in urban areas. Rural groups have limited access to services and resources. It is essential to identify and assess DV's current situation in rural areas, as this will lead agencies to tailor services to better treat those impacted by DV.

DOI: 10.4018/978-1-5225-0228-9.ch004

## BACKGROUND

Domestic violence is a pattern of behavior used by individuals to establish power and control over other human beings through the use of fear and intimidation. This pattern occurs within families, and it operates under the basis of the strong victimizing the weak. Other terms often used interchangeably to describe this pattern of behavior include interpersonal partner violence (IPV), battery, family violence, and spousal abuse. IPV encompasses abuse that is physical, emotional, verbal, psychological, sexual, and financial; it influences the persons it is directed against to change their actions as a result of the abuse directed toward them. Not all acts of domestic violence are defined as criminal acts; nevertheless, these are still acts of abuse. Victims may involve law enforcement for physical abuse, but the emotional and psychological aspects of their victimization are left untreated. Consequences experienced by victims of DV may include an increased risk of developing post-traumatic stress disorder (PTSD), depression, anxiety, low self-esteem, substance abuse problems, and suicide attempts. Further psychological effects on those being abused include fear, difficulty with trust and intimacy, problems with memory, difficulty concentrating, health concerns, anger and irritability, and cognitive confusion (Jordan, Nietzel, & Walker, 2004). These psychological effects are significantly affected by the severity and frequency of the abuse (Jordan et. al., 2004). Although terminating an abusive relationship may lead victims toward feelings of increased safety, thus decreasing some of those negative effects, there are still secondary stressors that occur as a result of this termination. Such stressors can include potential increase of physical abuse from the offender, financial difficulties, and parenting stressors; often times, the most dangerous time for victims is the period after they leave the offender (Jordan et al., 2004).

IPV, another term under the category of DV, can affect people from all walks of life; anyone can be a survivor regardless of age, gender, race, ethnicity, sexual identity, and socio economic status (Jordan et al., 2004). While the violence can be bidirectional—that is, occurring from male to female and female to male, this does not imply that the type and consequences of this violence is equal between the two. There are different consequences for men and women when violence is committed against them (Dasgupta, 1999). Physically, men tend to be stronger than women and, as a result, there is a higher chance for the female partner to be badly hurt and for her injuries to be more severe when her male abuser aggresses against her than vice versa. Women have higher lifetime rates of IPV: They experience greater frequency of assaults, suffer more severe injuries, and are also more likely to be hospitalized as a result of injuries and to be killed in IPV situations (Tjaden & Thoennes, 2000). Surveys show that rates for IPV can vary depending on how IPV is defined as well as what screening tools are used and questions asked. For example, the National Crime Victimization Survey (NCVS) combines multiple victimizations within a 6-month period, which leads to incidents being undercounted (Jordan et al., 2004). Screening tools that take precautions to protect confidentiality and the safety of the respondents indicate higher incidences of IPV being reported. The National Coalition Against Domestic Violence (NCADW) estimates that 1 out of 3 women and 1 out of 4 men have experienced rape, physical violence, or stalking by an intimate partner. Other statistics report that over 35% of women and up to 28% of men have reported physical assault, rape, and/or stalking by a current or former partner in their lifetime (Black, Basile, Breiding, Smith, Walters, Merrick, & Stevens, 2011). Over 70% of women who are diagnosed with a serious mental illness are involved in a domestically violent situation (Jordan et al., 2004).

Reports on different cultural groups have limited findings; Tjaden and Thoennes (2000) indicated that there is little to no significant differences between Hispanics, African Americans, and other racial and ethnic groups, while the NCVS indicated that between 1993 and 1998, African American women experienced IPV at a 35% rate higher than White women (Rennison & Welchans, 2000). Rates among Hispanic populations have varied, as these have been based on factors including country of origin and acculturation. American-born Mexican-American women have higher rates of IPV than Mexican-born Mexican American women (Sorenson & Telles, 1991). While there is limited research on IPV within the lesbian, gay, bisexual., and transgender communities, some studies have indicated that same-sex IPV occurs at a comparable rate to heterosexual partner violence (Tjaden & Thoennes, 2000a). Overall, the research indicates a significant portion of the population is impacted by IPV; it further indicates that there is an urgent need for more research on how characteristics of culture impact IPV and that studies need to focus on IPV assessment and treatment.

As awareness of the societal impact of IPV has increased, there has been a change over the past few decades within the legal system. Laws across the US have changed and adjusted to provide broader protections for victims of abuse. All states currently have a process where civil and criminal protective orders can be issued in IPV cases; all states have also implemented statutes allowing the state to file domestic violence charges on behalf of the victim, even when the victim wants to drop the charges (Rennison & Welchans, 2000). This has come about in response to victims of IPV dropping charges against their abusers due to their fear of their partners and dread of the consequences such legal action has on their lives. Consequences of legal action against abusers have included job loss, increased family stress and pressure, and financial loss due to the time lost from work and court fees. Fear of losing a partner whose income either contributes to the household or who is the sole provider can be one reason that victims rescind on charges against their partner. Family pressure to stay in a relationship, especially if the pair has children together, is another factor leading people to drop charges. Recent research has highlighted the impact IPV can have not only on the victim and their physical, emotional, and mental stability but on their children as well, as these may have been either directly or indirectly exposed to the violence. Days off from work and school, hospitalizations, medical care, impact on children, and lost revenue as a result of mental and physical injuries are some of the ways IPV impacts society and, as such, IPV is a public health concern (Logan et al., 2003). This realization has led to the public's increased recognition of the need for services such as crisis management services, shelters and transitional housing, legal action, and health care as a result of injuries.

Although IPV can and does occur across all socio-economic levels, numerous studies have indicated a higher representation of IPV in lower-income as compared to middle- and upper-income households (Logan et al., 2003). Although it would be simple to have a blanket statement correlating the two, it is important to remember that correlation does not equal causation. The reality is that there is a complex relationship between poverty and IPV; a person may not have the social supports or economic independence to leave, thereby leading this individual to feel trapped (Logan et al., 2003). Conversely, leaving a violent relationship can lead to financial losses, and this affects when the person leaves (Jordan et al., 2004). Factors such as a person's education level, children, work experiences, available community-wide resources, and substance use are often related difficulties a victim may also experience (Logan et al., 2003). Resources such as shelters, transitional housing, job development, and counseling services are oftentimes needed in order to successfully transition someone from a violent household (Postmus, Severson, Berry, & Yoo, 2009).

## RURAL CONSIDERATIONS TO PROVIDING TREATMENT

In 2000, the United States Census Bureau created new definitions for urban areas and urban clusters: These definitions apply for urban areas when such areas hold no more than 50,000 people, and they apply for urban clusters in such areas that hold no more than 2,500 people. Even though the Census does not define rural areas, it has been accepted that any area not considered urban is rural. Rural areas can have different configurations, from including an isolated family living miles from anyone else to an ethnically and racially homogenous community with limited resources. Overall, and, in essence, rural areas are those with low population densities. As of the most recent Census (2010), 19.3% of the US population currently lives in rural areas. The picture thus created is that of vast spaces populated sparsely with small communities with interdependent communities as compared to those living in urban areas.

Although there is literature and research on the effects of IPV in the general population, in comparison there is little research conducted on identifying the unique needs of IPV in rural areas. The findings that exist indicate that women experiencing IPV are impacted by isolation, high rates of poverty, and limited access to human services (Logan, Walker, Cole, Ratliff, & Leukefeld, 2003). Research has indicated a major factor affecting people living in rural communities is that the services needed are primarily located in urban areas and that shelters are almost twice as likely to turn away people from services due to lack of capacity in rural areas (Peek-Asa, Wallis, Harland, Beyer, Dickey, & Saftlas, 2011.) A person's ability to travel or to have access to transportation can place limits on the effectiveness of such programs in rural settings. Furthermore, fear of exposure to a smaller knit community and minimization of IPV as a community problem as well as financial stressors make it difficult for survivors of IPV to get the help they need for themselves or their families (Lewis, 2003). Mental health professionals working in rural areas may face unique challenges in that area that requires specific knowledge of how to address IPV in a rural setting. Some of these cultural traits have developed in response to their geographical remoteness, possible dependence on agriculture or mining, and interdependence fostered in response to their isolation. While rural communities differ from each other in history and culture, many share common traits including closer ties with family and friends, a simpler way of life, and lower costs of living. Rural areas can also have a cultural uniqueness to them which can carry implications for the delivery of services in terms of reporting, accountability, and service delivery (Lewis, 2003). Clinicians and service providers need to educate themselves on the intricacies of the areas they serve.

### Law Enforcement

*Julie didn't want to call the police unless it got serious. She had family members who were on the police force, and she didn't want her parents to know what was happening. She knew it would get back to them pretty fast.*

In rural areas, law enforcement officers are part of the community they serve, which leads to increased chances that they know the parties involved in an IPV situation. IPV, in general, is underreported, with as few as 7–14% of IPV assaults being reported (Kantor & Straus, 1987). There is limited research to find out how these rates compare to those in urban settings, but the general belief is that the rate of underreporting in rural settings is much higher (Lewis, 2003). Concern over involving someone with whom they know may deter people from reaching out and contacting law enforcement when needed, and people may be unwilling to seek help if they or others in their family have personal connections with the police or court system. The social and cultural norms of a rural area may include secrecy around sharing personal problems, which serves to prove that the "social climate may have the biggest impact on failure to report in rural areas" (Ruback & Menard, 2001). The close-knit nature of some rural communities combined with low population density may lead to a lack of anonymity that influences people's choice on reporting. Law enforcement officers may also be influenced by their actions based on the relationship they have with people in their communities. Typically, most rural police departments are small, and most of the officers are called to perform a variety of services within their communities; this leads to most law enforcement officers not having specialized training when working with IPV situations (Lewis, 2003). Lack of specialized training in recognizing and assessing domestic violence may lead to an increased risk of minimizing domestic violence, and this, in turn, may lead to offenders being less likely to be held accountable for their actions.

## Transportation

*Juanita was on her way to meet with a new family for the first time at their home. She had confirmed the appointment the day prior and had taken down the directions to their home that was an hour away from her office. She was running late due to driving on a dirt road the last few miles and having difficulty spotting the signs; Mary was unable to call the family to let them know about her lateness due to not having reception. After driving around one area several times, she was finally able to find the last road she needed. When she reached their home, it was only to find out that they had left.*

A typical characteristic of rural communities is their physical isolation; vast distances can discourage people from reaching out for help or attending services. One major barrier is transportation; people may not have private means to travel to attend services, such as not having a car or money for fuel, and there may be limited if any public transportation. Roads may not be well lit, barely maintained, and poorly marked. The geographical isolation can also mean poor cell phone reception in case of an emergency. The long distances can influence service providers in their ability to see families as often as needed, especially since more time is spent traveling between areas (Peek- Asa et al., 2011). As compared to urban areas, it costs more to provide services per family in rural communities due to the time and money needed for transportation. This, in turn, can pose a challenge, since oftentimes services are based on the number of people served (Lewis, 2003). Limited access to resources such as shelters and mental health clinics will affect the ability to utilize them to the extent needed. Furthermore, police and emergency responses to crises may have longer response times due to the travel, and the longer travel time in getting to a hospital can negatively impact an individual's health. Organizations and clinicians serving a rural community will need to account for the impact the increased distances have on offering needed services, and they have to budget more money to pay for increased transportation needs (Lewis, 2003).

## Poverty

*Mary didn't know how she would be able to pay the bills without Dennis. They were barely making it as is, and the majority of their fights seemed to start off with how she overspent. They weren't able to make the payments on their car and ended up losing it. Her parents were able to help with an older one, but she wasn't sure how long it would last either. He seemed to hold that against her.*

While IPV can occur across all socioeconomic classes, there is a relationship that exists between poverty and domestic violence. Numerous studies have documented the overrepresentation of IPV in poor households (Tjaden & Thoennes, 2000). Poverty can greatly impact a family with regards to additional stress and inability to leave a relationship. Education level appears to be a stronger predictor of IPV than employment status, but financial stress leading to deprivation is also a predictor (Cunradi, Caetano, & Schafer, 2002). Poverty impacts a family's ability to access services, especially with members who have limited access to insurance, such as undocumented immigrants. On the whole, rural areas have higher rates of poverty and few opportunities to become independent of an abusive partner (Logan et al., 2003).

## Other Barriers

Rural areas can be more insular, with the unspoken expectation of not speaking about or involving others in family problems; some people have chosen to live isolated lives due to wanting privacy and solitude. They may be hesitant to reach out and connect to resources and help within the nearest community or may be suspicious of outsiders coming into their homes (Lewis, 2003; Logan et al., 2003). New programs or organizations starting up in an area may have to do a lot of groundwork over time in connecting with the community. Discomfort in accessing a service for the first time or being seen utilizing a support service may affect people in connecting to available resources (Lewis, 2003). Another trait that rural communities share includes less development of social programs. As mentioned earlier, it can be more expensive to provide services in rural areas due to the distances involved and having to fund transportation for people who may not have access to services otherwise (Lewis, 2003). Furthermore, there may be a lack of qualified service providers who have the training to work on domestic violence issues with both offenders and survivors of different ages. Finally, a specific rural area may have significant populations of non-English speakers, which may present a limitation in terms of services offered.

## Overcoming Challenges

Intimate partner violence and child abuse are often intertwined, and both lead to different institutional responses. Typically, child abuse leads to the involvement of child protection safety workers, who advocate for child safety and the preservation of the family unit whenever possible. Services are put into place, including counseling, parenting classes, and crisis management services. The typical response to issues of IPV has included legal involvement and has focused on helping the victim leave an abusive relationship. The offending partner is often asked to leave the home and not have further contact with the family. These responses have typically not lent themselves to collaboration between the two types of services in rural areas. Furthermore, there are major barriers that exist in rural areas which impact reporting, accountability, and service delivery. Although, overall, more incidents of IPV occur in urban areas, based on the number of people living in rural areas, the rates of IPV tend to be higher in rural areas. Several factors play into this, including clear association with family isolation; factors that impact this include lack of ties within communities as well as decreased affiliations with religious and community organizations (Gelles & Cornell, 1990).

*James, who facilitated a Domestic Violence group for Men, found the weekly meetings he had with the probation office as well as the advocate from the shelter helped him in holding group members accountable. The advocate would let him know what was being reported from the victim with regards to contact and incidents of IPV, while the probation officer let him know of new charges or any substance use that came up during testing. In turn James was able to keep them informed of how group members were taking responsibility for their actions and speaking about the violence they had committed.*

IPV is a social problem that needs to be addressed at the community level. There are several ways this can be brought about; many urban areas have worked on establishing Coordinating Community Responses (CCR), which have assisted in increasing communication and collaboration in many areas between different services such as the court system, social services, and community and religious groups. This collaboration has led to shared goals, a willingness to work to understand each other's roles, and a willingness to work to put together a plan regarding how to address violence in the community. Rural areas, if they haven't already implemented such a plan, will benefit by coordinating services to both victims and offenders. Such coordination of services may not always be available in isolation. A domestic violence facilitator will not be able to hold an offender accountable without full knowledge of the extent of the violence committed against that offender's partner. Providing services in isolation without this coordination could lead to ineffective treatment. Clinicians would benefit from access to court and police reports of the incidents that occurred, both to work with the offender as well as to provide a complete picture of what has occurred with the adults and children involved (Jordan et al., 2004). Communities would benefit from organizational outreach around education and advocacy. Organizations can provide community training on the importance of assessing and identifying signs of IPV, and they can also encourage spiritual and community leaders to speak up on the impact violence can have on families.

As mentioned earlier, many rural areas have law enforcement officers as well as health care providers who may not be trained in identifying signs of IPV or who may be unwilling to intercede in a smaller community. Such training is focused on the impact IPV can have on children and individuals, and it stresses the importance early intervention can have on the safety of those involved. In an age of increasing integrated care, it is also recommended that medical providers be trained in assessing and screening children and adults for IPV in health care settings. Survivors of IPV may have obvious injuries as a result of physical or sexual abuse; however, indicators such as psychosomatic and somatic complaints have also been associated with victimization. Primary care physicians, nurses, and emergency rooms are more likely to be utilized by victims than non-victims and can screen for IPV (Jordan et al., 2004). Medical workers can play a major role by identifying IPV to implement appropriate services. Furthermore, services such as shelters and housing are needed for survivors to transition to becoming more independent after leaving a domestically violent relationship (Postmus et al., 2009).

Organizations would also benefit from establishing preventative programs that have had positive outcome studies, such as the Family-Nurse Partnership (NFP) programs that are offered to vulnerable first-time mothers. One of the major components of this program is that community nurses are able to offer regular in-home visits starting from prior to the birth up to the first two years of a child's life. These visits are for the purpose of improving the health of both children and mothers, who are vulnerable by being low-income first-time pregnant women (Olds, 2008). The program focuses on improving outcomes of pregnancy by improving prenatal care, by building a healthy secure attachment between parent and child, and by improving the parents' life course by discussing education, future children, and finding work (Olds, 2008). Overall, the results of FNP programs have shown success with pregnancy and health outcomes, with decreased incidences of child abuse and neglect, and with less reported delays in social and language functioning (Olds, 2008).

## IMPACT OF INTIMATE PARTNER VIOLENCE ON CHILDREN

Intimate partner violence impacts over 3 million children a year. Estimates based on the National Family Violence Survey indicate that over 10 million children have been exposed to IPV (Straus, 1992). The trauma that witnessing or being a victim of IPV can have on a child can be lifelong. Although all family members are impacted, children are especially vulnerable as they develop physically, emotionally, and cognitively. The statistics paint a grim picture: Children who witness IPV are more likely to be victims of abuse and neglect at higher rates than those who haven't been exposed (Tajima, 2002; Holt et al., 2008); they are also more likely to be exposed to multiple occurrences of violence (Straus, 1992). IPV has been shown to occur disproportionately in homes with children under 5 years old (Jordan et al., 2004). Research has indicated that women who experience violence during pregnancy are at an increased risk of homicide and that physical abuse during pregnancy is associated with more severe abuse from partners (Jordan et al., 2004). Overall, children who are exposed to violence are at greater risk of being negatively impacted by exposure to IPV.

Witnessing IPV can comprise a variety of things including a child's exposure through watching or hearing what is happening, direct involvement, seeing the aftereffects of physical injuries, property destruction, or observing the impact on the abused parent (Fantuzzo & Mohr, 1999). Children are affected by IPV both by exposure to its impact on a parent (seeing a fearful parent and/or obvious signs of injuries such as bruises and broken bones), observing violence between parents, or by being the recipients of the violence. Children are also at risk of being used by abusers as a way to control and abuse their partners (Beeble, Bybee, & Sullivan, 2007). Increased risk of child abuse when IPV is present can occur either intentionally or accidently; understanding the child's role during the violent incident can help respondents assess the situation more thoroughly. Children often get involved when they attempt to stop the violence directly by intervening, through calling law enforcement, or when they attempt to protect family members who are the recipients of the violence. Children are more likely to be hurt when attempting to protect their mothers by intervening; female children, as well as older children, are at increased risk of abuse by fathers (Logan et al., 2003). Studies indicate that there is a relationship between witnessing and experiencing violence in the home (Litrownik, Newton, Hunter, English, & Everson, 2003).

IPV has been shown to impact all areas of childhood development, from a child's ability to learn, to connect to others, and to enjoy physical health. Some children exposed to IPV internalize the effects that come out as increased depression, anxiety, and low self-esteem, or they externalize through aggressive behaviors (Graham-Bermann, 1998). Other children externalize their reactions to IPV by modeling the behavior of either parent, either becoming aggressive toward family and peers or by having behavioral problems such as substance use and delinquency (O'Keefe, 1995). Children may also experience an increase of somatic disorders such as difficulty sleeping and eating as well as increased emotional difficulties, leading to an impact on social development (Fantuzzo & Mohr, 1999). Overall, there are adverse outcomes on development due to exposure to domestic violence ranging from a child still in utero through infancy, childhood, and adolescence.

### Preterm, Infancy, and Toddlerhood

When a pregnant woman is in a domestic violence situation, she will experience increased stress in her body, which can impact her in a myriad of ways. One such consequence is the increased production of the stress hormone cortisol. Cortisol is a hormone that helps regulates stress and which has been shown to have a negative impact on a developing fetus. Violence before and during pregnancy has been associated with increased risk of miscarriage as well as low birth weight (McFarlane, Parker, & Soeken, 1996). After a child is born, one of the most important tasks within that first year is to attach to a parent figure; healthy attachment is important due to the fact that it provides a child with a sense of safety about its place in the world as well as that it serves as the template by which that child will relate to others. A parent's task is to provide the child with a sense of security and comfort in a consistent and reliable fashion; children at this age are fully dependent on their caregivers to have all their needs met. When there is IPV present in the home, this will affect the caregivers who handle the infant. A caretaker may not have the ability to soothe an infant consistently and to provide a safe environment. An infant's awareness can pick up stress through seeing or hearing the fear in its caretakers, hearing or seeing evidence of the violence, feeling abandoned and uncared for, or having the abuse perpetrated on them. When a child feels increased stress, this activates their brain to release cortisol to prepare for the fight/flight/freeze response to occur. Constant exposure to this will impact brain development, which is critical during the first three years of life (Jordan et al., 2004). There are programs that address the effect chronic stress has on developing children. As mentioned above, many areas have started nurse family partnerships to provide preventative services to first-time vulnerable mothers throughout their pregnancies and up to when their child is 2 years old, in order to educate parents on the impact IPV can have.

## Early and Later Childhood

Children who are exposed to IPV at other stages of life will continue to have increased cortisol levels in their body. This may cause mood swings, hyper-vigilance, and chronic fear. Their bodies experience this somatically through increased irritability, a decreased immune system leading to increased illnesses, and sleep disturbances (Moylan, Herrenkohl, Sousa, Tajima, Herrenkohl, & Russo, 2010). This impacts their ability to concentrate and pay attention and increases their inability to connect to playmates. Toddlers may start to externalize through acting out, having tantrums, and being hostile with adults and peers. School-aged children may demonstrate negative effects such as difficulty with schoolwork; lower scores in verbal, motor, and cognitive tests; as well as an impaired ability to concentrate and learn (Fantuzzo & Mohr, 1999).

## Adolescence

Teenagers are particularly vulnerable due to their ability to act out in more destructive ways as well as their increased potential to be the target of IPV. Adolescents exposed to IPV are more likely to run away, use violence against family members including their parents, and use violence against their dating partners (Moylan et al., 2010). They may be more likely to become targets of the abuse, especially if they attempt to intercede or protect the parent being offended. This leads to a higher prevalence of them being at risk for not only exposure to domestic violence but to be victims of child abuse as well. This double risk has implications for increased vulnerability to internalizing behaviors such as increased depression and anxiety as well externalizing behaviors such as aggressiveness (Moylan et al., 2010). Teens growing up exposed to domestic violence may have increased engagement in risky behaviors such as sexually acting out, experimenting in drug use, and escaping through gang involvement and criminal activity. The Center for Disease Control and Prevention (CDC) funded the Adverse Childhood Experiences Study (ACE) and found that adults who have survived childhood domestic violence, as well as childhood abuse, neglect, and other traumatic stressors, have a higher risk of developing physical and mental health issues.

## CONSIDERATIONS IN ASSESSMENT AND TREATMENT

Exposure to domestic violence has major repercussions on child development. While there are many programs and treatment models that have been developed to address those effects, the difficulty has been in implementing them in areas that are underserved and addressing the barriers discussed earlier in this paper. Assessment of domestic violence can be difficult due to factors including failure of clinicians to ask about abuse, lack of training on clinical indicators of abuse, institutional minimization of abuse, and relegating it to a secondary concern behind mental health diagnosis. Furthermore, there is a reluctance of victims and offenders to be open about IPV and a tendency to overlook certain types of victims such as the elderly and LGBT clients (Jory, 2014). Families living in rural areas may be more distrustful of those considered as outsiders and may take more time to build trust with them. It is important that a clinician have education and training in understanding what constitutes IPV to better serve children and families. A major consideration is assessing the culture in that particular community. Clinicians will not only be assessing family culture but will gain an awareness of the history and culture of the community they are serving in. As mentioned previously, some rural communities are racially and ethnically homogenous, and a willingness to learn about the specific culture in that area may lead to increased connection with clients (Lewis, 2003).

When assessing adults, recommendations include normalizing the questions by starting off with a general statement about the prevalence of violence in society—for example, "Reports indicate that violence can be common in relationships, so I like to ask all my clients about this" and by asking specific questions such as "Do you feel safe at home?" or "Does your partner ever hurt you?" Factors that impact someone disclosing violence in their relationship can include the sensitivity of the interviewer, which can be perceived by their tone of voice; by providing privacy; and by portraying a lack of judgment (Fife & Schrager, 2012). With both adults and children, an assessment must be conducted on what has been witnessed to understand the impact of their experiences on them. The initial intake of a child to a mental health agency needs to screen specifically for trauma. Once IPV is identified as having occurred, this can trigger a more in-depth evaluation of the effects of IPV. An abuse history needs to be taken, and important questions need to be asked to decide if the child saw the violent incident as well as to determine the chronicity and severity of the incident (Walker, 1996). The information can be gathered from second-hand sources such as the non-offending parent and court reports and documentation. It is important to keep in mind that the experiences of the child may be different from that of the parent, and their responses to DV may also be different from other children. Once a child who witnessed violence is identified, careful assessment is needed that gathers information about the child, their family, and their supports. Assessment should factor in the child's stage of development and the symptoms they are exhibiting and look for resiliency factors that are present in the family and community.

The appropriateness of family therapy depends on the stage that other members of the family are in. Once an offending parent has completed treatment, families may ask for family therapy. Even if a couple decides to separate, they may still have a co-parenting relationship with the children they have together. Careful assessment would need to be conducted to ensure that the offending parent has successfully completed treatment, is not using family therapy as a way to gain access to his former partner or children, and that there is no abuse that is occurring (Walker, 1996). Walker (1993b) created a check list to determine when family therapy is appropriate. It asks for the batterer to have accepted full responsibility for the violence and to have stopped all stalking, harassing behaviors, obsessive thinking, and compulsive behavior. It furthermore assesses if an offender has learned skills to manage control needs and manage anger. One of the goals which family therapy needs to include involves identifying risk factors for the transmission of violence to the next generation and promoting nonviolent ways to manage conflict (Walker, 1996). As mentioned earlier, children exposed to IPV are more likely to have learned negative role-modeling from their parents, and early intervention may help mitigate some of those effects. Several models that will be discussed are especially appropriate for children in rural areas due to the effectiveness they have demonstrated within a specific and time limited format.

## Trauma-Focused Cognitive Behavior Therapy

There are several models and techniques that have been found to be effective in treating children and families where IPV is present. One type of therapy is Trauma-Focused Cognitive Behavioral Therapy (TF-CBT). TF-CBT is a therapy model that incorporates elements of CBT, attachment, and family therapy models. Although originally developed to work with children who have experienced child sexual abuse, recent research has shown its effectiveness in treating a variety of trauma-related issues as a result of IPV and child abuse. The TF-CBT research has indicated positive outcomes with treating depression, anxiety, and behavior problems. A caveat is that children who are experiencing acute suicidality and serious self-harm participate in other services to stabilize them prior to moving forward with TF-CBT. Overall, children receiving TF-CBT had better outcomes as compared to other treatments such as play therapy, supportive therapy, or child-centered therapy and that it works in as few as 12 to 16 sessions. Providers may continue to provide up to 25 sessions for the full protocol if needed (Cohen, 2006). This is an important consideration when providing services in rural areas, where it is a hardship for families to travel for the therapy or where a traveling clinician would have to have a smaller case load due to the distances involved.

TF-CBT includes individual sessions for the child and family/caregiver as well as conjoint sessions between the two. There are seven primary components of the therapy, which include psychoeducation on the impact of trauma; parenting skills for the family/caregiver; relaxation and stress management skills; emotional regulation to help children and parents cope with the range of emotions expressed; cognitive processing; creating a trauma narrative; in vivo mastery of trauma triggers; family therapy sessions to increase communication between the child and caregiver; and continuing to develop future plans for safety and continuing growth (Cohen, 2006). One contraindication of working through the trauma narrative is if the child continues to live in an unsafe and triggering environment.

One of the primary reasons that TF-CBT would be useful in rural areas is its focus on fostering cultural competence as well as specific protocol and successful outcomes within a relatively brief number of sessions. Research has indicated TF-CBT's success in reducing PTSD in children from a large diversity of cultural backgrounds and that it is considered a highly collaborative therapy approach (Cohen, 2006). A focus of the therapy is to ask clinicians who are utilizing this to educate themselves on the specific cultural group as well as learning more about the family culture involved. A key concept of TF-CBT is that parents/caregivers are considered experts on their children and are therefore encouraged to take leadership roles in conjoint sessions.

## Eye Movement Desensitization and Reprocessing

Eye Movement Desensitization and Reprocessing (EMDR) is a therapy developed by Francine Shapiro that posits that disturbing memories are the root of psychopathology. When traumas occur, a person's ability to process, move past, and cope may be severely impacted; this in turn can lead to the development of disorders including PTSD. The overall idea behind EMDR is that the mind moves towards healing itself automatically once the blocks caused by painful memories are removed. Overall, a key concept of EMDR is that it doesn't assume pathology; the mind is already trying to heal itself, and the interventions used in EMDR help facilitate that process. There are 8 phases of the therapy that address specific areas in turn. These phases include building groundwork to conduct the processing; identifying the negative cognitions a person has developed as well as identifying a positive cognition to install in its place; processing traumatic memories while experiencing bilateral stimulation; and inserting positive cognitions within the individual about themselves. Bilateral stimulation typically takes place through a series of eye movements, or less commonly through sound or repetitive motions (Shapiro, 2001).

Multiple studies have been conducted that have indicated consistent results with the effectiveness of EMDR as compared to traditional talk therapy. Studies focused on EMDR's effect on children have yielded similar results; EMDR has been found to be especially effective with children who have difficulty verbalizing the experiences they have gone through (Rodenburg, Benjamin, De Roos, Meijer, & Stams, 2009). EMDR is a well-researched treatment model capable of addressing multiple incidents of trauma simultaneously. Similarly to TF-CBT, it has a specific protocol and provides stable treatment effects within a short period.

# CONCLUSION

Intimate personal violence is a societal issue that has repercussions on communities, families, and individuals. Furthermore, it is apparent that IPV in rural areas is a problem that is underreported as well as underserved. Children are extremely vulnerable due to the different challenges that exist in rural areas which prevent their access to services. Training rural health care providers on screening for IPV as well as connecting families to the appropriate community organizations is one way to start the shift away from secrecy. Community organization around creating more resources and ways to access them would continue this process. Educating all service providers on the signs and treatment concerns with IPV would put more focus on the safety and health of the survivors. Although some communities have started implementing the recommendations listed to mitigate the barriers that exist, more awareness needs to occur to continue the process. More research needs to be conducted on IPV in rural communities, on how IPV may uniquely impact children living in those communicates, as well as interventions that would be specifically geared towards this population.

# REFERENCES

Beeble, M., Bybee, D., & Sullivan, C. (2007). Abusive men's use of children to control their partners and ex-partners. *European Psychologist*, *12*(1), 54–61. doi:10.1027/1016-9040.12.1.54

Beyer, K. M., Layde, P. M., Hamberger, L. K., & Laud, P. L. (2013). Characteristics of the residential neighborhood environment differentiate intimate partner femicide in urban versus rural settings. *The Journal of Rural Health, 29*(3), 281–293. doi:10.1111/j.1748-0361.2012.00448.x PMID:23802930

Black, M. C., Basile, K. C., Breiding, M. J., Smith, S. G., Walters, M. L., & Merrick, M. T. (2011). *The National Intimate Partner and Sexual Violence Survey (NISVS): 2010 summary report*. Atlanta, GA: National Center for Injury Prevention and Control, Centers for Disease Control and Prevention.

Campbell, J. C., Glass, N., Sharps, P. W., Laughon, K., & Bloom, T. (2007). Intimate partner homicide: Review and implications of research and policy. *Trauma, Violence & Abuse, 8*(3), 246–269. doi:10.1177/1524838007303505 PMID:17596343

Campbell, J. C., Webster, D., Koziol-McLain, J., Block, C., Campbell, D., Curry, M. A., & Laughon, K. et al. (2003). Risk factors for femicide in abusive relationships: Results from a multisite case control study. *American Journal of Public Health, 93*(7), 1089–1097. doi:10.2105/AJPH.93.7.1089 PMID:12835191

Cohen, J., Mannarino, A. P., & Deblinger, E. (2006). *Treating trauma and traumatic grief in children and adolescents*. New York, NY: Guilford Press.

Cunradi, C. B., Caetano, R., & Schafer, J. (2002). Socioeconomic predictors of intimate partner violence among White, Black, and Hispanic couples in the United States. *Journal of Family Violence, 17*(4), 377–389. doi:10.1023/A:1020374617328

Dasgupta, S. D. (1999). Just like men? A critical view of violence by women. In M. F. Shepard & E. L. Pence (Eds.), *Coordinating community responses to domestic violence: Lessons from Duluth and beyond* (pp. 195–222). Thousand Oaks, CA: Sage. doi:10.4135/9781452231952.n10

Fantuzzo, J., McDermott, P., & Lutz, M. N. (1999). Clinical issues in the assessment of family violence involving children. In R. T. Ammerman & M. Hersen (Eds.), *Assessment of family violence: A clinical and legal sourcebook* (2nd ed.; pp. 10–23). Baltimore, MD: John Wiley and Sons.

Fantuzzo, J., & Mohr, W. (1999). Prevalence and effects of child exposure to domestic violence. *The Future of Children: Domestic Violence and Children, 9*(3), 21–32. doi:10.2307/1602779 PMID:10777998

Gelles, R. J., & Cornell, C. P. (1990). *Intimate violence in families*. Newbury Park, CA: Sage.

Graham-Berman, S. A. (1998). The impact of woman abuse on children's social development. In G. W. Holden, R. Geffner, & E. N. Jouriles (Eds.), *Children exposed to marital violence: Theory, research, and applied issues* (pp. 21–54). Washington, DC: American Psychological Society. doi:10.1037/10257-001

Holt, S., Buckley, H., & Whelan, S. (2008). The impact of exposure to domestic violence on children and young people: A review of the literature. *Child Abuse and Neglect: The International Journal, 32*(8), 797–810. doi:10.1016/j.chiabu.2008.02.004 PMID:18752848

Jordan, C. E., Nietzel, M. T., Walker, R., & Logan, T. K. (2004). *Intimate partner violence: a clinical training guide for mental health professionals*. New York, NY: Springer Publishing Company.

Jorey, B. (2004). The intimate justice scale: An instrument to screen for psychological abuse and physical violence in clinical practice. *Journal of Marital and Family Therapy, 30*(1), 29–44. doi:10.1111/j.1752-0606.2004.tb01220.x PMID:14763207

Kantor, G. K., & Straus, M. A. (1987). The "Drunken Bum" theory of wife beating. *Social Problems*, *34*(3), 213–231. doi:10.2307/800763

Lewis, S. H. (2003). *Unspoken crimes: sexual assault in rural America.* National Sexual Violence Resource Center. Retrieved from http://www.nsvrc.org/publications/booklets/rural_txt.htm

Litrownik, A. J., Newton, R., Hunter, W. M., English, D., & Everson, M. D. (2003). Exposure to family violence in young at-risk children: A longitudinal look at the effects of victimization and witnessed physical and psychological aggression. *Journal of Family Violence*, *18*(10), 59–73. doi:10.1023/A:1021405515323

Logan, T. K., Walker, R., Cole, J., Ratliff, S., & Leukefeld, C. (2003). Qualitative differences among rural and urban intimate violence victimization experiences and consequences: A pilot study. *Journal of Family Violence*, *18*(2), 83–86. doi:10.1023/A:1022837114205

McFarlan, J., Parker, B., & Soeken, K. (1996). Physical abuse, smoking, and substance use during pregnancy: Prevalence, interrelationships effects on birth weight. *Journal of Obstetric, Gynecologic, and Neonatal Nursing*, *25*(4), 313–320. doi:10.1111/j.1552-6909.1996.tb02577.x PMID:8708832

Moylan, C. A., Herrenkohl, T. I., Sousa, C., Tajima, E. A., Herrenkohl, R. C., & Russo, M. J. (2010). The effects of child abuse and exposure to domestic violence on adolescent internalizing and externalizing behavior problems. *Journal of Family Violence*, *25*(1), 53–63. doi:10.1007/s10896-009-9269-9 PMID:20495613

Olds, D. L. (2008). Preventing child maltreatment and crime with prenatal and infancy support of parents: The nurse-family partnership. *Journal of Scandinavian Studies in Criminology and Crime Prevention*, *9*(1), 2–24. doi:10.1080/14043850802450096 PMID:20885797

Peek-Asa, C., Wallis, A., Harland, K., Beyer, K., Dickey, P., & Saftlas, A. (2011). Rural disparity in domestic violence prevalence and access to resources. *Journal of Women's Health*, *11*(11), 1743–1749. doi:10.1089/jwh.2011.2891 PMID:21919777

Postmus, J. L., Severson, M., Berry, M., & Yoo, J. A. (2009). Women's experiences of violence and seeking help. *Violence Against Women*, *15*(7), 852–868. doi:10.1177/1077801209334445 PMID:19458091

Rennison, C. M., & Welchans, S. (2000). *Bureau of Justice statistics special report: Intimate partner violence*. Washington, DC: U.S. Department of Justice.

Rodenburg, R., Benjamin, A., De Roos, C., Meijer, A. M., & Stams, G. J. (2009). Efficacy of EMDR in children: A meta-analysis. *Clinical Psychology Review*, *29*(7), 599–606. doi:10.1016/j.cpr.2009.06.008 PMID:19616353

Ruback, B. R., & Menard, K. S. (2001). Rural-urban differences in sexual victimization and reporting: Analyses using UCR and Crisis Center data. *Criminal Justice and Behavior*, *28*(2), 131–155. doi:10.1177/0093854801028002001

Shapiro, F. (2001). *Eye movement desensitization and reprocessing* (2nd ed.). New York, NY: Guilford Press.

Sorenson, S. B., & Telles, C. A. (1991). Self-reports of spousal violence in a Mexican-American and non-Hispanic White population. *Violence and Victims*, *6*(1), 3–15. PMID:1859804

Storer, H. L., Lindhorst, T., & Starr, K. (2013). The domestic violence fatality review: Can it mobilize community-wide change? *Homicide Studies*, *17*(4), 418–435. doi:10.1177/1088767913494202 PMID:25741174

Tajima, E. A. (2013). Risk factors for violence against children: Comparing homes with and without wife abuse. *Journal of Interpersonal Violence*, *17*(2), 122–149. doi:10.1177/0886260502017002002

Thelen, R. (2000). *Advocacy in a coordinated community response: overview and highlights of three programs*. Clearwater, MN: Gender Violence Institute.

Tjaden, P., & Thoennes, N. (2000a). *Extent, nature, and consequences of intimate partner violence: Findings from the National Violence Against Women Survey* (NCJ No. 181867). Retrieved from http://www.ncjrs.org/pdffiles1/nij/181867.pdf

Tjaden, P., & Thoennes, N. (2000b). Prevalence and consequences of male to female and female to male intimate partner violence as measured by the National Violence Against Women Survey. *Violence Against Women*, *6*(2), 124–142. doi:10.1177/10778010022181769

Walker, L. E. A. (1993b). *Survivor therapy: Clinical assessment and intervention workbook*. Denver, CO: Endolor Communications.

Walker, L. E. A. (1996). Assessment of abusive spousal relationships. In F. W. Kaslow (Ed.), *Handbook of relational diagnosis and dysfunctional family patterns* (pp. 338–356). New York, NY: John Wiley & Sons, Inc.

# Chapter 5
# Treating Child Sexual Abuse in Rural Communities

**Leah Genieve Kenyon-George**
*Fielding Graduate University, USA*

## ABSTRACT

*The focus of this chapter will be to discuss the treatment of child sexual abuse in a rural setting. Children in rural communities who have experienced such traumas are entitled to the same access and quality of services available in urban centres. Although the rates of trauma are similar in urban and rural settings, rural centres often lack adequate mental health services for children and families. According to Jones and colleagues (2014), each year in the United States approximately 22% of children between the ages of two and seventeen experience trauma. As we know, the impacts of trauma on the developing brain are significant, as are the negative outcomes on affective, behavioral and cognitive functioning (Cohen, Mannarino, & Deblinger, 2006). Mental health service providers face unique challenges in terms of practicing in rural or remote communities. Multiple barriers exist to practice in these communities, including lack of resources, lack of specialist knowledge, and the training and supervision of professionals, to name a few.*

## INTRODUCTION

Each year in the United States, approximately 22 percent of children between the ages of 2 and 17 experience trauma (Jones et al., 2014). As we know, the impacts of trauma on the developing brain are significant, as are the negative outcomes on affective, behavioral, and cognitive functioning (Cohen, Mannarino, & Deblinger, 2006). Although the rates of trauma are similar in urban and rural settings, rural centres often lack specialized resources and clinicians who can provide specialized treatment. Children in rural communities who have experienced such traumas are entitled to the same access and quality of services as those that are available in urban centres.

Certainly the issue of child sexual abuse is an international one, and international rates of abuse parallel those in the United States and in Canada. One example of this is a 2009 study which occurred as a continuation of Finkelhor's initial 1994 analysis of international prevalence rates (Pereda, Guilera, Forns,

DOI: 10.4018/978-1-5225-0228-9.ch005

& Bomez-Benito, 2009). Pereda and colleagues' study compared the rates of prevalence of child sexual abuse from recent publications to Finkelhor's 1994 findings. The study included thirty eight articles, involving thirty nine studies, all addressing child sexual abuse. Twenty one countries were included across continents and in many ways, the study replicated Finkelhor's results, only twelve years later. Unfortunately, the authors illustrated that the international prevalence of child sexual abuse remained fairly constant, demonstrated a warning that little had changed since the previous decade.

Some interesting findings from Pereda and colleagues' study included that the adults across different countries had developed increased comfort in discussing the topic. Also noteworthy was that the prevalence rate was higher among male children (at sixty percent), as opposed to female children (fifty three percent). The differences in prevalence rates and gender are suspected to be a result of differing methodology from Finkelhorn's study, however Pereda and colleagues suggest that it may be that male participants were more comfortable in reporting. A common factor among the families of the children were that many children came from single parent families, and often with the absence of an adult male (Pereda et al.). It is important to acknowledge some of the internationally-focused research in this area, particularly as it demonstrates parallel themes to North American studies. For the purpose of this chapter, we will focus on treatment within Canada and the United States.

Mental health service providers face unique challenges when practicing in rural or remote communities. Practice in these communities must overcome multiple barriers, including (among others) the lack of resources and specialist knowledge, and the training and supervision of professionals that is required. This chapter will address some of the specific barriers involved in treating child sexual abuse in rural settings, as well as possible strategies for improving treatment service provision to children who have experienced such trauma.

For the purposes of this chapter, it is critical to define child sexual abuse as a form of abuse involving any of the following: sexual molestation, sexual assault, exposure, child pornography, and child prostitution. This chapter will discuss the prevalence of child abuse in rural communities, followed by some of the challenges and barriers these settings present. Following this, the chapter will discuss both broad and more specific cultural components of rural settings, along with some of the most current research on various evidence-based practices for child sexual abuse treatment. The chapter will examine three areas of practice in treating child sexual abuse in rural settings: private or community-based centres, school-based settings, and specialized treatment settings.

## BACKGROUND

The national prevalence of child sexual abuse in the United States is estimated to be 16 percent of men and between 25 and 27 percent of women (Perez-Fuentes et al., 2013). According to the US Department of Health and Human Services (2011), nine percent of Child Protective Services cases are child sexual abuse investigations. These estimates of child sexual abuse are difficult to obtain: many victims and families do not report abuse to the authorities, and child protection agencies can only report the information that they have obtained through victims, witnesses, and professionals. Self-report surveys, sometimes involving parental interviews, are often biased, particularly if a parent was the perpetrator (Menard & Ruback, 2003).

The associated impact of child sexual abuse and psychological disorders, including suicidal ideation and suicide attempts, is high. In a recent national study, 34,000 adult participants were interviewed face to face in a survey conducted in 2004–2005 (Perez-Fuentes et al., 2013). The data indicated that the prevalence of child sexual abuse was just over 10 percent among participants; of these, one quarter (25 percent) were male, while three quarters (75 percent) were female. High correlations of psychopathology and suicide attempts were also demonstrated in the findings.

Urban settings are commonly perceived to have higher rates of crime than rural settings. Despite this perception, researchers have demonstrated (Menard & Ruback, 2003) that factors related to crime (including poverty and unemployment) tend to be higher in rural communities. This context is important in understanding some of the issues that put children at risk of abuse, including poverty and family structure. Drake and Pandey (1996) found that child sexual abuse is more commonly experienced by children from dysfunctional families, as well as those from lower socioeconomic backgrounds. One suspected difference between settings may be that crime is reported less in rural areas compared to urban ones. The tendency to conceal problems, particularly personal problems, tends to be higher in rural regions.

Menard and Ruback (2003) propose that, due to 1) the unique social norms within rural settings, 2) the higher levels of poverty and unemployment, and 3) the use of more informal means of social control, rural regions may in fact experience greater levels of child sexual abuse. In their study, Menard and Ruback did find that, according to their data (which was gathered by the Pennsylvania Children and Youth Services), a higher rate of child sexual abuse occurred within rural communities than within urban communities. The authors put forth the possibility that this may be due to population dispersion in rural communities, along with social interaction that occurs within greater "acquaintance"-type relationships.

Given that child sexual abuse tends to be perpetrated by an acquaintance of the child, this may explain why rural regions demonstrated a slightly higher level of abuse. A second possibility is due to some of the social norms found within rural regions, particularly regarding the tendency to keep personal matters private or secret. The geographic isolation, combined with social norms regarding secrecy, may play a role in higher levels of child sexual abuse. The implications of this research are important, as they demonstrate that this type of offence is in fact greater in rural communities. This further stresses the need for preventative measures in such communities, and for children and families to have access to evidence-based treatment options.

## ISSUES, CONTROVERSIES, AND PROBLEMS

Therapeutic treatment in general faces a number of unique challenges within rural settings. The impact of geography—which is the primary factor—can vary, depending on the proximity of a rural community to its nearest urban centre. Due to privacy-related social norms, families sometimes choose to seek treatment in a nearby community (Menard & Ruback, 2003). It is important to consider that even seemingly short distances can have a large impact on treatment, particularly if a child is taking part in weekly therapy sessions in a neighboring community. Providing or obtaining this transportation can be challenging for parents or guardians, and it requires both financial and time-related resources.

The issue of geography becomes particularly challenging for communities in places such as northern Canada and Alaska. Bubar and Bundy-Fazioli (2011) discuss the general lack of resources available in rural Alaskan communities, which makes the coordination and facilitation of treatment very challenging. Furthermore, weather conditions in these northern communities often makes it difficult for families to obtain access to basic services, let alone mental health services. Due to geographic factors, collaborative, flexible, and creative efforts are needed among community leadership and medical, educational, and mental health service providers to ensure that both preventative and treatment measures are available.

## Confidentiality

Children who receive treatment for sexual abuse within their own communities also face other challenges, such as privacy and confidentiality. Confidentiality in the mental health field can generally pose a challenge for smaller communities. The use of greater levels of professional caution is often necessary due to the dual roles that can take place; the issue of child sexual abuse requires a high level of sensitivity, particularly in environments where dual roles may exist. Although national and provincial/state ethical codes and standards do not differ among professionals who work in these settings, professionals' sensitive navigation within such environments is critical. This is particularly true, for example, when a child or family encounters a mental health provider at the grocery store, or when the child's best friend is a neighbor of the therapist. Multitudes of such scenarios may be experienced within rural communities.

What Anderson (1999) stresses about child sexual abuse and professional boundaries in rural communities is poignant; she discusses the problematic patterns and confusion inherent among incestuous families. These patterns only further demonstrate the need for professionals not to further traumatize clients and their families by setting clear boundaries, communicating clearly, and not participating in secrecy or minimization of any kind. A professional's response to child sexual abuse disclosure or treatment can otherwise demonstrate a parallel process to the patterns that occur within a child's family. Some of the most common systems components of families where child sexual abuse has occurred include patterns of isolation, secrecy, denial, blurred boundaries, and role reversal (Anderson, 1999).

Anderson proposes that when mental health professionals engage in blurred boundaries (such as by associating together socially), this essentially re-creates some of the patterns that occur within families. In order to address these challenges, she suggests the role-modeling of boundaries, clearly defined roles, open direct communication, and confidentiality among professionals. In addition, a clear protocol for such cases can facilitate healthy collaboration among professionals, thus avoiding blurred and dual professional/personal roles.

Service providers in rural communities face the dialectic of aiming to be inclusive, respected community members who will foster a level of trust among residents. On the other hand, being an insider can lead to concerns of being silenced by the larger community (Bubar & Bundy-Fazioli, 2011), which may result in dual role and confidentiality concerns. Being considered an outsider has both advantages and disadvantages, especially when aiming for collaboration. Service providers' careful navigation of the outsider/insider role requires personal awareness and insight.

## Rural Service Providers

Another dilemma that is unique to rural settings relates to obtaining, fostering, and sustaining skilled mental health service providers. Those clinicians who work within rural settings must be comfortable with the independent nature of their roles, as they are often the sole clinical providers in the community. Locating employee candidates who have trauma-informed knowledge and skills may present a challenge within the rural setting. Many rural mental health practitioners are often generalists, and may lack specialized knowledge about the treatment of children, and specifically the treatment of child sexual abuse.

Depending on the setting, it is likely that clinicians in such communities will see some of the more common presenting problems, such as depression, anxiety, and substance abuse; they may also tend to see adults more frequently than they see children. Identifying clinicians who are equipped to support the needs of sexually abused children and adolescents can be difficult: particularly those professionals who can navigate some of the nuances within rural communities.

Another obstacle such professionals face is that they may have less frequent exposure to and experience with cases that involve child sexual abuse. (On the other hand, certain rural communities may exhibit a greater prevalence of such abuse, and the clinician may become more specialized in the area.) As noted earlier, child sexual abuse includes sexual molestation, sexual assault, exposure, child pornography, and child prostitution. The scope is large; because child sexual abuse could range from infant abuse to human trafficking in adolescence, clinicians in rural communities may encounter any range of presentations.

## Supervision and Consultation

The challenge for the rural clinician of obtaining ongoing supervision and consultation is also an important consideration. If it is not possible to consult with nearby colleagues, it is critical that mental health practitioners in rural communities obtain regular and frequent supervision/consultation via telephone- and web-based media. Identifying an individual with specialized training and experience with the treatment of child sexual abuse for consultation—whether in person or via other methods—is good practice.

Depending on the practice setting, because clinicians may not know when they may encounter a child sexual abuse case, it is crucial for them to identify early on in the process a specialist for consultation or supervision. Another consideration for rural practitioners is web-based practice groups, whereby regular and ongoing consultation occurs via platforms such as WebEx or Go-To-Meeting. This reduces the time and resources necessary for travel, and provides regularly scheduled consultation times for several practitioners.

## Staying Current

Rural clinicians can also prepare themselves by staying up to date with the most current research in the area of child sexual abuse. Whether this is through division memberships or journal subscriptions, it is important for rural practitioners to be aware of the current literature on child maltreatment. It is also critical for rural practitioners to be aware of the signs of child sexual abuse, and the state/provincial laws regarding the reporting of such abuse.

Due to the growing use of online platforms, child sexual exploitation is beginning to grow in social media via websites such as Facebook, Kijiji, and MSN. Furthermore, dating websites such as Plenty of Fish and Lava Life are often used to prey on adolescents; such environments can enable grooming, abuse, and exploitation. The majority of the youth treated by this author became involved with (or further involved in) sexual exploitation through the use of social media. For some young people, their involvement with sexual exploitation begins through a social media site before moving on to dating or pornographic websites. Initial contact and grooming can progress through these venues, thus resulting in face to face contact. Some youth described their experiences with their perpetrators; their abusers drove to the youths' rural communities and became involved in sexual abuse and exploitation, even at the adolescents' homes.

An awareness of the dangers of online environments is necessary for any rural practitioners who provide treatment to children and adolescents. The notion that rural communities are inherently safe is false in many regards; with the availability and exposure inherent in online media, perpetrators can enter a child's world through a computer, tablet, or phone—even an iPod. In order to prevent and treat child sexual abuse, clinicians who work in rural communities must have an understanding of the context of web-based interactions.

## SOLUTIONS AND RECOMMENDATIONS

Despite these possible challenges, practice within rural communities can have unexpected advantages, and can prove to be beneficial for children and families who are affected by child sexual abuse. One such advantage is that smaller communities can sometimes provide reduced levels of stress for families. The sense of community can be both an advantage and a disadvantage; while it provides support to children and families, the sense of community also means there is less anonymity.

One perhaps less considered advantage is the opportunity for rural treatment centres to host opportunities for alternative therapeutic options, specifically equine-assisted therapy or other animal-assisted therapy programs. In addition, outdoor-based, experiential opportunities for treatment programs tend to be located near rural centres. While it is important to consider some of the challenges of treating child sexual abuse within rural communities, it is also necessary to consider some of the other perspectives of receiving alternative treatment in this type of environment.

### Understanding the Rural Setting

Mental health providers who work in rural communities must be able to practice independently within their clinical roles while also working closely with the authorities. Calvert and Munsie-Benson (1999) conducted a survey in a rural community in Oregon, in which they surveyed 246 participants about general knowledge and attitudes about child sexual abuse. Their findings suggested that the respondents were most likely to report child sexual abuse to a physician or the police, which suggests that rural mental health practitioners must be skilled in collaboration with other large systems. Nevertheless, some rural northern communities do not have a police presence, whether state troopers or Royal Canadian Mounted Police. Some tribal communities have public safety officers; they are unarmed and lack the training received by other officials (Bubar & Bundy-Fazioli, 2011). Having a specific understanding of these systems is beneficial for working with all clients in these communities, but particularly for sensitive cases such as those that involve child sexual abuse.

Because rural communities often value relationships, clinicians need to build a rapport with rural police, physicians, and child welfare/emergency services. Interdisciplinary teams that provide child advocacy can be effective in both treating and preventing child sexual abuse. The role of physicians is particularly important due to the high frequency of reporting to physicians/pediatricians (Finkel, 2012). In addition to the diagnosis, treatment, and resourcing related to child sexual abuse, physicians can also have an impact on preventative measures by educating children about boundaries, appropriate touch, and personal privacy. Again, this illustrates the importance of both the "village" in rural communities and the collaborative approach.

In their study, Sprang and colleagues (G. Sprang et al., 2013) discuss the common reluctance in rural communities to seek help from professional sources such as clinicians and medical professionals. Among the authors' suggestions are that treatment efforts should be targeted at locations where these children and families tend to feel comfortable, and that identifying key, trusted individuals in the community (local leaders or professionals) who can assist with the screening or initial introduction to treatment can be beneficial. For example, in a First Nations community, this may involve enlisting some of the community elders to promote and encourage the benefits of treatment.

In addition to having knowledge about the cultural groups within a community, mental health service providers can also benefit from gaining a relevant understanding of the community's history and main industries. Gaining insights into a community's traditions, celebrations, stressors, and challenges gives providers a common ground when working with families who may well be apprehensive of sharing their 'secrets' with a clinician. Knowledge of the community's main facilities and the locations of important clubs or groups (as well as core influential subgroups such as faith-based influences) is necessary to both understand and provide treatment. While therapists may provide Cognitive Behavioral Therapy (CBT) to address the trauma, they may also recommend other therapeutic and healthy activities, such as involving other supports in a child's life (e.g. his or her Sunday school teacher, if appropriate) or encouraging the child to take part in spiritual or physical activity at a local community centre.

## Cultural Competence

Having an awareness of a rural region's cultural groups is paramount. This is critical in cases where the clinician also belongs to a community's largest cultural group, as well as when the cultural group is different from his or her own. Mental health clinicians in rural regions can prepare themselves by developing knowledge about the unique experiences of cultural groups specific to those regions. It is important to remain aware that some rural communities are comprised of multiple cultural groups. If a clinician is working with a First Nations community, for example, the specific cultural distinctions unique to the tribe and the tribe's location are both important. In Canada, working with First Nations populations requires a sound understanding of the multigenerational impact of the residential school system, and the Sixties Scoop (Sinclair, 2007) during which aboriginal children were "scooped" from their homes and placed, most often against their will, in institutional care. Without knowledge of the multi-generational impact of residential schools, clinicians may struggle to understand the complexities of child sexual abuse within this cultural backdrop.

Bubar and Bundy-Fazioli (2011) conducted an exploratory study of some of the beliefs about child sexual abuse, socioeconomic status, culture, and race among Native and non-Native Alaskans within a rural community. The authors included fifteen participants, including both Native and non-Native multidisciplinary professionals who were involved in law enforcement; mental health, medical, social service, and victim services; and the Indian child welfare professions. The authors found that three themes were predominant: the reporting of child sexual abuse, cultural dissonance, and systemic challenges. This speaks to the multifaceted nature of child sexual abuse within these isolated and rural settings.

The question about whose perspective is valued, "insiders" or "outsiders" is an interesting one, and as Bubar & Bundy-Fazioli discuss, advantages and disadvantages exist for both roles. Furthermore, what constitutes a "long term resident", is this a one year, five year or multi-generational residence in the region? One solution that the authors suggest is an open dialogue about the "insider"/ "outsider" concept, which is likely to vary in each rural community. Given the likelihood of outsiders to be unaware of their lack of power in an area, this open communication would provide more information and awareness to this group. Generally, it would increase intercommunity and intergovernmental collaboration in child sexual abuse cases.

## Multigenerational Trauma

Multigenerational trauma is a topic of current research in several communities. When parenting stress is elevated, one possibility can be that the parent is suffering from traumatic exposure or post-traumatic stress disorder (PTSD). Both family therapy and individualized therapy for the caregiver can be effective in intervening before the next generation is affected (G. Sprang et al., 2013). Screening for parenting stress is generally recommended, both to detect elevated parenting stress (which may have an impact on a parent's ability to prevent child sexual abuse) and also to reduce the chance that trauma may "cascade" to the younger generation.

Sprang and colleagues recommend a number of specialized interventions to reduce and prevent multigenerational trauma (G. Sprang et al., 2013). Some examples of such interventions include parent training programs and programs aimed to address stress management for caregivers; safety skills training for children may also help to prevent abuse within these vulnerable families. Parenting stress is already high in these communities, and if child sexual abuse is not detected or treated, the multigenerational cycle will most likely continue.

## Preventative Measures

Although the focus of this chapter is primarily on treatment interventions for children who have already been sexually abused, it is also necessary to consider some of the preventative measures that have been found to be effective in this area. Some examples of possible preventative measures include public service announcements, media campaigns, educational workshops, online and print flyers and brochures, self-report surveys, and school- or health centre–based presentations. The goal of such preventative approaches is typically to increase public knowledge about the issue of child sexual abuse.

Self-Brown, Rheingold, Campbell, and de Arellano (2008) suggest that the most effective prevention methods are those that include multimodal approaches and that directly target the behaviors and beliefs of prospective offenders. The authors conducted a quantitative self-report survey that examined participants' knowledge gain, comfort levels, and behavioral changes after responding to a media campaign about child sexual abuse. The findings suggested that across ethnic groups, those who took part in the survey demonstrated increased knowledge of and comfort in discussing the topic; thus, public knowledge about child sexual abuse also increased.

A national Canadian example of a preventative organization is the Little Warriors, whose aim is to promote awareness, prevention, and treatment of child sexual abuse (www.littlewarriors.ca/prevention). The program offers a workshop called Prevent It!, which is directed at educating adults on how to prevent and stop child sexual abuse. The three-hour workshop is available at no cost throughout Canada, and will soon be available in an online format. Support resources and treatment options are also available through the organization.

## Evidence-Based Treatments for Children Affected by Trauma

With the APA's emphasis on evidence-based practice in psychology (EBPP), the best available research, along with clinical observations of effective strategies for the child and adolescent population will be examined (Levant, 2005). The American Psychiatric Association's (2004) practice guidelines advocate the implementation of CBT for the treatment of PTSD; specifically the use of cognitive behavior therapy and exposure therapy. Similarly, the National Child Traumatic Stress Network provides a comprehensive list of forty three empirically supported treatments to address child trauma. These treatments range from the Attachment, to Self-Regulation and Competence (ARC) model, to Child-Parent Psychotherapy (CPP), and Psychological First Aid. The inclusive guide provides information about the target population, treatment modality as well as culture-specific fact sheets, and can be found at: www.nctsnet.org/resources/topics/treatments-that-work/promising-practices.

Before considering the unique cultural and regional factors related to a rural setting, it is important to consider some of the general empirical evidence that has been found on the treatment of child trauma and maltreatment. Multiple impacts can occur from trauma in general, many of which are consistent with childhood sexual trauma. For example, some of the related psychopathologies include PTSD, anxiety, suicidal ideation, substance abuse, aggressive or violent behavior, and depression. Cognitive behavior therapy (CBT), with an abuse-focused component, is considered to be an empirically supported treatment for both children and adolescents who have experienced child sexual abuse.

CBT has been demonstrated to be effective for children as young as 3 years old, and has been especially effective when implemented early on, particularly during Acute Stress Disorder, and prior to a child developing PTSD (Drury & Henry). The other advantage of CBT is that it can be adapted to be age-appropriate for younger clients, or for those clients with cognitive or processing speed challenges. One consideration, particularly in rural regions where Fetal Alcohol Spectrum Disorder may be prevalent, is to modify CBT treatment to be provided in a concrete manner. The Substance Abuse Mental Health Service Administration (SAMHSA) Fetal Alcohol Spectrum Disorders (FASD) Centre for Excellence offers a no cost, online training program for mental health service providers. *FASD, The Course* consists of seven modules, which can be completed at the participant's pace, and has a central module which explores diagnosis and treatment options (www.fasdcenter.samhsa.gov/educationTraining/courses). For professionals working who encounter clients who may be affected by FASD, becoming more familiar with specialized treatment interventions is critical.

In a recent systematic review, Leenarts, Diehle, Doreleijers, Jansma, and Lindauer (2013) reviewed the evidence-based treatments for child trauma and trauma-related disorders. They examined twenty-six randomized controlled clinical trials, as well as seven non-randomized clinical trials, between 2000 and 2012; both maltreated and sexually abused children were included in this sample. The psychotherapeutic treatments that the authors reviewed included several trauma-specific treatments, including Eye Movement Desensitization and Reprocessing (EMDR); various forms of CBT, including Trauma-focused Cognitive Behavioral Therapy (TF-CBT); various arts-based therapies; Child–Parent Psychotherapy; and Psycho-educational / teaching-based approaches. The authors also reviewed other (non-PTSD-based) therapies, including imagery rehearsal therapy, "CBT, and group therapy.

The findings of this systematic review demonstrated that TF-CBT was the best-supported treatment of children exposed to trauma. The authors also suggest, however, that given the increasing observance of complex trauma, a "phase-oriented" approach should also be implemented. This study examined child maltreatment and trauma, as well as related pathology, and thus it should be noted that it did not exclusively emphasize child sexual abuse; still, the phase-oriented approach does present a valuable treatment option that has demonstrated its efficacy.

Although there are numerous evidence-based treatments for treating child trauma (Leenarts et al., 2013), many of these interventions are inaccessible in rural communities (Paul, Gray, Elhai, Massad, & Stamm, 2006). Several evidence-based therapies such as TF-CBT can be applied to the rural setting, however, due to the financial feasibility of such treatments and the online format that is available to practitioners. As was discussed earlier in this chapter, TF-CBT has been demonstrated to be highly effective for treating child sexual abuse. Other therapies such as EMDR may be more difficult to provide via online methods, although researchers are working to find solutions to this problem. Despite this, recently EMDR iPhone "Aps" have been emerging for consumers to use independently. It is unknown at this time if research has been conducted on these types of applications.

The appropriateness of the TF-CBT format within rural environments is due to its availability as a free, web-based learning course for therapists who want to obtain training in the method. The online module includes nine categories:

1. Psychoeducation,
2. Stress management,
3. Affect expression and modulation,
4. Cognitive coping,
5. The creation of the trauma narrative,
6. Cognitive processing,
7. Behavior management training,
8. Parent–child sessions, and
9. Evaluation (National Child Traumatic Stress Network, 2015).

The training is provided through a conglomeration of several organizations, including the National Child Traumatic Stress Network.

A relevant broad clinical concern and one worth mentioning about the treatment of child sexual abuse is the extent to which community-based clinicians implement evidence-based practices (EBPS). Czincz & Romano (2013) discuss the issue of the lack of training in EBPS for clinicians treating children for sexual abuse. In their study, located in Ontario, Canada, two hundred and thirty one psychologists completed a self-report questionnaire about their treatment strategies, attitudes toward EBPS, training experience, and information about the community population in which they work. The psychologists were not students; in fact, were registered psychologists with the College of Psychologists of Ontario.

The authors discovered that in total, only five percent of the psychologists included in the study had received specific training in trauma-focused CBT. Alternatively, seventy eight percent of these clinicians indicated that they had never received specialized training in the area of specific treatment approaches to child sexual abuse (Czincz & Romano, 2013). Needless to say, this study demonstrates issues with, as they describe 'real world' community practice, and ethical concerns around psychologists working with this population with neither training nor supervision. Other than in community counselling settings, it is not clear which type of region that the psychologists were practicing in. Nonetheless, the implications of these findings are still relevant to rural practitioners.

## Alternative Treatment Options

A great deal of controversy surrounds the approach of Eye Movement Desensitization and Reduction (EMDR), developed by Dr. Francine Shapiro. The treatment combines aspects of CBT with mindfulness and integrated body approaches, and it is applied using a specific protocol to address particular targets. Bilateral stimulation is a key component, often occurring in the form of tracking using finger movements by the therapist. Visual imagery and relaxation techniques are also incorporated into the structured protocol. While many studies illustrate positive client outcomes after EMDR treatment, some of the specific components are yet to be evaluated, including the specific effects of bilateral stimulation (Sharpless & Barber). Some debate has led to inquiries about the possible mechanism of change, in fact, being that of exposure.

Bradley and colleagues' (2005) meta-analysis demonstrated the efficacy of EMDR in treating patients with PTSD, as approximately fifty percent of patients within the studies experienced an improvement. Kavakci, Dogan and Kugu (2010) describe some of the hypothesized neurological models of EMDR, such as possible changes to the anterior cingulate cortex, an inhibition model, changes to the limbic system and so forth (p. 202). Bergman (2010) has proposed that bilateral stimulation assists in the communication between the hemispheres, and released his findings from decades of research, which involved neuroimaging studies. These studies illustrated improvements in emotional regulation, memory, concentration, and a reduction in disturbing thoughts/ memories among patients who received EMDR.

Research with children and this form of treatment (implementing a modified therapeutic protocol) also appear to be promising, based on a significant number of studies (Fleming, 2012). Although promising, further research is needed for the use of EMDR with children, and about its mechanisms of change. One advantage of this form of therapy with children is that it can be flexibly integrated with a cognitive behavioral approach. Some clinicians use EMDR pulsars, placed on a child's lap or in their socks, while engaging in CBT or alternative forms of therapy. Future research regarding EMDR and iPOD "Aps" would also be helpful, particularly as this application would potentially be effective for adolescent clients.

## Psychopharmacology

In conjunction with a physician or psychiatrist, psychopharmacology can be helpful in treating symptoms related to PTSD, such as depression, and anxiety. As Drury and Henry (2012) discuss, there is insufficient evidence to support psychopharmacology as a first line of treatment intervention for child sexual abuse. Case studies and anecdotal evidence from psychiatrists suggest that psychopharmacological options can be helpful, perhaps to reduce distress enough to tolerate other forms of cognitive behavioral treatment. Further research is needed both comparing and combining Cognitive Behavioral Therapies and psychopharmacology. For practitioners in rural regions, it is important recognize the efficacy of this option for some children and adolescents, perhaps with more severe symptomatology. Given the challenges of treating PTSD among developing children with psychopharmacological interventions, close collaboration with the child's physician is recommended, many of which provide tele-health options in rural communities.

Alternative evidence-based therapies relevant to treating child-sexual abuse include other types of cognitive-behavioral therapies, though it is important not to overlook play and arts-based interventions, which can be used on their own or in conjunction with traditional CBT approaches. These types of narrative-influenced approaches can allow children to address child sexual abuse less directly, and with less dialogue about the subject matter. Furthermore, sand tray and play therapy options are appropriate for younger children, and those who prefer a narrative approach such as First Nations Children (Quinn, 2007). Lewis and Goodyear (2011) provide a thoughtful overview of sand tray interventions with children who have experienced sexual abuse. For rural psychologists commuting to rural regions to provide treatment, it is helpful to create mobile sand tray and expressive-arts kits, which can be easily transported, but also contain the central materials required for treatment. Other creative ideas are to create "coping kits" with children, which consist of selecting specific soothing objects which they can then use outside of the therapy session.

Therapeutic stories can also be beneficial for children and their families affected by child sexual abuse. One seminal book of stories is the compilation by Nancy Davis, PhD, whose most recent collection of therapeutic stories includes over one hundred stories for young children ranging to older adolescents, and even adults. Each story is identified with the appropriate age group intended, as well as the relevant issue and themes, such as PTSD, and grief and loss (Davis, 1996). Many of these interventions can also be helpful when working from a family-systems perspective, inviting (non-offending) parents/ guardians to be involved in sessions.

It is important to acknowledge some of the alternative treatment approaches to working with children living in different rural regions, particularly those treatments associated with the child's culture. For example, in a First Nations community, smudging and sweat lodge experiences are important healing rituals, as is involving elders in a child's treatment (Wilson, 2003). Clinicians working in these communities can support a child by assisting in making connections to their community and culture, and for some, in becoming competent in facilitating a smudge. Oftentimes, less formalized support groups for sexual abuse can be beneficial for adolescents. Although not necessarily facilitated by a psychologist, these options can still be beneficial, particularly as they create connection and normalize some of the associated challenges. By joining as an ally with elders and by supporting alternative, traditional community rituals, rural psychologists can broaden a client's opportunities for recovery from child sexual abuse.

## Practice in a Rural Community Setting

The first rural setting that will be discussed is the community or private practice setting. These settings may be located in a private office, or attached to a community location such as a hospital or community centre. Some practitioners commute from other communities or larger centres to provide coverage to rural communities on an "as needed" basis. If the clinician is commuting, again it can be helpful to have portable play therapies (such as arts-based or sand tray–based therapies) as well as portable files containing worksheets, handouts, and assessments tools.

A growing option in the mental health field is the application of technology in providing mental health services. Although the medical and psychiatric fields have had this in place for several years in many communities, it is a growing area in psychology; this has both practical and ethical considerations, particularly when working with children. Some of the current strategies employed in rural communities include tele-health direct service delivery by service providers, and telephone- or web-based training, supervision, and workshops for rural-based mental health professionals. The field of medicine is also implementing telemedicine service provision for child sexual abuse victims in rural communities, and has been found to be an effective strategy (Miyamoto et al., 2014).

Like other mental health service providers, clinicians in rural private or community settings can benefit from the use of "telemental" health programs. This is a current area of interest in the field of mental health that seeks to understand how the application of various technologies can benefit the provision of services. A recent study by Jones and colleagues (2014) discusses the implementation of a telemental health program within an already-established community outreach program. The authors identify some of the barriers to service access for trauma-exposed children and families, including reduced anonymity; few after-hours services, evidence-based treatments, and specialty clinics; and greater demands for travel, time away from work, and childcare (Jones et al., 2014).

Some of the major components of implementing such programs that the authors discuss include establishing and using community partnerships; for example, this can include connecting with other rural service providers in order to share in the provision of after-hours services. The authors recommend that the equipment for the remote service should be established within community organizations such as child advocacy centres, community centres, or schools. The financial costs can be reduced by utilizing already-existing equipment, if available. Jones et al. also discuss several types of videoconferencing software that are able to fulfill respective national privacy regulations, such as the Health Insurance Portability and Accountability Act (HIPPA) in the United States or the Personal Information Protection and Electronic Documents Act (PIPEDA) in Canada. The authors also consider additional practical considerations for telemental health programs, such as creating physical setups that are similar to therapy rooms, and finding the best ways to conduct clinic administration. In general, the authors suggest the inclusion of a liaison who can facilitate technical components and also assist with client scheduling and administration.

Jones and colleagues discuss at length the process of providing therapy via an online platform, which is particularly useful information for clinicians who work with youth. The authors in particular recommend TF-CBT, given its application to children aged 3–17. Fidelity can be maintained through this type of implementation, though the authors do acknowledge that some modifications will need to be made; for example, a family's access to informational handouts and worksheets will be necessary. While some aspects of this practice are no different than working with children and families in person, it is necessary to pay attention to a few of these minor differences.

## Practice in a Rural Educational Setting

The school setting is often where child sexual abuse is initially disclosed, and where mental health clinicians affiliated with academic settings can have an enormous and immediate impact. According to the US Department of Health and Human Services' Administration on Children, Youth and Families (2010), approximately 16 percent of all reported child maltreatment cases are reported to teachers. Along with physicians, teachers are among the professional groups most likely to report child maltreatment like child sexual abuse.

Similarly, the Public Health Agency of Canada (2010) reports that teachers and other school staff account for 24 percent of all child maltreatment reports, making this the single largest group to whom reports are initially made. Considering the rural community's role—and teachers' or other school personnel's roles—in a child's life, it is understandable why the educational setting is paramount. For this reason, school counsellors and teachers can collaborate effectively to intervene, since in many cases it is the teacher who first brings up concerns about a student. Two recent in-school efforts to address child sexual abuse have taken place in rural educational settings (Morsette et al., 2009; Hansel et al., 2010); the studies demonstrated how two unique efforts were made to assist underserviced children in the environment that was most familiar to them.

Service providers who work in rural educational settings often encounter many of the same issues as those who work in urban areas. One of the key differences, however, is the isolation that school counsellors can often experience when working in rural communities. By employing some of the abovementioned strategies (such as by creating consultation groups), rural school counsellors can broaden their consultation networks. Furthermore, because it is not uncommon for children who live in one community to attend a school in another, rural school counsellors must delicately balance their consultation with standards of confidentiality.

Some schools, particularly in communities where mutigenerational trauma has occurred, provide additional supports within the school program. This may include family support workers or groups that are provided to teach cognitive and behavioral skills. One example of a cognitive behavioral intervention in a school setting is a pilot of the CBITS (Cognitive Behavioral Intervention for Trauma in Schools) program, which took place within an American Indian school (Morsette et al., 2009; National Child Traumatic Stress Network). CBITS is a manualized cognitive behavioral program aimed at reducing trauma systems among students. Although it was initially implemented in urban schools with diverse cultural groups, with some modification, the protocol has also proven to be promising for applications in rural communities with diverse cultural groups.

The group, which was comprised of youth living on the reservation who presented with signs of PTSD, took place over ten weeks. The findings indicated that 75 percent of the youth who completed the program had a decrease in PTSD symptoms and depression. Several cultural modifications were made to include prayers from the specific American Indian tribe. Among the challenges that Morsette and colleagues identified was obtaining parental consents for students to participate in the groups; another was the attrition rate, although the authors wondered if perhaps providing make-up sessions in the future could assist with this particular barrier. The advantages of these types of school-based interventions are their relative cost-effectiveness and their brief duration (ten weeks). Because youths already spend the majority of their time at school, it becomes more feasible for families to take part in them if these types of programs can be employed in an educational setting.

Another example of a rural school-based trauma treatment program was demonstrated in Louisiana (2010) by Hansel and colleagues. The authors evaluated a rural school-based trauma treatment program among 115 student participants. They implemented a three-tiered approach, including relationship building, trauma training, and related trauma services; the authors found that the program did reduce the symptoms of trauma among participants. While this is another example of the advantage of offering treatment in school settings, the authors do acknowledge several challenges with this venue. One challenge, even for rural communities, can be overcrowding in schools, which can lead to a lack of appropriate and available space for ensuring confidentiality. The timing of such groups is also a consideration, particularly if youth are required to return to a class after a difficult session. Despite these challenges, the evidence suggests that treating child trauma can be effective in rural schools.

## Practice in a Rural Treatment Setting

The third section of this chapter concerns the rural treatment of child sexual abuse in a specialized treatment setting. Because less research has been conducted on these settings, the author will draw from personal experiences in this type of environment. Although these types of programs typically involve adolescents, programs of this type may include children in a residential / group home setting.

One such example of a rural treatment program for child sexual abuse is the Be Brave Ranch in Alberta, Canada. A program facilitated by the aforementioned Little Warriors program, the ranch offers an evidence-based treatment program for children ages 8–12. This camp-like program begins with a month-long residential stay that involves multiple treatment approaches, including TF-CBT, art and play therapies, EMDR, recreational activities, and peer support. Following this residential stay, the clients take part in three additional two-week-long stays to continue with their therapy. In total, the program is one year long and consists of over two hundred hours of therapy. A family-centred approach also allows for ongoing clinical support to be available to parents and guardians, who can stay overnight at the ranch during their children's treatment. (www.bebraveranch.littlewarriors.ca/)

Another example is Grimmon House Residential Treatment Program, which aims to create safety by removing adolescent clients from urban environments and the associated risks often found there, including sexual perpetrators, drugs, and alcohol. (http://www.boysandgirlsclubsofcalgary.ca/programs/community-based-care-supports/grimmon-house). The geographic removal, combined with limited and supervised access to social media, often effectively halts all contact with peers and perpetrators, thus eliminating the chance for further traumatization. This move also provides the clients with an opportunity to experience a safe place (often for the first time), and exposes them to positive adult mentors and influences. The holistic program, located in a rural community of Alberta, provides youth with residential treatment, where they can remain for several months; it is aimed at assisting female youth who have experienced (or are considered at risk of) sexual exploitation. As discussed previously, sexual exploitation is a form of child abuse, which, according to the Protection of Sexually Exploited Children's Act of Alberta, involves abuse on all of the following levels: severe physical, emotional, and psychological abuse; sexual mistreatment; and lack of care that results in damage to the child (Government of Alberta, 2010). The majority of clients have a history of child sexual abuse prior to being considered at risk of sexual exploitation.

Given the co-morbidity between sexual abuse and addictions (Briere & Runtz, 1987) Grimmon House offers both a full-time therapist and an addictions counsellor, in addition to a full residential staff team of case managers and support workers. The intake process is arranged so that youth can arrive as soon as possible, as many arrive directly from crisis and emergency situations. Because it is not uncommon for youth to arrive after being apprehended from a prostitution or pornography "trick pad," the need for the program to respond immediately is thus essential. Given the level of risk experienced by many of these adolescents, they require significant medical, emotional, and legal support; the transition to a rural community can provide physical and emotional safety that would not otherwise be available at urban treatment centres.

On the other hand, the transition of these adolescents from an urban to a rural setting may remove them from their support systems and families. The geographic location of Grimmon House can make family therapy challenging, let alone family visits. Maintaining or building the client's significant relationships therefore requires creative planning and quite often the use of telephone-based and various online means of communication. Although the youth are temporarily removed from a high-risk urban environment, they must later work to prepare to leave the rural community and its comforts.

Another unique challenge to this type of residential treatment setting is that despite the community's knowledge and overall support of the program, youth can be exposed to discrimination through name calling and subtle forms of judgement from some community members. For this reason, building relationships within the community is essential for reducing the stigma about sexual exploitation and abuse. This can occur by educating key community centres and leaders about the program and its goals. Furthermore, arranging long-term relationships with medical clinics, as well as volunteer or employment sites for the youth is beneficial. Grimmon House has been successful in part due to its location in a rural location.

## FUTURE RESEARCH DIRECTIONS

Many of the future research directions have been discussed throughout the chapter. Mainly, continued research examining the treatment efficacy of treatments for children who have experienced child sexual abuse are necessary. This can be challenging in part due to stigma and reporting obstacles. More specifically, research in treating child sexual abuse in rural communities is necessary, and was challenging to obtain, even for the purpose of this chapter. Ideally, having research specific to key geographic and cultural regions would assist rural mental health providers in adopting specialized-approaches within their own communities.

Another suggested area of research is that of programs which provide mobile assessment and treatment in rural communities with mental health providers communing to these areas. This is perhaps a cost-effective approach, which would allow for multiple regions to receive treatment, as opposed to having one therapist designated to each location. Furthermore, it would enable clinicians with specialized training and experience in child sexual abuse the mobility to provide service to remote areas. Finally, given the quickly developing field of web-based psychotherapeutic options such as iPhone "Aps" and online counselling, this is a critical area to be examined, particularly given its potential benefits for rural children and families. Although many ethical and best practice concerns arise, these options offer unique possibilities which traditional therapy may not provide in a rural setting.

## CONCLUSION

The identification and treatment of child sexual abuse requires sensitivity, experience, knowledge, and skill. It also requires that clinicians are able to manage relationships in a manner that is appropriate, respectful, and therapeutic to the child and his or her family. Whether or not they are members of the community, rural mental health providers must be aware of their own role in the community, and how this may ultimately affect their practice. Finding creative means to provide service—such as through the use of telemental health services or having portable therapeutic tools—is beneficial in this regard.

Furthermore, it is crucial to develop knowledge about communities' main industries, cultural groups, and norms. It is also vital to understand some of the larger stressors on families and the practical challenges of weather or transportation, and to devise creative means for providing service: perhaps through clinicians who can commute or provide in-home services. Children in rural communities who have experienced such traumas are entitled to the same access and quality of services that are available in urban centres.

Among the therapies discussed within this chapter, certainly evidence-based approaches are recommended, given the existing literature and demonstrated efficacy to date. Having said that, it is the opinion of this author that given what we know about psychotherapy and the common factors, we must not discard the value of relationship, particularly when treating a vulnerable population for a sensitive issue such as sexual abuse (Duncan, Hubble & Miller, 2010). In addition to this, it is necessary for clinicians to use their clinical judgement when practicing within their own geographic region. Their knowledge of the region's industries, culture and language will help guide their practice and treatment approach.

Therefore, the best form of therapy provided to children and families in rural communities is that which integrates EBPPs with creative and integrative and relational- approaches. This method, involving such things as arts-based, sand tray, cultural components, along with aspects of CBT or EMDR can perhaps dialectically meet the needs of these children. Due to the value of relationships within rural communities, it is critical that this be at the forefront of any intervention. It is this author's hope that this chapter will benefit service providers who participate in the privileged and vital clinical work of treating traumatized children in their communities.

## REFERENCES

American Psychiatric Association. (2004). Practice guidelines for the treatment of patients with acute stress disorder and posttraumatic stress disorder. *The American Journal of Psychiatry*, 16.

Anderson, D. M. (2008). Sexual abuse, professional boundaries, and the rural world. *Journal of Child Sexual Abuse*, *8*(3), 85–93. doi:10.1300/J070v08n03_05

Bergman, U. (2010). Neurobiological mechanisms of action: A survey of 20 years of searching. *Journal of EMDR Practice and Research*, *4*(1), 22–42. doi:10.1891/1933-3196.4.1.22

Bolen, R., & Scannpieco, M. (1999). Prevalence of child sexual abuse: A corrective meta-analysis. *The Social Service Review*, *73*(3), 281–313. doi:10.1086/514425

Boys and Girls Clubs of Calgary. (2015). *Grimmon House*. Retrieved December 14, 2015, http://www.boysandgirlsclubsofcalgary.ca/programs/community-based-care-supports/grimmon-house

Bradley, R., Greene, J., Russ, E., Dutral, L., & Westen, D. (2005). A multi-dimensional metaanalysis of psychotherapy for PTSD. *The American Journal of Psychiatry*, *16*(2), 214–227. doi:10.1176/appi.ajp.162.2.214 PMID:15677582

Briere, J., & Runtz, M. (1987). Post sexual abuse trauma: Data and implications for clinical practice. *Journal of Interpersonal Violence*, *2*(4), 367–379. doi:10.1177/088626058700200403

Bubar, R., & Bundy-Fazioli, K. (2011). Unpacking race, culture and class in rural Alaska: Native and non-Native multidisciplinary professionals' perceptions of child sexual abuse. *Journal of Ethnic & Cultural Diversity in Social Work*, *20*(1), 1–19. doi:10.1080/15313204.2011.545941

Calvert, J. F. Jr, & Munsie-Benson, M. (1999). Public opinion and knowledge about child sexual abuse in a rural community. *Child Abuse & Neglect*, *23*(7), 671–682. doi:10.1016/S0145-2134(99)00038-1 PMID:10442832

Cohen, J. A., Deblinger, E., Mannarino, A. P., & Deblinger, E. (2006). *Treating trauma and traumatic grief in children and adolescents*. New York: Guilford Press.

Czincz, J., & Romano, E. (2013). Childhood sexual abuse: Community-based treatment practices and predictors of use of evidence-based practices. *Child and Adolescent Mental Health*, *18*(4), 240–246.

Davis, N. (1996). Once upon a time: Therapeutic stories that teach and heal. Burke, VA: Nancy Davis.

Drake, B., & Pandey, S. (1996). Understanding the relationship between neighborhood poverty and specific types of child maltreatment. *Child Abuse & Neglect*, *20*(11), 1003–1018. doi:10.1016/0145-2134(96)00091-9 PMID:8958452

Drury, S. S., & Henry, C. (2012). Evidence-based treatment of PTSD in children and adolescents: Where does psychopharmacology fit? *Child and Adolescent Psychopharmacology News*, *17*(3), 1–9. doi:10.1521/capn.2012.17.3.1

Duncan, B., Hubble, M., & Miller, S. (Eds.). (2010). *The heart and soul of change: Delivering what works in therapy* (2nd ed.). Washington, DC: American Psychological Association. doi:10.1037/12075-000

Finkel, M. (2012). Children's disclosures of child sexual abuse. *Pediatric Annals*, *41*(12), 1–6. doi:10.3928/00904481-20121126-10 PMID:23205659

Finkelhor, D. (1994). The international epidemiology of child sexual abuse. *Child Abuse & Neglect*, *18*(5), 409–417. doi:10.1016/0145-2134(94)90026-4 PMID:8032971

Fleming, J. (2012). The effectiveness of eye movement desensitization and reprocessing in the treatment of traumatized children and youth. *Journal of EMDR Practice and Research*, *6*(1), 16–26. doi:10.1891/1933-3196.6.1.16

Goodyear-Brown, P. (Ed.). (2011). *Handbook of child sexual abuse: Identification, assessment, and treatment*. Hoboken, NJ: John Wiley & Sons. doi:10.1002/9781118094822

Government of Alberta. (2010). *Protection of sexually exploited children and youth*. Edmonton: The Crown in Right of the Government of Alberta.

Hansel, T. C., Osofsky, H. J., Osofsky, J. D., Costa, R. N., Kronenberg, M. E., & Selby, M. L. (2010). Attention to process and clinical outcomes of implementing a rural school-based trauma treatment program. *Journal of Traumatic Stress*, *23*(6), 708–715. doi:10.1002/jts.20595 PMID:21171131

Jones, A. M., Shealy, K. M., Reid-Quinones, K., Moreland, A. D., Davidson, T. M., Lopez, C. M., & de Arellano, M. A. et al. (2014). Guidelines for establishing a telemental health program to provide evidence-based therapy for trauma- exposed children and families. *Psychological Services*, *11*(4), 398–409. doi:10.1037/a0034963 PMID:24320994

Kaduson, H. G., & Schaefer, C. E. (Eds.). (2006). *Short-term play therapy for children*. New York: Guilford Press.

Leenarts, L. E. W., Diehle, J., Doreleijers, T. A. H., Jansma, E. P., & Lindauer, R. J. L. (2013). Evidence-based treatments for children with trauma-related psychopathology as a result of childhood maltreatment: A systematic review. *European Child & Adolescent Psychiatry*, *22*(5), 269–283. doi:10.1007/s00787-012-0367-5 PMID:23266844

Levant, R. F. (Ed.). (2005). Report of the 2005 presidential task force on evidence- based practice. American Psychological Association.

Little Warriors. (2015). *The Little Warriors Be Brave Ranch.* Retrieved November 5, 2015, from http://littlewarriors.ca/

Little Warriors. (2015). *Helping prevent children from child sexual abuse.* Retrieved November 5, 2015, from http://littlewarriors.ca/

Menard, K. S., & Ruback, R. B. (2003). Prevalence and processing of child sexual abuse: A multi-data-set analysis of urban and rural counties. *Law and Human Behavior*, *27*(4), 385–402. doi:10.1023/A:1024084916626 PMID:12916227

Miyamoto, S., Dharmar, M., Boyle, C., Yang, N. H., MacLeod, K., Rogers, K., & Marcin, J. P. et al. (2014). Impact of telemedicine on the quality of forensic sexual abuse examinations in rural communities. *Child Abuse & Neglect*, *38*(9), 1533–1539. doi:10.1016/j.chiabu.2014.04.015 PMID:24841062

Morsette, A., Swaney, G., Stolle, D., Schuldberg, D., van den Pol, R., & Young, M. (2009). Cognitive Behavioral Intervention for Trauma in Schools (CBITS): School-based treatment on a rural American Indian reservation. *Journal of Behavior Therapy and Experimental Psychiatry*, *40*(1), 169–178. doi:10.1016/j.jbtep.2008.07.006 PMID:18835478

National Child Traumatic Stress Network. (2015). *TF-CBT Web: A trauma-based learning course for Trauma-focused Cognitive-behavioral Therapy.* Retrieved November 13 from: http://tfcbt.musc.edu/

National Child Traumatic Stress Network. (2015). *National Child Traumatic Stress Network Empirically Supported Treatments and Promising Practices.* Retrieved November 13th from http://nctsnet.org/resources/topics/treatments-that-work/promising-practices

Paul, L. A., Gray, M. J., Elhai, J. D., Massad, P. M., & Stamm, B. H. (2006). Promotion of evidence-based practices for child traumatic stress in rural populations: Identification of barriers and promising solutions. *Trauma, Violence & Abuse*, *7*(4), 260–273. doi:10.1177/1524838006292521 PMID:17065547

Pereda, N., Guilera, G., Forns, M., & Gomez-Benito, J. (2009). The international epidemiology of child sexual abuse: A continuation of Finkelhor (1994). *Child Abuse & Neglect*, *33*(6), 331–342. doi:10.1016/j.chiabu.2008.07.007 PMID:19477003

Perez-Fuentes, G., Olfson, M., Villegas, L., Morcillo, C., Wang, S., & Blanco, C. (2013). Prevalence and correlates of child sexual abuse: A national study. *Comprehensive Psychiatry*, *54*(1), 16–27. doi:10.1016/j.comppsych.2012.05.010 PMID:22854279

Public Health Agency of Canada. (2010). *Canadian incidence study of reported child abuse and neglect–2008: Major findings.* Ottawa, CA: Public Health Agency of Canada.

Quinn, A. (2007). Reflections on intergenerational trauma: Healing as a critical intervention. *First Peoples Child & Family Review*, *3*(4), 72–82.

Self-Brown, S., Rheingold, A. A., Campbell, C., & de Aellano, M. (2008). A media campaign prevention program for child sexual abuse: Community members' perspectives. *Journal of Interpersonal Violence*, *23*(6), 728–743. doi:10.1177/0886260507313946 PMID:18378812

Sinclair, R. (2007). Identity lost and found: Lessons from the sixties scoop. *First Peoples Child & Family Review*, *3*(1), 65–82.

Sprang, G., Staton-Tindall, M., Gustman, B., Freer, B., Clark, J. J., Dye, H., & Sprang, K. (2013). The impact of trauma exposure on parenting stress in rural America. *Journal of Child & Adolescent Trauma*, *6*(4), 287–300. doi:10.1080/19361521.2013.836585

US Department of Health and Human Services, Administration for Children, Youth and Families, Children's Bureau. (2011). *Child maltreatment*. Retrieved November 7, 2015, from http://www.acf.hhs.gov/sites/default/files/cb/cm11.pdf#page=28

Walsh, K., Matthews, B., Rassafiani, M., Farrell, A., & Butler, D. (2012). Understanding teachers' reporting of child sexual abuse: Measurement methods matter. *Children and Youth Services Review*, *34*(9), 1937–1946. doi:10.1016/j.childyouth.2012.06.004

Wilson, K. (2003). Therapeutic landscapes and First Nations people: An exploration of culture, health and place. *Health & Place*, *9*(2), 83–93. doi:10.1016/S1353-8292(02)00016-3 PMID:12753791

# Chapter 6
# School Violence among Children and Adolescents in Rural Communities

**Michelle F. Wright**
*Masaryk University, Czech Republic*

## ABSTRACT

*School violence gained increased attention after highly publicized school shootings occurred in a variety of different school districts across the United States. Some of these school shootings occurred in non-urban communities, suggesting that such violence can occur in all areas, even those originally thought to be immune to such violence. As a result of these incidences, more research was conducted on school violence in nonurban communities and it quickly became clear that children and adolescents from rural school districts were often exposed to school violence at similar levels as those children and adolescents from urban areas. The aim of this chapter was to review research concerning school violence among children and adolescents in rural school districts, and to make recommendations for policy and school violence reduction programs as well as future research.*

## INTRODUCTION

About 20% of the people in the United States live in rural areas (United States Census, 2010). Research also indicates that joblessness, lower employment wages, poverty, and school violence is growing faster in rural communities than in urban areas (Atav & Spencer, 2002; Bachman, 1992; Bachus, 1994; Donnermeyer, 1994; Hodgkinson, 1994; Monsey, Owen, Zierman, Lambert, & Hyman, 1995; Prothrow-Stith & Quaday, 1996; Slovak & Singer, 2001). These communities also lag behind in terms of opportunities for higher education and well-paying occupations as well as having less opportunities for job and income growth (Bachman, 1992; Hobbs, 1994; Osgood & Chambers, 2003; Sherman, 1992; Stein, Jaycox, Kataoka, Rhodes, & Vestal, 2003; Weist, Myers, Danforth, McNeil, Ollendick, & Hawkins, 2000). In addition, the available jobs in rural communities require few skills and pay poorly. Consequently, highly educated youth from rural areas are leaving these communities for better educational and employment

DOI: 10.4018/978-1-5225-0228-9.ch006

opportunities (Hobbs, 1994). Therefore, considerable attention has been given to the role of rural public schools in educating the next generation for college and university enrollment as well as preparing children from rural communities for future, gainful employment.

Roughly 57% of regular school districts operate in rural areas, especially in the North Central, Southern, and Western parts of the United States, with many of these schools having smaller budgets and fewer resources (McLean & Ross, 1994; U.S. Department of Education, 2013). Despite having less funding, operational costs are sometimes slightly higher than state averages, most likely as a result of the misguided belief that these schools do not have as many problems as urban schools, which has a variety of implications for children's and adolescents' academic achievement, educational attainment, and their behaviors (Schroth & Fishbaugh, 2000). Rural schools are typically hypothesized to protect children and adolescents from school violence, racism, and general decay present in metropolitan areas (Friday, 1996; Schroth & Fishbaugh, 2000). However, research has begun to challenge this assumption, with findings indicating that rural children and adolescents are frequently exposed to high levels of school violence and that these schools no longer have the influence that they once had (Hobbs, 1994; Osgood & Chambers, 2003; Petersen, Beekley, Speaker, & Pietrzak, 1998; Slovak & Singer, 2001; Slovak & Singer, 2002). In particular, adolescents from rural schools in New York were significantly more likely than adolescents from urban schools to engage in school bullying, to carry a weapon to school, and to use drugs, tobacco, and alcohol (Atav & Spencer, 2002). Although student achievement is slightly higher than achievement from disadvantaged urban schools, achievement is lower than in more advantaged urban areas (U.S. Department of Education, 1994). Furthermore, school administrators from rural school districts report that parental involvement and supervision have diminished over the last few years, leading to poorer academic achievement and increases in school violence (Petersen et al., 1998; Stephens, 1994). Also contributing to the increase in school violence are family violence and unstable family structures (Petersen et al., 1998). Research findings also suggest that rural school districts that are close to large cities have more incidences of school violence than the national average (Kingery, Mirzaee, Pruitt, & Hurley, 1990). Despite such findings, published research on school violence in rural school districts has been slow to develop, leading to the mistaken attitude that such schools are safe, which prevents policy-making and intervention efforts. Therefore, a synthesis of the literature on school violence in rural school districts is needed in order to describe the importance and timeliness of investigating this topic as well as providing information concerning the gaps in the literature and proposing considerations for policy and future research.

The purpose of this chapter is to review literature on school violence among children and adolescents in rural school districts, including elementary, middle, and high schools. This chapter has six main purposes, including:

1. Explaining the nature of school violence;
2. Describing the prevalence and consequences of school violence in rural school districts;
3. Exploring the role of the social context in school violence – providing comparisons of school violence among children and adolescents from urban, suburban, and rural communities;
4. Explaining solutions and recommendations;
5. Proposing future research directions - describing future research on school violence among children and adolescents in rural school districts;
6. Conclusions – final remarks regarding the literature on school violence among children and adolescents in rural communities.

The chapter draws on multidisciplinary qualitative, quantitative, and mixed-design research methodologies from psychology, sociology, social work, and criminology. Furthermore, the chapter incorporates both cross-sectional and longitudinal research designs.

## The Nature of School Violence

School violence has received increased attention from educators, parents, researchers, and the general public after the Columbine School Shooting in 1999 (Greene, 2005; Snell, Bailey, Barona, & Mebane, 2002; Veltkamp & Lawson, 2008). Because the Columbine School Shooting occurred in a predominantly white, middle-class school, the general public began to believe that school violence was not localized to only urban areas, and that such events could happen anywhere in the United States. The general public also became very concerned that similar shootings could occur in their neighborhood school, despite school shootings being very rare (Anderson et al., 2001; Brooks et al., 2000; DeVoe, Peter, Noonan, Snyder, & Baum, 2005; Greene, 2005; Wilcox, Augustine, Bryan, & Roberts, 2005). As a result of school shootings, the media began to increasingly cover these events and other types of school violence (e.g., gang activity, fighting), and the government and school districts established specific policies and objectives in an effort to reduce physical fighting and carrying weapons to school (Brooks, Schiraldi, & Ziuedenberg, 2000; Elliott, Hamburg, & Williams, 1998; Herda-Rapp, 2003; Lawrence, 2000; Maeroff, 2000; Office of Disease Prevention and Health Promotion, 2005; Snyder & Sickmund, 1999; Sugai, Sprague, Horner, & Walker, 2000). Many of these objectives and policies are undergoing transformations, particularly as new forms of school violence, like some forms of cyberbullying, receive increasing attention. Research evidence also suggests that school violence is not only a problem in the United States, and that it is a serious global problem occurring in various countries throughout the world, which affects the core institutions of modern society (Akiba, LeTendre, Baker, & Goesling, 2002; Chen & Astor, 2009; Due et al., 2005; Due, Merlo, Harel-Fisch, & Damsgaard, 2009; Eslea, Menesant, Morita, O'Moore, Mora-Merchan, Perera, & Smith, 2003; Farrington & Ttoti, 2009; Kachur et al., 1996; Obeidat, 1997; Smith, Madsen, & Mood, 1999).

School violence is defined as youth violence perpetrated in an educational setting, either on school property, on the way to or from school, during or on the way to or from a school-sponsored event, and it takes the form of bullying, cyberbullying, assaults by fighting or using weapons, rape, threats, psychological stress, and gang violence (Anderson, 1998; Furlong, Pavelski, & Saxton, 2002; Gladstein & Slater, 1988; Gottfredson, 2001; Heaviside, Rowand, Williams, & Farris, 1998; McCabe & Martin, 2004; Reiss & Roth, 1993; Vossekuil, Fein, Reddy, Borum, & Modzeleski, 2002). It includes unwanted physical force or power directed to another person or group with the intention to cause physical injury and/or psychological harm (Aspy, Oman, Vesely, McLeroy, Rodine, & Marshall, 2004; Greene, 2000; Miller & Kraus, 2008; Thompson, Burcham, & McLaughlin, 2008). Although the majority of school violence occurs in late childhood and adolescence, it can also begin in early childhood (Centers for Disease Control and Prevention, 2014; Noonan & Vavra, 2007; Resnick et al., 1997; Sprott, 2004). Perpetrating school violence in early childhood is a strong predictor of engaging in these behaviors during adolescence and adulthood. In one study on school violence, 33.2% of adolescents were involved in a physical fight in the last 12 months, 17.4% thought about carrying a weapon to school in the last 30 days (6.4% actually carried a weapon), 9.5% experienced dating violence, and 8.9% were threatened or injured with a weapon at school in the last 12 months (Grunbaum, Kann, Kinchen, Ross, Lowry, & Kolbe, 2002). Rates of witnessing violence at school are greater than being directly victimized. For instance, 79% of children and adolescents from one sample reported to having witnessed someone being threatened at school and 71% reported to having witnessed someone being "beaten-up" at school (Flannery, Wester, & Singer, 2004). In addition, teachers were not exempt from experiencing violence at school, with 9% reporting that they have been threatened by a student from their school, and 5% reporting that they have been physically attacked by a student at their school (Robers, Kemp, Rathbun, & Morgan). Despite variations in the rates of school violence, it is clear that many individuals involved in the school system, including students and teachers, are involved in these behaviors, whether directly or indirectly.

Researchers are particularly concerned with school violence as it limits children's and adolescents' available coping strategies, which thereby inhibits the educational process and contributes to a variety of negative outcomes. For example, school violence predicts a variety of negative consequences, including future delinquency, school failure, school absences, and substance abuse (Bowen & Bowen, 1999; Cairns, Cairns, Neckerman, & Gariepy, 1989; Cunningham & Henggeler, 2001; Dishion, Eddy, Haas, Li, & Spracklen, 1997; Durant, Kahn, Beckford, & Woods, 1997; Loeber & Dishion, 1983; Parker & Slaby, 1983). These consequences are particularly damaging and they affect children and adolescents psychologically, including increasing their anxiety and depressive symptoms, as well as contributing to increases in violent behaviors and drug use (Slovak & Singer, 2002). Furthermore, children's and adolescents' exposure to school violence increased their risk of developing psychiatric disorders, including posttraumatic stress disorder and major depression, and substance abuse problems (Dukarm, Byrd, Auinger, & Weitzman, 1996; Kilpatrick, Ruggiero, Acierno, Saunders, Resnick, & Best, 2003; Vermeiren, Schwab-Stone, Deboutte, Leckman, & Ruchkin, 2003). Exposure to violence also increased children's and adolescents' victimization by school bullying and dissatisfaction with life (Nansel, Overpectk, Haynie, Ruan, & Scheidt, 2003; Valois, Zullig, Huebner, & Drane, 2001). Gun violence exposure also increased children's and adolescents' anger, dissociation, posttraumatic stress, and overall trauma when compared to those children and adolescents not exposed to gun violence (Slovak & Singer, 2001). As researchers' understanding of school violence increases, they began to recognize the importance of considering children's and adolescents' exposure to negative school behaviors in multiple environments. Therefore, researchers began to direct their attention to school violence occurring in rural communities as rural children and adolescents are often exposed to high levels of these behaviors (Osgood & Chambers, 2003; Slovak & Singer, 2001; Slovak & Singer, 2002).

## Prevalence and Consequences of School Violence in Rural School Districts

Although the bulk of research concerning school violence has focused on children and adolescents in urban and suburban communities, researchers are beginning to direct their attention to school violence exposure in rural communities as they began to recognize the importance of understanding such exposure in a variety of social contexts (Atav & Spencer, 2002; Mink, Moore, Johnson, Probst, & Martin, 2005). In one study, 25% of rural children and adolescents reported having been exposed to gun violence at least once (Slovak & Singer, 2001). Furthermore, more than half of the boys in one sample of 7th through 12th graders in rural school districts in Texas were involved in a physical fight with fists or weapons during the past school year (Kingery, Pruitt, Heuberger, & Brizzolara, 1995; Mink et al., 2005). Half of the boys had carried a knife at school, while 18% carried a handgun at school. In addition, 16% of the students in the sample had been robbed at school, with 37% having been threatened, 15% reporting that they were attacked, and 10% reporting that someone tried to force them to have sex against their will while at school. Gender differences also exist in rural adolescents' exposure to violence. In particular, adolescent males were more likely to use weapons at school, be threatened at school, and engage in fighting behaviors when compared to females who were more likely to be coerced into sex and engage in suicidal behaviors (Kingery et al., 1995; Mink et al., 2005). These statistics clearly indicate that school violence is a concern in rural communities, warranting additional attention by school personnel, parents, policy makers, and researchers.

Although research on the prevalence of school violence in rural communities is scarce, there is less research focused on the consequences of children's and adolescents' exposure to these behaviors. In this research, school violence perpetration and exposure are linked to internalizing (e.g., depression, anxiety, loneliness) and externalizing problems (e.g., bullying, delinquency) among rural children and adolescents (Kingery et al., 1990). Their exposure to school violence is linked to substance use and positive attitudes toward violence as well as less prosocial behavior (Womble & D'Amico, 1994). Furthermore, gun violence exposure is related to anger, dissociation, and posttraumatic stress disorder as well as higher levels of violent behaviors (Slovak & Singer, 2001). Gun violence exposure increased children's and adolescents' likelihood of experiencing other forms of school violence. In addition, being victimized by crimes at school was more common for rural adolescents who had lower levels of attachment to their peers and higher levels of isolation (Farrell & Sullivan, 2004; Wallace & May, 2005). School violence also interrupts the educational process. Exposure to high levels of school violence among rural children and adolescents contributed to lower literacy rates as a result of fear, which reduces their ability to learn and concentrate (Kingery, Coggeshall, & Alford, 1998). School violence also diminishes their academic performance and increased school absences (Farrell & Sullivan, 2004).

Similar to research on school violence in rural communities, little attention has been given to school bullying, a subtype of school violence, among children and adolescents in these communities. Like the definition of school violence, school bullying is defined as the intentional use of physical force or power, and it includes direct (i.e., physical aggression in which the victim is openly attacked) and indirect (i.e., social exclusion or social rejection) forms (Espelage & Swearer, 2003; Hemphill, Tollit, Kotevski, & Florent, 2015; Hong, Peguero, Choi, Lanesskog, Espelage, & Lee, 2014; Olweus, 1993). It also involves four types, including physical (e.g., pushing, hitting), verbal (e.g., name-calling), relational (e.g., exclusion, spreading rumors), and damage to property (Olthof & Goossens, 2008; Wang, Iannotti, Luk, & Nansel, 2010). Research evidence revealed that school bullying is perceived as a problem by rural children and adolescents as well as school personnel, further supporting the need for additional investigations on this topic (Isernhagen & Harris, 2004; Thomlison, Thomlison, Sowers, Theriot, & Dulmus, 2004). In one study, 60% to 82% of rural children and adolescents reported experiencing some form of bullying at school in the past three months (Dulmus, Theriot, Sowers, & Blackburn, 2004; Hoover, Oliver, & Hazler, 1992; Stockdale, Hangaduambo, Duys, Larson, & Sarvela, 2002). This prevalence rate was noted as being substantially higher than rates of school bullying in other communities throughout the United States. In particular, researchers typically report prevalence rates of 10% to 20% among children and adolescents from urban and suburban schools (Dake, Price, & Telljohann, 2003; Nansel et al., 2001; Perry, Kusel, & Perry, 1988; Twemlow & Sacco, 1996). Research on school bullying in rural school districts has also focused on cyberbullying, a new form of school bullying, involving harm carried out through information and communication technologies (e.g., cell phones, computers). In a rural sample of adolescents in Arizona, Bauman (2010) found that 1.5% participated in cyberbullying perpetration, 3% were classified as cybervictims, and 8.6% were cyberbully-cybervictims. Further investigating cyberbullying among rural adolescents, Burton and colleagues (2013) classified adolescents into uninvolved, cyberbullies, and cyberbully-cybervictims. Findings revealed that cyberbully-cybervictims had higher levels of reactive and proactive forms of cyberbullying when compared to cyberbullies and uninvolved adolescents. Being a bystander is another role that children and adolescents can have in school bullying involvement. In one of the few studies to investigate bystander behavior in rural communities, Hamby et al. (2015) found that bystanders were present in most situations involving peer victimization, and that bystanders typically involved friends or acquaintances.

Other research focuses on the causes and consequences associated with school bullying in rural communities. Children and adolescents from these communities who experience school bullying are more likely to report school adjustment difficulties, including an increased risk for school failure and school dropout (Cairns & Cairns, 1994; Estell, Farmer, Irvin, Thompson, Hutchins, & McDonough, 2007; Roscigno & Crowley, 2001). In addition, persistent peer victimization among rural children and adolescents is linked to low levels of school satisfaction, social support, less optimism, and lower self-esteem (Evans, Smokowski, & Cotter, 2014). Such victims also reported the highest levels of school hassles, peer rejection, anxiety, and depression as well as externalizing difficulties, like anger and aggression. Among rural youths, peer victimization is also linked to post-traumatic stress symptomatology and lower levels of attachment to peers (Crosby, Oehler, & Capaccioli, 2010; Scott & Friedli, 2002; Wallace & May, 2005).

Based on the literature reviewed in this section, it is clear that school violence is a concern in rural school districts, and that more research attention should be given to further understanding children's and adolescents' exposure to these behaviors. To better understand school violence in rural communities, it is important to understand research on differences in these behaviors among rural, urban, and suburban children and adolescents.

## The Role of the Social Context in School Violence

Children and adolescents from rural and urban schools are equally as likely to be victims of school violence in any given year (Kingery, Mirzaee, Pruitt, Hurley, & Heuberger, 1991). However, urban children and adolescents in this sample reported having experienced more incidences during that year. Rural adolescents also experienced and engaged in certain types of school violence-related behaviors more frequently than urban and suburban adolescents. In particular, rural adolescents were more likely to be exposed to gun violence and be victims of dating violence when compared to urban adolescents (Slovak & Singer, 2001; Spencer & Byrant, 2000). Additionally, they were more likely to carry a weapon to school within the last 30 days when compared to urban and suburban adolescents. Other research indicated that student-to-student violent behavior was the highest in rural schools when compared this type of violent behavior in urban and suburban schools, where it ranked as number three (Petersen et al., 2007). Although the previously reviewed literature utilized children's and adolescents' self-reports of school violence, other research has relied on principals' and teachers' reports of students' involvement in these behaviors at their school. Findings from this research revealed that teachers and administrators from rural school districts were more likely to report arson at their schools. Verbal threats, pushing, shoving, punching, and hitting were ranked as the most frequently occurring behaviors at all rural schools in the sample. In addition, rural educators were more concerned with their personal safety as they feared verbal threats and attacks from students and parents when compared to educators from suburban and urban communities. Some educators from rural school districts had even experienced school violence in the past two years. Researchers have also focused on differences in children's and adolescents' exposure to school violence as uninvolved, witnesses. Findings suggest that adolescents from both urban and rural schools reported witnessing similar levels of serious acts of violence (Farrell & Sullivan, 2004). Other research focuses on the locations within schools that increase incidences of school violence. In this literature, findings suggest that school violence can occur in many locations, but some locations are more often sites of such behavior. In rural schools, violence more often occurred in hallways and restrooms as well as at extracurricular events (Petersen et al., 1998). However, incidences of violence more often occurred in the classroom in suburban and urban schools.

It is often believed that gang violence is not a problem in rural communities, especially in the local schools. However, available research suggests that this perception is not entirely accurate. More specifically, the pressure to join a gang does not differ between rural and urban adolescents and neither does gang membership (Evans, Fitzgeral, Weigel, & Chvilicek, 1999). Adolescents from both communities were equally likely to carry weapons and get into physical fights at school. However, urban adolescents were more likely to have friends in gangs and to be threatened by gangs when compared to rural adolescents.

There are also similarities and differences between urban and rural children and adolescents concerning externalizing and internalizing problems at school. Urban adolescents reported more externalizing problems compared to adolescents from rural communities (Hope & Bierman, 1998). However, rural and urban adolescents did not differ in the amounts of internalizing problems. Rural adolescents are more likely to engage in high-risk behaviors, like bringing a weapon to school, and they are also at risk for poorer educational outcomes when compared to suburban and urban adolescents (Atav & Spencer, 2002; Witherspoon & Ennett, 2011).

## SOLUTIONS AND RECOMMENDATIONS

Most research attention has been given to school violence in urban and suburban areas, with research on such violence in rural schools being scarcer. Research should focus on school violence in rural schools, and, in order to conduct such research, federal programs should be developed to help with funding this research (Flynt & Morton, 2007). Such funding is important as research serves an important function in the development of school violence prevention programs. This funding should be better allocated to fund such research, and to ensure that children and adolescents from rural communities are included in efforts to reduce school violence in their communities. To aid in these efforts, schools should development a system to notify parents of incidences involving school violence in the school district. Not only would such a system notify parents of their children's involvement in an incident, but it would also notify parents when other children were involved in school violence. School policies of rural schools should also be revised in an effort to develop less punitive strategies for dealing with discipline (Mink et al., 2005). These policies should be modified to be more preventive as successful implementation of these policies could reduce incidences of school violence and increase the successful treatment of such violence and the associated negative consequences. There are few programs developed to accommodate children and adolescents from rural communities. Most programs aimed at prevention and intervention are not empirically evaluated for application to children and adolescents from rural communities. More prevention programs should be developed and tested to determine the benefits of reducing school violence in these communities. In addition, rural schools tend to have lower levels of funding, despite having slightly higher operating costs when compared to state averages (Schroth & Fishbaugh, 2000). A lack of perceived need contributes to a lack of resources, such as violence-related services, which makes it difficult to implement effective policies and strategies for dealing with school violence in rural communities. More funding should be allocated to ensure that rural schools have proper mental health services to address violence through prevention and treatment options.

## FUTURE RESEARCH DIRECTIONS

There are some noticeable gaps in the literature concerning school violence among children and adolescents in rural communities, and future research should aim to address these gaps. Many of the studies reviewed in this chapter involve cross-sectional research designs. Such designs make it difficult to draw conclusions about the long-term extent, causes, and consequences of school violence among rural children and adolescents. Longitudinal research designs can be employed to determine the risk and protective factors associated with school violence perpetration and exposure, with particular attention to the long-term consequences of involvement in these behavior. This research will also help to determine whether there are more severe consequences associated with rural children's and adolescents' involvement in school violence when compared to other children and adolescents from urban and suburban areas. Many of the studies conducted on school violence in rural communities do not take into account income levels or ethnicities. Just like with all communities, people of various racial and ethnic backgrounds are more advantaged or disadvantaged than others. Therefore, future research should focus on school violence by also taking into account income levels and different racial and ethnic backgrounds among children and adolescents in rural communities. Such a focus is important as the diverse backgrounds of children and adolescents from rural schools might differentially relate to different risks for school violence involvement.

## CONCLUSION

In summary, the purpose of this chapter was to review literature revealing that school violence is a concern in rural communities. Taken together, the literature provides evidence supporting children and adolescents in these communities' involvement in school violence. Additionally, the research suggests that some aspects of school violence are greater in rural communities, such as carrying weapons or being exposed to weapons at school. Rural school districts also receive less funding and more funding could better aid in developing, implementing, and maintaining school violence reduction initiatives. This is a significant issue as exposure and perpetration of school violence among children and adolescents in rural communities predicts a variety of negative consequences. More research should be conducted on school violence among rural children and adolescents in an effort to develop effective policies and prevention programs aimed at reducing their involvement in these behaviors.

## REFERENCES

Akiba, M., Letendre, G. K., Baker, D. P., & Goesling, B. (2002). Student victimization: National and school systems effects on school violence in 37 nations. *American Educational Research Journal*, *39*(4), 829–853. doi:10.3102/00028312039004829

Anderson, D. (1998). Curriculum, culture, and community: The challenge of school violence. In M. Tonry & M. Moore (Eds.), *Youth violence* (pp. 318–363). Chicago, IL: University of Chicago Press. doi:10.1086/449282

Anderson, M., Kaufman, J., Simon, T. R., Barrios, L., Paulozzi, L., Ryan, G., & Potter, L. et al. (2001). School-associated violent deaths in the United States, 1994-1999.[JAMA]. *Journal of the American Medical Association*, *286*(21), 2695–2702. doi:10.1001/jama.286.21.2695 PMID:11730445

Aspy, C. B., Oman, R. F., Vesely, S. K., McLeroy, K., Rodine, S., & Marshall, L. (2004). Adolescent violence: The protective effects of youth assets. *Journal of Counseling and Development*, *82*(3), 268–276. doi:10.1002/j.1556-6678.2004.tb00310.x

Astor, R. A., Benbenishty, R., Zeira, A., & Vinokur, A. (2002). School climate, observed risky behaviors, and victimization as predictors of high school students' fear and judgments of school violence as a problem. *Health Education & Behavior*, *29*(6), 716–736. doi:10.1177/109019802237940 PMID:12456131

Atav, S., & Spencer, G. A. (2002). Health risk behaviors among adolescents attending rural, suburban, and urban schools: A comparative study. *Family & Community Health*, *25*(2), 53–64. doi:10.1097/00003727-200207000-00007 PMID:12010115

Bachman, R. (1992). Crime in non metropolitan America: A national accounting of trends, incidence rates, and idiosyncratic vulnerabilities. *Rural Sociology*, *57*(4), 546–560. doi:10.1111/j.1549-0831.1992.tb00479.x

Bachus, G. (1994). Violence is no stranger in rural schools. *School Administrator*, *51*(4), 18–22.

Bauman, S. (2010). Cyberbullying in a rural intermediate school: An exploratory study. *The Journal of Early Adolescence*, *30*(6), 803–833. doi:10.1177/0272431609350927

Bowen, N. K., & Bowen, G. L. (1999). Effects of crime and violence in neighborhoods and schools on the school behavior and performance of adolescents. *Journal of Adolescent Research*, *14*(3), 319–342. doi:10.1177/0743558499143003

Brooks, K., Schiraldi, V., & Ziedenberg, J. (2000). School house hype: Two years later. Washington, DC: Justice Policy Institute/Children's Law Center. Retrieved from http://www.cjcj.org/schoolhousehype/shh2.html

Burton, K. A., Florell, D., & Gore, J. S. (2013). Differences in proactive and reactive aggression in traditional bullies and cyberbullies. *Journal of Aggression, Maltreatment & Trauma*, *22*(3), 316–328. doi:10.1080/10926771.2013.743938

Cairns, R. B., & Cairns, B. D. (1994). *Lifelines and risks: Pathways of youth in our time*. New York: Cambridge University Press.

Cairns, R. B., Cairns, B. D., Neckerman, H. J., & Gariepy, J. L. (1989). Growth and aggression: 1. Childhood to early adolescence. *Developmental Psychology*, *25*(2), 1–30. doi:10.1037/0012-1649.25.2.320

Centers for Disease Control and Prevention. (2014). *Youth risk behavior surveillance—United States, 2013*. Retrieved from: www.cdc.gov/mmwr/pdf/ss/ss6304.pdf

Chen, J. K., & Astor, R. A. (2009). The perpetration of school violence in Taiwan: An analysis of gender, grade level, school type. *School Psychology International*, *30*(6), 568–584. doi:10.1177/0143034309107076

Crosby, J. W., Oehler, J., & Capaccioli, K. (2010). The relationship between peer victimization and posttraumatic stress symptomatology in a rural sample. *Psychology in the Schools*, *47*(3), 297–310.

Cunningham, P. B., & Henggeler, S. W. (2001). Implementation of empirically based drug and violence prevention and intervention programs in public school settings. *Journal of Clinical Child Psychology*, *30*(1), 221–232. doi:10.1207/S15374424JCCP3002_9 PMID:11393922

Dake, J. A., Price, J. H., & Telljohann, S. K. (2003). The nature and extent of bullying at school. *The Journal of School Health*, *73*(5), 173–180. doi:10.1111/j.1746-1561.2003.tb03599.x PMID:12793102

DeVoe, J. F., Peter, K., Noonan, M., Snyder, T. D., & Baum, K. (2005). *Indicators of school crime and safety: 2005. U.S. Departments of Education and Justice*. Washington, DC: U.S. Government Printing Office.

Dishion, T. J., Eddy, J. M., Haas, E., Li, F., & Spracklen, K. (1997). Friendships and violent behavior during adolescence. *Social Development*, *6*(2), 207–223. doi:10.1111/j.1467-9507.1997.tb00102.x

Donnermeyer, J. F. (1994). Crime and violence in rural communities. In M. Womble & J. D'Amico (Eds.), *Perspectives on violence and substance use in rural America* (pp. 27–64). Oak Brook, IL: North Central Regional Educational Laboratory.

Due, P., Holstein, B. E., Lynch, J., Diderichsen, F., Gabhain, S. N., Scheidt, P., & Currie, C.The Health Behavior in School-Aged Children Bullying Working Group. (2005). Bullying and symptom among school-aged children: International comparative cross sectional study in 28 countries. *European Journal of Public Health*, *15*(2), 128–132. doi:10.1093/eurpub/cki105 PMID:15755782

Due, P., Merlo, J., Harel-Fisch, Y., Damsgaard, M. T., soc, M., Holstein, B. E., & Lynch, J. et al. (2009). Socioeconomic inequality in exposure to bullying during adolescence: A comparative, cross-sectional, multilevel study in 35 countries. *American Journal of Public Health*, *99*(5), 907–914. doi:10.2105/AJPH.2008.139303 PMID:19299676

Dukarm, C. P., Byrd, R. S., Auinger, P., & Weitzman, M. (1996). Illicit substance use, gender, and the risk of violent behavior among adolescents. *Pediatrics & Adolescent Medicine*, *150*(8), 797–801. doi:10.1001/archpedi.1996.02170330023004 PMID:8704884

Dulmus, C. N., Theriot, M. T., Sowers, K. M., & Blackburn, J. A. (2004). Student reports of peer bullying victimization in a rural school. *Stress, Trauma and Crisis*, *7*(1), 1–16. doi:10.1080/15434610490281093

DuRant, R. H., Kahn, J., Beckford, P. H., & Woods, E. R. (1997). The association of weapon carrying and fighting on school property and other health risk and problem behaviors among high school students. *Archives of Pediatrics & Adolescent Medicine*, *151*(4), 360–366. doi:10.1001/archpedi.1997.02170410034004 PMID:9111434

Elliott, D. S., Hamburg, B. A., & Williams, K. R. (1998). Violence in American schools: An overview. In D. Elliott, B. Hamburg, & K. Williams (Eds.), *Violence in American schools* (pp. 3–28). Cambridge, UK: Cambridge University Press.

Eslea, M., Menesant, E., Morita, Y., O'Moore, M., Mora-Merchan, J. A., Perera, B., & Smith, P. K. (2003). Friendship and loneliness among bullies and victims: Data from seven countries. *Aggressive Behavior*, *30*(1), 71–83. doi:10.1002/ab.20006

Espelage, D. L., & Swearer, S. M. (2003). Research on school bullying and victimization: What have we learned and where do we go from here? *School Psychology Review*, *32*, 365–383.

Estell, D. B., Farmer, T. W., & Cairns, B. D. (2007). Bullies and victims in rural African American youth: Behavioral characteristics and social network placement. *Aggressive Behavior*, *33*(2), 145–159. doi:10.1002/ab.20176 PMID:17441015

Estell, D. B., Farmer, T. W., Irvin, M. J., Thompson, J. H., Hutchins, B. C., & McDonough, E. M. (2007). Patterns of middle school adjustment and ninth grade adaptation of rural African American youth: Grades and substance use. *Journal of Youth and Adolescence*, *36*(4), 477–487. doi:10.1007/s10964-007-9167-5

Evans, C. B. R., Smokowski, P. R., & Cotter, K. L. (2014). Cumulative bullying victimization: An investigation of the dose-response relationship between victimization and the associated mental health outcomes, social supports, and school experiences of rural adolescents. *Children and Youth Services Review*, *44*, 256–264. doi:10.1016/j.childyouth.2014.06.021

Evans, W. P., Fitzgerald, C., Weigel, D., & Chvilicek, S. (1999). Are rural gang members similar to their urban peers? Implications for rural communities. *Youth & Society*, *30*(3), 267–282. doi:10.1177/0044118X99030003001

Farmer, T. W., Estell, D. B., Bishop, J. L., O'Neal, K. K., & Cairns, B. D. (2003). Rejected bullies or popular leaders? The social relations of aggressive subtypes of rural African American early adolescents. *Developmental Psychology*, *39*(6), 992–1004. doi:10.1037/0012-1649.39.6.992 PMID:14584980

Farmer, T. W., Irvin, M. J., Sgammato, A., Dadisman, K., & Thompson, J. H. (2009). Interpersonal competence configurations in rural Appalachian fifth graders: Academic achievement and associated adjustment factors. *The Elementary School Journal*, *109*(3), 301–321. doi:10.1086/592309

Farrell, A. D., & Sullivan, T. N. (2004). Impact of witnessing violence on growth curves for problem behaviors among early adolescents in urban and rural settings. *Journal of Community Psychology*, *32*(5), 505–525. doi:10.1002/jcop.20016

Farrington, D. P., & Ttoti, M. M. (2009). School-based programs to reduce bullying and victimization. *Campbell Systematic Reviews*, 6.

Flannery, D. J., Wester, K. L., & Singer, M. I. (2004). Impact of exposure to violence in school on child and adolescent mental health and behavior. *Journal of Community Psychology*, *32*(5), 559–573. doi:10.1002/jcop.20019

Flynt, S. W., & Morton, R. C. (2007). Bullying prevention and students with disabilities. *National Forum of Special Education Journal, 19*(1), 1-6.

Friday, J. C. (1996). Weapon-carrying in schools. In A. M. Hoffman (Ed.), *Schools, violence, and society* (pp. 21–32). Westport, CT: Praeger.

Furlong, M. J., Pavelski, R., & Saxton, J. (2002). The prevention of school violence. In S. Brock. P. Lazarus, & S. Jimerson (Eds.), Best practices in crisis intervention (pp. 131–149). Bethesda, MD: National Association of School Psychologists.

Gladstein, J., & Slater, E. J. (1988). Inner city teenagers' exposure to violence: A prevalence study. *Maryland Medical Journal (Baltimore, Md.)*, *37*(12), 951–954. PMID:3231019

Gottfredson, D. C. (2001). *Schools and delinquency*. New York: Cambridge University Press.

Greene, M. B. (2000). Bullying and harassment in schools. In R. S. Moser & C. E. Frantz (Eds.), *Shocking violence* (pp. 72–101). Springfield, IL: Charles C Thomas.

Greene, M. B. (2005). Reducing violence and aggression in schools. *Trauma, Violence & Abuse*, *6*(3), 236–253. doi:10.1177/1524838005277406 PMID:16237157

Grunbaum, J. A., Kann, L., Kinchen, S. A., Ross, W. B., Lowry, R., & Kolbe, L. (2002). Youth risk behavior surveillance - United States, 2001. *MMWR. Surveillance Summaries*, *51*, 1–62. PMID:12102329

Hamby, S., Weber, M. C., Grych, J., & Banyard, V. (2015). What difference do bystanders make? The association of bystander involvement with victim outcomes in a community sample. *Psychology of Violence.*

Heaviside, S., Rowand, C., Williams, C., & Farris, E. (1998). *Violence and discipline problems in U.S. public schools: 1996-1997.* Washington, DC: U.S. Department of Education, National Center for Education Statistics.

Hemphill, S. A., Tollit, M., Kotevski, A., & Florent, A. (2015). Bullying in schools: Rates, correlates and impact on mental health. In J. Lindert & I. Itzhak (Eds.), *Violence and mental health: Its manifold faces* (pp. 185–205). Springer. doi:10.1007/978-94-017-8999-8_9

Herda-Rapp, H. (2003). The social construction of local school violence threats by the news media and professional organizations. *Sociological Enquiry*, *73*(4), 545–574. doi:10.1111/1475-682X.00071

Hobbs, D. (1994). The rural context for education: Adjusting the images. In M. Womble & J. D'Amico (Eds.), *Perspectives on violence and substance use in rural America* (pp. 5–26). Oak Brook, IL: North Central Regional Educational Laboratory.

Hodgkinson, H. (1994). *The invisible poor: Rural youth in America*. Washington, D.C.: Institute for Educational Leadership, Center for Demographic Policy.

Hong, J. S., Davis, J. P., Sterzing, P. R., Yoon, J., Choi, S., & Smith, D. C. (2014). A conceptual framework for understanding the association between school bullying victimization and substance misuse. *The American Journal of Orthopsychiatry*, *84*(6), 696–710. doi:10.1037/ort0000036 PMID:25545436

Hoover, J. H., Oliver, R., & Hazler, R. J. (1992). Bullying: Perceptions of adolescent victims in the midwestern USA. *School Psychology International*, *13*(1), 5–16. doi:10.1177/0143034392131001

Hope, T. L., & Bierman, K. L. (1998). Patterns of home and school behavior problems in rural and urban settings. *Journal of School Psychology*, *36*(1), 45–58. doi:10.1016/S0022-4405(97)00049-6 PMID:19834584

Isernhagen, J., & Harris, S. (2004). A comparison of bullying in four rural middle and high schools. *Rural Educator*, *25*, 5–13.

Kachur, S. P., Stennies, G. M., Powell, K. E., Modzeleski, W., Stephens, R., Murphy, R., & Lowry, R. et al. (1996). School-associated violent deaths in the United States, 1992 to 1994. *Journal of the American Medical Association*, *274*(22), 1729–1733. doi:10.1001/jama.1996.03530460033027 PMID:8637169

Kilpatrick, D. G., Ruggiero, K. J., Acierno, R., Saunders, B. E., Resnick, H. S., & Best, C. L. (2003). Violence and risk of PTSD, major depression, substance abuse/dependence, and comorbidity: Results from the national survey of adolescents. *Journal of Consulting and Clinical Psychology*, *71*(4), 692–700. doi:10.1037/0022-006X.71.4.692 PMID:12924674

Kingery, P., Mirzaee, E., Pruitt, B. E., & Hurley, R. S. (1990). Town and country violence. *School Safety*, 22-25.

Kingery, P. M., Coggeshall, M. B., & Alford, A. A. (1998). Violence at school: Recent evidence from four national surveys. *Psychology in the Schools*, *35*(33), 247–258. doi:10.1002/(SICI)1520-6807(199807)35:3<247::AID-PITS5>3.0.CO;2-K

Kingery, P. M., Mirzaee, E., Pruitt, B. E., Hurley, R. S., & Heuberger, G. (1991). Rural communities near large metropolitan areas: Safe havens from adolescent violence and drug use? *Health Values*, *15*(4), 39–48.

Kingery, P. M., Priutt, B. E., Heuberger, G., & Brizzolara, J. A. (1995). Violence in rural schools. *School Psychology International*, *16*(4), 335–344. doi:10.1177/0143034395164002

Lawrence, R. (2000). School violence, the media, and the ACJS. ACJS Today, 20, 4-6.

Loeber, R., & Dishion, T. (1983). Early predictors of male delinquency: A review. *Psychological Bulletin*, *94*(1), 68–99. doi:10.1037/0033-2909.94.1.68 PMID:6353467

Maeroff, G. I. (2000). A symbiosis of sorts: School violence and the media. *Choice Briefs*, *7*, 1–9.

McCabe, K. A., & Martin, G. M. (2004). *School violence, the media, and criminal justice responses (studies in crime & punishment)*. Berne, Switzerland: Peter Lang International Academic Publishers.

McLean, J. E., & Ross, S. M. (1994, October). *The urban-rural funding disparity*. Paper presented at the annual meeting of the National Rural Education Association, Tuscaloosa, AL.

Miller, T. W., & Kraus, R. F. (2008). School-related violence: Definition, scope, and prevention goals. In T. W. Miller (Ed.), *School violence and primary prevention* (pp. 15–24). New York, NY: Springer Publisher. doi:10.1007/978-0-387-77119-9_2

Mink, M. D., Moore, C. G., Johnson, A., Probst, J. C., & Martin, A. (2005). *Violence and rural teens: Teen violence, drug use, and school-based prevention services in rural America*. Washington, DC: U.S. Department of Health and Human Services, Office of Rural Health Policy.

Monsey, B., Owen, G., Zierman, C., Lambert, L., & Hyman, V. (1995). *What works in preventing rural violence*. St. Paul, MN: Amherst H. Wilder Foundation.

Nansel, T. R., Overpeck, M. D., Haynie, D. L., Ruan, W. J., & Scheidt, P. C. (2003). Relationship between bullying and violence among US youth. *Archives of Pediatrics & Adolescent Medicine*, *157*(4), 348–353. doi:10.1001/archpedi.157.4.348 PMID:12695230

Noonan, J. H., & Vavra, M. C. (2007). *A study of offenders and arrestees reported via national incident-based reporting system data*. Retrieved from: http://www.fbi.gov/about-us/cjis/ucr/nibrs/crime-in-schools-and-colleges-pdf

Obeidat, Z. (1997). Bullying and violence in the Jordanian school. In T. Obsako (Ed.), *Violence at school: Global issues and interventions* (pp. 20–35). Paris, France: UNESCO.

Office of Disease Prevention and Health Promotion. (2005). *Healthy People 2010. US Department of Health and Human Service*. Retrieved from: http://www.healthypeople.gov/document/HTML/Volume2/15Injury.htm#_Toc490549392

Olthof, T., & Goossens, F. A. (2008). Bullying and the need to belong: Early adolescents' bullying-related behavior and the acceptance they desire and receive from particular classmates. *Social Development*, *17*(1), 24–46.

Olweus, D. (1993). *Bullying at school: What we know and what we can do*. Blackwell Publishing.

Osgood, D. W., & Chambers, J. M. (2003). Community correlates of rural youth violence. *Juvenile Justice Bulletin*. Retrieved from: http://www.ncjrs.org/html/ojjdp/193591/contents.html

Parker, R. D., & Slaby, R. G. (1983). The development of aggression. In E. M. Hetherington & P. H. Mussen (Eds.), Handbook of child psychology: Vol. 4. *Socialization, personality, and social development* (pp. 547–642). New York: Wiley.

Perry, D. G., Kusel, S. J., & Perry, L. C. (1988). Victims of peer aggression. *Developmental Psychology*, *24*(6), 807–814. doi:10.1037/0012-1649.24.6.807

Petersen, G. J., Beekley, C. Z., Speaker, K. M., & Pietrzak, D. (1998). An examination of violence in three rural school districts. *Journal for Rural and Small Schools*, *19*(3), 25–38.

Prothrow-Stith, D., & Quaday, S. (1996). Communities, schools, and violence. In A. M. Hoffman (Ed.), *Schools, violence, and society* (pp. 153–161). Westport, CT: Praeger.

Reiss, A., & Roth, J. A. (Eds.). (1993). *Understanding and preventing violence*. Washington, DC: National Academy Press.

Resnick, M. D., Bearman, R. W., Blum, K. E., Bauman, K. M., Harris, J., Jones, J., & Udry, J. R. et al. (1997). Protecting adolescents from harm: Findings from the National Longitudinal Study of Adolescent Health.[JAMA]. *Journal of the American Medical Association*, *178*(10), 823–832. doi:10.1001/jama.1997.03550100049038 PMID:9293990

Robers, S., Kemp, J., Rathbun, A., & Morgan, R. E. (2014). *Indicators of school crime and safety*. Washington, DC: National Center for Education Statistics.

Roscigno, V. J., & Crowley, M. L. (2001). Rurality, institutional disadvantage, and achievement/attainment. *Rural Sociology*, *66*(2), 268–293. doi:10.1111/j.1549-0831.2001.tb00067.x

Scott, D. M., & Friedli, D. (2002). Attendance problems and disciplinary procedures in Nebraska schools. *Journal of Drug Education*, *32*(2), 149–165. doi:10.2190/JTR4-6L61-4Q2K-WDEN PMID:12206064

Sherman, A. (1992). *Falling by the wayside: Children in rural America*. Washington, DC: The Children's Defense Fund.

Slovak, K., & Singer, M. I. (2001). Gun violence exposure and trauma among rural youth. *Violence and Victims*, *16*, 389–400. PMID:11506448

Slovak, K., & Singer, M. I. (2002). Children and violence: Findings and implications from a rural community. *Child & Adolescent Social Work Journal*, *19*(1), 35–56. doi:10.1023/A:1014003306441

Smith, P. K., Madsen, K. C., & Moody, J. C. (1999). What causes the age decline in reports of being bullied at school: Towards a developmental analysis of risks of being bullied. *Educational Researcher*, *41*(3), 267–285. doi:10.1080/0013188990410303

Snell, C., Bailey, C., Carona, A., & Mebane, D. (2002). School crime policy changes: The impact of recent highly publicized crimes. *American Journal of Criminal Justice*, *26*(2), 269–285. doi:10.1007/BF02887831

Snyder, H. N., & Sickmund, M. (1999). *Juvenile offenders and victims: 1999 national report*. Washington, DC: Office of Juvenile Justice and Delinquency Prevention, U.S. Department of Justice.

Spencer, G. A., & Byrant, S. A. (2000). Dating violence: A comparison of rural, suburban, and urban teens. *The Journal of Adolescent Health*, *27*(5), 302–305. doi:10.1016/S1054-139X(00)00125-7 PMID:11044701

Sprott, J. B. (2004). The development of early delinquency: Can classroom and school climates make a difference? *Canadian Journal of Criminology and Criminal Justice*, *46*(5), 553–572. doi:10.3138/cjccj.46.5.553

Stein, B. D., Jaycox, L. H., Kataoka, S., Rhodes, H. J., & Vestal, K. D. (2003). Prevalence of child and adolescent exposure to community violence. *Clinical Child and Family Psychology Review*, *6*(4), 247–264. doi:10.1023/B:CCFP.0000006292.61072.d2 PMID:14719637

Stephens, R. D. (1994). Gangs, guns and school violence. *USA Today, 122*(25584), 29-32.

Stockdale, M. S., Hangaduambo, S., Duys, D., Larson, K., & Sarvela, P. D. (2002). Rural elementary students', parents', and teachers' perceptions of bullying. *American Journal of Health Behavior*, *26*(4), 266–277. doi:10.5993/AJHB.26.4.3 PMID:12081359

Sugai, G., Sprague, J. R., Horner, R., & Walker, H. M. (2000). Preventing school violence: The use of office discipline referrals to assess and monitor school-wide discipline interventions. *Journal of Emotional and Behavioral Disorders*, *8*(2), 94–101. doi:10.1177/106342660000800205

Thomlison, R. J., Thomlison, B., Sowers, K. M., Theriot, M. T., & Dulmus, C. N. (2004). School personnel's observations of bullying and victimization among rural elementary and middle school children. In C. N. Dulmus & K. M. Sowers (Eds.), *Kids and violence: The invisible school experience* (pp. 25–43). Binghamton, NY: Haworth Press.

Thompson, M., Burcham, B., & McLaughlin, K. (2008). Violence in our schools. In T. W. Miller (Ed.), *School violence and primary prevention* (pp. 229–248). New York, NY: Springer Publisher. doi:10.1007/978-0-387-77119-9_12

Twemlow, S., & Sacco, F. (1996). Peacekeeping and peacemaking: The conceptual foundations of a plan to reduce violence and improve the quality of life in a midsized community in Jamaica. *Psychiatry*, *59*, 156–175. PMID:8837176

United States Census. (2010). *Urban and rural classification*. Retrieved from: https://www.census.gov/geo/reference/urban-rural.html

U.S. Department of Education. (1994). *The condition of education in rural schools*. Washington, D.C.: U.S. Government Printing Office.

U.S. Department of Education. (2014). *Leadership by principle: How rural values contribute to success in the classroom*. Washington, DC: U.S. Government Printing Office.

Valois, R. F., Zullig, K. J., Huebner, E. S., & Drane, J. W. (2001). Relationships between life satisfaction and violent behaviors among adolescents. *American Journal of Health Behavior*, *25*(4), 353–366. doi:10.5993/AJHB.25.4.1 PMID:11488546

Veltkamp, L. J., & Lawson, A. (2008). Impact of trauma in school violence on the victim and the perpetrator: A mental health perspective. In T. W. Miller (Ed.), *School violence and primary prevention* (pp. 185–200). New York, NY: Springer Publisher. doi:10.1007/978-0-387-77119-9_9

Vermeiren, R., Schwab-Stone, M., Deboutte, D., Leckman, P. E., & Ruchkin, V. (2003). Violence exposure and substance use in adolescents: Findings from three countries. *Pediatrics*, *111*(3), 535–540. doi:10.1542/peds.111.3.535 PMID:12612233

Vossekuil, B., Fein, R., Reddy, M., Borum, R., & Modzeleski, W. (2002). *The final report and findings of the safe school initiative: Implications for the prevention of school attacks in the United States*. Washington, DC: U.S. Department of Education.

Wallace, L., & May, D. C. (2005). The impact of parental attachment and feelings of isolation on adolescent fear of crime at school. *Adolescence*, *40*, 457–474. PMID:16268126

Wang, J., Iannotti, R. J., Luk, J. W., & Nansel, T. R. (2010). Co-occurrence of victimization from five subtypes of bullying: Physical, verbal, social exclusion, spreading rumors, and cyber. *Journal of Pediatric Psychology*, *35*(10), 1103–1112. doi:10.1093/jpepsy/jsq048 PMID:20488883

Weist, M. D., Myers, C. P., Danforth, J., McNeil, D. W., Ollendick, T. H., & Hawkins, R. (2000). Expanded school mental health services: Assessing needs related to school level and geography. *Community Mental Health Journal*, *36*(3), 259–273. doi:10.1023/A:1001957130982 PMID:10933243

Wilcox, P., Campbell, M., Bryan, J. P., & Roberts, S. (2005). The "reality" of middle-school crime: Objective vs. subjective experiences among a sample of Kentucky youth. *Journal of School Violence*, *4*(2), 3–27. doi:10.1300/J202v04n02_02

Witherspoon, D., & Ennett, S. (2011). An examination of social disorganization and pluralistic neighborhood theories with rural mothers and their adolescents. *Journal of Youth and Adolescence*, *40*(9), 1243–1253. doi:10.1007/s10964-009-9499-4 PMID:20047085

Womble, M., & D'Amico, J. J. (Eds.). (1994). *Perspectives on violence and substance use in rural America*. Oak Brook, IL: North Central Regional Educational Laboratory.

## KEY TERMS AND DEFINITIONS

**Cyberbullying:** A new form of bullying, which can also be perpetrated or experienced by peers at one's school, involving harm through information and communication technologies, like cell phones and the internet.

**Direct Bullying:** A form of school bullying that involves physical aggression in which the victim is openly attacked.

**Indirect Bullying:** A form of school bullying involves social exclusion or social rejection.

**Physical Bullying:** A type of school bullying that includes physical forms of bullying, such as pushing, hitting, kicking, and punching.

**Relational Bullying:** A type of school bullying that includes the desire to damage or disrupts social relationships, and it includes spreading rumors, gossiping, social exclusion, and social rejection.

**Rural Communities:** These are geographic areas located outside of cities and towns. They have lower levels of population density than urban areas.

**School Bullying:** School bullying is defined as the intentional use of physical force or power, and it includes direct and indirect forms.

**School Violence:** School violence is defined as youth violence perpetrated in an educational setting, either on school property, on the way to or from school, during or on the way to or from a school-sponsored event, and it takes the form of bullying, cyberbullying, assaults by fighting or weapons, rape, threats, psychological stress, and gang violence.

**Verbal Bullying:** A type of school bullying involving name-calling or making threats of physical harm or the intent to do harm.

# Chapter 7
# When the System Fails:
## Challenges of Child Trauma on Adoptive Families' Social and Emotional System

**Jacqueline Y. Ford**
*Walden University, USA*


## ABSTRACT

*Guided by the lens of psychodynamic theory, Ford (2015) investigated the challenges faced by adoptive families of traumatized children. Fifteen families were randomly selected to participate in this study from a group of 30 parents who adopted traumatized children in Arizona. Thematic categories were drawn and summarized. Textual descriptions evolved from the thematic groups acknowledging their experiences and how these lived experiences guided their decision to adopt a traumatized child. Verification techniques, data mining, journaling, clustering, brainstorming, and peer reviews were used to ensure the quality of data. Emergent themes emphasized the need for adoption-focused training specific to traumatized children. Ford's (2015) study revealed that these adoptive families desired to be equipped with specialized therapeutic training before and after their adoptions.*


## INTRODUCTION

Adoption in the United States has become one of the most instrumental tools to alleviate the increasing number of children raised within the public welfare system. Adoption has an impact on everyone involved, and there are many benefits to adoption (Child Welfare Information Gateway, 2012). The benefits resulting from adoption tend to vary. The child perceives a sense of hope, love, and a sense of belonging and a place to call home (Child Welfare Information Gateway, 2012). The adopting parents view adoption as a solution (i.e., solution for their inability to bear a child or the desire to help a child). The community's perception of the adoptive family differs (Wegar, 2000). Adoption causes a reduction in homelessness, teenage pregnancy, addiction, criminal behavior, and suicide (World Association for Children & Parents, 2012). Therefore, adoption affects everyone involved.

DOI: 10.4018/978-1-5225-0228-9.ch007

The effects of adoption tend to change after its finalization (Child Welfare Information Gateway, 2013). Support, services, and resources that once existed are no longer available to the newly adoptive parent. Adoptive families struggle to find the necessary resources needed in raising their newly adopted child. Meyers (2011) suggested that sometimes adoptive parents are unable to meet their child's needs because they are too damaged. Post (2013) suggested that prior adoptive trauma has a negative effect on the adoptive family while they are attempting to create an ideal and harmonious family unit. Although prior adoptive trauma can affect the parents' ability to establish permanency for the traumatized child, researchers have addressed ways to train and equip adoptive parents in meeting this challenge.

Ford's goal was to understand the challenges faced by the adoptive families in order to empower them in finding solutions to help the child in bonding within the new family unit. With the increasing number of children exposed to traumatic experiences, finding more effective strategies to support the adoptive family is imperative (Child Welfare, 2012; James, 1994).

Adoptive families agree that emergency foster placement is necessary; however, they perceive the necessity of finding a permanent home outweighs temporary placement. According to the U.S. Department of Human Health Services (2013), 94,626 of the 400,540 children were adopted from the public welfare system. The permanency placement of some children was not always successful (Child Welfare, 2010; Festinger & Maza, 2001; McDonald, Propp, & Murphy, 2001; Ruggiero, 2010). The urgency for placement cannot outweigh permanency. More emphasis must be placed on adoption (Mapes, 2012; McDonald et al., 2001; Smith, 2010). Preservation of the adoptive family can occur when placement supports exist (Forbes, 2008; Mapes, 2012; Smith, 2010). Barriers exist among professionals who provide direct and indirect services (e.g., therapy, support, and subsidy) to adoptive families (Casey Family Services, 2003b; Mapes, 2012; Smith, 2010). These barriers continue to challenge the successful adoption of traumatized children. When any serious disturbance and trauma exist within the nucleus of the family, the child may suffer from attachment issues to the adoptive parent (James, 1994; Pickert & Shuster, 2012).

The risk of adoption failure has increased among adoptive families of traumatized children (Brodzinsky, 1992; Casey Family Services, 2003b). Agency adoption failure can occur before or after it is legally finalized. Meyers (2011) revealed that disrupted adoption occurs before the adoption is legally finalized. The rate of "disruption is 10% to 20%" (Meyers, 2011, p.83). Dissolution occurs after the child has been legally adopted. The approximate "dissolution rate is 1% to 10% "(Meyers, 2011, p.83). In both cases, failure occurs, and the child is returned to the public welfare system (Brodzinsky, Smith, & Brodzinsky, 1998; Grotevant & McDermott, 2014; M. A. Baker, personal communication, August 15, 2013; Mapes, 2012; Meyers, 2011; Smith, 2010; Wilke-Deaton, 2005). Such results could be due to the lack of services and resources readily available in meeting the adoptive family's needs (McDonald, 2001). A lack of supportive services may impede successful adoption outcomes (Child Welfare, 2013; Mapes, 2012; McDonald, 2001; Pickert, 2010). Adoption permanency of traumatized children is the least studied by researchers (Brodzinsky, 1992; McCormick, 1991; McDonald, 2001; Pickert, 2010). In order to address the factors associated with thriving post adoptive experience, more research is required in cultivating healthy relationship among adoptive families. James (1994) suggested that many adoptive parents do not understand what it takes to care for the traumatized child. It takes more than the will to survive and thrive in challenging adoptions. James noted that, as the fetus must be in the womb to survive, so must a child have human attachment relations in which to develop, feel protected, nurtured, and become a productive human. Healthy human attachment develops as the child's circle of security grows through the trust with their new primary care giver. As the relationship develops, the child can master this developmental stage.

## BACKGROUND

Many researchers have sought to understand the challenges that disrupt the developmental balance in the child's ability to form healthy attachments. Scholars question whether the problem lies in the child's behavior or the adoptive family's parenting style (Brodzinsky et al., 1998; Grotevant & McDermott, 2014; M. A. Baker, personal communication, August 15, 2013; Ruggerio, 2012; Wilke-Deaton, 2005). Children removed from their original caregivers tend to present with challenges in adjusting to or establishing a new attachment (Brodzinsky et al., 1998; Grotevant & McDermott, 2014; M. A. Baker, personal communication, August 15, 2013; McDonald, 2001; Pickert & Shuster, 2010; Wilke-Deaton, 2005). Some children perceive the loss of their primary caregiver as devastating and confusing. They tend to be in denial. They perceive their loss as a "loss of love, safety, protection, even life itself, and prolonged unavailability of the primary attachment" (James, 1994, p. 7). Some children tend to question their importance in the eyes of their parents. Some question what they did and if they are able to change what went wrong. Unfortunately, the mind of the child is still developing. Therefore, their internal perceptions of why the loss occurred maybe convoluted or fragmented. Their first primary attachment no longer is available to them and thus the child denies their emotional responsiveness which causes the relational hub to become damaged. The relationship between the child and its primary caregiver is crucial. Bowlby (1969) claimed intimate attachment between human beings acts as the "hub" from which a person's life revolves. Bowlby suggested that these same dynamics are true of other attachment relationships in life. Humans require intimacy. Bergin (2009) indicated that attachment is the foundation of the child's socioemotional well-being. Intimate socialization promotes healthy and secure relationships in life.

Secured, attached relationships allow the child the opportunity to balance their need, exploration, and growth within their environment (The Early Years Foundation, 2007). Bowlby (1969) suggested that healthy child and parent (caregiver) relationships are essential. Relationships are the foundational threshold that allows the child to formulate healthy attachments through which the child is able to gain a secure base in order for exploration both physically and emotionally (Schore, 2003a, 2003b). Bowlby focused on helping children through the attachment process while helping the parents (Bretherton, 1992). Bowlby (1958) explored the difference between insecurity and attachment and the beginning of attachment theory and questioned the first developmental stage as being oral and the first relationship as being analytic. The attachment theory, in essence, describes the long-term interpersonal relationship that exists between humans. Bowlby (1958) attempted to understand separation anxiety and distress in children when they were separated from the mother (primary caregiver). Children develop cognitive impressions through early experiences and attachment to their primary caregiver. When the child is removed from their caregiver, they present threatened and lost. Separation anxiety is a result of unconscious internal conflicts. Bowlby (1958) viewed the reaction of a child being separated from their primary caregiver evolves in three stages: protestation (adult anxiety); desperation (depression); and detachment.

The exploration of early relationships between the mother and child was viewed from various perspectives. Child development in attachment theory includes the interaction between the environments, as well as genetic predispositions (Hart, 2011). In the past, the effects of child trauma and adoption were well-researched topics. Researchers sought to understand that phenomena using a systematic and psychodynamic theoretical approach. The psychodynamic approach that is used with traumatized children generally is cognitive behavior therapy (CBT). Cognitive Behavioral Therapy is used to promote safety and stabilization. The psychodynamic approach helps the child in processing their traumatic memories.

Many organizations have attempted to resolve the issues in child trauma and adoption by providing resources and rendering support through psycho-education to adoptive parents (Adoption Learning Partners, 2010; APAC-Alabama Post-Adoption Connection, 2010; Casey Foundation, 2010). Scholarly articles have been replaced with blogs on the challenges of child trauma on the adoptive family's social and emotional system that leads to disruption/dissolution. Berger (2012) discovered that no national data exist on disruption/dissolution in adoptions. There is a need to equip adoptive families in overcoming the challenges of failed adoption (i.e., disruption/dissolution) continues to exist.

Adoptive families, along with the adopted children, face many challenges. Actual challenges formulate when the child has experienced traumatic events during his or her life prior to adoption (Brodzinsky et al., 1998; Grotevant & McDermott, 2014; Mapes, 2012; Wilke-Deaton, 2005). Most adoptive families do not fully understand the requirements of raising a traumatized child (James, 1994; Mapes, 2012; Pickert & Shuster, 2010; Post, 2006; Ruggerio, 2010). Once the adoption is completed and challenges begin to arise, many adoptive families realize that they are not fully equipped to handle the reality of the presenting issues (James, 1994; Pickert, 2010; Post, 2013; Ruggerio, 2010). The newly adopted child, now living apart from his or her biological parents, tend to struggle with forming new attachments as the child wrestles with questions of disloyalty and estrangement (Forbes, 2008; Park, 2010; Ruggerio, 2010).

Adoptive parents revealed they sought out professional services to address the child's pre adoptive traumatic challenges, as these factors have an impact on the entire family (Ford, 2015; Park, 2010). Cohen, Coyne, and Duvall (1993) suggested that adoptive parents tend to refer their adopted children for clinical services, which are unrelated to general marital or family dysfunction. Miller, Finn, and Grotevant (2000) noted that many adoptive parents refer their adoptive children for clinical services at a higher rate than nonadoptive parents. Adoptive families face many challenges when attempting to work through their child's issues with the assistance of clinical services. Some parents found the only solution was to remove the child from the home (Cohen et al., 1993; Grotevant & McDermott, 2014; Mapes, 2012; Pickert, 2010).

Foster, pre adoptive, and adoptive parents undergo a rigorous amount of training to become a foster parent. Training includes first aid, CPR, disciplining, love and logical, mini map, and other state-required classes. Adoptive parents do not receive many of the needed specialized classes. Classes on attachment, crisis response, parenting the traumatized child, grief and loss, and working with neglected/abused children are rarely given. Adoptive parents struggle to find courses to address these concerns (Child Welfare Information Gateway, 2013). These specialized trainings are essential to help maintain permanency when working with adoptive families and traumatized children (Casey, 2003). Adoptive families require both professional and natural supports in order to be prepared for this challenge. Professional services such as therapy, respite care, crisis intervention, psycho-education courses, and direct family support helps the family work throughout difficult adjustment periods (Child Welfare Information Gateway, 2013). The traumatized child tends to lack sensitive responsiveness, especially when he or she has been a part of the child welfare system. Secure attachments develops internal working models which direct the child's thoughts, feelings, and emotions and helps in their future relationships (Grotevant, 2014; Hartman, 1984; M. A. Baker, personal communication, August 15, 2013; McDonald et al., 2011; Post, 2006, 2013).

Adoption in and of itself can be a powerful tool for social change because the adoption process allows the individuals involved the opportunity to grow into a new family unit. The number of children exposed to domestic violence, physical abuse, sexual abuse, and neglect has increased. It is imperative to find more effective strategies to support the adoptive family in assisting the child (Child Welfare League of America, 2010, 2013; Post, 2013; Smith, 2012, 2013).

Adoptive families may find themselves being challenged more than ever before. One experienced area they are challenged in is failed adoption. Failed adoption (disruption/dissolution) affects the adopting family and child, as well as the community. Homes, schools, and community settings have been affected by the increase in the number of children being removed from their biological homes and being placed into the public foster care system. Failed adoption builds a pressure within the family unit to conform to the expectations and requirements of Child Protective Services (CPS) while facing scrutiny and stereotyping from society.

Failed adoption can be explained through the psychodynamic theory. In the area of psychotherapy, the psychodynamic theory was considered to be the most dominant school of thought among clinical psychology and psychiatry practice in the early 20th century. This approach includes a focus on the unconscious thoughts of the individual in order to formulate an understanding of his or her relationships, experiences, and how he or she sees the world. Failed adoption (disruption/dissolution) and the psychodynamic theory are connected through the examination of the adoptive family's unresolved conflicts and symptoms that arise from dysfunctional relationships, which may lead to a dissolved adoption. Adoptive families may find themselves being challenged more than ever before. Failed adoptions occur by the child's inability to attach to their new family.

The attachment theory is widely used to explain relationship development between a child and its primary caregiver. Bowlby's (1969) theory of attachment derives from the psychodynamic theory. According to the theory of attachment, the infant/toddler must develop a secure base with a primary caregiver before age 2-years-old. Thus, adoptive parents who are ill-equipped or non-versed (e.g., lacking information necessary) to understand and approach the child's needs unconsciously find themselves harboring painful and vulnerable feelings. These thoughts may stay in the unconscious because they are too difficult to deal with (James, 1994; Hushion, Sherman, & Siskind, 2006). This maladaptive process of repression, denial, and rationalization develop as a means to defend oneself and tend to cause the adoptive parent more harm than good. Adoptive parents need to examine their perspective or understanding of grief and possible narcissistic injury, while consistently remaining in tuned to their child's lived experience as an adoptee (Marsh & Ruth, 2008).

According to the psychodynamic theory, human behaviors and feelings are impacted by unconscious motives rooted in childhood experiences. The psychodynamic approach used in the area of adoption is Bowlby's (1969) theory of attachment. Attachment theorists illustrate the dynamics of maintained long-term human relationships. In this theory, Bowlby examined the relationship development between the infant/toddler and at least one primary caregiver by age 2-years-old. Bowlby and Ainsworth (1969, 1973) addressed the dynamics of long-term human relationships and explained the importance of the parent/primary caregiver's role, especially during the social and emotional stages of the infant/child. Bowlby (1969) suggested that child relationships are essential. Attachment theorists suggest that, in healthy child development, it is imperative that interaction take place in various environments (Hart, 2011). Understanding the attachment element experienced from the adoptive parent's perspective could enhance the therapeutic alliance. The therapeutic alliance is what Sonkin (2005) revealed about the therapist attachment development while building an alliance in the therapeutic relationship. In providing the child an opportunity to learn to trust again within a healthy relationship, he or she is afforded a chance to attach to his or her new caregiver. Bowlby believed that this form of attachment figure could happen without the child's awareness. The attachment theory includes four characteristics: proximity maintenance, separation distress, haven, and secure base (Hazan & Zeifman, 1999). Bowlby suggested that these same dynamics are true of other close attachment relationships in life.

Attachment theory is used to clarify how the parental relationship influences the child's development. The traumatized child lacks in sensitive responsiveness, especially when he or she has been a part of the child welfare system (Child Welfare, 2010; Grotevant & McDermott, 2014; M. A. Baker, personal communication, August 15, 2013; National Child Traumatic Stress Network [NCTSN], 2005, 2012). These children are not afforded the opportunity to consistently attach to a secure base because they are moved from house to house, causing an unsecure base for exploration. Secure attachments help the child to develop internal working models which direct the child's thoughts, feelings, emotions, and hope in their future relationships (Grotevant & McDermott, 2014; M. A. Baker, personal communication, August 15, 2013). Attachment is one area that challenges the adoptive parent.

Traumatized children and their adoptive families are more at risk for failure due to a lack of services and resources readily available in meeting the needs of the child and family (Casey Family, 2003). More independent studies need to be conducted to understand the issues that the adoptive families experience (Keck & Kupecky, 2009; Post, 2013; Smith, 2010). Forbes (2008) revealed that the adoptive parent must live at a higher level of consciousness when parenting the traumatized child in order to stay attuned to their emotional state. Forbes suggested that the only way bonding and attachment can occur was by maintaining positive emotional experiences, which can allow the healing process to take place. Professionals question what can be done to help adoptive parents in gaining more understanding and confidence in raising their newly adopted child. Brodzinsky's (1998) stress and coping theory is used to screen adoptive families to ensure the existence of compatibility (good fit) and to make certain that the adoptive family is emotionally regulated. Bowlby's (1969) attachment theory places emphasis on the primary caregiver's responsiveness to the child's needs. Bowlby's attachment theory explores proximity maintenance, safe haven, and secure base (ensuring closeness or a type of intimacy where the child can explore from and return to) as well as separation anxiety, which is considered to be normal and adaptive in infants and is a part of their survival tools (Collins & Feeney, 2000).

The number of children being adopted from the public foster care system has increased. In the Adoption and Foster Care Analysis and Reporting System (AFCARS), the U.S. Department of Human Health Services (2013) revealed that 94,626 of the 400,540 children in the foster care system were adopted through the public welfare system. This number does not include the 14,213 children designated to pre adoptive licensed homes possessing a signed agreement with the state to foster and adopt (U.S. Department of Health and Human Services, 2013). However, the number of children adopted from the public welfare agency during 2011 was 50,516 (U.S. Department of Health and Human Services, 2013). In the past, the criteria for adopting a child differed then the criteria that is in place today, and the characteristics of the adoptive parent were primarily of middle socioeconomic status, upper-socioeconomic status, married, infertile, and nondisabled European American couples between the ages of 30s to 40s (Brodzinsky, Patterson, & Vaziri, 2001; Derdeyn, 1990).

The characteristics of adoptive parents have expanded to include individuals from low-income families, older individuals, single parents, and same-sex couples (Brodzinsky et al., 2001; Derdeyn, 1990; Smith, 2011). These changes surfaced due to the Adoption Assistance and Child Welfare Act (1980) and The Adoption and Safe Families Act (1997). The Child Welfare Act afforded an opportunity for special needs children (i.e., older age at placement, minority, racial, status, multiple sibling group, exposed to neglect and/or abuse, chronic medical problems, and mental and psychological disturbance) along with non-traumatized children to be adopted (Administration for Children and Families, 1980). The Adoption and Safe Families Act was passed with the purpose of reaffirming a commitment to permanency planning for foster children through reunification with the birth family or a concurrent plan for severance and adoption. From the standpoint of the adopted family, the reasons why they may struggle in receiving professional alliance within the home, school, and community, all of which are essential in order to survive and thrive in the midst of a difficult adoption. Providing knowledge from the adopted family's perspective renders additional insight into an effective intervention that takes into account the challenges that trauma etches on the adoptive family's social and emotional system (Adoption and Safe Families Act, 1997). With the increasing number of children exposed to domestic violence, physical abuse, sexual abuse, and neglect, finding more effective strategies to support their adoptive family in assisting their child, not only to survive but also to thrive, is imperative (Brodzinsky, 1992; James, 1994; Mapes, 2012; McDonald, 2001; Pickert, 2010; Ruggerio, 2010; Smith, 2010).

- **Disruption/Dissolution:** Refers to interruption within the family unit. A disruption occurs before the adoption has been legally finalized resulting in the child returning to the foster care system (Child Welfare, 2012; Meyers, 2011). Dissolution occurs when the legal relationship between the adoptive parents and the adopted child is severed, either voluntarily or involuntarily after the adoption is legally finalized (Child Welfare, 2012).
- **Pre Adoptive Placement:** "The placement of a foster child, for whom the permanency plan is adoption, with people who have been approved as an adoptive resource, pending the child becomes legally free for adoption" (Adoption Legal Risk- Child and Family Policy Manual, 2007, p. 1).
- **Unprivileged Information:** Complete medical, mental health, developmental, psychological, educational, and social information about the child and his or her biological family (Child Welfare Information Gateway, 2013).
- **Well-Informed/Unprivileged Information:** Information given or received by potential adoptive parents before making a legally finalized decision to adopt (Child Welfare Information Gateway, 2013).
- **Wrongful Adoption:** Accusations of undisclosed information withheld from adoptive parents by adoption agencies leading to an adoption. Undisclosed information can include a variety of things, such as serious physical emotional or psychological defects or deficiency (Meyers, 2011; National Adoption Information Clearinghouse, 2012).

Trauma is unique. Every individual who experienced such an event experiences it differently (Lee & James, 2011). Trauma is defined as any event that imposed a life altering or life threatening experience in such a way that the individual is deemed unable to function (Smith, 2012). The United States experienced an increase in children being placed in the public welfare system due to various traumatic situations of violence, neglect, and abuse. Foster children in the United States escalated over the last two decades making up the vast number of children adopted (Child Welfare Information Gateway, 2013; Smith, 2010). Adoption is used to reduce the number of children growing up in the public welfare system.

Adoption continues to be a valuable solution for the growing number of children living within the public foster care system. The U.S. Department of Human Health Services (2012) reported that over 400,540 children were adopted from the public welfare system. This number does not include the 14,213 children who were designated to pre adoptive homes (U.S. Department of Health and Human Services, 2012). In September 2012, the number of children in the foster care system reached 399,546 (Children's Bureau, 2013). In 2012, over 83,905 children were adopted in the United States alone (Children's Bureau, 2013). The number of children being adopted from the foster care system reveals adoption is one valuable solution. The desire is to have children raised in a loving and caring environment and not the foster care system.

In the adoption literature, failed adoptions are referred to as disruptions. While these acts were found to be complex and emotionally charged, they have occurred more often than reported (Mapes, 2012; Smith, 2010). Although statistical data may vary, the University of Minnesota and Hennepin County (2010) conducted a study of the U.S. adoption practices and found that between 6 to 11% of all adoptions faced disruption before the adoption was finalized. The University of Minnesota and Hennepin County revealed that age was one critical variable in the rate of disruption. Children older than age 3 had a likelihood of disruption between the ranges of 10 to 16% (The University of Minnesota and Hennepin County, 2010). The rate of disruption is worse for teens, ranging as high as 24%, or 1 in 4 adoptions (Barth, Berry, Carson, & Goodfield, 1986; Festinger, 1990; Schmidt, Rosenthal, & Bombeck, 1988; Westhues & Cohen, 1990).

Researchers have attempted to determine the cause of disrupted adoptions. Barth and Berry (1988) suggested that older children were washed over from the initial success of permanency planning. Grotevant and McDermott (2014) revealed that, when disruptions or dissolution occurred in the adoptive home, the child is then at a higher risk for problems with adaptation, especially in the area of internalizing, externalizing, and attention. Another layer of trauma occurs in the area of trust, bonding, and attachment. Foster children develop negative behavior associated with bonding and attachment due to loss, deprivation, abuse, and physical development problems (Keck & Kupecky, 2009; Rushton & Monck, 2009; Spangler, Johann, Ronai, & Zimmermann, 2009; Wilke-Deaton, 2005). Trauma is defined as any stressful event, which was prolonged, overwhelming, or unpredictable (Lee & James, 2011; Post, 2012; Smith, 2012; Wilke-Deaton, 2005). Trauma can also be defined as a life-threatening and life-altering set of events or experiences in which the individual has no control over and is an actual or perceived threat of danger where the individual feels overwhelmed and/or in an incapacitated state in which he or she is unable to cope as usual (Brodzinsky et al., 1998; James, 1994; Karp & Butler, 1996).

Non infant foster children are categorized as special needs due to age and racial characteristics in various entities (Brodzinsky et al., 1998; Children's Bureau, 2013; Forbes & Dziegielewski, 2003; James, 1994; Karp & Butler, 1996; NCTSN; 2012; Smith, 2010; Wilke-Deaton, 2005). Lived experiences are causational factors that escalated the child's confrontational reasoning ability with their newly adoptive parents (Brodzinsky, 2008; Brodzinsky et al., 1998; Grotevant & McDermott, 2014; Smith, 2012). Adoptive parents of these children may be at a disadvantage from the onset. They adopted more than the child itself; they took on the child's pre adoptive experiences as well (Forbes & Dziegielewski, 2003). As the traumatized child attempts to bond, he or she tends to struggle with mistrust and uncertainty, which is embossed on the forefront of their mind from past experiences (Wilke-Deaton, 2005). When mistrust and uncertainty transfers into placement the effect impacts the adoptive family's relationship as well (Brodzinsky, 2008; Brodzinsky et al., 1998; Grotevant & McDermott, 2014; Smith, 2012). While the adoptive family attempts to engage the child in their family, the child continues to struggle with past inner conflicts, which make parenting the child more difficult (Smith & Howard, 1998).

## MAIN FOCUS OF THE CHAPTER

### Challenges in Attachment

*Case Scenario: A married couple adopted a child (age 7) from the foster care system. The child presented with attachment issues. He had already formulated a healthy bond to his biological mother. The couple refused to stop loving the child although the child stated he could not call them mom and dad. These parents indicated that they had no professional training or alliance within the adoption/mental health arena. They primarily relied on friends and family members from their church for encouragement and direction. For years, they were challenged with rejection from their son. Finally, around age 16, the child realized that his parents really cared for him. He began calling them mom and dad. The husband recalled, "We faced a number of challenges that others might have walked away from. But we were committed to him way before he committed to us!"*

The development of human attachment begins within the first years of life. Bowlby (1969) suggested that the relationships between the child and the primary caregivers are essential. Relationships are seen as the foundational threshold that allows the child to formulate healthy attachments (Brodzinsky et al., 1998; Grotevant & McDermott, 2014; Schore, 2003a, 2003b; Wilke-Deaton, 2005). As the secure base is instilled for exploration, the child's increased need and ability to navigate in both the psychological and physical world develops (Schore, 2003a, 2003b).

Bowlby suggested helping children to find their way while helping the parents to feel secure was vital (Bretherton, 1992). From this point on, a difference between insecurity and attachment between the mother and child was explored (Bowlby, 1958). According to the attachment theory, the development of childhood includes the interaction between environments as well as genetic predisposition (Hart, 2011). Understanding the attachment element experienced from the adoptive parent's perspective was vital to enhance the therapeutic alliance. In fact, Bowlby (1969) felt that the intimate attachment between human beings acted as the hub from which a person's life revolved.

It is those initial relationships that Bowlby believed the individual attached to a personal therapist. Bowlby (1969) noted that attachment happened without the child's awareness, and the attachment theory developed four characteristics: proximity maintenance, separation distress, haven, and secure base. Bowlby suggested that these same dynamics were true of other close attachment relationships in life. Wilke-Deaton (2005) suggested that when the professional is looking to understand attachment theories or even attachment, in general, it is important to realize that children tend to have more than one primary caregiver. Past researchers focused on the relationship with the mother and child. Yet this has been noted as only one of the primary caregivers (Brodzinsky, 2008; Grotevant & McDermott, 2014; Smith, 2012; Wilke-Deaton, 2005).

Attachment theory is used to clarify the impact on how the parental relationship influences the child's development. Traumatized children tend to lack in sensitive responsiveness when raised in the foster care system (M. A. Baker, personal communication, August 15, 2013; Wilke-Deaton, 2005). These children lack a secure base because they moved from house-to-house, causing an unsecure base from which they can explore (Brodzinsky, 1992; McCormick, 1991; McDonald, 2001; Pickert, 2010; Rushton & Monck, 2009). Secured attachments help the child to develop internal working models that direct the child's thoughts, feelings, emotions, and hope in his or her future relationships (Brodzinsky et al., 1998; Grotevant & McDermott, 2014; M. A. Baker, personal communication, August 15, 2013;

Wilke-Deaton, 2005). The internal working model of each traumatic event influences the outcome of the organization and functional capacity of the adoptive family's outcome depending on the complexity or longevity of each experience (Grotevant & McDermott, 2014).

Within attachment theory, James (1994) defined attachment as a reciprocal process by which the child and his or her caregiver endure emotions and physical affiliation. In addition the reciprocal processes engage each party (caregiver and child) into the bonding and attachment approach (Wilke-Deaton, 2005). One facet of the reciprocal approach resembles the action of the primary caregiver establishing or instilling trust, morals, beliefs, and love in the form of bonding, which allows the child to begin to formulate an attachment relationship with the caregiver (Wilke-Deaton, 2005). When applied to traumatize children, it is easier to understand why children who are removed from their original caregivers tend to present as challenged in adjustment or establishment of new attachments.

When the attachment is severely disrupted, the child's physical, social, and mental developmental balances are interrupted as well (Grotevant & McDermott, 2014). These disruptions are displayed in academia and other school areas, adjustment within various environmental settings, externalizing and impulsive displayed symptoms, hyperactive behavior, conduct problems, and substance abuse issues (Anda et al., 2006). These misunderstood challenges stigmatize the adoptive family unit and render many of them ill-equipped because these families tend to lack information about their child's past traumatic experiences which is required to advocate for the needs of their new family. The lack of background information and parental stressors are the strongest service-related predictors of disruption (Groze, 1996; Rosenthal, 1993). Family preservation is crucial in order to maintain the relationship of the pre-existing family unit and provide the child with stabilization and permanency in a safe and secured environment (Brodzinsky, 1992, 2008; Grotevant & McDermott, 2014; James, 1994; McDonald, 2001; Smith, 2012; Wilke-Deaton, 2005). Therefore, it is necessary that placement supports be established allowing the child to generate a new bond of trust with his or her new caregiver. When the circle of security (trust) is generated, and a healthy relationship (nurturance and protection) with the caregiver is created, the child's psychological human development is constructed (James, 1994).

## Challenges of Well-Informed Decision Making

*Case Scenario: A married couple adopted another child. "We adopted this little girl straight out of the hospital. We did it because we had already adopted her brothers a few years back. We thought that we knew what we were getting ourselves into because we had her brothers. We knew that the mother had been on drugs. However, we were not prepared at all to deal with these challenges. Our daughter presented with life-threatening medical issues. She presented with sensory, speech, attachment, and behavior issues that were magnified to the tenth power. We were not given any information to make a well-informed decision."*

Research is needed to explore evidence-based strategies for working with adoptive parents of traumatized children. Adoptive parents may not receive well-informed documentation about the child before the adoption was finalized. Agencies may withhold vital information as seen in *(Burr v. Board of County Commissioners of Stark County, 1986).* Funding needs to be allocated for preadoption training to ensure the adoptive parents are equipped with understanding and knowledge of the challenges that present in adopting traumatized children. Postadoption services (therapies, respite care, subsidies, and support groups) must exist to empower the stability of the parent and the family unit as a whole. Of particular importance is the need for the awareness of the knowledge and understanding of the challenges of child trauma on the adoptive family's social and emotional system. As the child's social, emotional, and behavioral problems manifest, the parents' unrealistic expectations of the child may cause disruptions within the new family unit (Barth & Berry; 1988). These gaps laid the foundation for this study by pointing out the challenges that adoptive parents faced in the area of attachment. Adoptive families are apt to be challenged with new stressors just to face the child's rejecting behavior (Barth & Berry, 1988; Wilke-Deaton, 2005).

All states suggest that adoptive families receive information about the potential adopted child and the circumstances that placed him or her in the welfare system. However, receipt of such information happens less often (B. Troupe, personal communication, April 16, 2014; National Adoption Information Clearinghouse, 2013). To make well-informed decisions on whether to adopt or not, this information has been found to be essential (B. Troupe, personal communication, April 16, 2014 (National Adoption Information Clearinghouse, 2013). According to the Child's Bureau (2012), accurate information about a child's background, to the extent allowed by law, should be shared. Initially, this is done with an introduction of a limited scope of information. If the family still shows interest, then the limited scope is continued through full disclosure of obtainable information (Child's Welfare Information Gateway, 2012; Mapes, 2012; Smith, 2012).

Well-informed decision making is a realistic exploration of adoption. The Child Welfare Information Gateway (2010) revealed that this process is a relevant resource for ensuring a legal permanent, nurturing family for every child. When such information is received, the adoptive families are equipped with information on how to advocate for the needs of their potential child. Also, some foster care and adoption agencies have used such information to cross-match potential adoptive families to certain adoptive children. Adopting parents have the opportunity to preview potential genetic defects, generation, and environmental experienced events. Such genetic defects could have an impact on the child's medical, behavioral, social, and emotional mental health. Therefore, such information needs to be shared before the adoptive parent commits to a life-long relationship with the child. Some agencies find this to be a detrimental step in finding a good home for some children. However, it is not enough just to place the child in a home where disruption or dissolution can take place. The goal of this decision-making process is to alleviate further potential trauma. Adoptive families cannot meet the needs of the adopted child being ill-equipped (Child Welfare Gateway, 2010, 2012; Forbes & Dziegielewski, 2003; Grotevant & McDermott, 2014; Smith, 2012; Wilke-Deaton, 2005). When the informed decision-making process is carried out, it allows the potential adoptive family the chance to obtain the necessary training to raise a traumatized child (Child Welfare Gateway, 2010, 2012).

Such training can be in various areas. Training in adopting traumatized children is required for there to be stability and permanency (Brodzinsky, 2008; Forbes & Dziegielewski, 2003; Grotevant & McDermott, 2014; Smith, 2012). The National Academy of Sciences reported the consequences of abuse (trauma) has been found to reshape the brain of the traumatized child. The results of this reshaping leave a long-lasting effect, especially when the child is untreated (Schulte, 2013). The effects influence the child's physical behaviors as well as their mental health behaviors (Schulte, 2013). In fact, many states require adoption agencies and attorneys to collect medical and genetic information on the child that can be shared with the adoptive parent (Dinwoode, 2014).

In adoptions, the adopting parent is required to sign consent where they agree to take and raise the child with the same privileges as their birth child (Child Welfare Gateway, 2010, 2012). Every state regulates their consent to adopt. Consent to adopt is not governed by federal laws. However, consents to adopt are required by all states (Children's Bureau, 2013).

Although adoption consent is designed to ensure the protection of all parties involved (child, birth parent, and adopting parent), it was not designed to protect adoptive parents from wrongful adoption. Wrongful Adoption is a legal term that refers to the failure of an adoption agency or worker to disclose known information about a child to the prospective adoptive parents (Child Welfare Information Gateway, 2013). Valuable information which includes known medical or psychiatric. Wrongful adoption occurs when adoption workers stand unclear on adoption law and what is to be disclosed. Many adoption agencies are attempting to obtain placement of the child in a permanent home. Although unprivileged information regarding the child is required at the time of placement, sometimes the pertinent information has been knowingly omitted. Some families receive less than accurate preplacement (well-informed/unprivileged) information (Arizona Revised Statues, 2013). Well-informed decisions are only capable of being made when adoptive parents receive all relevant information about the child. Well-informed decisions derive from information gathered on the child and his or her biological family. The Child Welfare League of America (CWLA, 2013) proposed that a standard of excellence be in place for all adoption services. The adoptive family should receive complete unprivileged information on the child, their birth family and other birth relatives two generations back (CWLA, 2013). Therefore, included in the well-informed decision-making process is unprivileged information. The Arizona's Revised Statues 8-514 (2013) viewed unprivileged information to include but was not limited to: demographic information; type of custody and previous placement; pertinent family information including the names of family members who, by court order, may not visit the child; known or available medical history including but not limited to (a) allergies, (b) immunizations, (c) childhood diseases, (d) physical handicaps, (e) other idiosyncrasies (e.g., psychological, mental health, etc.), and (f) the child's last doctor; and a summary of the child's history of adjudication on acts of delinquency, as may be public record and available in the file of the clerk of the superior court (pp. 1-3).

Sometimes adoption agencies have limited knowledge of the child's past traumatic experiences. Therefore, they too are challenged with understanding the complexity of the child's trauma (Wilke-Deaton, 2005). Many adoption agencies have learned that all prospective parents are required to have disclosed non-identifying information where with an informed decision to adopt can be made. Adoptive parents are commissioned not to assume they received all medical, psychiatric, and social information about their potential adopted child (Child Welfare Information Gateway, 2013; Riggs & Kroll, 2004). One historical case of a wrongful adoption was Burr vs. Board of County Commissioners of Stark County (1986) in Ohio. In this case, the adoptive parents struggled with challenges of their child. It was discovered that known; unprivileged information was purposefully withheld about the birthmother's mental illness. The agency's worker knowingly withheld information and misrepresented the child as a child who was healthy (Combs, 1986). The adoptive parents were led to believe that the 17-month old baby was being placed up for adoption by his 18-year-old mother. Allegedly, the grandparents were said to have abused the child and the mother's desire to make a better life for herself in another state (Combs, 1986). The adoptive parents immediately proceeded with the adoption based off of the information received. Their lives and that of their sons throughout his childhood indicted a myriad of physical and mental health problems. This case pointed out how necessary it was for adoptive parents to inquire about their child's past in order to have obtained child abuse, medical, psychiatric, and placement history.

Adoptive parents need to advocate to receive complete historical information, both known and unprivileged, to formulate a well-informed decision about adoption. Such information includes medical and mental health issues, social and emotional, behavioral, educational, legal, and any genetic predisposition information that could have an adverse effect on the development of the child and the stability of the new family. All of this information should be granted prior to the finalization of the adoption to alleviate any further disruptions in the child's life or dissolution of the new family unit. When knowledge of the child's past is received, the adoptive parents are equipped in making well-informed decisions in adopting. This knowledge prepares the adoptive parents and allows for them to advocate for the needs of their child, thus reducing the challenges associated with adopting a traumatized child.

Due to the increase in the number of children in the public welfare system and in out of home placement, child protection agents may strive for placement over permanency when they seek out residency for a child. The gaps in the research laid the foundation for this study by pointing out the challenges that adoptive parents face in the area of well-informed documentation. When the release of medical and mental health disclosures is not discovered until after the adoption finalized, the adoptive family is challenged. Disclosure failure could result from a lack of undocumented information unrevealed even to the child protection service workers.

## Challenge of Placement versus Permanency

*Case Scenario: A single mother shared her story about adopting her son. She stated "In the beginning it they just wanted me to keep my son and work with him on his problems. I was his home because he had nowhere else to go. No one wanted him. But I grew to love him. He had been in so many placements, He had experienced years of rejection, and abandonment issues from various foster families in addition to his own." The re-traumatization this child experienced continues to wreak devastation. "To some, it was about placement, but as I grew to love him it was all about giving this child something he has never experienced......a permanent place to call home!"*

Permanency is stemmed from active participation between a youth and an adult who have searched in finding a permanent connection. The adult is committed to providing the youth with a safe, secure, and stable relationship demonstrated with unconditional love and lifelong support (Brodzinsky et al., 1988; Forbes & Dziegielewski, 2003; M. A. Baker, personal communication, August 15, 2013; Smith, 2012).

Over the last 2 decades, the number of adoptions from the public welfare system in the United States has increased (Child Welfare Information Gateway, 2013). The Children's Bureau (2013) reported that on September 30, 2012, there were an estimated 399,546 children in the public foster care system. Close to half of those children (47%) resided in nonrelative placement, and of this 47%, 24% of these children had a goal of adoption (Children's Bureau, 2013). There must be a paradigm shift from placement towards the direction of achieved permanency and assured supports, which are needed to transition these children from disrupted relationships to a healthy adulthood outcome (Donaldson, 2010). This shift is needed because many children are placed in homes that are not equipped to deal with the challenges these children present, such as abuse, neglect, multiple placements, and other preadoption experiences that inflict physical, psychological, emotional, and developmental harm on them (Donaldson, 2010).

There are few families that willing to adopt traumatized children. With the number of children who are still waiting to find their forever home, these homes are fewer. These special needs children require specialized parenting once they are adopted into their permanent home (Forbes & Dziegielewski, 2003;

Keck & Kupecky, 2009; Smith, 2012). Forbes and Dziegielewski (2003) claimed that there are many reasons provided required for specialized parenting; however, the common thread is found in the mental and behavioral health arena. Mental and behavioral health issues, such as oppositional defiant disorder (ODD), conduct disorder (CD), reactive attachment disorder (RAD), posttraumatic stress disorder (PTSD), and/or depression are common in special needs children (Forbes & Dziegielewski, 2003).

The child welfare system is mandated with the responsibility of placement of children who are wards of the state (National Association of Social Workers, 2009). The Adoption Assistance and Child Welfare Act (1980) renders the goals of family preservation and permanency as priority goals (National Association of Social Workers, 2009). Every adoptive home is required to be screened before placement and supervised monthly while the child is placed in the home. Although, in the beginning, the targeted objective is placement, researchers have shown that this not sufficient enough (Barth & Berry, 1988; Forbes & Dziegielewski, 2003; James, 1994). Best practices for adoption entail not only establishing the formulation of the family, but also cultivating their success (Donaldson, 2010). However, in order for this goal to be carried out, policy makers and professionals must revisit state and national priorities to strengthen and sustain the adoptive family (Keck & Kupecky, 2009; Petra & Kohl, 2010; Randall, 2009; Smith, 2012).

Professionals and policy makers must define, alter, and advocate for the resources necessary to strengthen and sustain the adoptive family unit. Through obtained knowledge and supportive resources, the adoptive parents will be equipped with the essential tools needed to assist their child in enjoining the family unit, causing stabilization to take place on the child and family. This knowledge prepares the adoptive parents and allows for them to advocate for the needs of their child, reducing the challenges associated with adopting a traumatized child (B. Troupe, personal communication, May 2, 2014; Barth & Berry1988; Brodzinsky et al., 1988; Forbes & Dziegielewski, 2003; James, 1994; Keck & Kupecky, 2009; M. A. Baker, personal communication, August 15, 2013; Petra & Kohl, 2010; Randall, 2009; Smith, 2012; Wilke-Deaton, 2005).

Many adoptive parents lack understanding of the various forms of the trauma their adopted child may have experienced. Prolonged exposure to neglect, domestic violence, multiple placement, and trauma within the home and system become a challenge for these parents (James, 1994; Wilke-Deaton, 2005). The adoptive parents face challenges in the area of placement versus permanency. Placement is not enough (Brodzinsky et al., 1988). Policy makers, along with other federal officials, must begin to look at the long-term effects that trauma has on the child, as well as the family unit as a whole. Forbes and Dziegielewski (2003) revealed that researchers have not examined the outcomes or effects on the adoptive family. Yet, understanding the challenges and perspectives of adopting children of trauma needs to be studied in order for the adoptive parent to obtain the specialized training in parenting traumatized children (Forbes & Dziegielewski, 2003).

## Challenges in Understanding Endured Trauma

*Case Scenario: "As an adoptive parent of four different adopted children, I never understood the forms of trauma which abused children endured. Every child I adopted had experienced sexual trauma, abandonment, their biological parents were substance abuse. These children did not attach to their families. Each one presented with attention seeking cravings. They presented victims from within. Due to the sexual abuse of the girls, the family was challenged with vindictive and hurtful scapegoat behaviors towards all males. Until they grow up, I realized that they present with a 'you owe me' mentality instead of seeing everything that I have sacrificed for them."*

Researchers found that the direct impact of experienced trauma from 40% of CPS cases was unknown (U.S. Department of Health & Human Services, ACF, 2010). Acts towards children produce complex traumatic experiences with extended consequences. These acts affect the child, their families, and the community (English, 2005; Higgins & McCabe, 2003; Sabol, Coulton, & Polousky, 2004; Wulczyn, 2009; Zielinski, 2009). These children often experience multiple forms and incidents of abuse or neglect. The National Child Abuse and Neglect Data System (NCANDS) revealed that 40% of the substantiated victims received preventative services within their homes (U.S. Department of Health & Human Services, ACF, 2010). Researchers have revealed the events in which children are traumatically affected. Although these events cause psychological-threatening or physical threats that fuel the child to launch their flight, fight or freeze responses, the child may not qualify for the diagnosis of PTSD (American Psychiatric Association, 2000; James, 1994; M. A. Baker, personal communication, August 15, 2013; Wilke-Deaton, 2005). PTSD in these children occurs because the child's neurophysiological responses continue to linger in a chronically aroused state, even though the intimidation, risk, or danger has ended (Terr, 1992). Traumatic events, such as domestic violence, car accidents, neglect, physical and sexual abuse, national disasters, or even medical procedural trauma cause lingering effects which incapacitate the child's ability to function or self-regulate physically and emotionally (Brodzinsky, 1992; Grotevant, & McDermott, 2014; James, 1994; M. A. Baker, personal communication, December 15, 2013; McDonald, 2001; Pickert, 2010; Ruggiero, 2010). In their presentation, physical and emotional dysregulation are masked by a range of behaviors, which include the following: dissociation, enuresis, eating issues, hyper arousal, heightened startle response, elimination issues, focusing/concentration challenges, sleeping problems, sensory issues, and isolation and attachment issues (Grotevant & McDermott, 2014).

In the past, the criteria for adopting a child differed then the criteria that is in place today (Adoption Assistance and Child Welfare Act (1980). In the past, the adoptive parents were primarily middle socioeconomic status, upper socioeconomic status, married, infertile, and European American couples ages 30s to 40s without any form of disability (Brodzinsky et al., 2001; Derdeyn 1990). In the past, when a couple went to adopt a child, their reasons may have stemmed due to their inability to conceive a child. Today, individuals from low-income families, older individuals, single parents, and same-sex couples adopt children from the public welfare system (Brodzinsky et al., 2001; Derdeyn 1990). These changes surfaced with the Adoption Assistance and Child Welfare Act (1980). This act afforded an opportunity for special needs children (i.e., older age at placement, minority, racial, status, multiple sibling group, exposed to neglect and/or abuse, chronic medical problems, mental and psychological disturbance) along with non-traumatized children to be adopted (Administration for Children and Families, 1980). The Adoption and Safe Families Act (1987) passed with the purpose of reaffirming a commitment to permanency planning for foster children through reunification with the birth family or a concurrent plan for severance and adoption.

Many parents fail to understand or gain the knowledge about the challenges endured when adopting a traumatized child. The basic training that families receive only begins to scratch the surface of what is to come. Lavner, Waterman, and Peplau (2014) suggested that the services rendered to adoptive parents should be required throughout the transition to parenthood. These services need to promote the well-being of the family unit as well as the child. James (1994) revealed that it is not enough to merely survive and thrive in difficult adoptions; adoptive families needed to understand how equipped they must be to establish a healthy relationship when parenting the traumatized child.

*I remember going through the basic training, which didn't teach me about anything that I was going to experience with raising other people's children as my own. I have been horrified at some of the things that I have experienced and appalled at other things. Basic training is not enough! Taking on children is one thing, but when they have gone through so many layers of trauma, it has been another. I had no one to help me. As a single full-time working mother barriers were faced especially when the professional providing direct and indirect services failed to meet the needs of my family .i sought and received support outside of the professional arena in order to meet the needs of my family. Yet this is not the way the challenges of postadoption services should have been met. As an adoptive parent, I was doing a service to the state in addition to making a contractual commitment to love another's child as my own. No I would not change anything that I have experienced. I have learned a lot while on this journey. My four children have taught me life's lessons of what it means to raise and stand beside an individual who has experienced childhood trauma. Before them, I thought my life was 'normal' yet going through the roller coaster ride of life with them, I gained the necessary knowledge to help teach other adoptive parents how to help their adopted children to maintain permanency while being members of a supportive network. I am sincerely grateful to all of the foster parents, kinship placements, and adoptive parents who decided to take on the rewarding challenge of providing a traumatized child a chance at a new life, in a new environment where the risk of trauma recurring is reduced. And to all of the adopted children who have experienced childhood trauma and have learned to trust again, your strength and experiences are there to help another child in overcoming their past and achieve new life within their new families.*

Many adoptive families experience more challenges in the lack of postadoption services. According to Casey Family Services (2003b), continuous barriers exist among professionals who provide direct and indirect (e.g., therapy, support, and subsidy) services to traumatized children and their adoptive families. Ruggiero (2010) believed that families face three challenges in attempting to parent traumatized children. Two of these challenges deal primarily with the foundation that equips the parent for his or her new task. Ruggiero suggested that adoptive parents are unprepared in the preadoption phase for raising children who struggle emotionally from traumatizing experiences; currently, there is a lack of postadoption services, especially in the area of behavior supports. These children and their adoptive families are at risk for failure. Failure in an adoptive home is perceived as the child being admitted in long-term therapeutic placement or even being returned to the welfare system (Casey, 2003b). Such results may be due to the lack of services and resources readily available in meeting the needs of the children and their families. Forbes (2008) acknowledged that parenting traumatized children are different from parenting non-traumatized children. Forbes contended that adoptive parents often face various issues that have a connection to the child's past traumatic experience or event. These challenges often are the cause of a significant alteration of the family's life, which causes an imbalance. Forbes revealed that stress and demands of special needs adoption range around 1/5 to 1/4 of the unsatisfactory reported adoptions. This contributes to 10% of disruptive adoptions which leads to the child returning to the foster care system. These hurdles highlighted some of the critical issues in adoption failure. Constant challenges in adoption permanency (e.g., remaining, maintaining, and integrating as an active member of the new family) of the traumatized child are the least studied. Therefore, researchers must address the needs and factors associated with strong, vigorous, and thriving post adoptive experiences (Forbes, 2008; James, 1994).

Researchers have looked to understand the issues or challenges that disrupt the developmental balance in the child's ability to form healthy attachments instead of viewing the challenges through the lens of the adoptive family. McGlone, Santos, Kazama, Fong, and Mueller (2003) conducted a study to understand the nature and the extent of parental stress endured by adoptive parents of special needs children. Adoptive parents revealed that they sought out clinical services to address their child's pre-adoptive factors (e.g., biological and earlier experiences or abuse and neglect), which had an influential impact on the entire family. Adoptive families face challenges where the only solution to the problem was to remove the child from the home (Cohen, Coyne, & Duvall, 1993). Multiple placements increase additional layers of trauma.

## SOLUTIONS AND RECOMMENDATIONS

Researchers have examined the challenges that adoptive parents have faced when adopting a child who has experienced trauma. However, scholars must also understand from the adoptive family's perspective and not just the child's perspective of the causes of failed adoption. Scholars have provided insight to the challenges of child trauma on the adoptive family social and emotional system. Researchers have revealed the importance of the foundation for human preservation within the family unit. Research is needed to explore evidence-based strategies for working with adoptive parents of traumatized children. The ultimate goal of prevention services appears to center around the child and family's environment. Here the catalyst is focused on positive changes among the primary family. The traumatic effects that an adoptive child experience affect the entire family unit; therefore, professional services are required for the whole family (Higgins & McCabe, 2003).

The significance of this topic aims to understand, from the perspective of the adopted family and their children, the reasons why they may be challenged with receiving professional alliance within the home, school, and community. The results added additional insight to actual knowledge for intervention while taking into account the impact of trauma etched on the adoptive family's social and emotional system. Adoption can be a powerful tool for social change. With the increasing number of children exposed to domestic violence, physical abuse, sexual abuse, and neglect, finding more efficient strategies to support their adoptive family in assisting their child, not only to survive but also to thrive, is imperative.

## FUTURE RESEARCH DIRECTIONS

Adoption in and of itself can be a powerful tool for social change (Meyers, 2011). The number of children exposed to domestic violence, physical abuse, sexual abuse, and neglect has increased (Child Welfare League of America. 2010, 2013; Post, 2013; Smith, 2012, 2013). There is a need for more individuals to take on the challenge of adoption. There are many individuals who are willing to take on this challenge. However, it is important for adoption workers to understand that family unity does not always occur once the adoption paperwork is completed. In fact, this is often the time when many of the social and emotional challenges begin (Donaldson, 2013). Desire is not enough. It is imperative for individuals to be equipped with knowledge, coping skills, and support. Thus moving families beyond thriving to surviving in difficult adoptions (Child League of America, 1996; James 1994). Understanding the adoptive family's perspective could contribute to providing more effective treatment and supports. This population of individuals is in need of psychoeducation, supportive services, insurances and financial subsidies. Such positive outcomes can promote permanency in their adoptive homes after placement (Child Welfare, 2010, 2012; McDonald, 2001; Rushton & Monck, 2009).

## CONCLUSION

Many adoptive parents are willing to take on the challenge of raising a child who has experience trauma. However, they desire to be trained and to have supportive resources in place to take on the task. Adoptive parents are committed to raising the children that they have adopted. Adoptive parents desire to be informed of the trauma the children have faced. Supportive resources prepare the adoptive parent for potential challenges that they will face. Social change begins with one action. The ripples of change could extend to professional agencies and down into these homes by equipping adoptive parents with essential tools. These adoptive families can begin to reach out and form bonds that originate trust and attachment between the adult and child within the family unit. As attachments adhere, the family unit thrives and survives within difficult adoptions.

## REFERENCES

Adoption and Safe Families Act of 1997. Pub. L. No.105-89, 42 U.S.C. §§ 620-679 (1997).

Adoption Assistance and Child Welfare Act of 1980 P. L. 96-272

*Adoption Learning Partners*. (2010). Retrieved from http://www.adoptionlearningpartners.org

Ainsworth, M. D. S., Blehar, M. C., Waters, E., & Wall, S. (1978). *Patterns of attachment: A psychological study of the strange situation*. Hillsdale, NJ: Erlbaum.

American Academy of Pediatrics. (2010). *Section on adoption and foster care. Adoption directory membership list*. Retrieved on July 8, 2014, from http://www.aap.org/en-us/professional-resources/publications-and-journals/Pages/Publications-and-Journals.aspx

American Psychiatric Association. (2000). *Diagnostic and statistical manual of mental disorders* (4th ed.). Washington, DC: Author.

Anda, R. F., Felitti, V. J., Bremner, J. D., Walker, J. D., Whitfield, C., Perry, B. D., & Giles, W. H. et al. (2006). The enduring effects of abuse and related adverse experiences in childhood: A convergence of evidence from neurobiology and epidemiology. *European Archives of Psychiatry and Clinical Neuroscience*, *256*(3), 174–186. doi:10.1007/s00406-005-0624-4 PMID:16311898

Annie E. Casey Foundation. (2010). *Funding permanency services: A guide to leveraging federal, state, and local dollars*. Baltimore: Annie E Casey Foundation.

*APAC-Alabama Post-Adoption Connections*. (2010). Retrieved July 8, 2014, from http://www.casapac.org/index.shtml

*Arizona Revised Statures*. (2013). Retrieved from www.Azleg.gov

Aronson, J. (2010). *Impact of adoption on adoptive parents*. Retrieved from www.childwelfare.gov

Barth, R., & Berry, M. (1988). *Adoption and disruption: Rates, risks, and responses*. New York, NY: Aldine de Gruyter.

Barth, R., & Berry, M. (1994). Adoption of drug-exposed children. In R. P. Barth, J. D. Berrick, & N. Gilbert (Eds.), *Child welfare research review* (Vol. 1, pp. 273–294). New York, NY: Columbia University Press.

Barth, R. P., & Miller, J. M. (2000). Building effective post-adoption services: What is the empirical foundation? *Family Relations*, *49*(4), 447–455. doi:10.1111/j.1741-3729.2000.00447.x

Basit, T. N. (2003). Manual or electronic? The role of coding in qualitative data analysis. *Educational Research*, *45*(2), 143–154. doi:10.1080/0013188032000133548

Bernzies, K., & Mychasiuk, R. (2009). Fostering family resiliency: A review of the key protective factors. *Child & Family Social Work*, *14*(1), 103–114. doi:10.1111/j.1365-2206.2008.00586.x

Bertaux, D. (1981). From the life-history approach to the transformation of sociological practice. In D. Bertaux (Ed.), *Biography and society: The life history approach in the social sciences* (pp. 29–45). London, England: Sage.

Blaustein, M., & Kinniburgh, K. (2010). *Treating traumatic stress in children and adolescents: How to foster resilience through attachment, self-regulation, and competency*. New York, NY: Guilford Press.

Booth, P. B., & Jernberg, A. M. (2010). *Theraplay: Helping parents and children build better relationships through attachment-based play* (3rd ed.). San Francisco, CA: John Wiley.

Borgatta, E. F., & Borgatta, R. V. (1992). *Encyclopedia of sociology* (Vol. 4). Retrieved from http://www.sesp.northwestern.edu/docs/publications/16511665225230b3b2ad63d.pdf

Bourdon, S. (2002). The integration of qualitative data analysis software in research strategies: Resistance and possibilities. *Forum Qualitative Sozialforschung / Forum: Qualitative. Social Research*, *3*(2), 11. Retrieved from http://nbn-resolving.de/urn:nbn:de:0114-fqs0202118

Bowlby, J. (1969). *Attachment and loss*. Retrieved from http://www.scribd.com/doc/46786672/Bowlby-1969-Attachment-and-Loss-Volume-1-Attachment

Bowlby, J. (1969). Attachment and loss: Vol. 1. *Attachment* (2nd ed.). London, England: Hogarth Press.

Bowlby, J. (1973). Attachment and loss: Vol. 2. *Separation*. New York, NY: Basic.

Bowlby, J. (1988). *Secure base: Clinical applications of attachment theory*. London, England: Routledge.

Bretherton, I. (1992). The origins of attachment theory-psychology. *Developmental Psychology*, *28*, 759–775. doi:10.1037/0012-1649.28.5.759

Briere, J. (1996). *Trauma Symptom Checklist Children (TSCC)*. Odessa, FL: Psychological Assessment Resources.

Briere, J. (2005). *Trauma Symptom Checklist for Young Children (TSCYC)*. Odessa, FL: Psychological Assessment Resources.

Brodzinsky, D. M. (1990). A stress and coping model of adoption adjustment. *The Psychology of Adoption*, *3*(1), 3–24.

Brodzinsky, D. M. (1992). The impact of family structure on the adjustment of adopted children. *Child Welfare*, *71*(1), 69–76. PMID:1737523

Brodzinsky, D. M. (1993). Long-term outcomes in adoption. *The Future of Children*, *3*(1), 153–166. doi:10.2307/1602410

Brodzinsky, D. M. (2005). Reconceptualizing openness in adoption: Implications for theory, research, and practice. *Psychological issues in adoption: Research and Practice*, 145-166.

Brodzinsky, D. M. (2008). *Adoptive parent preparation: Meeting the mental health and developmental needs of adopted children*. Retrieved July 4, 2014, from: www.adoptioninstitute.org/policy/2008_02parent_prep.php

Brodzinsky, D. M., & Huffman, L. (1988). Transition to adoptive parenthood. *Marriage & Family Review*, *12*(3-4), 267–286. doi:10.1300/J002v12n03_13

Brodzinsky, D. M., & Phinderhughes, E. (2002). Parenting and child development in adoptive families. In M. Bornstein (Ed.), *Handbook of parenting*. Retrieved from http://www.adoptioninstitute.org/publications/2008_02_Parent_Preparation.pdf

Brodzinsky, D. M., Smith, D. W., & Brodzinsky, A. B. (1998). *Children's adjustment to adoption: Developmental and clinical issues*. Thousand Oaks, CA: Sage.

Byrne, M. M. (2001). Evaluating the findings of qualitative research. *AORN Journal*, *3*, 1-3. Doi:(06)61966-210.1016/S0001-2092

Casey Family Services. (2003). *Strengthening families and communities: Promising practices for adoption-competent mental health services.* A white paper. Retrieved from www.caseyfamilyservices.org/pdfs/casey_mhpaper_sum.pdf

Chambers, R., & Potter, C. (2009). A typology of family needs in child neglect cases. *Families in Society*, *89*(5), 18–27. doi:10.1606/1044-3894.3841

Cherry, K. A. (2006). *What is attachment theory?* Retrieved from http://psychology.about.com/od/loveandattraction/a/attachment01.htm

Child Welfare Information Gateway. (2010). *Impact of adoption on adoptive parents*. Retrieved from www.childwelfare.gov

Child Welfare Information Gateway. (2011). *Parenting after adoption*. Retrieved from www.childwelfare.gov

Child Welfare Information Gateway. (2012). *Finding and using postadoption services*. Retrieved from www.childwelfare.gov

Child Welfare Information Gateway. (2012). *Foster parents considering adoption*. Washington, DC: U.S. Department of Health and Human Services, Children's Bureau.

Child Welfare Information Gateway. (2013). *Disruption and dissolution in adoption*. Retrieved from www.childwelfare.gov

Child Welfare Information Gateway. (2013). *Consent to adoption*. Washington, DC: US Department of Health and Human Services, Children's Bureau.

*Children's Bureau*. (2013). Retrieved from http://www.acf.hhs.gov/programs/cb/research-data-technology/statistics-research

Chorpita, B. F., & Daleiden, E. L. (2009). Mapping evidence-based treatments for children and adolescents: Application of the distillation and matching model to 615 treatments from 322 randomized trails. *Journal of Counseling and Clinical Psychology*, *77*(3), 566–579. doi:10.1037/a0014565 PMID:19485596

Combs, C. G. (1986). Case note: Wrongful adoption: Adoption agency held liable for fraudulent representations: Burr v. Stark County Board of Commissioners, Ohio St. 3d 69 491 N. E. 2d 1101. *University of Cincinnati Law Review*.

Cook, A., Spinnazzola, J., Ford, J. A., Lanktree, C., Blaustein, M., Cloitre, M., & Van der kolk, B. (2005). Complex trauma in children and adolescents. *Psychiatric S Annals, 35*, 390-398.

Cradle. (2010). *Post-adoption services*. Retrieved July 2, 2014, from http://www.cradle.ord/postadopt_home.html

Creswell, J. W. (2002). *Educational research: Planning, conducting, and evaluating quantitative and qualitative research*. Upper Saddle River, NJ: Merrill Prentice Hall.

Creswell, J. W. (2003). *Research design: Qualitative, quantitative and mixed methods approaches* (2nd ed.). Thousand Oaks, CA: Sage.

Creswell, J. W. (2007). *Qualitative inquiry & research design: Choosing among five approaches* (2nd ed.). Los Angeles, CA: Sage.

Early Years Foundation. (2007). *Child development overview*. Retrieved from http://webarchive.nationalarchives.gov.uk/20130401151715/http://www.education.gov.uk/publications/eOrderingDownload/eyfs_cards_0001207.pdf

Eth, S., & Pynoos, R. S. (1985). *Posttraumatic stress disorder in children (Progress inPsychiatry Series)*. Washington, DC: American Psychiatric Association.

Evan B. Donaldson Adoption Institute. (2010). *Keeping the promise: The critical need for post-adoption services to enable children and families to succeed*. Retrieved from http://life.familyeducation.com/adoption/adoptive-parents/45782html#ixzz2srEgs9bLhtml#ixzz2srEgs9bL

Family Preservation and Support Services Act of 1993, P. L. 103-66.

Fay, J., Fay, C., & Cline, F. (2010). *Becoming a love and logic parent curriculum*. Golden, CO: Love and Logic Institute.

Fellows, R., & Liu, A. (2008). *Research methods for construction*. New York, NY: John Wiley & Sons.

Festinger, T., & Maza, P. (2009). Displacement or post-adoption? A research note. *Journal of Public Child Welfare*, *3*(3), 275–286. doi:10.1080/15548730903129889

Finkelhor, D., Turner, H., Ormrod, R., & Hamby, S. L. (2010). Trends in childhood violence and abuse exposure: Evidence from 2 national surveys. *Pediatrics & Adolescent Medicine, 238-242*. doi:10.1001/archpediatric.2009.283 PMID:20194256

Finkelhor, D., Turner, H. A., Ormrod, R., & Hamby, S. L. (2009). Violence, abuse, and crime exposure in a national sample of children and youth. *Pediatrics*, *124*(5), 1411–1423. doi:10.1542/peds.2009-0467 PMID:19805459

Forbes, H., & Dziegielewski, S. F. (2003). Issues facing adoptive mothers of children with special needs. *Journal of Social Work*, *3*(3), 301–320. doi:10.1177/146801730333003

Ford, J. (2015). *Challenges of Child Trauma on Adoptive Families' Social and Emotional System.* ProQuest LLC. UMI Dissertation Publishing 3707129.

Fuller, T., Brulin, C., Cohen, L., Lis, M., Rollock, N., & Sheridan, K. (2006). *Supporting adoptions and guardianships in Illinois: An analysis of subsidies, services and spending*. Urbana-Champaign, IL: University of Illinois. Retrieved July 11, 2014, from http://cfrc.illinois.edu/pubs/rp_20070901_ConditionsOfChildrenBH2006.pdf

Golafshani, N. (2003). Understanding reliability and validity in qualitative research. *Qualitative Report*, *8*(4), 597–607.

Greely, H. T. (2001). Informed consent and other ethical issues in human population genetics. *Annual Review of Genetics*, *35*(1), 785–800. doi:10.1146/annurev.genet.35.102401.091453 PMID:11700299

Grotevant, H., & McDermott, J. (2014). Adoption: Biological and social process linked to adaptation. *Annual Review of Psychology*, *65*(1), 235–265. doi:10.1146/annurev-psych-010213-115020 PMID:24016275

Grotevant, H. D. (2009). Emotional disturbance regulation over the life course in adoptive kinship networks. In G. M. Wrobel & E. Neil (Eds.), *International advances in adoption research for practice* (pp. 295–316). London: Wiley-Blackwell.

Groze, V. (1996a). A 1 and 2 year follow-up study of adoptive families and special needs children. *Children and Youth Services Review, 18*, 57-82. Doi:(95)00054-210.1016/0190-7409

Groze, V. (1996b). *Successful adoptive families*. Westport, CT: Praeger.

Groze, V., & Rosenthal, J. A. (1993). Attachment theory and the adoption of children with special needs. *Social Welfare Research and Abstracts*, *29*(2), 5–12. doi:10.1093/swra/29.2.5

Hartmann, A. (1984). *Working with adoptive families beyond placement.* New York, NY: Child Welfare League of America.

Hazan, C., & Zeifman, D. (1999). Pair bonds as attachments: Evaluating the evidence. In J. Cassidy & P. R. Shaver (Eds.), *Handbook of attachment: Theory, research, and clinical applications* (pp. 336–354). New York, NY: Guilford Press.

Higgins, D. J., & McCabe, M. (2003). Maltreatment and family dysfunction in childhood and the subsequent adjustment of children and adults. *Journal of Family Violence*, *18*(2), 107–120. doi:10.1023/A:1022841215113

Higgins, D. J., & McCabe, M. P. (2000). Multiple forms of child abuse and neglect: Adult retrospective reports. *Aggression and Violent Behavior*, *6*(6), 547–578. doi:10.1016/S1359-1789(00)00030-6

Hoepfl, M. C. (1997). Choosing qualitative research: A primer for technology education researchers. *Journal of Technology Education*, *9*(1), 47–63.

Hushion, K., Sherman, S. B., & Siskind, D. (Eds.). (2006). *Understanding adoption: clinical work with adults, children, and parents*. Rowman & Littlefield.

Jacob, E., Miller, L. C., & Tirella, L. G. (2010). Developmental and behavioral performance of internationally adopted preschoolers: A pilot study. *Child Psychiatry and Human Development*, *41*(1), 15–29. doi:10.1007/s10578-009-0149-6 PMID:19593639

James, B. (1994). *Handbook for treatment of attachment-trauma problems in children*. New York, NY: The Free Press.

Jones, J. (2009). *Who adopts? Characteristics of women and men who have adopted children, NCHS Data Brief, No. 12. Center for Disease Control and Prevention*. National Center for Health Statistics.

Jones, L. M., & Finkelhor, D. (2007). *Updated trends in child maltreatment*. Retrieved from http://www.unh.edu/ccrc/pdf/Updated%20Trends%20in%20Child%20Maltreatment%202007.pdf

Karen, R. (1998). *Becoming attached: First relationships and how they shape our capacity to love*. New York, NY: Oxford University Press.

Karen, R. (1998). *Becoming attached: First relationships and how they shape our capacity to love*. New York, NY: Oxford University Press.

Karp, C. L., & Butler, T. L. (1996). *Treatment strategies for abused children: From victim to survivor*. Thousand Oaks, CA: Sage Publications.

Keck, G. C., & Kupecky, R. M. (2009). *Parenting the hurt child: Helping adoptive families heal and grow*. Colorado Springs, CO: NavPress.

Lavner, J. A., Waterman, J., & Peplau, L. A. (2014). Parent adjustment over time in gay, lesbian, and heterosexual parent families adopting from foster care. *The American Journal of Orthopsychiatry*, *84*(1), 46–53. doi:10.1037/h0098853 PMID:24826826

Lincoln, Y. S., & Guba, E. G. (1985). *Naturalistic inquiry*. Newbury Park, CA: Sage.

Mapes, D. (2012). It takes more than love: What happens when adoption fails? *Today Moms*. Retrieved from http://www.today.com/moms/it-takes-more-love-what-happens-when-adoption-fails-918076

Marshall, M. N. (1996). Sampling for qualitative research. *Family Practice*, *13*(3), 522–525. doi:10.1093/fampra/13.6.522 PMID:9023528

McCann, I. L., & Pearlman, L. A. (1990). Vicarious traumatization: A framework for understanding the psychological effects of working with victims. *Journal of Traumatic Stress*, *3*(1), 131–149. doi:10.1007/BF00975140

McCaslin, M., & Scott, K. W. (2003). The five-question method for framing a qualitative research study. *Qualitative Report*, *8*(3), 447–461.

McCormick, J., & Wingert, P. (1991). Whose child am I anyway? *Newsweek*, p. 58.

McDonald, T. P., Propp, J. R., & Murphy, K. (2001). The postadoption experience: Child, parent, and family predictors of family adjustment to adoption. *Child Welfare. Child Welfare League of America.* Retrieved from http://www.highbeam.com/doc/1P3-67282959.htm

McGlone, K., Santos, L., Kazama, L., Fong, R., & Mueller, C. (2003). *Developmental disabilities: Theory, research, and intervention.* New York, NY: Praeger.

Merriam, S. B. (1998). *Qualitative research and case study applications in education.* San Francisco, CA: Jossey -Bass Publishers.

Merriam, S. B. (2009). *Qualitative research: A guide to design and implementation.* San Francisco, CA: Jossey-Bass.

Metz, E. C., & McCall, R. B. (2010). Behavior problems in children adopted from psychosocially depriving institutions. *Journal of Abnormal Child Psychology*, *38*(4), 459–470. doi:10.1007/s10802-009-9383-4 PMID:20084451

Meyers, J. E. B. (2011). *The APSAC Handbook on child maltreatment* (3rd ed.). Thousand Oaks, CA: Sage.

Morse, J. M. (1994). Designing funded qualitative research. In N. K. Denzin & Y. S. Lincoln (Eds.), *Handbook of qualitative research* (2nd ed.; pp. 220–235). Thousand Oaks, CA: Sage.

National Child Traumatic Stress Network. (2005). *Understanding child traumatic stress.* Retrieved from www.nctsnet.org

National Child Traumatic Stress Network. (2012). *The 12 core concepts: Concerns for understanding traumatic stress responses in children and families.* Retrieved from www.nctsnet.org

*New Jersey Adoption Resource Clearing House.* (2010). Retrieved from http://www.njarch.org

North American Council on Adoptable Children. (2009). *Developing a parent-to-parent support network.* Retrieved July 10, 2014, from: http://www.nacac.org/adoptalk/parent2parentnetwork.pdf

Palacios, J., Wrobel, G. M., & Neil, E. (2009). The ecology of adoption. *International advances in adoption research for practice*, 71-94.

Patton, M. Q. (1990). *Qualitative evaluation methods* (2nd ed.). Thousand Oaks, CA: Sage.

Paulsen, C., & Merighi, J. (2009). Adoption preparedness, cultural engagement, and parental satisfaction in inter-country adoption. *Adoption Quarterly*, *12*(1), 1–18. doi:10.1080/10926750902791540

Petra, M., & Kohl, P. (2010). Triple P and the child welfare system: A promising fit. *Children and Youth Services Review*, *32*(4), 611–618. doi:10.1016/j.childyouth.2009.12.008 PMID:20419078

Pickert, K., & Shuster, S. (2010). When the adopted can't adapt. *Time International (South Pacific Edition, 176*(2), 22-27.

Post, B. (2006). *The adopted child: Trauma and its impact*. Retrieved from http://www.streetdirectory.com/travel_guide/201812/child_adoptions/the_adopted_child_trauma_and_its_impact.htm

Post, B. (2013). *The adopted child: Trauma and its impact*. Retrieved from http://postinstitute.com/blog/2013/11/06/the-adopted-child-trauma-and-its-impact-bryan-post/

Prinz, R. (2009). Dissemination of a multilevel evidence based system of parenting interventions with broad application to child welfare populations. *Child Welfare*, *88*(1), 127–132. PMID:19653456

Randall, J. (2009). Towards a better understanding of the needs of children currently adopted from care: An analysis of placements 2003-2006. *Adoption & Fostering*, *33*(1), 44–55. doi:10.1177/030857590903300105

Robison, M., Lindeman, S. L., Clemmons, M. P., Doyle-Buckwalter, K., & Ryan, M. (2009). I deserve a family ll: The evolution of an adolescent's behavior and beliefs about himself and others when treated with therapy in residential care. *Child & Adolescent Social Work Journal*, *26*(4), 291–306. doi:10.1007/s10560-009-0177-x

Rosenberg, M. B. (1989). *Growing up adopted*. New York: Bradbury Press.

Ruggiero, J. A. (2010). When adoption isn't easy. *Newsweek, 155*(17), 14.

Rushton, A., & Monck, E. (2009). Adopters' experiences of preparation to parent children with serious difficulties. *Adoption & Fostering*, *33*(2), 4–12. doi:10.1177/030857590903300202

Sabol, W., Coulton, C., & Polousky, E. (2004). Measuring child maltreatment risk in communities: A life table approach. *Child Abuse & Neglect*, *28*(9), 967–983. doi:10.1016/j.chiabu.2004.03.014 PMID:15450762

Schore, A. N. (2003a). *Affect dysregulation and disorders of the self*. New York, NY: Norton.

Schore, A. N. (2003b). *Affect regulation and the repair of the self*. New York, NY: Norton.

Schulte, B. (2013). Child abuse's long-lasting effects. *Arizona Daily Star.*

Shaver, P. R., & Mikulincer, M. (2002.) *Adult attachment strategies and regulation of emotion*. Retrieved from http://1st-socrates.berkeley.edu:bobley/images/affective%20science%20readings/Shaver/20100309110651377pdf

Smith, S. (2010). *Keeping the promise: The critical need for post-adoption services to enable children and families to succeed*. Evan B. Donaldson Adoption Institute. Retrieved from http://adoptioninstitute.org/pubs_cat/adoption-support-and-preservation

Smith, S. (2011). *Expanding resources for children III: Research based best practices in adoption by gays and lesbians*. Evan B. Donaldson Adoption Institute. Retrieved from http://adoptioninstitute.org/pubs_cat/adoption-support-and-preservation

Smith, S. (2012). *New: Untangling the web; the Internet's transformative impact on adoption*. Evan B. Donaldson Adoption Institute. Retrieved from http://adoptioninstitute.org/pubs_

Smith, S. (2012). *The vital role of adoption subsidies: Increasing permanency and improving children's lives*. Evan B. Donaldson Adoption Institute. Retrieved from http://adoptioninstitute.org/pubs_keeping-thepromise

Sonkin, D. J. (1999). *Domestic violence and attachment theory: Clinical application to treatment with perpetrators*. Volcano, CA: Volcano Press.

Sonkin, D. J., & Durphy, M. (1997). *Learning to live without violence: A handbook for men* (Rev. Ed.). Volcano, CA: Volcano Press.

Spangler, G., Johann, M., Ronai, Z., & Zimmermann, P. (2009). Genetic and environmental influence on attachment disorganization. *Journal of Child Psychology and Psychiatry, and Allied Disciplines*, *50*(8), 952–961. doi:10.1111/j.1469-7610.2008.02054.x PMID:19673052

*Strengthening Families and Communities: Promising Practices for Adoption-Competent Mental Health services*. (2003). A white paper. Retrieved from www.caseyfamilyservices.org/pdfs/casey_mhpaper_sum.pdf

Terr, L. (1992). *Too scared to cry: Psychic trauma in childhood*. New York, NY: Basic Books.

U.S. Department of Health and Human Services. (2010). *Adoption Assistance and Child Welfare Act of 1980*. Retrieved from https://www.childwelfare.gov/systemwide/laws_policies/federal/index.cfm?event=federalLegislation.viewLegis&id=22

U.S. Department of Health and Human Services, Administration for Children and Families, Administration on Children, Youth and Families, Children's Bureau. (2013). *The adoption and foster care analysis and reporting system (AFCARS) report - no. 20*. Retrieved from www.acf.hhs.gov/sites/default/files/cb/afcarsreport19.pdf

Wegar, K. (2000). Adoption, family ideology, and social stigma: Bias in community attitudes, adoption research, and practice. *Family Relations*, *49*(4), 363–369. doi:10.1111/j.1741-3729.2000.00363.x

Wilke-Deaton, J. (2005). *Attachment and bonding: Effective strategies that work*. Eau Claire, WI: Pesi HealthCare.

World Association for Children and Parents. (2012). *WACAP named 2012 Evergreen Award Winner*. Retrieved from www.wacap.org

Wulczyn, F. (2003). Closing the gap: Are changing exit patterns reducing the time African American children spend in foster care relative to Caucasian children? *Children and Youth Services Review, 25*(5/6), 431-462. Doi:(03)00030-610.1016/S0190-7409

Wulczyn, F. (2004). Family reunification. *The Future of Children*, *14*(1), 95–110. doi:10.2307/1602756 PMID:15072020

Wulczyn, F. (2009). Epidemiological perspectives on maltreatment prevention. *The Future of Children*, *19*(2), 39–66. doi:10.1353/foc.0.0029 PMID:19719022

# Chapter 8
# Assessment of Childhood Trauma in Rural Settings

**Apryl A. Alexander**
*Auburn University, USA*

**Megan E. Harrelson**
*Auburn University, USA*

## ABSTRACT

*Childhood exposure to trauma is prevalent and has been shown to contribute to both immediate and long-term psychological distress and functional impairment. Most mental health professionals will encounter trauma-related issues in their work, regardless of their specialty or the context in which they work, however, in rural communities it may be difficult for mental health practitioners to seek specialty training in working with survivors of trauma. The aim of this chapter is to provide practitioners with basic knowledge about the effects of trauma on children and adolescents, clinical skills and available measures designed to appropriately assess exposure to trauma and subsequent trauma-related symptoms, and ethical and cultural considerations required when assessing trauma in children and adolescents in rural communities.*

## INTRODUCTION

Childhood exposure to trauma is prevalent and has been shown to contribute to both immediate and long-term psychological distress and functional impairment. Thus, most mental health professionals will encounter trauma-related issues in their work, regardless of their specialty or the context in which they work. Clinical interviews and psychological assessments of individuals in rural settings who have experienced trauma may be affected by bias, and such bias can result in the over-, under-, or misdiagnosis of trauma-related symptomatology and posttraumatic stress disorder (PTSD). Accurate assessment of individuals in these communities must take into account the norms of the population and combine informed clinical judgment with objective measures of trauma-related symptoms. Such accurate trauma-informed assessment helps to inform individualized treatment goals and guide treatment.

DOI: 10.4018/978-1-5225-0228-9.ch008

The aim of this chapter is to provide practitioners with basic knowledge about the effects of trauma on children and adolescents, clinical skills and available measures designed to appropriately assess exposure to trauma and subsequent trauma-related symptoms, and ethical and cultural considerations required when assessing trauma in children and adolescents in rural communities.

## BACKGROUND

Despite the need for culturally responsive and empirically supported care for childhood trauma survivors, trauma education and training vary greatly for practitioners (DePrince & Newman, 2011). Although our understanding of trauma and violence exposure in rural communities is limited in part by a general paucity of research, there is some evidence to suggest that exposure to traumatic events, such as sexual abuse, is as prominent in rural communities as it is in urban areas (Finkelhor, 1978; Leistyna, 1980; Schultz & Jones, 1983). The trauma-exposed individuals in rural communities, however, often lack specialty services that are designed to both assess and treat trauma victims. Increased emphasis is being placed on providing trauma-informed care to patients. Trauma-informed care is an approach to engaging individuals with histories of trauma that recognizes traumatic symptoms and acknowledges the role that trauma has played in each person's life. Trauma-informed assessment involves evaluating the ways in which a youth's functioning might have been affected by the experience of trauma (Kerig, 2013).

Accurately evaluating responses to trauma is essential for a comprehensive psychological assessment. Thus, clinicians must be able to recognize both typical and atypical responses to trauma. In children and adolescents, trauma symptoms are often expressed differently than they are in adults. Younger children especially may not have the vocabulary or cognitive ability to articulate the nature of their traumatic experience (e.g., sexual abuse) or recognize that their symptoms are connected to the traumatic event. Therefore, it is important to recognize common responses to trauma. Following a traumatic event, children and adolescents can experience a number of cognitive, behavioral, affective, and physical responses or symptoms.

*Table 1. Common responses to traumatic events*

| Initial/Short-Term | Delayed/Cumulative |
|---|---|
| • Shakiness, dizziness, numbness<br>• Crying or tearfulness<br>• Sleep disturbances<br>• Increased irritability and anger<br>• Withdrawal<br>• Avoidance of event reminders<br>• Somatic/physical symptoms<br>• Anxiety<br>• Thoughts of death/dying<br>• Flashbacks/nightmares<br>• Initiating or increasing substance use<br>• Dissociation<br>• Sexualized behaviors | • Preoccupation with the event to the exclusion of life activities<br>• Avoidance of event reminders<br>• Ongoing fatigue<br>• Feelings of hopelessness, powerlessness, worthlessness<br>• Forgetfulness<br>• Flashbacks/nightmares<br>• Sense of not being "all there"<br>• Inability to leave home and feel safe<br>• Suicidal thinking/planning<br>• Dissociation |

Posttraumatic stress disorder (PTSD) is a disorder that may develop as a result of exposure to a traumatic event. The fifth edition of the *Diagnostic and Statistical Manual for Mental Disorders* (*DSM-5*; American Psychiatric Association, 2013) defines trauma in PTSD as exposure to death, threatened death, actual or threatened serious injury, or actual or threatened sexual violence, as follows (one required):

- Direct exposure.
- Witnessing, in person.
- Indirect exposure, by learning that a close relative or close friend was exposed to trauma. If the event involved actual or threatened death, it must have been violent or accidental.
- Repeated or extreme indirect exposure to aversive details of the event(s), usually in the course of professional duties (e.g., first responders, collecting body parts, professionals repeatedly exposed to details of child abuse). This does not include indirect nonprofessional exposure through electronic media, television, movies, or pictures.

In addition, the traumatic event must be persistently reexperienced through intrusive memories, traumatic nightmares, or marked physiological reactivity after exposure to a trauma-related stimulus. The individual makes efforts to avoid trauma-related stimuli, including trauma-related thoughts or feelings or external reminders of the trauma. Individuals diagnosed with PTSD also experience alterations in cognition or mood, which may include an inability to recall features of the traumatic event, persistent negative beliefs about the world, marked diminished interest in activities, feelings of alienation from others, and constricted affect. These symptoms must cause clinically significant distress or impairment in individuals' social interactions, ability to work, or other important areas of functioning. In order to meet criteria for PTSD, the symptoms must be present for at least 4 weeks.

It should be noted that not all individuals who experience what could be considered a traumatic event have trauma-related symptoms or develop PTSD. In fact, several studies that assessed trauma-related symptoms in sexually abused children found that between 21% and 49% of children were asymptomatic at the time of their assessment (Caffaro-Rouget, Lang, & vanSanten, 1989; Conte & Schuerman, 1987; Mannarino & Cohen, 1986; Tong, Oates, & McDowdell, 1987). There have been several explanations for this finding. Two studies found that at an 18-month follow-up, approximately 30% of the asymptomatic children had eventually developed symptoms (Gomes-Schwartz, Horowitz, Cardarelli, & Sauzier, 1990; Saywitz, Mannarino, Berliner, & Cohen, 2000). There are several reasons children may present as asymptomatic. First, many studies administer measures soon after the disclosure of abuse or trauma, or admission into treatment. It is possible that these children have yet to manifest symptoms at the time of the test administration. Second, given the broad definition of abuse, some children may not display symptoms because the event was less severe and not viewed as traumatic (Saywitz et al., 2000).

In rural communities, death by suicide, as well as occurrence of suicidal behavior, has been found to be much higher than in urban areas, particularly among adult males and children (Hirsch & Cukrowicz, 2014). Geographic isolation, access to firearms, economic difficulties, and lack of access to mental health services are all likely contributors to the higher suicide risk in rural populations. On the contrary, Hirsch and Cukrowicz (2014) note that personal and family honor and community cohesion are potential buffers against suicidal behavior. When assessing for other trauma-related symptoms, clinicians should evaluate the client's history of suicide attempts or self-injurious behaviors as well as the individual's current mental state, querying statements such as "I wish I were no longer here."

Although literature has focused on the effects of specific traumas in children (e.g., sexual abuse, traumatic loss, witnessing violence), victimizing experiences often do not occur in isolation but rather exist as components of larger complex trauma (Banyard, Williams, & Siegel, 2001; Finkelhor et al., 2005a; Higgins & McCabe, 2001). In the last decade, researchers have shifted their focus to evaluating the effects of cumulative trauma, sometimes called poly-victimization, on the long-term well-being of trauma survivors. A study by Turner, Finkelhor, and Ormrod (2010) found that in a survey of 4,053 respondents between the ages of 2 and 17, 80% were exposed to at least one type of victimization in their lifetime; 66% were exposed to more than one type, 30% to five or more types, and 10% to eleven or more different forms of victimization over the lifetime. In turn, participants with greater cumulative traumas displayed more distress symptoms and higher rates of psychopathology than those with fewer traumas (Finkelhor, Ormrod, & Turner, 2009; Finkelhor, Turner, Hamby, & Ormrod, 2011; Turner et al., 2010). Previously victimized children are at greater risk for not only subsequent traumas, but also different types of traumatic experiences (Finkelhor et al., 2011). Poly-victimized youth are found to exhibit more internalized anxiety, depression, and trauma symptoms as well as more aggression and conduct issues than nonvictimized youth (Burk & Burkhart 2003; Cohen, Mannarino, Kliethermes, & Murray, 2012; Finkelhor et al., 2011; Hyde, Bentovim, & Monck, 1995).

## IMPORTANT CONSIDERATIONS IN ASSESSMENT OF CHILDHOOD TRAUMA IN RURAL SETTINGS

Not only do children experience and express trauma-related symptoms differently than adults, but the effects of childhood trauma can also differ depending on a child's age and developmental stage. In younger children with limited verbal skills, feelings of helplessness and anxiety resulting from trauma are often expressed through regressive behaviors or loss of acquired developmental skills. They may have difficulty falling asleep, have nightmares or night terrors, have regressed speech and toileting skills, and have difficulty separating from their primary caregiver. Younger children may also engage in traumatic play—a repetitive and less imaginative play that can represent either the child's perseveration on the trauma or an attempt to change a negative outcome from a traumatic event. Because symptom expression is closely tied to development in young children, the *DSM-5* has added Posttraumatic Stress Disorder for Children 6 years and Younger, which was not in previous editions of the text. School-age children may report concerns over their own safety and the safety of others. They often experience guilt or shame regarding their actions during the event, specifically what they did or did not do during the trauma. School-age children might also engage in retelling of the traumatic event and may describe themselves as being overwhelmed by feelings of fear or sadness. Finally, adolescents tend to be more self-conscious after experiencing a traumatic event. They often exhibit feelings of fear and vulnerability and worry that others will perceive or treat them differently because of the trauma, leading them to withdraw from peers and family. Adolescents may also experience feelings of shame and guilt about the traumatic event and may even express fantasies about revenge toward and retribution from the perpetrator.

Along with age-related factors, when thinking about the assessment of trauma in rural settings, it is important to note that children can respond very differently to the same traumatic events based on individual factors including cultural background, gender, biological vulnerability or predisposition to stress, and social and community support. For instance, externalizing symptoms have been found to be related to the victim's gender, as boys demonstrate more externalizing symptoms than girls (Deblinger et al., 1997). Overall, these individual and contextual variables can influence the intensity, severity, and duration of trauma-related symptoms.

## Clinical Interviewing

Appropriate clinical interviewing of a child following a traumatic event is critical. It is important to distinguish clinical interviews from forensic interviews. A clinical interview is more focused on the child's health and safety. The key question from this interview is "Do we need to worry?" In a forensic interview, the purpose is to learn the truth, meaning to discover whether a traumatic experience or abuse has occurred. These types of interviews are often requested by law enforcement or the legal system and are typically conducted by trained professionals. Medical evaluations are generally required in these cases because the information gathered in these interviews may be used as evidence in court. It is important for the clinician to know at the beginning of the assessment what type of interview he or she will be conducting.

There are several important strategies for gathering accurate information during the clinical interview. When conducting a clinical interview, rapport building is essential. Along with traditional barriers that prevent effective trauma assessment (e.g., stigma, lack of community resources), mistrust is a barrier that is often associated with individuals in rural settings. Various forms of distrust have been documented in minority and marginalized communities, including rural communities, and mistrust can have an impact on how children and adolescents disclose traumatic events and reveal traumatic symptoms (Bonham & Nathan, 2002). Children and adolescents might be shy or ashamed, or they may express feelings of guilt regarding their abuse. Furthermore, in some cases the child has told other professionals about the abuse several times and may be reluctant to do so again.

After developing rapport with the child, it is important to assess his or her competency to answer questions. Some clinicians ask a child to tell them the story. This technique allows the clinician to assess the child's storytelling abilities, particularly how well the child can describe events. For example, some children have difficulties telling stories in a linear fashion. This may indicate to the clinician that when the child is discussing the traumatic incident, the timeline may not be accurate. For younger children it is also important to assess their ability to differentiate between telling the truth and telling a lie. Informing children and adolescents that they can answer questions with "I don't know" or "I don't understand" if they do not know the answer to a question is also essential for gathering accurate information. When conducting an interview with a child who may have experienced sexual abuse, the clinician should assess the child's knowledge of sex and ascertain how the child describes anatomy. When asking about the traumatic event, a free-recall approach can be helpful in the initial stages. During this time, the clinician should be engaging and demonstrate active listening and appropriate empathy. Afterwards, asking *Who*, *Where*, *When*, *What*, and *How* questions can help the clinician gather more detailed information. As readers will note, *Why* questions were not included. *Why* questions sometimes come across as judgmental. Furthermore, children may have trouble interpreting or adequately explaining the events that happened to them. Clinicians should also avoid asking leading questions. These are questions that may force interpretations or elicit inaccurate information. Also, yes or no questions should be avoided, especially with younger children who may have an acquiescent response tendency and highly suggestible. For diagnostic purposes, it is important to observe the child's behaviors during the interview, as this

*Table 2. Key components of a clinical interview*

| | |
|---|---|
| **Key Strategies** | • Build rapport<br>• Comprehension of a truth vs. lie<br>• Test child's story-telling abilities/knowledge of sex<br>• Use free recall/open-ended questions<br>• Engage in active listening<br>• Use developmentally appropriate questions or phrases<br>• Assess suggestibility |
| **Avoid** | • Leading questions<br>• Judgmental statements or body language<br>• Quizzing the child<br>• Close-ended questions that elicit a yes/no response<br>• Avoid 'why' questions/accusatory tones<br>• Touch without consent (i.e. hugs) |

may provide insight into his or her symptoms. Again, younger children might not have the vocabulary to express their symptoms. Clinicians may have to be creative by asking how they feel when they experience stress or worry and whether they experience physical symptoms such as headaches or an upset stomach.

To close the interview, the clinician should allow the child to ask questions and to voice any concerns that he or she may have. Keeping the child informed by providing information about what may come next in treatment will allow the child to feel some comfort. Table 2 provides a quick reference of important strategies to use or avoid when conducting a clinical interview.

Poor interviewing practices and techniques can lead to a number of iatrogenic consequences. Children can be highly suggestible, and practitioners need to be aware of how others (e.g., caregivers, law enforcement officials) may affect the quantity and quality of the child's disclosure. Careful interviewing strategies are also important because children, like adults, are capable of giving inaccurate or false reports of traumatic events, particularly their history of abuse. While some children may have very good recall of distressing events, not all children are able to give accurate reports. Children may misunderstand the question being asked, particularly if they have limited verbal skills. Other children and adolescents may intentionally lie, report misperceptions of events, or report fantasies as if they were actual events happening. Thus, the skills previously described, such as avoiding leading questions and repeated questioning of children about events, are important in order to obtain accurate descriptions of the abuse or trauma that has occurred.

Alternative assessment methods used with children include using anatomical dolls to assess sexual abuse, observational play, and analysis of drawings. These methods are typically implemented to gather information from children who might have been sexually assaulted. However, there is little evidence to show the benefits of these procedures, and methods are not standardized. Moreover, the inferences gathered from assessing trauma through play, drawings, and anatomical doll interviews could be harmful. Historically, some clinicians have made inaccurate inferences from these approaches. Lipovsky (1992) cautions that interactions with anatomical dolls or behaviors observed during play cannot be taken at face value. Individuals using these types of methods for trauma assessment should be aware of the controversy surrounding them. Therefore, it is advisable to read further about these alternative methods to assess trauma in children and adolescents and to emphasize more evidence-based approaches.

## Assessment Measures of Childhood Trauma

Since the 1990s, a number of psychological measures have been developed and validated to assess trauma-related symptoms and PTSD in children and adolescents. These include child self-report measures, semi-structured clinical interviews, and caregiver- and teacher-report measures. As noted by Kerig (2013), most of the existing, well-validated trauma assessment instruments focus on single-event traumas and the subsequent symptoms of "classic" PTSD because measures assessing complex PTSD have yet to be developed and/or validated. While all of the following measures possess limitations, they are the most accurate and empirically supported trauma assessments to date and are preferred when assessing children and adolescents from rural communities.

### Child's Reaction to Traumatic Events Scale—Revised (CRTES-R)

The Child's Reaction to Trauma Events Scale—Revised (CRTES-R; Jones, Fletcher, & Ribbe, 2002) is a measure based on the Horowitz Impact of Events Scale (HIES; Horowitz, Wilner, & Alvaraz, 1979), which was modified from its original version, the CRTES, to assess intrusion and avoidance symptoms based on the *Diagnostic and Statistical Manual of Mental Disorders* (3rd ed., revised) PTSD criteria. The CRTES was further modified to include the assessment of arousal and to update the items to align with the *Diagnostic and Statistical Manual of Mental Disorders* (4th ed.) criteria. The CRTES-R is a 23-item self-report measure designed to assess psychological responses to stressful life events. Scoring is based on a 4-point scale: 0 (not at all), 1 (rarely), 3 (sometimes), or 5 (often). The child is asked to rate the frequency of experiences that have occurred in the past 7 days. The measure can be administered in both English and Spanish and is intended to assess children and adolescents from 6 to 18 years of age.

### Child Sexual Behavior Inventory (CSBI)

The Child Sexual Behavior Inventory (CSBI; Friedrich, 1997) has been used to determined normative sexual behaviors of young children. Researchers using the CSBI have demonstrated that certain sexual behaviors, such as showing one's genitals to others and looking at (or trying to look at) another's genitals, are commonly observed, especially among preschool-aged children (Friedrich et al., 2001; Friedrich, Grambsch, Broughton, Kuiper, & Beilke, 1991; Friedrich et al., 1992; Friedrich & Trane, 2002). The CSBI is written at a fifth grade reading level and is completed by the mother or other primary female caregiver. The CSBI covers nine major domains: Boundary Issues; Gender Role Behavior; Sexual Interest; Sexual Knowledge; Exhibitionism; Self-Stimulation; Sexual Intrusiveness; Voyeuristic Behavior; and Sexual Anxiety. The primary female caregiver indicates how often she has observed each of the listed behaviors during the preceding 6 months. The CSBI Total scale indicates the overall level of sexual behavior the child exhibits. There is also a Developmentally Related Sexual Behavior scale, which indicates sexual behaviors that can be considered normative for the child's age and gender, and a Sexual Abuse Specific Items scale, which indicates sexual behaviors that can be viewed as relatively atypical for the child's age and gender and thus should raise suspicion of possible sexual abuse. The CBSI was normed on 1,114 children from a wide range of socioeconomic backgrounds in the general population. CSBI data from 512 children assessed at child abuse centers is also available and can provide helpful information regarding normative sexual behavior in young children.

## Juvenile Victimization Questionnaire (JVQ)

The Juvenile Victimization Questionnaire (JVQ; Hamby, Finkelhor, Ormrod, & Turner, 2004a) is a comprehensive 34-item self-report questionnaire designed to gather information from adolescents and their caregivers on a broad range of victimization occurring during childhood. (Hamby et al., 2004b). The adult retrospective version contains behaviorally specific questions regarding 34 individual types of victimization that participants may have experienced during their childhood. The types of victimization assessed vary in terms of both the frequency and the severity of the experience. For example, some questions assess relatively common yet potentially lower severity experiences (e.g., theft of personal items), while others assess relatively infrequent yet higher severity events (e.g., exposure to war). Although some types of victimization assessed are not inherently criminal and might not be considered serious by many people (e.g., assaults by peers or siblings), Finkelhor et al. (2005b) reported that they are included on the JVQ in light of evidence that such victimization experiences may nonetheless have serious consequences for some children. Participants report the number of times they experienced each offense from the time they were born until 17 years of age on a 6-point scale (none, 1 time, 2 times, 3 times, 4 times, or 5 or more times).

Six aggregate categories of victimization described by Finkelhor et al. (2007) were constructed to indicate whether participants had experienced any victimization within each category (i.e., property crime, physical assault, child maltreatment, peer/sibling victimization, sexual victimization, and witnessed/indirect victimization). Scoring is dichotomized into 1 (yes, the participant answered "1 time" or more to at least one of the questions making up the aggregate) or 0 (the participant answered no to all questions making up the aggregate). This dichotomous scoring approach reports the occurrence of *any* victimization within each aggregate and was utilized by Finkelhor et al. (2005a) "because of potential overlap among items within an aggregate domain" (p. 393). Although one limitation of this approach to classifying victimization categories, as reported in some studies (e.g., Higgins & McCabe, 2000), is that it does not allow for examination of the severity of the victimization experience, it does allow clinicians to determine potential sources of distress symptoms in traumatized clients (Finkelhor et al., 2007).

## Trauma Symptom Checklist for Children (TSCC) and Trauma Symptom Checklist for Young Children (TSCYC)

The Trauma Symptom Checklist for Children (TSCC; Briere, 1996) and Trauma Symptom Checklist for Young Children (TSCYC; Briere, 2005) are measures of trauma-related symptoms in young children and adolescents. The TSCC is a 54-item self-report scale originally designed to assess trauma symptoms related to sexual abuse and other traumatic events. It is comprised of two validity scales (indicating over- and underreporting of symptoms) and six clinical scales (Anxiety, Depression, Posttraumatic Stress, Sexual Concerns, Dissociation, and Anger). The child is presented with a list of thoughts, feelings, and behaviors and is asked to mark how often he or she experiences each. Items are rated on a 4-point scale: 0 (never) to 3 (almost all the time). A 44-item alternate version (TSCC-A) is available that makes no reference to sexual issues. Administration time is approximately 15 to 20 minutes and hand scoring takes approximately 5 to 10 minutes. The instrument is suitable for individual or group administration in both English and Spanish. The TSCC is written at an 8-year-old reading level and has been normed for boys and girls between the ages of 8 and 16. Overall, the TSCC is useful in evaluating children who have experienced traumatic events including physical and sexual assault, victimization by peers, major losses, the witnessing of violence toward others, and natural disasters.

The TSCYC is a 90-item caretaker-report instrument that can be used to assess PTSD symptoms in children between 3 and 12 years of age. It comprises eight clinical scales (Anxiety, Depression, Anger/Aggression, Posttraumatic Stress—Intrusion, Posttraumatic Stress—Avoidance, Posttraumatic Stress—Arousal, Dissociation, and Sexual Concerns) as well as a summary PTSD Scale (PTSD Total). A PTSD diagnostic worksheet provides a possible PTSD diagnosis in children ages 5 and over. The TSCYC also contains two validity scales to assess caretaker over- and underreporting of the child's symptoms. Items are rated on a 4-point scale from 1 (not at all) to 4 (very often) in reference to the previous month. The TSCYC can be administered by both professionals and paraprofessionals and takes approximately 15 to 20 minutes to administer and 20 minutes to hand score. The TSCYC is normed separately for boys and girls within three separate age groups (3–4, 5–9, and 10–12 years old). In a published study of traumatized children, TSCYC scale patterns have been found to predict different forms of trauma exposure.

### UCLA PTSD Reaction Index for DSM-5

The UCLA PTSD Index for *DSM-5* (UPID; Rodriguez, Steinberg, & Pynoos, 1999) is a revision of the Child PTSD Reaction Index (CPTS-RI). It is an instrument used to screen for trauma exposure and assess *DSM-5* PTSD symptoms in children over age 6. The first part of the measure is a clinician-administered trauma exposure screener, which prompts the clinician to assess age and features of exposure to various traumatic events. Clinicians should use all available sources of information (e.g., self-report trauma screener, caregiver interviews, and social services reports) to properly assess the child's symptoms. To assess progress in treatment, the measure can be completed at intake and updated over the course of treatment. The second part of the instrument is a self-report screener for history of trauma exposure that can be completed independently by the child or adolescent. The screener assesses 14 types of trauma exposure by using a yes/no format and allows the child to write a brief description of the trauma. If multiple types of trauma exposure are endorsed, the child can indicate which type is currently the most bothersome and when it occurred. The clinician can then write a brief description of this bothersome trauma if it is different from the child's original description. Lastly, the UPID has a symptom scale comprising 27 items that assess PTSD symptoms and four additional items that assess dissociative symptoms. The symptom scale can be administered verbally or completed independently by the child or adolescent. When answering the questions, the child is asked to think about the traumatic event endorsed as currently most bothersome to him or her and to rate the frequency of symptoms during the last month.

## Cultural Factors in Assessment of Trauma

Cultural factors need to be considered when conducting trauma-informed assessments in rural communities. Cultural norms in rural communities must be taken into account when evaluating exposure to trauma and violence in order to properly assess contextual factors and limit bias. For example, individuals may believe exposure to guns could be a predictor of witnessing violence or could contribute to trauma exposure. However, gun ownership within rural communities is quite the norm, with one study finding 62% of individuals in rural communities report having a gun in their homes compared to 25% of individuals in cities (Maguire & Pastore, 1996). Thus, this information would be more important to know when conducting an assessment of safety or suicide risk in rural communities.

Professionals working in rural communities must be aware of the cultural diversity in the area. Jones, Hadder, Carvajal, Chapman, & Alexander (2006) note that one of the greatest barriers for both researchers and clinicians is a lack of trust when working with minority and marginalized communities. Mistrust of physicians, cultural misunderstanding, misdiagnoses of illness, and financial constraints can contribute to mistrust in marginalized communities. For example, undocumented citizens may not seek to receive services in fear of deportation. In some rural communities, there is a high percentage of racial and ethnic minorities or immigrant populations. It will be important for the clinician to learn the customs, beliefs, values, and norms of these traditionally underserved populations. The rapport-building stage noted in the clinical interviewing section is especially important when working in these rural communities.

In some rural communities, there may be only one mental health professional. In this case, the clinician might face some difficult challenges in conducting a proper trauma assessment. For example, availability of interpreters in rural communities may be limited, which would be problematic if the clinician does not speak the language(s) spoken in the community. Consequences of linguistic problems have resulted in misdiagnosis and poor quality of treatment (Norris & Alegria, 2005). Clinicians should be aware that some psychological assessment instruments have been criticized for being culturally biased; such bias can result in misdiagnosis. When conducting any type of assessment, it is important to note its limitations. Seeking additional supervision and consultation may also be necessary in order to complete an adequate assessment. Building connections with stakeholders in certain communities may also prove beneficial. For example, spiritual leaders in Native American cultures may recommend incorporating their traditional practices in treating illnesses with conventional trauma treatment. Thus, being aware of cultural norms and practices and finding other professionals would enhance the assessment and treatment.

Essentially, it is important for practitioners in rural communities to become culturally-responsive and competent. Sue (1998) notes that cultural competence "is the belief that people should not only appreciate and recognize other cultural groups but also be able to effectively work with them" (p. 440). As stated previously, being aware of the norms, values, and beliefs of cultures within a community is important in being an informed clinician, particularly a trauma-informed clinician. If a clinician is working with a culture that is unfamiliar or different from his or her own, it is important to seek consultation, supervision, or additional education in order to be a competent and ethical professional. In rural communities, it will also be important for the clinician to become immersed in the culture to further develop knowledge of the culture and trust of the community members.

## Ethical Considerations

Psychologists in rural areas regularly confront unique ethical challenges. Researchers have previously argued that much of the ethics literature and ethics codes appear to be based on urban areas. The limited literature on ethics associated with rural mental health practice commonly identifies competence, multiple relationships, and confidentiality as primary ethical concerns (Werth, Hastings, & Riding-Malon, 2010). The limits associated with these factors must be taken into consideration in trauma-informed assessment.

In rural areas, as noted above, it is important to become involved in the community in order to gain trust with the population one is serving. However, this could result in multiple relationships with clients. Rural practitioners often face isolation because of the areas in which they work and the paucity of resources available to them. Furthermore, they can only rely on informal networks with general healthcare professionals in their communities. Because psychologists in rural areas may be the only mental health professional in that community or even the entire county, difficulties often occur regarding referrals to other mental health services, consultation with other practitioners, and availability for clients. Additionally, rural mental health professionals face unique challenges in obtaining specialized areas of competence. Rural practitioners tend to operate as generalists rather than specialists in order to treat rural populations and not deprive the community of access to mental health resources. If clients are experiencing unique problems, their options for psychologists may be limited. Therefore, all mental health professionals can inform their ethical decisions by abiding by the principle of nonmalfeasance, or minimizing harm. If the risk of harm to the client is low and the possibility of benefiting the client is high, then the intervention or assessment may be done in the best interest of the client. With regard to trauma-informed assessment, there may only be a few psychologists available with specialized trauma treatment skills. Hence, practitioners acting as generalists need to be informed about trauma-related symptoms and appropriate techniques for assessment. These practitioners may have to seek additional training and consultation in order to provide ethically competent practice.

Rural communities present special challenges with regard to maintaining privacy and confidentiality. It is likely that residents may know one another more intimately than residents in urban communities. Clerical staff at mental health facilities, for instance, may go to church with clients, have children that go to school with the children of their clients, or run into clients at the grocery store. Therefore, it is critical for clinicians and their staff members in rural settings to understand the limits of confidentiality and maintain the boundaries of the therapy office. This is especially important in maintaining the privacy of trauma victims and survivors.

Another issue that may occur in rural settings is setting appropriate fees. Early versions of the American Psychological Association (APA) ethics code discouraged bartering. However, the current APA ethics code allows bartering if it is not clinically contraindicated and if the resulting arrangement is not exploited (APA, 2010). Thus, entering into a bartering arrangement is not necessarily unethical; however, practitioners must be careful to minimize the chances that the exchange could be unfair. It is recommended that barter involve goods, not services, and that others appraise the value of the goods.

Psychologists should refrain from providing services when it is likely that their personal problems will interfere with their competence or performance. Psychologists should make efforts to maintain their own psychological health by being cognizant of their own health and well-being and seeking their own mental health care, if needed. Clinicians who work with trauma survivors may experience vicarious traumatization at some point in their career. Vicarious traumatization occurs when professionals are affected by their clients' traumatic experiences. Repeatedly hearing about clients' traumas can take its toll on some clinicians. Clinicians may experience symptoms similar to those of their clients such as physiological arousal, depression, and anxiety. In severe cases, they may experience professional burnout. Clinicians must distance themselves from their clients' stories and develop their own coping skills to deal with the stories. It is important for clinicians to monitor their own well-being and engage in effective self-care. Maintaining a healthy work-life balance by developing a support network, both personal and professional, is important in reducing burnout.

## CONCLUSION

This chapter provided an overview of trauma-informed assessment of children and adolescents in rural settings. Given that individuals in rural communities often lack available trauma specialists, mental health and medical professionals must be equipped with empirically based information on how to detect trauma-related symptoms in children and adolescents, be knowledgeable about effective measurement tools, and consider the important cultural and ethical issues in conducting an assessment of trauma exposure and its related symptoms.

## REFERENCES

American Psychiatric Association. (2013). *Diagnostic and statistical manual of mental disorders* (5th ed.). Arlington, VA: American Psychiatric Publishing.

American Psychological Association. (2010). *American Psychological Association ethical principles of psychologists and code of conduct*. Retrieved May 1, 2015, from http://www.apa.org/ethics/code/

Banyard, V. L., Williams, L. M., & Siegel, J. A. (2001). The long-term mental health consequences of child sexual abuse: An exploratory study of the impact of multiple traumas in a sample of women. *Journal of Traumatic Stress*, *14*(4), 697–715. doi:10.1023/A:1013085904337 PMID:11776418

Bohnam, V. L., & Nathan, V. R. (2002). Environmental public health research: Engaging communities. *International Journal of Hygiene and Environmental Health*, *205*(1-2), 11–18. doi:10.1078/1438-4639-00125 PMID:12018003

Briere, J. (1996). *Trauma Symptom Inventory professional manual*. Odessa, FL: Psychological Assessment Resources.

Briere, J. (2005). *Trauma Symptom Checklist for Young Children: Professional manual*. Odessa, FL: Psychological Assessment Resources.

Burk, L., & Burkhart, B. (2003). Disorganized attachment as a diathesis for sexual deviance. *Aggression and Violent Behavior*, *8*(5), 487–511. doi:10.1016/S1359-1789(02)00076-9

Caffaro-Rouget, A., Lang, R. A., & van Santen, V. (1989). The impact of child sexual abuse. *Annals of Sex Research*, *2*(1), 29–47. doi:10.1177/107906328900200102

Cohen, J. A., Mannarino, A. P., Kliethermes, M., & Murray, L. A. (2012). Trauma-focused CBT for youth with complex trauma. *Child Abuse & Neglect*, *36*(6), 528–541. doi:10.1016/j.chiabu.2012.03.007 PMID:22749612

Conte, J., & Schuerman, J. (1987). The effects of sexual abuse on children: A multidimensional view. *Journal of Interpersonal Violence*, *2*(4), 380–390. doi:10.1177/088626058700200404

Deblinger, E., Taub, B., Maedel, A. B., Lippmann, J., & Stauffer, L. B. (1997). Psychosocial factors predicting parent reported symptomatology in sexually abused children. *Journal of Child Sexual Abuse*, *6*(4), 35–49. doi:10.1300/J070v06n04_03

DePrince, A. P., & Newman, E. (2011). The art and science of trauma-focused training and education. *Psychological Trauma: Theory. Research Policy*, *3*, 213–214. doi:10.1037/a0024640

Finkelhor, D. (1978). Psychological, cultural, and family factors in incest and family sexual abuse. *Journal of Marriage and Family Counseling*, *4*(4), 41–49. doi:10.1111/j.1752-0606.1978.tb00539.x

Finkelhor, D., Hamby, S. L., Ormrod, R., & Turner, H. (2005b). The Juvenile Victimization Questionnaire: Reliability, validity, and national norms. *Child Abuse & Neglect*, *29*(4), 383–412. doi:10.1016/j.chiabu.2004.11.001 PMID:15917079

Finkelhor, D., Ormrod, R. K., & Turner, H. A. (2007). Polyvictimization and trauma in a national longitudinal cohort. *Development and Psychopathology*, *19*(01), 149–166. doi:10.1017/S0954579407070083 PMID:17241488

Finkelhor, D., Ormrod, R. K., & Turner, H. A. (2009). Lifetime assessment of poly-victimization in a national sample of children and youth. *Child Abuse & Neglect*, *33*(7), 403–411. doi:10.1016/j.chiabu.2008.09.012 PMID:19589596

Finkelhor, D., Ormrod, R. K., Turner, H. A., & Hamby, S. L. (2005a). Measuring poly-victimization using the Juvenile Victimization Questionnaire. *Child Abuse & Neglect*, *29*(11), 1297–1312. doi:10.1016/j.chiabu.2005.06.005 PMID:16274741

Finkelhor, D., Turner, H., Hamby, S., & Ormrod, R. (2011). Poly-victimization: Children's exposure to multiple types of violence, crime, and abuse. *Free Inquiry in Creative Sociology*, *39*, 24–34.

Friedrich, W. N. (1997). *Child Sexual Behavior Inventory professional manual*. Lutz, FL: Psychological Assessment Resources, Inc.

Friedrich, W. N., Fisher, J. L., Dittner, C. A., Acton, R., Berliner, L., Butler, J., & Wright, J. et al. (2001). Child Sexual Behavior Inventory: Normative, psychiatric, and sexual abuse comparisons. *Child Maltreatment*, *6*(1), 37–49. doi:10.1177/1077559501006001004 PMID:11217169

Friedrich, W. N., Grambsch, P., Broughton, D., Kuiper, J., & Beilke, R. L. (1991). Normative sexual behavior in children. *Pediatrics*, *101*, 456–464. PMID:1881723

Friedrich, W. N., Grambsch, P., Damon, L., Hewitt, S. K., Koverola, C., Lang, R. A., & Broughton, D. et al. (1992). Child Sexual Behavior Inventory: Normative and clinical comparisons. *Psychological Assessment*, *4*(3), 303–311. doi:10.1037/1040-3590.4.3.303

Friedrich, W. N., & Trane, S. T. (2002). Sexual behavior in children across multiple settings. *Child Abuse & Neglect*, *26*(3), 243–245. doi:10.1016/S0145-2134(01)00322-2 PMID:12013056

Gomes-Schwartz, B., Horowitz, J. M., Carderelli, A. P., & Sauzier, M. (1990). The aftermath of child sexual abuse: 18 months later. In B. Gomes-Schwartz, J. M. Horowitz, & A. P. Cardarelli (Eds.), *Child sexual abuse: The initial effects* (pp. 132–152). Newbury Park, CA: Sage.

Hamby, S. L., Finkelhor, D., Ormrod, R. K., & Turner, H. A. (2004a). The Juvenile Victimization Questionnaire (JVQ): Administration & scoring manual. Durham, NH: Crimes against Children Research Center.

Hamby, S. L., Finkelhor, D., Ormrod, R. K., & Turner, H. A. (2004b). The Juvenile Victimization Questionnaire (JVQ): Child Self-Report Version. Durham, NH: Crimes against Children Research Center.

Higgins, D. J., & McCabe, M. P. (2000). Multi-type maltreatment and long-term adjustment of adults. *Child Abuse Review*, *9*(1), 6–18. doi:10.1002/(SICI)1099-0852(200001/02)9:1<6::AID-CAR579>3.0.CO;2-W

Higgins, D. J., & McCabe, M. P. (2001). Multiple forms of child abuse and neglect: Adult retrospective reports. *Aggression and Violent Behavior*, *6*(6), 547–578. doi:10.1016/S1359-1789(00)00030-6

Hirsch, J. K., & Cukrowicz, K. C. (2014). Suicide in rural areas: An updated review of the literature. *Journal of Rural Mental Health*, *38*(2), 65–78. doi:10.1037/rmh0000018

Horowitz, M. J., Wilner, N., & Alvarez, W. (1979). Impact of events scale: A measure of subjective stress. *Psychosomatic Medicine*, *41*(3), 209–218. doi:10.1097/00006842-197905000-00004 PMID:472086

Hyde, C., Bentovim, A., & Monck, E. (1995). Some clinical and methodological implications of a treatment outcome study of sexually abused children. *Child Abuse & Neglect*, *19*(11), 1387–1399. doi:10.1016/0145-2134(95)00096-Q PMID:8591095

Jones, R. T., Fletcher, K., & Ribbe, D. R. (2002). *Child's Reaction to Traumatic Events Scale—Revised: A self-report traumatic stress measure*. Unpublished manuscript, Virginia Polytechnic Institute and State University, Virginia.

Jones, R. T., Hadder, J., Carvajal, F., Chapman, S., & Alexander, A. (2006). Conducting research on diverse, minority, and marginalized communities. In F. Norris, M. Friedman, D. Reissman, & P. Watson (Eds.), *Research methods for studying mental health after disasters and terrorism: Community and public approaches* (pp. 265–277). New York: Guilford Press.

Kerig, P. K. (2013). *Trauma informed assessment and intervention*. Los Angeles, CA: National Center for Child Traumatic Stress.

Leistyna, J. (1980). Advocacy for the abused rural child. In H. Johnson (Ed.), *Rural human services: A book of readings* (pp. 92–96). Itasca, IL: Peacock.

Lipovsky, J. A. (1992). Assessment and treatment of post-traumatic stress disorder in child survivors of sexual assault. In D. W. Foy (Ed.), *Treating PTSD: Cognitive-behavioral strategies* (pp. 127–164). New York: Guilford Press.

Maguire, K., & Pastore, A. L. (Eds.). (1996). *Sourcebook of criminal justice statistics*. Available at: http://www.albany.edu/sourcebook

Mannarino, A. P., & Cohen, J. A. (1986). A clinical-demographic study of sexually abused children. *Child Abuse & Neglect*, *10*(1), 17–23. doi:10.1016/0145-2134(86)90027-X PMID:3955424

Norris, E., & Alegria, M. (2005). Mental health care for ethnic minority individuals and communities in the aftermath of disasters and mass violence. *CNS Spectrums*, *10*, 132–140. PMID:15685124

Rodriguez, N., Steinberg, A. M., & Pynoos, R. S. (1999). *UCLA PTSD Index for DSM-IV*. Los Angeles, CA: University of California at Los Angeles Trauma Psychiatric Service.

Saywitz, K. J., Mannarino, A. P., Berliner, L., & Cohen, J. A. (2000). Treatment of sexually abused children and adolescents. *The American Psychologist*, *55*(9), 1040–1049. doi:10.1037/0003-066X.55.9.1040 PMID:11036707

Schultz, L., & Jones, P. (1983). Sexual abuse of children: Issues. *Child Welfare*, *62*, 99–108. PMID:6831979

Sue, S. (1998). In search of cultural competence in psychotherapy and counseling. *The American Psychologist*, *43*(4), 440–448. doi:10.1037/0003-066X.53.4.440 PMID:9572007

Tong, L., Oates, K., & McDowell, M. (1987). Personality development following sexual abuse. *Child Abuse & Neglect*, *11*(3), 371–383. doi:10.1016/0145-2134(87)90011-1 PMID:3676894

Turner, H. A., Finkelhor, D., & Ormrod, R. (2010). Poly-victimization in a national sample of children and youth. *American Journal of Preventive Medicine*, *38*(3), 323–330. doi:10.1016/j.amepre.2009.11.012 PMID:20171535

Werth, J. L., Hastings, S. L., & Riding-Malon, R. (2010). Ethical challenges of practicing in rural areas. *Journal of Clinical Psychology: In Session*, *66*, 537–548. doi:10.1002/jclp.20681 PMID:20222121

## KEY TERMS AND DEFINITIONS

**Assessment:** A process of evaluation that uses a combination of self-report, objective, and/or projective techniques to help inform diagnosis and treatment for mental disorders.

**Culture:** Ideas, beliefs, customs, values, and knowledge handed down from one generation to another, or that distinguish one group of people from another.

***DSM-5*:** The *Diagnostic and Statistical Manual of Mental Disorders* (5th edition), developed by the American Psychiatric Association, widely regarded as one of the most authoritative reference works on the definition and classification of mental disorders.

**Ethics:** Guidelines and principles that inform professionals to ensure competent practice and promote values of fairness and beneficence.

**Posttraumatic Stress Disorder (PTSD):** A disorder arising after experiencing or witnessing a traumatic event involving actual or threatened death or serious injury. It is characterized by intense fear, helplessness, or horror lasting more than four weeks and by the traumatic event being persistently reexperienced in the form of distressing thoughts, recurrent dreams, or sensations of reliving the experience.

**Poly-Victimization:** The experiencing of multiple victimizations of different types, such as sexual assault, bullying, and witnessing violence.

**Symptom:** A subjective indication of a disorder reported by the person rather than being observed by someone else.

**Trauma:** A physical injury or wound or a powerful psychological shock that has long-standing effects.

**Vicarious Traumatization:** The impact of clients' traumatic experiences on professionals who are uninvolved in the trauma.

# Chapter 9
# What If a Whole Community Came Together?
## Collaborating to Ensure No Wrong Door to Services

**Rebecca Hoffmann Frances**
*Maine Behavioral Healthcare, USA*

## ABSTRACT

*Isolation is often a key factor and contributor to childhood trauma in rural communities. Not only does it potentially mean that there are less "eyes" on a family but it also means less supports and positive connections for a family. It means less ways out of the maze of childhood trauma and poverty. This chapter will explore how to build community in rural areas so that families feel connected and supported. It will give tools and tips for engaging traditional and non-traditional partners to create a web of support for families. It will call upon research and scientifically proven tactics for community engagement as well as more grass roots efforts that work in rural communities. In addition the article will give real life examples from some of the most rural areas in the state of Maine of how communities have come together to support children and ensure better screening, intervention and treatment.*

## INTRODUCTION

Children living in rural communities are exposed to trauma at higher rates than children who live in suburban or urban communities. Although services are sparser, there are resources and solutions within the community that can be developed and implemented to counteract this problem. This chapter will explore how to build community in rural areas so that families feel connected and supported. It will give tools and tips for engaging traditional and nontraditional partners to create a web of support for families experiencing who have experienced trauma and adversity. This chapter will also use examples from rural Maine and other areas to demonstrate methods for engaging with rural communities to address child trauma.

DOI: 10.4018/978-1-5225-0228-9.ch009

## BACKGROUND

Twenty percent of the US population lives in rural America (Clay, 2014). When coupled with other adverse experiences like poverty and isolation, trauma can be even more dangerous for children. Research tells us that a supportive community and caring adults can be the safeguard for children. These adults and the extended community can act as a buffer and build resilience in children so that they are able to withstand adverse experiences and grow from them. Further, these caring adults can often identify when there is a problem and possibly intervene on behalf of the child or children.

As John Adams once said, "As much as I converse with sages and heroes, they have very little of my love and admiration. I long for rural and domestic scene, for the warbling of birds and the prattling of my children." The picture of blissful childhoods filled with exploration and safety in rural America differs from reality. In fact, many children living in adversity in rural settings are suffering silently in isolation, with no access to help and seemingly no way to alter or escape their realities. There are solutions to this problem and these solutions can be found within the community and infrastructure that already exists in rural America.

Living in a rural setting presents a host of positive attributes for children, including community connections and relationships, less exposure to community and gang violence, and a lower cost of living. In addition, there are risk factors that living in a rural area brings that can cause challenges for children, such as

- Poverty,
- Isolation,
- Privacy and Stigma,
- Higher rates of trauma,
- Historical/Intergenerational trauma—that is, no knowledge/awareness of a different way of living,
- Lack of service/response system.

## MAIN FOCUS OF THE CHAPTER

### Issues, Controversies, Problems

There are a host of issues at play in rural communities such as poverty, isolation, historical trauma, lack of privacy, stigma, and weak response system. These issues can negatively impact the experience of exposure to trauma. In addition, whether the issues underlying or compounding, they act as barriers to healing from trauma. They are also fuel for symptomology and traumatization.

### Poverty

*Almost half of the population of the world lives in rural regions and mostly in a state of poverty. Such inequalities in human development have been one of the primary reasons for unrest and, in some parts of the world, even violence. — A. P. J. Abdul Kalam*

According to Size (2015), rural residents tend to be poorer. On the average, per capita income is $7,417 lower than urban areas, and rural Americans are more likely to live below the poverty level. The disparity in incomes is even greater for minorities living in rural areas. Nearly 24% of rural children live in poverty. Poverty does not necessarily cause trauma but is surely a contributing factor (Feder et al., 2009; Kato Klebanov, Brooks-Gunn, & Duncan 1994). According to the National Center for Children and Poverty this can be particularly dangerous during one of the critical brain growth periods in a child's life (ages 0–3). Certain environmental factors can pose a greater risk to brain development. These factors include inadequate nutrition, substance abuse, maternal depression, exposure to environmental toxins, trauma/abuse, and quality of daily care. Additionally, it has been found that children who live in poverty are generally more likely to drop out of school, have developmental delays, behavioral issues, and health problems (National Center for Children and Poverty, 1999).

Groundbreaking studies on adverse childhood experiences conducted in partnership by the US Centers for Disease Control and Kaiser Permanente by Vincent Felitti and Robert Anda (Felitti et al., 1998) determined that poverty in and of itself was a stressful enough life experience in children to be correlated to negative health outcomes as adults. Poverty is one of ten categories of adverse childhood experiences that one can experience. The Adverse Childhood Experience (ACE) study found a correlation between the number of ACEs and negative health outcomes later in life such as heart disease, liver disease, and substance abuse. In addition, the exposure to this toxic stress in childhood affects memory and the ability to learn, therefore impacting the trajectory of success in school and in the workplace. Economists have estimated that childhood poverty costs the US economy $500 billion a year (National Center for Children and Poverty, 1999). Therefore to reduce poverty is a profound intervention in and of itself.

Not only are children in poverty at risk for trauma, they also suffer from lack of resources that are necessary to recover. Systems of support that are available to communities with financial means do not exist for those in poverty.

## Isolation

*Do you know, Watson, said he, that it is one of the curses of a mind with a turn like mine that I must look at everything with reference to my own special subject. You look at these scattered houses, and you are impressed by their beauty. I look at them, and the only thought which comes to me is a feeling of their isolation and of the impunity with which crime may be committed there. — Arthur Conan Doyle, Sherlock Holmes: The Complete Novels and Stories, Volume I*

Social ties are fundamental to mental health (Kawachi & Berkman, 2001). Social ties are also key factors in identifying and supporting at risk families. When living in rural communities the nearest neighbor may be miles away. There is nowhere to run to safety or get help; no neighbor to see or hear what is going on in a home; and no one to ensure that a child is safe and has food to eat. In urban communities an adult is not far away. In rural communities the only adults in a child's life—from birth until school age—may be their parent or parents. Isolation is a confounding factor with trauma and poverty. In addition, families living in isolation and under stress may have few resources to call upon when needed. This isolated and stressful way of life becomes the norm. Parents and children become immune to the situation as they know it and grow accustomed to their isolation. The coupling of trauma and isolation is not just an issue for families. Service providers in those areas, such as police officers, highway workers, and other governmental employees often witness traumatic events and are alone when left to deal with these incidents (Hunter, 2006). They then become victims or witnesses of trauma themselves.

## Privacy and Stigma

*In small towns, news travels at the speed of boredom. — Carlos Ruiz Zafón*

In small towns and other rural settings, the converse issue to isolation is the issue of privacy and confidentiality. In small rural towns there is a high likelihood that someone will encounter someone they know in the grocery store, the doctor's office, or the counseling center. And with closely linked communities, word travels quickly. When a family experiences challenges or a child is exposed to trauma there may be reluctance or a fear of sharing this information because the family does not want others to know about it or may have a fear of being judged. When this fear of "airing the dirty laundry" is coupled with the stigma attached to poverty and trauma it creates a powerful barrier to accessing services. There is a certain type of anonymity in an urban area—"a face in the crowd"—that is absent in smaller communities. In addition, since families live there generation after generation, the knowledge and stories are passed down from generation to generation.

Additionally, a family may know someone personally at the police department, which can lead to a fear sharing too much information and a general reluctance to call 9-1-1 (Slovak, & Singer, 2002) or a fear of collusion between the police officer with the offender. If small town police departments have not been trained for this sensitivity the officers may unknowingly be are creating barriers to access for families. In addition, there are sometimes perceptions from the community about whether these departments and their officers are friend or foe. This can impact whether the police are called to help.

## Higher Rates of Trauma

For those exposed to trauma, this exposure occurs at higher rates in rural areas than in urban areas. Recent statewide studies in both Maine and California have found this (Puccia, 2015; Center for Youth Wellness, 2015). The Maine Children's Trauma Response Initiative, a federally funded project through the Substance Abuse and Mental Health Services Administration found that the children seeking trauma treatment in the more urban counties in Maine had experienced an average of four different types of trauma, where children in the rural counties in Maine had experienced an average of seven different types of trauma.

Similarly in California, the Center for Youth Wellness in San Francisco found that the poor, primarily Caucasian counties had higher rates of trauma than the more urban multicultural counties (Center for Youth Wellness, 2015). This is especially alarming given the fewer number of service providers in rural areas. This may be due to the lack of caring adults who are supporting children in a rural area and the isolation in which families live but it also may be due to historical trauma. Either way, trauma gets woven into the very web of a family's culture and the risk is that it becomes the norm. Research has also found that violent crime is increasing in rural areas but when policy makers and service providers think of violent crime, they often consider urban environments and don't plan for rural environments (Slovak & Singer, 2002; Lee & Bartkowski, 2004).

Treatment for trauma may require specialized mental health care, and in particular evidence-based treatment. This type of treatment can also be sparse in rural regions. Often care for specialty mental health issues is either provided by primary care providers (specifically when medication is needed) or is not provided at all (Pearson, Hines-Martin, Evans, York, Kane & Yearwood, 2014).

## Historical Trauma

*All of us grow up in particular realities—a home, family, a clan, a small town, a neighborhood. Depending upon how we're brought up, we are either deeply aware of the particular reading of reality into which we are born, or we are peripherally aware of it.—Chaim Potok*

Historical or intergenerational trauma refers to trauma that has occurred across more than one generation. This may be trauma that a certain cultural group has experienced across generations, such as racism and oppression, or it may be a type of trauma that a family has experienced generation after generation, such as domestic violence. Historical trauma is cumulative (SAMHSA GAINS Center) and the effects become part of the family's or community's culture. This type of trauma is passed down as a way of life. For example, if children learn to solve problems through domestic violence, and they see no other way to solve problems, this is passed down through generations. The unfortunate risk, then, is that they think this is the norm. There is an expectation that this is how life is for everyone. When it is cultural trauma and oppression this pain is carried from generation to generation and is often still perpetrated on a given community. The trauma is collective and chronic and continues. Children will see this as the norm but may not have skills to deal with the anger and sorrow that they feel as a result of it.

Additionally, children of the survivors of direct historical trauma may actually exhibit symptoms even though they themselves have not been directly exposed (SAMHSA GAINS Center). Parents with histories of trauma also exhibit symptoms of emotional dysregulation and aggression, which can affect their ability to parent (Collins et al., 2010). Again, this behavior and these reactions to stressed are learned by their children and hence passed on to that generation. In addition, the growing field of epigenetics studies how gene expressions change over time, possibly due to the environment. Epigenetics applies to the field of traumatology as well. Exposure to trauma can permanently alter gene function, which is passed on to further generations (Yehuda & Bierer, 2005).

## Lack of Service/Response System

Not only do rural areas lack the sheer number of resources that urban areas have but these communities also geographically may be located far from those who seek them. When poverty and lack of transportation are issues, this distance could be insurmountable. In some areas, even a police response could take fifteen minutes to half an hour. Consider what this means for someone who experiences domestic violence. The risk of making the call and then having to wait that lengthy period of time may be lethal. Again, this could feel insurmountable and could therefore be a barrier to requesting help.

In addition, the system itself may be a stressed and overburdened. Providers in child welfare, police officers, and other first responders in rural communities are often faced with the danger of encountering family and community issues, which are or may turn violent on their own (Hunter, 2006). This in and of itself may produce trauma in these service providers and impact service delivery. If a provider has faced danger and trauma on the job, they may walk into a home ready for this again. This readiness may be sensed from families as aggressiveness, danger, distrust, or disbelief. This shapes the interaction from the very beginning.

## SOLUTIONS AND RECOMMENDATIONS

### Poverty/Basic Needs Interventions

When poverty is addressed, childhood trauma will be reduced. When the levels of toxic stress and adversity are lifted from families, they will have the inner resources to better cope and find a way out of the maze of poverty and oppression. When they can afford the basic needs for their family, they will be able to pay for safer childcare, safer transportation, and more expensive, healthier food (Duva & Metzger, 2010).

Yale University conducted a peer-reviewed study on diaper insecurity, (Smith, Kruse, Weir, & Goldblum, 2013). Their goal was to determine if diaper need was correlated to psychosocial issues faced by low-income families. Diapers are notoriously expensive and are not covered by many assistance programs (e.g., food stamp programs). This study found that 30 percent of families reported an inadequate supply of diapers, and that women with mental health needs were much more likely to report diaper need. Almost a third of these families reported stretching out the supply by changing diapers less frequently in order to have enough. The danger in this approach is that babies in wet diapers will more likely develop diaper rashes and urinary tract infections. This might cause the baby to be physically uncomfortable and cry. In homes with other psychosocial stressors and possibly untreated maternal mental illness, the baby might be at risk for abuse. Also, many Laundromats will not let you wash cloth diapers (for sanitary reasons). So unless you have an at-home washing machine you have to pay for diapers. If diaper insecurity is truly a stressor that is correlated to other stressors such as maternal mental health, poverty, and child well-being there are numerous solutions that would solve this issue. There are a growing number of diaper banks that exist across the country. Making these available in rural areas where people congregate—such as grocery stores, doctor's offices, or churches—could provide access to a much needed resource.

The solution to reducing childhood poverty in rural areas exists in the very fabric of the community and needs to be built from within the community. When an outside resource is needed, it is imperative that this resource be "culturally competent" to rural life and poverty in order to build trust in a community. They need to understand the strengths of those living in rural communities and the nuances of how they interact and communicate. It is also important that providers understand that poverty is not a choice for families. It is passed down from generation to generation and is very difficult to break free from. When this "poverty-informed" lens is taken, providers will be better able to connect with families.

### Provider Solutions

- **Training Providers:** In the medical field, it has been found that by training doctors to provide care in rural communities they are much more likely to settle in a rural community. The practice of rural medicine is different enough than traditional medical practice that training is actually needed for specific rural skills (Strasser, 2010). This training in providing rural medicine is rare. Unless a doctor conducts their residency in a rural location, they may not gain the skills necessary to work successfully in such a location. Therefore, working with medical and mental health postgraduate education systems to train their emerging practitioners in rural care would allow for providers to embrace it as a model. In rural Ontario, Canada, medical schools are actually providing intensive training to their practitioners in rural care by embedding them in rural communities (with a host family) and having them provide care there. The authors describe this as a social accountability to improving community health (Strasser, 2010). The authors also found that the practitioners who were from rural areas are more likely to settle in rural areas. This may seem self-explanatory in terms of the comfort of the practitioner but is also speaks to the comfort of the community in accepting that practitioner as a trusted community member. If there were more active recruitment and incentivizing for medical students from rural communities, there may be a difference over time in how many serve rural communities.

Community engagement in many university settings has become a priority (Weerts & Sandmann, 2010). Colleges and universities are seeking ways to partner more with their surrounding communities and also to serve them better. Land grant universities in particular have a sensitivity to the community and in particular the rural communities. Many students there are from rural areas and can be an asset to finding new and innovative ways to serve the community. Universities have resources and technology that many communities do not have. These resources and technology could be used to support the needs of the rural community.

It is important to remember that these relationships are not easily built and require thought and skill on both the university side and the community side to engage together. As Weerts and Sandmann (2010) describe, it is important to determine who your "boundary spanners" are and how the "boundary spanning" will be done. Boundary spanning is a concept developed by Friedman and Podolny (1992) and refers to the idea that when two parties engage in a relationship it is spanning a boundary and it is important to do this with care. By choosing the best person within your organization to span that boundary and build a relationship you are increasing your chances of success. It is also important to ensure that communication is well thought out when spanning boundaries (Weerts & Sandmann 2010). This is especially true in rural communities where trust of outsiders may be an issue. It is important to choose the person who will make that connection as someone who is a good communicator and who understands rural living. It is also vital for the university to see the community is an important contributor to the process.

- **Service Location, Mobile Services, and Telehealth:** Connections to services are critical for children and families living in rural areas, and especially those who live in poverty (Edmund & Bland, 2011). Untreated medical conditions and legal issues are often present as well as the need for financial advocacy. Organizations may have determined ways to meet the needs of the community through tele-video, satellite offices, co-location, or mobile units but because they don't have brick and mortar locations, their presence is not overtly felt by the citizens. For instance, the Veteran's Affairs Vet Centers in many states operate their services through motorized vehicle (www.vetcenter.va.gov). These mobile vet centers (MVCs) travel from location to location to ensure counseling services and other resources to veterans in the most far-reaching rural areas. Mobile services have had a positive impact on the issue of isolation and geographic distance but a downside is that MVC assistance may only be in a specific community once a month or even less frequently. Therefore rural areas have had to think of new ways to access resources. Tele-video has provided a way to receive services when and where these services are needed. This is done by using a television with specific equipment and now is even done by computer or tablet. An opportunity and need for growth is in the area of billing. In some states, many services (such as certain types of mental health treatment) are not billable by way of telehealth. This is a financial barrier for the provider and an access barrier for the patient.

Furthermore, locating services in places that children already are such as school-based health and counseling has been highly effective because it is very accessible, and built into the fabric of an institution that they frequent. In rural communities in particular, school can be an important location to engage parents in services. It has been found that when cross system supports occur, such as school supporting health and parents supporting academics, children see higher levels of success in these areas (Semke & Sheridan, 2012). In addition, integrating mental health into pediatric and family medicine practices has also been a mechanism for providing services, since many families regularly see their doctor.

Family treatment has been found to be effective for families facing multiple adversities such as trauma and poverty (Collins et al., 2010). The entire family is facing this adversity and runs the risk of becoming organized around their adversities. For example, if a child has suffered sexual abuse by an extended family member this can affect the whole family. Feelings of shame, guilt, anger, and sadness can affect every family member, not just the victim. Without support for the entire family, this can lead to a decline in the functioning of the family unit.

## Innovative Practices

It is important to respect the autonomy of rural families (Edmund & Bland, 2011). Many are hardworking, proud individuals and want to actively participate in strategies to make their situations better. They have relied on themselves for many generations and are often sensitive to others telling them how to live. Automated and uniform services may not work. More "kitchen table counseling" (more casual interactions or in more comfortable locations rather than the traditional office-based counseling) may need to occur or conversations in other locations other than the counseling office. Reminding people of the importance and existence of confidentiality regulations will be important to build trust. In addition, specialized training in working in rural settings is imperative. Research has shown that engagement at community mental health centers is lower in rural areas than in other areas (Greeno, Anderson, Shear, & Gerard, 1999). This may be due to a cultural divide between practitioner and consumer.

In addition, home-based treatment is very common in rural areas because the distance may be prohibitive to an office- based practice. Travel times may be too long or cost prohibitive for families. This can be very effective not only because it is private and convenient for the family but also because it allows the clinician to observe and work with families in their own environment.

- **Social Support Interventions:** Since isolation is such a major factor for rural families, and social support is known to combat this factor (Kawachi & Berkman, 2001), social support interventions, even the most basic, may be of assistance. Churches used to perform this function well. Churches were a gathering and connecting place for community members. In a time when the role of churches and other religious institutions are less prominent, other means for connection need to be made in small communities. This could be as simple as a knitting group or a cooking class or a sustainable agriculture lesson, where wellbeing interventions are built into the programming. That could include a parenting class focused on antiviolence curriculum and the means for managing difficult child behavior. This type of intervention could be a valuable way to teach healthy skills to community members and also reduce isolation.

- **Community Collaboratives:** One of the problems in tackling the issue of childhood trauma is that it is such a pervasive issue, which makes it seem insurmountable. In addition, no one person (other than the perpetrators) is responsible for fixing the overall problem. We as a community are all responsible for fixing it. And with no one in charge and no clear answer, people feel disempowered. By developing a community-based committee, assigning a leader, and meeting regularly, much can be accomplished. Community-based meetings have been highly effective in Maine in determining who has a stake in the issue of childhood trauma, what the gaps are to services and how they can be solved (Puccia et al., 2012). Many people have a stake in childhood trauma: schools, police, healthcare providers, mental health practitioners, early childcare providers, advocacy agencies, and businesses. Most of these exist in all communities, whether big or small, urban or rural. These entities have a stake in making the issue better. They can tackle a small issue (like a diaper bank) that impacts the larger issue. By including family members and consumers of these committees, stakeholders can learn what works and what doesn't.

Research has shown that these collaborative partnerships are correlated to community health improvement. According to Roussos and Fawcett (2000) it is important to set these committees up for success. It is important to identify stakeholders who are passionate about the issue, are decision makers at their own agencies, and if possible, have access to financial support or grant writers. In addition, research has shown that community participation is integral to determining successful solutions for health inequities, particularly in rural areas (Kenney, Hyett, Sawtell, Dickson-Swift, Farmer, & O'Meara 2013). In rural areas community participation is often at lower levels than in urban areas, but these are the areas where it is most vital. Health solutions need to be tailored to the individual community culture, especially in rural areas. For these communities, that so often feel disenfranchised, drawing in local social capital is extremely important to creating an empowered community (Kenney, Hyett, Sawtell, Dickson-Swift, Farmer, & O'Meara 2013).

Furthermore, helping the community to buy into this issue is critical. When it is thought of as someone else's issue and hence someone else's problem to fix it, the problem becomes a hot potato, easily passed on to the next person to solve. For example, when medical providers see childhood trauma as a mental health issue and one in which they do not have the tools or knowledge to deal with, there is a risk that the problem never gets addressed. Trauma and its subsequent sequelae or an issue of health and medical providers have a duty to address issues of health of their patients. In Maine, through the Portland Defending Childhood project (2015), pediatric providers are tackling this issue (in the largest health system that serves the majority of the population in the state). Children are screened at regular intervals for adverse experiences and symptoms. They are given anticipatory guidance or if symptomology exists, a referral to mental health. In addition they are given discharge instructions (much like if they had an infection) for what symptoms to look for, how to help, and where to access help. They are also, as a universal prevention technique, given handouts at each well-child visit about healthy parenting, healthy relationships, and violence prevention information. This is an example of a provider who could say that childhood trauma is not their problem, but instead chose to make it their problem and tackle it.

Additionally, other providers who have not traditionally been focused on childhood but have been a safe haven for children, like schools and police officers, can be involved. For example group interventions in schools have been shown to be effective post community trauma (Openshaw, 2013). Furthermore, the evidence-based practice, Cognitive Behavioral Intervention for Trauma in Schools (CBITS) has been found to be highly effective and has been used in rural settings such as American Indian reservations

(Morsette, Swaney, Stolle, Schuldberg, van den Pol, & Young, 2009). By embedding services in schools, children have access to them, and the therapist can work in conjunction with other supportive adults such as school counselors, school nurses, and teachers.

*In poverty and other misfortunes of life, true friends are a sure refuge. The young they keep out of mischief; to the old they are a comfort and aid in their weakness, and those in the prime of life they incite to noble deeds.—Aristotle*

The most impactful intervention in rural America may be the idea of the *one caring adult* (National Scientific Council on the Developing Child, 2015). One caring adult can make an impact on a child suffering from trauma. Whether this person is a parent, a relative, a mentor, someone in the community, or the person who delivers the mail does not matter. Resilience is built in children through positive relationships, which can happen through one caring adult. If an adult takes an interest in a child, teaches them what self-esteem, health, and healthy relationships look like, this may buffer them from the stressors (National Scientific Council on the Developing Child, 2015).

## FUTURE RESEARCH DIRECTIONS

There is still very little research in the area of rural childhood trauma and on quantifying the impact on trauma symptomology. In addition, many innovative practices have not been tested. They are anecdotally useful but have not been researched. More focus needs to be put on what actually works in communities, especially rural resource-poor communities.

## CONCLUSION

Rural communities face childhood trauma at higher rates than their suburban and urban counterparts. This is mostly due to confounding factors such as poverty, historical trauma, and isolation. There is no one solution to tackling this issue but the community must be part of the solution. Engaging the community into being part of the solution is important and also remembering that small interventions have large impact in rural communities. The service system is not likely to change drastically but the trajectory of a child's life may change with one small, quality intervention.

## REFERENCES

Administration of Children and Families Office of Planning Research & Evaluation (ACF-OPRE). (2006). *Research to Practice: Depression in the Lives of Early Head Start Families*. Washington, DC: U.S. Department of Health and Human Services.

Center for Youth Wellness. (2014). *Data Report: A Hidden Crisis, Findings on Adverse Childhood Experiences in California*. Retrieved from https://app.box.com/s/nf7lw36bjjr5kdfx4ct9 on 5/27/15

Clay, R. A. (2014). Reducing Rural Suicide: Psychologists are finding innovative ways to reach out to people in isolated communities. American Psychological Association, 45(4), 36.

Collins, K., Connors, K., Davis, S., Donohue, A., Gardner, S., Goldblatt, E., . . . Thompson, E. (2010). Understanding the Impact of Trauma and Urban Poverty on Family Systems: Risks, Resilience, and Interventions. Family Informed Trauma Treatment Center, 1–117.

Conan Doyle, A. (1986). *Sherlock Holmes: The Complete Novels and Stories* (Vol. I). New York, NY: Random House Inc.

Duva, J., & Metzger, S. (2010). Addressing Poverty as a Major Risk Factor in Child Neglect: Promising Policy and Practice. *Protecting Children*, *25*(1), 63–74.

Edmund, D. S., & Bland, P. J. (2011). Poverty and Trauma. From Real Tools: Responding to Multi-Abuse Trauma. *Alaska Network on Domestic Violence and Sexual Abuse,* Retrieved from http://www.apa.org/pi/families/poverty.aspx on 5/27/15

Feder, A., Alonso, A., Tang, M., Liriano, W., Warner, V., Pilowsky, D., & Weissman, M. et al. (2009). Children of Low-Income Depressed Mothers: Psychiatric Disorders and Social Adjustment. *Depression and Anxiety*, *26*(6), 513–520. PMID:19016460

Felitti, V. J., Anda, R. F., Nordenberg, D., Williamson, D. F., Spitz, A. M., Edwards, V., & Marks, J. S. et al. (1998). Relationship of Childhood Abuse and Household Dysfunction to Many of the Leading Causes of Death in Adults. *American Journal of Preventive Medicine*, *14*(4), 245–258. doi:10.1016/S0749-3797(98)00017-8 PMID:9635069

Friedman, R. A., & Podolny, J. (1992). Differentiation of Boundary Spanning Roles: Labor Negotiations and Implications for Role Conflict. *Administrative Science Quarterly*, *37*(1), 28–47. doi:10.2307/2393532

Gerson, M. (2015, March 16). The Effects of Inequality on America's Kids. *The Washington Post.*

Greeno, C. G., Anderson, C. M., Shear, M. K., & Gerard, M. (1999). Initial Treatment Engagement in a Rural Community Mental Health Center. *Psychiatric Services (Washington, D.C.)*, *50*(12), 1634–1636. doi:10.1176/ps.50.12.1634 PMID:10577887

Hunter, M. E. (2006). Mental Health Care in Rural and Isolated Areas: Lessons from Northern British Columbia. *British Columbia Medical Journal*, *48*(4), 174–177.

Kato Klebanov, P., Brooks-Gunn, J., & Duncan, G. (1994). Does Neighborhood and Family Poverty Affect Mothers' Parenting, Mental Health, and Social Support? *Journal of Marriage and the Family*, *56*(2), 441–455. doi:10.2307/353111

Kawachi, I., & Berkman, L. F. (2001). Social Ties and Mental Health. *Journal of Urban Health: Bulletin of the New York Academy of Medicine*, *78*(3), 458–467. doi:10.1093/jurban/78.3.458 PMID:11564849

Kenny, A., Hyett, N., Sawtell, J., Dickson-Swift, V., Farmer, J., & O'Meara, P. (2013). Community participation in rural health: A scoping review. *BMC Health Services Research*, *13*(1), 64. doi:10.1186/1472-6963-13-64 PMID:23414561

Lee, M., & Bartkowski, J. P. (2004). Love Thy Neighbor? Moral Communities, Civic Engagement, and Juvenile Homicide in Rural Areas. *Project Muse*, *82*(3), 1001–1035.

Morsette, A., Swaney, G., Stolle, D., Schuldberg, D., van den Pol, R., & Young, M. (2009). Cognitive Behavioral Intervention for Trauma in Schools (CBITS): School-Based Treatment on a Rural American Indian Reservation. *Journal of Behavior Therapy and Experimental Psychiatry*, *40*(1), 169–178. doi:10.1016/j.jbtep.2008.07.006 PMID:18835478

National Center for Children in Poverty. (1999). Poverty and Brain Development in early Childhood. New York, NY: Author.

National Scientific Council on the Developing Child. (2015). *Supportive Relationships and Active Skill-Building Strengthen the Foundations of Resilience: Working Paper 13*. Retrieved from http://www.developingchild.harvard.edu

Openshaw, L. L. (2013). Group Interventions in Rural Schools to Assist with a Community Trauma. *Contemporary Rural Social Work*, *5*, 110–124.

Pearson, G. S., Hines-Martin, V. P., Evans, L. K., York, J. A., Kane, C. F., & Yearwood, E. L. (2014). Addressing Gaps in Mental Health Needs of Diverse, At-Risk, Underserved, and Disenfranchised Populations: A Call for Nursing Action. *Archives of Psychiatric Nursing*. PMID:25634869

Policy Research Associates, Inc. (n.d.). Substance Abuse and Mental Health Services Administration GAINS Center. *Fact Sheet: Historical Trauma*.

Puccia, E. (2015). *Evaluation report of the Maine Children's Trauma Response Initiative*. Substance Abuse and Mental Health Services Administration Grant #5U79SM062112-08 (Unpublished Report). Portland, Maine.

Puccia, E., Redding, T. M., Brown, R. S., Gwynn, P. A., Hirsh, A. B., Hoffmann Frances, R., & Morrison, B. (2012). Using Community Outreach and Evidenced-Based Treatment to Address Domestic Violence Issues. *Social Work in Mental Health*, *10*(2), 104–126. doi:10.1080/15332985.2011.601704

Roussos, S. T., & Fawcett, S. B. (2000). A Review of Collaborative Partnerships as a Strategy for Improving Community Health. *Annual Review of Public Health*, *21*(1), 369–402. doi:10.1146/annurev.publhealth.21.1.369 PMID:10884958

SAMHSA's GAINS Center. (n.d.). *How Being Trauma-Informed Improves Criminal Justice System Responses. Historical Fact Sheet*. Policy Research Associates .

Semke, C., & Sheridan, S. (2012). Family-School Connections inRural Educational Settings: A Systematic Review of the Empirical Literature. *School Community Journal*, *22*(1), 21–48.

Size, T. (n.d.). *Rural Health Can Lead the Way*. Retrieved from http://www.ruralhealthweb.org/go/left/about-rural-health on 5/20/15

Slovak, K., & Singer, M. I. (2002). Children and Violence: Findings and Implications from a Rural Community. *Child & Adolescent Social Work Journal*, *19*(1), 35–56. doi:10.1023/A:1014003306441

Smith, M. V., Kruse, A., Weir, A., & Goldblum, J. (2013). Diaper Need and Its Impact on Child Health. *Pediatrics*, *132*(2), 253–259. doi:10.1542/peds.2013-0597 PMID:23897910

Strasser, R. P. (2010). Community Engagement: A Key to Successful Rural Clinical Education. *Rural and Remote Health*, *10*, 1–7. PMID:20815653

Weerts, D. J., & Sandmann, L. R. (2010). Community Engagement and Boundary-Spanning Roles at Research Universities. *The Journal of Higher Education*, *81*(6), 702–727.

Yehuda, R., & Bierer, L. (2009). The Relevance of Epigenetics to PTSD: Implications for the DSM-V. *Journal of Traumatic Stress*, *22*(5), 427–434. doi:10.1002/jts.20448 PMID:19813242

## KEY TERMS AND DEFINITIONS

**Adverse Childhood Experiences:** A set of ten different possible experiences a person may have in their childhood that may have been traumatic, as defined by the work of Vincent Felitti and Robert Anda.

**Community Engagement:** Involving stakeholders in a similar geographic region in a process.

**Historical Trauma:** Trauma that is multigenerational in nature, existing within a family or cultural group and that carries with it beliefs, feelings, and even psychological symptoms.

**Isolation:** Separation from others.

**Poverty:** Living without basic needs being met, such as food, clothing, and shelter.

**Resilience:** The ability to recover from something or adjust easily to a misfortune or trauma.

**Telehealth:** Healthcare delivered through telephone and/or video.

**Toxic Stress:** Stress that overwhelms the body's ability to cope, which over time may cause psychological symptoms.

# Chapter 10
# Spirituality:
## A Path to Healing for Children in Rural Communities

**Sandra Barnes**
*Fielding Graduate University, USA*

**Tosin Alabi**
*Fielding Graduate University, USA*

## ABSTRACT

*Religion appears to shape the daily lives of most children in America; the influence of religion often serves as a template for making decisions, establishing relationships, comprehending the world, and finding meaning in confusing and/or traumatic situations that children may encounter. To ignore the role of religion and spirituality in behavioral and mental health treatment is to dismiss a central domain of child and adolescent development as well as a potential path to healing. In this chapter, we discuss the role of spirituality and religion in children in rural communities and how they can be integrated into counseling and therapy as a path to healing.*

## INTRODUCTION

According to Pew Forum on Religious and Public Life (2008), the United States stands out as one of the most religious nations in the developed world. Given the high levels of religiosity in America, it is not surprising that the vast majority of adolescents in this country, approximately 87%, tend to affiliate with one particular religious group (Smith & Denton, 2005). In addition, research suggests that children and adolescents living in less densely populated and more rural areas of the country have a greater association with religiousness than their peers in other parts of the country (Smith & Denton, 2005.)

Religion shapes the daily lives of most children in America; religious influence often serves as a template for making decisions, establishing relationships, comprehending the world, and finding meaning in confusing and/or traumatic situations that children may encounter (Smith & Denton, 2005). To ignore the role of religion and spirituality in behavioral and mental health treatment is to dismiss a central

DOI: 10.4018/978-1-5225-0228-9.ch010

domain of child and adolescent development, as well as a potential path to healing. In this chapter, we discuss the role of spirituality and religion in children in rural communities and how to integrate them into counseling and therapy as a path to healing.

## Definitions

Religiousness and spirituality are similar and overlapping constructs; however, different connotations are developing in U.S. culture to describe these terms. Religion is described as an organized system of beliefs, practices, rituals, and symbols designed to:

1. Facilitate closeness to the sacred or transcendent (higher power), and
2. Foster an understanding of one's relationship and responsibility to others within a community (Koenig, McCullough, & Larson, 2001).

Spirituality, as defined by Koenig and colleagues (2001), is the personal quest for understanding answers to ultimate questions about life, meaning, and relationship to the sacred or transcendent, which may (or may not) lead to or arise from the development of religious rituals and the formation of community.

As noted, religion and spirituality are broad concepts that can very often use overlapping terminology. There is much controversy regarding definitions of spirituality and religion, even within the religion and mental health fields (Moreira-Almeida & Koenig, 2006). For the purposes of this review, religion will refer to an organized system of beliefs, rituals, practices, and community, oriented toward the sacred. Spirituality will refer to more personal experiences of or searches for ultimate reality or the transcendent that are not necessarily institutionally connected (Josephson & Dell, 2004). Because of controversy over precise definitions, no attempt will be made here to distinguish these two concepts. Inasmuch as the terms are commonly used together, the generic term, religion/spirituality, is used in many places throughout this chapter to capture an often overlooked variable that helps shape identity in children.

## INTEGRATING SPIRITUALITY AND PSYCHOTHERAPY

There is a significant need for mental health services in rural America. Research suggests that, in comparison to children in urban areas, children living in rural areas have a small, but significantly higher prevalence of mental health problems (Lenardson et al., 2010). Also, in comparison to urban peers, there is a greater proportion of children with mental health problems compounded with behavioral problems in rural areas. However, studies further reflect much lower access to needed healthcare for children in rural communities (Lenardson et al., 2010). As mentioned, more rural areas of the country have a greater association with religiousness (Smith & Denton, 2005). As service providers become more sensitive to the role of religion/spirituality in the lives of rural children, mental health evaluations can broaden to address religious issues as a serious component of their well-being. When service providers do not ask clients about their spiritual life and religious background, an opportunity to leverage a powerful resource to help clients process their trauma or give meaning to the difficulties of their lives may be lost (Grame, Totorici, Healey, Dillingham, & Winkebaur, 1999). A client's spiritual experience or religious background can be used as a healing resource.

The physical, sexual, or emotional abuse that occurs in childhood can be so severe that it leads to posttraumatic stress disorder (PTSD). Butler (1996) describes several symptoms of PTSD, including having an exaggerated startle response, sleeplessness, hypervigilance alternating with numbness and withdrawal that may disrupt relationships, and profound distortions of memory. Herman (1992) purports that traumatic events can very often undermine an individual's belief system or violate a person's faith in a natural or divine order. McBride (1998) adds that traumatic events can impact one's spiritual life and cause a deep sense of alienation or spiritual emptiness. Therefore, the overall goal of focusing on the spiritual in therapy with traumatized children should be regaining of hope, as well as reestablishing a constructive relationship with the sacred and self (Tortorici, 1993).

Psychological trauma in children can be understood through the framework of several psychotherapy and religion theories. Grame and colleagues (1999) provide a brief overview of four such theories, which will be highlighted below: (1) attachment theory, (2) self-psychology theory, (3) Thomas Aquina's theology of embodiment, and (4) object relations theory.

The underlying premise of Bowlby's (1998) attachment theory is that the success of all relationships or "attachments" in life is dependent upon the success of the first one; namely, the bond between the infant or small child and his mother or primary caregiver. During infancy and childhood, caregivers are looked to for protection, comfort, and support. The capacity to later form intimate emotional bonds in the roles of caregiver or care seeker is considered a primary feature in healthy personality functioning and good mental health. Abused children, like most children, have a need for closeness; however, in the face of trauma, this need for closeness in abused children is coupled with fear of abandonment or fear of being hurt (Grame et al., 1999).

Kohut's (1971) self-psychology theory holds that it is necessary for a child to have empathic caregivers who perform functions that the child is not able to perform for himself or herself. As the child grows and develops, these functions become internalized into the child's self. If a child suffers a traumatic loss of his or her caregiver, then internalization is disrupted and does not meet its optimal state in the child. Grame et al. (1999) argue that the traumatized child does not acquire the needed internal structure; thus, the child will need therapists and/or clergy to respond in affirming and reassuring ways.

The underpinning of Thomas Aquina's theology of embodiment is that "the rational soul has no being apart from the being of the body." There is unity between these entities; whereby each has a bidirectional impact on the other. Aquina posited that the body is not able to suffer pain without the soul also suffering pain. As physical or sexual assaults violate the child's body, such trauma also deforms the child's soul.

Object relations theory maintains that a person's mind develops as a direct result of formidable relationships, and primary motivational factors in one's life are based on human relationships. Objects refer to people, parts of people, or physical items that symbolically represent what is perceived as good or bad. Object relations theorists posit that God images serve as "transitional objects" that can reduce attachment insecurity as the child develops more independence from caregivers. Evidence shows that many young people in the U.S. and around the world report relationships with God (Gallup International Association, 1999; Smith & Denton, 2005) and that, as distance from parents increases, intimacy with God increases (Dickie et al., 1997). Furthermore, there is some evidence of important changes in conceptions of God toward a more relational view during adolescence.

Because traumatic experiences damage relationships, a supportive response from a therapist can mitigate the impact of the trauma. Healy (1993) states that the object relations approach is useful in gathering information to gain insight on the whole person. Not only does the therapist learn about the traumatized child's relationships to others in general but also about his or her relationship with God and members of the religious community.

Integrating a spiritual approach to treating traumatized children in rural areas is conducive to forming a more comprehensive sense of what might be the source of suffering. It is believed that proper attention to spirituality will result in more insightful approaches to treatment and effective interventions. Ai and Park (2005) maintain that researchers and practitioners should shift sole attention from the traditional focus on the negative and pathological aspects of trauma to a more balanced view of assessing the potentially positive aspects of protection, resilience, and growth that many trauma survivors also experience. The researchers note three interrelated trends that can be incorporated in mental health to broaden the view of trauma being seen as a case of victimization and pathology. The trends include:

1. The positive psychology movement,
2. The recognition of the role of spirituality and religion in health and mental well-being, and
3. Stress-related growth (Ai & Park, 2005).

Positive psychology, initiated by Seligman, is a movement that advocates attending to the positive aspects of the human condition as well as the negative, including qualities such as "well-being, hope and optimism, and positive emotions; capacities for love, courage, interpersonal skill, perseverance, forgiveness, and wisdom; and civic virtues and institutions such as responsibility, nurturance, altruism, civility, and tolerance" (Ai & Parker, 2005, p. 243; Peterson & Seligman, 2004; Seligman & Csikszentmihalyi, 2000). For example, in a study of 475 students following the 9/11 attacks, hope and spiritual meaning were found to be associated with fewer psychological symptoms (Ai, Cascio, Santangelo, & Evans-Camball, 2005). In addition, optimism was found to be inversely related to posttraumatic stress, specifically for those who knew someone who died in the attacks (Ai, Evans-Campbell, Santangelo, & Cascio, 2006).

The second trend is the role of spirituality and religion in coping with adversity. Since trauma can challenge an individual's core values and raise questions about meaning and purpose in life (Janoff-Bulman & Frantz, 1997), it is believed that faith-related phenomena can buttress mental resources (Ai & Park, 2005). A study conducted by Pargament, Smith, Koenig, and Perez (1998) reflected two patterns of religious/spiritual coping after participants experienced trauma from the Oklahoma bombings. The positive pattern indicated includes forgiveness, seeking spiritual support, collaborative religious coping, spiritual connection, religious purification, and benevolent religious reappraisal. The negative pattern highlighted consists of spiritual discontent, punishing God reappraisals (such as viewing God as vengeful and unforgiving), interpersonal religious discontent, demonic reappraisal, and reappraisal of God's powers (Pargament et al., 1998).

The third trend highlighted by Ai and Park (2005) involves positive changes known as stress-related growth. The process of dealing with traumatic events may help develop new coping skills, as well as personal and social resources. Ai and Park (2005) cite several studies of positive adjustments and benefits after experiencing various types of traumas, including those who survived a tornado, a mass killing, a plane crash (McMillen, Smith, & Fisher, 1997), and sexual assault (Frazier, Tashiro, Berman, Steger, & Long, 2004). Positive changes included handling stress, self-care, clearer focus and identity, closer relationship with God, greater appreciation of life, and the courage to try new things (Ai & Park, 2005).

While some of these changes may seem small, they are nontheless important. Evidence suggests that those who perceive growth shortly after the trauma also experience better mental health (Park, 2004). These trends, although interrelated, should be leveraged when working with adolescents who have experienced trauma.

## Religion and Spirituality as a Coping Mechanism

In the last century, the connection between religious establishments and providers of mental healthcare appeared to be largely ignored. However, within the last few decades, there has been a dramatic increase in scientific investigations linking an association of mental health to spirituality and religiousness (Dew et al., 2008).

Smith and Denton (2005) report that about half of all U.S. adolescents (ages 13–17 years) indicate a strong, positive orientation to matters of religion, faith, and religious experience in their lives. Children and adolescents are known to use religion and spirituality as a coping mechanism. Religious coping can be defined as a search for significance in times of stress in ways related to the sacred (Pargament, 2007); that is, some adolescents will use religious and spiritual knowledge and imagery in their search for the *causes of* and *ways of responding to* stress and traumatic events.

In addition, religion and spirituality can be conceptualized as an attributional meaning system that addresses inexplicable events; that is, when natural explanations prove unsatisfactory in justifying grief and loss, trauma or suffering, such as physical and sexual abuse, then spirituality and religion may be sources of hope that can counter feelings of depression, hopelessness, and loneliness (Smith & Denton, 2005).

Pargament (2007) posits that some adolescents may use religion and spiritual knowledge to interpret the causes of certain life stressors in terms of "sanctification"—a challenging experience that is in some way "God given." Pargament (2007) further notes that spiritual knowledge may also be used as a means of addressing life stress. In such cases, not only is stress attributed as God given, but stressors are reframed in a positive light such that they are spiritual tests or learning experiences associated with suffering.

In studying religious coping within the youth population, Dubow, Pargament, Boxer, and Tarakeshwar (2000) found that Jewish adolescents used three different kinds of religious coping strategies in the face of stressors:

1. Asking God for help in times of need,
2. Seeking support from Jewish culture and social relationships, and
3. Seeing difficulties in a spiritual light.

Eck (2007) found that minority and immigrant youth used religion as a buffer against racial and ethnic discrimination. Coping strategies involving spirituality have been an important resource for the African American community for much of its history (King & Roeser, 2008). For example, Brega and Coleman (1999) found that, in a sample of 50 African American high school-aged adolescents, those who were more religious were less likely to internalize stigmatizing messages in the wider society about African Americans.

It appears that some people who experience overwhelming threats tend to pursue support from a higher power. Heckhausen and Schulz (1995) refer to this style of coping as vicarious control, which is a secondary control strategy. Accordingly, researchers have found that spiritual coping may increase with distress as a sign of crisis-related resource mobilization (Ai & Park, 2005). While there have been mixed findings on the relationship between religiousness and coping after trauma, some studies have found a positive relationship. For example, Smith, Pargament, Brant, and Oliver (2000) studied survivors of the1993 Midwest flood and found the association between religiousness and positive religious coping to include better adjustment. In addition, the study also showed religious coping mediated the influence of religiousness on adjustment. There is also some indication that there may possibly be a bidirectional influence between spirituality and trauma. According to Peterson and Seligman (2003), positive psychologists used a Web-based, large sample study to compare data collected before and after the 9/11 terrorist attacks. Researchers found seven character strengths that encompass theological virtues, including gratitude, hope, kindness, leadership, love, faith, and teamwork increased among Americans. However, secular strengths remained unchanged (Peterson & Seligman, 2003).

## Protective Factors and Risk Factors of Religion and Spirituality

Empirical research of traumatic events has advanced our understanding of the nature of posttraumatic distress disorder (PTSD) and other psychological sequelae of experiencing or witnessing life-threatening events, such as combat, natural disasters, violent assaults, serious accidents, and physical trauma (Ai & Park, 2005). In addition, the emergence of international violence around the globe has escalated concerns about violence and its often-traumatic aftermath. Certainly, not everyone who experiences or witnesses a violent act develops PTSD or other psychological pathology; and indeed, questions arise as to how some people are more resilient than others. More specifically, researchers are beginning to explore the question of what characteristics help people prevail in the aftermath of violence and traumatic events? This inquiry has birthed new investigations that affirm positive aspects of human functioning and mental health in the face of pathology, such as resilience, wellness, and fulfillment. In addition, there is growing evidence that supports religion and spirituality as a shield against maladaptive behavior in children and adolescents. In this section, we will discuss research findings that highlight the protective factors of religion and spirituality.

The relationship between religiosity and mental health has been clearly demonstrated in adolescents. For example, adolescent religiosity, assessed in terms of church attendance and reported importance of religion, has been shown to be inversely related with feelings of depression, hopelessness, and loneliness and positively related to life satisfaction (Sinha, Cnaan, & Gelles, 2007; Smith & Denton, 2005). In another study of 615 ethnically and denominationally diverse adolescents, Kelley and Miller (2007) found that frequency of spiritual experiences in the context of daily life (e.g., seeing the sacred in others) was associated with life satisfaction. Further, in a study of 134 college students, Leake, DeNeve, and Greteman (2007) found that youth who reported spiritual strivings were more likely to experience positive emotions, such as vitality and zest, in addition to greater psychological health as operationalized by tendencies toward self-actualization and achieved identity status. The one exception to these trends are pregnant adolescent girls, who may be more likely to experience feelings of shame or guilt, perhaps as a result of their pregnancies being incongruent with religious or moral beliefs.

Studies that document a relationship among religious involvement, less psychological distress; and greater positive emotional experience, esteem, and life satisfaction also extend to international youth and immigrant youth. Research from studies performed outside of the U.S., including adolescents in

Germany and Spain, indicates that adolescent religiosity, assessed in terms of church attendance and reported importance of religion, was positively related to self-esteem (Donahue & Benson, 1995). In a national U.S. study of adolescent health, Harker (2001) found that immigrant adolescents experience less depression and greater positive well-being than their native-born peers from similar demographic and family backgrounds.

The risk for suicide is heightened when adolescents experience feelings of worthlessness and depression that may result from traumatic events. Studies by Gartner, Larson, and Allen (1991), as well as Trovato (1992) reflect a relationship between having a religious affiliation and lower rates of suicide in both male and female adolescents. In a large representative samples of American adolescents in grades 6–12, Jamieson and Romer (2008) indicated that religiosity (attendance, importance) are associated with lower levels of fatalism and suicidal ideation and fewer suicide attempts.

The literature also shows a strong body of evidence chronicling a negative relationship between adolescent religious and/or spiritual development and engagement in risk-taking behavior, such as substance use and sexual activity. It appears that while the religious child and adolescent populations do not totally abstain from risky behavior, engagement happens at a lesser extent in comparison to nonreligious/spiritual youth (Smith & Denton, 2005). Studies by Bartkowski and Xu (2007) and Sinha et al. (2007) present evidence that spirituality in heterosexual teens is negatively related to their use of marijuana, tobacco, steroids, and alcohol.

In addition, Smith and Denton (2005) reported striking differences in teens' sexual attitudes based on their level of religious involvement and religious commitment. According to the researchers, a national longitudinal study conducted by Rostosky, Regnerus, and Wright (2003) found that adolescent religiosity at age 15 predicted delayed onset of sexual activity for both males and females. This study consisted of 3,691 adolescents assessed at age 15 (time 1) and age 21 (time 2), and it accounted for factors such as adolescents' demographic background and number of romantic partners.

As a balanced perspective, we would be remiss in not also pointing out risk factors of religion and spirituality. Although there is a plethora of evidence that supports the beneficial role of religion and spirituality in optimal adolescent development, concern for risk can be associated with distorted or inappropriately applied religious practices. For example, religious traditions that emphasize the faith community without valuing a youth's individual uniqueness pose the risk of depriving the youth of developing a personal identity. As an illustration, King and Roeser (2008) describe spiritual groups that demand their members dress alike. In addition, acts such as suicide bombings, whereby devastation occurs because the beliefs and goals of the religious sect are valued more than an individual's life also pose a threat.

In contrast to these examples, religious and spiritual platforms that exalt the individual over the greater good of the community can promote narcissism, entitlement, and lack of connectedness and/or civic duty toward global efforts (King & Roeser, 2008). Such approaches could breed prejudices or ethnocentrism, which is detrimental to others.

In summary, studies have revealed that religious and spiritual youth have lower risk behaviors such as delinquency, substance abuse, violence, risk-taking behaviors such as sexual activity, and suicide (Smith & Denton, 2005; Bartkowski & Xu, 2007; Jamieson & Romer, 2008); however religion should not be used to foster guilt and shame, prejudices, or to justify violent acts.

## Barriers and Solutions to the Integration of Spirituality/Religion and Psychotherapy

The extant literature reflects several obstacles that hinder service providers in assimilating children's spiritual beliefs in treatment. Grame et al. (1999) present the following reasons that will be discussed: therapists do not always agree with how clients make sense of their lives spiritually; some service providers have a bias against religion; there is difficulty in assessment and discomfort in discussing religion; there are ethical concerns and fear of overstepping boundaries; and mental healthcare professionals have little training in addressing religious issues in therapy. Additional barriers that have been reported by other researchers include lack of time and experience, difficulty identifying patients who want to discuss spirituality, and the belief that addressing spiritual concerns is not a therapist's responsibility (Saguil & Phelps, 2012).

The increasing expectation for service providers to be open to understanding a client's religious/spiritual belief system is the impetus for becoming more culturally competent. There is a need for specific training programs for therapists on religious diversity. One way to gain an understanding of various religious beliefs is through cooperative relationships between therapists and religious leaders. Workshops and symposia involving representation from both disciplines can provide solutions to the integration difficulties. When leaders in both domains interact, stereotypes and unfounded biases can be reduced, the process of referrals can be eased, and inner healing can be promoted (Miller, 1992).

Plante (2008) provides a list of 13 spiritual tools that have been successfully implemented throughout the ages. In his study, the author briefly described each spiritual and religious tool and presented a clinical example of their use in psychotherapy. The tools include meditation, prayer, vocation, meaning, purpose and calling in life, acceptance of self and others (even with faults), ethical values and behaviors being part of something larger and greater than oneself, forgiveness, gratitude, love, kindness, compassion, volunteerism, charity ritual and community support, social justice, spiritual models, bibliotherapy, and sacredness of life. Plante (2008) argues that these tools can be useful to psychologists regardless of their interest or lack of interest in specific religious faith traditions.

While gaining an understanding of our society's diverse religious practices is helpful, it is important to remember, however, that clients may not adhere to each specific belief or practice of their faith. Therefore, therapists should avoid making generalized assumptions about a client's spiritual beliefs. Instead, the proper approach is to conduct an individual assessment that incorporates spiritual and/or religious background and current beliefs and practices (Saguil & Phelps, 2012).

## Cultural Assessment and Treatment

The DSM-5 includes spirituality as a critical factor in culture. The American Psychological Association ethically mandates its members to consider religion in the treatment of a patient's health. The spiritual assessment allows therapists to support patients as they employ empathetic listening, while documenting spiritual preferences for future sessions. When therapists incorporate a patient's faith traditions into treatment plans, patients are encouraged to use the resources of their spiritual traditions and communities for overall wellness. Conducting the spiritual assessment may also help strengthen the therapeutic relationship by building trust and rapport. In addition, it may offer therapists an opportunity for personal renewal, resiliency, and growth (Saguil & Phelps, 2012).

While it is important to assess the role of religion and spirituality with all clients, it is especially imperative to evaluate spirituality with children who have experienced abuse or trauma. There is a large and growing body of research documenting that many abused children are not only impacted physically and emotionally but also spiritually. This population may be grappling with good versus evil, shame and guilt, or struggling with forgiveness.

Of primary importance to any assessment is the taking of a comprehensive history. Studies suggest that attempts should not be made to address spiritual issues without first gathering historical data on the client's religious background (Grame et al., 1999). Such information will yield insight into the client's emotional tone regarding religious experiences and any connection among religion, abuse, and trauma.

According to Bowman (1989), an assessment of religious history should include current denominational affiliation; religious training; frequency of attendance at religious services during childhood; frequency of parents' or caregivers' attendance at religious services; client's opinion about parents' beliefs and practices; and client's view of God, Supreme Being, and prayer. Bowman (1989) further states that any question is useful if it helps the therapist understand the client's relationship with God or Supreme Being in terms of how the client feels about this Deity or how the Deity feels about and treats him or her. In addition, assessment tools, such as the FICA, the HOPE questions, and the Open Invite, provide efficient means of eliciting patients' thoughts on spirituality. Each assessment tool is briefly explained.

An acronym is used in the FICA Spiritual History Tool to help guide mental health professionals through a series of questions that are designed to gather information on patient spirituality and its potential effect on healthcare. Queries include questions about faith and belief, importance of faith and belief to the patient, the patient's community of faith, and how the patient wishes the therapist to address spirituality in his or her treatment (Saguil & Phelps, 2012).

Questions in the HOPE assessment tool elicit answers that lead the therapist from general concepts to specific applications by asking about patients' sources of hope and meaning, whether they belong to an organized religion, their personal spirituality and practices, and what effect their spirituality may have on treatment (Saguil & Phelps, 2012).

The Open Invite is yet another client spirituality assessment tool. It utilizes natural and conversational questions that are designed to provoke spiritual dialogue while being respectful and nonthreatening (Saguil & Phelps, 2012). The Open Invite is structured to allow patients who are spiritual to speak further, and to allow those who are not to easily opt out. For example, a therapist may ask, "Is there a way in which you would like for me to account for your spirituality in your treatment?"

If spiritual values are important to the client and for case formulation, then these values should be integrated into treatment. Saguil and Phelps (2012) note that, before conducting a spiritual assessment, therapists should consider their own personal faith tradition, beliefs, and practices as well as positive and negative religious experiences. Understanding personal beliefs will help determine how treatment may be influenced. Viewing the spiritual assessment as another means of gathering historical data to provide quality, comprehensive mental healthcare treatment should alleviate discomfort in broaching the topic of spirituality.

Research and practice support the benefits of integrating spirituality into psychological treatment. However, some critics have cautioned that such integration is ethically, professionally, and scientifically dangerous (Sloan, Bagiella, & Powell, 2001). With this concern in mind, therapists who practice an approach of incorporating a client's spiritual values into practice must be aware of potential pitfalls. Plante (2007) warns of the following four dangers:

1. Integrity issues regarding blurred boundaries and dual relationships may cause conflicts when a therapist is also a member of the clergy. For example, a therapist is mandated to report when a client is in serious and immediate danger to self and others; however, this mandated reporting responsibility may very well not be required for clergy members acting in their pastoral role.
2. Respect issues arise when there is spiritual and religious bias; therefore, it is important for professionals to keep their own potential biases in check, especially when they are not knowledgeable or even antagonistic toward particular religious traditions and denominations.
3. Competence issues come into place when a therapist is a member of a faith tradition and regards himself or herself as an expert. Therapists must not usurp the role of clergy in their psychotherapeutic work. They must avoid falling into pastoral care, spiritual direction, or theological consultation if they are not in that role.
4. Concern issues are in the forefront when religious beliefs and behaviors are destructive. While the APA ethics codes require professionals to be respectful of faith and religious traditions and beliefs, therapists cannot condone destructive thoughts, feelings, and behaviors associated with religion, especially when they result in significant physical or mental harm, abuse, or neglect as defined by both legal and ethical definitions (Plante, 2007).

## FUTURE DIRECTION

The difficulty in defining religion and spirituality makes it challenging to present reliable measurements. In different studies, religion has been operationalized as church attendance, personal devotion, religious beliefs, or a composite variable made up of responses to several items (Dew et al., 2008). Such variability leads to heterogeneity in findings, differences in interpretations, and also difficulty in drawing conclusions across studies. Dew and colleagues (2008) state that heterogeneity of measurement approaches makes it hard to isolate which precise religious variable (i.e., service attendance, prayer, devotion) is most associated with positive health findings. More specificity in measurement is needed to determine which dimensions of religion/spirituality—church attendance, private prayer, and belief in God, etc.—are most important to measure when studying particular mental health outcomes.

Comparing distinct religious variables could also possibly shed light on precise mechanisms through which religion may influence mental health outcomes in adolescents. George and Ellison (2002) cite improved health behaviors regarding substance abuse and establishing a sense of meaning in life as proposed mechanisms for adults. It is not clear whether this directly translates to adolescents because of developmental concerns. Regarding youth, Nooney (2005) found social support as a mechanism; whereas, Smith (2003) purports that lifestyle choices and learning experiences, such as leadership skills, ways to cope, and cultural knowledge afforded by religious institutions, are mechanisms.

Religion, spirituality, and mental health appear to interact in complex ways that vary among cultures, denominations, families, and individuals (Dew et al., 2008). As indicated in some longitudinal studies, religious behaviors may likely both impact and be impacted by mental health status. With this understanding, there is much investigation that can and should be done. For example, there is substantial evidence that teenage substance use and religion/spirituality are related. This knowledge should be leveraged in future studies to gain greater clarity on the relationship between religion/spirituality and other public health concerns like depression, anxiety, and suicidality. Such studies will help facilitate the determination of specific dimensions of religion/spirituality that may serve as protective factors in mental health of children and adolescents as well as the mechanisms through which they act. A better understanding of the true relationship of religiosity and mental health could have far-reaching implications for treatment.

First, this research suggests that faith communities may be appropriate and effective bases for preventive healthcare efforts. Knowing that religiousness may positively impact the mental health of adolescents may help churches, synagogues, and other religious organizations focus on this objective and address prevention of mental health problems more directly (Dew et al., 2008).

Second, the link between mental health and religion/spirituality is an impetus for clinicians to increase their awareness and sensitivity to the role of religion/spirituality in their patients' lives. While ethical objections regarding the integration of religion and secular healthcare remains a contention, basic elements of alternative therapeutic approaches, such as knowing one's purpose in life, meditation, altruism, group activities, and social support, may prove invaluable.

## CONCLUSION

In summary, the objective of this chapter is to discuss the role of spirituality and religion in children in rural communities. It is important to evaluate a child's religiousness/spirituality as another domain in treatment that could be either problematic or conducive to good mental health, depending on the child's religious experience.

Spirituality is central to many of the daily decisions children in rural communities make about their own development, including that of whether or not to participate in risky behavior. Spirituality and religious practices are often utilized as coping mechanisms, allowing traumatized children and adolescents to make meaning of confusing events or to reframe stressors into positive events for personal growth. In addition, studies indicate that spirituality and religion have served as potential protective factors, given the documented relationship between religious involvement and less psychological distress, less risk-taking behaviors, and greater positive emotional experience. While spirituality and religiosity appear to benefit youth, they should not be viewed as panaceas. Therapists should also be aware of any evidence that suggests religious distortions or inappropriate practices that cause harm to clients or others.

There are several barriers to integrating spirituality and psychotherapy, including lack of training or therapists' incompetence, difficulty identifying patients who want to discuss spirituality, and the belief that addressing spiritual concerns is not a therapist's responsibility (Saguil & Phelps, 2012). These concerns can be countered by attending workshops that promote cooperative relations between therapists and religious leaders. The use of assessment tools, such as FICA, HOPE, and Open Invite, can help determine a client's religious background, the opinion and/or relationship with Deity, or whether or not a client would like to have his or her spiritual values incorporated in treatment. In addition, there are several spiritual tools that have been effectively blended with evidence-based techniques, regardless of their interest or lack of interest in specific religious faith traditions (Plante, 2008).

While the inclusion of spirituality into clinical care with children in rural settings may be challenging, it can serve as a leverage to tap into whatever strength, power, and hope that spiritual beliefs provide the client. Further, it can foster a deeper therapeutic alliance and enhance therapeutic outcomes.

## REFERENCES

Ai, A. L., Cascio, T., Santangelo, L. K., & Evans-Camball, T. (2005). Hope, meaning, and growth following 9-11. *Journal of Interpersonal Violence*, *20*(2), 523–547. doi:10.1177/0886260504272896 PMID:15601799

Ai, A. L., Evans-Campbell, T., Santangelo, L. K., & Cascio, T. (2006). The traumatic impact of September 11 terrorist attack and potential protection of optimism: Implications for profession. *Journal of Interpersonal Violence*, *21*(5), 689–700. doi:10.1177/0886260506287245 PMID:16574640

Ai, A. L., & Park, C. L. (2005). Possibilities of the positive following violence and trauma: Informing the coming decade of research. *Journal of Interpersonal Violence*, *20*(2), 242–250. doi:10.1177/0886260504267746 PMID:15601799

Bartkowski, J. P., & Xu, X. (2007). Religiosity and teen drug use reconsidered: A social capital perspective. *American Journal of Preventive Medicine*, *32*(6), 182–194. doi:10.1016/j.amepre.2007.03.001 PMID:17543710

Bowlby, J. (1988). *A secure base: Parent-child attachment and healthy human development*. New York: Basic Books.

Bowman, E. S. (1989). Understanding and responding to religious material in the therapy of multiple personality disorders. *Dissociation*, *2*(4), 231–238.

Brega, A. G., & Coleman, L. M. (1999). Effects of religiosity and racial socialization on subjective stigmatization in African-American adolescents. *Journal of Adolescence*, *22*(2), 223–242. doi:10.1006/jado.1999.0213 PMID:10089121

Butler, K. (1996). The biology of fear. *The Family Therapy Networker*, *20*(4), 38–45.

Dew, R. E., Daniel, S. S., Armstrong, T. D., Goldston, D. B., Triplett, M. F., & Koenig, H. G. (2008). Religion/spirituality and adolescent psychiatric symptoms: A review. *Child Psychiatry and Human Development*, *39*(4), 381–398. doi:10.1007/s10578-007-0093-2 PMID:18219572

Dickie, J. R., Eshleman, A. K., Merasco, D. M., Shepard, A., Vander Wilt, M., & Johnson, M. (1997). Parent – child relationships and children's images of God. *Journal for the Scientific Study of Religion*, *36*(1), 25–43. doi:10.2307/1387880

Donahue, M. J., & Benson, P. L. (1995). Religion and the well being of adolescents. *The Journal of Social Issues*, *51*(2), 145–160. doi:10.1111/j.1540-4560.1995.tb01328.x

Dubow, E. F., Pargament, K. I., Boxer, P., & Tarakeshwar, N. (2000). Initial investigation of Jewish early adolescents' ethnic identity, stress, and coping. *The Journal of Early Adolescence*, *20*(4), 418–441. doi:10.1177/0272431600020004003

Eck, D. (2007). Religion. In M. C. Waters & R. Ueda (Eds.), The new Americans: A guide to immigration since 1965, (pp. 214–227). Cambridge, MA: Harvard University Press.

Frazier, P., Tashiro, T., Berman, M., Steger, M., & Long, J. (2004). Correlates of levels and patterns of positive life changes following sexual assault. *Journal of Consulting and Clinical Psychology*, *72*(1), 19–30. doi:10.1037/0022-006X.72.1.19 PMID:14756611

Gallup International Association. (1999). *Gallup international millennium survey*. Retrieved from www.gallup-international.com/surveys1.html

Gartner, J., Larson, D. B., & Allen, G. D. (1991). Religious commitment and mental health: A review of the empirical literature. *Journal of Psychology and Theology*, *19*, 6–25.

George, L. K., Ellison, C. G., & Larson, D. B. (2002). Explaining the relationships between religious involvement and health. *Psychological Inquiry*, *13*(3), 190–200. doi:10.1207/S15327965PLI1303_04

Grame, C. J., Tortorici, J. S., Healey, B. J., Dillingham, J. H., & Winklebaur, P. (1999). Addressing spiritual and religious issues of clients with a history of psychological trauma. *Bulletin of the Menninger Clinic*, *63*(2), 223.

Harker, K. (2001). Immigrant generation, assimilation and adolescent psychological well-being. *Social Forces*, *79*(3), 969–1004. doi:10.1353/sof.2001.0010

Healy, B. (1993). Psychotherapy and religious experience: Integrating psychoanalytic psychotherapy with Christian religious experience. In G. Stricker & J. Gold (Eds.), *Comprehensive handbook of psychotherapy integration*. New York: Plenum. doi:10.1007/978-1-4757-9782-4_18

Heckhausen, J., & Schulz, R. (1995). A life-span theory of control. *Psychological Review*, *102*(2), 284–304. doi:10.1037/0033-295X.102.2.284 PMID:7740091

Herman, J. L. (1992). *Trauma and recovery*. New York: Basic Books.

Jamieson, P. E., & Romer, D. (2008). Unrealistic fatalism in U.S. youth ages 14 to 22: Prevalence and characteristics. *The Journal of Adolescent Health*, *42*(2), 154–160. doi:10.1016/j.jadohealth.2007.07.010 PMID:18207093

Josephson, A. M., & Dell, M. L. (2004). Religion and spirituality in child and adolescent psychiatry: A new frontier. *Child and Adolescent Psychiatric Clinics of North America*, *13*(1), 1–15. doi:10.1016/S1056-4993(03)00099-3 PMID:14723297

Kelley, B. S., & Miller, L. (2007). Life satisfaction and spirituality in adolescents. *Research in the Social Scientific Study of Religion*, *18*, 233–261. doi:10.1163/ej.9789004158511.i-301.91

King, P. E., & Roeser, R. W. (2008). In R. M. Lerner & L. D. Steinberg (Eds.), Handbook of adolescent psychology: Vol. 435–478. *Religion and spirituality in adolescent development*. Hoboken, NJ: Wiley.

Koenig, H., McCullough, M., & Larson, D. (2001). *Handbook of religion and health*. New York, NY: Oxford University Press. doi:10.1093/acprof:oso/9780195118667.001.0001

Kohut, H. (1971). *The analysis of self*. Madison, CT: International Universities Press.

Leake, G. K., DeNeve, K. M., & Greteman, A. J. (2007). The relationship between spirituality, assessed through self–transcendent goal strivings, and positive psychological attributes. *Research in the Social Scientific Study of Religion*, *18*, 263–279. doi:10.1163/ej.9789004158511.i-301.102

Lenardson, J. D., Ziller, E. C., Lambert, D., Race, M. M., & Yousefian, A. (2010). Access to mental health services and family impact of rural children with mental health problems. Maine Rural Health Research Center, 45, 1–15.

McBride, J. L. (1998). *Spiritual crisis. Surviving traumas to the soul.* New York: Haworth.

McMillen, J. C., Smith, E. M., & Fisher, R. H. (1997). Perceived benefit and mental health after three types of disaster. *Journal of Consulting and Clinical Psychology*, *65*(5), 733–739. doi:10.1037/0022-006X.65.5.733 PMID:9337492

Miller, G. A. (1992). Integrating religion and psychology in therapy: Issues and recommendations. *Counseling and Values*, *36*(2), 112–122. doi:10.1002/j.2161-007X.1991.tb00968.x

Moreira-Almeida, A., & Koenig, H. G. (2006). Retaining the meaning of the words religiousness and spirituality: A commentary on the WHOQOL SRPB group's ''A cross-cultural study of spirituality, religion, and personal beliefs as components of quality of life''. *Social Science & Medicine*, *63*(4), 843–845. doi:10.1016/j.socscimed.2006.03.001 PMID:16650515

Nooney, J. G. (2005). Religion, stress, and mental health in adolescence: Findings from Add Health. *Review of Religious Research*, *46*(4), 341–354. doi:10.2307/3512165

Pargament, K. I. (2007). *Spiritually integrated psychotherapy: Understanding and addressing the sacred.* New York: Guilford.

Pargament, K. I., Smith, B. W., Koenig, H. G., & Perez, L. (1998). Patterns of positive and negative religious coping with major life stressors. *Journal for the Scientific Study of Religion*, *37*(4), 710–724. doi:10.2307/1388152

Park, C. L. (2004). The notion of stress-related growth: Problems and prospects. *Psychological Inquiry*, *15*, 69–76.

Peterson, C., & Seligman, M. E. P. (2003). Character strengths before and after September 11. *Psychological Science*, *14*(4), 381–384. doi:10.1111/1467-9280.24482 PMID:12807415

Peterson, C., & Seligman, M. E. P. (2004). *Character strengths and virtues: A classification and handbook. Washington, DC: American Psychological Association.* Oxford, UK: University Press.

Pew Forum on Religion and Public Life. (2008). *U.S. religious landscape survey*. Washington, DC: Pew Research Center.

Plante, T. G. (2007). Integrating spirituality and psychotherapy: Ethical issues and principles to consider. *Journal of Clinical Psychology*, *63*(9), 891–902. doi:10.1002/jclp.20383 PMID:17674403

Plante, T. G. (2008). What do the spiritual and religious traditions offer the practicing psychologist? *Pastoral Psychology*, *56*(4), 429–444. doi:10.1007/s11089-008-0119-0

Rostosky, S. S., Regnerus, M. D., & Wright, M. L. C. (2003). Coital debut: The role of religiosity and sex attitudes in the add health survey. *Journal of Sex Research*, *40*(4), 358–367. doi:10.1080/00224490209552202 PMID:14735410

Saguil, A., & Phelps, K. (2012). The spiritual assessment. *American Family Physician*, *86*(6), 546–550. PMID:23062046

Seligman, M., & Csikszentmihalyi, M. (2000). Positive psychology: An introduction. *The American Psychologist*, *55*(1), 5–14. doi:10.1037/0003-066X.55.1.5 PMID:11392865

Sinha, J. W., Cnaan, R. A., & Gelles, R. J. (2007). Adolescent risk behaviors and religion: Findings from a national study. *Journal of Adolescence*, *30*(2), 231–249. doi:10.1016/j.adolescence.2006.02.005 PMID:16677701

Sloan, R. P., Bagiella, E., & Powell, T. (2001). Without a prayer: Methodological problems, ethical challenges, and misrepresentations in the study of religion, spirituality, and medicine. In T. G. Plante & A. C. Sherman (Eds.), Faith and health: Psychological perspectives, (pp. 339–354). New York: Guilford Press.

Smith, B. W., Pargament, K. I., Brant, C., & Oliver, J. M. (2000). Noah revisited: Religious coping by church members and the impact of the 1993 Midwest flood. *Journal of Community Psychology*, *28*(2), 169–186. doi:10.1002/(SICI)1520-6629(200003)28:2<169::AID-JCOP5>3.0.CO;2-I

Smith, C. (2003). Theorizing religious effects among American adolescents. *Journal for the Scientific Study of Religion*, *42*(1), 17–30. doi:10.1111/1468-5906.t01-1-00158

Smith, C., & Denton, M. (2005). *Soul searching: The religious and spiritual lives of American teenagers*. New York: Oxford University Press. doi:10.1093/019518095X.001.0001

Tortorici, J. (1993). *Abuse of the sacred and the need for spiritual healing in the treatment of MPD*. Paper presented at a Menninger conference on Dissociative States: Multiple Personality and Other Trauma-related Disorders, Topeka, KS.

Trovato, F. (1992). A Durkheimian analysis of youth suicide: Canada, 1971 and 1981. *Suicide & Life-Threatening Behavior*, *22*, 413–427. PMID:1488788

## KEY TERMS AND DEFINITIONS

**FICA:** An assessment tool used to gain information about a patient's spiritual history. The acronym FICA stands for faith and belief; importance; community; address in care.

**HOPE:** A practical approach to spiritual assessment, whereby HOPE stands for the following: H--sources of hope, strength, comfort, meaning, peace, love and connection, O--the role of organized religion for the patient, P--personal spirituality and practices, E--effects on medical care and end-of-life decisions.

**Open Invite:** A patient-focused approach to encouraging a spiritual dialogue, whereby the therapist asks questions that open the door for conversation and invites patients to discuss spiritual needs.

**Rural Communities:** A community within a country of origin that does not have services, resources, or amenities similar to those in the neighboring city or town.

# Chapter 11
# "Rural–Specific" Types of Childhood Trauma in Rural Communities

**Roberto Jose Velasquez**
*New Mexico State University, USA*

**Yadira Juarez**
*San Diego State University, USA*

## ABSTRACT

*In this chapter, the authors discuss eight types of trauma that Latino children are likely to encounter by residing in rural or geographically-isolated communities. The authors contend that there exist more "rural-specific" types of childhood trauma that Latino children are at-risk for when compared to "urban-specific" types of trauma. For example, Latino children who reside in rural communities are more likely to traumatized by parental deportation, migrating from one town to another because parents follow the harvest, language brokering or translating for their parents, experiencing or witnessing farming accidents, relocating from the city to the country, isolation from extended family, pesticide poisoning of the child or a family member, and living in labor camps or substandard housing. It is important to note that Latino children, like children from other cultural, racial, and ethnic backgrounds, can experience all types of trauma irrespective of whether they reside in urban or rural settings.*

## INTRODUCTION

The primary aim of this chapter is to discuss eight common types of trauma that Latino children are likely to encounter by residing in rural or geographically-isolated communities. A secondary aim is to briefly discuss some interventions that can be used with traumatized Latino children. A third aim is to present some directions for future research on childhood trauma in Latino children who reside in rural and geographically-isolated communities.

A systematic review of the scientific literature indicates that there is a growing body of research on trauma in Latino children, with the majority of the research conducted in large urban or metropolitan

DOI: 10.4018/978-1-5225-0228-9.ch011

communities. As the Latino population grows and continues to spread across the country, including into rural and geographically-isolated communities, there is also an increasing awareness of the mental health needs of Latino families and their children. In urban communities, Latino families and their children are at-risk for "urban-specific" forms of trauma and in rural communities they are likely to encounter different types of trauma.

It is the contention of these authors, that childhood trauma can be viewed from the perspective of urban versus rural types of trauma, especially in Latino children because of the social, economic, and political circumstances of Latino families. While Latino children are not immune from the infinitesimal types of trauma that can occur to them by living in either type of setting, there are some forms of trauma that are more likely to occur when living in rural communities. Below are some examples of the types of trauma that Latino children are at-risk for in these communities.

- *Luis recently witnessed the arrest of his father at gunpoint in rural Oregon. Luis, who is 10 years old, saw his father beaten by the police and believed that his father was going to die. He is now very angry at the authorities and has constant nightmares about this incident.*
- *Mayte, a 10 year old undocumented female was in school when her parents were arrested at work and immediately placed in deportation proceedings. She was placed under the care of child protective services in Iowa where she has no family. She quickly became traumatized and began to have severe psychotic symptoms. She also faces deportation because of her legal status.*
- *Julio is a 17-year-old undocumented Guatemalan who came to the U.S. three years ago. He went to work at a meat packing plant in Nebraska. He was recently apprehended during an ICE raid and is now facing deportation. He fled his country after his parents were murdered by drug dealers and now fears that he will be killed when he is returned home. While in custody, he has become very paranoid and suspicious.*
- *Susana and her sister Eva , both 14 years old, crossed into the United States from Mexico after traveling from their country of El Salvador in the summer of 2014. They came to the U. S.in search of their parents. During their journey to the United States, both had been raped on numerous occasions, and now experience severe trauma including suicidal ideations.*
- *Roberto, who is 16 years old, worked alongside of his parents for many years in farms across rural California. When he was 14 years old, he began to have seizures and problems learning at school. He was later diagnosed with an inoperable brain tumor. He prognosis is very poor and is very afraid of dying and never being able to help his family.*
- *Elizabeth , a 13-year-old Mexican American lived with her family in rural Georgia. She witnessed the suicide of her older brother after her family moved from a large metropolitan city to a small rural town in Georgia. Sandra is now very depressed and anxious, and feels responsible for not preventing the suicide. She stated that her brother had difficulty adjusting to the rural community after living in the city.*
- *Margarita is an 11-year-old child of Guatemalan descent whose family moved to a rural community in Arizona. She was bitten by a rattlesnake in her back yard and traumatized by this event. For many months, she refused to leave her house and developed and constantly clung to her parents. She also refused to go to school for one month.*
- *Johnny , who is 8 years old, witnessed the amputation of his father's arm in a hay baler accident during a recent harvest and saw him die as medical assistance arrived too late. He has experienced significant flashbacks, nightmares, dissociation, and guilt.*

- *Silvia is 16-year-old and is the oldest of four children in her family. She has always served the language broker for family translator for her family. Her aunt, whom she translated for at the hospital recently died. Silvia was devastated and felt responsible for the death of her aunt because she feels that she did not translate her medical complaint in a correct or accurate manner. She also reported feeling tired and angry for having to also be a "third parent in the family".*
- *Octavio is 17 years and has cared for his father for five years after he developed several medical conditions due to pesticide poisoning. His father recently died and Octavio is now afraid that his mother, who worked alongside his father in the fields in rural California, has begun to display the same medical symptoms. He has five younger siblings and fears that he will have to raise his siblings if his mother should die. He continues to grieve his father's death and has nightmares of the day his father died. He cannot concentrate at school and is considering dropping out to go to work to help his family.*

Latino children, like children from other cultural, racial, and ethnic backgrounds, are at-risk for different types or sources of "childhood trauma" (Blaustein & Kinniburgh, 2010; Silva, 2004). The trauma can be mild or severe; transient or paralyzing; and/or short-lived or permanent (Kay, Burt, Eth, & Phillips, 2001). The trauma can significantly affect one aspect of a child's life, such as school performance, or it can be all-encompassing (Greenwald, 2015). Childhood trauma can change a child's life from joy to desperation, impact a child's personality development, and/or color their world-view forever (Ford & Curtois, 2013). The effects of psychological trauma can impact the child at the cognitive, affective, behavioral, and somatic- physiological levels, and can become intergenerational (Armsworth & Holaday, 1993). The symptoms of the trauma that a Latino child exhibits can be common or universal (e.g., fear, crying spells, nightmares, clinging, etc.) or culture-bound (e.g., *susto*, *ataque de nervios*, *bilis*, etc.). The child can be diagnosed with acute stress disorder, depression, anxiety disorder, and/or posttraumatic stress disorder, or PTSD (American Psychiatric Association, 2013; Ford & Curtois, 2013). The trauma can scar a child for life and impact how the child relates to other persons including loved ones, cause severe depression and suicide, promote serious mental and substance abuse disorders in adulthood, or be a healing and inoculating experience that makes the child highly resilient to the many stressors and problems that are likely to occur later in life as a result of simply living (Greenwald, 2015).

The most common types of childhood trauma that Latino children are at-risk for, and that have received some attention in the research literature, can range from child abuse and neglect (e.g., Coohey, 2001; Damashek, Nelson, & Bonner, 2013; Flores, Ciccheti, & Rogosch, 2005; Fontes, 2002; Lipschitz, Winegar, Nicolau, Harthick, Wolfson, & Southwick, 1999), sexual molestation (e.g., Fontes, 2007; Fontes, Cruz, & Tabachnick, 2001; Moisan, Sanders-Phillips, & Moisan, 1997), incest (e.g., Bass, Taylor, Knudson-Martin, & Huenergardt, 2006; Flores-Oritz, 1997), exposure to domestic violence and parental partner abuse (Fantuzzo & Mohr, 1999; Klevens, 2007; McFarlane, Groff, O'Brien, & Watson, 2003; Mattson & Ruiz, 2005; Rodriguez, Heileman, Fielder, Ang, Nevarez, & Mangione, 2008), parental substance abuse (Hanson, Self-Brown, Fricker-Elhai, Kilpatrick, Saunders, & Resnick, 2006; Van De Mark, Russell, O'Keefe, Finkelstein, Noether, & Gampbel, 2005), and parental abandonment (e.g., Burnette, 1999; Cabrera, Ryan, Mitchell, Shannon, & Tamis-LeMonda, 2008; Cervantes, Mejia, & Mena, 2010).

Latino children, like all other children, are also at-risk for other types of childhood trauma including being traumatized by parental divorce (Ayoub, Deutsch, & Maraganore, 1999; Dreman, 1991; Johnston, 2005; Shooter, 1997), auto accidents (Meiser-Stedman, Yule, Smith, Glucksman, & Dalgleish, 2005), animal bites (Peters, Sottiaux, Appelboom, & Kahn, 2004), natural disasters (Evans & Oehler-Stinnett,

2006), parental illness (Huizinga, Visser, van der Graff, Hoekstra, Klip, Pras, & Hoekstra-Weebers, 2005), dental interventions (Onetto, Flores, & Garbino, 1994), body burns (Saxe, Stoddard, & Sheridan, 1988), terrorism including bombings (Pfefferbaum, Nixon, Tucker, Tivis, Moore, Gurwitch, Pynoos, & Geis, 1999), school shootings (Schwarz & Kowalski, 1991), and many other types of trauma.

## Urban-Specific Types of Childhood Trauma for Latino Children

In urban or metropolitan settings, Latino children can be at high risk for "urban-specific" types of trauma. These are the types of childhood trauma that are likely to occur because of the social, economic (including poverty), physical, cultural, political (including disenfranchisement of the populace), and spatial conditions of urban communities. This can include trauma triggered by neighborhood or *barrio* violence (Aisenberg & Herrenkohl, 2008; Ceballo, Dahl, Aretakis, & Ramirez, 2001; Clauss-Ehlers & Levi, 2002; Gorman-Smith, Henry, & Tolan, 2010; Kataoka, Stein, Jaycox, Wong, Escudero, Tu, & Fink, 2003), gang violence (Mendoza-Denton, 2014; Katz, 1997; Romero, 2000; Stodolska, Acevedo, & Shinew, 2009; Vigil, 2003; Wilson & Rosenthal, 2003; Zatz & Portillos, 2000), homicide (Martinez, 2000, 2014; Freeman, Shaffer, & Smith, 1996), overcrowding and urban blight (Bradman, Chevrier, Tager, Lipsett, Sedgwick, Macher, & Eskenazi, 2005; Evans & Lepore, 1993; Memken & Canabal, 1994; Sampson & Raudenbush, 2004), human trafficking and prostitution (Baldwin, Eisenman, Sayles, Ryan, & Chung, 2011; Cicero-Dominguez, 2005; Ugarte, Zarate, & Farley, 2004), victimization by peers in the *'hood* and bullying at school (Peguero, 2009; Shetgiri, Lin, Avila, & Flores, 2012; Yabko, Hakoda, & Ulloa, 2008) and neighborhood crime (Aisenberg, Trickett, Mennen, Saltzman, & Zayas, 2007; Barron-McKeagney, Woody, & D'Souza, 2002; Torres & Vogel, 2001).

In more recent years, Latino children have also become at-risk for trauma related to the mass incarceration of Latino men and women, many of whom are parents (Foster & Hagan, 2009; Genty, 2002; Krisberg & Temin, 2001; Glaze & Maruschak, 2008; Pattillo, Western, & Weiman, 2004; Reed & Reed, 1997; Sanchez, Funes, & Velasquez, in press; Springer, Lynch, & Rubin, 2000; Swisher & Waller, 2008; Urbina, 2012; Velasquez & Funes, 2014). In 2003, The Sentencing Project reported that one in three persons in federal prisons were Latino, with an astounding increase of 219% of Latinos in both state and federal prisons between the years 1985 and 1995. In a 2009 report, The Sentencing Project found that 1 in 42 Latino children had a parent in prison. Today, 1 in 28 Latino children have at least one parent in prison. There is no doubt that many of these children are at-risk for or have already experienced the trauma of being separated from one or both parents because of parental incarceration (Gabel & Johnston, 1995).

## Latinos in Rural America Today

Latinos are not only the fastest growing ethnic minority group in the United States, but also in rural America (Ennis, Rios-Vargas, & Albert, 2011; Humes, Jones, & Ramirez, 2011; Passel, Cohn, & Lopez, 2011). Since the 1980s, the Latino population has increased dramatically to the point that they have surpassed African Americans as the largest ethnic/racial minority group in rural America (Rochin, 1995; Saenz & Torres, 2003; Smith & Furuseth, 2006; Zuniga, & Hernandez-Leon, 2005). In the 1980s, the Latino population in rural and geographically- isolated parts of the country increased by 27% and exploded to 67% in the 1990s (Kandel & Cromartie, 2004). According to the most recent census (United States Census Bureau, 2010), the Latino rural population increased by almost 2 million between 2000 and 2010, with the total population of Latinos in rural communities reaching six million. Overall, while

Latinos are urban dwellers, with 91% of the total population residing in cities and metropolitan areas, 9% of the population resides in rural and settings. Even the 9% remains constant over the next 35 years, up to 11 million Latinos will reside in rural America by the year 2050.

In total, Latinos represent 17% of the total U.S. population with a current population of 54 million (U.S. Census Bureau, 2013), and an estimated population of 112 million by the year 2050. As of 2014, there were 17.5 million Latino children in the United States, with 90% having been born in the United States and 70% being of Mexican descent (Murphey, Guzman, & Torres, 2014). The National Center for Education Statistics (2013) reported that 23% of all students in rural schools were of Latino descent and only 16% were African American during the 2010-2011 academic year. This suggests that the population of Latinos, especially children, is increasing in rural America, and is likely to remain as residents in these communities.

At the same time, it is very important to emphasize in 2012 the Housing Assistance Council found that 27.3% of the rural Latino population lived in poverty, which in turn, has a strong causal link to multiple social and psychological problems in Latino families and their children including childhood trauma (Brown & Swanson, 2010; Crowley, Lichter, & Qian, 2006; Saenz, 1997; Taylor, Martin, Fix, & Alarcon, 1997). Murphrey, Guzman, and Torres (2014) observed that 62% of all Latino children in the United States lived with low-income families, while 33% of Latino children lived in poverty. These researchers also found that 37% of Latino children lived in communities with "concentrated poverty".

While there has always been a very strong representation of Latinos, predominantly of Mexican and Central American descent, in rural communities as migrant (and non-migrant farmworkers) for many decades, other Latinos and their families have purposely moved to rural communities in search of an increased quality of life (Crowley & Lichter, 2009; Dalla, Ellis, & Cramer, 2005; Fraga & Garcia, 2010; Kandel & Cromartie, 2004; Torres, Popke, & Hapke, 2010). In fleeing from large and congested urban/metropolitan communities, these families have attempted to provide a better life for their children free of gang violence, substance abuse, victimization, bullying, inner-city violence, etc. Other Latino families, especially those with undocumented family members, have move to or settled in rural communities for, albeit tenuous, safe haven from the immigration authorities (Arbona, Olvera, Rodriguez, Hagan, Linares, & Wiesner, 2010; Cantu, 1995; Raffaelli & Wiley, 2013; Gouveia, 2005).

Yet, in spite of leaving behind many social problems related to urban life, Latino families cannot fully escape from the problems and challenges that accompany living in rural communities. For example, researchers have studied some problems that Latinos and their children are likely to encounter in rural communities. These include marginal health status (Casey, Blewett, & Call, 2004; Hubert, Snider, & Winkleby, 2005; Sherrill, Crew, Mayo, Rogers, & Haynes, 2005), work-related accidents on ranches and farms (Walter, Bourgois, & Loinaz, 2004), pesticide poisoning (Arcury, Marin, Snively, Hernandez-Pelletier, & Quandt, 2009; Halfacre-Hitchcock, McCarthy, Burkett, & Carvajal, 2006; LePrevost, Storm, Blanchard, Asuje, & Cope, 2013), substance abuse (Garcia, 2007; Loury & Kulbok, 2007; Quintero, Lilliott, & Willging, 2007), domestic and partner violence (Ames, Hancock, & Behnke, 2011; Gonzalez-Guarda, Florom-Smith, & Thomas, 2011; Kim-Godwin & Fox, 2009; Morraco, Hilton, Hodges, & Frasier, 2005), language barriers in accessing health care (Berdahl, Kirby, & Stone, 2007; Cristancho, Graces, Peters, & Mueller, 2008; Timmins, 2002; gang violence (Moreno, 2006; Tapia, 2014; Warthan,, Mortimer, & Allard, 2011), mental illness (Folsom, Gilmer, Barrio, Moore, Bucardo, Lindamer, Garcia, & Jeste, 2007; Grzywacz, Quandt, Early, Tapia, Graham, & Arcury, 2006; Hiott, Grzywacz, Davis, Quandt, & Arcury, 2008; Petterson, Williams, Havenstein, Rounyak, & Merwin, 2009), grandparents raising children in rural communities, (Bullock, 2007), and educational attainment and high school drop-out rates (Behnke, Gonzalez, & Cox, 2010; Hondo, Gardiner, & Sapien, 2008).

Other studies have examined the stress of being undocumented in rural communities (Arbona, Olvera, Rodriguez, Hagan, Linares, & Weisner, 2010; Cantu, 1995; Gouveia, 2005; Raffaelli & Wiley, 2013) and overall quality of life for Latinos in rural America (Allensworth & Rochin, 1996; Dalla & Christensen, 2005; Dalla, Ellis, & Cramer, 2005; Crowley & Lichter, 2009; Fraga & Garcia, 2010; Kandel & Cromartie, 2004; Torres, Popke, & Hapke, 2006). Still other investigations have examined the high rates of obesity among Latino children who reside in rural communities in the United States (Eichner, Moore, Perveen, Kobza, Abbott, & Stephens, 2012; Liu, Bennett, Harun, & Probst, 2008; Wickrama, Elder, & Abraham, 2007)

## Rural-Specific Types of Childhood Trauma for Latino Children

As previously noted, and irrespective of whether Latino children reside in urban or rural communities, they remain at-risk for a myriad of different types of childhood trauma. Yet, the following sources of trauma are more likely to occur to Latino children in rural communities because of many reasons ranging from geographic isolation, poverty, broken or separated families, substandard housing including living in labor camps, constant migration and relocation, recurring uprooting, and isolation from social support networks including extended families (e.g., Hovey & Magana, 2002; Landale & Lichter, 1997; Ward, 2010). The following are some of the most common types of childhood trauma that Latino children are likely to encounter in rural or geographically-isolated communities. The first type of trauma is "parental deportation". While it may not be the most common, it is clearly growing every day as more and more Latino adults are being arrested, detained, and deported back to their country of origin. Many of these children are born in this country and more importantly, are U. S. citizens (Osterberg, 2009; Zayas, Aguilar-Gaxiola, Yoon, & Rey, 2015).

## Parental Deportation Trauma

Many Latino families move to rural or geographically-isolated communities in order to avoid detection by immigration authorities because of their illegal or undocumented status (Brabeck & Xu, 2010; Chaudry, Capps, Pedroza, Castaneda, Santos, & Scott, 2010; Dreby, 2012; Garrison, Roy, & Azar, 1999; Golash-Boza & Hondagneu-Sotelo, 2013; Hagan, Castro, & Rodrgiuez, 2010; Mendoza & Olivos, 2009). In many ways, the further away they live from metropolitan areas, the less likely these families are at-risk for being detected, apprehended, and deported. Yet, as in the case of *Mayte*, her parents were eventually arrested at work and deported. She had to be placed under the care of the Iowa child protective services and eventually became so severely traumatized that she experienced psychotic episodes. Dreby (2012) noted that parental deportation not only affects a child, but the rest of the family and the greater community.

Given the large number of deportations, especially under the Obama administration over the past five years, more and more research has addressed the psychological effects of parental deportation on children (e.g., Allen, Cisneros, & Tellez, 2013; Brabeck, Lykes, & Hunter, 2014; Gonzalez, 2015; Henderson & Baily, 2013; Homer, Saunders, Martinez, Doering-White, Lopez, & Delva, 2014; McLeigh, 2010; Osterberg, 2009; Suarez-Orozco, Yoshikawa, Teranishi, & Suarez-Orozco, 2001; Zayas, Aguilar-Gaxiola, Yoon, & Rey, 2015). For example, Brabeck, Lykes, and Lustig (2013) noted that between July 2010 and September 2012, a total of 205,000 Latino deportees reported having at least one U. S. citizen child.

Velasquez and Funes (2014) recently observed that ranking second to parental deportation, is probably parental incarceration, especially in light of the massive growth of the prison and immigration industrial complexes in recent decades and the "war on drugs" and the criminalization of undocumented persons.

Collectively, these studies suggest that deportations are highly damaging to Latino children to the point that the trauma is likely to have not only psychological effects, but also interrupt key developmental periods in the child (Suarez-Orozco, Yoshikawa, Teranishi, & Suarez-Orozco, 2001). The trauma caused on these children is connected to many factors including the sudden and unexpected arrest or disappearance of the parent(s), the broken attachment or bond that had existed between the child and the parent(s), imposed family separation, fears related to the deportation of the parents and never having contact with them again, anxiety and fear by the child over their unknown fate, and consternation over the possibility of having to move to the parents' country in order to be with them (Brabeck, Lykes, & Lustig, 2013; Henderson & Baily, 2013; Zayas, Aguilar-Gaxiola, Yoon, & Rey, 2015).

Capps, Castaneda, Chaudry, and Santos (2007) discussed how the actual arrest, oftentimes at gunpoint, of a parent in front of the child can leave a lasting effect. In the case of *Luis*, whose father was beaten by the police, he was significantly traumatized with his attitude toward the police authorities changing completely. While there is an absence of research on how Latino children respond to their parents' apprehension by immigration officials at gunpoint or through the use of force, children who undergo such trauma are also likely to quickly develop depression, loneliness, and anxiety at not knowing the fate of their parent(s). Depending on the age of the child, the response to such a trauma, as seen through the presentation of clinical symptoms is likely to be most severe in children who have developed a verbal and visual bond with their parents, and who have had a very close and healthy relationship. In the end, the biggest problem for these children is parental separation and imposed abandonment, and what life will be without their parents in their lives.

Allen, Cisneros, and Tellez (2013) noted that children who are left behind (in this country) because of their parents' deportation experience the type of trauma than easily meets the criteria for PTSD. In addition to having symptoms of trauma, they are also likely to have separation anxiety, severe depression, and at-riskness for substance abuse later in life. Brabeck, Lykes, and Lustig (2013) observed that "adverse effects from a single event, such as a parent's deportation, are more likely to result in negative outcomes when they occur against the backdrop of multiple risk factors". Thus, for many of these children, multiple risk factors include isolation, poverty, poor housing, and even food insecurity.

## Geographic-Isolation Trauma

As more Latino families move from urban to rural settings, children are at greater risk for trauma associated with having to adjust from one environment to another (Crowley & Lichter, 2010; Dalla & Chistensen, 2005; Nelson & Hiemstra, 2008; Schultz, 2008). While some children may embrace rural life, other children may view relocation as not only negative but over time very traumatic. Just as families who relocate from rural to urban settings have to undergo a period of adjustment, so do families who move from urban to rural communities. Difficulty in adjustment may also be linked to moving to a geographically-isolated community such as the desert, mountains, ranches, or farmland.

While there is an absence of research on the psychological adjustment of Latino children who live in rural and geographically-isolated communities, it is clear that many Latino children are likely to be at-risk for not only adjustment disorders and acculturative stress, but also for more severe trauma. This is especially the case for Latino children who have lived for a greater part of their lives in more urban or metropolitan communities and have now moved with their families to rural communities (Landale & Lichter, 1997; Ward, 2010). These children are likely to leave behind family, strong friendships and a social support network, and strong ties to their community or neighborhood. They are likely to encounter a different type of environment from urban life and over time may feel intense levels of boredom because of the lack of social and intellectual stimulation. The may also begin to feel like a numerical minority for the first time in their lives, especially if they lived in a city where Latinos were the majority. This shift from being a member of the majority to minority may place the child at-risk for increased sensitivity to not only feeling out of place, but also for racism and prejudice.

These children may also resent the relocation of the family to a rural community and may develop homesickness for the past urban home. At school, these children may have problems in adjusting to the new school environment including friendships with peers. They may develop significant academic problems with a heightened risk of dropping out of school. The case of *Elizabeth*, who witnessed the suicide of her brother because of his dislike of living in a rural community, is an example of the seriousness of geographic-isolation trauma. The case of *Margarita*, who was bitten by a rattlesnake, is an example of the types of ecological dangers that a child is more likely to encounter when living in a rural as opposed to an urban community.

## Pesticide Poisoning Trauma

The late Cesar Chavez, leader of the United Farmworkers of America, was one of the first Latino leaders to openly talk about the dangers of pesticides, especially with Latino migrant farmworkers in rural communities across the United States. Chavez recognized that more and more Latino workers and their families were developing severe medical conditions because of chemical poisoning. Today, more and more studies have documented the detrimental effects of various chemicals that are used on farms and ranches (e.g., Arcury, Grzywacz, Barr, Tapia, Chen, & Quandt, 2007; Hohl, Gonzalez, Carosso, Ibarra, & Thompson, 2014; Mc Cauley, Laserer, Higgins, Rothlein, Muniz, Ebbert, & Phillips, 2001; Quant, 2009). Collectively, while these studies focus on more on the effects of these chemicals on the physical well-being of Latinos, including children, there is clearly a need for studies that examine how these children react, on an emotional level, when they are found to have a medical illness caused by high levels of chemical toxicity, or when they have to help care for a parent who has developed a medical problem.

The case of *Roberto* is an example of the emotional trauma that he experienced in not only developing a severe medical condition but in knowing that he would likely die at a very young age. The case of *Octavio* illustrates the trauma that a Latino adolescent can experience with the death of a parent due to pesticide poisoning, and with another parent beginning to exhibit the same types of symptoms. In addition, this latter case reflects the importance of family members in the Latino family. In this case, *Octavio* is the oldest of six children and has always been expected to care for his younger siblings even after all have grown up. As the oldest child, he is also expected to take on a parental role should one or both of his parents die. Thus, while he was anointed with this important role shortly after the birth of the second child, Octavio has always taken this role and responsibility very seriously. Yet, this type of role responsibility, coupled with the death of one parent and the imminent death of the other parents makes Octavio at high-risk for difficulty in coping with future trauma.

## Language Broker Trauma

While usually not thought of a stressful event in a child's life, or series of events, language brokering or translating/interpreting for non-English-speaking parents can be very stressful and under some circumstances, very traumatic (Castaneda, 1998; Love & Buriel, 2007; Martinez, McClure, & Eddy, 2008; Morales, Yakushko, & Castro, 2012; Orellana, 2009; Tilghman-Osborne, Bamaca-Colbert, Witherspoon, Wadsworth, & Hecht, 2015; Valenzuela, 1999; Weiskirch, 2005; Weisskirch, & Alva, 2002). Researchers who have investigated children who serve as language brokers have found these children to be anxious, nervouss, and depressed. These children have also been found to very afraid of becoming "parentified" or placed in the position of having to act highly responsible and very mature at a very young age. These children are also afraid of incorrectly translating for their parents and relatives as they do not want to be the sources of greater problems. Such potential problems can include not being accurate or precise in describing a parent's medical condition to a doctor or making a mistake in communicating a parent's feelings to a therapist.

Language broker trauma can also push children to become psychologically enmeshed with a parent or parents and the parents to become highly dependent on their children. That is, the children begin to act like adults and parents while the adults begin to act more like children. Depending on the age of the child, this dependence can overwhelm the child who is the family language broker and make them lose their focus and motivation away from school. The child may also take on the position of feeling and acting like a parent, which in turn can bring instability to the rest of the family. The case of *Sylvia* illustrates the importance of being a language broker in a Latino family but also the huge responsibility that is attached to this family role. In the case of *Sylvia*, she felt very guilty and responsible for the death of her aunt. *Sylvia* in therapy talked about how much she hated being the family language broker as she felt that her childhood was "robbed" by her parents because of their dependence on her.

While the first time that the child is called upon to translate may not necessarily be traumatic or highly stressful for the child, this is the type of condition that can become more stressful over the years, especially when the child is an adolescent and beginning to spend more time at school and with peers or when they grow and elderly parents continue to remain highly dependent and needy. Love and Buriel (2007) found very high rates of depression among Latino adolescents who served as language brokers, with acculturation serving as a moderating variable. They also found that high levels of depression placed these children at higher risk for traumatic injury.

## Migration Trauma

There are different types of migration trauma that can negatively impact Latino children (Hovey & Magana, 2002). The first type is where a child and their family migrate from another country to the United States, usually with the aid of a *coyote*. Depending on the route taken by the parents, many of these children witness death and dying, physical aggression, and murder while on their journey. Others have to travel through very dangerous territories, especially in Mexico, on their way to the United States and also witness high levels of aggression including murder and rapes. The second type of migration trauma relates to traveling or migrating within the United States from one region of the country to another and having to endure the long days and nights on the road, extreme weather conditions, poor nutrition, and constant reestablishment of one's home. In this type of migration, families and children are never able to set roots in a particular community that they can call their town and instead experience a personal history of having very poor, shallow, or limited attachments to others including peers at school. Other consequences to migration trauma can include the lack of a strong and consistent educational experience, high drop-out rates for these children, a lack of social support network, and a poor connection with extended family (Behnke, Gonzalez, Lin, & Cox, 2010; Hampton, Ekboir, & Rochin, 1995; Hondo, Gardiner, & Sapien, 2008; Rodriguez, Rodriguez, & Davis, 2006). Hampton, Ekboir, and Rochin (1995) found significant drops in test scores of Latino school children in rural communities, with higher rates of migration as a mediating factor.

The third type of migration trauma refers to recent migrations of children, primarily from Central American countries. For example, in the fiscal 2014 year, over 68,500 unaccompanied children arrived in the United States from Central America, with 75% coming from El Salvador, Guatemala, and Honduras (Meyer, Seelke, Taft-Morales, & Margesson, 2015). Many of these children began their long trek to the United States by illegally boarding trains in Southern Mexico and traveling all the way to the U. S.-Mexico border. Gonzalez (2015), in a recent doctoral dissertation, recorded the narratives of many of these children, as well as children who were separated from their parents because of deportation proceedings.

The case of *Susana* and her sister *Eva* illustrate the horrors that Latino children can experience in their long trek to the United States. In the case of these sisters, both were raped on numerous occasions on their trip and both became more traumatized after each event. In addition to enduring the long trip from their country, they also endured starvation, lack of access to medical care, especially after the rapes, sleep deprivation, and no contact with their parents or family back home. Both children were placed in an INS program for unaccompanied minors where they experienced extreme psychological hardships including bullying by other children, lack of mental health counseling services, poor food and nutrition, and no legal representation for many months. Eventually both *Susana* and *Eva* were deported back to their country and have yet to locate their parents.

## School to School Trauma

Related to migration trauma is school to school trauma. In this type of trauma, migrant families who have to move from rural community to rural community because they follow diverse harvest seasons are likely to place their children at-risk for trauma related to shifting from school to school. This inconsistency in education is bound to catch-up with the child over the years and likely to place the child at-risk for problems in learning and dropping out from school. For example, a child with constant school interruptions is likely to develop a patchwork of learning concepts with some that are essential and missing. In many cases, Latino children are always having to "catch-up" as they move from one school to another. In turn, this is likely to produce a child who will be at-risk for underachievement, low self-esteem, and poor self-efficacy.

The child is also likely to have problems in attaining a comprehensive educational experience that will prepare the child for the future, difficulties in developing appropriate social and academic skills, and problems in having healthy attachment and bonding relationships with peers. In some cases, these children are also at-risk for victimization and bullying because they are minorities within the school and community. In addition, because of an inconsistent educational track record, they may be at-risk to be misdiagnosed by a school psychologist and placed in special education-type classes. Oftentimes, children who are labeled as special education students are victimized by other students and peers.

It is not unusual for many migrant families to enroll their children in more than a dozen schools in one year as they move from one part of the country to another in following different harvests. The trauma may not necessarily occur during the first-ever shift from one school to another, but may occur any time during the education of the child, especially if they begin to develop a sense of rootedness and connectedness to a particular school and community (e.g., Hampton, Ekboir, & Rochin, 1995; Rodriguez, Rodriguez, & Davis, 2006).

In the case of school to school to trauma, it is likely that Latino children will develop a history of cumulative mini-traumatic experiences that can eventually lead to a more well-defined and permanent trauma. In turn, one of the most common symptoms in these children would be a diminished interest in school, an increasing desire to stay at home, and discomfort in being in the presence of other children. In other words, they are at-risk for also developing a school phobia.

## Labor Camp Trauma

Labor camps, trailer parks, and other types of labor-related housing are some of the most difficult places for Latino children to adjust to because the physical conditions of these facilities. It is not unusual for these places to be disorganized, infested with rodents, dirty, and poor sanitation facilities. In addition, another stressor to Latino parents and their children relates to the types of persons who may be living next door. While some of these persons may be good citizens, others may have past criminal records. Also, it is very common for labor camps and other living facilities for migrant camps to be overpopulated by men who are prone to use alcohol and drugs and bring prostitutes to these places. In other words, many parents become easily stressed over having to keep constant watch over their children in these locations.

A systematic review of the research literature on this topic yielded some limited studies that have examined the strain, stress, and potential trauma that Latino children may experience in labor or work camps (Arcury, Weir, Chen, Summers, Pelletier, Galvan, & Quandt, 2012; Benson, 2008; Cravey, 1997; Atiles & Bohon, 2003; McConnell & Miraftab, 2010). In general, these studies found that poor quality of life, overrepresentation of single men, high rates of substance abuse, and the presence of prostitutes in these camps likely increased the conditions that could be traumatizing to a Latino child. In addition, the researchers also found that high levels of poverty in these camps coupled with crowding, noise, and social disorganization also placed Latino children at-risk for trauma.

## Farm Equipment Accident Trauma

The case of *Johnny* best illustrates farm equipment accident trauma. While not yet fully documented, there are bound to be many cases of trauma related to children either being hurt by farm equipment of all types to witnessing a family member who is a victim of an accident due to farming equipment. In this case, Johnny not only witnessed the bloody amputation of his father's arm while working on a baling machine, he also witnessed his death as the accident occurred in a very geographically-isolated farm.

A comprehensive review of the research literature on this type of trauma suggests that there is a wealth of research on farming accidents in children in the United States (Bayard, Gilbert, James, & Lipsett, 1999; Cogbill, Busch, & Stiers, 1985; Meiers & Baerg, 2001; Pickett, Brison, Berg, Zentner, Linneman, & Marlenga, 2005; Swanson, Sachs, Dahlgren, & Tinguely, 1987). The results of these studies, collectively, suggest that childhood trauma on farms and ranches in rural areas is more common than one would expect, with traumatic events ranging from trauma caused by farm animals to injuries from different types of farm equipment including tractors and trucks to fatalities. Unfortunately, there is an absence of research which takes into account ethnicity or race of these children, or studies which take into consideration the trauma caused to a child who witnesses farm accidents. Yet, because of the growing Latino population in rural communities, it is critical that research take into consideration the ethnicity of the children who are victims of physical or psychological trauma.

In the case of *Johnny*, it appears that the trauma of witnessing the injury and death of his father was such a severe form of trauma that the prognosis would appear to be poor for an extended period of time, and without any type of intervention, the event would probably affect him for the rest of his life.

## Rural-Specific Types of Childhood Trauma: Identification of Cardinal Symptoms

As discussed at the beginning of this chapter, researchers and clinicians have identified both universal and culture-bound symptoms of childhood trauma. In fact, as the DSM system has evolved through the current DSM-V (2013), more and more attention has been paid to both recognizing and treating symptoms that are more likely to be defined by culture. While it is beyond the scope of this chapter to discuss in great detail the many symptoms that children who are traumatized by different sources of trauma are likely to experience, it is important to briefly discuss some of the most common symptoms observed childhood trauma, whether in urban or rural communities.

Some of the classic symptoms of childhood trauma that can be expected in Latino children (as in other children) who reside in rural and geographically-isolated communities include, but are not limited, to depression, fear, anger, confusion, poor concentration, social anxiety, alienation, flashbacks of the traumatic event, nightmares, enuresis and encopresis, clinging, insomnia, apathy, aggression, needy and dependent behaviors, crying spells, self-harming behaviors including cutting, guilt, hypervigilance, suspiciousness and mistrust, dissociation, and terror (see Blaustein & Kinnibrough, 2010; Cohen, Mannarino, & Deblinger, 2006; Ford & Courtois, 2013; Greenwald, 2015; Kay, Burt, Eth, & Phillips, 2001; Silva, 2004).

It is important to note that the extent to which a Latino child can successfully cope with the impact of a traumatic event is related to their past history of trauma and whether the trauma has been cumulative, the quality of the bonding or attachment relationship of the child to one or both parents, the age and gender of the child, the quality of relationships among family members including siblings, the level of maturity in the child, the presence or absence of acculturative stress in the child and family's life, degree of poverty and a marginalized life, parental education, connectedness with extended *familia* including grandparents, and the role of formal religious practices within the family. Other key factors include language of parents, access to mental health and medical sources, and access to health insurance.

## Conclusion: Barriers to the Effective Treatment of Rural-specific Trauma in Latino Children

Our review of the research literature in the identification, treatment, and prevention of childhood trauma in Latino children who reside in rural communities led us to conclude that there remain many barriers for these children and their families. The following are some of the most obvious barriers:

1. There is a continuing absence of research on rural-specific types of trauma in Latino children. In our systematic review of the literature, we found a scattering of studies on trauma and mental illness in Latino children in rural communities, but the majority of the research continues to be conducted in urban settings. While there is no doubt that some of the findings from these studies, especially those related to the detection and treatment of trauma are applicable to Latino children in rural communities, there is a significant need to conduct more research, especially in light of the fact that the Latino population has grown in rural communities and geographically-isolated regions of this country.
2. There is a lack of Latino mental health professionals in rural and geographically-isolated communities who can treat Latino children who have diverse mental health needs including trauma related to living in these communities. While the shortage of Latino mental health professionals may not be so evident in some urban and metropolitan parts, there is still clearly a need for professionals to expand into rural communities.
3. Consistent with the above barrier, there is still an absence of Spanish-speaking professionals who can assist in the treatment of traumatized Latino children in rural communities. Research studies related to the recent U. S. census suggest that the rates of retention of Spanish by U.S. born children remain high as parents value that their children are bilingual.
4. There is an absence of Latino oriented community-based organizations, support networks, or agencies that can advocate for the identification, treatment, and prevention of childhood trauma in rural communities. In urban and large metropolitan communities, these organizations have helped parents find the necessary resources to assist their children. This is still lacking in rural communities across the country.

## REFERENCES

Aisenberg, E., & Herrenkohl, T. (2008). Community violence in context risk and resilience in children and families. *Journal of Interpersonal Violence*, *23*(3), 296–315. doi:10.1177/0886260507312287 PMID:18245570

Aisenberg, E., Trickett, P. R., Mennen, F. E., Saltzman, W., & Zayas, L. H. (2007). Maternal depression and adolescent behavior problems: An examination of mediation among Latino immigrant mothers and their adolescent children exposed to community violence. *Journal of Interpersonal Violence*, *22*(10), 1227–1249. doi:10.1177/0886260507304292 PMID:17766724

Allen, B., Cisneros, E. M., & Tellez, A. (2013). The children left behind: The impact of parental deportation on mental health. *Journal of Child and Family Studies*, *24*(2), 386–392. doi:10.1007/s10826-013-9848-5

Allensworth, E. M., & Rochin, R. I. (1996). *White exodus, Latino repopulation, and community well-being: Trends in California's rural communities*. Julian Samora Research Institute, Michigan State University.

American Psychiatric Association. (2013). *Diagnostic and statistical manual of mental disorders: DSM-5* (5th ed.). Washington, DC: American Psychiatric Publishing.

Ames, N., Hancock, T. V., & Behnke, A. (2011). Latino church leaders and domestic violence: Attitudes and knowledge. *Families in Society*, *92*(2), 161–167. doi:10.1606/1044-3894.4093

Androff, D. K., Ayon, C., Becerra, D., & Gurrola, M. (2011). U.S. immigration policy and immigrant children's well-being: The impact of policy shifts. *Journal of Sociology and Social Welfare*, *38*, 77.

Arbona, C., Olvera, N., Rodrgiguez, N., Hagan, J., Linares, A., & Weisner, M. (2010). Acculturative stress among documented and undocumented Latino immigrants in the United States. *Hispanic Journal of Behavioral Sciences*, *32*(3), 362–384. doi:10.1177/0739986310373210 PMID:25484488

Arcury, T. A., Grzywacz, J. G., Barr, D. B., Tapia, J., Chen, H., & Quandt, S. A. (2007). Pesticide urinary metabolite levels of children in Eastern North Carolina farmworker households. *Environmental Health Perspectives*, *115*(8), 1254–1260. doi:10.1289/ehp.9975 PMID:17687456

Arcury, T. A., Marin, A., Snively, B. M., Hernandez-Pelletier, J., & Quandt, S. A. (2009). Reducing farmworker residential pesticide exposure: Evaluation of a lay health advisor intervention. *Health Promotion Practice*, *10*(3), 447–455. doi:10.1177/1524839907301409 PMID:18287581

Arcury, T. A., Weir, M., Chen, H., Summers, P., Pelletier, L. E., Galvan, L., & Quandt, S. A. (2012). Migrant farmworker housing regulation violations in North Carolina. *Journal of Industrial Medicine*, *55*(3), 191–204. doi:10.1002/ajim.22011 PMID:22237961

Armsworth, M. W., & Holaday, M. (1993). The effects of psychological trauma on children and adolescents. *Journal of Counseling and Development*, *72*(1), 49–56. doi:10.1002/j.1556-6676.1993.tb02276.x

Atiles, J. H., & Bohon, S. A. (2003). Camas calientes: Housing adjustments and barriers to social and economic adaptation among Georgia's rural Latinos. *Rural Sociology*, *19*, 97–122.

Ayoub, C. C., Deutsch, R. M., & Maraganore, A. (1999). Emotional distress in children of high conflict divorce. *Family Court Review*, *37*(3), 297–315. doi:10.1111/j.174-1617.1999.tb01307.x

Baldwin, S. B., Eisenman, D. P., Sayles, J. N., Ryan, G., & Chung, K. S. (2011). Identification of human trafficking victims in health care settings. *Health and Human Rights*, *13*, 36–49. PMID:22772961

Barron-McKeagney, T., Woody, J., & D'Souza, H. (2002). Mentoring at-risk Latino children and their parents: Analysis of the parent-child relationship and family strength. *Families in Society*, *83*(3), 285–292. doi:10.1606/1044-3894.19

Bass, L. B., Taylor, B. A., Knudson-Martin, C., & Huenergardt, D. (2006). Making sense of abuse: Case studies in sibling incest. *Contemporary Family Therapy*, *28*(1), 87–109. doi:10.1007/s10591-006-9697-0

Behnke, A. O., Gonzalez, L. M., & Cox, R. B. (2008). Latino students in new arrival states: Factors and service to prevent youth from dropping out. *Hispanic Journal of Behavioral Sciences*, *32*(3), 385–409. doi:10.1177/0739986310374025

Benson, P. (2008). El campo: Facility and structural violence in farm labor camps. *Cultural Anthropology*, *23*(4), 589–629. doi:10.1111/j.1548-1360.2008.00020.x

Berdahl, T. A., Kirby, J. B., & Stone, R. A. T. (2007). Access to health care for nonmetro and metro Latinos of Mexican origin in the United States. *Medical Care*, *45*(7), 647–657. doi:10.1097/MLR.0b013e3180536734 PMID:17571013

Blaustein, M. E., & Kinniburgh, K. M. (2010). *Traumatic stress in children and adolescents: How to foster resilience through attachment, self-regulation, and competency*. New York: The Guilford Press.

Brabeck, K., & Xu, Q. (2010). The impact of deportation on Latino immigrant children and families: A quantitative exploration. *Hispanic Journal of Behavioral Sciences*, *32*(3), 341–361. doi:10.1177/0739986310374053

Brabeck, K. M., Lykes, M. B., & Hunter, C. (2014). The psychosocial impact of detention and deportation on U. S. migrant children and families. *Journal of Orthopsychiatry*, *84*(5), 496–505. doi:10.1037/ort0000011 PMID:25110972

Brabeck, K. M., Lykes, M. B., & Lustig, S. L. (2013). *The psychological impact of detention and deportation on U. S. migrant children and families: A report to the Interamerican human rights court.* Academic Press.

Bradman, A., Chevrier, J., Tager, I., Lipsett, M., Sedgwick, J., Macher, J., & Eskanazi, B. (2005). Association of housing disrepair indicators in a cohort of pregnant Latina women and their children. *Environmental Health Perspectives*, 1795–1801. doi:10.1289/ehp.7588 PMID:16330367

Brown, D., & Swanson, L. E. (2010). *Challenges for rural America in the twenty-first century*. Pennsylvania State Press.

Bullock, K. (2005). Chapter 7: Ahora le voy a cuidar a mis nietos: Rural Latino grandparents raising grandchildren of alcohol and other drug abusing parents. *Alcoholism Treatment Quarterly*, *23*(2-3), 107–130. doi:10.1300/J020v23n02_07

Burnette, D. (1999). Social relationships of Latino grandparent caregivers: A role theory perspective. *The Gerontologist*, *39*(1), 49–58. doi:10.1093/geront/39.1.49 PMID:10028770

Byard, R. W., Gilbert, J., James, R., & Lipsett, J. (1999). Pathologic features of farm and tractor-related fatalities in children. *The American Journal of Forensic Medicine and Pathology*, *20*(1), 73–77. doi:10.1097/00000433-199903000-00018 PMID:10208343

Cabrera, N. J., Ryan, R. M., Mitchell, S. J., Shannon, J. D., & Tamis-LeMonda, C. S. (2008). Low-income, non-resident, and father involvement with their toddlers: Variation by fathers' race and ethnicity. *Journal of Family Psychology*, *22*(4), 643–647. doi:10.1037/0893-3200.22.3.643 PMID:18729678

Cantu, L. (1995). The peripheralization of rural America: A case study of Latino migrants in America's heartland. *Sociological Perspectives*, *38*(3), 399–414. doi:10.2307/1389434

Capps, R., Castaneda, R. M., Chaudry, A., & Santos, R. (2007). *Paying the price: The impact of immigration raids on America's children*. Washington, DC: Urban Institute.

Casey, M. M., Blewett, L. A., & Call, K. T. (2004). Providing health care to Latino immigrants: Community-based efforts in the rural Midwest. *American Journal of Public Health*, *94*(10), 1709–1711. doi:10.2105/AJPH.94.10.1709 PMID:15451737

Castaneda, R. S., & Alva, S. A. (2002). Language brokering the acculturation of Latino children. *Hispanic Journal of Behavioral Sciences*, *24*(3), 369–378. doi:10.1177/0739986302024003007

Ceballo, R., Dahl, T. A., Aretakis, M. T., & Ramirez, C. (2001). Inner-city children's exposure to community violence: How much do parents know? *Journal of Marriage and the Family*, *63*(4), 927–940. doi:10.1111/j.1741-3737.2001.00927.x

Cervantes, J. M., Mejia, O. L., & Mena, A. G. (2010). Serial migration and the assessment of extreme and unusual hardship with undocumented Latina/o families. *Hispanic Journal of Behavioral Sciences*, *32*(2), 275–291. doi:10.1177/0739986310366286

Chaudry, A., Capps, R., Pedroza, J., Castaneda, R. M., Santos, R., & Scott, M. M. (2010). *Facing our future: Children in the aftermath of immigration enforcement*. Washington, DC: Urban Institute.

Christancho, S., Garces, D. M., Peters, K., & Mueller, B. C. (2008). Listening to rural Hispanic immigrants in the Midwest: A community-based participatory assessment of barriers to health care access and use. *Qualitative Health Research*, *18*(5), 633–646. doi:10.1177/1049732308316669 PMID:18420537

Cicero-Dominguez, S. A. (2005). Assessing the U.S.-Mexico fight against human trafficking and smuggling: Unintended results of U.S. immigration policy. *Northwestern University Journal of International Human Rights*, *4*, 303.

Clauss-Ehlers, C. S., & Levi, L. L. (2002). Violence and community, terms in conflict: An ecological approach to resilience. *Journal of Social Distress and the Homeless*, *11*(4), 265–278. doi:10.1023/A:1016804930977

Cogbill, T. H., Busch, H. m., & Stiers, G. R. (1985). Farm accidents in children. *Pediatrics*, *76*, 562–566. PMID:4047799

Cohen, J. A., Mannarino, A. P., & Deblinger, E. (2006). *Treating trauma and traumatic grief in children and adolescents*. New York: Guilford Press.

Coohey, C. (2001). The relationship between familism and child maltreatment in Latino and Anglo families. *Child Maltreatment*, *6*(2), 130–142. doi:10.1177/1077559501006002005 PMID:16705788

Cravey, A. J. (1997). Latino labor and poultry production in rural North Carolina. *Southeastern Geographer*, *37*(2), 295–300. doi:10.1353/sgo.1997.0001

Crowley, M., & Lichter, D. T. (2009). Social disorganization in new Latino destinations? *Rural Sociology*, *74*(4), 573–604. doi:10.1526/003601109789864026

Crowley, M., & Lichter, D. T. (2010). Social disorganization in new Latino destinations? *Rural Sociology*, *74*(4), 573–604. doi:10.1111/j.1549-0831.2009.tb00705.x

Crowley, M., Lichter, D. T., & Qian, Z. (2006). Beyond gateway cities: Economic restructuring and poverty among immigrant families and children. *Family Relations*, *55*(3), 345–360. doi:10.1111/j.1741-3729.2006.00407.x

Dalla, R. L., & Chirstensen, A. (2005). Latino immigrants describe residence in rural Midwestern communities: A longitudinal assessment of social and economic change. *Hispanic Journal of Behavioral Sciences*, *27*(1), 23–42. doi:10.1177/0739986304272354

Dalla, R. L., Ellis, A., & Cramer, S. C. (2005). Immigration and rural America: Latinos' perceptions of work and residence in three meat packing communities. *Community Work & Family*, *8*(2), 163–185. doi:10.1080/13668800500049639

Damashek, A., Nelson, M. M., & Bonner, B. L. (2013). Fatal child maltreatment: Characteristics of death from physical abuse versus neglect. *Child Abuse & Neglect*, *37*, 735–744. PMID:23768940

Dreby, J. (2012). The burden of deportation on children in Mexican immigrant families. *Journal of Marriage and the Family*, *74*(4), 829–845. doi:10.1111/j.1741-3737.2012.00989.x

Dreby, J. (2012). *How today's immigration enforcement policies impact children, families, and communities: A view from the ground.* Center for American Progress.

Dreman, S. (1991). Coping with the trauma of divorce. *Journal of Traumatic Stress*, *4*(1), 113–121. doi:10.1002/jts.2490040109

Eichner, J. E., Moore, W. E., Perveen, G., Kobza, C. E., Abbott, K. E., & Stephens, A. L. (2012). Overweight and obesity in an ethnically diverse rural school district: The Healthy Kids Project. *Obesity (Silver Spring, Md.)*, *16*(2), 501–504. doi:10.1038/oby.2007.60 PMID:18239668

Ennis, S. R., Rios-Vargas, M., & Albert, N. G. (2011). *The Hispanic population: 2010.* U. S. Department of Commerce, Economics and Statistics Administration, U. S. Census Bureau.

Evans, G. W., & Lepore, S. J. (1993). Household crowding and social support: A quasi-experimental analysis. *Journal of Personality and Social Psychology*, *65*(2), 308–316. doi:10.1037/0022-3514.65.2.308 PMID:8366422

Evans, L. G., & Oehler-Stinnett, J. (2006). Structure and prevalence of PTSD symptomatology in children who have experienced a severe tornado. *Psychology in the Schools*, *43*(3), 283–295. doi:10.1002/pits.20150

Fantuzzo, J. W., & Mohr, W. K. (1999). Prevalence and effects of child exposure to domestic violence. *The Future of Children*, *9*(3), 21–32. doi:10.2307/1602779 PMID:10777998

Flores, E., Cicchetti, D., & Rogosch, F. A. (2005). Predictors of resilience in maltreated and nonmaltreated Latino children. *Developmental Psychology*, *41*(2), 338–351. doi:10.1037/0012-1649.41.2.338 PMID:15769190

Flores-Ortiz, Y. G. (1997). The broken covenant: Incest in Latino family. Voces: A Journal of Chicana. *Latino Studies*, 48–70.

Folsom, D. P., Gilmer, T., Barrio, C., Moore, D. J., Bucardo, J., Lindamer, L. A., & Jeste, D. V. (2007). A longitudinal study of the use of mental health services by persons with serious mental illness: Do Spanish-speaking Latinos differ from English-speaking Latinos and Caucasians? *The American Journal of Psychiatry*, *164*(8), 1173–1180. doi:10.1176/appi.ajp.2007.06071239 PMID:17671279

Fontes, L. A. (2002). Child discipline and physical abuse in immigrant Latino families: Reducing violence and misunderstandings. *Journal of Counseling and Development*, *80*(1), 31–40. doi:10.1002/j.1556-6678.2002.tb00163.x

Fontes, L. A. (2007). Sin verguenza: Addressing shame with Latino victims of child sexual abuse and their families. *Journal of Child Sexual Abuse*, *16*(1), 61–83. doi:10.1300/J070v16n01_04 PMID:17255077

Fontes, L. A., Cruz, M., & Tabachnick, J. (2001). Views of child sexual abuse in two cultural communities: An exploratory study among African Americans and Latinos. *Child Maltreatment*, *6*(2), 103–117. doi:10.1177/1077559501006002003 PMID:16705786

Ford, J. D., & Courtois, C. A. (2013). *Treating complex stress traumatic stress disorders in children and adolescents: Scientific foundations and therapeutic models*. New York: Guilford Press.

Foster, H., & Hagan, J. (2009). The mass incarceration of parents in America: Issues of race/ethnicity, collateral damage to children, and prisoner reentry. *The Annals of the American Academy of Political and Social Science*, *623*(1), 179–194. doi:10.1177/0002716208331123

Fraga, L., & Garcia, J. A. (2010). *New patterns of Hispanic settlement in rural America*. Washington, D. C.: U. S. Department of Agriculture, Economic Research Service.

Freeman, L. N., Shaffer, D., & Smith, H. (1996). Neglected victims of homicide: The needs of young siblings of murder victims. *The American Journal of Orthopsychiatry*, *66*(3), 337–345. doi:10.1037/h0080184 PMID:8827257

Gabel, K., & Johnston, D. (1995). *Children of incarcerated parents*. New York: Lexington Books.

Garcia, V. (2007). Meeting binational research challenge: Substance abuse among transnational farmworkers in the United States. *The Journal of Rural Health*, *31*(s1), 61–67. doi:10.1111/j.1748-0361.2007.00125.x PMID:18237326

Garrison, E. G., Roy, I. S., & Azar, V. (1999). Responding to the mental health needs of Latino children and families through school-based services. *Clinical Psychology Review*, *19*(2), 199–219. doi:10.1016/S0272-7358(98)00070-1 PMID:10078420

Genty, P. M. (2002). Damage to family relationships as a collateral consequence of parental incarceration. *The Fordham Urban Law Journal*, *30*, 1671.

Glaze, L. E., & Maruschak, L. M. (2008). *Parents in prison and their minor children*. Washington, D. C.: Department of Justice, Office of Justice Programs. doi:10.1037/e513862010-001

Golash-Boza, T., & Hondagneu-Sotelo, P. (2013). Latino immigrant men and the deportation crisis: A gendered racial removal program. *Latino Studies*, *11*(3), 271–292. doi:10.1057/lst.2013.14

Gonzalez, M. A. (2015). Stories of separation: Impact of detention and deportation on Latino children's attachment representation. *Dissertation Abstracts International.*

Gonzalez-Guarda, R. M., Florom-Smith, A. L., & Thomas, T. (2011). A synthetic model of substance abuse, intimate partner violence, HIV infection, and mental health among Hispanics. *Public Health Nursing (Boston, Mass.)*, *28*(4), 366–378. doi:10.1111/j.1525-1446.2010.00928.x PMID:21736615

Gorman-Smith, D., Henry, D. B., & Tolan, P. H. (2010). Exposure to community violence and violence perpetration: The protective effects of family functioning. *Journal of Clinical and Adolescent Psychology*, *33*(3), 439–449. doi:10.1207/s15374424jccp3303_2 PMID:15271602

Gouveia, L. (2005). Latinos in rural America and U. S. agriculture: From pioneers to new arrivals. *The Journal of Latino-Latin American Studies*, *1*(4), 1–24. doi:10.18085/llas.1.4.g863048x3k152w82

Greenwald, R. (2015). *Child trauma handbook: A guide for helping trauma-exposed children and adolescents*. New York: Routledge.

Grzywacz, J. G., Quandt, S. A., Early, J., Tapia, J., Graham, C. N., & Arcury, T. A. (2006). Leaving family for work: Ambivalence and mental health among Mexican migrant farmworker men. *Journal of Health Care for the Poor and Underserved*, *20*, 662. PMID:19835002

Hagan, J., Castro, B., & Rodriguez, N. (2010). The effects of deportation policies on immigrant families and communities: Cross-border perspectives. *North Carolina Law Review*, *88*, 1799–1884.

Halfacre-Hitchcock, A., McCarthy, D., Burkett, T., & Carvajal, A. (2006). Latino immigrant farmworkers in low country South Carolina: A demographic profile and an examination of pesticide perception and protection in two pilot case studies. *Human Organization*, *65*(1), 55–71. doi:10.17730/humo.65.1.6cc5wqtvpw5xku4j

Hampton, S., Ekboir, J. M., & Rochin, R. I. (1995). The performance of Latinos in rural public schools: A comparative analysis of test scores in grades 3, 6, and 12. *Hispanic Journal of Behavioral Sciences*, *17*(4), 480–498. doi:10.1177/07399863950174005

Hanson, R. F., Self-Brown, S., Fricker-Elhai, A., Kilpatrick, D. G., Saunders, B. E., & Resnick, H. (2006). Relations among parental substance abuse, violence exposure and mental health: The national survey of adolescents. *Addictive Behaviors*, *31*(11), 1988–2001. doi:10.1016/j.addbeh.2006.01.012 PMID:16503092

Henderson, S. W., & Baily, C. D. R. (2013). Parental deportation, families, and mental health. *Journal of the American Academy of Child and Adolescent Psychiatry*, *52*(5), 451–453. doi:10.1016/j.jaac.2013.01.007 PMID:23622844

Hiott, A. E., Grzywacz, J. G., Davis, S. W., Quandt, S. A., & Arcury, T. A. (2008). Migrant farmworker stress: Mental health implications. *The Journal of Rural Health*, *24*(1), 32–39. doi:10.1111/j.1748-0361.2008.00134.x PMID:18257868

Hohl, S. D., Gonzalez, C., Carusso, E., Ibarra, G., & Thompson, B. (2014). "I did it for us and I would do it again": Perspectives of rural Latinos on providing biospecimens for research. *American Journal of Public Health*, *104*(5), 911–916. doi:10.2105/AJPH.2013.301726 PMID:24625153

Homer, P., Sanders, L., Martinez, R., Doering-White, J., Lopez, W., & Delva, J. (2014). "I put the mask on": The human side of deportation efforts on Latino youth. *Journal of Social Welfare and Human Rights*, *2*, 33–47.

Hondo, C., Gardiner, M. E., & Sapien, Y. (2008). *Latino dropouts in rural America: Realities and possibilities*. Albany, N. Y.: State University of New York Press.

Housing Assistance Council. (2012). *Rural research brief: Poverty in rural America*. Washington, D. C.: Housing Assistance Council.

Hovey, J. D., & Magana, C. G. (2002). Psychosocial predictors of anxiety among immigrant Mexican migrant farmworkers: Implications for prevention and treatment. *Cultural Diversity and Ethnic Minority Mental Health*, *8*(3), 274–289. doi:10.1037/1099-9809.8.3.274 PMID:12143104

Hubert, H. B., Snider, J., & Winkleby, M. A. (2005). Health status, health behaviors, and acculturation factors associated with overweight and obesity in Latinos from a community and agricultural labor camp survey. *Preventive Medicine*, *40*(6), 642–651. doi:10.1016/j.ypmed.2004.09.001 PMID:15850860

Huizinga, G. A., Visser, A., van der Graff, W. T., Hoekstra, H. J., Klip, E. C., Pras, E., & Hoekstra-Weebers, J. E. (2005). Stress response symptoms in adolescent and young children of parents diagnosed with cancer. *European Journal of Cancer*, *41*(2), 288–295. doi:10.1016/j.ejca.2004.10.005 PMID:15661555

Humes, K., Jones, N. A., & Ramirez, R. R. (2011). *Overview of race and Hispanic origin, 2010*. U. S. Department of Commerce, Economics and Statistics Administration, U. S. Census Bureau.

Johnston, J. R. (2005). Children of divorce who reject a parent and refuse visitation: Recent research and social policy implications for the alienated child. *Family Law Quarterly*, 757–775.

Kandel, W., & Cromartie, J. (2004). *New patterns of Hispanic settlement in rural America*. U. S. Department of Agriculture, Economic Research Service.

Kataoka, S. H., Stein, B. D., Jaycox, L. H., Wong, M., Escudero, P., Tu, W., & Fink, A. (2003). A school-based mental health program for traumatized Latino immigrant children. *Journal of the American Academy of Child and Adolescent Psychiatry*, *42*(3), 311–318. doi:10.1097/00004583-200303000-00011 PMID:12595784

Katz, S. R. (1997). Presumed guilty: How schools criminalize Latino youth. *Social Justice (San Francisco, Calif.)*, 77–95.

Kay, J., Burt, V. K., Eth, S., & Phillips, K. A. (2001). *PTSD in children and adolescents*. New York: American Psychiatric Publishers.

Kim-Godwin, Y. S., & Fox, J. A. (2009). Gender differences in intimate partner violence and alcohol use among Latino-migrant and seasonal farmworkers in rural Southeastern South Carolina. *Journal of Community Health Nursing*, *26*(3), 131–142. doi:10.1080/07370010903034474 PMID:19662561

Klevens, J. (2007). An overview of intimate partner violence among Latinos. *Violence Against Women*, *13*(2), 111–122. doi:10.1177/1077801206296979 PMID:17251500

Krisberg, B. A., & Temin, C. E. (2001). *Plight of children whose parents are in prison*. Oakland, CA: National Council on Crime and Delinquency.

Landale, N. S., & Lichter, D. T. (1997). Gegoraphy and the etiology of poverty among Latino children. *Social Science Quarterly*, *78*, 874–894.

Le Prevost, C. E., Storm, J. F., Blanchard, M. R., Asuje, C. R., & Cope, W. G. (2013). Engaging Latino farmworkers in the development of symbols to improve pesticide safety and health education and risk communication. *Journal of Immigrant and Minority Health*, *15*(5), 975–981. doi:10.1007/s10903-012-9685-4 PMID:22833257

Lipschitz, D. S., Winegar, R. K., Nicolau, A. L., Hartnick, E., Wolfson, M., & Southwick, S. M. (1999). Perceived abuse and neglect at risk factors for suicidal behavior in adolescent inpatients. *The Journal of Nervous and Mental Disease*, *187*(1), 32–39. doi:10.1097/00005053-199901000-00006 PMID:9952251

Liu, J., Bennett, K. J., Harun, N., & Probst, J. C. (2008). Urban-rural differences in overweight status and physical inactivity among U. S. children aged 10-17 years. *The Journal of Rural Health*, *24*(4), 407–415. doi:10.1111/j.1748-0361.2008.00188.x PMID:19007396

Loury, S., & Kulbok, P. (2007). Correlates of alcohol and tobacco use among immrigants in rural North Carolina. *Family & Community Health*, *30*(3), 247–256. doi:10.1097/01.FCH.0000277767.00526.f1 PMID:17563486

Love, J. A., & Buriel, R. (2007). Language brokering and depression: autonomy, parent-child bonding, biculturalism, and depression: A study of Mexican American adolescents from immigrant families. *Hispanic Journal of Behavioral Sciences*, *29*(4), 472–491. doi:10.1177/0739986307307229

Martinez, C. R., McClure, H., & Eddy, J. (2008). Language brokering contexts and behavioral and emotional adjustment among Latino parents and adolescents. *The Journal of Early Adolescence*, *29*(1), 71–98. doi:10.1177/0272431608324477 PMID:19898605

Martinez, R. (2000). Immigration and urban violence: The link between immigrant Latinos and types of homicide. *Social Science Quarterly*, 363–374.

Martinez, R. (2014). *Latino homicide: Immigration, violence, and community*. New York: Routledge.

Mattson, S., & Ruiz, E. (2005). Intimate partner violence in the Latino community and its effect on children. *Health Care for Women International*, *26*(6), 523–529. doi:10.1080/07399330590962627 PMID:16020019

McCauley, L. A., Laserer, M. R., Higgins, G., Rothlein, J., Muniz, J., Ebbert, C., & Phillips, J. (2001). Work characteristics and pesticide exposure among migrant agricultural families: A community-based research approach. *Environmental Health Perspectives*, *109*(5), 533–538. doi:10.1289/ehp.01109533 PMID:11401767

McConnell, E. D., & Miraftab, F. (2010). Sundown town to "Little Mexico": Old-timers and newcomers in an American small town. *Rural Sociology*, *74*(4), 605–629. doi:10.1111/j.1549-0831.2009.tb00706.x

McFarlane, J. M., Groff, J. Y., O'Brien, J. A., & Watson, K. (2003). Behaviors of children who are exposed to intimate partner violence: An analysis of 330 Black, White, and Hispanic children. *Pediatrics*, *112*(3), 202–207. doi:10.1542/peds.112.3.e202 PMID:12949313

McLeigh, J. D. (2010). How do immigration and customs enforcement (ICE) practices affect the mental health of children? *The American Journal of Orthopsychiatry*, *80*(1), 96–100. doi:10.1111/j.1939-0025.2010.01011.x PMID:20397993

Meiers, S., & Baerg, J. (2001). Farm accidents in children: Eleven years of experience. *Journal of Pediatric Surgery*, *36*(5), 726–729. doi:10.1053/jpsu.2001.22946 PMID:11329575

Meiser-Stedman, R., Yule, W., Smith, P., Glucksman, E., & Dalgleish, T. (2005). Acute stress disorder and posttraumatic stress disorder in children and adolescents involved in assaults or motor vehicle accidents. *The American Journal of Psychiatry*, *162*(7), 1381–1383. doi:10.1176/appi.ajp.162.7.1381 PMID:15994725

Memken, J. A., & Canabal, M. E. (1994). Housing tenure, structure, and crowding among Latino households. *Journal of Family and Economic Issues*, *15*(4), 349–365. doi:10.1007/BF02353810

Mendoza, M., & Olivos, E. M. (2009). Advocating for control with compassion: The impacts of raids and deportations on children and families. *Oregon Review of International Law*, *11*, 111.

Mendoza-Denton, N. (2014). *Homegirls: Language and cultural practice among Latina youth gangs*. New York: John Wiley & Sons.

Moisan, P. A., Sanders-Phillips, K., & Moisan, P. M. (1997). Ethnic differences in circumstances of abuse and anger among sexually abused Black and Latino boys. *Child Abuse & Neglect*, *21*, 473–488. doi:10.1016/S0145-2134(97)00007-0 PMID:9158907

Moracco, K. E., Hilton, A., Hodges, K. G., & Frasier, P. Y. (2005). Knowledge and attitudes about intimate partner violence among immigrant Latinos in rural North Carolina baseline information and implications for research. *Violence Against Women*, *11*(3), 337–352. doi:10.1177/1077801204273296 PMID:16043553

Morales, A., Yakushko, O. F., & Castro, A. J. (2012). Language brokering among Mexican-immigrant families in the Midwest: A multiple case study. *The Counseling Psychologist*, *40*(4), 520–553. doi:10.1177/0011000011417312

Moreno, E. M. (2006). Mexican American street gangs, migration, violence in the Yakima Valley. *Pacific Northwest Quarterly*, 131–138.

Murphey, D., Guzman, L., & Torres, A. (2014). *America's Hispanic children: Gaining ground, looking forward*. Academic Press.

Nelson, L., & Hiemstra, N. (2008). Latino immigrants and the renegotiation of place and belonging in small town America. *Social & Cultural Geography*, *9*(3), 319–342. doi:10.1080/14649360801990538

Onetto, J. E., Flores, M. T., & Garbino, M. L. (1994). Dental trauma in children and adolescents in Valparaiso, Chile. *Dental Traumatology*, *10*(5), 223–227. doi:10.1111/j.1600-9657.1994.tb00074.x PMID:7843064

Orellana, M. F. (2009). *Translating childhood: Immigrant youth, language, and culture*. Rutgers University Press.

Osterberg, A. M. (2009). Removing the dead hand on the future: Recognizing citizen children's right against parental deportation. *Lewis and Clark Law Review*, *13*, 751.

Passel, J. S., Cohn, D., & Lopez, M. H. (2011). *Hispanics account for more than half of the nation's growth in past decade*. Washington, DC: Pew Hispanic Center.

Pattillo, M., Western, B., & Weiman, D. (2004). *Imprisoning America: The social effects of mass incarceration*. Russell Sage Foundation.

Peguero, A. A. (2009). Victimizing the children of immigrants: Latino and Asian American student victimization. *Youth & Society*, *41*(2), 186–208. doi:10.1177/0044118X09333646

Peters, V., Sottiaux, M., Appelboom, J., & Kahn, A. (2004). Posttraumatic stress disorder after dog bites in children. *The Journal of Pediatrics*, *144*(1), 121–122. doi:10.1016/j.jpeds.2003.10.024 PMID:14722529

Pfefferbaum, B., Nixon, S. J., Tucker, P. M., Tivis, R. D., Moore, V. L., Gurwitch, R. H., & Geis, H. K. et al. (1999). Posttraumatic stress responses in bereaved children after the Oklahoma City bombing. *Journal of the American Academy of Child and Adolescent Psychology*, *38*(11), 1372–1379. doi:10.1097/00004583-199911000-00011 PMID:10560223

Pickett, W., Brison, R. J., Berg, R. L., Zentner, J., Linneman, J., & Marlenga, B. (2005). Pediatric farm injuries involving non-working children injured by a farm work hazard: Five priorities for primary prevention. *Injury Prevention*, *11*(1), 6–11. doi:10.1136/ip.2004.005769 PMID:15691981

Quandt, S. A. (2009). Health of children and women in the farmworker community in eastern United States. In S. A. Quandt & T. A. Arcury (Eds.), *Latino farmworkers in the eastern United States* (pp. 173–200). New York: Springer. doi:10.1007/978-0-387-88347-2_8

Quintero, G. A., Lilliot, E., & Willging, C. (2007). Substance abuse treatment provider views of "culture" for behavioral health care in rural settings. *Qualitative Health Research*, *17*(9), 1256–1267. doi:10.1177/1049732307307757 PMID:17968042

Raffaelli, M., & Wiley, A. R. (2013). Challenges and strengths of immigrant families in the rural Midwest. *Journal of Family Issues*, *34*(3), 347–372. doi:10.1177/0192513X11432422

Reed, D. F. & Reed, E. L. (1997). Children of incarcerated parents. *Social Justice/Global Options, 24*, 152-169.

Rochin, R. I. (1995). *Rural Latinos: Evolving conditions and issues: The changing American countryside: Rural people and places*. Lawrence, KS: The University Press of Kansas.

Rodriguez, M. A., Heileman, M. V., Fielder, E., Ang, A., Nevarez, F., & Mangione, C. M. (2008). Intimate partner violence, depression, and PTSD among pregnant Latina women. *Annals of Family Medicine*, *6*(1), 44–52. doi:10.1370/afm.743 PMID:18195314

Rodriguez, M. D., Rodriguez, J., & Davis, M. (2006). Recruitment of first generation Latinos in a rural community: The essential nature of personal contact. *Family Process*, *45*(1), 87–100. doi:10.1111/j.1545-5300.2006.00082.x PMID:16615255

Romero, M. (2000). State violence and the social and legal construction of Latino criminality: From el bandido to gang member. *Denver University Law Review*, *78*, 1081.

Saenz, R. (1997). Ethnic concentration and Chicano poverty: A comparative approach. *Social Science Research*, *26*(2), 205–228. doi:10.1006/ssre.1997.0595

Saenz, R., & Torres, C. C. (2003). Latinos in rural America. In Challenges for rural America in the twenty-first century (pp. 57-70). Academic Press.

Sampson, R. J., & Raudenbush, S. W. (2004). Seeing disorder: Neighborhood stigma and the social construction of "broken windows". *Social Psychology Quarterly*, *67*(4), 319–342. doi:10.1177/019027250406700401

Sanchez, O., Funes, S. M., & Velasquez, R. J. (in press). The mass incarceration of Latinos and Latinas in the United States: A binational-transborder mental health perspective. *Journal of Transborder Studies: Research and Practice.*

Sanders-Phillips, K., Moisan, P. A., Wadlington, S., Morgan, S., & English, K. (1995). Ethnic differences in psychological functioning among Black and Latino sexually abused girls. *Child Abuse & Neglect*, *19*(6), 691–706. doi:10.1016/0145-2134(95)00027-6 PMID:7552838

Saxe, G. N., Stoddard, F. J., & Sheridan, R. L. (1988). PTSD in children with burns: A longitudinal study. *Journal of Burn Care & Research; Official Publication of the American Burn Association*, 19.

Schultz, B. (2008). Inside the gilded cage: The lives of Latino immigrant males in rural Kentucky. *Southeastern Geographer*, *48*(2), 201–218. doi:10.1353/sgo.0.0024

Schwarz, E. D., & Kowalski, J. M. (1991). Malignant memories: PTSD in children and adults after a school shooting. *Journal of the American Academy of Child and Adolescent Psychiatry*, *30*(6), 936–944. doi:10.1097/00004583-199111000-00011 PMID:1757443

Sherrill, W. W., Crew, L., Mayo, R., Rogers, B. L., & Haynes, D. F. (2005). Educational and health services innovation to improve care for rural Hispanic communities in the U. S. *Education for Health, 18*, 356-367.

Shetgiri, R., Lin, H., Avila, R. M., & Flores, G. (2012). Parental characteristics associated with bullying perpetration in U. S. children aged 10 to 17 years. *American Journal of Public Health, 102*(12), 2280–2286. doi:10.2105/AJPH.2012.300725 PMID:23078471

Shooter, M. (1997). The impact of death, divorce, and disaster on young people. *Current Opinion in Psychiatry*, *10*(4), 268–274. doi:10.1097/00001504-199707000-00003

Silva, R. R. (2004). *Posttraumatic stress disorders in children and adolescents: Handbook.* New York: W. W. Norton & Company.

Smith, H. A., & Furuseth, O. J. (2006). *Latinos in the new South: Transformations of place*. Ashgate Publishing Ltd.

Springer, D. W., Courtney, L., & Rubin, A. (2000). Effects of a solution-focused mutual aid group for Hispanic children of incarcerated parents. *Child & Adolescent Social Work Journal, 17*(6), 431–442. doi:10.1023/A:1026479727159

Stodolska, M., Acevedo, J. C., & Shinew, K. J. (2009). Gangs of Chicago: Perceptions of crime and its effect on the recreation behavior of Latino residents in urban communities. *Leisure Sciences*, *31*(5), 466–482. doi:10.1080/01490400903199773

Suarez-Orozco, C., Yoshikawa, H., Teranishi, R., & Suarez-Orozco, M. (2011). Growing up in the shadows: The developmental implications of unauthorized status. *Harvard Educational Review*, *81*(3), 438–472. doi:10.17763/haer.81.3.g23x203763783m75

Swanson, J. A., Sachs, M., Dahlgren, K. A., & Tinguely, J. J. (1987). Accidental farm injuries in children. *American Journal of Diseases of Children*, *141*, 1276–1279. PMID:3687867

Swisher, R. R., & Waller, M. R. (2008). Confining fatherhood incarceration and paternal involvement among non-resident White, African American, and Latino fathers. *Journal of Family Issues*, *29*(8), 1067–1088. doi:10.1177/0192513X08316273

Tapia, M. (2014). Latino street gang emergence in the Midwest: Strategic franchising or natural migration. *Crime and Delinquency*, *60*(4), 592–618. doi:10.1177/0011128712458750

Taylor, J. E., Martin, P. L., Fix, M., & Alarcon, R. (1997). *Poverty amid prosperity: Immigration and the changing face of rural California*. The Urban Institute.

The Sentencing Project. (2003). *Hispanic prisoners in the United States*. Washington, DC: The Sentencing Project.

The Sentencing Project. (2009). *Incarcerated parents and their children: Trends 1991-2007*. Washington, DC: The Sentencing Project.

Tilghman-Osborne, E. M., Bamaca-Colbert, M., Witherspoon, D., Wadsworth, M. E., & Hecht, M. L. (2015). Longitudinal associations of language brokering and parent-adolescent closeness in immigrant Latino families. *The Journal of Early Adolescence*.

Timmis, C. (2002). The impact of language barriers in the health care of Latinos in the United States: A review of the literature and guidelines for practice. *Journal of Midwifery & Women's Health*, *47*(2), 80–96. doi:10.1016/S1526-9523(02)00218-0 PMID:12019990

Torres, R. M., Popke, E. J., & Hapke, H. M. (2006). The South's silent bargain: Rural restructuring, Latino labor, and the ambiguities of migrant experience. In The New South: Latinos and transformation of place (pp. 37-68). Academic Press.

Torres, S. & Vogel, R. E. (2001). Pre- and post-test differences between Vietnamese and Latino residents involved in a community policing experiment reducing fear of crime and improving attitudes toward the police. *Journal of Police Strategies and Management*, 40-55.

Ugarte, M. B., Zarate, L., & Farley, M. (2004). Prostitution and trafficking of women and children from Mexico to the United States. *Journal of Trauma Practice*, *2*(3-4), 147–165. doi:10.1300/J189v02n03_08

Urbina, M. G. (2012). *Hispanics in the U. S. criminal justice system: The new American demography*. Springfield, IL: Charles C. Thomas Publisher.

Valenzuela, A. (1999). Gender roles and settlement activities among children and their families. *The American Behavioral Scientist*, *42*(4), 720–772. doi:10.1177/0002764299042004009

Van De Mark, X., Russell, L. A., O'Keefe, M., Finkelstein, N., Noether, C. D., & Gampbel, J. C. (2005). Children of mothers with histories of substance abuse, mental illness, and trauma. *Journal of Community Psychology*, *33*(4), 445–459. doi:10.1002/jcop.20062

Velasquez, R. J., & Funes, S. M. (2014). The Mass Incarceration of Latinos in the United States: Looking ahead to the year 2050. In S. W. Bowman (Ed.), *Color behind bars: Racism in the U. S. prison system* (pp. 273–289). Santa Barbara, CA: Praeger.

Vigil, J. D. (2003). Urban violence and street gangs. *Annual Review of Anthropology*, *32*(1), 225–242. doi:10.1146/annurev.anthro.32.061002.093426

Waldoff, R. A. (2008). Arrested contact: The criminal justice system, race, and father engagement. *The Prison Journal*, *88*(2), 179–206. doi:10.1177/0032885508319154

Walters, N., Bourgois, P., & Loinaz, H. M. (2004). Masculinity and undocumented labor migration: Injured day laborers in San Francisco. *Social Science & Medicine*, *59*(6), 1159–1168. doi:10.1016/j.socscimed.2003.12.013 PMID:15210088

Ward, L. S. (2010). Farmworkers at risk: The costs of family separation. *Journal of Immigrant and Minority Health*, *12*(5), 672–677. doi:10.1007/s10903-008-9207-6 PMID:18987973

Warthan, S., Mortimer, K., & Allard, E. (2011). Homies in the new Latino diaspora. *Language & Communication*, *31*(3), 191–202. doi:10.1016/j.langcom.2011.02.007

Weisskirch, R. S. (2005). The relationship of language brokering to ethnic identity for Latino early adolescents. *Hispanic Journal of Behavioral Sciences*, *27*(3), 286–299. doi:10.1177/0739986305277931

Weisskirch, R. S., & Alva, S. A. (2002). Language brokering and the acculturation of Latino children. *Hispanic Journal of Behavioral Sciences*, *24*(3), 369–378. doi:10.1177/0739986302024003007

Wickrama, K. A. S., Elder, G. H., & Arabaham, W. T. (2007). Rurality and ethnicity in adolescent physical illness: Are children of the growing rural Latino population at excess health risk? *The Journal of Rural Health*, *23*(3), 228–237. doi:10.1111/j.1748-0361.2007.00095.x PMID:17565523

Wilson, W. C., & Rosenthal, B. S. (2003). The relationship between exposure to community violence and psychological distress among adolescents: A meta-analysis. *Violence and Victims*, *18*(3), 335–352. doi:10.1891/vivi.2003.18.3.335 PMID:12968662

Yabko, B. A., Hakoda, A., & Ulloa, E. C. (2008). Depression as a mediator between family factors and peer-bullying victimization in Latino adolescents. *Violence and Victims*, *23*(6), 727–742. doi:10.1891/0886-6708.23.6.727 PMID:19069564

Zatz, M. S., & Portillos, E. L. (2000). Voices from the barrio: Chicano/a gangs, families, and communities. *Criminology*, *8*(2), 369–402. doi:10.1111/j.1745-9125.2000.tb00894.x

Zayas, L. H., Aguilar-Gaxiola, S., Yoon, H., & Rey, G. N. (2015). The distress of citizen children with detained and deported parents. *Journal of Child and Family Studies*, 1–11. PMID:26640358

Zuniga, V., & Hernandez-Leon, R. (2005). *New destinations: Mexican immigration in the United States*. Russell Sage Foundation.

# Chapter 12

# Clinical Forensic Issues in Child Trauma Stemming from Juvenile Fire Setting and Bomb Making:

## Culturally Responsive Risk Assessment and Treatment Paradigm for Rural Settings

**Ronn Johnson**
*University of San Diego, USA*

**Eric Jacobs**
*University of San Diego, USA*

**Karla Klas**
*University of Michigan, USA*

**Elizabeth Grace**
*University of San Diego, USA*

**Alejandra Murillo**
*University of San Diego, USA*

## ABSTRACT

*Internationally, burns stemming from Juvenile Fire Setting and Bomb Making (JFSB) represent a major healthcare problem as signaled by traumatic deaths and injuries sustained by youth involved in these unfortunate incidents. While JFSB incidents may occur with greater frequency in non-rural locales, emerging evidence shows that the clinical forensic issues secondary to these burn cases can be surprisingly more complex in rural settings. The treatment challenges that rural areas have are fueled by a limited availability of mental health emergency resources. Further compounding it, the treatment professionals accessible to families often have insufficient experience or qualifications for competently managing the traumatic issues presented by combined JFSB/Burn Survivor (BS-JFSB) cases. This chapter aims to demonstrate how trauma-focused approaches can be integrated into existing clinical forensic practices in rural settings. The treatment requires altering how the concerns presented by these BS-JFSB children are addressed within a risk assessment paradigm.*

DOI: 10.4018/978-1-5225-0228-9.ch012

## INTRODUCTION

Children in rural settings are not immune to the negative healthcare impact resulting from explosions, electrical accidents, and fires. Such injuries are frequently experienced as traumatic psychological events by child burn survivors and their families (Askay, Wiechman & Magyar-Russell, 2009; Mashreky, 2009). Burn Survivors and Juvenile Fire Setting and Bomb Making (BS-JFSB) refers to any person that builds, creates or ignites an explosive or incendiary device that caused self-injury requiring significant medical attention. The assessment, diagnosis and treatment of BS-JFSB are an ongoing challenge in rural settings because of a blend of clinical forensic issues found in these cases. For example, youth involved in BS-JFSB could be in an unwanted legal situation as a result of significant property damage, death or injuries to others (Johnson & Jones, 2014). The rates of BS-JFSB are rapidly climbing in urban areas. However, for rural settings, providing services for BS-JFSB can be complicated because of lower budgets for emergency healthcare (Lee, Jiang, Phillips, & Ohsfeldt, 2014). The blend of JFSB and BS-JFSB also presents as an important determinant for intervention services. In this case, comprehensive BS-JFSB services can be defined along a continuum and differently for several overlapping disciplines (e.g., fire service, healthcare providers, schools, counseling, psychology and the criminal justice system). From a BS-JFSB trauma perspective in rural settings, this also means that it is essential to adopt a culturally responsive healthcare model that includes establishing treatment protocols, developing diagnostic impressions, collecting psychosocial histories, using psychoeducation, and incorporating research-based methods. For rural settings, BS-JFSB requires the orchestration and management of interdisciplinary interventions for the clinical forensic trauma issues that often accompany these cases. For example, some of these clinical forensic issues include low budgets for emergency mental health care; lack of mental health providers experienced in the unique treatment aspects of both BS and JFSB. These same clinical forensic issues fuel the need for engaging multiple disciplines/agencies in the collaborative culturally responsive treatment intervention as well as the importance of assisting with school/community reintegration and survivor support.

### Overview of Child Burn Survivors (BS) and Clinical Forensic Trauma Issues Stemming from JFSB

From a clinical forensic perspective, BS-JFSB youth must cope with their burn injuries along with the distress associated with any pending legal charges related to their misconduct. Much of the clinical mental health research so far has primarily focused on the post-incident distress and disability of child BS by applying interventions for the Post Traumatic Stress Disorder (PTSD) symptom clusters found in the *Diagnostic and Statistical Manual of Mental Disorders (5th ed.; DSM–5; American Psychiatric Association, 2013)*. The diagnostically relevant cluster of symptoms in such BS-JFSB cases can include avoidance, depression, fear of death, flashbacks, nightmares, pain, and phobias; each can assume an important role for long-term adjustment. Diagnostically, while there is no shortage of criticism of the DSM-5, its use with PTSD likely offers the best culturally responsive tool for assessing the complex trauma experiences of child burn survivors (Young & Johnson, 2010; Johnson, 2013; Barglow, 2011, 2013). That is, burn survivors frequently enter treatment with diverse risk assessment factors (e.g., developmental concerns, cultural, family circumstances, and preexisting mental problems) that must be clinically addressed. At the same time, licensed clinical mental health professionals must remain cognizant of the risks posed by the stages and multiple layers of trauma that are associated with child burn survivors (Johnson, 2010).

For example, for BS the risks can be: anxiety/trauma/stress from the actual traumatic event that caused the burn injury; guilt related to being responsible for the injury (especially in the BS-JFSB); anxiety/fear related to the very real threat of legal, financial, and social ramifications from participating in a likely illegal activity; bullying/teasing/staring challenges all along the burn survivor experience, (i.e. initial reintegration after the injury, upon changing grades or schools, during new social encounters, etc.). To no surprise, inadequate management of the BS-JFSB trauma is a significant problem in all aspects of healthcare in rural settings (Erickson, Hedges, Call, & Bair, 2013; Axinn, 2013). In every clinical situation that has been studied, the full scope of clinical forensic issues of children often receives far less attention than that of adults (Jensen, et al., 2011; Ames, 2008). For example, a representative group of primary care providers are untrained and unequipped to promote health by preventing risk factors or screening asymptomatic patients, and health clinics and health information systems are not organized enough to promote continuity of care across either the patient or trauma life-cycles of BS-JFSB. In actuality, it's often the rural community/public health and restorative juvenile justice systems that are either simply absent or aren't at a high-functioning level to be able to provide the necessary support and treatment intervention for BS-JFSB. Nowhere is this situation more unfortunate, however, than in management of the expansive range of behavioral and emotional reactions associated with BS-JFSB.

At a minimum, a BS-JFSB has to be able to manage the traumatic life-altering burn injury that is mixed with knowledge that they are responsible for their self-inflicted injuries (Franchitto, et al., 2011; Bakker, Maertens, Van Son, & Van Loey, 2013). For instance, there are several unique aspects that have an impact on the involved child's quality of life, such as: the impairments that present in BS-JFSB. For example, some of the problems include split families, chaotic home environment, increased incidence of pre-existing ADHD and mental health conditions, high rate of abuse/neglect/maltreatment, etc.) and behavior problems (e.g., anger management, impulsivity, underdeveloped or ineffective social skills, etc.) that are major issues. Furthermore, burns in particular are associated with psychological distress and reduced quality of life for family members as well. For example, parents of children with burns are at increased risk for stress, PTSD, and/or exacerbation of mental health problems when compared with parents of children with other illnesses (Lawrence, et al., 2010; Lawrence et al., 2011; Quezada, Gonzalez, & Mecott, 2015). Recent research indicates that pediatric burn survivors' resilience and psychological outcomes are associated with if their caregivers develop PTSD symptoms (Quezada, Gonzalez, & Mecott, 2015). Although less marked, siblings of children with burns also appear to be at increased risk for behavior problems themselves (Landolt, Buehlmann, Maag, & Schiestl, 2009). Given the difficulties experienced by children with burns and their family members, there has been considerable interest in crafting interventions that simultaneously improve the child's functioning, while positively affecting their family members' psychosocial life course.

Working with BS-JFSB requires careful use of a psychosocial history and timeline to discern whether post-incident psychological symptoms are reflective of premorbid illness or are the product of current stressors. Mental health conditions and poly-substance use are common pre-existing issues in the burn-injured patient population. However, gathering an accurate psychosocial history from BS-JFSB may be more difficult to acquire because of poor communication skills, fear of disclosing information that may have unwanted ramifications for a pending legal case, limited sources of collateral information, absence of records, and a general lack of cooperation. In some BS-JFSB cases, youth may even be instructed by their attorneys to not to speak with healthcare providers about the incident or their reactions. Medical care priorities must take priority over attempts to collect any additional JFSB incident information (Schofield & Bourgeois, 2010; Aftyka, Rybojad, & Rudnicka-Drozak, 2014).

Scene rescue, emergent burn treatment, hospitalization or other medical services themselves can contribute to the exacerbation of mental illness of the BS-JFSB. Nonetheless, when assessing mental illness in a BS-JFSB population, it is critical to consider the impact of the following potential risk factors:

1. A significant number of JFSB suffer from mental illness prior to these incidents.
2. Depending on the nature of the JFSB incident, some form of diversion or therapeutic jurisprudence may be used as an alternative to incarceration for these youth (Johnson, Beckenbach & Killbourne, 2013).
3. Resulting punitive and legal actions can be traumatizing, and require psychological sensitivity.

More than anything else, for BS-JFSB cases, innovative assessment and interventions are a cornerstone for providing culturally responsive services in rural settings (Chatterjee, Chatterjee, & Jain, 2003; Johnson, Beckenbach, & Killbourne, 2013). It is important to note that for rural settings, culture functions as an important lens that offers a considerable vantage point through which healthcare providers can assess and assimilate the insights required for working with BS-JFSB. Perhaps the largest takeaway message here for rural settings is recognizing the inevitable interconnectedness of the various disciplines that must be involved in these clinical forensic trauma cases (Cornish, Church, Callanan, Bethune, Robbins, & Miller, R., 2003; Fertman, Dotson, Mazzocco, & Reitz, 2005).

## Shifts in Clinical Forensic Thinking Regarding Trauma Treatment for Children in Rural Settings

The improper or under-treated BS-JFSB case remains a leading cause of repeat recidivism or post-incident adjustment difficulties for these youth. BS-JFSB are less likely than suburbanites to receive a psychological screening and are therefore more likely to be diagnosed with underlying contributing mental and behavioral conditions at a later stage, when the clinical symptom pattern is more advanced and difficult to reverse from a psychological treatment standpoint (Mann, Crawford, Wilson, & McDermott, 2008; McMorris, Cox, Hudson, Liu, & Bebko, 2013). The multiple barriers to care can be identified by healthcare providers, patients and their families. For example, some of these barriers could include understanding and navigating a confusing mental health network system, accessing mental who are specifically experienced in BS-JFSB, costs/reimbursement, length of treatment, unrealistic expectations of treatment/intervention outcomes (especially related to medications and the length of time for effectiveness), transportation, etc.).

To enable a shift within the practicalities of BS-JFSB care is, in many respects, a challenge. Changing the attitudes of rural healthcare clinicians to realize the importance of providing education to patients in a non-scare-tactics method or approach may pose a problem. For example, healthcare providers must implement proven effective strategies in assessing BS-JFSB patients, such as using open-ended questions when questioning patients about their behaviors leading up to the incident and subsequent reactions. These provide an informational-rich foundation base for all disciplines working with the case. This information is what can guide subsequent educational sessions relative to a youth's thinking errors, social/relationship skills, or gaps in knowledge. At the same time, this information can be quite instructive in supporting the BS-JFSB family and intervention team with cultural or language interpreters. Specifically in BS-JFSB cases, healthcare providers must learn the importance of using a treatment strategy that involves multi-agency collaboration, with goal-directed timelines related to various clinical or forensic issues (Palanisamy & Verville, 2015; Chong, Aslani, & Chen, 2013). The inherent complexity of BS-JFSB cases requires an interdisciplinary, collaborative approach in order to reduce confusion that can occur as a result of conflicting guidance. For example, a primary care provider's failure to refer to mental health (or a YFS intervention program) when it is required may be out of ignorance or due to anxiety about possibly losing a patient. From a behavioral perspective, there is a balancing of boundaries that must be tempered by full awareness of comorbidity (e.g., multiple mental health issues simultaneously) in BS-JFSB. Effective comorbidity treatment requires coping skills development that may be beyond the expertise of any one rural service provider.

While BS-JSFB treatment and forensic issues often overlap, it is critical to keep them separate. Ethically, mental health professionals are prohibited from dual relationships with patients, i.e., clinical treatment and forensic evaluative or dual identity provider (APA, 2010; ACA, 2014). For example, a clinical patient may not be as forthcoming with vital information in therapy if they suspect such data will be used to conduct a forensic evaluation. At the same time, a therapeutic provider may be more vulnerable to being accused of slanting a forensic evaluation as a result of a desire to assist the BS-JFSB patient.

More than anything else, the aforementioned introduction section speaks volumes about the complex and multidimensional experiences of BS-JFSB in rural settings. This reinforces the need for healthcare providers to be attuned to the clinical forensic issues presented by these cases. The extant literature on BS-JFSB has produced important and significant information that can help fill the void by creating a framework "scaffolding" to better understand BS-JFSB. The chapter starts by providing an overview of child burn survivor trauma stemming from JFSB. Next, risk assessment factors that can have a preventative and culturally responsive therapeutic result for these children are discussed. The following two sections respectively cover the necessity of evidence-based, trauma-focused treatment into the entire continuum of care. Finally, implications for clinical mental health practice and research are examined.

## Children, Burn Injury Frequency, and Etiology

Unintentional injuries are one of the leading causes of death for children worldwide, and burns are a common injury (World Health Organization, 2008). Burns are considered one of the most serious types of injury, as they often lead to both acute and chronic illness (De Young et al., 2012). Severe burns often meet the criteria for a traumatic event (American Psychiatric Association, 2000) and are not only distressing at the time of the event, but may result in long-term physical, psychological, and financial hardships for both BS-JFSB and family members (De Young et al., 2012).

In the United States, Nearly one-half million burn injuries serious enough to require medical treatment occur in the United States each year (American Burn Association. Burn incident and treatment in the United States: 2015 fact sheet. Chicago: American Burn Association; 2015). In a single year, an estimated 131,419 children (aged 19 years and under) are injured and 430 die from fire and burns. [These data are from Centers for Disease Control and Prevention, National Center for Injury Prevention and Control, 2010. Web-based Injury Statistics Query and Reporting System (WISQARS). Children under the age of 19 years represent approximately one-third of all admissions to U.S. burn center hospitals. (American Burn Association. National burn repository 2015: report of data from 2005–2014. Chicago: American Burn Association; 2015). Specifically for burns, nearly one-half million injuries serious enough to require medical treatment occur in the United States each year (ABA, 2015a). Children under the age of 19 years represent one-third of admissions to burn center hospitals (ABA, 2015b). Overall, approximately 93 percent of burn injuries are thermally induced (i.e., flame, scald, contact), with chemical and electrical burns accounting for the remaining 7 percent of injuries (ABA, 2015b). Scald injury from hot liquids and steam cause the overwhelming majority of burns to young children. Flame/Fire is the primary burn etiology in older children and teens.

While specific data on BS-JFSB are extremely sparse, unpublished data on the patient is typically an older child or teen. The type of injury sustained is usually flame/flash burns (from the explosion or secondary ignition of clothing), chemical burns (from making chemically reactive explosive devices), blast injuries (from the bomb explosion; these can include instantaneous amputations, fractures, or significant wounds), or penetrating injuries (from shrapnel). These types of mechanisms often lead to an increased severity of burn injury. JFSB-related injuries most commonly occur to the eyes, face, hands, and extremities. This becomes especially significant during the clinical forensic and trauma-based treatment course, as the resulting injuries, scars, deformities, and physical impairments are likely visible to others. Visible differences represent a unique challenge that the multidisciplinary treatment team must address during the child's community and school reintegration, post-injury. Improvements in burn medical care over the past several decades have made survival an expected outcome, thus there is a new emphasis on quality of life and psychosocial aspects in treatment plans. The most beneficial interventions are based on individual assessments and incorporate cultural traditions. Clinicians and caregivers can utilize easily-accessible support programs to positively facilitate a burn-injured child's return to society, family, and school such as: The Phoenix Society for Burn Survivors (www.phoenix-society.org); survivor peer support (e.g., Survivors Offering Assistance In Recovery – SOAR: www.phoenix-society.org/programs/soar/); Model Systems Knowledge Translation Center (www.msktc.org/burn); pediatric burn survivor camps; and school reintegration programs (e.g., The Journey Back at www.phoenix-society.org/our-programs/kids/school-reentry and Return to Education and Continued Healing – REACH at http://reach.traumaburn.org/). Pediatric burn survivor support and community/school reintegration is most successful when collaboration occurs with medical and mental health professionals, school personnel, parents/caregivers, family, and the involved child.

Although many children recover from traumatic injury events, a significant number of children and family members develop severe emotional symptoms (Winston et al., 2002; Marsac et al., 2011; Quezada, Gonzalez, & Mecott, 2015). Research suggests that following a burn injury, approximately 6-47 percent of children and adolescents develop acute stress disorder (ASD; Fukunishi, 1998; Saxe et al., 2005), posttraumatic stress disorder (PTSD; Landolt, Buehlmann, Maag, & Schiestl, 2009) and anxiety disorder (Stoddard, Norman, Murphy, & Beardslee, 1989; De Young et al., 2012).

ASD appears to be a probable and expected outcome of burn-injury trauma. Stoddard et al. (2006) report that 29 percent of burn victims between the ages of 12 and 48 months experienced symptoms of ASD within the first month of injury (De Young et al., 2012). Licensed mental health practitioners should be aware of and vigilant in assessing for the potential prodromal phases associated with ASD when treating this specific patient population. Long-term psychological effects relating to traumatic burn injury and BS-JFSB have been identified with a 45.5 percent psychiatric disorder prevalence rate in young adults who experienced burns as children (De Young et al., 2012). Early intervention strategies should be implemented in order to aid in the prevention of long-term psychological deficits for both burn trauma survivors and their family members.

## Outreach and Collaboration with Parents and the Community

Pediatric burns occur relatively often in young children under the age of 5 due to their vulnerability and developmental ability (American Burn Association, 2015; Klas et al., 2015; Vloemans et al., 2011). While BS-JFSB incidents typically involve older children, younger children and other bystanders can be inadvertently or intentionally injured. Young children are particularly dependent on their parents or other adult primary caregivers for all physical, emotional and psychological needs and safety (Bakker, 2013; Klas et al., 2015). Many firesetting youth and pediatric burn patients are cared for by people other than their birth parents….this is another culturally sensitive treatment issue that needs to be considered. Parents play a crucial role in their children's health care treatment including scheduling, appointment attendance, financial requirements, and treatment compliance. Regardless of trauma severity, younger children are more dependent upon their parents' overt reactions to the traumatic event and internalize their parents' reactions (Arceneaux & Meyer, 2009). Research has recognized a positive relation between high levels of parenting stress and the use of emergency and medical services (Raphael, Zhang, Liu, & Giardino, 2010) or primary care services (Janicke & Finney, 2003) for children (Marsac et al., 2011). Parents' personal acute stress appears to be a key determinant of whether parents reached out for help for their child (Marsac et al., 2011) and whether their child develops ASD/PTSD symptoms (Quezada, Gonzalez, & Mecott, 2015). In addition to parenting stress, poorer emotional functioning in mothers and children has been related to an increase in overall health care utilization (Janicke, Finney, & Riley, 2001; Marsac et al., 2011).

Parents' perception of their own symptoms appear to be a greater influence than their child's overt symptoms when determining whether to seek treatment from professional sources (Marsac et al., 2011; Johnson & Jones, 2014). Parents generally seek assistance for their child if traumatic stress symptoms were indicated, however they are even more likely to seek treatment when they themselves experience significant early traumatic stress (Marsac et al., 2011). Parents' own acute stress should be adequately addressed by medical and professional staff both in hospital and emergency care settings. Medical agencies may benefit from incorporating a parental acute stress assessment in order to provide sufficient family-centered care (Marsac et al., 2011; Quezada, Gonzalez, & Mecott, 2015).

In contrast to parental stress as an influential factor for child trauma treatment, a healthy family environment has been identified as one of the most significant pre-existing factors for child burn injury in regards to coping and adjustment post trauma (Barakat & Kazak, 1999; Tarnowski & Brown, 2003). Social support has been identified as a protective factor in helping reduce and prevent severity after a child has been exposed to a traumatic burn event (Barakat & Linney, 1992; Kazak et al., 1997; Ozer & Weinstein, 2004; Quezada, Gonzalez, & Mecott, 2015; Wooding & Raphael, 2004; Marsac et al., 2011). Addressing parental stress and subsequently fostering psychological well-being cannot be emphasized enough (Johnson & Jones, 2014; Quezada, Gonzalez, & Mecott, 2015). Parents who are able to demonstrate an ability to cope well are less likely to have children experience prolonged traumatic symptoms (Laor, Wolmer, & Cohen, 2001; Quezada, Gonzalez, & Mecott, 2015). Psychoeducation as well as stress-reduction treatment should be readily available to parents and families in conjunction with the child's treatment.

A critical component to successful BS-JFSB treatment, outreach, and caregiver collaboration is providing culturally sensitive school and community reintegration. Underlying issues and motivating factors contributing to the JFSB incident must be considered, such as: social (e.g., bullying, teasing, peer-induced isolation, etc.); behavioral (e.g., poor impulse control, anger management issues, underdeveloped interrelationship skills, etc.); and mental conditions (e.g., ADHD, depression, etc.). These can have specific treatment implications and require individualized care. Pre-existing conditions can complicate recovery and community/peer-acceptance. For example, if social issues such as bullying/teasing were occurring before the BS-JFSB event, they will likely be amplified when the injured child returns to school. Social isolation and rejection can be especially problematic in JFSB, due to associated legal ramifications, property destruction, financial cost, or victimization of community members. Another important treatment consideration is identifying and understanding any unique characteristics of the culture and community in which the child resides that may potentially impact his recovery. Some cultures publically ostracize and socially isolate members of their community who have scars or disfigurements. All of these factors must be addressed and incorporated into the comprehensive treatment plan of the BS-JFSB.

## Medical and Professional Collaboration

In order to effectively treat children who have experienced burn-related trauma, an interdisciplinary approach should be established to include outreach and collaboration with care providers. This approach facilitates time management, effective communication, and treatment consistency throughout various treatment specialties. Arceneaux and Meyer (2009) recommend implementing a daily routine schedule in the child's hospital room to help the child establish consistency, as well as foster communication throughout various staff members working on the client's treatment team.

Family doctors and pediatricians are often a common source of professional assistance for children who have experienced trauma. It is essential that pediatric physicians, family practitioners, emergency departments, and medical personnel have sufficient training and understanding of trauma informed care. Research suggests higher instances of emergency department visits correlated with heightened PTSD symptoms in children. For example, Shemesh et al., (2003) assessed children in a pediatric emergency department and found a relationship between current PTSD symptoms and an increase in recent emergency department visits (Marsac et al., 2011). Due to the high level of emergency department services, it is crucial that medical personnel are competent in trauma care, especially in rural settings where it may be comparatively less available. This includes the ability to identify and recognize posttraumatic symptomatology, dual diagnoses, and evidence-based treatment protocol.

It is important to note that not all children who experience a burn injury will develop symptoms of traumatic stress. Assuming trauma or acute stress without proper assessment may lead to unnecessary complications in the child's treatment and overlooking the actual presenting problem. Children generally have the strength of resiliency. Several factors contribute to positive adjustment and resiliency post-burn injury including: the child's developmental level; inherent or learned coping skills; and strong sources of emotional, social and physical support (Arceneaux & Meyer, 2009; Quezada, Gonzalez, & Mecott, 2015).

Once a child burn survivor has been assessed and post-traumatic stress symptoms have been accurately identified, treatment providers should acknowledge factors, which may contribute to the complexity of the trauma case. For example, anxiety and mood disorders often present in children as a psychological response to the trauma, and subsequent treatment of the burn injury. Pre-existing conditions that are especially important to identify in the treatment of child burn victims are anxiety, conduct disorders, attention deficit hyperactivity disorder (ADHD), depression and other mental illnesses (Arceneaux & Meyer, 2009). These diagnoses may exacerbate the traumatic state or interfere with the medical treatment (Arceneaux & Meyer, 2009). Trauma symptoms include cognitive, physical, emotional, and behavioral challenges. BS-JFSB who have experienced a traumatic event may undergo a drastic change in their perception of self and the immediate world in which they experience. In younger populations, fear, anxiety and pain often have similar symptoms that may contribute to diagnostic ambiguity (Arceneaux & Meyer, 2009). Proper assessment by a licensed mental health professional is essential in order to provide effective treatment and rule out differential diagnoses.

It is important that treatment specialists are aware of both the physical and mental state of the child burn survivor. BS-JFSB are often concerned about medical procedures, family interactions, scheduling events, bathing and meals, receiving medication, and the ability to play naturally (Arceneaux & Meyer, 2009). Panic attacks may manifest as a result of anticipation, consistent and painful treatments, or other medical procedures such as physical therapy or surgery. In addition, obsessive compulsive disorder may be exhibited by hand washing and cleanliness around burn wounds especially following discharge from the hospital (Arceneaux & Meyer, 2009).

BS-JFSB may demonstrate avoidance towards reminders and situations relating to a traumatic event. Children may develop an absence of emotional responses, and appear unaware of their surroundings. Children may also have attachment issues with their primary care givers, irritability or temper tantrums, forgetfulness, helplessness, and other symptoms indicative of distress (Arceneaux & Meyer, 2009). Novel symptoms may manifest during the course of care that are not congruent with symptoms of traumatic stress, or are believed to be caused by the treatment environment. Treatment-induced symptoms should be addressed immediately, and communication across the interdisciplinary treatment team should be established to adjust the intervention protocol if needed.

## Treatment Considerations

Medical providers may increase trauma detection by implementing routine screening and offering psychoeducation, as well as preventative measures when indicated as necessary (Marsac et al., 2011). It may be beneficial for care providers to identify symptoms linked to the injury event in order to decrease long-term consequences of traumatic stress in BS-JFSB (Marsac et al., 2011).

Interventions rendered immediately after the traumatic event should focus on mental status, management of pain, and nutritional intake (Tarnowski & Brown, 2003). Pain management for the child burn survivor should include both pharmacological management to treat pain, as well as evidence-based therapeutic pain distraction techniques (Arceneaux & Meyer, 2009). Distraction-based cognitive-behavioral interventions have been formulated specifically to treat burn victims. The most common distraction interventions utilized in burn care are virtual reality, social support, play and music therapy, cartoon or television viewing, and guided imagery. A combination of these interventions may be utilized in treatment depending on the child's specific needs and interests.

Cognitive Behavioral Therapy in addition to supportive family therapy has been effective for the treatment of child burn survivors (Silverman, Pina, & Viswesvaran, 2008). If a BS-JFSB meets DSM-5 criteria for major depression, antidepressant pharmacology may be considered as a treatment medium. There is scarcity of psychotropic medications approved for use in children, however, select serotonin reuptake inhibitors (SSRIs) including Sertraline and Fluoxetine have been approved for use in children and adolescents (Thomas, Meyer, & Blakeney, 2007). Antidepressant pharmacology should be considered in conjunction with psychotherapy as well as parental psychoeducation regarding dosage, risk factors, and side effects.

## Trauma-Informed Care

In order to ensure proper treatment and promote the welfare of the BS-JFSB, trauma informed care should be implemented by professional staff on the interdisciplinary team. Competency in trauma work will ensure best practice and ethical treatment of the trauma-exposed child and family members.

Trauma informed care emphasizes the health care provider's approach to the trauma situation, rather than focusing solely on treatment strategies and interventions. Informed providers understand barriers that trauma creates in the client's ability to succeed in treatment, and seeks to avoid subjecting patients to re-traumatization through inadvertent experiences. Practitioners of this approach recognize the prevalence of trauma among child survivors and are aware of potential trauma history while interacting with clients from all backgrounds.

The tenants of trauma informed care focuses on "what has happened to you" vs. the traditional psychoanalytic perspective, "what is wrong with you." Trauma-specific intervention programs recognize the survivor's need to be respected and informed regarding their recovery. Practitioners aim to conceptualize a holistic perspective of a patient's individually unique situation, taking into account factors that contribute to the case complexity such as history, socio-economic factors, pre-existing medical and psychological illnesses, and family systems. In addition, focus is given to symptoms of trauma such as anxiety and depression (SAMHSA, 2015). An interdisciplinary approach is essential in order to ensure proper diagnosis and subsequent treatment for the child burn victim.

Many communities, especially those in rural settings, lack informed trauma-based providers who are trained in evidence-based treatment for child burn victims (Chadwick Center for Children and Families, 2004; Chaffin & Friedrich, 2004; Ko et al., 2008). This lack of awareness and training in trauma informed care may result in the practitioner to not fully or accurately conceptualize the client's presenting problem, failure to make appropriate referrals, and can lead to direct harm to the client through re-traumatization (Butler et al., 2011).

The NCTSN Child Welfare Trauma Training Toolkit identifies essential elements of trauma-informed care for health care practitioners including focus on: increasing the child's sense of safety, fostering emotional regulation, coordinating with other agencies, implementing a complete assessment of the child's trauma experiences, promoting positive relationships and social support, and managing stress (Ko et al., 2008). The incorporation of these elements promotes a well-rounded and competent practitioner who is able to ensure the standard of care for the child burn survivor.

## Risk Assessment Factors for Child Burn Survivors and JFSB

Trauma experienced by BS-JFSB is subjective and manifests in several different presentations. People experience trauma in combat, through sexual assault, abuse, natural disasters, acts of terrorism, fires, etc. However, exposure to trauma, directly or vicariously, does not always result in unwanted mental health symptoms or anxiety disorders. This leaves us with the questions surrounding how to determine if someone that is exposed to a trauma will develop symptoms that require intervention from a mental health professional. This section focuses on how to assess for this risk with child burn survivors juvenile fire setters and bomb makers.

In the healthcare settings, the pediatric burn population has the longest length of stay, outnumbering all other admissions (Benjamin & Herndon, 2002.). Burns are painful both initially and throughout the long healing process, they sometimes leave permanent scarring or loss of function, and the incident surrounding their origin can be traumatic in and of itself. Trauma can manifest in many different ways in child burn survivors, leading to anxiety disorders such as ASD or PTSD, which are the most common in post-trauma scenarios (Toon et al., 2011).

As briefly explored previously, ASD and PTSD are the most common mental diagnoses following a traumatic event, and this holds true when the trauma survivor is a child. ASD is a trauma and stressor related disorder in the DSM-5. For a child to be diagnosed with this disorder, the child does not have to directly experience the traumatic event. The child needs only to have witnessed the event, learned the event happened to a close family member, or have repeated or extreme exposure to the details of the trauma. While in the case of child burn survivors it is direct exposure to the event, in the case of JFSB related trauma that is not necessarily so (e.g., a child could witness another person start a fire that burns a person or destroys property). Symptoms of ASD vary and include several different categories of symptoms (i.e., intrusion, negative mood, dissociative, avoidant, and arousal). Intrusive symptoms include recurrent involuntary memories and/or dreams related to the event, disassociate reactions, and intense or prolonged psychological stress. With children, they may experience frightening dreams that do not contain recognizable content. Negative mood involves the inability to experience positive emotions (Dalgleish et al., 2015). Dissociative symptoms are when the child experiences an altered sense of reality of their surroundings or self, and/or the inability to remember important aspects of the traumatic event. Avoidant symptoms occur when the child undergoes efforts to avoid distressing memories, thoughts, or feelings, as well as external reminders of the traumatic event (Gigengack, Meijel, Alisic, & Lindauer, 2015). Finally, arousal symptoms might manifest as sleep disturbances, irritable behavior, hypervigilance, problems with concentration, and an exaggerated startle response. These symptoms typically begin immediately after the traumatic event, and some of these symptoms are even considered normal reactions to a trauma. However, if the symptoms persist for three days, up to a month after the event, or cause a clinically significant disturbance to the child, then it can become ASD (American Psychiatric Association, 2013).

In previous editions of the DSM, PTSD descriptions focused primarily on adult clients. However, in the 5$^{th}$ edition of the DSM greater attention was given to how symptoms may manifest in children and adolescents (Dalgleish et al., 2015). PTSD contains many of the same symptoms as ASD. However with PTSD, symptoms must continue after a month following the traumatic event. While there are similar symptoms, there are some differences to note. PTSD symptoms include dissociative reactions such as flashbacks to the traumatic event. In the case of children in particular, this can sometimes manifest as trauma-specific reenactment that occurs through play or drawing (Schimmenti & Caretti, 2014). This trauma play opens the door to psychological interventions that we will explore in the next section. In addition to reenacting the event, trauma play may include themes of trauma during play. This is often seen with children aged six and above. With children under six, symptoms can manifest as extreme temper tantrums and constriction in play. It is also important to note that at times symptoms may not occur more than six months after the traumatic event (American Psychiatric Association, 2013). In this case, it means symptoms may not occur until up to 6 months after the injury event. Or if they last longer than 6 months, then it is differentially diagnosed.

In addition to ASD and PTSD, depression can occur with a traumatized child, which can have a profound impact on the way they see themselves and the way they see the world. While ASD and PTSD are more common, it is important to understand how depressive symptoms can manifest in slightly different ways within children (Stark and Laurent, 2001; American Psychiatric Association, 2013). For example, in adults one would identify a depressed mood that lasts most of the day, however in children symptoms can manifest as an irritable mood, angry outbursts, hyperactivity, disobedience, or cutting behaviors (www.seans-story.org/supplemental-materials/mental-behavioral-health). Additionally, while children may not have significant weight loss as you may find in a depressed adult, children might instead fail to meet their expected weight gain (American Psychiatric Association, 2013).

The task for mental health practitioners then becomes one of identifying which children are at risk of developing dysfunctional symptomology or an anxiety disorder. To understand that, we must break assessing for risk down into the researched characteristics (i.e., trauma severity, disassociation at time of event, social support). Many researchers have found that both preexisting characteristics and those that involve the trauma event and increase the chance that an individual will develop anxiety disorder symptoms. Initially, there is a dose-response relationship between the severity of the traumatic event and the likelihood that one could develop anxiety related symptoms such as the ones outlined above (Rodriguez, van de Kemp, & Foy, 1998). There is also evidence to support that traumatic events involving injury are malicious events, where the client was directly exposed to the trauma as opposed to a witness, and disassociation at the time of the trauma are more likely to result in the trauma survivor experiencing a dysfunctional response (Briere, Scott & Weathers, 2014). In the case of child burn survivors, burns can satisfy much of these criteria. Disassociation at the time of the event has been shown to be one of the primary indicators that symptoms of an anxiety disorder could arise after trauma exposure (Ozer et al., 2003). Researchers also found through a meta-analysis, that preexisting attributes can exist. Preexisting trauma has been shown to increase the chances of developing harmful symptoms, as well as female gender, lack of access to mental health services (e.g., rural areas), lower socioeconomic status (SES), lower education, lower intelligence, and racial minority status (Lonigan, Shannon, Taylor, Finch, & Sallee, 1994; Brewin et al., 2000).

Beyond the trauma event, and the events of the individual's life leading up to it, there are risk factor characteristics to examine after the event has occurred. Initially, a lack of social support has been found to be a strong indicator of developing adverse anxiety symptoms after a trauma (Brewin et al., 2000). With children, this social support often comes in the form of their immediate and extended family, teachers, and other adults in the child's life. The next section examines the importance of rapport building with the child and family as paramount to all treatment modalities, and the beginning stages of rapport involves psychoeducation. This will be the time to inform the family of the importance of their role as the child's support system, and educating them on how to assist the child most effectively. In terms of rural areas where families can be isolated from others, familiar support becomes even more important (Henderson, Crotty, Fuller, & Martinez, 2014).

Additionally, in the same vein as familial support, is the presence of additional life stressors as a risk factor (Brewin et al., 2000). In children this is related to the family as well, as they are the people largely in control of what life stressors the child is exposed to. While some life stressors might be inherent in the family (e.g., low SES), other stressors can be directly controlled by the family (e.g., expressing anger). Pine and Cohen (2002), found that when the victim of the trauma is a child, family cohesion played a significant role in the risk assessment of the child. This again highlights the importance that the caregivers of the child play in the aftermath of a trauma and in the development of anxiety symptoms. While factors have been shown to indicate a higher level of risk in developing anxiety symptoms, there is still not an exact checklist to make such a determination.

## Evidence Based Trauma Focused Treatment in Rural Settings

There are many challenges that exist when treating trauma victims. Trauma impacts individuals in a multitude of ways ranging from sleep and appetite disturbances to crippling fear and anxiety (American Psychiatric Association, 2013). Adding to the difficulties of treatment are factors such as younger ages and possible physical reminders in the form of scarring that can sometimes present in child burn survivors. Moreover, an individual's access to services becomes a factor in recovery. Therefore, children and families that reside in rural areas are at increased risk of an inability to access mental health professionals skilled in evidence based treatment (Oetinger, Flanagan, & Weaver, 2014). However, several approaches to effectively treating child burn survivors exist, and can be effectively utilized in various settings.

At the onset of treatment with any client it is critical to first develop rapport and trust in the therapeutic relationship. This critical aspect is also present when working with children exposed to trauma, firesetting youth with pre-existing mental conditions (such as oppositional defiance or conduct disorder), and JFSB who have encountered the juvenile justice system. In all of the evidence-based approaches below, the initial step will be establishing this healthy therapeutic relationship. Keep in mind, that BS-JFSB cases require working with the child and parents, caregivers, extended family, teachers, etc. involved in their lives (Baker-Ericzén, Jenkins, & Haine-Schlagel, 2013). These other individuals must actively participate and be invested in treatment in order for these approaches to be culturally responsive and effective.

## Culturally Responsive Trauma Focused Cognitive Behavioral Therapy (TF-CBT)

Trauma Focused Cognitive Behavioral Therapy (TF-CBT) is a form of CBT developed for use to treat trauma victims, and has been shown to have positive results with children and adults alike. When applying TF-CBT to work with children, there are five main components: psychoeducation, stress inoculation training, trauma narrative processing, cognitive processing, and a parental treatment component (Vogt, King, & King, 2007). These five components are specifically designed for working with youth, and research indicates that inclusion of these components will produce the best outcomes. Research also indicates that the best approach for TF-CBT is through a three phase-based system: stabilizing, processing, and integration (Cohen, 2012). This five component and three-phase system approach of TF-CBT has simple guidelines that can be followed by most properly credentialed mental health professionals.

To best utilize this model, Cohen et al. (2012) recommend using the acronym PRACTICE to navigate the three phases containing the essential components outlined above. In the first phase (i.e., coping skills), the first letter represents psychoeducation and parenting skills. With psychoeducation the mental health practitioner will provide the child's caregivers with information on trauma, the TF-CBT process, as well as answer any of their questions. This will also be the opportunity to educate on parenting skills that will be utilized during and after treatment. Not only are these aspects of the process important for the sharing of information, but they are also paramount to the rapport building process. Additionally, psychoeducation will be provided to the youth in developmentally appropriate ways.

The next letters of the acronym is representative of "relaxation, affective, and cognitive coping skills, respectively," (Cohen et al., 2012). In this early stage, the child may have severe symptomology and find it difficult to come down from their elevated state. For this reason, educating and practicing relaxation exercises (e.g., progressive muscle relaxation) with the child is beneficial. At this time it may be counter-indicated to associate the relaxation skills with the traumatic event. Simply deescalating the child and providing them with the tools they need to apply relaxations themselves is the best initial approach. Once this is achieved, the mental health professional can then encourage the child to utilize the relaxation skills when they experience anxiety at other times. From this point, the therapist could begin to introduce other coping skills, such as mindfulness or visualization (Cohen et al., 2012).

Phase two is classified as "trauma narration and processing," which also is represented by the "T" in the acronym. Trauma narratives are utilized in trauma processing, as individuals that have experienced a trauma often avoid places, people, or thoughts related to the trauma. Creating a trauma narrative allows the child to unpack the traumatic event, and begin to process it with a mental health professional (Mott, Galovski, Walsh, & Elwood, 2015). When working with children, it is sometimes better to create a "life narrative" instead, as children can have fragmented or non-linier recall of traumatic events (Cohen et al., 2012). It is also encouraged that once the narrative is complete, the child share the story with their caregiver; however if the child is not ready for this step, it should not be pushed.

The last part of phase two is "in vivo mastery of trauma reminders." To complete this, the child and the therapist will work together to create a hierarchy of feared stimuli (e.g., places, items, people, etc.). Next, utilizing gradual exposure therapy, work with the child to slowly expose them to the ranked stimuli, beginning with the least feared, while utilizing the coping skills master in the previous phase of treatment. This may take several sessions depending on the size of the feared stimuli list. Once this step is complete, the child and therapist move on to phase three, "consolidation and closure" (Frye & Spates, 2012).

Beginning with sharing the narrative, the child should participate in three or four conjoined sessions with the caregiver. The purposes of these sessions will be for the child and the caregiver to have open discussions about the traumatic event. This will accomplish two things. First, the child will continue to expose his or her self to the trauma narrative, confronting the trauma instead of thought blocking. Secondly, the child will experience the caregiver hearing about the trauma and reacting in a supportive way. This will begin to ease the child's reluctance to share the trauma and open communication with the caregiver (Cohen et al, 2012).

The final step is "enhancing safety and trust." In this, the therapist and child will explore avenues in which to expand the feelings of safety and trust felt with the therapist and caregiver to new situations and people. In the case of pediatric burn survivors, the child may possess a scar or physical disability from the injury, creating anxiety around meeting new people, which might lead to reliving the trauma through a narrative. However, with the skills learned in previous steps, and with the love and support of the caregiver and therapist, the child will have the tools to gradually grow this area. Continued practice, trial, and error are the only ways to advance and begin to terminate therapy (Cohen, et al., 2012).

## Trauma Focused Art Therapy (TF-ART)

Depending on the chronological or developmental age of the child, it is sometimes indicated to utilize Trauma Focused Art Therapy as the means of treatment. Perrin, Smith, and Yule (2000) found that children manifest their trauma in different ways compared to adults or older youths. The symptoms in children will manifest in more abstract ways, such as through play, drawing, or storytelling. TF-ART utilizes this avenue of expression in children by tapping into how the symptoms manifest, and therapeutically guiding them through the processing of their trauma.

Lyshak-Stelzer et al. (2007) utilized several approaches to TR-ART in their study to determine the effectiveness of the approach in a group setting. The authors incorporated more traditional processing via drawing or collage. In this sixteen-session model, a topic was chosen for each session and began with an emotion check-in by each child. The group then spent approximately twenty minutes discussing the topic of the day, and processing as a group. Next, the children were all allowed to spend the majority of the remaining time on their drawings. At the end of the session, children were encouraged to share and discuss their art with the group, however this was not required. The end result was a book of drawings and collages that were titled "My Life" for each child. The authors found children who participated in TF-ART had a greater reduction in trauma symptoms compared to other forms of treatment.

TF-ART incorporates the importance of processing the trauma in a safe place, reinforcing children's natural tendency to express their feelings and emotions through abstract means like art and play. This model also lends itself well to group settings, which in rural settings creates a cost-effective approach that mental health professionals can utilize with minimal additional training.

## Play Therapy

Play Therapy begins with the understanding that children have an innate ability to learn, grow, and heal from traumatic events they have experienced (Lendeth, 2012). The Association for Play Therapy (2013) defines play therapy as "the systematic use of a theoretical model to establish an interpersonal process wherein trained play therapists use the therapeutic powers of play to help clients prevent or resolve psychosocial difficulties and achieve optimal growth and development." Similar to TF-ART, play therapy utilizes a child's natural tendencies to express themselves in more abstract ways, such as imaginative play. After a trauma is experienced children (ages 2-10) will often engage in post-traumatic play, as they are still developing concrete operations (Jordan, Perryman, & Anderson, 2013). This population often utilizes post-traumatic play through the use of toys to represent events, anger, and fear.

As children already possess this natural ability to play in a symbolic way, a mental health professional can provide some guidance to the play to allow for processing of the trauma. Through this play children can explore the trauma in a safe place, without having to re-expose themselves completely to the trauma (Crenshaw & Hardy, 2007). Axline (1947) has outlined eight aspects of Play Therapy for it to be effective:

1. Must develop a warm and friendly relationship with the child.
2. Accept the child as she or he is.
3. Establish a feeling of permissiveness in the relationship so that the child feels free to express her feelings completely.
4. Recognize the feelings the child is expressing and reflect these feelings back in such a manner that the child gains insight into his or her behavior.
5. Maintain a deep respect for the child's ability to solve his or her problems and give the child the opportunity to do so. The responsibility to make choices and to institute change is the child's.
6. Does not attempt to direct the child's actions or conversations in any manner. The child leads the way, the therapist follows.
7. Does not attempt to hurry the therapy along. It is a gradual process and must be recognized as such by the therapist.
8. Only establish those limitations necessary to anchor the therapy to the world of reality and to make the child aware of his or her responsibility in the relationship

Ultimately, Play Therapy allows children to regain a sense of control over their environment and their trauma in the form of manipulation of toys. This allows for processing the trauma without the child having to fully confront the trauma head on. Not only does the child gain a sense of independence from the activity of play, the child also leads the way of the process with little direction from the mental health professional. As touched on at the beginning of this section, this taps into the child's natural ability to process and heal with a little guidance (Jordan, Perryman, & Anderson, 2013).

## Implications for Clinical Mental Health Practice and Research

Treating BS-JFSB in rural settings requires rethinking of who and how care will be delivered. This motivation for the shift in thinking is reinforced by statistics suggesting that people residing in rural settings is approaching 50 percent (Chong, Aslani, & Chen, 2013). Therefore the number alone buttresses the motivation and priority for expanding resources in rural settings. From a clinical mental health perspective, the expansion of psychological screening that includes diagnosis will be essential for BS-JFSB. The clinical practice model promoted in this paper stresses the strong preference for an interdisciplinary approach that underscores a desire for collaboration among healthcare providers. This collaboration among providers also encompasses the BS-JFSB patient and their families. For example, burn care nurses play a key role in providing education to children and their families, as well as all members of the interdisciplinary healthcare team. In additional, nurses may also offer coping strategies for children and their families that are culturally responsive.

In terms of research, there is a dearth of evidence that exists related to BS-JFSB, which highlights the importance of future clinical forensic research in this area. For example, subsequent research could explore PTSD assessment and management strategies for BS-JFSB. Longitudinal studies on PTSD in BS-JFSB would be beneficial to elucidate how symptoms change overtime. At the same time, trauma-focused research should also explore the influence of gender, age, cultural, ethnoracial, and socioeconomic factors. BS-JFSB have many clinical forensic facets that are relevant to assessing and treating trauma in rural settings. Advanced knowledge associated with BS-JFSB empowers diverse healthcare providers to deliver an optimal level of care to this unique population.

## REFERENCES

Aftyka, A., Rybojad, B., & Rudnicka-Drozak, E. (2014). Are there any differences in medical emergency team interventions between rural and urban areas? A single-centre cohort study. *The Australian Journal of Rural Health*, *22*(5), 223–228. doi:10.1111/ajr.12108 PMID:25303413

American Burn Association. (2015a). Burn incident and treatment in the United States: 2015 fact sheet. Chicago: American Burn Association.

American Burn Association. (2015b). National burn repository 2015: report of data from 2005–2014. Chicago: American Burn Association.

*American Counseling Association*. (2014). Washington, DC: Ethical Guidelines of the American Counseling Association.

Ames, N. (2008). Medically underserved children's access to health care: A review of the literature. *Journal of Human Behavior in the Social Environment*, *18*(1), 64–77. doi:10.1080/10911350802266334

Arceneaux, L. L., & Meyer, W. J. III. (2009). Treatments for common psychiatric conditions among children and adolescents during acute rehabilitation and reintegration phases of burn injury. *International Review of Psychiatry (Abingdon, England)*, *21*(6), 549–558. doi:10.3109/09540260903343984 PMID:19919208

Askay-Wiechman, S., & Magyar-Russell, G. (2009). Post-traumatic growth and spirituality in burn recovery. *International Review of Psychiatry (Abingdon, England)*, *21*(6), 570–579. doi:10.3109/09540260903344107 PMID:19919210

Association for Play Therapy. (2013). *About play therapy overview*. Retrieved from http://www.a4pt.org/ps.playtherapy.cfm?ID1158

Author. (2010). *APA's Ethical Principles of Psychologists and Code of Conduct*. Washington, DC: American Psychological Association.

Axinn, W. G., Ghimire, D. J., Williams, N. E., & Scott, K. M. (2013). Gender, traumatic events, and mental health disorders in a rural Asian setting. *Journal of Health and Social Behavior*, *54*(4), 444–461. doi:10.1177/0022146513501518 PMID:24311755

Axline, V. (1947). *Play therapy*. Boston, MA: Houghton Mifflin.

Benjamin, D., & Herndon, D. N. (2002). Special considerations of age: The pediatric burned patient. In *Total Burn Care* (2nd ed.). London: W.B. Saunders.

Baker-Ericzén, M. M., Jenkins, M., & Haine-Schlagel, R. (2013). Therapist, parent, and youth perspectives of treatment barriers to family-focused community outpatient mental health services. *Journal of Child and Family Studies*, *22*(6), 854–868. doi:10.1007/s10826-012-9644-7 PMID:24019737

Bakker, A., Maertens, K. J. P., Van Son Maarten, J. M., & Van Loey, N. E. E. (2013). Clinical Psychological consequences of pediatric burns from a child and family perspective: A review of the empirical literature. *Psychological Review*, *33*(3), 361–371. PMID:23410718

Bakker, A., Van der Heijden, P. M., Van Son, M. M., & Van Loey, N. E. (2013). Course of traumatic stress reactions in couples after a burn event to their young child. *Health Psychology*, *32*(10), 1076–1083. doi:10.1037/a0033983 PMID:23957899

Barglow, P. (2011). We can't treat soldiers' PTSD without a better diagnosis. *Skeptical Inquirer*, *36*(3), 42–49.

Barglow, P. (2013). A rose is a rose is a rose? *The American Journal of Psychiatry*, *170*(6), 680–681. doi:10.1176/appi.ajp.2013.13010087 PMID:23732969

Brewin, C. R., Andrews, B., & Valentine, J. D. (2000). Meta-analysis of risk factors for posttraumatic stress disorder in trauma-exposed adults. *Journal of Consulting and Clinical Psychology*, *68*(5), 748–766. doi:10.1037/0022-006X.68.5.748 PMID:11068961

Briere, J., Scott, C., & Weathers, F. (2014). Peritraumatic and persistent dissociation in the presumed etiology of PTSD. *The American Journal of Psychiatry*, *162*(12), 2295–2301. doi:10.1176/appi.ajp.162.12.2295 PMID:16330593

Butler, L., Critelli, F., & Rinfrette, E. S. (2011). Trauma-informed care and mental health. *Directions in Psychiatry*, *31*(3), 197–212.

Chatterjee, S., Chatterjee, A., & Jain, S. (2003). Developing community-based services for serious mental illness in a rural setting. In Meeting the mental health needs of developing countries: NGO innovations in India. Sage Publications, Inc.

Chong, W. W., Aslani, P., & Chen, T. F. (2013). Shared decision-making and interprofessional collaboration in mental healthcare: A qualitative study exploring perceptions of barriers and facilitators. *Journal of Interprofessional Care*, *27*(5), 373–379. doi:10.3109/13561820.2013.785503 PMID:23679672

Cohen, J. A., Berliner, L., & Mannarino, A. P. (2010). Trauma-focused CBT for children with co-occurring trauma and behavior problems. *Child Abuse & Neglect*, *34*(4), 215–224. doi:10.1016/j.chiabu.2009.12.003 PMID:20304489

Cohen, J. A., & Mannarino, A. P. (2008). Trauma-focused cognitive behavioural therapy for children and parents. *Child and Adolescent Mental Health*, *13*(4), 158–162. doi:10.1111/j.1475-3588.2008.00502.x

Cohen, J. A., Scheid, J., & Gerson, R. (2014). Transforming Trajectories for Traumatized Children. *Journal of the American Academy of Child and Adolescent Psychiatry*, *53*(1), 9–13. doi:10.1016/j.jaac.2013.10.004 PMID:24342380

Cornish, P. A., Church, P. A., Callanan, T., Bethune, C., Robbins, C., & Miller, R. (2003). Rural interdisciplinary mental health team building via satellite: a demonstration project. Special Issue: Success Stories in Telemedicine: Some Empirical Evidence. *Telemedicine Journal and e-Health*, *9*(1), 63–71. doi:10.1089/153056203763317666 PMID:12699609

Crenshaw, D., & Hardy, K. V. (2007). The crucial role of empathy in breaking the silence of traumatized children in play therapy. *International Journal of Play Therapy, 16,* 160-175.

Dalgleish, T., Goodall, B., Chadwick, I., Werner-Seidler, A., McKinnon, A., Morant, A., & Meiser-Stedman, R. et al. (2015). Trauma-focused cognitive behaviour therapy versus treatment as usual for post-traumatic stress disorder (PTSD) in young children aged 3 to 8 years: Study protocol for a randomised controlled trial. *Trials*, *16*(1), 116. doi:10.1186/s13063-015-0632-2 PMID:25872653

Deblinger, E., Mannarino, A. P., Cohen, J. A., Runyon, M. K., & Steer, R. A. (2011). Trauma-focused cognitive behavioral therapy for children: Impact of the trauma narrative and treatment length. *Depression and Anxiety*, *28*(1), 67–75. doi:10.1002/da.20744 PMID:20830695

Degraw, M., Hicks, R. A., & Lindberg, D. (2010). Incidence of fractures among children with burns with concern regarding abuse. *Pediatrics*, *125*(2), 295–259.

D'Souza, A. L., Nelson, N. G., & McKenzie, L. B. (2009). Pediatric burn injuries treated in US emergency departments between 1990 and 2006. *Pediatrics*, *124*(5), 1424–1430. doi:10.1542/peds.2008-2802 PMID:19805456

De Young, A. C., Kenardy, J. A., Cobham, V. E., & Kimble, R. (2012). Prevalence, comorbidity and course of trauma reactions in young burn-injured children. *Journal of Child Psychology and Psychiatry, and Allied Disciplines*, *53*(1), 56–63. doi:10.1111/j.1469-7610.2011.02431.x PMID:21671940

Erickson, L. D., Hedges, D. W., Call, V. R. A., & Bair, B. (2013). Prevalence of and factors associated with subclinical posttraumatic stress symptoms and PTSD in urban and rural areas of Montana: A cross-sectional study. *The Journal of Rural Health*, *29*(4), 403–412. PMID:24088214

Feather, J. S., & Ronan, K. R. (2009). Trauma-focused CBT with maltreated children: A clinic-based evaluation of a new treatment manual. *Australian Psychologist*, *44*(3), 174–194. doi:10.1080/00050060903147083

Fertman, C. I., Dotson, S., Mazzocco, G. O., & Reitz, S. (2005). Maggie challenges of preparing allied health professionals for interdisciplinary practice in rural areas. *Journal of Allied Health*, *34*(3), 163–168. PMID:16252679

Franchitto, N., Faurie, C., Franchitto, L., Minville, V., Telmon, N., & Rouge, D. (2011). Self-inflicted burns: The value of collaboration between medicine and law. *Journal of Forensic Sciences*, *56*(3), 638–642. doi:10.1111/j.1556-4029.2011.01706.x PMID:21361934

Frye, L. A., & Spates, C. R. (2012). Prolonged exposure, mindfulness, and emotion regulation for the treatment of PTSD. *Clinical Case Studies*, *11*(3), 184–200. doi:10.1177/1534650112446850

Gigengack, M. R., van Meijel, E. P., Alisic, E., & Lindauer, R. J. (2015). Comparing three diagnostic algorithms of posttraumatic stress in young children exposed to accidental trauma: An exploratory study. *Child and Adolescent Psychiatry and Mental Health*, *9*(1), 14. doi:10.1186/s13034-015-0046-7 PMID:25984233

Henderson, J., Crotty, M. M., Fuller, J., & Martinez, L. (2014). Meeting unmet needs? The role of a rural mental health service for older people. *Advances in Mental Health*, *12*(3), 182–191. doi:10.1080/18374905.2014.11081896

Hoagwood, K. E. (2006). *Final report on the child and adolescent trauma treatment consortium (cats) project.* SAMHSA, Unpublished report.

Jensen, P. S., Goldman, E., Offord, D., Costello, E. J., Friedman, R., Huff, B., & Roberts, R. et al. (2011). Overlooked and underserved: 'Action signs' for identifying children with unmet mental health needs. *Pediatrics*, *128*(5), 970–979. PMID:22025589

Johnson, R. (2010). Forensic assessment and clinical intervention for juvenile firesetters: The San Diego model. *Matchbook: Journal on the Prevention & Treatment of Juvenile Firesetting*, *2*, 14–16.

Johnson, R. (2013). Using the DSM-5 and ICD-11 in forensic and clinical applications with children across racial and ethnic lines. In G. P. Koocher, J. C. Norcross, & B. A. Greene (Eds.), *Psychologists' Desk Reference* (3rd ed.). New York: Oxford University Press. doi:10.1093/med:psych/9780199845491.003.0010

Johnson, R., Beckenbach, H., & Killbourne, S. (2013). Forensic psychological public safety risk assessment integrated with culturally responsive treatment for juvenile fire setters: DSM-5 implications. *Journal of Criminal Psychology*, *3*(1), 49–65. doi:10.1108/20093821311307767

Jordan, B., Perryman, K., & Anderson, L. (2013). A case for child-centered play therapy with natural disaster and catastrophic event survivors. *International Journal of Play Therapy, 22*(4), 219–230. doi:10.1037/a0034637

Klas, K. S., Vlahos, P. G., McCully, M., Piche, D. R., & Wang, S. C. (2015). School-based prevention program associated with increased short- and long-term retention of safety knowledge. *Journal of Burn Care & Research; Official Publication of the American Burn Association, 36*(3), 387–393. doi:10.1097/BCR.0000000000000151 PMID:25159554

Ko, S. J., Ford, J. D., Kassam-Adams, N., Berkowitz, S. J., Wilson, C., Wong, M., & Layne, C. M. et al. (2008). Creating trauma-informed systems: Child welfare, education, first responders, health care, and juvenile justice. *Professional Psychology, Research and Practice, 39*(4), 396–404. doi:10.1037/0735-7028.39.4.396

Landolt, M. A., Buehlmann, C., Maag, T., & Schiestl, C. (2009). Brief report: Quality of life is impaired in pediatric burn survivors with posttraumatic stress disorder. *Journal of Pediatric Psychology, 34*(1), 14–21. doi:10.1093/jpepsy/jsm088 PMID:17890286

Landreth, G. L. (2012). *Play therapy: The art of the relationship* (2nd ed.). New York, NY: Brunner Rutledge.

Lawrence, J. W., Rosenberg, L., Mason, S. & Fauerbach, J. A. (2011). *Comparing parent and child perceptions of stigmatizing behavior experienced by children with burn scars*. Academic Press.

Lawrence, J. W., Rosenberg, L., Rimmer, R. B., Thombs, B. D., & Fauerbach, J. A. (2010). Perceived stigmatization and social comfort: Validating the constructs and their measure ment among pediatric burn survivors. *Rehabilitation Psychology, 55*(4), 360–371. doi:10.1037/a0021674 PMID:21171795

Lee, W. C., Luohua, J., Phillips, C. D., & Ohsfeldt, R. L. (2014). Rural-urban differences in health care expenditures: Empirical data from us households. *Advances in Public Health, 2014*. doi:10.1155/2014/435780

Lonigan, C. J., Shannon, M. P., Taylor, C. M., Finch, A. J. Jr, & Sallee, F. R. (1994). Children exposed to disaster: II. Risk factors for the development of post-traumatic symptomatology. *Journal of the American Academy of Child and Adolescent Psychiatry, 33*(1), 94–105. doi:10.1097/00004583-199401000-00013 PMID:8138526

Lyshak-Stelzer, F., Singer, P., St. John, P., & Chemtob, C. M. (2007). Art therapy for adolescents with posttraumatic stress disorder symptoms: A pilot study. *Art Therapy: Journal of the American Art Therapy Association, 24*(4), 163–169. doi:10.1080/07421656.2007.10129474

Mann, J. R., Crawford, S., Wilson, L., & McDermott, S. (2008). Does race influence age of diagnosis for children with developmental delay? *Disability and Health Journal, 1*(3), 157–162. doi:10.1016/j.dhjo.2008.04.002 PMID:21122725

Marsac, M. L., Cirilli, C., Kassam-Adams, N., & Winston, F. K. (2011). Post-injury medical and psychosocial care in children: Impact of traumatic stress symptoms. *Children's Health Care, 40*(2), 116–129. doi:10.1080/02739615.2011.564564

Mashreky, S. R., Rahman, A., Chowdhury, S. M., Svanstrom, L., Linnan, M., Shafinaz, S., & Rahman, F. et al. (2009). Perceptions of rural people about childhood burns and their prevention: A basis for developing a childhood burn prevention programme in Bangladesh. *Public Health*, *123*(8), 568–572. doi:10.1016/j.puhe.2009.06.014 PMID:19665740

McMorris, C. A., Cox, E., Hudson, M., Liu, X., & Bebko, J. M. (2013). The diagnostic process of children with autism spectrum disorder: Implications for early identification and intervention. *Journal on Developmental Disabilities*, *19*(2), 42–49.

Mott, J. M., Galovski, T. E., Walsh, R. M., & Elwood, L. S. (2015). Change in trauma narratives and perceived recall ability over a course of cognitive processing therapy for PTSD. *Traumatology*, *21*(1), 47–54. doi:10.1037/trm0000012 PMID:26005396

Oetinger, M. A., Flanagan, K. S., & Weaver, I. D. (2014). The decision and rewards of working as a mental health professional in a rural area. *Journal of Rural Mental Health*, *38*(1), 50–60. doi:10.1037/rmh0000011

Ozer, E. J., Best, S. R., Lipsey, T. L., & Weiss, D. S. (2008, August). Predictors of posttraumatic stress disorder and symptoms in adults: a meta-analysis. In *Annual Meeting of the International Society for Traumatic Stress Studies*. Educational Publishing Foundation. doi:10.1037/1942-9681.S.1.3

Palanisamy, R., & Verville, J. (2015). Factors enabling communication-based collaboration in interprofessional healthcare practice: A case study. *International Journal of e-Collaboration*, *11*(2), 8–27. doi:10.4018/ijec.2015040102

Pine, D. S., & Cohen, J. A. (2002). Trauma in children and adolescents: Risk and treatment of psychiatric sequelae. *Biological Psychiatry*, *51*(7), 519–531. doi:10.1016/S0006-3223(01)01352-X PMID:11950454

Quezada, L., Gonzalez, M. T., & Mecott, G. A. (in press). Explanatory model of resilience in pediatric burn survivors. *Journal of Burn Care & Research; Official Publication of the American Burn Association*. PMID:26056758

Rodriguez, N., van de Kemp, H., & Foy, D. W. (1998). Post traumatic stress disorder in survivors of childhood sexual abuse: A critical review of the empirical research. *Journal of Child Sexual Abuse*, *7*(2), 17–45. doi:10.1300/J070v07n02_02

Schimmenti, A., & Caretti, V. (2014). Linking the overwhelming with the unbearable: Developmental trauma, dissociation, and the disconnected self. *Psychoanalytic Psychology*. doi:10.1037/a0038019

Schofield, A., & Bourgeois, D. (2010). Socially responsible medical education: Innovations and challenges in a minority setting. *Medical Education*, *44*(3), 263–271. doi:10.1111/j.1365-2923.2009.03573.x PMID:20444057

Shemesh, E., Keshavarz, R., Leightling, N. K., Weinberg, E., Mousavi, A., Sadow, K., & Yehuda, R. et al. (2003). Pediatric emergency department assessment of psychological trauma and posttraumatic stress. *Psychiatric Services (Washington, D.C.)*, *54*(9), 1277–1281. doi:10.1176/appi.ps.54.9.1277 PMID:12954946

Shen, Y. (2002). Short-term group play therapy with Chinese earthquake victims: Effects on anxiety, depression, and adjustment. *International Journal of Play Therapy*, *11*(1), 43–63. doi:10.1037/h0088856

Stark, K. D., & Laurent, J. (2001). Joint Factor Analysis of the Children's Depression Inventory and the Revised Children's Manifest Anxiety Scale. *Journal of Clinical Child Psychology*, *30*(4), 552–567.

Toon, M. H. (2011). Children with burn injuries-assessment of trauma, neglect, violence and abuse. *Journal of Injury & Violence Research*, *3*(2), 98–110.

*Trauma-Informed Approach and Trauma-Specific Interventions*. (n.d.). Retrieved June 18, 2015 from: http://www.samhsa.gov/nctic/trauma-interventions

Vogt, D. S., King, D. W., & King, L. A. (2007). Risk pathways for PTSD. In Handbook of PTSD: Science and Practice, (pp. 99-115). Academic Press.

Wethington, H. R., Hahn, R. A., Fuqua-Whitley, D. S., Sipe, T. A., Crosby, A. E., Johnson, R. L., & Chattopadhyay, S. K. et al. (2008). The effectiveness of interventions to reduce psychological harm from traumatic events among children and adolescents: A systematic review. *American Journal of Preventive Medicine*, *35*(3), 287–313. doi:10.1016/j.amepre.2008.06.024 PMID:18692745

Young, G., & Johnson, R. (2010). Post-Traumatic Stress Disorder in the DSM-5: Group Difference Commentary. *Psychology Injury and the Law*, *3*(4), 314–319. doi:10.1007/s12207-010-9093-9

# Chapter 13
# Childhood Trauma and Barriers in a Rural Setting:
## My Experience with Childhood Trauma and Barriers in a Rural Setting

**Sonja Lee Salcido**
*Center of Hope, USA*

## ABSTRACT

*This chapter details the experiences author had while attempting to obtain medical and psychological help for her children while living in a rural area. This chapter, per the author's request, addresses childhood trauma and barriers that need to be broken down so that emotional healing can begin. This submission is personal, and real occurrences. Rural areas generally have less resources available and because rural areas are sometimes remote, financial resources may not be available for a parent or caregiver to travel to obtain the needed help. Rural towns are normally condensed. This means that there is less privacy, and more ways for perpetrators to work a system of abuse within the schools, community, and churches in order to continue "getting to" the victim-- the child, or in this submission, child and parent. Healing from trauma can only begin when the barriers are recognized, broken down, and eliminated.*

## INTRODUCTION

The outside of a house looks much different than the inside, it is no different in the life, or lives of victims of abuse. The intention of this chapter is to give a close look at the inside of what life can be like for the victim. A sort of "walking tour" of the world that can easily encompass them and keep the locked up, unable to leave. Barriers must be broken down, but in order to do that successfully, one must first identify and address each barrier individually. Rural barriers can be much different than most others, and this chapter shall identify and address each one and how they can be broken down so that the victim can live in peace, begin to heal, and be a victim no more. It is important for the counselor to understand to quickly and appropriately identify the source of the issues and act appropriately and diligently without delay.

DOI: 10.4018/978-1-5225-0228-9.ch013

## BACKGROUND

I am the mother of ten children (all my own), and I have navigated my large family through 15 years of extensive and outstanding emotional, financial, legal, professional, and social sabotage-- not always successfully, but always persistently. Nine of my children are from a twenty-year marriage. Their ages now range from 18 to 34 years old. My youngest child, who is now 14 years old, is from a second marriage that lasted nine years. *It is her situation that this chapter is primarily about, because we succeeded, with our therapist, in ending the abuse that was making my daughter physically ill.*

## MAIN FOCUS

This chapter focuses on what I have learned while trying to obtain help for my children in a convoluted system of government red tape. I am not a trained psychologist, nor a counselor; what I learned about this subject came from years of first-hand experience. It has not been an education that I could have learned from a book, nor is it the kind of education that I would have sought by my own volition. I will explain our situation in the following synopsis. I will then discuss a few barriers that we were able to overcome, and I will list the barriers that we needed someone professional to help us--for I was not equipped to handle everything on my own. Some barriers I never was able to overcome, partly due to our remote location, and partly due to the lack the resources needed to seek help. Sometimes the help that I did find, turned out to be a negative influence.

## MY STORY

The first 17 years of parenting were easy. Our home was joyful in Minnesota, where the first nine of my children resided with their father and me. We had a strong sense of community, because we were actively involved in it in many positive ways. We were highly respected among our peers, involved in church and community clubs, and we also had extended family support. We raised animals and a garden, we took meals to new parents, shut ins, and the ill, we produced a home-school newsletter which had subscribers all over, including Canada, New Zealand and England. We often visited residents of a local nursing home, and entertained orphaned children once a week.

So how did all of that goodness come to an end? It all began with an 1,800 mile relocation to the Southwest in 1998. The culture and social shock of the move laid the foundation for the problems and a divorce, remarriage, another baby, surgeries, loss of a home, and another divorce built the framework of the stress and drama of everyday life. Little did I know that there was more yet to come; not so much because of relocating and having "bad things" happen, but because of the men that fathered my children. And not just those men (even though they were the *source*), but also much misery came by way of the people that were enlisted to help my ex-husbands with their personal vendettas against me and our children.

It is almost unbelievable when I look back on the extent of the misery. In fact, I probably would not believe it, had it not happened to my family and me.

The beginning of the end of our struggles started with our finding a new therapist, after having gone to many others. I thank God every day for the day when she accepted our case. Was it by chance, persistence, or the Hand of God? Probably all of the above. Whatever it was that brought her to us, we will always be thankful that it finally happened after years of unsuccessful attempts at finding help. Without her involvement, we would not be where we are today. It makes me shudder to think what our future would have been like, and what we would be dealing with today.

I was trying to think of the right word for our therapist's participation in our case. The word, "ability" kept coming to mind but did not seem like a good enough word, probably because it is so commonly used. So I went to my "Visual Thesaurus" to find a better word. It turned out that "ability" is the best word to use. According to "Visual Thesaurus", 'ability' only has one other word like it, "power". Their definition of ability is:

*The quality of being able to perform; a quality that permits or facilitates achievement or accomplishment; possession of the qualities (especially mental qualities) required to do something or get something done; Adjectives: (usually followed by 'to) having the necessary means or skill or know-how or authority to do something.*

This is exactly her role in our dilemma and her role in aiding us to finally gain peace of mind.

It is unfortunate that my life turned out to be a stockpile of events leading up to needing professional help. Up until my late 30's, I had always been able to overcome obstacles, trials, disappointments, and abusive situations. The only one thing that I can attribute to the entire list of inauspicious occurrences is that I trusted people who should not be trusted, and I did it for far too many years. However, I will not accept any blame, because a perpetrator is a perpetrator and a victim is a victim. Even if a victim is enabling an abuser, they are still a victim; that is the bottom line. Over the years I have heard this from victims, counselors, and many other people in the field of psychology. Sadly, it often takes a victim of abuse years to realize their predicament. And once they find themselves caught in a web of deception and ill-treatment (once they finally identify it for what it is), it can take them years to get untangled from it, if ever; especially when children are involved.

The situation in which I found myself brought on years of trauma for my children and is rather unique in the fact that there were so many people involved and that it went on for many, many years. I attribute a lot of that to where we live. Our rural setting made room for barriers that stopped or hindered my ability to get immediate help for my children and me. A good example would be trying to seek help in a church of our faith. When there are only three churches nearby, and the abuser is involved with the leadership and members of all three, and the next church is 50 miles away, access to that kind of support is non-existent if one has a very limited budget.

Most anyone who works in the health care system would agree that ALL children should have immediate help with emotional and physical trauma. Sadly, that is not how the system generally works, and that is not how a church works. Nobody wants to get involved when it comes to abuse of a child in a home. Every effort that I made to get the needed help would take a huge amount of time and cost money that I did not have; only to end with no progress made. As I said, some of the reason for the inability to get the proper help for such a long period of time was because of where we lived. The lack of good-paying jobs, or any job at all, lack of funds, and the long distances to drive to counselors prevented me from getting the needed help. And some of the reason that it took so long to find the right help was because of the incompetent and unprofessional people that I trusted to help us. It also takes time and money to find this out one by one, filtering through multiple counselors in counseling centers. Although many of the barriers that we faced were associated with living in a rural community, some of them can be found in any community, because whenever we are involved with people, we are susceptible to dealing with their shortcomings. These shortcomings can cause a lot of obstacles which can turn into barriers for the one seeking help. The poor in rural areas find that limitations are almost too many to overcome. So when we find ourselves involved with incompetent professionals who cause more damage than do good, we fear that the chances of finding the proper help is narrowed even more, and may be impossible. This can lead to many years of living in a terrible situation, or giving up altogether.

Another main problem that I faced with living in a rural area was the inability to stop "visitation abuse" for my youngest child. The remote location actually aided her father and those who supported his opprobrious behavior towards me, and our daughter. Further along in this chapter I will go into that in more detail.

There is an upside and a downside to rural living. First, I will discuss the positive aspects of rural living.

I cannot say that rural life was completely bad for us, because rural life was, and is, good in many ways. It gave the children a place to play and be loud, with less onlookers and complaining neighbors. It allowed for late-night bonfires and roasting marshmallows, planting things that grew to become large, established trees and vines (a sign that we kept busy with the goodness of life). It opened up to them a world of animal stewardship which brought them much joy and rewards by raising rabbits, cats, dogs, cavies, pigeons and many other pets. They also had two horses (both, given to us). And in time, they obtained go-karts to race on our acreage and a trampoline to jump upon. We played ball, hit golf balls and threw Frisbees in the yard. We also had a swimming pool and a tent that gave them many years of fun and laughter.

There is a negative aspect of rural living, especially when a child is being traumatized and help must be found. One of the downside factors to rural living is the lack of a "sense of community", especially when the small community that we had was turned against us. And, as mentioned before, it made for difficulties, such as limited access to the help that we needed when dealing with abusive relationships in which we found ourselves. Other factors were the lack of ability to find a good-paying job, and when I did find one, time issues arose. While I was working 50 miles away from home, scheduling problems with work and school were consistent. And when I wasn't working, the lack of funds for gasoline caused issues (it can take many trips to find a good counselor).

I have parented in city and rural settings, using charter and public schools, and I homeschooled some of the children, on and off, for 25 years. I have brought up ten children, over three decades of social and personal changes, including two divorces. I have parented my children through times of plenty, and in times where there was not enough for everyone. We did live in poverty for a number of years. There were years when I had to stand in food lines in 100 degree weather, just to get a few meals for a few days following. Brown vegetables and stale bread were not uncommon and a commodity chicken for a holiday was a thankful addition to the table. In 2001, when the poverty began, I turned to every charity and state department that I could think of. It was not until 2005 that we were able to get consistent state aid, and no charity helped us.

How could a mother of (by then) seven minor children, be refused state aid after filling out several applications over several years? What was the barrier? The barrier turned out to be a supervisor in the local DES office who was friends with my second husband's ex-wife (that was what I learned after it was over). She was throwing our applications away and refusing to communicate with me. When I would insist on an answer as to why we were being denied aid, I was told to reapply. This was all before online applications. This was when applying for state aid meant that I had to gather up every birth certificate, bank statement, utility bill, social security card, and statements from neighbors, and almost everyone living under my roof. I had to fill out eight pages of information about my family and me, which would take up to five hours, drop it off at the local office, and then call an 800 number and sit on hold for two hours for a 30 minute interview.

It wasn't until one of my daughters was caught shoplifting in Tucson that I became friends with the officer involved. I told him our situation, and he encouraged the store not to prosecute my daughter. Then he kindly suggested that I contact the Phoenix DES office and tell them my situation and how many times I had applied for state aid. I did, and in less than a month that supervisor was no longer at the local office and we finally had some relief.

It was not easy for me to accept that kind of help because the father of the nine children, the one who convinced me to leave Minnesota and then divorced me on our 20th anniversary, two years after the move, was making over $90,000 a year and refused to help financially. He had tricked me into signing a divorce decree that left us nearly homeless, but neighbors and the children told me that he sat in church on Sunday asking for "prayers for" his finances. Because of his actions, or lack of action, we did become homeless in 2003, and that was yet another barrier that I had to overcome. I will not go into how I handled that here.

Because I have spent many years in an oppressive, and lonely environment of a rural location, I am quite outspoken about the trauma and barriers that were involved. This is because rural locations work out quite well for those who seek to abuse their family. This explains why my first husband made promises to get us to move so far away from our community and family support in Minnesota, (with no intention to keep those promises) because we had no one to turn to here; we were isolated. It also explains why my second husband and his family lived behind a locked gate on his family's ranch before we were forced to move his house off of the ranch property. I soon found out the extent of abuse that went on behind that gate before my children and I ever arrived.

Does this mean that country life, privacy, and locked gates are bad? No, it just means that they are yet another tool that abusive people use. Obviously, they do not "need" those tools because there is plenty of abuse that goes on in apartments in city settings.

It is common knowledge that isolation is a favorite tool for those who wish to abuse their family and it can be achieved anywhere. I also learned that abusive people tend to build up their own social circle of support, without the knowledge of the immediate family. I learned this the hard way because it happened to me. The way that my ex-husbands used our small community to build a support circle for themselves was so that when I realized that I needed help, there was no place for me to turn that was not hostile or suspicious of me. In a case like this, a victim will have a very difficult time finding support, and an even more difficult time convincing the abuser's supporters that abuse is happening to them.

I learned through trial and error that it is only when the victims of the abuse are able to separate themselves from the damaging relationship(s) and from everyone, and everything, connected and associated with the negativity in their lives, that they can finally begin to build a life apart from that awful, lonely, and oppressive world. Then they can begin to heal. One cannot heal emotionally in the midst of aggression and violence. We might be able to endure, but we cannot heal. If the victim does not move away from the source, (mentally, socially, and usually physically, through ending a relationship, or many relationships or physically relocating, which is very hard to do on limited funds) it can overcome them and they can lose hope of ever living a life of peace and progress. I was almost at the place of losing hope when we finally found our therapist.

We were lucky because I was able to stay put in our home, and eventually turn a hostile rural setting into a favorable place to live. This took many years and much effort, but it is now a kind of 'sanctuary'; a place where friends and family want to travel to, so that they can rest, relax, visit, and spend time away from the hustle of a busy city. It wasn't easy for me to do, but it was accomplished with the help of people who were willing and able to get involved and help me make it happen. Our therapist, a friend of the family, and a few supporters in the community who stopped gossip about our situation when they would hear it, helped to change our situation.

This is my story. This is how I, and the others who helped us, were able to break down the barriers and turn our life in a rural setting into a sanctuary of peace and progress. This place where we reside, is now a quiet, controlled setting. And although the memories of the past trauma still lingers, healing is active and ongoing. The bad memories are fading and many good ones are replacing them.

My daughter's and my experience to overcome the, "Childhood Trauma and Barriers in a Rural Setting", happened to us in a small town outside of a large city. She is my youngest child, eight years old at the time, when I separated from her father in 2009. In the beginning, at the time of our separation, I encouraged her visits with him. I did not see any signs of abuse toward her, during the marriage. It was important to me that she continue her close relationship to her daddy. I did not realize that he would turn his aggression toward me onto her. Up until the time after the divorce in 2010, I had not been aware of him ever abusing her. I had only witnessed a strong love-bond between them. Since then, I have found just how common this kind of abuse is through other parents who have gone through the same horrific occurrences following divorce.

Once I realized that abuse was taking place during his parenting time, the struggle to free our daughter from it began for me. Sadly, for two more years, I was to face horrific obstacles and barriers, trying to make that happen. To an onlooker, and to the system in which we became entangled, two years may not seem like a long time. But the counselors and the Courts need to understand that two years of abuse to a child could seem like forever. To a child, one month can feel like one year. And to a parent who is trying to end abuse for their child, one minute can feel like an eternity.

The father's abuse toward me and our daughter, continued for several years after the divorce. He enlisted many helpers in his effort to make our lives difficult, including his girlfriend at the time, some people who worked in the school administration, friends of our family, a half-sister (who we barely knew but hoped to become close to), several private businesses, a Superior Court Judge (who was eventually taken off of the case), a private counselor who was appointed by that judge, a second Superior Court Judge who did not want to believe that the father was using his parenting time in such a harmful way, neighbors and private business owners in our neighborhood, and a local town. Had we lived in a larger city, would it have been easier to deal with? I believe in some ways, maybe, because we might have been able to expand our circle of influence. As it was, in the setting that we were in, it seemed like the whole world was against us.

Although it is not common to stop a parent's access to a child, I believe that in certain cases like ours, it is necessary. The abuse from my daughter's father finally came to an end through my persistent, and vigorous efforts, the help of a family friend, and the professional approach of our therapist who is now a Doctor of Psychology; and proudly, with the help of my daughter herself. My daughter told the truth and did not play any games.

Freedom from the direct abuse by her father was solidified by the Ruling of a Superior Court in 2012 when it was ordered that the court-ordered visitations with him would no longer be expected. She would no longer be forced to spend time with him alone. This order came after our therapist submitted a letter to the court, stating what my child's wishes were. Such a simple act! But one that is almost impossible to achieve alone, within the system of Family Law.

Without her help, I doubt that the madness ever would have ended and I am positive that if there were no therapists like her in the world, there would be no hope for anyone in a situation such as ours.

This is because as in many cases just like ours, the shameful, antagonizing, and abusive actions are fueled to continue on, by way of the system, the courts, and the community. Those who "sided" with the abusive father, via the court, the school, through local businesses, and through friends of our families, were allowed to continue to sabotage our social standing and rob us of peace within the community and in our home. The only one that I was able to stop quickly was the half-sister by using an "Order of Protection".

These very real barriers are difficult to break through. But, the breakthrough did happen!

While dealing with all of the above, the other father of the other nine children also continued his abuse long past the divorce and on into the children's adult lives, but I was never able to get the needed help for that (not for lack of trying, I can assure you). Perhaps it was because much of it had to do with living in a rural setting. The isolation from large numbers of people, accessibility to support groups, and inability to obtain the funds needed for the many miles of travel that was involved in seeking counsel and court filings and hearings prohibited getting the needed help. Also, at the time of our divorce in 2000 and until 2006, the only vehicle that I had to transport the number of children that I had from our rural setting to the needed help, was a fifteen-passenger one-ton van to take the kids to appointments. I did try using the 800 abuse hot-line numbers to seek help and advice, but usually the person on the other end did not have experience with the enormity of my situation. But instead of taking the responsibility completely upon myself, perhaps all that it would have taken is for a willing therapist to become involved.

When I was new to all of this, I was appalled to find that when a counselor or a counseling service cannot interpret the truths at hand, quite often they will turn the blame onto the victim or victims. This is also true for the courts and the GAL (a Guardian ad Litem, who the court sometimes appoints to represent the best interests of a child or children in a divorce or parental rights case). After all, why was I in the situation in the first place? I was actually asked that several times by people and professionals who could have helped me stop the abusers! This can be a very dangerous assertion toward one who is trying to help a child escape from an abusive relationship or situation, and who is usually a victim of the same abuse themselves. Had I not been as stable as I was throughout these years, that kind of accusation (or even the hint of an implication of guilt) could have had extreme, detrimental, and possibly permanent consequences for me and my children. I have seen it happen to others.

How did I manage? Sometimes I ask myself that question. But if I make a list of reasons that I did not give up or collapse, I come up with a list that I give to others. Here are some managing tools that I used to cope:

- Joining online victim's network who would listen and advise.
- Online friends who had the similar family and social issues:
    - cafemom.com was the best.
    - lovefraud.com was another.
- Growing plants, flowers and vegetables with the children.
- Taking outings with the children: hiking, picnics etc.
- A pet or several pets to care for with the children.
- Keeping a journal of positive occurrences (not just the negative).
- Reading books about people who survived abuse.
- Sharing with strangers that I would meet while traveling.
- Finding humor in most situations and using that humor to make people laugh.

At 53 years old, as I look back on my life-experiences to include my own childhood trauma, I have found that childhood trauma is much more common than most people want to admit. I call it, "typical and natural trauma". The kind of upsets and challenges that happen out of our control and are a part of life and living. When we refuse to admit that this trauma exists, we form an unrealistic view of what childhood should be, rather than what childhood really is. This can lead to heavy disappointment, resulting in inability to overcome, achieve, and succeed as an adult.

I have also found that it is almost impossible to prevent negative occurrences in childhood, even by the most attentive and loving parents. And when we find that we have produced children with a partner who insists on disturbing a life that would otherwise have been manageable, we find ourselves dealing with much more than just typical, natural, childhood trauma. We eventually have to stand up to, and fight against, the abuse.

Over the 34 years that I have been a parent, sadly, I have seen more abuse, neglect, and antagonizing of children than can be imagined. Life is hard enough. Why do these people get away with years and years of abuse towards those who depend upon them? Until the system improves, and the time that it takes to help victims is decreased, and until counselors and courts learn to do it the first time and do it right, that question will always be number one in my mind, and in the mind of other victims whom I have conversed with about that subject. I have met many survivors of abuse on this journey. Thankfully, I have been able to use what I learned to help others and to help those in the system. I have sometimes been able to help young adults who found themselves with no parent or guardian to advise them.

When barriers arise between a traumatized child and a parent, the non-abusive parent usually attempts to seek help outside of the family. All too often they fail. The effort to find help can be difficult enough in any setting. But in a rural area, and when funds are limited as they usually are, things such as gasoline or a vehicle to put it in is too expensive, so the number of trips to find the needed help is unobtainable. Also, if the parent works full time, it is usually a 50-hour week or more when the driving time is factored into a week. Many jobs do not allow for a parent to take time off for running around finding a counselor. And securing a future apart from abuse will almost always have to involve the Court. This means more expense and missing work. And many times, the Court has trouble "seeing" the truth of a situation, which makes for on-going hearings. I think that I had to attend 12 hearings, 100 miles round trip from our home, before it finally ended. That was not counting the trips to an attorney's office, and then when I began representing myself, the additional trips to the Courthouse to file the necessary paperwork. All of this running around puts a humongous financial and time-burden on the parent fighting for freedom from abuse.

If the parent does not have the stamina that it takes to break down and overcome all of the barriers stacked up in front of them, many times they will give up, turn to substance abuse or worse. This is why it is so important for the counselor to understand how important it is to quickly identify the source of the issues and act appropriately and diligently without delay.

When I was a young mother, I was convinced that if a parent would just set up a good environment, good would come from that. It was so simple! Unfortunately, for all too many parents including myself, numerous difficult and unforeseen occurrences intrude on everyday life. Over time, these obstacles cause changes in the family unit and become a part of everyday living. All too often, they become a foundation for barriers to build upon and these barriers between the parent and child, or between siblings, strengthen over time. Events such as a divorce, a big move, loss of a pet or a loved-one, an illness or accident, psychological and physical abuse (from trusted family members or society) which could include neglect and bullying from a long list of sources can be traumatic to children and contribute to barriers.

Any kind of rejection-- or perceived rejection--is one of the most difficult things a child faces. Thus, a barrier is built between that child and the rejecting person or the feeling of rejection. Sometimes we have to find out what it is, and then help them know when it is imagined and when it is real.

When it is real and not imagined, the parent must involve themselves with the situation. Sometimes it is a matter of removing whatever or whomever is provoking them. This is not always possible, but when it is, it must be done no matter how inconvenient for the parent. That may mean a move, changing of schools, finding new friends, trying a different social activity, changing churches, or divorcing.

I have found that some of my children, and children that I have helped with, have been resilient and some have not. What makes a child resilient? We may never know for sure, but one thing that I did find out, is that resiliency can come natural, which is easiest for the parent, or be taught (but not always). When it comes natural, resiliency can be seen from the toddler years. If it is nurtured continuously, that child usually does not lose the natural ability to overcome difficulties. However, as in a few of my children, when there is harsh, direct abuse, or sneaky, psychological abuse, over a long period of time, they sometimes would develop a habit of negative thinking and that leads to negative actions. If the child did not have anyone to nurture their resiliency, sometimes they did not recover, and any resiliency was not obvious again. Sometimes children and adults will turn to chemical forms of relief, when they feel that there is no hope in an abusive situation. Sometimes when they do not understand that it is an abusive situation that they are in, their actions may resemble the actions of their abuser. They cannot overcome any of their troubles until they understand that they are a victim and not a perpetrator. In a rural setting, it is easy to become isolated. Obtaining the resources to overcome the abuse is sometimes impossible because of the limited accessibility to find the help needed.

The barriers between the traumatized and the professional are usually more manageable and easier to overcome because of the authority that comes with the professional's title. The fact is, parents and children have little to no authority when it comes to the system. A therapist who is able to recognize that, has the power to take the proper steps and actions to achieve positive and healing results for the victims.

So let's take a look at a list of the typical barriers facing traumatized children in a rural setting:

- **Accessibility:** It is important for Mental Health Care Professionals to be available and for rural residents to have access to their services.
- **Finding Unbiased Support:** It can be nearly impossible to find support when ex-spouses lie and manipulate people within the schools, churches, and neighborhoods so that the traumatized people have nowhere to turn for unbiased support.

- **Finances:** I was on a very limited budget, so driving 90 miles round-trip to Tucson and/or Sierra Vista, was nearly impossible.
- **Privacy:** When it was possible to find the funds for gas, I found yet another barrier blocking my path anyway. All it took was one phone call or one meeting (from the father) with the Counselor or Psychologist, and suddenly my efforts to get the proper help became convoluted.
- **Time:** Most parents work at least 40 hours a week, and providers are not generally available on weekends, so it is not affordable or possible to travel 90 miles round trip, going from provider to provider and looking for proper help for a child. The intake can take weeks, the first few sessions can take months, and by that time, if the counselor, therapist, or psychologist is not on track, the parent seeking help has to start the process all over again with a new provider.

*A year or more can go by*, before the child gets a chance for proper counseling. For a child to have to meet new and multiple providers and explain their traumatic experiences all over again adds to their anxiety.

As I stated before, from 2009 until we met our final therapist in 2010, my youngest daughter was suffering abuse by her father during visitations. Even though she missed 30 days of school a year due to bloody noses, diarrhea, headaches, and immune deficiencies, I had no way to prove to the court that her father's abuse was the direct source of her poor physical condition. It was he who was instigating and enlisting others to aid him with his agenda to punish us, which led to even larger barriers between her and any hope for healing.

Recently, I took her to her doctor for something unrelated. He was looking at her chart and asked if her stomach issues and headaches were ever resolved. We both answered, "Yes!" and we explained to him that all of her physical ailments that he was seeing on her history had stopped when her father was put out of her life by his own actions, just three years ago. It is a harsh reality of life: There is no life when living with an abuser, especially for a defenseless child. (More about the benefit of her physical improvement, at the end of this chapter).

So, let me sum up the Barriers in a Rural Setting:

- **Perpetrators:** The school counselor (as well as some teachers, staff, and the principal) was friends with her father, and would add to her stress during school hours by admonishing her for not wanting to see her father.
- **Limitations of Practitioners:** Our family practitioner could only assume that her physical problems were stress-related. He could not make a psychological determination. All that he could offer us, were prescription medications and notes for school absences.
- **The Half-Sister:** Whenever we went to a local store where that sister worked, or if she happened to be at any local business when we were there, she would try to get my daughter alone, and then admonish and scold her for not wanting to see her father. This would confuse my nine-year-old daughter, because she wanted to see her father. She just did not want to be with him if he was going to abuse her. This was confusing to me because that half-sister, when she was 12 years old, helped her mother get a court order keeping her father away from her until she was 18. Why did she expect her little half-sister to do anything different?

- **The Judge:** The "Court" believed that I was a negative influence on the father/daughter relationship. I guess that I was, because it was not a "relationship" but rather an abusive playground for the father. I tried to explain to the "court" that her health was deteriorating, her vision was blurring, and her attendance and grades at school were plummeting. I tried to explain that when she would come home from "visiting" her father, it took several days for the diarrhea to go away, and for her cheerful spirit to return. I tried to convince the "court" that, if she loved to visit her father, if she flourished in his presence, that I would gladly encourage him to have her more time with her, than me, and that I would gladly pay him child support. I was shocked to be reprimanded by the "court" for, "Being the kind of mother that would cast off their child in that way."

A private counselor, who was a friend of the judge, was appointed to our daughter by the judge. I could not afford the $1,000 per session fees but that did not matter to the "court". The counselor immediately befriended her father and then began to manipulate our daughter. He tried to manipulate the 'friend of the family', me, and the case; going so far as to take our daughter off of our property for a private "session". He also obtained sealed documents (probably given to him by the father) from my first divorce and then writing a long report against me, and getting my first name wrong, calling me "Lisa", over 200 times in his report. This kind of "counselor" can cause all kinds of damage.

- **The System:** After several sessions with the court-appointed counselor, we ended the association with him and reported him to his Board. A family friend who had been helping with the case and I even attended a hearing in Phoenix to discipline the counselor, but nothing came of it.
- **The Second Judge:** Eventually, we were given a new judge.

I finally got the counselor ordered off of the case, and was able to obtain an order allowing me to seek out a new counselor on my own. It was up to me to find someone who could break down the barriers and end the horrible cycle that my daughter and I were caught in. I knew that if I could obtain a Superior Court Order, that the forced visitations would end between father and daughter and healing could begin. My daughter would be free to be herself. It was enough that her life had changed, that she had lost her family unit, and it was absolutely ridiculous that all of the trauma following the divorce was even happening to her. I knew without a doubt that if this cycle did not end soon, the long-term damage done to her might be permanent, and follow her into her adult years.

## Breaking the Barriers

Our therapist became involved through a local, small, Behavioral Health Center (SEABHS) as was recommended by our family practitioner (once I obtained the Order to seek our own counselor). The minute we met her, we knew by her presence that we were finally going to get the needed help.

The therapist did a full intake first with my child, and then with me. Within days, someone at SEABHS was leaking information to my daughter's father about her visits with our therapist. I know this because he had no other way of knowing who was the new counselor, I had 30 days to report it to him and was not going to until day 30. As soon as he found it out, he went to the counseling center with an envelope to try and get the therapist to read the inaccurate and unprofessional "report" against me by the first court-appointed counselor (the report that had my first name wrong over 200 times). She refused. Her approach was, child first, and everyone else after that, and first things first.

True to her professionalism, our therapist blocked a barrier that was meant to prevent progress for our daughter. She ignored the father's attempts to manipulate our case while she took an immediate and professional position as my daughter's Personal Therapist. We now knew that we could trust her. The father was not the one seeking help, and his input was not going to be taken into account unless there was reason other than his demanding it.

### Breaking a Barrier

Once the father realized that he was not going to be able to influence our therapist in a negative way, he went away and stayed away from the counseling center. Even though we tried to set up supervised visitation with him and our daughter, he would not show for that. He will never be accountable to any counselor for himself or for the means to see his daughter.

Since that very first day that my daughter had a session with our latest therapist, she showed remarkable improvement. It all began with trust. Once trust was established, there was a firm foundation for hope.

## The Proof that Ending Abuse Has Positive Results

The troubled little girl who had so many health issues and who was getting D's and F's on her report cards and who had missed 90 days of school out of three years, is now not only an amazing teenager, but is also an 'A' student and has broken the record at her middle school for three years of perfect attendance. She is presently working on a fourth year of perfect attendance. She says that she is very thankful for finally getting the help that we needed. And even though it is painful for her to be missing a loving, nurturing father-daughter relationship, she is able to manage a life free from the stress and hopelessness of abuse.

Our therapist's ability to handle our case was obvious right away. Her professional ability to listen to our daughter first, and then to me and to our family friend was crucial to solving the issues that we faced. She gave my daughter creative ways to work out her emotions and she listened. What was most important, was that she did not allow the father to interfere with the process. Our daughter felt safe with her. Finally, her honest communication to the Court broke down yet another barrier; my inability to present and express the truth of what was happening, and the truth of what the solution was.

For my daughter, healing began immediately with the knowing that she finally had someone in her life who had the power to help eliminate the stress. She finally had someone outside of the family who understood what the source was and did not blame her for it, or seek ways to blame her mother for it, but speedily addressed a solution. It was significant that our therapist did not expect her to, "get along with", or find a way to deal with her father's abuse, which is all too commonly forced upon victims of abuse. There is no "getting along" with an abuser.

At the time when we met our therapist, we both had become very fragile. We were at the breaking point. That point where a victim of abuse reaches after trying every option available. This is common for most victims of abuse, and most are already at a breaking point before they even try to find help. For us, our therapist was our last chance, because I had exhausted every other resource that I could think of.

I was relieved to find that her professional abilities far surpassed the efforts of anyone that I had ever met in the field of, Mental Health Care. I only wish that I had had her for the other children, and my case with their father. Perhaps she could have set that GAL on the right path, perhaps she could have helped the kids to identify what kind of abuse they were dealing with, and how to handle it. The problem that arises when a family member is abusive is the victims of their abuse tend to try to win them in any way possible. This leads to years and years of a vicious cycle that has no ending. The only way to stop it is to end the relationship. But everyone knows, when that kind of advice comes from the "other" parent, it is not taken seriously or it is taken with hostility. And as I stated before, most counselors only focus on "coping" with an abuser, and they do not seek a permanent solution to end it. Maybe our therapist could have helped prevent the stress that is still going on with my other children, because now that they are adults, they are carrying the damage on with them as they continue to try to have a relationship with their father, who only sees them as a means to work out his detrimental manipulations. I know this because they have come to me with their complaints and asked me for solutions.

In conclusion, I would like to state that even though a rural setting can pose challenges that are different and sometimes more difficult than other settings, and even though a rural setting has its own, unique barriers concerning childhood trauma, it only takes one professional like we finally found, to break down the barriers.

If our therapist broke down the barriers in a complicated situation like ours, many other therapists could do the same. She helped us break barriers in the system and addressed and resolved many barriers in my child's life and in my life. This had a chain-reaction because once the abuse ended, once the door of access to the victim was shut, the community supporters for the abuser began to go away. Today, are nearly all gone and my daughter and I are finding many, many positive people who support her at school, and in friendship. We are finally building a "sense of community", which is something that had been barred from us for a very long time. Right now as I write this, there is a 7th Warrant out for her father's arrest, for nothing more than refusing to communicate with the Court. Time always reveals the truth, and the truth is, she is at her peak right now, without his influence on her life.

Every year on our daughter's birthday, a friend and I offer to pay for a dinner with her dad (with me and my friend sitting outside, not far from the restaurant), but every year, she says, "No. I'm good. I really don't want to start that problem up again. Not now. I'm doing too good." She thinks, that when she is older, and she can drive away, she might visit with her dad, but she also knows that once he is back into her life, she will be opening a door that she may not want opened again. It is unfortunate that sometimes children have to sever relationships with a parent, in order to be free from abuse, but counselors and the courts must understand the importance of doing so, when necessary. It is not the child's responsibility to manage an abusive parent.

Our therapist not only became a positive force in our case, but she helped turn my daughter's and my life around, so that healing was able to get a foothold. I don't think that anyone can ever fully recover from harsh trauma and it may take a lifetime to heal from all that we have been through, because one can rarely forget; but at least now, there is a chance of total healing.

There is hope. The world surely needs more like her, in the field of counseling.

I would like to thank and congratulate our therapist, Jacqueline Ford for her ability to listen and help us, and also on her recent accomplishment of becoming, Dr. Ford.

She will definitely make a huge, positive impact on the world.

# Chapter 14
# The Contagion of Trauma: Exploring Attachment through the Book Love Lessons

**James Dumesnil**
*Independent Researcher, USA*


## ABSTRACT

*Research has been increasingly clear regarding the critical importance of the first years of life, especially the first three years, on personality development and the ability to adapt and adjust throughout life. Children with histories of traumas such as abuse, neglect, drug exposure, inconsistent caregiving, or violence during these critical early years can have profound disruptions in their development, including severe behavioral and emotional problems. The parents who adopt a child with a history of trauma are vulnerable to developing their own vicarious, or secondary trauma. This chapter explores this contagion of trauma within adoptive families, following the story of one such affected family. Treatment has focused on the needs of the traumatized child individually and through behaviorally-based parenting interventions. The individual clinical needs of the attachment figures, the parents, have not received the attention they deserve. These needs are as critical as addressing the child's trauma in order to allow for creation of a secure attachment with the child.*


A family's journey.
A child's pain.
A mother's heart broken.
A child who thinks she is protecting herself.

In this chapter, we will explore one family's journey of understanding the effect of trauma on their adopted child[1]. Families who adopt children through domestic or foreign agencies may be ill prepared for the harm and the scars that earlier life trauma and deprivation have left on their child. They may even be more ill prepared for the scars that the child's earlier trauma and deprivation will leave on them, their family and their children. Families may not know or understand what trauma their child has already

DOI: 10.4018/978-1-5225-0228-9.ch014

suffered, and how the effects of this trauma will continue to manifest in their lives and in their homes. Instead of being able to restore their child to safety, the adoptive family can end up suffering with Post Traumatic Stress Disorder similar or secondary to their child's complex PTSD diagnosis.

The consequences of institutionalized care and maternal deprivation early in life have been extensively documented (Bowlby, 1988, 1990; Fonagy et. al. 1991; Main & Hesse, 1990). Institutionalized children are behind on all physical as well as emotional indicators (Juffer et al., 2011; van der Dries et al., 2009; Merz & McCall, 2010; Zeanah & Gleason, 2014). They are below levels of non-institutionalized children in their physical growth, cognition, and general behavioral development (Zeanah et al., 2011). Their attachment and social-emotional development are mostly disorganized and delayed (Bakermans-Kranenburg et. al., 2012). Almost 3/4 of institutionalized children display insecure disorganized attachment behavior: (Main & Hesse, 1990). This is consistent with the neglectful environments and the lack of sensitive, responsive, consistent caregiving that most of these children experience (Bakermans-Kranenburg et al., 2012).

Palacios and Brodzinsky (2010) have documented a substantial and rapid "catch-up" in development for post-institutionalized children adopted by typically advantaged families. However, catch-up is not always complete. Social, cognitive and behavioral developments and especially attachment continue to lag behind (Van den Dries, Juffer, van IJzendoorn, & Bakermans-Kranenburg, 2009).

Even after spending years in an advantaged adoptive family, adopted children continue to have severe behavioral and emotional problems, especially with adjustment and attachment issues. Problems are much more severe for children adopted after the age of one year old (Bakermans-Kranenburg, 2009; Palacios & Brodzinsky, 2010). Certainly the outcomes for adopted children in typically advantaged families are better than for those, who remain in orphanages and in foster care. However, adopted children do not completely "catch up" with parent-reared peers. Some would have us believe that many of these issues will work themselves out, as the child becomes an adult. Unfortunately, studies indicate these problems do not simply represent an extremely troublesome adolescent period but persist in one form or another into adulthood (Van der Vegt et al., 2009; Bakermans-Kranenburg et. al., 2012). In adulthood, adoptees, especially males, were found to have more psychiatric disorders than nonadopted individuals. Furthermore, the experience of multiple early adversities significantly increased the chances of poorer adjustment outcomes and health outcomes (Palacios & Brodzinsky, 2010; Felitti et al., 1998).

A frequently cited study from the annual Untied States Department of Health and Human Services Adoption and Foster Care Analysis and Reporting System (AFCARS, 2006) reported that children in foster care and adoption have more PTSD and mood disorders than our soldiers returning from war. "A recent study by Harvard University and the Casey Family Programs reported that over half of the children in foster care leave with an anxiety disorder. They have twice the rate of traumatic stress (PTSD) as compared to Vietnam veterans" (AFCARS, 2006; Gray, 2007).

The preponderance of the research is clear. Children with early deprivation have profound attachment issues. While they may "catch up" with physical parameters (Palacios & Brodzinsky, 2010) neurological and cognitive issues and attachment issues can persist into adulthood (Zeanah et al., 2011). Adoptive families aspire to mediate and modify these effects of trauma. Unfortunately, the trauma may be too much for many parents. Purvis (2008) and Lieberman (2008) are two who speak to parents being "overmatched" by the child's history and pathology.

Families adopting "a child from a hard place" (Purvis et al., 2008), a child with Developmental Trauma Disorder due to repeated exposure to sanctuary trauma (van der Kolk & D'Andrea, 2010), a child with a history of repeated Adverse Childhood Experiences (Felitti et al., 1997; Szalavitz & Perry,

2010) may not be prepared to handle the ongoing effects of the child's earlier life trauma. Parents may quickly begin to feel very overwhelmed and isolated. Oftentimes even those closest to them question their parenting strategies. Families begin to lose allies. At church and family gatherings they must manage humiliation and frustration, as they receive unsolicited advice and disapproving looks from well-intentioned friends and family. Adoptive families everywhere report they cannot get the help or support they so desperately need.

*Love Lessons,* an autobiography written by an adoptive mother, portrays a family's journey to love a wounded child. The family appears to be as ready, solid, and strong as any family could be. Jodi and Jay Bean have been happily married for 11 years. They have three healthy, thriving sons. Their support system is complete and intact and includes regular weekly worship services and gatherings with loving extended family. The parents are well educated and successful. They are able to provide emotional connection, intellectual stimulation, and all the educational and recreational opportunities growing children need. They appear ready to address any challenges that arise for family and child. What a great foundation! What a great beginning!

They go to great lengths to bring Victoria home. Victoria is nearly four years old, and has spent her life in a foreign orphanage. She needs a loving family, which the Beans are eager and prepared to provide for her. When Jodi and Jay meet Victoria, she threw her arms around them screaming "Mama and Papa," showing no "stranger anxiety" at all. Being indiscriminately affectionate is a common trait of attachment deprived and traumatized children (Bowlby, 1990; Bruce et. al., 2009; Maclean, 1998). She is ready to leave the orphanage, and the staff and children are ready for her to leave as well.

Within the first moments of meeting her it is apparent she is more interested in things than people. "The water bottle mattered most of all" (p. 33). Things were given to her to share with other children in the orphanage. It was clear she could not do that. Other children even called her mean and selfish. "Take your crackers and go to America" (p. 33) was what one boy told her when she refused to share. Orphanage staff said the same about Victoria. It would be unfair to make conclusions at that time about Victoria. She had been so deprived. She was starving, thirsty, and neglected in every way that matters. Her actions were understandable. She had suffered extensive trauma and deprivation. Therefore her behaviors actually were adaptive and made sense given her traumatic history of neglect and abuse (Fonagy, 2015).

The Beans proceeded to try to give her all they provided to their three biological children: love, care, safety, security, guidance, teaching, forgiveness, and the opportunity for second chances. Yet, without a full understanding of the effects of trauma, they were not able to reach Victoria. Victoria was not able to receive the gifts and the loving leadership offered. The "honeymoon" was very short-lived, or nonexistent. Love was rejected. The ability to trust and to receive love cannot be expected from a child with her early life experiences of rejection, neglect, abuse, and trauma. Her cautious distance and need to retain some control were adaptive in the orphanage. They no longer served her in a loving family home, but how is a three year old with a history of trauma to understand that?

*Love Lessons* is not an academic or research-based book. It is one adoptive mother's story. It recounts the oftentimes gut-wrenching journey of self-examination, self-realization, struggle, redemption, and recovery of one child and one family. While it is not research-based, it provides a real story consistent with current research in attachment theory and complex trauma of early childhood. We explore the impact and demands of such a journey on many, if not most, adoptive parents of traumatized children.

## Coming Home: What Happened?

Upon coming home, Victoria's patterns and tendencies observed in the orphanage continued and intensified. Jodi snuggled and cuddled her daily. Victoria seemed eager to hug any and every one. She "looked" attached. She wore a smile for four years. However, her behaviors were passive-aggressive. Once home, she rejected guidance from her parents. Non-compliance and non-cooperation became the norm. Teaching her was an ordeal. Asking obvious questions to which she already knew the answer was a game she played without pause. She would deliberately get answers wrong when she knew what was right.

Motivational Interviewing has taught therapists to be aware of the "righting reflex" —the automatic tendency to provide correction to a patient's thoughts and set them promptly on a better course, relying in particular on directing (Miller & Rollnick, 2012). It is not helpful in therapy. It tends to set up an oppositional pattern of conversation. What is particularly paradoxical about children like Victoria is that they seem to "set up" adults, especially parents to routinely employ the "righting reflex." If adults unwittingly, and we do, stumble into offering such automatic corrections, the children appear to believe they are in control of the adults. For example, interrupting her mom and teachers, getting them to repeat themselves by pretending that she did not hear them were all ways that she demonstrated she (believed) she was in control of every interaction. Victoria stole and lied routinely, apparently to confirm to herself that she could not trust others; paradoxical and true.

For the first three years, Jodi reports she spent all her time trying to reason with Victoria, trying to get the truth out of her, trying to give her love, trying to have teaching opportunities with her—all strategies that worked so well with her three oldest sons.

One day when Jodi went to Victoria's kindergarten class, a little boy came up to Jodi and said, "You are Victoria's mother, aren't you?" "Yes," Jodi replied. "She is the meanest girl in the class. She is evil." For three years Jodi had felt the same way (p. 94). Yet, she could hardly believe that she felt this way about any child, much less her own daughter!

Years later, Jodi was able to recognize that "Victoria's defiance was not blatant. It was tactical and subtle" (p. 41).

*Once, while visiting friends, Victoria came up to me on the couch and was being very affectionate. This was unusual at this point. When we got into the car to leave, I asked what that was all about. She replied, "I wanted them to think I was nice to you." Her attempts at affection were staged and ill-timed. She knew how to appear affectionate. She did not know how to be affectionate. (p. 66)*

On another occasion while visiting family:

*The extended family had gotten together for dinner. Victoria had been wearing glasses, and she was constantly rubbing them with spit. We finally stopped asking her to keep them clean and just left them dirty. Right before dinner started, my sister-in-law asked, "Why don't you keep Victoria's glasses clean?"*

*That was a fair enough question, but she didn't know what a source of contention the glasses had been for us over the past months. And this was just one of many where Victoria drew attention to herself over controlling behaviors at home. Instead of directing the question back onto Victoria, I reacted with disgust, "UGH!" because I didn't want to have to try to explain it and mostly because Victoria was getting the negative attention she was looking for. My sister-in-law responded, "Oh now we can't even talk about the glasses."*

*"No you can't," I defensively replied.*

*I knew it was reactionary the moment I said it, but the pressure I was under, especially at family events, and the misunderstanding that surrounded me, made me feel like I couldn't ever make them understand. (p. 151)*

And difficulties arose even with professionals in the community:

*I was getting suspecting looks from the teacher's aide that felt like she needed to provide Victoria with everything it appeared she wasn't getting at home. This was a familiar response to me, even from my own family members. I knew it was difficult to understand from the outside looking in, but the suspicion was hurtful. So as hard as it was, for me, it was the right thing to pull her out of the last few months of school. What it simply came down to was this: I couldn't compete with anyone else. I would always lose to the shallowness of attention. Victoria always chose the schoolteacher, the Sunday school teacher, the smiling stranger, primarily because they were unsuspecting. She could draw attention out of them and not have to give anything in return. My love was scary to her. My love wanted to give and take. Reciprocity was required. (p. 123)*

Instead of love, Jodi "spent far too many hours trying to get the truth out of her. It would drive me to a rage" (p. 48). Later, Jodi was able to realize that "Fighting her for control only enraged both of us, and that was her goal" (p. 47).

The struggle resulted in Jodi feeling like she had lost control of herself. By losing control of her reactions to Victoria, she reports feeling completely out of control herself. Maintaining control of one's affect and reactions can be impossible or at the very least, exhausting. "The self-control required to ignore a child that seemed to be peeing out of malice was exhausting" (p. 47).

*I spent so much time being impatient and mean to her. I never wanted to give her anything. She didn't appreciate or care about anything… I didn't know what was going on, and I hated my reactions to her. This wasn't who I was. And Victoria accepted this. She didn't like it, but I think she felt she deserved it. (p. 69)*

The mother is in anguish, while the child's first orphanage experiences with inadequate, incapable, neglectful and abusive caretakers are repeated. It may be true that such conflict and rejection is "expected" if only on an unconscious level by the child. Repetition compulsion, the compulsion to repeat earlier life trauma (Freud, 1922; Gay, 1998) has been understood and accepted in psychology for close to a century or even longer (Ellenberger, 1970). "Trauma-informed" therapy and care informs us that the child has a core belief or implicit memory (Ecker et al., 2012; van der Kolk & D'Andrea, 2010; Siegel, 1999). The core belief or Internal Working Model (IWM) formed at the beginning of the child's life is stronger, more rigid, and unchanging than the love, forgiveness, and acceptance of today's adoptive family. The IWM forged in trauma is stronger than today's truth. It is more compelling to the traumatized child. Threat demands more attention (Perry, 2006). The expectations dictated by the IWM demand more of the child's attention than the unthreatening and loving adoptive family (Porges, 2009; Szalavitz & Perry, 2010). It is attuned to the threat that almost annihilated the child's life in the beginning when life was fragile and survival dependent on care from others. The child fears and believes that annihilation is still immanent, unavoidable, even deserved. We may even imagine that for the child, the possibility of "survival and having another chance with a safe, loving and caring family," is what is unbelievable—a promise which would be a mistake to trust. Therefore the child must, not by choice and certainly not consciously, hold that the original threat—adults cannot be trusted and are not dependable; they don't love me; I don't deserve to be loved—remains true. They believe that adults will again reject and not care for them. Trauma-informed therapies guide us to recognize that this is the driving force behind the child's actions, reactions, perceptions, and interpretations of all subsequent relationships (Schladale, 2010). Thus, Victoria could not accept or trust love and comfort from Jodi or any "real" mother/attachment figure.

Problems and pain are sure to follow. Lieberman (2008) points out that the parent and child have two different agendas. Problems occur as the parent cannot see the child's agenda, and the child cannot see the parent's agenda. It is the role of the therapist to help each see the other's agenda. In this case, the agendas diverge and create a profound tension. Even after the family begins to understand the source of their difficulties, the hurt does not necessarily go away. Jodi comes to understand she cannot quickly and automatically change the way that she feels toward Victoria. The pain and dissension caused by conflicting agendas can intensify.

*By the time I realized that her need for control would never subside, by the time I realized her sincerity was all an act, by the time I realized she saved her worst self for me, ignoring her was out of the question. I demanded justice. I thought I could "make" her experience remorse for her actions. But there was nothing. No amount of punishment, no matter what kind, changed Victoria's behavior. (p. 54)*

*Victoria's brain really wouldn't allow her to make the right choice. The only choice she had was the one that left her feeling in control, which was usually the most damaging one. (p. 66)*

As Jodi Bean states, she became frightened of her own reactions, of her own anger and rage, of her own feelings of hatred toward her daughter.

*I had virtually no patience with her and found myself yelling at all the kids. For me this was so disappointing, because it meant I was out of control. I realize now it was more than a lack of control. I was suffering from Post-Traumatic Stress Disorder (PTSD) as she was systematically targeting all of my weaknesses and trauma. (p. 52)*

Trauma does not only affect the child. Parents may end up suffering from secondary, or vicarious, trauma as well. They will be diagnosed as suffering from Post-Traumatic Stress Disorder. Under the new diagnostic criteria in the DSM-V, PTSD can result from indirect exposure to an event (involving actual or threatened death, serious injury, or sexual violence) through a close family member or repeated or extreme indirect exposure to disturbing details of traumatic events. Even parents who don't have unresolved trauma or unresolved attachment issues from earlier in life can develop PTSD from the indirect, daily exposure to the trauma the child has suffered. This may come from direct threats to the parents or to other children or often from hearing of all of the threats the child has endured.

Many of the children do threaten grave bodily harm, and some later act on these threats. Parents begin to feel responsible for and trapped by the child's behavior (Foli & Thompson, 2004). They fear that the child's acting out is a reflection on their inability and inadequacy as parents (van Gulden &

Bartels-Rabb, 2002: Berthelot et al., 2015). Thus, they can feel controlled by the child's "out of control" behavior, sometimes held hostage by public tantrums (Purvis, 2008). The pattern the child appears to resort to, or stumbles into, is exploitation through dysregulation and decompensation.

Because of the experience and ongoing threat of public tantrums, as well as false allegations, parents and families can become isolated. They perceive that others will blame them for the child's struggles. Thus, they feel compelled to keep secrets about the child's behavior. They can begin to fear that if Children's Protective Services hears the allegations and the blame that the child routinely articulates and vents about the family to the school, relatives, or anyone who acts sympathetic, that they will be blamed and punished. They fear the traumatized child will hurt other children. They fear Protective Services may conclude that the parents cannot keep their other children safe, and other children will be removed from the home. They fear that getting adequate treatment may cost an enormous amount of money and create further neglect of their other children and family. In summary, they blame themselves for the chaos and crisis that has gradually become the norm in their home. Many of these fears are similar to those commonly reported by the protective parents in domestic violence relationships. Another similarity with domestic violence is how gradual and insidious the process is. Jodi states she had to compare what was going on today to what things were like in the beginning. Compared to what happened yesterday, it was not noticeable. The child almost takes on omniscient qualities, as if they have some hold on the parents and family.

*Love Lessons* helps us to see how painful, intense, dramatic, insidious, far-reaching, family threatening, and sanity-threatening this journey to heal a traumatized child can be. Most books on attachment and adoption, and there are many very good books,[2] acknowledge that the primary attachment figure/caregiver, which usually means the mother, will need to resolve their own trauma history and attachment patterns in order to be able to help a traumatized child to heal. Yet, few are able to help us appreciate how unexpected, intense, and painful this proposition is for the mother of the traumatized child. When Karyn Purvis acknowledges that it will take a brutally and fiercely honest round of psychotherapy lasting from six months to two years (Purvis, 2008), we start to get a realistic picture of what is demanded. It is brutal, as this requires confronting issues that we normally avoid and perhaps have been avoiding successfully without any previous negative impacts on our lives or the lives of our biological children. When parenting a traumatized child, however, anything less than confronting and addressing our own trauma history and attachment pattern will not suffice. For a lot of parents this is a lot to ask, often too much.

Do we realize what many parents have to do to achieve an "earned Healthy, Secure Attachment pattern?" How many professionals have been willing to undergo such painful self-analysis for two years in order to be able to keep their job? Furthermore, parents are not paid for their work.

We have a trauma-informed approach to the children's history, appropriately so given the magnitude of suffering many of these children have endured by their first or second birthday. But we also need the same trauma-informed approach to the parents who bring these children home. They will often suffer a similar or secondary PTSD. The pain of the exposure, scrutiny, and doubt they will be subjected to will only be surpassed by the pain of the child's early trauma history. Parents have to be willing to look at their own attachment patterns, the origins of their own trauma, see their own trauma cues and trauma echoes (Schladale, 2011), and begin to resolve them.

Many experts in the field of trauma state that an individual needs to have safety in their world today before they can start to try to resolve the trauma from the past (Goulding & Schwartz, 2002). Today's threats have to be managed, preferably eliminated, before a person is safe enough to resolve yesterday's threats and trauma. Many clinicians will not encourage a patient to look at unresolved past threats when they are currently under threat—for example, if they are currently in a relationship with an abusive partner. Rather, adults would be advised and supported to secure safety, remove current / future threats from others, before working on a history of unresolved trauma. This can be viewed as good, prudent, best practice guidelines. For many adoptive parents, this may not be practical. They are under threat from their adoptive child and cannot remove themselves from this context in order to resolve old hurts.

Three of the hallmarks of domestic violence victimization are isolation from others, including from those that may provide support; attempts to deny and hide the violence, often for fear of separation from children; and the feeling that the abuser is omniscient or all-powerful, making reaching out for help a seemingly, and often legitimately, dangerous and impossible task. While there are many differences between domestic violence and parenting traumatized children in relation to oppression, power, and control, a similar effect can be seen in parents and siblings of traumatized children: They feel trapped; they socially isolate themselves to hide the dysfunction in their home; they fear that disclosing the problems, often including violence, and reaching out for help will put them and their families at greater risk, including risk of separation. In this way, the traumatized child can start to feel omniscient to the family. While there are many differences, it is helpful to recognize similar patterns.

When there is unresolved trauma in the history of the primary caregiver, when past trauma has led to feelings of rage, isolation, or insecurity, then we can see how this history and the child's trauma can truly conspire to create overwhelming experiences of powerlessness, helplessness, hopelessness, and even flashbacks, regressions, and abreactions on the part of the caregiver (Main, 1970). Dysregulated and disorganized reactions are sure to follow.

*Love Lessons* helps us to see what that journey really looks like and how painfully unavoidable it can be. The self-hatred, self-criticism, and self-doubt can be much greater than what parents feel from others. As Jodi said, several months after she took Victoria into her home, "I wasn't just a bad mother, I was a bad person" (p. 58).

*My fear of what was happening to me, and my hurt, were nearly as big as hers. I went from intense and purposeful love to intense and purposeful hate. (p. 61)*

*I needed answers to my reactions and tools… (p. 63)*

## Changing Course

Understanding and treating what has been variously known as Complex Post-Traumatic Stress Disorder of Early Childhood, Reactive Attachment Disorder, Developmental Trauma Disorder, have had a short and at times controversial history in mental health treatment. Reactive Attachment Disorder first appeared in the DSM-III in 1980 (Zeanah & Gleason, 2014). Research has focused on attachment as a relationship between two people, particularly on the psychological adjustment of the caregiver. On the other hand the treatment community and the parent support networks have tended to place the onus of change on the traumatized child. It is a false dichotomy. Each influences the other, for better or worse, creating protective factors or vulnerabilities in the child to later forming psychiatric disorders, character disorders, and anti-social behavior (Schore, 1994).

As the book is structured, so went the healing process. The Bean family did find a therapist that understood adoption and attachment issues. When they began it was not easy. The therapist explained Victoria's needs for safety and for attachment, including affection, healthy touch, and even snuggle time. Jodi thought:

*This was a problem. Any trust we formed early in her arrival had been destroyed by our ignorance, inconsistency, and impatience. Max (the therapist) really didn't have anything to work with. Not only was the child damaged, the mom was depleted and the dad just trying to make sense of what this girl was doing to his wife. ... I had given so much to Victoria in those first few years that I began to shut down. The abuse of my trust, my love and the guilt ... there are not words to describe the burden I felt, to know how I should feel toward my daughter, when I couldn't. And it is this that is so painful: even after I learned the motivations behind her behaviors, my heart continued to lag behind. (p. 95)*

Once therapy began for Victoria, changing the parenting strategies and interventions became an immediate priority. Jodi and Jay needed to begin to "respond and not to react." They had to implement their own form of therapeutic parenting (Thomas, 1997). We can think of therapeutic parenting for traumatized children as what Karyn Purvis (2008) called "The Investment Model of Parenting."

*There will be times when you leave a full cart of groceries in the grocery store... The child needs to learn that he or she does not have you over a barrel and can't control you with public tantrums... If you are out in public, you have to be prepared to drop whatever you're doing immediately and tend to defiance or behavioral retraining needs... It's high-investment, high-yield parenting. If you fail to pay now, you'll pay later, and the interest is steep. (Purvis et al., 2008, p. 132)*

The structural changes do place great demands on the parents. They are not able to react as one would normally or naturally react. Jodi realized,

*Now I don't even confront her about many of her provocative behaviors... for example, "Victoria, when you steal food and leave the wrappers in the same 'secret hiding place' every time, it just shows me you are not ready to trust yet and receive privileges... I learned that peeing everywhere was another behavior I had to approach with indifference. (p. 85)*

The parents learned to exert a great deal more control over Victoria's environment, including her interactions with others, as well as her interactions with Jodi and Jay and the family. They stopped her access to others she could manipulate, control, and lie to. Most critically, Jodi and Jay stopped her ability to manipulate and control their moods and reactions. They learned to develop mastery over their own reactions. Thus, Victoria's IWM that others, especially parents and family, would reject her, as her first family did, which she (thought she) could prove by getting parents and families to reject her, was starting to be disproved.

New strategies began to prevail. Old ways of reacting disappeared. It was not easy. Learning to ignore, "peeing out of malice" everywhere but the toilet bowl, is extremely exhausting for parents. Learning to respond and not react is a lot to ask of parents. Jodi understood that "Victoria needed to know that I accepted her the way she was and that I could handle whatever she did. If she didn't experience this in me, she could never trust me" (p. 84).

Parents have to be able to ignore and manage provocative behaviors. They have to learn to control emotions so that they can match the intensity of the child, but in a benevolent way (Lieberman & Van Horn, 2008; Purvis, 2007).

*To build trust my mind worked as hard as hers to anticipate… and ignore deliberate negative behavior, trying to find the sincerity in the positive, deciding what to respond to or not and stay consistent. It was hard. It is time consuming. I had to constantly be thinking one step ahead of her. It didn't allow me to be the mother I wanted to be to my other children, or truthfully, a great wife, friend, sister, or daughter. But I knew it would not last forever, And when that time came, I would have already learned so many lessons, that I would be a far better mother, wife, friend, sister, and daughter than I could've ever hoped to be. (p. 85)*

This is exactly what Purvis (2007) means by "The Investment Model of Parenting." Jodi Bean knew she had to be the one to be able to handle all of Victoria: the provocative behaviors and the threatening disclosures. "In fact, she couldn't get any better until my heart was free to help hers. It was personal" (p. 133). She is right (Hafetz, 2008; Ecker et al., 2012; Siegel & Hartzell, 2003).

Parents (and therapists) need to resolve attachment style and trauma history so that the children are no longer able to trigger these unresolved issues. Parents need to be in a place of healthy, secure attachment in order to be able to help heal a child who comes from a hard place (Purvis, 2008). Purvis demonstrates that the child will feel safe when the child can no longer control the moods of the adult(s) in her life. When I begin work with families, I often state that, "The silver lining to the cloud of all the trauma your child brings into your heart and into your home is that you will have no unresolved issues left in your life." If parents can laugh at this statement, it is a positive prognostic indicator. Any "buttons" the child can push, including unfinished conversations with one's spouse/partner, have to be resolved. If the child can no longer make the adult feel "out of control," then the child will feel safe enough to be honest about harm done to the child and by the child. The Beans discovered the same:

*Things finally began to make sense when she told me how often she thought about destroying her room, ripping up my clothes, and breaking everything. She told me she hated everyone in the family. I was so relieved. … I had felt this from her, but nothing she said ever indicated it. I had no idea these thoughts and others were even possible in a tiny child… our thoughts become our actions, so it was no surprise that her destructive behaviors were predicated upon a very destructive mental process. But I still didn't have the knowledge of how this was all related to attachment disorders. I still believed she had a choice and she always made the wrong one. Intentionally. (p. 65)*

The anger and hostility and fantasies about harming family, pets, and home may be hard for loving parents to hear. At the same time, it can be a relief for parents to hear such honesty. Parents have sensed that the child has fantasized about harming the family. However, it was never acknowledged. The child never admitted it. Thus, it is a huge breakthrough when she feels safe enough to disclose what she has done and what she has schemed and fantasized to do.

By contrast, what is far more destructive to the family is when others, especially expert professionals or well-meaning family and friends, minimize the child's pathology to the parent, especially in front of the child. To do this in front of the child emboldens the child's pathology. They become ever more allied with their pathological coping mechanisms, false independence, epistemic hypervigilance and faulty Internal working modal and more adversarial to the parents' agenda for success for the child and the family. The parents feel ever more isolated and defeated and ever more reluctant to ask for help. They know there is something really wrong, but others don't see it, acknowledge it, or believe it. The self-doubt is excruciating, and parents wonder if they are overly sensitive. As Jodi observes:

*I can look back and see in our first years together that Victoria's brain really wouldn't allow her to make the right choice. The only choice she had was the one that left her feeling in control, which was usually the most damaging one. (p. 66)*

Yet before Jodi understood this, she could only feel that something was wrong with her.

*I wasn't just a bad mother. I was a bad person. (p. 58)*

Many parents will have a very hard time recovering from seemingly deliberate attempts to sabotage their best efforts. They have summoned all their resources and are giving the child everything a child needs; everything common sense, research, and the experts state that the child needs. Everything the parents themselves needed as children and may not have received. There is not a "thanks Mom, thanks Dad." Instead, the parents see manipulation and attempts to control or intimidate with temper tantrums, false allegations and threats of destruction of property and threats of harm and violence toward pets and children who are too small to defend themselves. One family even coined the term "attackatory" for the defenses used by the traumatized children; the children themselves came up with the term.

*This is one of the controversies surrounding attachment disorder—how much of their thought processing is a can't or a won't? It wasn't until later, when I began to build a foundation of trust with Victoria that new pathways in her brain were created that allowed her to make decisions safely. (p. 65)*

If the behavior is a "*won't,*" then natural, normal responses might be appropriate, such as talking it through, loss of privileges, consequences, and restitution. Thusly, parents can regain control and leadership of the home.

Unfortunately, if the child "*can't*" make the right choice, such reactions reinforce the child's belief, that control is all that matters. The child believes, "I have to figure out how to get control before they do, how to get more than they have; it is the only currency of any value. I will only have value when I am in control of others. It is clearly all that matters."

A trauma-informed approach helps us to understand the child's perspective. Trauma informed programs (CPP, Lieberman, & Van Horn, 2008; TBRI, Purvis, & Cross, 2007; ARC, Blaustein, & Kinniburgh, 2010; Coherence Therapy, Ecker et al., 2012)[3] coach parents and therapists to achieve a balanced middle ground and even to see negative behavior as an opportunity for healing (Ecker et al., 2012). Parents can evaluate if they might be too strict or too lenient (Purvis, 2007). Parents can learn to match the intensity of the child but in a benevolent way, without becoming emotionally reactive (Lieberman & van Horn, 2008; Szalavitz & Perry, 2010). Trauma-informed care helps us to realize that the child's control battles and hypervigilance originate in neglect, betrayal and exploitation (Fonagy & Campbell, 2015). The traumatized child's "control issues" are essentially "trust issues"; she is not really seeking "attention" but is suffering from a lack of "connection." They exist because of past exploitation, not because s/he is a "control freak."

Once Victoria started to trust Jodi, she began to disclose all of the toxic thoughts and feelings that riddled her wounded mind and spirit. Victoria admitted that she felt like killing Jodi.

*... Every day ... about 20 times a day ... with a knife behind my back. I would sneak up and put it right in your stomach... I could also take a big rock and throw it at your forehead ... or just use scissors... I would kill the whole family so I could have Finn (our dog). I would take his cage, toys and for sure his leash. We would go live at my friend's house. (p. 110)*

Jodi reports this was the smoothest conversation she had ever had with Victoria! It just came pouring forth. Note how matter-of-fact Victoria is. She thinks of what she needs for the dog and where they will live, all within the same context and the same breath as her thoughts of killing her family. Yes, we can see why there is great concern that these children lack conscience (Cline, 1995; Magid & McKelvey, 1989) and how they could develop into anti-social personality disorders (Schore & Schore, 2008).

For some parents, such disclosures and revelations are harder to handle than the provocations, which preceded them. Prudence teaches us to wait and to not react (Provence, 1977). We are taught "The first affect to regulate in the room is our own" (Lieberman & Van Horn, 2008).

Thus, when the children get honest about what they have done—and about what they have thought about doing and have wanted to do—parents and therapists need to be ready to accept this truth; not only accept the truth, but also even powerfully reward and reinforce the great risk taken by the child in order to tell the truth. "Good job telling the truth! Good job cleaning that out. I am so sad for you that you did that, but I am so happy for you that you are ready to work on it." Healing requires the child to speak the unspeakable (Lieberman & Van Horn, 2008) about what they have done and what was done to them. Parents may have to love the unlovable, and forgive the unforgivable. This is a very challenging stage in the process for most families, and especially for the primary attachment figure, most often the mother. Some families cannot accept what the child has done.

It would be natural for parents to stumble here. "Your brothers love you. Why do you want to hurt them?" It would be very easy to panic. What a difficult positions for families to be in! Can we appreciate what a terrible bind these parents are in? We need to.

Trained professional clinicians must develop an ability to not emotionally react to unexpected disclosures. Cultivating this skill is not completed in graduate school. It is ongoing throughout one's career. It is also not possible for professionals to do unless they have "earned a Healthy, Secure Attachment Pattern" (Purvis, 2008). As professionals, we must hone our own skills and relentlessly work to remove personal reactions to actions and disclosures. Then we can begin to appreciate how hard it is for parents to do the same—especially when the parents are the targets and victims of the provocations. As Sally Provence advised, therapists need to "not just do something; stand there" (Provence, 1977). As Lieberman states, "This wise admonition reminds clinicians that watching and waiting may be more therapeutic than impulsive intervention when they are uncertain of what will help" (Lieberman & Van Horn, 2008). When we are uncertain of what to say, we can give "generic gestures of reassurance, which are not helpful" (Lieberman, 2015).

When Victoria admitted she thought about killing Jodi daily, even 20 times a day, and then got very excited reporting the different ways she would do it, Jodi had to tell someone "ASAP! I told Jay, and he was very upset. Jay was so upset that I knew I couldn't tell him about any more of the disturbing experiences I had with Victoria. He didn't want to hear them, and he had a hard time handling them" (p. 111).

Jay's reaction is understandable and quite normal; trauma is a normal reaction to abnormal circumstances (Gray, 2007; Schooler et al., 2009). It is not normal to hear that your child wants to stab your wife and kill your family. "Having a hard time handling this information" can be considered a healthy reaction from a loving parent or spouse. Thus, the primary attachment figure, usually mother, who will most likely receive all of this toxic trauma as well as the toxic coping behaviors and strategies, must be able to be firmly grounded— unshakably grounded (Purvis, 2007, p. 120).

Jodi states she knew she had to be the one to accept Victoria and all of her disturbing disclosures and provocative behaviors.

"I began to realize I could not do anything until I was whole" (p. 97). At the beginning of therapy a quiet, small suggestion had been made by the therapist for Jodi to explore forgiveness toward Victoria. There had been so much hurt and betrayal.

Purvis acknowledges that parents often feel outmatched by the child's history and pathology (2010). She states that parents often bump into the child's history, and sometimes the child bumps into the parent's history. Parents need to not take it personally. In fact, analyses of brain chemistry performed by the lab at Texas Christian University's Institute for Child Development indicate that the "parent's brain chemistry is just as fried and burnt out as the child's" (Purvis, 2010). Purvis therefore prescribes a "fierce program of self-care" for adoptive parents. She acknowledges we will need a change in our mental health, child protection, foster and adoption agencies—a change in our culture to support these parents. She acknowledges that parents have to do the brutal work of resolving past trauma and attachment issues, with an "eye towards forgiveness." For Jodi, "exploring forgiveness" almost felt like a betrayal of herself. She had been profoundly wounded, as her efforts to love Victoria had been twisted and thwarted. Instead, Victoria had been able to create doubt toward Jodi and Jay with close family and friends. The hurt was deep and it seemed it would never subside. As she said, her intense love for the child had turned to intense hatred. Now she was asked to look at exploring forgiveness.

*It was so hard! I had to convince my heart she truly did not know what she was doing and to let it all go. It was such a weight, and I had carried it around for so long I didn't even realize how heavy it was until I began to feel my heart mend. I was ready to let it go. But in letting go I had to tell myself that moving forward and leaving the resentment and bitterness behind did not diminish what I had endured. (p. 94)*

The experience was too intense to bear alone. She needed help. She returned to the therapist for her own support. She did not like the way she felt. She did not like her own thoughts. She did not like the anger and the hurt she had for Victoria. She wrote a letter to Victoria. It was a therapy assignment, not necessarily to be read or shared, but just to get it down on paper. It was torture for Jodi to do. It took months to complete. She hated what she wrote and what she felt. She hated how hard it was for her to forgive and to love Victoria again. She hated herself.

She needed trauma resolution, choosing Eye Movement Desensitization and Reprocessing (EMDR) specifically, in order to openly share the letter even with her therapist. As far as Jodi was concerned, the letter was that bad. It showed how awful she herself was. "There are not words to describe the burden I felt, to know how I should feel toward my daughter, when I could not" (p. 95). She was able, with EMDR, to regulate affect sufficiently, to soothe her emotional disturbance of arousal to openly share her hurt, betrayal, and anger and rage, helplessness, and pain. She was able to see how Victoria had triggered her. Looking at her feelings for Victoria created such a disturbance of arousal that she needed trauma therapy before she could begin to face Victoria's trauma.

She was able to see that she had stumbling blocks. She was able to see that past trauma from her life was actually resurfacing due to Victoria. Around 10 years of age there were two traumatic events in Jodi's life. Her dearly beloved father left her mother rather abruptly, and around the same time Jodi suffered sexual assault. Life had been fairly well organized for Jodi prior to this. She was able to somehow push through and keep things organized and goal-oriented after these events. She continued with academic and athletic accomplishments. Social and spiritual life were still pillars in a life that was going well. Friends were strong. She was able to marry and to form a healthy, secure attachment with her husband. Her three sons were able to form a healthy secure attachment with her and with Jay. Prior trauma had not derailed her. As long as her efforts to love, lead, and guide were well received, past trauma was just that: past.

When her adopted child was not able to receive Jodi's loving leadership, the trauma echo (Schladale, 2010) of experiencing rejection, abandonment, and isolation resurfaced. She discovered, "what she could not have known, what the therapist did not know: that traumatized children, with all their mechanisms for survival, often aggravate unresolved trauma that occurred in the mother's life" (p. 100).

*So much of the pain Victoria has borne, I had endured during my childhood. I could not make sense of the trauma and hurt inflicted on my young heart. Neither could she. I had no one to relieve the hurt. Neither did she. I took it all and carefully folded it up and tucked it away. I began to protect myself from it ever happening again. So did she. (p. 105)*

Jodi began to see how trauma had affected both herself and her daughter. She began to accept and reflect on her own trauma. She knew that Victoria was not the only one with unresolved trauma impairing the family relationships. She was able to take the next very challenging step. She recognized that her own trauma and past hurts were triggered by Victoria (Main, 1990; Fonagy et al., 1991), and furthermore could begin to understand, accept, and forgive the hurt that Victoria had done to her and to her family. Such self-acceptance and forgiveness of self is transformative. The transformation cannot likely happen unless the forgiveness and understanding is felt toward both self and child.

When a parent is not able to *see* the child and attune to the child's perceptions and the child's agenda, it is because they are often only able to see their frustration, failure, and disappointment. "Loss of the 'wished for adoption, wished for child' may emerge" (Gray, 2007, p. 469). It is one source of grief for parents. Unresolved past trauma is another source of grief. Parents who have not resolved past trauma will often react with distress to their child's distress.

Fonagy and colleagues have found that a mother's inability to develop mentalization or reflective function about past trauma will create insecure and disorganized attachment in her child (Fonagy et al., 1991; Main & Hesse, 1990; Berthelot et al., 2015). Reflective function about past trauma or mentalization is described as "the capacity to think about oneself and others as psychological beings and to consider underlying mental states and motivations when interpreting behaviors in attachment contexts" (Choi-Kain & Gunderson, 2008; Berthelot et al., 2015).

Research findings do not suggest that mothers with unresolved child abuse and neglect will display global failures in sensitivity towards their children, but rather that there "may be momentary displays of inadequately modulated aggression or affectively inappropriate and mismatched reactions to the child's distress" (Berthelot et al., 2015). While these displays are only momentary, such mismatched or incongruent "reactions such as smiling when the infant is distressed, have far more important implications for infant attachment disorganization than previously expected" (Beebe et al., 2010; Berthelot et al., 2015). If a parent is able to imagine accurately the mental world of one's child, then the parent will be better able to "go with" the distress of the child and engage in behaviors soothing to the child. When the child experiences that his mind is known by the mind of another through such attunement, then the child will develop epistemic trust (Fonagy & Campbell, 2015).

Thus, it is not a history of trauma per se in the mother that created insecure or disorganized attachment in her child. Instead it is the inability to talk about past trauma and remain coherent, organized, and regulated that will likely create insecure or disorganized attachment in a child. Mothers who can remain coherent and organized even when addressing, discussing, or thinking about past trauma could respond to their child's stress without themselves feeling stressed or threatened and reacting with rigidity or inflexibility in their response to their child's stress. Thus, Daniel Siegel (1999) has concluded that "The Coherent Narrative" of the primary attachment figure is the single greatest factor that determines the child's ability to develop a healthy, secure attachment pattern.

Once Jodi was able to adequately resolve past trauma, she could see how hurt Victoria was. She could see how broken she had been. She was humbled to be her mother. Helping the child to acknowledge, experience, express, and release these feelings safely is often the real reason parents open their hearts to the children.

*She finally reached a place where the emotion, anger for now, was so real and so big. It was humbling that I am her caregiver, responsible for someone so hurt and broken. Her revelations were nearly as freeing for me as they were for her. I wish I could have known sooner… I was glad that I was still here and she was still here. It was nothing short of a miracle. (p. 131)*

What started to happen next is what everyone wants to happen. Jodi's acceptance of self and of Victoria led to much more honesty from Victoria. As Jodi broke down her walls, Victoria was more able and ready to break down her walls. In therapy and out of therapy, she began to say much more to her mother. Jodi was able to see where Victoria's anger was directed: at "the hurt and betrayal from her birth mother." Jodi was also able to see how that anger had been displaced toward Victoria's adoptive mother and adoptive family.

As Jodi discovered and reports, "It is amazing what can happen when your heart is in the right place" (p. 124).

*It was so important for me to learn where the majority of her anger came from and that all of her subtle behaviors were means to get me to react and confirm how she was feeling. I fell right into the trap. (p. 130)*

In the end Jodi is finally able to know and to say,

*As soon as I began to learn the motivations behind her behaviors, the first thing I had to do was walk that ever-personal road of repentance and forgiveness. I, with miracles working in my heart, was able to completely forgive her for the things she was not even accountable for. … In fact she could not get better until my heart was free to help hers. It was personal. (p. 133)*

Most of us can appreciate the revelatory, redemptive, even spiritual nature of this stage of the process—how important and critical it is, and how elusive it can be. If anger and hurt still prevail in the parents' hearts, forgiveness and redemption are not possible.

Yet, even after all of this amazing and resounding therapeutic progress, forgiveness, reconciliation, bonding, attachment, trust, and even love—even after all of that—Victoria still tried to harm her mother and her family, and herself. Full disclosure does not prevent relapse, nor is it correlated with a higher likelihood of relapse prevention (Calder, 2011; Schladale, 2007). It does facilitate powerful and profound bonding experiences. It does facilitate reconciliation and reunification, especially if the child needed out-of-home treatment. It fosters Restorative Justice for the entire family system: victim, offender, and the family (Mendenhall & Dumesnil, 2006; Zehr, 2002). Sadly, it does not prevent a relapse into past behaviors.

Jodi's therapist told her to expect it. At least she was warned. "Maybe you will be the first to experience" no regression or relapse from your child. "We can always hope" (p. 138). It did come. What then can a parent do? "While I couldn't protect myself from the hurt and disappointment, I could protect myself from my anger that ensued" (p. 138).

For many parents, this seems like it is just not good enough. It is almost as if we can hear the very justified protest, "The goal and the reward are simply to protect myself from my anger when she hurts me again?" Jodi Bean and her family maintain that this is a victory. Jodi relates that even while struggles remain, she does not have to be in the struggle with Victoria. By maintaining her forgiveness and her peace of mind, she was able to remain the stable, secure attachment figure for Victoria. Regardless of Victoria's struggles, Jodi was now able to be the safe, stable secure attachment coach: unchanging, consistent, dependable, and affect-regulated (Leslie, 2002). She was able to remain open for connection. Thus whenever there was a need for correction, connection was already in place. She was able to naturally and seamlessly implement IDEAL-parenting interventions. Purvis and colleagues describe IDEAL interventions as immediate, direct, efficient, action-based, interventions leveled at the behavior and not at the child (Purvis et al., 2007). Reminders are provided to parents to stay cool, respond quickly, don't get into a discussion, and use few words to be instructive and corrective. Victoria may continue to have struggles, but Jodi is always there. That her presence minimizes, contains, and even manages Victoria's struggles and how bad they get is indisputable. There is a stable attachment figure or object. No matter what Victoria does, it does not threaten or compromise Jodi's central place in her life. Now, Victoria can and has started to integrate the important developmental concepts and experiences of object constancy and permanence (van Gulden & Bartels-Rabb, 2002; Blaustein & Kinniburgh, 2010) and even epistemic trust (Fonagy & Campbell, 2015). Anger will not make the nurturing mom disappear; neither Victoria's anger nor her mom's anger. Anger is no longer explosive or threatening to the mother–child relationship.

In summary, parents' narrative must be coherent (2006; Siegel & Harzell, 2007); they must develop meta-cognitive insight (Main & Hesse, 1990; Fonagy et al., 1991); and they must earn a healthy, secure attachment pattern (Purvis, 2008; Perry, 2012) to provide a secure base for the child with a history of sanctuary trauma or DTD (van der Kolk & d'Andrea, 2010). This appears to be a consistent echo from all others in the field (Hughes, 1998; Schooler et al., 2009). *Love Lessons* gives us an example of what that actually looks like. In a relatively circumspect and concise approximately 150 pages, detail is provided to flesh out and give meaning to the simple statement that "prospective adoptive parents need to resolve past trauma and attachment issues" (Schooler et al., 2009).

Yet another disservice that books and therapists such as myself can do is that we would have parents believe that now the work is done. The proverbial "happy ending" is at hand. All you have to do is work through your attachment history. Then support your child in resolving her past trauma and hurt and rage and forgive her for all the damage she did before her issues were resolved—then she will be an attached child without struggles.

Sadly, this is not true. Children may still resort to old patterns. Parents are not now completely protected from the hurt—which may actually feel even more poignant than before the great breakthroughs were made—but they can be protected from the anger that ensues. Sublime success.

Jodi wonders why, with all of the books on attachment and adoption that she read, she never read her story.

*I have felt naïve and ignorant. Is this a typical discovery of moms with RAD kids? Or is it just my story? I don't ever read about moms being as angry as I was. They were always just trying to do what is best for their child…Am I the only one with unresolved hurt that catapulted me into chaos? Am I the only one that continued to take things personally for so long? Am I the only one weak enough to think a five-year-old could intentionally victimize me? Am I the only one that was pushed to the edge of insanity because I couldn't make sense of her or eventually of myself? For a long time, I did feel like the only one (p. 159).*

This is a great disservice to families who are serving all of society. Without adequate treatment these children will continue to hurt themselves and others. Families in adoption and foster care are on the front line, and they are often our last best hope to stop the contagion of unresolved trauma. Therefore we absolutely must understand what they are going through and how we can help them. [4]

## REFERENCES

AACAP Official Action, . (2005). Practice Parameters for the Assessment and Treatment of Children & Adolescents with Reactive Attachment Disorder of Infancy and Early Childhood. *Journal of the American Academy of Child and Adolescent Psychiatry*, *44*(11), 1206–1219. doi:10.1097/01.chi.0000177056.41655.ce PMID:16239871

AFCARS Report # 13, Health and Human Services. (2006). *Administration for Children and Families, Administration on Children, Youth and Families, Children's Bureau*. Retrieved from www.acf.hhs.gv/gprograms/cb

American Psychological Association. (2013). *Guidelines for the practice of telepsychology*. Retrieved from http://www.apa.org/practice/guidelines/telepsychology.aspx

American Telemedicine Association. (2013). *Practice guidelines for video-based online mental health services*. Retrieved from http://www.americantelemed.org/docs/default-source/standards/practice-guidelines-for-video-based-online-mental-health-services.pdf?sfvrsn+6

Bakermans-Kranenburg, M. J., McCreery-Bunkers, K., Dobrova-Krol, N. A., & Zeanah, C. (n.d.). The Development and Care of Institutionally Reared Children: The Leiden Conference on the development and care of children without permanent parents. *Child Development Perspectives, 6*(2), 174-180.

Bavolek, S. J. (2007). *Nurturing Skills for Families: Parent Handbook*. Trenton, NJ: Family Development Resources.

Bean, J. (2010). *Love lessons: Understanding, learning, and finding purpose while raising challenging children*. Highland, UT: Love All Network.

Berthelot, N., Ensink, K., Bernazzani, O., Normandin, L., Luyten, P., & Fonagy, P. (2015). Intergenerational Transmission of Attachment in Abused and Neglected Mothers: The Role of Trauma-Specific Reflective Functioning. *Infant Mental Health Journal*, *36*(2), 1–13. doi:10.1002/imhj.21499 PMID:25694333

Blaustein, M. E., & Kinniburgh, K. (2010). *Treating Traumatic Stress in Children and Adolescents: How to Foster Resilience through Attachment, Self-Regulation and Competency*. New York: The Guilford Press.

Bowlby, J. (1988). *A Secure Base: Parent-Child Attachment and Healthy Human Development*. London: Routledge.

Bowlby, J. (1990). Attachment and Loss: Vol. III. *Loss*. New York, NY: Basic Books.

Bruce, J., Tarullo, A. R., & Gunnar, M. R. (2009). Disinhibited social behavior among internationally adopted children. *Development and Psychopathology*, *21*(1), 151–171. doi:10.1017/S0954579409000108 PMID:19144228

Calder, M. C. (2011). *Contemporary practice with young people who sexually abuse: Evidence based developments*. Holyoke, MA: NEARI press.

Choi-Kain, L. W., & Gunderson, J. G. (2008). Mentalization: Ontogeny, assessment, and application in the treatment of borderline personality disorder. *The American Journal of Psychiatry*, *165*(9), 1127–1135. doi:10.1176/appi.ajp.2008.07081360 PMID:18676591

Clinton, T., & Sibcy, G. (2002). *Attachments: Why You Love, Feel And Act The Way You Do*. Brentwood, TN: Thomas Nelson Publishers.

D'Andrea, W., Ford, J., Stolbach, B., Spinazzola, J., & van der Kolk, B. A. (2012). Understanding interpersonal trauma in children: Why we need a developmentally appropriate trauma diagnosis. *The American Journal of Orthopsychiatry*, *82*(2), 187–200. doi:10.1111/j.1939-0025.2012.01154.x PMID:22506521

Ecker, B., Ticic, R., & Hulley, L. (2012). *Unlocking the Emotional Brain: Eliminating Symptoms at Their Roots Using Memory Reconsolidation*. New York, NY: Routledge.

Felitti, V. J., Anda, R. F., Nordenberg, D., Williamson, D. F., Spitz, A. M., Edwards, V., & Marks, J. S. et al. (1998). Relationship of childhood abuse and household dysfunction to many of the leading causes of death in adults: The Adverse Childhood Experiences Study. *American Journal of Preventive Medicine*, *14*(4), 245–258. doi:10.1016/S0749-3797(98)00017-8 PMID:9635069

Foli, K. J., & Thompson, J. R. (2004). *The Post-Adoption Blues: Overcoming the Unforseen Challenges of Adoption*. Emmaus, PA: Rodale.

Fonagy, P., & Campbell, C. (2015). Bad blood revisited: Attachment and Pscychoanalysis, 2015. *British Journal of Psychotherapy*, *31*(2), 229–250. doi:10.1111/bjp.12150

Fonagy, P., Steele, M., Moran, G. S., & Higgitt, A. (1993). Measuring the ghost in the nursery: An empirical study of the relation between parents' mental representations of childhood experiences and theirinfants' security of attachment. *Journal of the American Psychoanalytic Association*, *41*(4), 957–989. doi:10.1177/000306519304100403 PMID:8282943

Fonagy, P., Steele, M., Steele, H., Moran, G. S., & Higgitt, A. C. (1991). The capacity for understanding mental states: The reflective self in parent and child and its significance for security of attachment. *Infant Mental Health Journal*, *12*(3), 201–218. doi:10.1002/1097-0355(199123)12:3<201::AID-IMHJ2280120307>3.0.CO;2-7

Fosha, D., Siegel, D. J., & Solomon, M. (2009). *The Healing Power of Emotion: Affective Neuroscience, Development & Clinical Practice*. New York: W.W. Norton & Company.

Fraiberg, S., Adelson, E., & Shapiro, V. (1975). Ghosts in the nursery: A psychoanalytic approach to the problems of impaired mother–infant relationships. *Journal of the American Academy of Child and Adolescent Psychiatry*, *14*(3), 387–422. doi:10.1016/S0002-7138(09)61442-4

Freud, S. (1990). *Beyond the Pleasure Principle*. New York: W.W. Norton & Company.

Goulding, R. A., & Schwartz, R. C. (2002). *The mosaic mind: Empowering the Tormented Self of Child Abuse Survivors*. Oak Park, IL: Trailheads Publications.

Gray, D. (2007). *Nurturing Adoptions: Creating Resilience after Neglect and Trauma*. Indianapolis, IN: Perspectives Press.

Hafetz, R. (2008). *Not Remembered, Never Forgotten*. Charleston, SC: Book Surge Publications.

Hughes, D. (1997). *Facilitating Developmental Attachment: The Road to Recovery and Behavioral Change in Foster and Adopted Children*. Lanham, MD: Rowman & Littlefield Publishers, Inc.

Hughes, D. (1998). *Building the Bonds of Attachment: Awakening Love in Deeply Troubled Children*. Northvale, NJ: Jason Aronson, Inc.

Jacobs, J.A. (2015). Legal and ethical guidance for the provision of teletherapy—more questions than answers. *The Colorado Psychologist, 4*, 4-5.

Karr-Morse, R., & Wiley, M. (1997). *Ghosts from the Nursery: Tracing the Roots of Violence*. New York, NY: The Atlantic Monthly Press.

Kinniburgh, K. J., Blaustein, M., Spinazzola, J., & van der Kolk, B. A. (2005, May). Attachment, Self-Regulation, and Competency. *Psychiatric Annals*, *35*(5), 424–430.

Leslie, K. (2002). *When a stranger calls you mom*. Pittsboro, NC: Brand New Day Publishing.

Lieberman, A. F. & Van Horn, P. (2008). *Psychotherapy with Infants and Young Children: Repairing the Effects of Stress and Trauma on Early Attachmen*t. Guilford Publications.

MacLean, K. (1998). A three year follow-up of attachment and indiscriminate friendliness in children adopted from Romanian orphanages. *Child Development*, *69*(4), 1092–1106. doi:10.1111/j.1467-8624.1998.tb06162.x PMID:9768488

Magid, K., & McKelvey, C. (1987). *High risk: children without a conscience*. New York, NY: Bantam Books.

Main, M., & Hesse, E. (1990). Parent's unresolved traumatic experiences are related to infant disorganized attachment status: Is frightened and/or frightening parental behavior the linking mechanism? In M. T. Greenberg, D. Cicchetti, & E. M. Cummings (Eds.), *Attachment in the preschool years: Theory, research, and intervention* (pp. 161–182). Chicago: University of Chicago Press.

Meins, E., Fernyhough, C., Fradley, E., & Tuckey, M. (2001). Rethinking maternal sensitivity: Mothers' comments on infants' mental processes predict security of attachment at 12 months. *Journal of Child Psychology and Psychiatry, and Allied Disciplines*, *42*(5), 637–648. doi:10.1111/1469-7610.00759 PMID:11464968

Mendenhall, B., & Dumesnil, J. (2006). Exploring Traditional Cultural Mechanisms of Conflict Resolution in American Indian Communities. In E. Jensen & J. Jepsen (Eds.), *Juvenile Law Violators, Human Rights, and the Development of New Juvenile Justice Systems* (pp. 341–372). Portland, OR: Hart Publishing.

Merz, E. C., & McCall, R. B. (2010a). Behavior problems in children adopted from socially-emotionally depriving institutions. *Journal of Abnormal Child Psychology*, *38*(4), 459–470. doi:10.1007/s10802-009-9383-4 PMID:20084451

Miller, W., & Rollnick, S. (2012). *Motivational Interviewing* (3rd ed.). New York, NY: The Guilford Press.

Nelsen, J. (2006). *Positive discipline*. New York, NY: Ballantine Books.

Palacios, J., & Brodzinsky, D. (2010). Adoption research: Trends, topics, outcomes. *International Journal of Behavioral Development*, *34*(3), 270–284. doi:10.1177/0165025410362837

Perry, B. (1997). Incubated in terror: Neurodevelopmental factors in the cycle of violence. In D. Osofsky (Ed.), *Children in a Violent Society* (pp. 124–149). New York, NY: The Guilford Press.

Perry, B. (2006). Applying principles of neurodevelopment to clinical work with maltreated and traumatized children: The neurosequential model of therapeutics. In N. B. Webb (Ed.), *Working with Traumatized Youth in Child Welfare* (pp. 27–52). New York, NY: The Guilford Press.

Provence, S. (1977). Developmental assessment. In M. Green & R. Haggerty (Eds.), *Ambulatory pediatrics* (pp. 374–383). Philadelphia: Saunders.

Purvis, K. (2010). *Empowering, Connecting & Correcting Principles: Healing Children Through Trust and Relationships.* [DVD]. Fort Worth, TX: Texas Christian Institute of Child Development.

Purvis, K. (2010). *Facilitating Behavioral Change.* [DVD]. Fort Worth, TX: Texas Christian Institute of Child Development.

Purvis, K. (2010). *The Attachment Dance.* [DVD]. Fort Worth, TX: Texas Christian Institute of Child Development.

Purvis, K., Cross, D., & Sunshine, W. (2007). *The connected child: bring hope and healing to your adoptive family*. New York: McGraw Hill.

Schladale, J. (2002). *The Trauma Outcome Process Workbook For Taming Violence and Sexual Aggression*. East Providence, RI: Signature Printing.

Schladale, J. (2007). A Collaborative Approach for Family Reconciliation and Reunification With Youth Who Have Caused Sexual Harm. In D. Prescott (Ed.), *Knowledge & Practice: Challenges in the Treatment and Supervision of Sexual Abusers*. Safer Society Press.

Schooler, J., Smalley, D., & Callahan, T. (2009). *Wounded children, Healing homes*. Colorado Springs, CO: NavPress.

Schore, A. N. (1994). *Affect regulation and the origin of the self: The neurobiology of emotional development*. Hillsdale, NJ: Erlbaum.

Schore, J. R., & Schore, A. N. (2008). Modern Attachment Theory: The Central Role of Affect Regulation in Development and Treatment. *Clinical Social Work Journal*, *36*(1), 9–20. doi:10.1007/s10615-007-0111-7

Schwartz, R. C. (1995). *Internal Family Systems therapy*. New York: Guilford Press.

Siegel, D. J. (1999). *The developing mind*. New York: Guilford Press.

Siegel, D. J., & Hartzell, M. (2004). *Parenting from the inside out*. New York: Tarcher.

Szalavitz, M., & Perry, B. (2010). *Born for love*. New York: William Morrow.

Thomas, J. (2014, July-August). Veterans Administration is leader in telemental health. The National Psychologist, 6.

Thomas, N. (1997). *When love is not enough*. Glenwood Springs, CO: Families by Design.

Van den Dries, L., Juffer, F., van IJzendoorn, M. H., & Bakermans-Kranenburg, M. J. (2009). Fostering security? A meta-analysis of attachment in adopted children. *Children and Youth Services Review*, *31*(3), 410–421. doi:10.1016/j.childyouth.2008.09.008

Van der Kolk, B., & D'Andrea, W. (2010). Towards a developmental trauma disorder diagnosis for childhood interpersonal trauma. In R. A. Lanius, E. Vermetien, & C. Pain (Eds.), *The Impact of Early Life Trauma on Health and Disease: The Hidden Epidemic* (pp. 57–68). Cambridge, UK: Cambridge University Press. doi:10.1017/CBO9780511777042.008

Van der Vegt, E. J. M., Van der Ende, J., Ferdinand, R. F., Verhulst, F. C., & Tiemeier, H. (2009). Early childhood adversities and trajectories of psychiatric problems in adoptees: Evidence for long lasting effects. *Journal of Abnormal Child Psychology*, *37*(2), 239–249. doi:10.1007/s10802-008-9272-2 PMID:18807165

Van Gulden, H., & Bartels-Rabb, L. M. (2002). *Real parents, real children: Parenting the adopted child*. New York, NY: Crossroads Publishing.

Zeanah, C. H., & Gleason, M. M. (2014). Annual research review: Attachment disorders in early childhood – Clinical presentation, causes, correlates and treatments. *Journal of Child Psychology and Psychiatry, 56*(3). Retrieved from www.researchgate.net/publication/267627731

Zeanah, C. H., Gunnar, M. R., McCall, R. B., Kreppner, J. M., & Fox, N. A. (2011). Sensitive periods. In R. B. McCall, M. H. van IJzendoorn, F. Juffer, C. J. Groark, & V. K. Groza (Eds.), Children without permanent parents: Research, practice, and policy. Academic Press.

Zehr, H. (2002). *The little book of restorative justice*. Intercourse, PA: Good Books.

## KEY TERMS AND DEFINITIONS

**ACEs:** Adverse Childhood Experiences a study by Kaiser Permanente, which began in 1995. 17,000 adults completed a questionnaire scoring the number and type of childhood stressors and traumas or ACEs, that they experienced. The participants' health continues to be tracked, making it one of the broadest longitudinal studies of health and trauma exposures ever undertaken. The data shows that the more ACEs a participant reports above 4, the more they have a significantly higher rate of chronic health conditions.

**Attachment Styles:** A pattern of engaging / disengaging with primary attachment figure and the world. For infants there are four patterns: Healthy Secure, Anxious Ambivalent, Anxious Avoidant and Disorganized or Unresolved. These correspond with four adult patterns of relationship.

**Coherent Narrative:** AKA Meta-cognitive insight. A concept that represents the ability to organize and integrate past history with continuity, directionality and meaning. Coherence allows one to not dysregulate when recalling past events even traumatic events. It also allows one to integrate new information into what is already known, processed and understood so that we can heal and move on.

**Epistemic Trust:** New findings indicate that epistemic trust not only makes a child open to attachment to the mother, but further that the child will be open to more information / direction from the mother. On the other hand, without the experience of one's mind being known by the mind of another, a child develops epistemic hypervigilance. Epistemic hypervigilance leads a child to not be open to new information from the attachment figure or from others.

**Implicit Memory:** Also known as Motor Memory, or unconscious memory, e.g. driving a car for someone, who has been doing it for decades. It can allow us to do many tasks without having to think about doing them. But it can also program certain responses, without being moderated or filtered through the pre-frontal cortex.

**Reflective Function: (RF):** Also known as Mentalizing refers to the ability to think about thinking. For parents, this indicates an ability to think about the mental process of their child. A low RF in mother is linked to infant attachment disorganization. Whereas mothers with higher RF about their children showed less hostility and intrusiveness in interaction with their infants, suggesting that mentalization buffers against affect dysregulation when mothers confront infant distress as described by Berthelot and colleagues.

**Repetition Compulsion:** A psychological phenomenon in which a person repeats a traumatic event or its circumstances over and over again. This includes reenacting the event or putting oneself in situations where the event is likely to happen again.

**Secondary Trauma:** A condition resulting from experiencing vicarious trauma. It has been used to describe the trauma suffered by children, even grandchildren of Holocaust survivors. The PTSD of Holocaust survivors affected their family members, who also showed signs of PTSD. The same happens for families, who adopt children who have been severely abused. It has also occurred in family members of survivors of the terror attacks of 9/11.

**Secure Base:** In attachment literature, this refers to the attachment figure or object that provides a foundation for the infant to establish and re-establish a sense of safety and security allowing the child to engage and re-engage in health exploratory behavior.

**Trauma Informed Care:** An approach to treatment of past trauma. In order to provide trauma-informed care to children, youth, and families, professionals must understand the impact of trauma on child development and learn how to effectively minimize and resolve its effects without causing additional trauma.

## ENDNOTES

1. The author wishes to thank Jodi Bean for her continued collaboration in support of adoptive families. All excerpts from the book "*Love Lessons*" are reprinted with permission from the author and publisher.
2. Clinton & Sibcy, 2002; Fosha et al., 2009; Gray, D., 2007; Hughes, D., 1997; Hughes, D., 1998; Leslie, K., 2002; Purvis et al., 2007; Schooler et al., 2009; Szalavitz & Perry, 2010; Van Gulden & Bartels-Rabb, 2002.
3. CPP—Child Parent Psychotherapy; ARC—Attachment, Self-Regulation, and Competency; TBRI—Trust Based Relational Intervention.
4. It is important to recognize that much of the support and education critical for families can be provided through telemental health services. In trying to prevent and treat trauma in rural and underserved areas telemental health therapy has proven to be very effective even when treating PTSD (Thomas, 2014; see also APA, 2013; ATA, 2013).

# Compilation of References


AACAP Official Action, . (2005). Practice Parameters for the Assessment and Treatment of Children & Adolescents with Reactive Attachment Disorder of Infancy and Early Childhood. *Journal of the American Academy of Child and Adolescent Psychiatry, 44*(11), 1206–1219. doi:10.1097/01.chi.0000177056.41655.ce PMID:16239871

Adams, G., & Markus, H. R. (2004). Toward a conception of culture suitable for a social psychology of culture. In M. Schaller & C. S. Crandall (Eds.), *The psychological foundations of culture* (pp. 335–360). Hillsdale, NJ: Erlbaum.

Administration of Children and Families Office of Planning Research & Evaluation (ACF-OPRE). (2006). *Research to Practice: Depression in the Lives of Early Head Start Families.* Washington, DC: U.S. Department of Health and Human Services.

Adoption and Safe Families Act of 1997. Pub. L. No.105-89, 42 U.S.C. §§ 620-679 (1997).

Adoption Assistance and Child Welfare Act of 1980 P. L. 96-272

*Adoption Learning Partners.* (2010). Retrieved from http://www.adoptionlearningpartners.org

AFCARS Report # 13, Health and Human Services. (2006). *Administration for Children and Families, Administration on Children, Youth and Families, Children's Bureau.* Retrieved from www.acf.hhs.gv/gprograms/cb

Aftyka, A., Rybojad, B., & Rudnicka-Drozak, E. (2014). Are there any differences in medical emergency team interventions between rural and urban areas? A single-centre cohort study. *The Australian Journal of Rural Health, 22*(5), 223–228. doi:10.1111/ajr.12108 PMID:25303413

Ai, A. L., Cascio, T., Santangelo, L. K., & Evans-Camball, T. (2005). Hope, meaning, and growth following 9-11. *Journal of Interpersonal Violence, 20*(2), 523–547. doi:10.1177/0886260504272896 PMID:15601799

Ai, A. L., Evans-Campbell, T., Santangelo, L. K., & Cascio, T. (2006). The traumatic impact of September 11 terrorist attack and potential protection of optimism: Implications for profession. *Journal of Interpersonal Violence, 21*(5), 689–700. doi:10.1177/0886260506287245 PMID:16574640

Ai, A. L., & Park, C. L. (2005). Possibilities of the positive following violence and trauma: Informing the coming decade of research. *Journal of Interpersonal Violence, 20*(2), 242–250. doi:10.1177/0886260504267746 PMID:15601799

Ainsworth, M. D. S., Blehar, M. C., Waters, E., & Wall, S. (1978). *Patterns of attachment: A psychological study of the strange situation.* Hillsdale, NJ: Erlbaum.

Aisenberg, E., & Herrenkohl, T. (2008). Community violence in context risk and resilience in children and families. *Journal of Interpersonal Violence, 23*(3), 296–315. doi:10.1177/0886260507312287 PMID:18245570

Aisenberg, E., Trickett, P. R., Mennen, F. E., Saltzman, W., & Zayas, L. H. (2007). Maternal depression and adolescent behavior problems: An examination of mediation among Latino immigrant mothers and their adolescent children exposed to community violence. *Journal of Interpersonal Violence*, *22*(10), 1227–1249. doi:10.1177/0886260507304292 PMID:17766724

Akiba, M., Letendre, G. K., Baker, D. P., & Goesling, B. (2002). Student victimization: National and school systems effects on school violence in 37 nations. *American Educational Research Journal*, *39*(4), 829–853. doi:10.3102/00028312039004829

Allen, B., Cisneros, E. M., & Tellez, A. (2013). The children left behind: The impact of parental deportation on mental health. *Journal of Child and Family Studies*, *24*(2), 386–392. doi:10.1007/s10826-013-9848-5

Allensworth, E. M., & Rochin, R. I. (1996). *White exodus, Latino repopulation, and community well-being: Trends in California's rural communities*. Julian Samora Research Institute, Michigan State University.

American Academy of Pediatrics. (2010). *Section on adoption and foster care. Adoption directory membership list*. Retrieved on July 8, 2014, from http://www.aap.org/en-us/professional-resources/publications-and-journals/Pages/Publications-and-Journals.aspx

American Burn Association. (2015a). Burn incident and treatment in the United States: 2015 fact sheet. Chicago: American Burn Association.

American Burn Association. (2015b). National burn repository 2015: report of data from 2005–2014. Chicago: American Burn Association.

*American Counseling Association*. (2014). Washington, DC: Ethical Guidelines of the American Counseling Association.

American Psychiatric Association. (2000). *Diagnostic and statistical manual of mental disorders* (4th ed.). Washington, DC: Author.

American Psychiatric Association. (2000). Diagnostic and Statistical Manual of Mental Disorders-text revision (DSM-TR-IV). Washington, DC: APA.

American Psychiatric Association. (2004). Practice guidelines for the treatment of patients with acute stress disorder and posttraumatic stress disorder. *The American Journal of Psychiatry*, 16.

American Psychiatric Association. (2013). *Diagnostic and statistical manual of mental disorders: DSM-5* (5th ed.). Washington, DC: American Psychiatric Publishing.

American Psychological Association. (2010). *American Psychological Association ethical principles of psychologists and code of conduct*. Retrieved May 1, 2015, from http://www.apa.org/ethics/code/

American Psychological Association. (2013). *Guidelines for the practice of telepsychology*. Retrieved from http://www.apa.org/practice/guidelines/telepsychology.aspx

American Telemedicine Association. (2013). *Practice guidelines for video-based online mental health services*. Retrieved from http://www.americantelemed.org/docs/default-source/standards/practice-guidelines-for-video-based-online-mental-health-services.pdf?sfvrsn+6

Ames, N. (2008). Medically underserved children's access to health care: A review of the literature. *Journal of Human Behavior in the Social Environment*, *18*(1), 64–77. doi:10.1080/10911350802266334

Ames, N., Hancock, T. V., & Behnke, A. (2011). Latino church leaders and domestic violence: Attitudes and knowledge. *Families in Society*, *92*(2), 161–167. doi:10.1606/1044-3894.4093

Anda, R. F., Felitti, V. J., Bremner, J. D., Walker, J. D., Whitfield, C., Perry, B. D., & Giles, W. H. et al. (2006). The enduring effects of abuse and related adverse experiences in childhood: A convergence of evidence from neurobiology and epidemiology. *European Archives of Psychiatry and Clinical Neuroscience*, *256*(3), 174–186. doi:10.1007/s00406-005-0624-4 PMID:16311898

Anderson, D. (1998). Curriculum, culture, and community: The challenge of school violence. In M. Tonry & M. Moore (Eds.), *Youth violence* (pp. 318–363). Chicago, IL: University of Chicago Press. doi:10.1086/449282

Anderson, D. M. (2008). Sexual abuse, professional boundaries, and the rural world. *Journal of Child Sexual Abuse*, *8*(3), 85–93. doi:10.1300/J070v08n03_05

Anderson, M., Kaufman, J., Simon, T. R., Barrios, L., Paulozzi, L., Ryan, G., & Potter, L. et al. (2001). School-associated violent deaths in the United States, 1994-1999.[JAMA]. *Journal of the American Medical Association*, *286*(21), 2695–2702. doi:10.1001/jama.286.21.2695 PMID:11730445

Androff, D. K., Ayon, C., Becerra, D., & Gurrola, M. (2011). U.S. immigration policy and immigrant children's well-being: The impact of policy shifts. *Journal of Sociology and Social Welfare*, *38*, 77.

Annie E. Casey Foundation. (2010). *Funding permanency services: A guide to leveraging federal, state, and local dollars*. Baltimore: Annie E Casey Foundation.

*APAC-Alabama Post-Adoption Connections*. (2010). Retrieved July 8, 2014, from http://www.casapac.org/index.shtml

Arbona, C., Olvera, N., Rodrgiguez, N., Hagan, J., Linares, A., & Weisner, M. (2010). Acculturative stress among documented and undocumented Latino immigrants in the United States. *Hispanic Journal of Behavioral Sciences*, *32*(3), 362–384. doi:10.1177/0739986310373210 PMID:25484488

Arceneaux, L. L., & Meyer, W. J. III. (2009). Treatments for common psychiatric conditions among children and adolescents during acute rehabilitation and reintegration phases of burn injury. *International Review of Psychiatry (Abingdon, England)*, *21*(6), 549–558. doi:10.3109/09540260903343984 PMID:19919208

Arcury, T. A., Grzywacz, J. G., Barr, D. B., Tapia, J., Chen, H., & Quandt, S. A. (2007). Pesticide urinary metabolite levels of children in Eastern North Carolina farmworker households. *Environmental Health Perspectives*, *115*(8), 1254–1260. doi:10.1289/ehp.9975 PMID:17687456

Arcury, T. A., Marin, A., Snively, B. M., Hernandez-Pelletier, J., & Quandt, S. A. (2009). Reducing farmworker residential pesticide exposure: Evaluation of a lay health advisor intervention. *Health Promotion Practice*, *10*(3), 447–455. doi:10.1177/1524839907301409 PMID:18287581

Arcury, T. A., Weir, M., Chen, H., Summers, P., Pelletier, L. E., Galvan, L., & Quandt, S. A. (2012). Migrant farmworker housing regulation violations in North Carolina. *Journal of Industrial Medicine*, *55*(3), 191–204. doi:10.1002/ajim.22011 PMID:22237961

*Arizona Revised Statures*. (2013). Retrieved from www.Azleg.gov

Armsworth, M. W., & Holaday, M. (1993). The effects of psychological trauma on children and adolescents. *Journal of Counseling and Development*, *72*(1), 49–56. doi:10.1002/j.1556-6676.1993.tb02276.x

Aronson, J. (2010). *Impact of adoption on adoptive parents*. Retrieved from www.childwelfare.gov

Askay-Wiechman, S., & Magyar-Russell, G. (2009). Post-traumatic growth and spirituality in burn recovery. *International Review of Psychiatry (Abingdon, England)*, *21*(6), 570–579. doi:10.3109/09540260903344107 PMID:19919210

Aspy, C. B., Oman, R. F., Vesely, S. K., McLeroy, K., Rodine, S., & Marshall, L. (2004). Adolescent violence: The protective effects of youth assets. *Journal of Counseling and Development*, *82*(3), 268–276. doi:10.1002/j.1556-6678.2004.tb00310.x

Association for Play Therapy. (2013). *About play therapy overview*. Retrieved from http://www.a4pt.org/ps.playtherapy.cfm?ID1158

Astor, R. A., Benbenishty, R., Zeira, A., & Vinokur, A. (2002). School climate, observed risky behaviors, and victimization as predictors of high school students' fear and judgments of school violence as a problem. *Health Education & Behavior*, *29*(6), 716–736. doi:10.1177/109019802237940 PMID:12456131

Atav, S., & Spencer, G. A. (2002). Health risk behaviors among adolescents attending rural, suburban, and urban schools: A comparative study. *Family & Community Health*, *25*(2), 53–64. doi:10.1097/00003727-200207000-00007 PMID:12010115

Atiles, J. H., & Bohon, S. A. (2003). Camas calientes: Housing adjustments and barriers to social and economic adaptation among Georgia's rural Latinos. *Rural Sociology*, *19*, 97–122.

Author. (2010). *APA's Ethical Principles of Psychologists and Code of Conduct*. Washington, DC: American Psychological Association.

Axinn, W. G., Ghimire, D. J., Williams, N. E., & Scott, K. M. (2013). Gender, traumatic events, and mental health disorders in a rural Asian setting. *Journal of Health and Social Behavior*, *54*(4), 444–461. doi:10.1177/0022146513501518 PMID:24311755

Axline, V. (1947). *Play therapy*. Boston, MA: Houghton Mifflin.

Ayoub, C. C., Deutsch, R. M., & Maraganore, A. (1999). Emotional distress in children of high conflict divorce. *Family Court Review*, *37*(3), 297–315. doi:10.1111/j.174-1617.1999.tb01307.x

Bachman, R. (1992). Crime in non metropolitan America: A national accounting of trends, incidence rates, and idiosyncratic vulnerabilities. *Rural Sociology*, *57*(4), 546–560. doi:10.1111/j.1549-0831.1992.tb00479.x

Bachus, G. (1994). Violence is no stranger in rural schools. *School Administrator*, *51*(4), 18–22.

Baker-Ericzén, M. M., Jenkins, M., & Haine-Schlagel, R. (2013). Therapist, parent, and youth perspectives of treatment barriers to family-focused community outpatient mental health services. *Journal of Child and Family Studies*, *22*(6), 854–868. doi:10.1007/s10826-012-9644-7 PMID:24019737

Bakermans-Kranenburg, M. J., McCreery-Bunkers, K., Dobrova-Krol, N. A., & Zeanah, C. (n.d.). The Development and Care of Institutionally Reared Children: The Leiden Conference on the development and care of children without permanent parents. *Child Development Perspectives, 6*(2), 174-180.

Bakker, A., Maertens, K. J. P., Van Son Maarten, J. M., & Van Loey, N. E. E. (2013). Clinical Psychological consequences of pediatric burns from a child and family perspective: A review of the empirical literature. *Psychological Review*, *33*(3), 361–371. PMID:23410718

Bakker, A., Van der Heijden, P. M., Van Son, M. M., & Van Loey, N. E. (2013). Course of traumatic stress reactions in couples after a burn event to their young child. *Health Psychology*, *32*(10), 1076–1083. doi:10.1037/a0033983 PMID:23957899

Baldwin, S. B., Eisenman, D. P., Sayles, J. N., Ryan, G., & Chung, K. S. (2011). Identification of human trafficking victims in health care settings. *Health and Human Rights*, *13*, 36–49. PMID:22772961

Banyard, V. L., Williams, L. M., & Siegel, J. A. (2001). The long-term mental health consequences of child sexual abuse: An exploratory study of the impact of multiple traumas in a sample of women. *Journal of Traumatic Stress*, *14*(4), 697–715. doi:10.1023/A:1013085904337 PMID:11776418

Barglow, P. (2011). We can't treat soldiers' PTSD without a better diagnosis. *Skeptical Inquirer*, *36*(3), 42–49.

Barglow, P. (2013). A rose is a rose is a rose? *The American Journal of Psychiatry*, *170*(6), 680–681. doi:10.1176/appi.ajp.2013.13010087 PMID:23732969

Barron-McKeagney, T., Woody, J., & D'Souza, H. (2002). Mentoring at-risk Latino children and their parents: Analysis of the parent-child relationship and family strength. *Families in Society*, *83*(3), 285–292. doi:10.1606/1044-3894.19

Barth, R. P., & Miller, J. M. (2000). Building effective post-adoption services: What is the empirical foundation? *Family Relations*, *49*(4), 447–455. doi:10.1111/j.1741-3729.2000.00447.x

Barth, R., & Berry, M. (1988). *Adoption and disruption: Rates, risks, and responses*. New York, NY: Aldine de Gruyter.

Barth, R., & Berry, M. (1994). Adoption of drug-exposed children. In R. P. Barth, J. D. Berrick, & N. Gilbert (Eds.), *Child welfare research review* (Vol. 1, pp. 273–294). New York, NY: Columbia University Press.

Bartkowski, J. P., & Xu, X. (2007). Religiosity and teen drug use reconsidered: A social capital perspective. *American Journal of Preventive Medicine*, *32*(6), 182–194. doi:10.1016/j.amepre.2007.03.001 PMID:17543710

Basit, T. N. (2003). Manual or electronic? The role of coding in qualitative data analysis. *Educational Research*, *45*(2), 143–154. doi:10.1080/0013188032000133548

Bass, L. B., Taylor, B. A., Knudson-Martin, C., & Huenergardt, D. (2006). Making sense of abuse: Case studies in sibling incest. *Contemporary Family Therapy*, *28*(1), 87–109. doi:10.1007/s10591-006-9697-0

Bauman, S. (2010). Cyberbullying in a rural intermediate school: An exploratory study. *The Journal of Early Adolescence*, *30*(6), 803–833. doi:10.1177/0272431609350927

Bavolek, S. J. (2007). *Nurturing Skills for Families: Parent Handbook*. Trenton, NJ: Family Development Resources.

Bean, J. (2010). *Love lessons: Understanding, learning, and finding purpose while raising challenging children*. Highland, UT: Love All Network.

Beckman, L. J., & Amaro, H. (1984). Patterns of women's use of alcohol treatment agencies. In S. C. Wilsnack & L. J. Beckman (Eds.), *Alcohol problems in women* (pp. 319–348). New York: Guilford Press.

Beeble, M., Bybee, D., & Sullivan, C. (2007). Abusive men's use of children to control their partners and ex-partners. *European Psychologist*, *12*(1), 54–61. doi:10.1027/1016-9040.12.1.54

Begle, A. M., Dumas, J. E., & Hanson, R. F. (2010). Predicting child abuse potential: An empirical investigation of two theoretical frameworks. *Journal of Clinical Child and Adolescent Psychology: The Official Journal for the Society of Clinical Child and Adolescent Psychology*, *39*(2), 208–219. doi:10.1080/15374410903532650

Behnke, A. O., Gonzalez, L. M., & Cox, R. B. (2008). Latino students in new arrival states: Factors and service to prevent youth from dropping out. *Hispanic Journal of Behavioral Sciences*, *32*(3), 385–409. doi:10.1177/0739986310374025

Benjamin, D., & Herndon, D. N. (2002). Special considerations of age: The pediatric burned patient. In *Total Burn Care* (2nd ed.). London: W.B. Saunders.

Benson, P. (2008). El campo: Facility and structural violence in farm labor camps. *Cultural Anthropology*, *23*(4), 589–629. doi:10.1111/j.1548-1360.2008.00020.x

Berdahl, T. A., Kirby, J. B., & Stone, R. A. T. (2007). Access to health care for nonmetro and metro Latinos of Mexican origin in the United States. *Medical Care*, *45*(7), 647–657. doi:10.1097/MLR.0b013e3180536734 PMID:17571013

Bergman, U. (2010). Neurobiological mechanisms of action: A survey of 20 years of searching. *Journal of EMDR Practice and Research*, *4*(1), 22–42. doi:10.1891/1933-3196.4.1.22

Bernzies, K., & Mychasiuk, R. (2009). Fostering family resiliency: A review of the key protective factors. *Child & Family Social Work*, *14*(1), 103–114. doi:10.1111/j.1365-2206.2008.00586.x

Bertaux, D. (1981). From the life-history approach to the transformation of sociological practice. In D. Bertaux (Ed.), *Biography and society: The life history approach in the social sciences* (pp. 29–45). London, England: Sage.

Berthelot, N., Ensink, K., Bernazzani, O., Normandin, L., Luyten, P., & Fonagy, P. (2015). Intergenerational Transmission of Attachment in Abused and Neglected Mothers: The Role of Trauma-Specific Reflective Functioning. *Infant Mental Health Journal*, *36*(2), 1–13. doi:10.1002/imhj.21499 PMID:25694333

Besharov, D. J. (Ed.). (1994). *When drug addicts have children: Reorienting child welfare's response*. Washington, DC: CWLA.

Beyer, K. M., Layde, P. M., Hamberger, L. K., & Laud, P. L. (2013). Characteristics of the residential neighborhood environment differentiate intimate partner femicide in urban versus rural settings. *The Journal of Rural Health*, *29*(3), 281–293. doi:10.1111/j.1748-0361.2012.00448.x PMID:23802930

Black, M. C., Basile, K. C., Breiding, M. J., Smith, S. G., Walters, M. L., & Merrick, M. T. (2011). *The National Intimate Partner and Sexual Violence Survey (NISVS): 2010 summary report*. Atlanta, GA: National Center for Injury Prevention and Control, Centers for Disease Control and Prevention.

Blaustein, M. E., & Kinniburgh, K. (2010). *Treating Traumatic Stress in Children and Adolescents: How to Foster Resilience through Attachment, Self-Regulation and Competency*. New York: The Guilford Press.

Blaustein, M. E., & Kinniburgh, K. M. (2010). *Traumatic stress in children and adolescents: How to foster resilience through attachment, self-regulation, and competency*. New York: The Guilford Press.

Blaustein, M., & Kinniburgh, K. (2010). *Treating traumatic stress in children and adolescents: How to foster resilience through attachment, self-regulation, and competency*. New York, NY: Guilford Press.

Bohnam, V. L., & Nathan, V. R. (2002). Environmental public health research: Engaging communities. *International Journal of Hygiene and Environmental Health*, *205*(1-2), 11–18. doi:10.1078/1438-4639-00125 PMID:12018003

Bolen, R., & Scannpieco, M. (1999). Prevalence of child sexual abuse: A corrective meta-analysis. *The Social Service Review*, *73*(3), 281–313. doi:10.1086/514425

Bolin, J. N., & Bellamy, G. (n.d.). *Rural healthy people 2020*. Retrieved from http://sph.tamhsc.edu/srhrc/docs/rhp2020.pdf

Booth, P. B., & Jernberg, A. M. (2010). *Theraplay: Helping parents and children build better relationships through attachment-based play* (3rd ed.). San Francisco, CA: John Wiley.

Borgatta, E. F., & Borgatta, R. V. (1992). *Encyclopedia of sociology* (Vol. 4). Retrieved from http://www.sesp.northwestern.edu/docs/publications/16511665225230b3b2ad63d.pdf

Bourdon, S. (2002). The integration of qualitative data analysis software in research strategies: Resistance and possibilities. *Forum Qualitative Sozialforschung / Forum: Qualitative. Social Research*, *3*(2), 11. Retrieved from http://nbn-resolving.de/urn:nbn:de:0114-fqs0202118

Bowen, N. K., & Bowen, G. L. (1999). Effects of crime and violence in neighborhoods and schools on the school behavior and performance of adolescents. *Journal of Adolescent Research*, *14*(3), 319–342. doi:10.1177/0743558499143003

Bowlby, J. (1969). *Attachment and loss*. Retrieved from http://www.scribd.com/doc/46786672/Bowlby-1969-Attachment-and-Loss-Volume-1-Attachment

Bowlby, J. (1969). Attachment and Loss: Vol. I. *Attachment*. London: The Hogarth Press.

Bowlby, J. (1973). Attachment and loss: Vol. 2. *Separation*. New York, NY: Basic.

Bowlby, J. (1988). *A Secure Base: Parent-Child Attachment and Healthy Human Development*. London: Routledge.

Bowlby, J. (1988). *A secure base: Parent-child attachment and healthy human development*. New York: Basic Books.

Bowlby, J. (1988). *Secure base: Clinical applications of attachment theory*. London, England: Routledge.

Bowlby, J. (1990). Attachment and Loss: Vol. III. *Loss*. New York, NY: Basic Books.

Bowman, E. S. (1989). Understanding and responding to religious material in the therapy of multiple personality disorders. *Dissociation*, *2*(4), 231–238.

Boys and Girls Clubs of Calgary. (2015). *Grimmon House*. Retrieved December 14, 2015, http://www.boysandgirlsclubsofcalgary.ca/programs/community-based-care-supports/grimmon-house

Brabeck, K. M., Lykes, M. B., & Lustig, S. L. (2013). *The psychological impact of detention and deportation on U. S. migrant children and families: A report to the Interamerican human rights court*. Academic Press.

Brabeck, K. M., Lykes, M. B., & Hunter, C. (2014). The psychosocial impact of detention and deportation on U. S. migrant children and families. *Journal of Orthopsychiatry*, *84*(5), 496–505. doi:10.1037/ort0000011 PMID:25110972

Brabeck, K., & Xu, Q. (2010). The impact of deportation on Latino immigrant children and families: A quantitative exploration. *Hispanic Journal of Behavioral Sciences*, *32*(3), 341–361. doi:10.1177/0739986310374053

Bracken, P. J., Giller, J. E., & Summerfield, D. (1995). Psychological responses to war and atrocity: The limitations of current concepts. *Social Science & Medicine*, *40*(8), 1073–1082. doi:10.1016/0277-9536(94)00181-R PMID:7597460

Bradley, R., Greene, J., Russ, E., Dutral, L., & Westen, D. (2005). A multi-dimensional metaanalysis of psychotherapy for PTSD. *The American Journal of Psychiatry*, *16*(2), 214–227. doi:10.1176/appi.ajp.162.2.214 PMID:15677582

Bradman, A., Chevrier, J., Tager, I., Lipsett, M., Sedgwick, J., Macher, J., & Eskanazi, B. (2005). Association of housing disrepair indicators in a cohort of pregnant Latina women and their children. *Environmental Health Perspectives*, 1795–1801. doi:10.1289/ehp.7588 PMID:16330367

Brega, A. G., & Coleman, L. M. (1999). Effects of religiosity and racial socialization on subjective stigmatization in African-American adolescents. *Journal of Adolescence*, *22*(2), 223–242. doi:10.1006/jado.1999.0213 PMID:10089121

Bremner, J. D. (2002). *Does stress damage the brain? Understanding trauma related disorders from a mind-body perspective*. New York: W.W. Norton.

Breslau, J. (2000). Globalizing Disaster Trauma: Science, Culture and Psychiatry after the Kobe Earthquake. *Ethos (Berkeley, Calif.)*, *28*(2), 174–197. doi:10.1525/eth.2000.28.2.174

Breslau, J. (2004). Cultures of Trauma: Anthropological Views of Post-traumatic Stress Disorders in International Health. *Culture, Medicine and Psychiatry*, *28*(2), 113–126. doi:10.1023/B:MEDI.0000034421.07612.c8 PMID:15470944

Breslau, N., & Kessler, R. C. (2001). The stressor criterion in DSMIV Post-traumatic stress disorder. *Biological Psychiatry, 50*, 699–704. doi:10.1016/S0006-3223(01)01167-2 PMID:11704077

Bretherton, I. (1992). The origins of attachment theory-psychology. *Developmental Psychology, 28*, 759–775. doi:10.1037/0012-1649.28.5.759

Brewin, C. R., Andrews, B., & Valentine, J. D. (2000). Meta-analysis of risk factors for posttraumatic stress disorder in trauma-exposed adults. *Journal of Consulting and Clinical Psychology, 68*(5), 748–766. doi:10.1037/0022-006X.68.5.748 PMID:11068961

Briere, J. (1996). *Trauma Symptom Checklist Children (TSCC)*. Odessa, FL: Psychological Assessment Resources.

Briere, J. (1996). *Trauma Symptom Inventory professional manual*. Odessa, FL: Psychological Assessment Resources.

Briere, J. (2005). *Trauma Symptom Checklist for Young Children (TSCYC)*. Odessa, FL: Psychological Assessment Resources.

Briere, J. (2005). *Trauma Symptom Checklist for Young Children: Professional manual*. Odessa, FL: Psychological Assessment Resources.

Briere, J., & Runtz, M. (1987). Post sexual abuse trauma: Data and implications for clinical practice. *Journal of Interpersonal Violence, 2*(4), 367–379. doi:10.1177/088626058700200403

Briere, J., Scott, C., & Weathers, F. (2014). Peritraumatic and persistent dissociation in the presumed etiology of PTSD. *The American Journal of Psychiatry, 162*(12), 2295–2301. doi:10.1176/appi.ajp.162.12.2295 PMID:16330593

Brison, K. J. (1995). You Will Never Forget: Narrative, Bereavement, and Worldview among Kwanga Women. *Ethos (Berkeley, Calif.), 23*(4), 474–488. doi:10.1525/eth.1995.23.4.02a00060

Brison, K. J., & Leavitt, S. C. (1995). Coping with Bereavement: Long-Term Persectives on Grief and Mourning. *Ethos (Berkeley, Calif.), 23*(4), 395–400. doi:10.1525/eth.1995.23.4.02a00010

Brodzinsky, D. M. (2005). Reconceptualizing openness in adoption: Implications for theory, research, and practice. *Psychological issues in adoption: Research and Practice*, 145-166.

Brodzinsky, D. M. (2008). *Adoptive parent preparation: Meeting the mental health and developmental needs of adopted children*. Retrieved July 4, 2014, from: www.adoptioninstitute.org/policy/2008_02parent_prep.php

Brodzinsky, D. M., & Phinderhughes, E. (2002). Parenting and child development in adoptive families. In M. Bornstein (Ed.), *Handbook of parenting*. Retrieved from http://www.adoptioninstitute.org/publications/2008_02_Parent_Preparation.pdf

Brodzinsky, D. M. (1990). A stress and coping model of adoption adjustment. *The Psychology of Adoption, 3*(1), 3–24.

Brodzinsky, D. M. (1992). The impact of family structure on the adjustment of adopted children. *Child Welfare, 71*(1), 69–76. PMID:1737523

Brodzinsky, D. M. (1993). Long-term outcomes in adoption. *The Future of Children, 3*(1), 153–166. doi:10.2307/1602410

Brodzinsky, D. M., & Huffman, L. (1988). Transition to adoptive parenthood. *Marriage & Family Review, 12*(3-4), 267–286. doi:10.1300/J002v12n03_13

Brodzinsky, D. M., Smith, D. W., & Brodzinsky, A. B. (1998). *Children's adjustment to adoption: Developmental and clinical issues*. Thousand Oaks, CA: Sage.

Brooks, K., Schiraldi, V., & Ziedenberg, J. (2000). School house hype: Two years later. Washington, DC: Justice Policy Institute/Children's Law Center. Retrieved from http://www.cjcj.org/schoolhousehype/shh2.html

Brown, D., & Swanson, L. E. (2010). *Challenges for rural America in the twenty-first century*. Pennsylvania State Press.

Bruce, J., Tarullo, A. R., & Gunnar, M. R. (2009). Disinhibited social behavior among internationally adopted children. *Development and Psychopathology*, *21*(1), 151–171. doi:10.1017/S0954579409000108 PMID:19144228

Bubar, R., & Bundy-Fazioli, K. (2011). Unpacking race, culture and class in rural Alaska: Native and non-Native multidisciplinary professionals' perceptions of child sexual abuse. *Journal of Ethnic & Cultural Diversity in Social Work*, *20*(1), 1–19. doi:10.1080/15313204.2011.545941

Bullock, K. (2005). Chapter 7: Ahora le voy a cuidar a mis nietos: Rural Latino grandparents raising grandchildren of alcohol and other drug abusing parents. *Alcoholism Treatment Quarterly*, *23*(2-3), 107–130. doi:10.1300/J020v23n02_07

Burk, L., & Burkhart, B. (2003). Disorganized attachment as a diathesis for sexual deviance. *Aggression and Violent Behavior*, *8*(5), 487–511. doi:10.1016/S1359-1789(02)00076-9

Burnette, D. (1999). Social relationships of Latino grandparent caregivers: A role theory perspective. *The Gerontologist*, *39*(1), 49–58. doi:10.1093/geront/39.1.49 PMID:10028770

Burton, K. A., Florell, D., & Gore, J. S. (2013). Differences in proactive and reactive aggression in traditional bullies and cyberbullies. *Journal of Aggression, Maltreatment & Trauma*, *22*(3), 316–328. doi:10.1080/10926771.2013.743938

Burton, L. M., Lichter, D. T., Baker, R. S., & Eason, J. M. (2013). Inequality, family processes, and health in the "new" rural America. *The American Behavioral Scientist*.

Butler, K. (1996). The biology of fear. *The Family Therapy Networker*, *20*(4), 38–45.

Butler, L., Critelli, F., & Rinfrette, E. S. (2011). Trauma-informed care and mental health. *Directions in Psychiatry*, *31*(3), 197–212.

Byard, R. W., Gilbert, J., James, R., & Lipsett, J. (1999). Pathologic features of farm and tractor-related fatalities in children. *The American Journal of Forensic Medicine and Pathology*, *20*(1), 73–77. doi:10.1097/00000433-199903000-00018 PMID:10208343

Byrne, M. M. (2001). Evaluating the findings of qualitative research. *AORN Journal, 3*, 1-3. Doi:(06)61966-210.1016/S0001-2092

Cabrera, N. J., Ryan, R. M., Mitchell, S. J., Shannon, J. D., & Tamis-LeMonda, C. S. (2008). Low-income, non-resident, and father involvement with their toddlers: Variation by fathers' race and ethnicity. *Journal of Family Psychology*, *22*(4), 643–647. doi:10.1037/0893-3200.22.3.643 PMID:18729678

Caffaro-Rouget, A., Lang, R. A., & van Santen, V. (1989). The impact of child sexual abuse. *Annals of Sex Research*, *2*(1), 29–47. doi:10.1177/107906328900200102

Cairns, R. B., & Cairns, B. D. (1994). *Lifelines and risks: Pathways of youth in our time*. New York: Cambridge University Press.

Cairns, R. B., Cairns, B. D., Neckerman, H. J., & Gariepy, J. L. (1989). Growth and aggression: 1. Childhood to early adolescence. *Developmental Psychology*, *25*(2), 1–30. doi:10.1037/0012-1649.25.2.320

Calder, M. C. (2011). *Contemporary practice with young people who sexually abuse: Evidence based developments*. Holyoke, MA: NEARI press.

Calvert, J. F. Jr, & Munsie-Benson, M. (1999). Public opinion and knowledge about child sexual abuse in a rural community. *Child Abuse & Neglect*, *23*(7), 671–682. doi:10.1016/S0145-2134(99)00038-1 PMID:10442832

Campbell, J. C., Glass, N., Sharps, P. W., Laughon, K., & Bloom, T. (2007). Intimate partner homicide: Review and implications of research and policy. *Trauma, Violence & Abuse*, *8*(3), 246–269. doi:10.1177/1524838007303505 PMID:17596343

Campbell, J. C., Webster, D., Koziol-McLain, J., Block, C., Campbell, D., Curry, M. A., & Laughon, K. et al. (2003). Risk factors for femicide in abusive relationships: Results from a multisite case control study. *American Journal of Public Health*, *93*(7), 1089–1097. doi:10.2105/AJPH.93.7.1089 PMID:12835191

Cantu, L. (1995). The peripheralization of rural America: A case study of Latino migrants in America's heartland. *Sociological Perspectives*, *38*(3), 399–414. doi:10.2307/1389434

Capps, R., Castaneda, R. M., Chaudry, A., & Santos, R. (2007). *Paying the price: The impact of immigration raids on America's children*. Washington, DC: Urban Institute.

Cardena. (2001). Psychiatric Disorders Among Tortured Bhutanese Refugees in Nepal. *Archives of General Psychiatry*, *58*(5), 475–482.

Casey Family Services. (2003). *Strengthening families and communities: Promising practices for adoption-competent mental health services*. A white paper. Retrieved from www.caseyfamilyservices.org/pdfs/casey_mhpaper_sum.pdf

Casey, M. M., Blewett, L. A., & Call, K. T. (2004). Providing health care to Latino immigrants: Community-based efforts in the rural Midwest. *American Journal of Public Health*, *94*(10), 1709–1711. doi:10.2105/AJPH.94.10.1709 PMID:15451737

Cassiman, S. A. (2005). Toward more inclusive poverty knowledge: Traumatological contributions to the poverty discourse. The Social Policy Journal, and. *Cutting Edge of Social Policy Research*, *4*, 93–106.

Castaneda, R. S., & Alva, S. A. (2002). Language brokering the acculturation of Latino children. *Hispanic Journal of Behavioral Sciences*, *24*(3), 369–378. doi:10.1177/0739986302024003007

Ceballo, R., Dahl, T. A., Aretakis, M. T., & Ramirez, C. (2001). Inner-city children's exposure to community violence: How much do parents know? *Journal of Marriage and the Family*, *63*(4), 927–940. doi:10.1111/j.1741-3737.2001.00927.x

Center for the Study of Social Policy. (2003). *Protective factors literature review: Early care and education programs and the prevention of child abuse and neglect*. Retrieved from http://www.cssp.org/reform/strengthening-families/resources/body/LiteratureReview.pdf

Center for Youth Wellness. (2014). *Data Report: A Hidden Crisis, Findings on Adverse Childhood Experiences in California*. Retrieved from https://app.box.com/s/nf7lw36bjjr5kdfx4ct9 on 5/27/15

Centers for Disease Control and Prevention. (2014). *Youth risk behavior surveillance—United States, 2013*. Retrieved from: www.cdc.gov/mmwr/pdf/ss/ss6304.pdf

Cervantes, J. M., Mejia, O. L., & Mena, A. G. (2010). Serial migration and the assessment of extreme and unusual hardship with undocumented Latina/o families. *Hispanic Journal of Behavioral Sciences*, *32*(2), 275–291. doi:10.1177/0739986310366286

Chaffin, M., Silovsky, J. F., Funderburk, B., Valle, L. A., Brestan, E. V., Balachova, T., & Bonner, B. L. (2004). Parent-child interaction therapy with physically abusive parents: Efficacy for reducing future abuse reports. *Journal of Consulting and Clinical Psychology*, *72*(3), 500–510. doi:10.1037/0022-006X.72.3.500 PMID:15279533

Chambers, R., & Potter, C. (2009). A typology of family needs in child neglect cases. *Families in Society*, *89*(5), 18–27. doi:10.1606/1044-3894.3841

Chatterjee, S., Chatterjee, A., & Jain, S. (2003). Developing community-based services for serious mental illness in a rural setting. In Meeting the mental health needs of developing countries: NGO innovations in India. Sage Publications, Inc.

Chaudry, A., Capps, R., Pedroza, J., Castaneda, R. M., Santos, R., & Scott, M. M. (2010). *Facing our future: Children in the aftermath of immigration enforcement*. Washington, DC: Urban Institute.

Chen, J. K., & Astor, R. A. (2009). The perpetration of school violence in Taiwan: An analysis of gender, grade level, school type. *School Psychology International*, *30*(6), 568–584. doi:10.1177/0143034309107076

Cherry, K. A. (2006). *What is attachment theory?* Retrieved from http://psychology.about.com/od/loveandattraction/a/attachment01.htm

Child Welfare Information Gateway. (2010). *Impact of adoption on adoptive parents*. Retrieved from www.childwelfare.gov

Child Welfare Information Gateway. (2011). *Child Maltreatment Prevention: Past, Present and Future*. Retrieved from https://www.childwelfare.gov/pubPDFs/ cm_prevention.pdf

Child Welfare Information Gateway. (2011). *Parenting after adoption*. Retrieved from www.childwelfare.gov

Child Welfare Information Gateway. (2012). *Finding and using postadoption services*. Retrieved from www.childwelfare.gov

Child Welfare Information Gateway. (2012). *Foster parents considering adoption*. Washington, DC: U.S. Department of Health and Human Services, Children's Bureau.

Child Welfare Information Gateway. (2013). *Consent to adoption*. Washington, DC: US Department of Health and Human Services, Children's Bureau.

Child Welfare Information Gateway. (2013). *Disruption and dissolution in adoption*. Retrieved from www.childwelfare.gov

Child Welfare Information Gateway. (n.d.). *What is prevention and why is it important?* Retrieved from https://www.childwelfare.gov/topics/preventing/overview/whatiscap/?hasBeenRedirected=1#one

Child Welfare League of America. (2001). *Alcohol, other drugs, & child welfare*. Washington, DC: Author. Retrieved from www.cwla.org/programs/bhd/aodbrochure.pdf

*Children's Bureau*. (2013). Retrieved from http://www.acf.hhs.gov/programs/cb/research-data-technology/statistics-research

Choi-Kain, L. W., & Gunderson, J. G. (2008). Mentalization: Ontogeny, assessment, and application in the treatment of borderline personality disorder. *The American Journal of Psychiatry*, *165*(9), 1127–1135. doi:10.1176/appi.ajp.2008.07081360 PMID:18676591

Chong, W. W., Aslani, P., & Chen, T. F. (2013). Shared decision-making and interprofessional collaboration in mental healthcare: A qualitative study exploring perceptions of barriers and facilitators. *Journal of Interprofessional Care*, *27*(5), 373–379. doi:10.3109/13561820.2013.785503 PMID:23679672

Chorpita, B. F., & Daleiden, E. L. (2009). Mapping evidence-based treatments for children and adolescents: Application of the distillation and matching model to 615 treatments from 322 randomized trails. *Journal of Counseling and Clinical Psychology*, *77*(3), 566–579. doi:10.1037/a0014565 PMID:19485596

Christancho, S., Garces, D. M., Peters, K., & Mueller, B. C. (2008). Listening to rural Hispanic immigrants in the Midwest: A community-based participatory assessment of barriers to health care access and use. *Qualitative Health Research*, *18*(5), 633–646. doi:10.1177/1049732308316669 PMID:18420537

Cicero-Dominguez, S. A. (2005). Assessing the U.S.-Mexico fight against human trafficking and smuggling: Unintended results of U.S. immigration policy. *Northwestern University Journal of International Human Rights*, *4*, 303.

Clauss-Ehlers, C. S., & Levi, L. L. (2002). Violence and community, terms in conflict: An ecological approach to resilience. *Journal of Social Distress and the Homeless*, *11*(4), 265–278. doi:10.1023/A:1016804930977

Clay, R. A. (2014). Reducing Rural Suicide: Psychologists are finding innovative ways to reach out to people in isolated communities. American Psychological Association, 45(4), 36.

Clinton, T., & Sibcy, G. (2002). *Attachments: Why You Love, Feel And Act The Way You Do*. Brentwood, TN: Thomas Nelson Publishers.

Cogbill, T. H., Busch, H. m., & Stiers, G. R. (1985). Farm accidents in children. *Pediatrics*, *76*, 562–566. PMID:4047799

Cohen, J. A., Berliner, L., & Mannarino, A. P. (2010). Trauma-focused CBT for children with co-occurring trauma and behavior problems. *Child Abuse & Neglect*, *34*(4), 215–224. doi:10.1016/j.chiabu.2009.12.003 PMID:20304489

Cohen, J. A., & Mannarino, A. P. (2008). Trauma-focused cognitive behavioural therapy for children and parents. *Child and Adolescent Mental Health*, *13*(4), 158–162. doi:10.1111/j.1475-3588.2008.00502.x

Cohen, J. A., Mannarino, A. P., Kliethermes, M., & Murray, L. A. (2012). Trauma-focused CBT for youth with complex trauma. *Child Abuse & Neglect*, *36*(6), 528–541. doi:10.1016/j.chiabu.2012.03.007 PMID:22749612

Cohen, J. A., Scheid, J., & Gerson, R. (2014). Transforming Trajectories for Traumatized Children. *Journal of the American Academy of Child and Adolescent Psychiatry*, *53*(1), 9–13. doi:10.1016/j.jaac.2013.10.004 PMID:24342380

Cohen, J., Mannarino, A. P., & Deblinger, E. (2006). *Treating trauma and traumatic grief in children and adolescents*. New York, NY: Guilford Press.

Collins, K., Connors, K., Davis, S., Donohue, A., Gardner, S., Goldblatt, E., . . . Thompson, E. (2010). Understanding the Impact of Trauma and Urban Poverty on Family Systems: Risks, Resilience, and Interventions. Family Informed Trauma Treatment Center, 1–117.

Combs, C. G. (1986). Case note: Wrongful adoption: Adoption agency held liable for fraudulent representations: Burr v. Stark County Board of Commissioners, Ohio St. 3d 69 491 N. E. 2d 1101. *University of Cincinnati Law Review*.

Conan Doyle, A. (1986). *Sherlock Holmes: The Complete Novels and Stories* (Vol. I). New York, NY: Random House Inc.

Conte, J., & Schuerman, J. (1987). The effects of sexual abuse on children: A multidimensional view. *Journal of Interpersonal Violence*, *2*(4), 380–390. doi:10.1177/088626058700200404

Coohey, C. (2001). The relationship between familism and child maltreatment in Latino and Anglo families. *Child Maltreatment*, *6*(2), 130–142. doi:10.1177/1077559501006002005 PMID:16705788

Cook, A., Spinnazzola, J., Ford, J. A., Lanktree, C., Blaustein, M., Cloitre, M., & Van der kolk, B. (2005). Complex trauma in children and adolescents. *Psychiatric S Annals, 35*, 390-398.

Cornish, P. A., Church, P. A., Callanan, T., Bethune, C., Robbins, C., & Miller, R. (2003). Rural interdisciplinary mental health team building via satellite: a demonstration project. Special Issue: Success Stories in Telemedicine: Some Empirical Evidence. *Telemedicine Journal and e-Health*, *9*(1), 63–71. doi:10.1089/153056203763317666 PMID:12699609

Counts, J. M., Buffington, E. S., Chang Rios, K., Rasmussen, H. N., & Preacher, K. J. (2010). The development and validation of the protective factors survey: A self-report measure of protective factors against child maltreatment. *Child Abuse & Neglect*, *34*(10), 762–772. doi:10.1016/j.chiabu.2010.03.003 PMID:20851466

Cowart-Osborne, M., Jackson, M., Chege, E., Baker, E., Whitaker, D., & Self-Brown, S. (2014). Technology-based innovations in child maltreatment prevention programs: Examples from SafeCare®. *Social Sciences*, *3*(3), 427–440. doi:10.3390/socsci3030427 PMID:25606347

Cradle. (2010). *Post-adoption services*. Retrieved July 2, 2014, from http://www.cradle.ord/postadopt_home.html

Cravey, A. J. (1997). Latino labor and poultry production in rural North Carolina. *Southeastern Geographer*, *37*(2), 295–300. doi:10.1353/sgo.1997.0001

Crenshaw, D., & Hardy, K. V. (2007). The crucial role of empathy in breaking the silence of traumatized children in play therapy. *International Journal of Play Therapy, 16,* 160-175.

Creswell, J. W. (2002). *Educational research: Planning, conducting, and evaluating quantitative and qualitative research*. Upper Saddle River, NJ: Merrill Prentice Hall.

Creswell, J. W. (2003). *Research design: Qualitative, quantitative and mixed methods approaches* (2nd ed.). Thousand Oaks, CA: Sage.

Creswell, J. W. (2007). *Qualitative inquiry & research design: Choosing among five approaches* (2nd ed.). Los Angeles, CA: Sage.

Crittenden, P. M., & Ainsworth, M. D. S. (1989). Child maltreatment and attachment theory. In D. Cicchetti & V. Carlson (Eds.), *Child Maltreatment: Theory and research on the causes and consequences of child abuse and neglect*. Cambridge, UK: University of Cambrindge. doi:10.1017/CBO9780511665707.015

Crosby, J. W., Oehler, J., & Capaccioli, K. (2010). The relationship between peer victimization and posttraumatic stress symptomatology in a rural sample. *Psychology in the Schools*, *47*(3), 297–310.

Crowley, M., & Lichter, D. T. (2009). Social disorganization in new Latino destinations? *Rural Sociology*, *74*(4), 573–604. doi:10.1526/003601109789864026

Crowley, M., Lichter, D. T., & Qian, Z. (2006). Beyond gateway cities: Economic restructuring and poverty among immigrant families and children. *Family Relations*, *55*(3), 345–360. doi:10.1111/j.1741-3729.2006.00407.x

Cullen, J. P., Ownbey, J. B., & Ownbey, M. A. (2010). The effects of the Healthy Families America Home Visitation Program on parenting attitudes and practices and child social and emotional competence. *Child & Adolescent Social Work Journal*, *27*(5), 335–354. doi:10.1007/s10560-010-0206-9

Cunningham, P. B., & Henggeler, S. W. (2001). Implementation of empirically based drug and violence prevention and intervention programs in public school settings. *Journal of Clinical Child Psychology*, *30*(1), 221–232. doi:10.1207/S15374424JCCP3002_9 PMID:11393922

Cunradi, C. B., Caetano, R., & Schafer, J. (2002). Socioeconomic predictors of intimate partner violence among White, Black, and Hispanic couples in the United States. *Journal of Family Violence*, *17*(4), 377–389. doi:10.1023/A:1020374617328

Czincz, J., & Romano, E. (2013). Childhood sexual abuse: Community-based treatment practices and predictors of use of evidence-based practices. *Child and Adolescent Mental Health*, *18*(4), 240–246.

D'Andrea, W., Ford, J., Stolbach, B., Spinazzola, J., & van der Kolk, B. A. (2012). Understanding interpersonal trauma in children: Why we need a developmentally appropriate trauma diagnosis. *The American Journal of Orthopsychiatry*, *82*(2), 187–200. doi:10.1111/j.1939-0025.2012.01154.x PMID:22506521

Dake, J. A., Price, J. H., & Telljohann, S. K. (2003). The nature and extent of bullying at school. *The Journal of School Health*, *73*(5), 173–180. doi:10.1111/j.1746-1561.2003.tb03599.x PMID:12793102

Dalgleish, T., Goodall, B., Chadwick, I., Werner-Seidler, A., McKinnon, A., Morant, A., & Meiser-Stedman, R. et al. (2015). Trauma-focused cognitive behaviour therapy versus treatment as usual for post-traumatic stress disorder (PTSD) in young children aged 3 to 8 years: Study protocol for a randomised controlled trial. *Trials*, *16*(1), 116. doi:10.1186/s13063-015-0632-2 PMID:25872653

Dalla, R. L., & Chirstensen, A. (2005). Latino immigrants describe residence in rural Midwestern communities: A longitudinal assessment of social and economic change. *Hispanic Journal of Behavioral Sciences*, *27*(1), 23–42. doi:10.1177/0739986304272354

Dalla, R. L., Ellis, A., & Cramer, S. C. (2005). Immigration and rural America: Latinos' perceptions of work and residence in three meat packing communities. *Community Work & Family*, *8*(2), 163–185. doi:10.1080/13668800500049639

Damashek, A., Doughty, D., Ware, L., & Silovsky, J. (2011). Predictors of client engagement and attrition in home-based child maltreatment prevention services. *Child Maltreatment*, *16*(1), 9–20. doi:10.1177/1077559510388507 PMID:21148600

Damashek, A., Nelson, M. M., & Bonner, B. L. (2013). Fatal child maltreatment: Characteristics of death from physical abuse versus neglect. *Child Abuse & Neglect*, *37*, 735–744. PMID:23768940

Dasgupta, S. D. (1999). Just like men? A critical view of violence by women. In M. F. Shepard & E. L. Pence (Eds.), *Coordinating community responses to domestic violence: Lessons from Duluth and beyond* (pp. 195–222). Thousand Oaks, CA: Sage. doi:10.4135/9781452231952.n10

Davis, N. (1996). Once upon a time: Therapeutic stories that teach and heal. Burke, VA: Nancy Davis.

De Jongh, A., Olff, M., van Hoolwerff, H., Aartman, I. H., Broekman, B., Lindauer, R., & Boer, F. (2008). Anxiety and Post-traumatic stress symptoms following wisdom tooth removal. *Behaviour Research and Therapy*, *46*(12), 1305–1310. doi:10.1016/j.brat.2008.09.004 PMID:18954863

De Jong, J. T. V. M. (2004). Public Mental Health and Culture: Disasters as a Challenge to Western Mental Health Care Models, the Self, and PTSD. In J. P. Wilson & B. Drozdek (Eds.), *Broken Spirits: The Treatment of Asylum Seekers and Refugees with PTSD* (pp. 157–176). New York: Brunner/Routledge.

De Jong, J. T. V. M., & Van Ommeren, M. H. (2002). Toward A Culture-informed Epidemiology: Combining Qualitative and Quantitative Research in Transcultural Contexts. *Transcultural Psychiatry*, *39*(4), 422–433. doi:10.1177/136346150203900402

De Young, A. C., Kenardy, J. A., Cobham, V. E., & Kimble, R. (2012). Prevalence, comorbidity and course of trauma reactions in young burn-injured children. *Journal of Child Psychology and Psychiatry, and Allied Disciplines*, *53*(1), 56–63. doi:10.1111/j.1469-7610.2011.02431.x PMID:21671940

Deblinger, E., Mannarino, A. P., Cohen, J. A., Runyon, M. K., & Steer, R. A. (2011). Trauma-focused cognitive behavioral therapy for children: Impact of the trauma narrative and treatment length. *Depression and Anxiety*, *28*(1), 67–75. doi:10.1002/da.20744 PMID:20830695

Deblinger, E., Taub, B., Maedel, A. B., Lippmann, J., & Stauffer, L. B. (1997). Psychosocial factors predicting parent reported symptomatology in sexually abused children. *Journal of Child Sexual Abuse*, *6*(4), 35–49. doi:10.1300/J070v06n04_03

Degraw, M., Hicks, R. A., & Lindberg, D. (2010). Incidence of fractures among children with burns with concern regarding abuse. *Pediatrics*, *125*(2), 295–259.

DePrince, A. P., & Newman, E. (2011). The art and science of trauma-focused training and education. *Psychological Trauma: Theory. Research Policy*, *3*, 213–214. doi:10.1037/a0024640

DeVoe, J. F., Peter, K., Noonan, M., Snyder, T. D., & Baum, K. (2005). *Indicators of school crime and safety: 2005. U.S. Departments of Education and Justice*. Washington, DC: U.S. Government Printing Office.

Dew, R. E., Daniel, S. S., Armstrong, T. D., Goldston, D. B., Triplett, M. F., & Koenig, H. G. (2008). Religion/spirituality and adolescent psychiatric symptoms: A review. *Child Psychiatry and Human Development*, *39*(4), 381–398. doi:10.1007/s10578-007-0093-2 PMID:18219572

Dickie, J. R., Eshleman, A. K., Merasco, D. M., Shepard, A., Vander Wilt, M., & Johnson, M. (1997). Parent – child relationships and children's images of God. *Journal for the Scientific Study of Religion*, *36*(1), 25–43. doi:10.2307/1387880

Dishion, T. J., Eddy, J. M., Haas, E., Li, F., & Spracklen, K. (1997). Friendships and violent behavior during adolescence. *Social Development*, *6*(2), 207–223. doi:10.1111/j.1467-9507.1997.tb00102.x

Donahue, M. J., & Benson, P. L. (1995). Religion and the well being of adolescents. *The Journal of Social Issues*, *51*(2), 145–160. doi:10.1111/j.1540-4560.1995.tb01328.x

Donnermeyer, J. F. (1994). Crime and violence in rural communities. In M. Womble & J. D'Amico (Eds.), *Perspectives on violence and substance use in rural America* (pp. 27–64). Oak Brook, IL: North Central Regional Educational Laboratory.

Drake, B., & Pandey, S. (1996). Understanding the relationship between neighborhood poverty and specific types of child maltreatment. *Child Abuse & Neglect*, *20*(11), 1003–1018. doi:10.1016/0145-2134(96)00091-9 PMID:8958452

Dreby, J. (2012). *How today's immigration enforcement policies impact children, families, and communities: A view from the ground*. Center for American Progress.

Dreby, J. (2012). The burden of deportation on children in Mexican immigrant families. *Journal of Marriage and the Family*, *74*(4), 829–845. doi:10.1111/j.1741-3737.2012.00989.x

Dreman, S. (1991). Coping with the trauma of divorce. *Journal of Traumatic Stress*, *4*(1), 113–121. doi:10.1002/jts.2490040109

Drury, S. S., & Henry, C. (2012). Evidence-based treatment of PTSD in children and adolescents: Where does psychopharmacology fit? *Child and Adolescent Psychopharmacology News*, *17*(3), 1–9. doi:10.1521/capn.2012.17.3.1

D'Souza, A. L., Nelson, N. G., & McKenzie, L. B. (2009). Pediatric burn injuries treated in US emergency departments between 1990 and 2006. *Pediatrics*, *124*(5), 1424–1430. doi:10.1542/peds.2008-2802 PMID:19805456

Dubow, E. F., Pargament, K. I., Boxer, P., & Tarakeshwar, N. (2000). Initial investigation of Jewish early adolescents' ethnic identity, stress, and coping. *The Journal of Early Adolescence*, *20*(4), 418–441. doi:10.1177/0272431600020004003

Due, P., Holstein, B. E., Lynch, J., Diderichsen, F., Gabhain, S. N., Scheidt, P., & Currie, C.The Health Behavior in School-Aged Children Bullying Working Group. (2005). Bullying and symptom among school-aged children: International comparative cross sectional study in 28 countries. *European Journal of Public Health*, *15*(2), 128–132. doi:10.1093/eurpub/cki105 PMID:15755782

Due, P., Merlo, J., Harel-Fisch, Y., Damsgaard, M. T., soc, M., Holstein, B. E., & Lynch, J. et al. (2009). Socioeconomic inequality in exposure to bullying during adolescence: A comparative, cross-sectional, multilevel study in 35 countries. *American Journal of Public Health*, *99*(5), 907–914. doi:10.2105/AJPH.2008.139303 PMID:19299676

Dukarm, C. P., Byrd, R. S., Auinger, P., & Weitzman, M. (1996). Illicit substance use, gender, and the risk of violent behavior among adolescents. *Pediatrics & Adolescent Medicine*, *150*(8), 797–801. doi:10.1001/archpedi.1996.02170330023004 PMID:8704884

Dulmus, C. N., Theriot, M. T., Sowers, K. M., & Blackburn, J. A. (2004). Student reports of peer bullying victimization in a rural school. *Stress, Trauma and Crisis*, *7*(1), 1–16. doi:10.1080/15434610490281093

Duncan, B., Hubble, M., & Miller, S. (Eds.). (2010). *The heart and soul of change: Delivering what works in therapy* (2nd ed.). Washington, DC: American Psychological Association. doi:10.1037/12075-000

DuRant, R. H., Kahn, J., Beckford, P. H., & Woods, E. R. (1997). The association of weapon carrying and fighting on school property and other health risk and problem behaviors among high school students. *Archives of Pediatrics & Adolescent Medicine*, *151*(4), 360–366. doi:10.1001/archpedi.1997.02170410034004 PMID:9111434

Duva, J., & Metzger, S. (2010). Addressing Poverty as a Major Risk Factor in Child Neglect: Promising Policy and Practice. *Protecting Children*, *25*(1), 63–74.

Early Years Foundation. (2007). *Child development overview*. Retrieved from http://webarchive.nationalarchives.gov.uk/20130401151715/http://www.education.gov.uk/publications/eOrderingDownload/eyfs_cards_0001207.pdf

Eck, D. (2007). Religion. In M. C. Waters & R. Ueda (Eds.), The new Americans: A guide to immigration since 1965, (pp. 214–227). Cambridge, MA: Harvard University Press.

Ecker, B., Ticic, R., & Hulley, L. (2012). *Unlocking the Emotional Brain: Eliminating Symptoms at Their Roots Using Memory Reconsolidation*. New York, NY: Routledge.

Edmund, D. S., & Bland, P. J. (2011). Poverty and Trauma. From Real Tools: Responding to Multi-Abuse Trauma. *Alaska Network on Domestic Violence and Sexual Abuse*, Retrieved from http://www.apa.org/pi/families/poverty.aspx on 5/27/15

Edwards, A., & Lutzker, J. R. (2008). Iterations of the SafeCare model: An evidence-based child maltreatment prevention program. *Behavior Modification*, *32*(5), 736–756. doi:10.1177/0145445508317137 PMID:18441332

Egeland, B., Bosquet, M., & Levy Chung, A. (2002). Continuities and Discontinuities in the Intergenerational Tranmission of Child Maltreatment: Implications for Breaking the Cycle of Abuse. In K. Browne et al. (Eds.), *Early Prediction and Prevention of Child Abuse: A Handbook*. John Wiley & Sons Ltd.

Eichner, J. E., Moore, W. E., Perveen, G., Kobza, C. E., Abbott, K. E., & Stephens, A. L. (2012). Overweight and obesity in an ethnically diverse rural school district: The Healthy Kids Project. *Obesity (Silver Spring, Md.)*, *16*(2), 501–504. doi:10.1038/oby.2007.60 PMID:18239668

Eisenbruch, M. (1990). The cultural bereavement interview: A new clinical and research approach with refugees. *The Psychiatric Clinics of North America*, *13*, 715–735. PMID:2281015

Eisenstadt, T. H., Eyberg, S., McNeil, C. B., Newcomb, K., & Funderburk, B. (1993). Parent-child interaction therapy with behavior problem children: Relative effectiveness of two stages and overall treatment outcome. *Journal of Clinical Child Psychology*, *22*(1), 42–51. doi:10.1207/s15374424jccp2201_4

Elliott, D. S., Hamburg, B. A., & Williams, K. R. (1998). Violence in American schools: An overview. In D. Elliott, B. Hamburg, & K. Williams (Eds.), *Violence in American schools* (pp. 3–28). Cambridge, UK: Cambridge University Press.

Ennis, S. R., Rios-Vargas, M., & Albert, N. G. (2011). *The Hispanic population: 2010.* U. S. Department of Commerce, Economics and Statistics Administration, U. S. Census Bureau.

Erickson, L. D., Hedges, D. W., Call, V. R. A., & Bair, B. (2013). Prevalence of and factors associated with subclinical posttraumatic stress symptoms and PTSD in urban and rural areas of Montana: A cross-sectional study. *The Journal of Rural Health*, *29*(4), 403–412. PMID:24088214

Eslea, M., Menesant, E., Morita, Y., O'Moore, M., Mora-Merchan, J. A., Perera, B., & Smith, P. K. (2003). Friendship and loneliness among bullies and victims: Data from seven countries. *Aggressive Behavior*, *30*(1), 71–83. doi:10.1002/ab.20006

Espelage, D. L., & Swearer, S. M. (2003). Research on school bullying and victimization: What have we learned and where do we go from here? *School Psychology Review*, *32*, 365–383.

Estell, D. B., Farmer, T. W., & Cairns, B. D. (2007). Bullies and victims in rural African American youth: Behavioral characteristics and social network placement. *Aggressive Behavior*, *33*(2), 145–159. doi:10.1002/ab.20176 PMID:17441015

Estell, D. B., Farmer, T. W., Irvin, M. J., Thompson, J. H., Hutchins, B. C., & McDonough, E. M. (2007). Patterns of middle school adjustment and ninth grade adaptation of rural African American youth: Grades and substance use. *Journal of Youth and Adolescence*, *36*(4), 477–487. doi:10.1007/s10964-007-9167-5

Eth, S., & Pynoos, R. S. (1985). *Posttraumatic stress disorder in children (Progress inPsychiatry Series).* Washington, DC: American Psychiatric Association.

Evan B. Donaldson Adoption Institute. (2010). *Keeping the promise: The critical need for post-adoption services to enable children and families to succeed.* Retrieved from http://life.familyeducation.com/adoption/adoptive-parents/45782html#ixzz2srEgs9bLhtml#ixzz2srEgs9bL

Evans, C. B. R., Smokowski, P. R., & Cotter, K. L. (2014). Cumulative bullying victimization: An investigation of the dose-response relationship between victimization and the associated mental health outcomes, social supports, and school experiences of rural adolescents. *Children and Youth Services Review*, *44*, 256–264. doi:10.1016/j.childyouth.2014.06.021

Evans, G. W., & Lepore, S. J. (1993). Household crowding and social support: A quasi-experimental analysis. *Journal of Personality and Social Psychology*, *65*(2), 308–316. doi:10.1037/0022-3514.65.2.308 PMID:8366422

Evans, L. G., & Oehler-Stinnett, J. (2006). Structure and prevalence of PTSD symptomatology in children who have experienced a severe tornado. *Psychology in the Schools*, *43*(3), 283–295. doi:10.1002/pits.20150

Evans, W. P., Fitzgerald, C., Weigel, D., & Chvilicek, S. (1999). Are rural gang members similar to their urban peers? Implications for rural communities. *Youth & Society*, *30*(3), 267–282. doi:10.1177/0044118X99030003001

Fallon, B., Trocmé, N., Fluke, J., MacLaurin, B., Tonmyr, L., & Yuan, Y. Y. (2010). Methodological challenges in measuring child maltreatment. *Child Abuse & Neglect*, *34*(1), 70–79. doi:10.1016/j.chiabu.2009.08.008 PMID:20053453

Family Preservation and Support Services Act of 1993, P. L. 103-66.

Fantuzzo, J., McDermott, P., & Lutz, M. N. (1999). Clinical issues in the assessment of family violence involving children. In R. T. Ammerman & M. Hersen (Eds.), *Assessment of family violence: A clinical and legal sourcebook* (2nd ed.; pp. 10–23). Baltimore, MD: John Wiley and Sons.

Fantuzzo, J., & Mohr, W. (1999). Prevalence and effects of child exposure to domestic violence. *The Future of Children: Domestic Violence and Children*, *9*(3), 21–32. doi:10.2307/1602779 PMID:10777998

Farmer, T. W., Estell, D. B., Bishop, J. L., O'Neal, K. K., & Cairns, B. D. (2003). Rejected bullies or popular leaders? The social relations of aggressive subtypes of rural African American early adolescents. *Developmental Psychology*, *39*(6), 992–1004. doi:10.1037/0012-1649.39.6.992 PMID:14584980

Farmer, T. W., Irvin, M. J., Sgammato, A., Dadisman, K., & Thompson, J. H. (2009). Interpersonal competence configurations in rural Appalachian fifth graders: Academic achievement and associated adjustment factors. *The Elementary School Journal*, *109*(3), 301–321. doi:10.1086/592309

Farrell, A. D., & Sullivan, T. N. (2004). Impact of witnessing violence on growth curves for problem behaviors among early adolescents in urban and rural settings. *Journal of Community Psychology*, *32*(5), 505–525. doi:10.1002/jcop.20016

Farrington, D. P., & Ttoti, M. M. (2009). School-based programs to reduce bullying and victimization. *Campbell Systematic Reviews*, 6.

Fawzi, M. C., Pham, T., Lin, L., Nguyen, T. V., Ngo, D., Murphy, E., & Mollica, R. (1997). The Validity of Post-traumatic Stress Disorder Among Vietnamese Refugees. *Journal of Traumatic Stress*, *10*(1), 101–108. doi:10.1002/jts.2490100109 PMID:9018680

Fay, J., Fay, C., & Cline, F. (2010). *Becoming a love and logic parent curriculum*. Golden, CO: Love and Logic Institute.

Feather, J. S., & Ronan, K. R. (2009). Trauma-focused CBT with maltreated children: A clinic-based evaluation of a new treatment manual. *Australian Psychologist*, *44*(3), 174–194. doi:10.1080/00050060903147083

Feder, A., Alonso, A., Tang, M., Liriano, W., Warner, V., Pilowsky, D., & Weissman, M. et al. (2009). Children of Low-Income Depressed Mothers: Psychiatric Disorders and Social Adjustment. *Depression and Anxiety*, *26*(6), 513–520. PMID:19016460

Felitti, V. J., Anda, R. F., Nordenberg, D., Williamson, D. F., Spitz, A. M., Edwards, V., & Marks, J. S. et al. (1998). Relationship of Childhood Abuse and Household Dysfunction to Many of the Leading Causes of Death in Adults. *American Journal of Preventive Medicine*, *14*(4), 245–258. doi:10.1016/S0749-3797(98)00017-8 PMID:9635069

Fellows, R., & Liu, A. (2008). *Research methods for construction*. New York, NY: John Wiley & Sons.

Fertman, C. I., Dotson, S., Mazzocco, G. O., & Reitz, S. (2005). Maggie challenges of preparing allied health professionals for interdisciplinary practice in rural areas. *Journal of Allied Health*, *34*(3), 163–168. PMID:16252679

Festinger, T., & Maza, P. (2009). Displacement or post-adoption? A research note. *Journal of Public Child Welfare*, *3*(3), 275–286. doi:10.1080/15548730903129889

Finkelhor, D. (1978). Psychological, cultural, and family factors in incest and family sexual abuse. *Journal of Marriage and Family Counseling*, *4*(4), 41–49. doi:10.1111/j.1752-0606.1978.tb00539.x

Finkelhor, D. (1994). The international epidemiology of child sexual abuse. *Child Abuse & Neglect*, *18*(5), 409–417. doi:10.1016/0145-2134(94)90026-4 PMID:8032971

Finkelhor, D., Hamby, S. L., Ormrod, R., & Turner, H. (2005b). The Juvenile Victimization Questionnaire: Reliability, validity, and national norms. *Child Abuse & Neglect*, *29*(4), 383–412. doi:10.1016/j.chiabu.2004.11.001 PMID:15917079

Finkelhor, D., & Jones, L. (2006). Why have child maltreatment and child victimization declined? *The Journal of Social Issues*, *62*(4), 685–716. doi:10.1111/j.1540-4560.2006.00483.x

Finkelhor, D., Ormrod, R. K., & Turner, H. A. (2007). Polyvictimization and trauma in a national longitudinal cohort. *Development and Psychopathology*, *19*(01), 149–166. doi:10.1017/S0954579407070083 PMID:17241488

Finkelhor, D., Ormrod, R. K., & Turner, H. A. (2009). Lifetime assessment of poly-victimization in a national sample of children and youth. *Child Abuse & Neglect*, *33*(7), 403–411. doi:10.1016/j.chiabu.2008.09.012 PMID:19589596

Finkelhor, D., Ormrod, R. K., Turner, H. A., & Hamby, S. L. (2005a). Measuring poly-victimization using the Juvenile Victimization Questionnaire. *Child Abuse & Neglect*, *29*(11), 1297–1312. doi:10.1016/j.chiabu.2005.06.005 PMID:16274741

Finkelhor, D., Turner, H. A., Ormrod, R., & Hamby, S. L. (2009). Violence, abuse, and crime exposure in a national sample of children and youth. *Pediatrics*, *124*(5), 1411–1423. doi:10.1542/peds.2009-0467 PMID:19805459

Finkelhor, D., Turner, H., Hamby, S., & Ormrod, R. (2011). Poly-victimization: Children's exposure to multiple types of violence, crime, and abuse. *Free Inquiry in Creative Sociology*, *39*, 24–34.

Finkelhor, D., Turner, H., Ormrod, R., & Hamby, S. L. (2010). Trends in childhood violence and abuse exposure: Evidence from 2 national surveys. *Pediatrics & Adolescent Medicine*, *238-242*. doi:10.1001/archpediatric.2009.283 PMID:20194256

Finkel, M. (2012). Children's disclosures of child sexual abuse. *Pediatric Annals*, *41*(12), 1–6. doi:10.3928/00904481-20121126-10 PMID:23205659

Finkelstein, N. (1994). Treatment issues for alcohol- and drug-dependent pregnant and parenting women. *Health & Social Work*, *19*(1), 7–15. PMID:8168782

Flannery, D. J., Wester, K. L., & Singer, M. I. (2004). Impact of exposure to violence in school on child and adolescent mental health and behavior. *Journal of Community Psychology*, *32*(5), 559–573. doi:10.1002/jcop.20019

Fleming, J. (2012). The effectiveness of eye movement desensitization and reprocessing in the treatment of traumatized children and youth. *Journal of EMDR Practice and Research*, *6*(1), 16–26. doi:10.1891/1933-3196.6.1.16

Flores, E., Cicchetti, D., & Rogosch, F. A. (2005). Predictors of resilience in maltreated and nonmaltreated Latino children. *Developmental Psychology*, *41*(2), 338–351. doi:10.1037/0012-1649.41.2.338 PMID:15769190

Flores-Ortiz, Y. G. (1997). The broken covenant: Incest in Latino family. Voces: A Journal of Chicana. *Latino Studies*, 48–70.

Flynt, S. W., & Morton, R. C. (2007). Bullying prevention and students with disabilities. *National Forum of Special Education Journal, 19*(1), 1-6.

Foli, K. J., & Thompson, J. R. (2004). *The Post-Adoption Blues: Overcoming the Unforseen Challenges of Adoption*. Emmaus, PA: Rodale.

Folsom, D. P., Gilmer, T., Barrio, C., Moore, D. J., Bucardo, J., Lindamer, L. A., & Jeste, D. V. (2007). A longitudinal study of the use of mental health services by persons with serious mental illness: Do Spanish-speaking Latinos differ from English-speaking Latinos and Caucasians? *The American Journal of Psychiatry*, *164*(8), 1173–1180. doi:10.1176/appi.ajp.2007.06071239 PMID:17671279

Fonagy, P., & Campbell, C. (2015). Bad blood revisited: Attachment and Pscychoanalysis, 2015. *British Journal of Psychotherapy*, *31*(2), 229–250. doi:10.1111/bjp.12150

Fonagy, P., Steele, M., Moran, G. S., & Higgitt, A. (1993). Measuring the ghost in the nursery: An empirical study of the relation between parents' mental representations of childhood experiences and theirinfants' security of attachment. *Journal of the American Psychoanalytic Association*, *41*(4), 957–989. doi:10.1177/000306519304100403 PMID:8282943

Fonagy, P., Steele, M., Steele, H., Moran, G. S., & Higgitt, A. C. (1991). The capacity for understanding mental states: The reflective self in parent and child and its significance for security of attachment. *Infant Mental Health Journal*, *12*(3), 201–218. doi:10.1002/1097-0355(199123)12:3<201::AID-IMHJ2280120307>3.0.CO;2-7

Fontes, L. A. (2002). Child discipline and physical abuse in immigrant Latino families: Reducing violence and misunderstandings. *Journal of Counseling and Development*, *80*(1), 31–40. doi:10.1002/j.1556-6678.2002.tb00163.x

Fontes, L. A. (2007). Sin verguenza: Addressing shame with Latino victims of child sexual abuse and their families. *Journal of Child Sexual Abuse*, *16*(1), 61–83. doi:10.1300/J070v16n01_04 PMID:17255077

Fontes, L. A., Cruz, M., & Tabachnick, J. (2001). Views of child sexual abuse in two cultural communities: An exploratory study among African Americans and Latinos. *Child Maltreatment*, *6*(2), 103–117. doi:10.1177/1077559501006002003 PMID:16705786

Forbes, H., & Dziegielewski, S. F. (2003). Issues facing adoptive mothers of children with special needs. *Journal of Social Work*, *3*(3), 301–320. doi:10.1177/146801730333003

Ford, J. (2015). *Challenges of Child Trauma on Adoptive Families' Social and Emotional System.* ProQuest LLC. UMI Dissertation Publishing 3707129.

Ford, J. D., & Courtois, C. A. (2013). *Treating complex stress traumatic stress disorders in children and adolescents: Scientific foundations and therapeutic models*. New York: Guilford Press.

Fosha, D., Siegel, D. J., & Solomon, M. (2009). *The Healing Power of Emotion: Affective Neuroscience, Development & Clinical Practice*. New York: W.W. Norton & Company.

Foster, H., & Hagan, J. (2009). The mass incarceration of parents in America: Issues of race/ethnicity, collateral damage to children, and prisoner reentry. *The Annals of the American Academy of Political and Social Science*, *623*(1), 179–194. doi:10.1177/0002716208331123

Fraga, L., & Garcia, J. A. (2010). *New patterns of Hispanic settlement in rural America*. Washington, D. C.: U. S. Department of Agriculture, Economic Research Service.

Fraiberg, S., Adelson, E., & Shapiro, V. (1975). Ghosts in the nursery: A psychoanalytic approach to the problems of impaired mother–infant relationships. *Journal of the American Academy of Child and Adolescent Psychiatry*, *14*(3), 387–422. doi:10.1016/S0002-7138(09)61442-4

Franchitto, N., Faurie, C., Franchitto, L., Minville, V., Telmon, N., & Rouge, D. (2011). Self-inflicted burns: The value of collaboration between medicine and law. *Journal of Forensic Sciences*, *56*(3), 638–642. doi:10.1111/j.1556-4029.2011.01706.x PMID:21361934

Frazier, P., Tashiro, T., Berman, M., Steger, M., & Long, J. (2004). Correlates of levels and patterns of positive life changes following sexual assault. *Journal of Consulting and Clinical Psychology*, *72*(1), 19–30. doi:10.1037/0022-006X.72.1.19 PMID:14756611

Freeman, L. N., Shaffer, D., & Smith, H. (1996). Neglected victims of homicide: The needs of young siblings of murder victims. *The American Journal of Orthopsychiatry*, *66*(3), 337–345. doi:10.1037/h0080184 PMID:8827257

Freud, S. (1990). *Beyond the Pleasure Principle*. New York: W.W. Norton & Company.

Friday, J. C. (1996). Weapon-carrying in schools. In A. M. Hoffman (Ed.), *Schools, violence, and society* (pp. 21–32). Westport, CT: Praeger.

Friedman, R. A., & Podolny, J. (1992). Differentiation of Boundary Spanning Roles: Labor Negotiations and Implications for Role Conflict. *Administrative Science Quarterly*, *37*(1), 28–47. doi:10.2307/2393532

Friedrich, W. N. (1997). *Child Sexual Behavior Inventory professional manual*. Lutz, FL: Psychological Assessment Resources, Inc.

Friedrich, W. N., Fisher, J. L., Dittner, C. A., Acton, R., Berliner, L., Butler, J., & Wright, J. et al. (2001). Child Sexual Behavior Inventory: Normative, psychiatric, and sexual abuse comparisons. *Child Maltreatment*, *6*(1), 37–49. doi:10.1177/1077559501006001004 PMID:11217169

Friedrich, W. N., Grambsch, P., Broughton, D., Kuiper, J., & Beilke, R. L. (1991). Normative sexual behavior in children. *Pediatrics*, *101*, 456–464. PMID:1881723

Friedrich, W. N., Grambsch, P., Damon, L., Hewitt, S. K., Koverola, C., Lang, R. A., & Broughton, D. et al. (1992). Child Sexual Behavior Inventory: Normative and clinical comparisons. *Psychological Assessment*, *4*(3), 303–311. doi:10.1037/1040-3590.4.3.303

Friedrich, W. N., & Trane, S. T. (2002). Sexual behavior in children across multiple settings. *Child Abuse & Neglect*, *26*(3), 243–245. doi:10.1016/S0145-2134(01)00322-2 PMID:12013056

Frye, L. A., & Spates, C. R. (2012). Prolonged exposure, mindfulness, and emotion regulation for the treatment of PTSD. *Clinical Case Studies*, *11*(3), 184–200. doi:10.1177/1534650112446850

Fuller, T., Brulin, C., Cohen, L., Lis, M., Rollock, N., & Sheridan, K. (2006). *Supporting adoptions and guardianships in Illinois: An analysis of subsidies, services and spending*. Urbana-Champaign, IL: University of Illinois. Retrieved July 11, 2014, from http://cfrc.illinois.edu/pubs/rp_20070901_ConditionsOfChildrenBH2006.pdf

Furlong, M. J., Pavelski, R., & Saxton, J. (2002). The prevention of school violence. In S. Brock. P. Lazarus, & S. Jimerson (Eds.), Best practices in crisis intervention (pp. 131–149). Bethesda, MD: National Association of School Psychologists.

Gabel, K., & Johnston, D. (1995). *Children of incarcerated parents*. New York: Lexington Books.

Gallup International Association. (1999). *Gallup international millennium survey*. Retrieved from www.gallup-international.com/surveys1.html

Garcia, V. (2007). Meeting binational research challenge: Substance abuse among transnational farmworkers in the United States. *The Journal of Rural Health*, *31*(s1), 61–67. doi:10.1111/j.1748-0361.2007.00125.x PMID:18237326

Garrison, E. G., Roy, I. S., & Azar, V. (1999). Responding to the mental health needs of Latino children and families through school-based services. *Clinical Psychology Review*, *19*(2), 199–219. doi:10.1016/S0272-7358(98)00070-1 PMID:10078420

Gartner, J., Larson, D. B., & Allen, G. D. (1991). Religious commitment and mental health: A review of the empirical literature. *Journal of Psychology and Theology*, *19*, 6–25.

Gelles, R. J., & Cornell, C. P. (1990). *Intimate violence in families*. Newbury Park, CA: Sage.

Genty, P. M. (2002). Damage to family relationships as a collateral consequence of parental incarceration. *The Fordham Urban Law Journal*, *30*, 1671.

George, A. A., & Tucker, J. A. (1996). Help-seeking for alcohol-related problems: Social contexts surrounding entry into alcoholism treatment or Alcoholics Anonymous. *Journal of Studies on Alcohol*, *57*(4), 449–457. doi:10.15288/jsa.1996.57.449 PMID:8776687

George, L. K., Ellison, C. G., & Larson, D. B. (2002). Explaining the relationships between religious involvement and health. *Psychological Inquiry*, *13*(3), 190–200. doi:10.1207/S15327965PLI1303_04

Gerson, M. (2015, March 16). The Effects of Inequality on America's Kids. *The Washington Post*.

Gigengack, M. R., van Meijel, E. P., Alisic, E., & Lindauer, R. J. (2015). Comparing three diagnostic algorithms of posttraumatic stress in young children exposed to accidental trauma: An exploratory study. *Child and Adolescent Psychiatry and Mental Health*, *9*(1), 14. doi:10.1186/s13034-015-0046-7 PMID:25984233

Gladstein, J., & Slater, E. J. (1988). Inner city teenagers' exposure to violence: A prevalence study. *Maryland Medical Journal (Baltimore, Md.)*, *37*(12), 951–954. PMID:3231019

Glaze, L. E., & Maruschak, L. M. (2008). *Parents in prison and their minor children*. Washington, D. C.: Department of Justice, Office of Justice Programs. doi:10.1037/e513862010-001

Golafshani, N. (2003). Understanding reliability and validity in qualitative research. *Qualitative Report*, *8*(4), 597–607.

Golash-Boza, T., & Hondagneu-Sotelo, P. (2013). Latino immigrant men and the deportation crisis: A gendered racial removal program. *Latino Studies*, *11*(3), 271–292. doi:10.1057/lst.2013.14

Gomes-Schwartz, B., Horowitz, J. M., Carderelli, A. P., & Sauzier, M. (1990). The aftermath of child sexual abuse: 18 months later. In B. Gomes-Schwartz, J. M. Horowitz, & A. P. Cardarelli (Eds.), *Child sexual abuse: The initial effects* (pp. 132–152). Newbury Park, CA: Sage.

Gonzalez-Guarda, R. M., Florom-Smith, A. L., & Thomas, T. (2011). A synthetic model of substance abuse, intimate partner violence, HIV infection, and mental health among Hispanics. *Public Health Nursing (Boston, Mass.)*, *28*(4), 366–378. doi:10.1111/j.1525-1446.2010.00928.x PMID:21736615

Gonzalez, M. A. (2015). Stories of separation: Impact of detention and deportation on Latino children's attachment representation. *Dissertation Abstracts International.*

Goodyear-Brown, P. (Ed.). (2011). *Handbook of child sexual abuse: Identification, assessment, and treatment*. Hoboken, NJ: John Wiley & Sons. doi:10.1002/9781118094822

Gorman-Smith, D., Henry, D. B., & Tolan, P. H. (2010). Exposure to community violence and violence perpetration: The protective effects of family functioning. *Journal of Clinical and Adolescent Psychology*, *33*(3), 439–449. doi:10.1207/s15374424jccp3303_2 PMID:15271602

Gottfredson, D. C. (2001). *Schools and delinquency*. New York: Cambridge University Press.

Goulding, R. A., & Schwartz, R. C. (2002). *The mosaic mind: Empowering the Tormented Self of Child Abuse Survivors*. Oak Park, IL: Trailheads Publications.

Gouveia, L. (2005). Latinos in rural America and U. S. agriculture: From pioneers to new arrivals. *The Journal of Latino-Latin American Studies*, *1*(4), 1–24. doi:10.18085/llas.1.4.g863048x3k152w82

Government of Alberta. (2010). *Protection of sexually exploited children and youth*. Edmonton: The Crown in Right of the Government of Alberta.

Graham-Berman, S. A. (1998). The impact of woman abuse on children's social development. In G. W. Holden, R. Geffner, & E. N. Jouriles (Eds.), *Children exposed to marital violence: Theory, research, and applied issues* (pp. 21–54). Washington, DC: American Psychological Society. doi:10.1037/10257-001

Grame, C. J., Tortorici, J. S., Healey, B. J., Dillingham, J. H., & Winklebaur, P. (1999). Addressing spiritual and religious issues of clients with a history of psychological trauma. *Bulletin of the Menninger Clinic*, *63*(2), 223.

Gray, D. (2007). *Nurturing Adoptions: Creating Resilience after Neglect and Trauma*. Indianapolis, IN: Perspectives Press.

Greely, H. T. (2001). Informed consent and other ethical issues in human population genetics. *Annual Review of Genetics*, *35*(1), 785–800. doi:10.1146/annurev.genet.35.102401.091453 PMID:11700299

Greene, M. B. (2000). Bullying and harassment in schools. In R. S. Moser & C. E. Frantz (Eds.), *Shocking violence* (pp. 72–101). Springfield, IL: Charles C Thomas.

Greene, M. B. (2005). Reducing violence and aggression in schools. *Trauma, Violence & Abuse*, *6*(3), 236–253. doi:10.1177/1524838005277406 PMID:16237157

Greeno, C. G., Anderson, C. M., Shear, M. K., & Gerard, M. (1999). Initial Treatment Engagement in a Rural Community Mental Health Center. *Psychiatric Services (Washington, D.C.)*, *50*(12), 1634–1636. doi:10.1176/ps.50.12.1634 PMID:10577887

Greenwald, R. (2015). *Child trauma handbook: A guide for helping trauma-exposed children and adolescents*. New York: Routledge.

Gregoire, K. A., & Schultz, D. J. (2001). Substance-abusing child welfare parents: Treatment and child placement outcomes. *Child Welfare*, *80*(4), 433–452. PMID:11480487

Grotevant, H. D. (2009). Emotional disturbance regulation over the life course in adoptive kinship networks. In G. M. Wrobel & E. Neil (Eds.), *International advances in adoption research for practice* (pp. 295–316). London: Wiley-Blackwell.

Grotevant, H., & McDermott, J. (2014). Adoption: Biological and social process linked to adaptation. *Annual Review of Psychology*, *65*(1), 235–265. doi:10.1146/annurev-psych-010213-115020 PMID:24016275

Groze, V. (1996a). A 1 and 2 year follow-up study of adoptive families and special needs children. *Children and Youth Services Review*, *18*, 57-82. Doi:(95)00054-210.1016/0190-7409

Groze, V. (1996b). *Successful adoptive families*. Westport, CT: Praeger.

Groze, V., & Rosenthal, J. A. (1993). Attachment theory and the adoption of children with special needs. *Social Welfare Research and Abstracts*, *29*(2), 5–12. doi:10.1093/swra/29.2.5

Grunbaum, J. A., Kann, L., Kinchen, S. A., Ross, W. B., Lowry, R., & Kolbe, L. (2002). Youth risk behavior surveillance - United States, 2001. *MMWR. Surveillance Summaries*, *51*, 1–62. PMID:12102329

Grzywacz, J. G., Quandt, S. A., Early, J., Tapia, J., Graham, C. N., & Arcury, T. A. (2006). Leaving family for work: Ambivalence and mental health among Mexican migrant farmworker men. *Journal of Health Care for the Poor and Underserved*, *20*, 662. PMID:19835002

Hafetz, R. (2008). *Not Remembered, Never Forgotten*. Charleston, SC: Book Surge Publications.

Hagan, J., Castro, B., & Rodriguez, N. (2010). The effects of deportation policies on immigrant families and communities: Cross-border perspectives. *North Carolina Law Review*, *88*, 1799–1884.

Halfacre-Hitchcock, A., McCarthy, D., Burkett, T., & Carvajal, A. (2006). Latino immigrant farmworkers in low country South Carolina: A demographic profile and an examination of pesticide perception and protection in two pilot case studies. *Human Organization*, *65*(1), 55–71. doi:10.17730/humo.65.1.6cc5wqtvpw5xku4j

Hamby, S. L., Finkelhor, D., Ormrod, R. K., & Turner, H. A. (2004a). The Juvenile Victimization Questionnaire (JVQ): Administration & scoring manual. Durham, NH: Crimes against Children Research Center.

Hamby, S. L., Finkelhor, D., Ormrod, R. K., & Turner, H. A. (2004b). The Juvenile Victimization Questionnaire (JVQ): Child Self-Report Version. Durham, NH: Crimes against Children Research Center.

Hamby, S., Weber, M. C., Grych, J., & Banyard, V. (2015). What difference do bystanders make? The association of bystander involvement with victim outcomes in a community sample. *Psychology of Violence*.

Hampton, S., Ekboir, J. M., & Rochin, R. I. (1995). The performance of Latinos in rural public schools: A comparative analysis of test scores in grades 3, 6, and 12. *Hispanic Journal of Behavioral Sciences*, *17*(4), 480–498. doi:10.1177/07399863950174005

Hansel, T. C., Osofsky, H. J., Osofsky, J. D., Costa, R. N., Kronenberg, M. E., & Selby, M. L. (2010). Attention to process and clinical outcomes of implementing a rural school-based trauma treatment program. *Journal of Traumatic Stress*, *23*(6), 708–715. doi:10.1002/jts.20595 PMID:21171131

Hanson, R. F., Self-Brown, S., Fricker-Elhai, A., Kilpatrick, D. G., Saunders, B. E., & Resnick, H. (2006). Relations among parental substance abuse, violence exposure and mental health: The national survey of adolescents. *Addictive Behaviors*, *31*(11), 1988–2001. doi:10.1016/j.addbeh.2006.01.012 PMID:16503092

Harker, K. (2001). Immigrant generation, assimilation and adolescent psychological well-being. *Social Forces*, *79*(3), 969–1004. doi:10.1353/sof.2001.0010

Hartmann, A. (1984). *Working with adoptive families beyond placement*. New York, NY: Child Welfare League of America.

Hazan, C., & Zeifman, D. (1999). Pair bonds as attachments: Evaluating the evidence. In J. Cassidy & P. R. Shaver (Eds.), *Handbook of attachment: Theory, research, and clinical applications* (pp. 336–354). New York, NY: Guilford Press.

Healy, B. (1993). Psychotherapy and religious experience: Integrating psychoanalytic psychotherapy with Christian religious experience. In G. Stricker & J. Gold (Eds.), *Comprehensive handbook of psychotherapy integration*. New York: Plenum. doi:10.1007/978-1-4757-9782-4_18

Heaviside, S., Rowand, C., Williams, C., & Farris, E. (1998). *Violence and discipline problems in U.S. public schools: 1996-1997*. Washington, DC: U.S. Department of Education, National Center for Education Statistics.

Heckhausen, J., & Schulz, R. (1995). A life-span theory of control. *Psychological Review*, *102*(2), 284–304. doi:10.1037/0033-295X.102.2.284 PMID:7740091

Helman, C. G. (2007). *Culture, Health, and Illness* (5th ed.). London: Hodder Arnold.

Hemphill, S. A., Tollit, M., Kotevski, A., & Florent, A. (2015). Bullying in schools: Rates, correlates and impact on mental health. In J. Lindert & I. Itzhak (Eds.), *Violence and mental health: Its manifold faces* (pp. 185–205). Springer. doi:10.1007/978-94-017-8999-8_9

Henderson, J., Crotty, M. M., Fuller, J., & Martinez, L. (2014). Meeting unmet needs? The role of a rural mental health service for older people. *Advances in Mental Health*, *12*(3), 182–191. doi:10.1080/18374905.2014.11081896

Henderson, S. W., & Baily, C. D. R. (2013). Parental deportation, families, and mental health. *Journal of the American Academy of Child and Adolescent Psychiatry*, *52*(5), 451–453. doi:10.1016/j.jaac.2013.01.007 PMID:23622844

Herda-Rapp, H. (2003). The social construction of local school violence threats by the news media and professional organizations. *Sociological Enquiry*, *73*(4), 545–574. doi:10.1111/1475-682X.00071

Herman, J. L. (1992). *Trauma and recovery*. New York: Basic Books.

Higgins, D. J., & McCabe, M. (2003). Maltreatment and family dysfunction in childhood and the subsequent adjustment of children and adults. *Journal of Family Violence*, *18*(2), 107–120. doi:10.1023/A:1022841215113

Higgins, D. J., & McCabe, M. P. (2000). Multiple forms of child abuse and neglect: Adult retrospective reports. *Aggression and Violent Behavior*, *6*(6), 547–578. doi:10.1016/S1359-1789(00)00030-6

Higgins, D. J., & McCabe, M. P. (2000). Multi-type maltreatment and long-term adjustment of adults. *Child Abuse Review*, *9*(1), 6–18. doi:10.1002/(SICI)1099-0852(200001/02)9:1<6::AID-CAR579>3.0.CO;2-W

Hiott, A. E., Grzywacz, J. G., Davis, S. W., Quandt, S. A., & Arcury, T. A. (2008). Migrant farmworker stress: Mental health implications. *The Journal of Rural Health*, *24*(1), 32–39. doi:10.1111/j.1748-0361.2008.00134.x PMID:18257868

Hirsch, J. K., & Cukrowicz, K. C. (2014). Suicide in rural areas: An updated review of the literature. *Journal of Rural Mental Health*, *38*(2), 65–78. doi:10.1037/rmh0000018

Hoagwood, K. E. (2006). *Final report on the child and adolescent trauma treatment consortium (cats) project*. SAMHSA, Unpublished report.

Hobbs, D. (1994). The rural context for education: Adjusting the images. In M. Womble & J. D'Amico (Eds.), *Perspectives on violence and substance use in rural America* (pp. 5–26). Oak Brook, IL: North Central Regional Educational Laboratory.

Hodgkinson, H. (1994). *The invisible poor: Rural youth in America*. Washington, D.C.: Institute for Educational Leadership, Center for Demographic Policy.

Hoepfl, M. C. (1997). Choosing qualitative research: A primer for technology education researchers. *Journal of Technology Education*, *9*(1), 47–63.

Hohl, S. D., Gonzalez, C., Carusso, E., Ibarra, G., & Thompson, B. (2014). "I did it for us and I would do it again": Perspectives of rural Latinos on providing biospecimens for research. *American Journal of Public Health*, *104*(5), 911–916. doi:10.2105/AJPH.2013.301726 PMID:24625153

Hollan, D. (1995). To the Afterworld and Back: Mourning and Dreams of the Dead among the Toraja. *Ethos (Berkeley, Calif.)*, *23*(4), 424–436. doi:10.1525/eth.1995.23.4.02a00030

Holmberg, T. (2003). *Lapsetjavanhempienpäihdeongelma: opasvanhemmille, lastensuojelunammattilaisillejamuillelastenkanssatyöskenteleville. Saarijärvi.* Saarijärven Offset.

Holt, S., Buckley, H., & Whelan, S. (2008). The impact of exposure to domestic violence on children and young people: A review of the literature. *Child Abuse and Neglect: The International Journal*, *32*(8), 797–810. doi:10.1016/j.chiabu.2008.02.004 PMID:18752848

Homer, P., Sanders, L., Martinez, R., Doering-White, J., Lopez, W., & Delva, J. (2014). "I put the mask on": The human side of deportation efforts on Latino youth. *Journal of Social Welfare and Human Rights*, *2*, 33–47.

Hondo, C., Gardiner, M. E., & Sapien, Y. (2008). *Latino dropouts in rural America: Realities and possibilities*. Albany, N. Y.: State University of New York Press.

Hong, J. S., Davis, J. P., Sterzing, P. R., Yoon, J., Choi, S., & Smith, D. C. (2014). A conceptual framework for understanding the association between school bullying victimization and substance misuse. *The American Journal of Orthopsychiatry*, *84*(6), 696–710. doi:10.1037/ort0000036 PMID:25545436

Hoover, J. H., Oliver, R., & Hazler, R. J. (1992). Bullying: Perceptions of adolescent victims in the midwestern USA. *School Psychology International*, *13*(1), 5–16. doi:10.1177/0143034392131001

Hope, T. L., & Bierman, K. L. (1998). Patterns of home and school behavior problems in rural and urban settings. *Journal of School Psychology*, *36*(1), 45–58. doi:10.1016/S0022-4405(97)00049-6 PMID:19834584

Horowitz, M. J., Wilner, N., & Alvarez, W. (1979). Impact of events scale: A measure of subjective stress. *Psychosomatic Medicine*, *41*(3), 209–218. doi:10.1097/00006842-197905000-00004 PMID:472086

Housing Assistance Council. (2012). *Rural research brief: Poverty in rural America*. Washington, D. C.: Housing Assistance Council.

Hovey, J. D., & Magana, C. G. (2002). Psychosocial predictors of anxiety among immigrant Mexican migrant farmworkers: Implications for prevention and treatment. *Cultural Diversity and Ethnic Minority Mental Health*, *8*(3), 274–289. doi:10.1037/1099-9809.8.3.274 PMID:12143104

Howard, W. T., Loberiza, R. F., Pfohl, B. M., Thorne, P. S., Magpantay, R. L., & Woolson, R. F. (1999). Initial Results, Reliability, and Validity of a Mental Health Survey of Mount Pinatubo Disaster Victims. *The Journal of Nervous and Mental Disease*, *187*(11), 661–672. doi:10.1097/00005053-199911000-00003 PMID:10579594

Hubert, H. B., Snider, J., & Winkleby, M. A. (2005). Health status, health behaviors, and acculturation factors associated with overweight and obesity in Latinos from a community and agricultural labor camp survey. *Preventive Medicine*, *40*(6), 642–651. doi:10.1016/j.ypmed.2004.09.001 PMID:15850860

Hughes, D. (1997). *Facilitating Developmental Attachment: The Road to Recovery and Behavioral Change in Foster and Adopted Children*. Lanham, MD: Rowman & Littlefield Publishers, Inc.

Hughes, D. (1998). *Building the Bonds of Attachment: Awakening Love in Deeply Troubled Children*. Northvale, NJ: Jason Aronson, Inc.

Huizinga, G. A., Visser, A., van der Graff, W. T., Hoekstra, H. J., Klip, E. C., Pras, E., & Hoekstra-Weebers, J. E. (2005). Stress response symptoms in adolescent and young children of parents diagnosed with cancer. *European Journal of Cancer*, *41*(2), 288–295. doi:10.1016/j.ejca.2004.10.005 PMID:15661555

Humes, K., Jones, N. A., & Ramirez, R. R. (2011). *Overview of race and Hispanic origin, 2010*. U. S. Department of Commerce, Economics and Statistics Administration, U. S. Census Bureau.

Hunter, M. E. (2006). Mental Health Care in Rural and Isolated Areas: Lessons from Northern British Columbia. *British Columbia Medical Journal*, *48*(4), 174–177.

Hushion, K., Sherman, S. B., & Siskind, D. (Eds.). (2006). *Understanding adoption: clinical work with adults, children, and parents*. Rowman & Littlefield.

Hyde, C., Bentovim, A., & Monck, E. (1995). Some clinical and methodological implications of a treatment outcome study of sexually abused children. *Child Abuse & Neglect*, *19*(11), 1387–1399. doi:10.1016/0145-2134(95)00096-Q PMID:8591095

Isernhagen, J., & Harris, S. (2004). A comparison of bullying in four rural middle and high schools. *Rural Educator*, *25*, 5–13.

Itäpuisto, M. (2008). *Pullonpohjimmaiset: lapsi, perhejaalkoholi*. Helsinki: Kirjapaja.

Jacob, E., Miller, L. C., & Tirella, L. G. (2010). Developmental and behavioral performance of internationally adopted preschoolers: A pilot study. *Child Psychiatry and Human Development*, *41*(1), 15–29. doi:10.1007/s10578-009-0149-6 PMID:19593639

Jacobs, J.A. (2015). Legal and ethical guidance for the provision of teletherapy—more questions than answers. *The Colorado Psychologist, 4*, 4-5.

Jakovljević, M., Brajković, L., Jakšić, N., Lončar, M., Aukst-Margetić, B., & Lasić, D. (2012). Postraumatic stress disorders (PTSD) from different perspectives: A transdisciplinary integrative approach. *Psychiatria Danubina*, *24*(3), 246–255. PMID:23013627

James, B. (1994). *Handbook for treatment of attachment-trauma problems in children*. New York, NY: The Free Press.

Jamieson, P. E., & Romer, D. (2008). Unrealistic fatalism in U.S. youth ages 14 to 22: Prevalence and characteristics. *The Journal of Adolescent Health, 42*(2), 154–160. doi:10.1016/j.jadohealth.2007.07.010 PMID:18207093

Jensen, P. S., Goldman, E., Offord, D., Costello, E. J., Friedman, R., Huff, B., & Roberts, R. et al. (2011). Overlooked and underserved: 'Action signs' for identifying children with unmet mental health needs. *Pediatrics, 128*(5), 970–979. PMID:22025589

Johnson, R. (2010). Forensic assessment and clinical intervention for juvenile firesetters: The San Diego model. *Matchbook: Journal on the Prevention & Treatment of Juvenile Firesetting, 2*, 14–16.

Johnson, R. (2013). Using the DSM-5 and ICD-11 in forensic and clinical applications with children across racial and ethnic lines. In G. P. Koocher, J. C. Norcross, & B. A. Greene (Eds.), *Psychologists' Desk Reference* (3rd ed.). New York: Oxford University Press. doi:10.1093/med:psych/9780199845491.003.0010

Johnson, R., Beckenbach, H., & Killbourne, S. (2013). Forensic psychological public safety risk assessment integrated with culturally responsive treatment for juvenile fire setters: DSM-5 implications. *Journal of Criminal Psychology, 3*(1), 49–65. doi:10.1108/20093821311307767

Johnston, J. R. (2005). Children of divorce who reject a parent and refuse visitation: Recent research and social policy implications for the alienated child. *Family Law Quarterly*, 757–775.

Jones, L. M., & Finkelhor, D. (2007). *Updated trends in child maltreatment.* Retrieved from http://www.unh.edu/ccrc/pdf/Updated%20Trends%20in%20Child%20Maltreatment%202007.pdf

Jones, R. T., Fletcher, K., & Ribbe, D. R. (2002). *Child's Reaction to Traumatic Events Scale—Revised: A self-report traumatic stress measure.* Unpublished manuscript, Virginia Polytechnic Institute and State University, Virginia.

Jones, A. M., Shealy, K. M., Reid-Quinones, K., Moreland, A. D., Davidson, T. M., Lopez, C. M., & de Arellano, M. A. et al. (2014). Guidelines for establishing a telemental health program to provide evidence-based therapy for trauma-exposed children and families. *Psychological Services, 11*(4), 398–409. doi:10.1037/a0034963 PMID:24320994

Jones, J. (2009). *Who adopts? Characteristics of women and men who have adopted children, NCHS Data Brief, No. 12. Center for Disease Control and Prevention.* National Center for Health Statistics.

Jones, M. C., Dauphinais, P., Sack, W., & Somervell, P. (1997). Trauma-Related Symptomatology Among American Indian Adolescents. *Journal of Traumatic Stress, 10*(2), 163–173. doi:10.1002/jts.2490100202 PMID:9136086

Jones, R. T., Hadder, J., Carvajal, F., Chapman, S., & Alexander, A. (2006). Conducting research on diverse, minority, and marginalized communities. In F. Norris, M. Friedman, D. Reissman, & P. Watson (Eds.), *Research methods for studying mental health after disasters and terrorism: Community and public approaches* (pp. 265–277). New York: Guilford Press.

Jordan, B., Perryman, K., & Anderson, L. (2013). A case for child-centered play therapy with natural disaster and catastrophic event survivors. *International Journal of Play Therapy, 22*(4), 219–230. doi:10.1037/a0034637

Jordan, C. E., Nietzel, M. T., Walker, R., & Logan, T. K. (2004). *Intimate partner violence: a clinical training guide for mental health professionals.* New York, NY: Springer Publishing Company.

Jorey, B. (2004). The intimate justice scale: An instrument to screen for psychological abuse and physical violence in clinical practice. *Journal of Marital and Family Therapy, 30*(1), 29–44. doi:10.1111/j.1752-0606.2004.tb01220.x PMID:14763207

Joseph, C. M. (1999). *Ethnic Conflict in Bhutan.* New Delhi: Nirala Publications.

Josephson, A. M., & Dell, M. L. (2004). Religion and spirituality in child and adolescent psychiatry: A new frontier. *Child and Adolescent Psychiatric Clinics of North America, 13*(1), 1–15. doi:10.1016/S1056-4993(03)00099-3 PMID:14723297

Kachur, S. P., Stennies, G. M., Powell, K. E., Modzeleski, W., Stephens, R., Murphy, R., & Lowry, R. et al. (1996). School-associated violent deaths in the United States, 1992 to 1994. *Journal of the American Medical Association, 274*(22), 1729–1733. doi:10.1001/jama.1996.03530460033027 PMID:8637169

Kaduson, H. G., & Schaefer, C. E. (Eds.). (2006). *Short-term play therapy for children.* New York: Guilford Press.

Kalland, M. (2005). Kiintymissuhdeteoriankliininenmerkitys: soveltaminenerityistilanteissa. In J. Sinkkonen & M. Kalland (Eds.), *Varhaisetihmissuhteetjaniidenhäiriintyminen.* Vantaa: Werner SöderströmOy.

Kane-Cavaiola, C., & Rullo-Cooney, D. (1991). Addicted women: Their families' effect on treatment outcome. *Journal of Chemical Dependency Treatment, 4*(1), 111–119. doi:10.1300/J034v04n01_08

Kantor, G. K., & Straus, M. A. (1987). The "Drunken Bum" theory of wife beating. *Social Problems, 34*(3), 213–231. doi:10.2307/800763

Karen, R. (1998). *Becoming attached: First relationships and how they shape our capacity to love.* New York, NY: Oxford University Press.

Karp, C. L., & Butler, T. L. (1996). *Treatment strategies for abused children: From victim to survivor.* Thousand Oaks, CA: Sage Publications.

Karr-Morse, R., & Wiley, M. (1997). *Ghosts from the Nursery: Tracing the Roots of Violence.* New York, NY: The Atlantic Monthly Press.

Kashima, Y. (2000). Conceptions of culture and person for psychology. *Journal of Cross-Cultural Psychology, 31*(1), 14–32. doi:10.1177/0022022100031001003

Kataoka, S. H., Stein, B. D., Jaycox, L. H., Wong, M., Escudero, P., Tu, W., & Fink, A. (2003). A school-based mental health program for traumatized Latino immigrant children. *Journal of the American Academy of Child and Adolescent Psychiatry, 42*(3), 311–318. doi:10.1097/00004583-200303000-00011 PMID:12595784

Kato Klebanov, P., Brooks-Gunn, J., & Duncan, G. (1994). Does Neighborhood and Family Poverty Affect Mothers' Parenting, Mental Health, and Social Support? *Journal of Marriage and the Family, 56*(2), 441–455. doi:10.2307/353111

Katz, S. R. (1997). Presumed guilty: How schools criminalize Latino youth. *Social Justice (San Francisco, Calif.)*, 77–95.

Kawachi, I., & Berkman, L. F. (2001). Social Ties and Mental Health. *Journal of Urban Health: Bulletin of the New York Academy of Medicine, 78*(3), 458–467. doi:10.1093/jurban/78.3.458 PMID:11564849

Kay, J., Burt, V. K., Eth, S., & Phillips, K. A. (2001). *PTSD in children and adolescents.* New York: American Psychiatric Publishers.

Keck, G. C., & Kupecky, R. M. (2009). *Parenting the hurt child: Helping adoptive families heal and grow.* Colorado Springs, CO: NavPress.

Kelley, B. S., & Miller, L. (2007). Life satisfaction and spirituality in adolescents. *Research in the Social Scientific Study of Religion, 18*, 233–261. doi:10.1163/ej.9789004158511.i-301.91

Kenny, A., Hyett, N., Sawtell, J., Dickson-Swift, V., Farmer, J., & O'Meara, P. (2013). Community participation in rural health: A scoping review. *BMC Health Services Research, 13*(1), 64. doi:10.1186/1472-6963-13-64 PMID:23414561

Kerig, P. K. (2013). *Trauma informed assessment and intervention.* Los Angeles, CA: National Center for Child Traumatic Stress.

Khaled, W. (2001). Lifetime Events and Post-traumatic Stress Disorder in Four Postconflict Settings. *Journal of the American Medical Association, 286*(5), 555–562. doi:10.1001/jama.286.5.555 PMID:11476657

Kilpatrick, D. G., Ruggiero, K. J., Acierno, R., Saunders, B. E., Resnick, H. S., & Best, C. L. (2003). Violence and risk of PTSD, major depression, substance abuse/dependence, and comorbidity: Results from the national survey of adolescents. *Journal of Consulting and Clinical Psychology, 71*(4), 692–700. doi:10.1037/0022-006X.71.4.692 PMID:12924674

Kim-Godwin, Y. S., & Fox, J. A. (2009). Gender differences in intimate partner violence and alcohol use among Latino-migrant and seasonal farmworkers in rural Southeastern South Carolina. *Journal of Community Health Nursing, 26*(3), 131–142. doi:10.1080/07370010903034474 PMID:19662561

Kingery, P., Mirzaee, E., Pruitt, B. E., & Hurley, R. S. (1990). Town and country violence. *School Safety,* 22-25.

Kingery, P. M., Coggeshall, M. B., & Alford, A. A. (1998). Violence at school: Recent evidence from four national surveys. *Psychology in the Schools, 35*(33), 247–258. doi:10.1002/(SICI)1520-6807(199807)35:3<247::AID-PITS5>3.0.CO;2-K

Kingery, P. M., Mirzaee, E., Pruitt, B. E., Hurley, R. S., & Heuberger, G. (1991). Rural communities near large metropolitan areas: Safe havens from adolescent violence and drug use? *Health Values, 15*(4), 39–48.

Kingery, P. M., Priutt, B. E., Heuberger, G., & Brizzolara, J. A. (1995). Violence in rural schools. *School Psychology International, 16*(4), 335–344. doi:10.1177/0143034395164002

King, P. E., & Roeser, R. W. (2008). In R. M. Lerner & L. D. Steinberg (Eds.), Handbook of adolescent psychology: Vol. 435–478. *Religion and spirituality in adolescent development.* Hoboken, NJ: Wiley.

Kinniburgh, K. J., Blaustein, M., Spinazzola, J., & van der Kolk, B. A. (2005, May). Attachment, Self-Regulation, and Competency. *Psychiatric Annals, 35*(5), 424–430.

Kira, I. A., Lewandowski, L., Templin, T. N., Ramaswamy, V., Chiodo, L. M., Ozkan, B., & Mohanesh, J. (2008b). *Measuring cumulative trauma dose, types, and profiles using a development-based taxonomy of traumas: The long version.* American Psychological Association.

Kirmayer, L., & Young, A. (1998). Culture and somatization: Clinical, epidemiological and ethnographic perspectives. *Psychosomatic Medicine, 60*(4), 420–429. doi:10.1097/00006842-199807000-00006 PMID:9710287

Klas, K. S., Vlahos, P. G., McCully, M., Piche, D. R., & Wang, S. C. (2015). School-based prevention program associated with increased short- and long-term retention of safety knowledge. *Journal of Burn Care & Research; Official Publication of the American Burn Association, 36*(3), 387–393. doi:10.1097/BCR.0000000000000151 PMID:25159554

Kleinman, A. (1988a). *The illness narratives: Suffering, healing and human condition.* New York: Basic Books.

Kleinman, A. (1988b). *Rethinking psychiatry: From cultural category to personal experience.* New York: The Free Press.

Klevens, J. (2007). An overview of intimate partner violence among Latinos. *Violence Against Women, 13*(2), 111–122. doi:10.1177/1077801206296979 PMID:17251500

Koenig, H., McCullough, M., & Larson, D. (2001). *Handbook of religion and health.* New York, NY: Oxford University Press. doi:10.1093/acprof:oso/9780195118667.001.0001

Kohut, H. (1971). *The analysis of self.* Madison, CT: International Universities Press.

Ko, S. J., Ford, J. D., Kassam-Adams, N., Berkowitz, S. J., Wilson, C., Wong, M., & Layne, C. M. et al. (2008). Creating trauma-informed systems: Child welfare, education, first responders, health care, and juvenile justice. *Professional Psychology, Research and Practice*, *39*(4), 396–404. doi:10.1037/0735-7028.39.4.396

Krisberg, B. A., & Temin, C. E. (2001). *Plight of children whose parents are in prison*. Oakland, CA: National Council on Crime and Delinquency.

Kujasalo, A., & Nykänen, H. (2005). *Viininviemää – Nainenalkoholinansassa. Hämeenlinna*. KaristoOy.

Landale, N. S., & Lichter, D. T. (1997). Gegoraphy and the etiology of poverty among Latino children. *Social Science Quarterly*, *78*, 874–894.

Landolt, M. A., Buehlmann, C., Maag, T., & Schiestl, C. (2009). Brief report: Quality of life is impaired in pediatric burn survivors with posttraumatic stress disorder. *Journal of Pediatric Psychology*, *34*(1), 14–21. doi:10.1093/jpepsy/jsm088 PMID:17890286

Landreth, G. L. (2012). *Play therapy: The art of the relationship* (2nd ed.). New York, NY: Brunner Rutledge.

Lavner, J. A., Waterman, J., & Peplau, L. A. (2014). Parent adjustment over time in gay, lesbian, and heterosexual parent families adopting from foster care. *The American Journal of Orthopsychiatry*, *84*(1), 46–53. doi:10.1037/h0098853 PMID:24826826

Lawrence, J. W., Rosenberg, L., Mason, S. & Fauerbach, J. A. (2011). *Comparing parent and child perceptions of stigmatizing behavior experienced by children with burn scars*. Academic Press.

Lawrence, R. (2000). School violence, the media, and the ACJS. ACJS Today, 20, 4-6.

Lawrence, J. W., Rosenberg, L., Rimmer, R. B., Thombs, B. D., & Fauerbach, J. A. (2010). Perceived stigmatization and social comfort: Validating the constructs and their measure ment among pediatric burn survivors. *Rehabilitation Psychology*, *55*(4), 360–371. doi:10.1037/a0021674 PMID:21171795

Le Prevost, C. E., Storm, J. F., Blanchard, M. R., Asuje, C. R., & Cope, W. G. (2013). Engaging Latino farmworkers in the development of symbols to improve pesticide safety and health education and risk communication. *Journal of Immigrant and Minority Health*, *15*(5), 975–981. doi:10.1007/s10903-012-9685-4 PMID:22833257

Leake, G. K., DeNeve, K. M., & Greteman, A. J. (2007). The relationship between spirituality, assessed through self–transcendent goal strivings, and positive psychological attributes. *Research in the Social Scientific Study of Religion*, *18*, 263–279. doi:10.1163/ej.9789004158511.i-301.102

Lee, M., & Bartkowski, J. P. (2004). Love Thy Neighbor? Moral Communities, Civic Engagement, and Juvenile Homicide in Rural Areas. *Project Muse*, *82*(3), 1001–1035.

Leenarts, L. E. W., Diehle, J., Doreleijers, T. A. H., Jansma, E. P., & Lindauer, R. J. L. (2013). Evidence-based treatments for children with trauma-related psychopathology as a result of childhood maltreatment: A systematic review. *European Child & Adolescent Psychiatry*, *22*(5), 269–283. doi:10.1007/s00787-012-0367-5 PMID:23266844

Lee, W. C., Luohua, J., Phillips, C. D., & Ohsfeldt, R. L. (2014). Rural-urban differences in health care expenditures: Empirical data from us households. *Advances in Public Health*, *2014*. doi:10.1155/2014/435780

Leistyna, J. (1980). Advocacy for the abused rural child. In H. Johnson (Ed.), *Rural human services: A book of readings* (pp. 92–96). Itasca, IL: Peacock.

Lenardson, J. D., Ziller, E. C., Lambert, D., Race, M. M., & Yousefian, A. (2010). Access to mental health services and family impact of rural children with mental health problems. Maine Rural Health Research Center, 45, 1–15.

Leslie, K. (2002). *When a stranger calls you mom.* Pittsboro, NC: Brand New Day Publishing.

Levant, R. F. (Ed.). (2005). Report of the 2005 presidential task force on evidence- based practice. American Psychological Association.

Lewis, S. H. (2003). *Unspoken crimes: sexual assault in rural America.* National Sexual Violence Resource Center. Retrieved from http://www.nsvrc.org/publications/booklets/rural_txt.htm

Lewis-Fernandez, R., & Kleinman, A. (1994). Culture, personality, and psychopathology. *Journal of Abnormal Psychology, 103*(1), 67–71. doi:10.1037/0021-843X.103.1.67 PMID:8040483

Lieberman, A. F. & Van Horn, P. (2008). *Psychotherapy with Infants and Young Children: Repairing the Effects of Stress and Trauma on Early Attachmen*t. Guilford Publications.

Lincoln, Y. S., & Guba, E. G. (1985). *Naturalistic inquiry.* Newbury Park, CA: Sage.

Lipovsky, J. A. (1992). Assessment and treatment of post-traumatic stress disorder in child survivors of sexual assault. In D. W. Foy (Ed.), *Treating PTSD: Cognitive-behavioral strategies* (pp. 127–164). New York: Guilford Press.

Lipschitz, D. S., Winegar, R. K., Nicolau, A. L., Hartnick, E., Wolfson, M., & Southwick, S. M. (1999). Perceived abuse and neglect at risk factors for suicidal behavior in adolescent inpatients. *The Journal of Nervous and Mental Disease, 187*(1), 32–39. doi:10.1097/00005053-199901000-00006 PMID:9952251

Litrownik, A. J., Newton, R., Hunter, W. M., English, D., & Everson, M. D. (2003). Exposure to family violence in young at-risk children: A longitudinal look at the effects of victimization and witnessed physical and psychological aggression. *Journal of Family Violence, 18*(10), 59–73. doi:10.1023/A:1021405515323

Little Warriors. (2015). *Helping prevent children from child sexual abuse.* Retrieved November 5, 2015, from http://littlewarriors.ca/

Little Warriors. (2015). *The Little Warriors Be Brave Ranch.* Retrieved November 5, 2015, from http://littlewarriors.ca/

Liu, J., Bennett, K. J., Harun, N., & Probst, J. C. (2008). Urban-rural differences in overweight status and physical inactivity among U. S. children aged 10-17 years. *The Journal of Rural Health, 24*(4), 407–415. doi:10.1111/j.1748-0361.2008.00188.x PMID:19007396

Loeber, R., & Dishion, T. (1983). Early predictors of male delinquency: A review. *Psychological Bulletin, 94*(1), 68–99. doi:10.1037/0033-2909.94.1.68 PMID:6353467

Logan, T. K., Walker, R., Cole, J., Ratliff, S., & Leukefeld, C. (2003). Qualitative differences among rural and urban intimate violence victimization experiences and consequences: A pilot study. *Journal of Family Violence, 18*(2), 83–86. doi:10.1023/A:1022837114205

Lonigan, C. J., Shannon, M. P., Taylor, C. M., Finch, A. J. Jr, & Sallee, F. R. (1994). Children exposed to disaster: II. Risk factors for the development of post-traumatic symptomatology. *Journal of the American Academy of Child and Adolescent Psychiatry, 33*(1), 94–105. doi:10.1097/00004583-199401000-00013 PMID:8138526

Loury, S., & Kulbok, P. (2007). Correlates of alcohol and tobacco use among immrigants in rural North Carolina. *Family & Community Health, 30*(3), 247–256. doi:10.1097/01.FCH.0000277767.00526.f1 PMID:17563486

Love, J. A., & Buriel, R. (2007). Language brokering and depression: autonomy, parent-child bonding, biculturalism, and depression: A study of Mexican American adolescents from immigrant families. *Hispanic Journal of Behavioral Sciences, 29*(4), 472–491. doi:10.1177/0739986307307229

Lyshak-Stelzer, F., Singer, P., St. John, P., & Chemtob, C. M. (2007). Art therapy for adolescents with posttraumatic stress disorder symptoms: A pilot study. *Art Therapy: Journal of the American Art Therapy Association*, *24*(4), 163–169. doi:10.1080/07421656.2007.10129474

MacKenzie, M. J., Kotch, J. B., & Lee, L. C. (2011). Toward a cumulative ecological risk model for the etiology of child maltreatment. *Children and Youth Services Review*, *33*(9), 1638–1647. doi:10.1016/j.childyouth.2011.04.018 PMID:24817777

MacLean, K. (1998). A three year follow-up of attachment and indiscriminate friendliness in children adopted from Romanian orphanages. *Child Development*, *69*(4), 1092–1106. doi:10.1111/j.1467-8624.1998.tb06162.x PMID:9768488

Maeroff, G. I. (2000). A symbiosis of sorts: School violence and the media. *Choice Briefs*, *7*, 1–9.

Magid, K., & McKelvey, C. (1987). *High risk: children without a conscience*. New York, NY: Bantam Books.

Maguire, K., & Pastore, A. L. (Eds.). (1996). *Sourcebook of criminal justice statistics.* Available at: http://www.albany.edu/sourcebook

Magura, S., & Laudet, A. B. (1996). Parental substance abuse and child maltreatment: Review and implications for intervention. *Children and Youth Services Review*, *18*(3), 193–220. doi:10.1016/0190-7409(96)00001-1

Main, M., & Hesse, E. (1990). Parent's unresolved traumatic experiences are related to infant disorganized attachment status: Is frightened and/or frightening parental behavior the linking mechanism? In M. T. Greenberg, D. Cicchetti, & E. M. Cummings (Eds.), *Attachment in the preschool years: Theory, research, and intervention* (pp. 161–182). Chicago: University of Chicago Press.

Mannarino, A. P., & Cohen, J. A. (1986). A clinical-demographic study of sexually abused children. *Child Abuse & Neglect*, *10*(1), 17–23. doi:10.1016/0145-2134(86)90027-X PMID:3955424

Mann, J. R., Crawford, S., Wilson, L., & McDermott, S. (2008). Does race influence age of diagnosis for children with developmental delay? *Disability and Health Journal*, *1*(3), 157–162. doi:10.1016/j.dhjo.2008.04.002 PMID:21122725

Mapes, D. (2012). It takes more than love: What happens when adoption fails? *Today Moms*. Retrieved from http://www.today.com/moms/it-takes-more-love-what-happens-when-adoption-fails-918076

Marsac, M. L., Cirilli, C., Kassam-Adams, N., & Winston, F. K. (2011). Post-injury medical and psychosocial care in children: Impact of traumatic stress symptoms. *Children's Health Care*, *40*(2), 116–129. doi:10.1080/02739615.2011.564564

Marshall, M. N. (1996). Sampling for qualitative research. *Family Practice*, *13*(3), 522–525. doi:10.1093/fampra/13.6.522 PMID:9023528

Martinez, C. R., McClure, H., & Eddy, J. (2008). Language brokering contexts and behavioral and emotional adjustment among Latino parents and adolescents. *The Journal of Early Adolescence*, *29*(1), 71–98. doi:10.1177/0272431608324477 PMID:19898605

Martinez, R. (2000). Immigration and urban violence: The link between immigrant Latinos and types of homicide. *Social Science Quarterly*, 363–374.

Martinez, R. (2014). *Latino homicide: Immigration, violence, and community*. New York: Routledge.

Mashreky, S. R., Rahman, A., Chowdhury, S. M., Svanstrom, L., Linnan, M., Shafinaz, S., & Rahman, F. et al. (2009). Perceptions of rural people about childhood burns and their prevention: A basis for developing a childhood burn prevention programme in Bangladesh. *Public Health*, *123*(8), 568–572. doi:10.1016/j.puhe.2009.06.014 PMID:19665740

Mattingly, M. J., & Walsh, W. A. (2010). *Rural families with a child abuse report are more likely headed by a single parent and endure economic and family stress (10)*. Durham, NH: Carsey Institute.

Mattson, S., & Ruiz, E. (2005). Intimate partner violence in the Latino community and its effect on children. *Health Care for Women International*, *26*(6), 523–529. doi:10.1080/07399330590962627 PMID:16020019

McBride, J. L. (1998). *Spiritual crisis. Surviving traumas to the soul*. New York: Haworth.

McCabe, K. A., & Martin, G. M. (2004). *School violence, the media, and criminal justice responses (studies in crime & punishment)*. Berne, Switzerland: Peter Lang International Academic Publishers.

McCann, I. L., & Pearlman, L. A. (1990). Vicarious traumatization: A framework for understanding the psychological effects of working with victims. *Journal of Traumatic Stress*, *3*(1), 131–149. doi:10.1007/BF00975140

McCaslin, M., & Scott, K. W. (2003). The five-question method for framing a qualitative research study. *Qualitative Report*, *8*(3), 447–461.

McCauley, L. A., Laserer, M. R., Higgins, G., Rothlein, J., Muniz, J., Ebbert, C., & Phillips, J. (2001). Work characteristics and pesticide exposure among migrant agricultural families: A community-based research approach. *Environmental Health Perspectives*, *109*(5), 533–538. doi:10.1289/ehp.01109533 PMID:11401767

McConnell, E. D., & Miraftab, F. (2010). Sundown town to "Little Mexico": Old-timers and newcomers in an American small town. *Rural Sociology*, *74*(4), 605–629. doi:10.1111/j.1549-0831.2009.tb00706.x

McCormick, J., & Wingert, P. (1991). Whose child am I anyway? *Newsweek*, p. 58.

McDonald, T. P., Propp, J. R., & Murphy, K. (2001). The postadoption experience: Child, parent, and family predictors of family adjustment to adoption. *Child Welfare. Child Welfare League of America*. Retrieved from http://www.highbeam.com/doc/1P3-67282959.htm

McDonald, J. J. Jr. (2003). Post-traumatic stress dishonesty. *Employee Relations Law Journal*, *28*, 93–111.

McFarlane, J. M., Groff, J. Y., O'Brien, J. A., & Watson, K. (2003). Behaviors of children who are exposed to intimate partner violence: An analysis of 330 Black, White, and Hispanic children. *Pediatrics*, *112*(3), 202–207. doi:10.1542/peds.112.3.e202 PMID:12949313

McFarlan, J., Parker, B., & Soeken, K. (1996). Physical abuse, smoking, and substance use during pregnancy: Prevalence, interrelationships effects on birth weight. *Journal of Obstetric, Gynecologic, and Neonatal Nursing*, *25*(4), 313–320. doi:10.1111/j.1552-6909.1996.tb02577.x PMID:8708832

McGlone, K., Santos, L., Kazama, L., Fong, R., & Mueller, C. (2003). *Developmental disabilities: Theory, research, and intervention*. New York, NY: Praeger.

McLean, J. E., & Ross, S. M. (1994, October). *The urban-rural funding disparity*. Paper presented at the annual meeting of the National Rural Education Association, Tuscaloosa, AL.

McLeigh, J. D. (2010). How do immigration and customs enforcement (ICE) practices affect the mental health of children? *The American Journal of Orthopsychiatry*, *80*(1), 96–100. doi:10.1111/j.1939-0025.2010.01011.x PMID:20397993

McMillen, J. C., Smith, E. M., & Fisher, R. H. (1997). Perceived benefit and mental health after three types of disaster. *Journal of Consulting and Clinical Psychology*, *65*(5), 733–739. doi:10.1037/0022-006X.65.5.733 PMID:9337492

McMorris, C. A., Cox, E., Hudson, M., Liu, X., & Bebko, J. M. (2013). The diagnostic process of children with autism spectrum disorder: Implications for early identification and intervention. *Journal on Developmental Disabilities*, *19*(2), 42–49.

Meiers, S., & Baerg, J. (2001). Farm accidents in children: Eleven years of experience. *Journal of Pediatric Surgery*, *36*(5), 726–729. doi:10.1053/jpsu.2001.22946 PMID:11329575

Meins, E., Fernyhough, C., Fradley, E., & Tuckey, M. (2001). Rethinking maternal sensitivity: Mothers' comments on infants' mental processes predict security of attachment at 12 months. *Journal of Child Psychology and Psychiatry, and Allied Disciplines*, *42*(5), 637–648. doi:10.1111/1469-7610.00759 PMID:11464968

Meiser-Stedman, R., Yule, W., Smith, P., Glucksman, E., & Dalgleish, T. (2005). Acute stress disorder and posttraumatic stress disorder in children and adolescents involved in assaults or motor vehicle accidents. *The American Journal of Psychiatry*, *162*(7), 1381–1383. doi:10.1176/appi.ajp.162.7.1381 PMID:15994725

Memken, J. A., & Canabal, M. E. (1994). Housing tenure, structure, and crowding among Latino households. *Journal of Family and Economic Issues*, *15*(4), 349–365. doi:10.1007/BF02353810

Menard, K. S., & Ruback, R. B. (2003). Prevalence and processing of child sexual abuse: A multi-data-set analysis of urban and rural counties. *Law and Human Behavior*, *27*(4), 385–402. doi:10.1023/A:1024084916626 PMID:12916227

Mendenhall, B., & Dumesnil, J. (2006). Exploring Traditional Cultural Mechanisms of Conflict Resolution in American Indian Communities. In E. Jensen & J. Jepsen (Eds.), *Juvenile Law Violators, Human Rights, and the Development of New Juvenile Justice Systems* (pp. 341–372). Portland, OR: Hart Publishing.

Mendoza-Denton, N. (2014). *Homegirls: Language and cultural practice among Latina youth gangs*. New York: John Wiley & Sons.

Mendoza, M., & Olivos, E. M. (2009). Advocating for control with compassion: The impacts of raids and deportations on children and families. *Oregon Review of International Law*, *11*, 111.

Merriam, S. B. (1998). *Qualitative research and case study applications in education*. San Francisco, CA: Jossey -Bass Publishers.

Merriam, S. B. (2009). *Qualitative research: A guide to design and implementation*. San Francisco, CA: Jossey-Bass.

Metz, E. C., & McCall, R. B. (2010). Behavior problems in children adopted from psychosocially depriving institutions. *Journal of Abnormal Child Psychology*, *38*(4), 459–470. doi:10.1007/s10802-009-9383-4 PMID:20084451

Meyers, J. E. B. (2011). *The APSAC Handbook on child maltreatment* (3rd ed.). Thousand Oaks, CA: Sage.

Mezzich, J. E., Kirmayer, L. J., Kleinman, A., Fabrega, H. Jr, Parron, D. L., Good, B. J., & Manson, S. M. et al. (1999). The place of culture in DSM-IV. *The Journal of Nervous and Mental Disease*, *187*(8), 457–464. doi:10.1097/00005053-199908000-00001 PMID:10463062

Miller, G. A. (1992). Integrating religion and psychology in therapy: Issues and recommendations. *Counseling and Values*, *36*(2), 112–122. doi:10.1002/j.2161-007X.1991.tb00968.x

Miller, T. W., & Kraus, R. F. (2008). School-related violence: Definition, scope, and prevention goals. In T. W. Miller (Ed.), *School violence and primary prevention* (pp. 15–24). New York, NY: Springer Publisher. doi:10.1007/978-0-387-77119-9_2

Miller, W., & Rollnick, S. (2012). *Motivational Interviewing* (3rd ed.). New York, NY: The Guilford Press.

Ministry of Social Affairs and Health. (2009). Raskaanaolevienpäihdeongelmaistennaistenhoidonvarmistaminen – työryhmänraportti. *Sosiaali-jaterveysministeriönselvityksiä*, *4*.

Mink, M. D., Moore, C. G., Johnson, A., Probst, J. C., & Martin, A. (2005). *Violence and rural teens: Teen violence, drug use, and school-based prevention services in rural America*. Washington, DC: U.S. Department of Health and Human Services, Office of Rural Health Policy.

Miyamoto, S., Dharmar, M., Boyle, C., Yang, N. H., MacLeod, K., Rogers, K., & Marcin, J. P. et al. (2014). Impact of telemedicine on the quality of forensic sexual abuse examinations in rural communities. *Child Abuse & Neglect*, *38*(9), 1533–1539. doi:10.1016/j.chiabu.2014.04.015 PMID:24841062

Moisan, P. A., Sanders-Phillips, K., & Moisan, P. M. (1997). Ethnic differences in circumstances of abuse and anger among sexually abused Black and Latino boys. *Child Abuse & Neglect*, *21*, 473–488. doi:10.1016/S0145-2134(97)00007-0 PMID:9158907

Mollica, R. F., Kikuchi, Y., Lavelle, J., & Allden, K. (1995). *The Invisible Human Crisis: Mental Health Recommendations for the Care of Persons Evacuated and Displaced by the Hanshin-Awaji (Kobe) Earthquake*. Boston: Harvard Program in Refugee Trauma.

Mol, S. S. L., Arntz, A., Metsemakers, J., Dinant, G. J., Vilters-Van Montfort, P. A., & Knottnerus, J. A. (2005). Symptoms of Post-traumatic stress disorder after nontraumatic events. *The British Journal of Psychiatry*, *186*, 494–499. doi:10.1192/bjp.186.6.494 PMID:15928360

Monsey, B., Owen, G., Zierman, C., Lambert, L., & Hyman, V. (1995). *What works in preventing rural violence*. St. Paul, MN: Amherst H. Wilder Foundation.

Moracco, K. E., Hilton, A., Hodges, K. G., & Frasier, P. Y. (2005). Knowledge and attitudes about intimate partner violence among immigrant Latinos in rural North Carolina baseline information and implications for research. *Violence Against Women*, *11*(3), 337–352. doi:10.1177/1077801204273296 PMID:16043553

Morales, A., Yakushko, O. F., & Castro, A. J. (2012). Language brokering among Mexican-immigrant families in the Midwest: A multiple case study. *The Counseling Psychologist*, *40*(4), 520–553. doi:10.1177/0011000011417312

Moreira-Almeida, A., & Koenig, H. G. (2006). Retaining the meaning of the words religiousness and spirituality: A commentary on the WHOQOL SRPB group's ''A cross-cultural study of spirituality, religion, and personal beliefs as components of quality of life''. *Social Science & Medicine*, *63*(4), 843–845. doi:10.1016/j.socscimed.2006.03.001 PMID:16650515

Moreno, E. M. (2006). Mexican American street gangs, migration, violence in the Yakima Valley. *Pacific Northwest Quarterly*, 131–138.

Morse, J. M. (1994). Designing funded qualitative research. In N. K. Denzin & Y. S. Lincoln (Eds.), *Handbook of qualitative research* (2nd ed.; pp. 220–235). Thousand Oaks, CA: Sage.

Morsette, A., Swaney, G., Stolle, D., Schuldberg, D., van den Pol, R., & Young, M. (2009). Cognitive Behavioral Intervention for Trauma in Schools (CBITS): School-based treatment on a rural American Indian reservation. *Journal of Behavior Therapy and Experimental Psychiatry*, *40*(1), 169–178. doi:10.1016/j.jbtep.2008.07.006 PMID:18835478

Mott, J. M., Galovski, T. E., Walsh, R. M., & Elwood, L. S. (2015). Change in trauma narratives and perceived recall ability over a course of cognitive processing therapy for PTSD. *Traumatology*, *21*(1), 47–54. doi:10.1037/trm0000012 PMID:26005396

Moylan, C. A., Herrenkohl, T. I., Sousa, C., Tajima, E. A., Herrenkohl, R. C., & Russo, M. J. (2010). The effects of child abuse and exposure to domestic violence on adolescent internalizing and externalizing behavior problems. *Journal of Family Violence*, *25*(1), 53–63. doi:10.1007/s10896-009-9269-9 PMID:20495613

Murphey, D., Guzman, L., & Torres, A. (2014). *America's Hispanic children: Gaining ground, looking forward*. Academic Press.

Nansel, T. R., Overpeck, M. D., Haynie, D. L., Ruan, W. J., & Scheidt, P. C. (2003). Relationship between bullying and violence among US youth. *Archives of Pediatrics & Adolescent Medicine*, *157*(4), 348–353. doi:10.1001/archpedi.157.4.348 PMID:12695230

National Center for Children in Poverty. (1999). Poverty and Brain Development in early Childhood. New York, NY: Author.

National Child Traumatic Stress Network. (2005). *Understanding child traumatic stress*. Retrieved from www.nctsnet.org

National Child Traumatic Stress Network. (2012). *The 12 core concepts: Concerns for understanding traumatic stress responses in children and families*. Retrieved from www.nctsnet.org

National Child Traumatic Stress Network. (2015). *National Child Traumatic Stress Network Empirically Supported Treatments and Promising Practices*. Retrieved November 13th from http://nctsnet.org/resources/topics/treatments-that-work/promising-practices

National Child Traumatic Stress Network. (2015). *TF-CBT Web: A trauma-based learning course for Trauma-focused Cognitive-behavioral Therapy*. Retrieved November 13 from: http://tfcbt.musc.edu/

National Scientific Council on the Developing Child. (2015). *Supportive Relationships and Active Skill-Building Strengthen the Foundations of Resilience: Working Paper 13*. Retrieved from http://www.developingchild.harvard.edu

Nelsen, J. (2006). *Positive discipline*. New York, NY: Ballantine Books.

Nelson, L., & Hiemstra, N. (2008). Latino immigrants and the renegotiation of place and belonging in small town America. *Social & Cultural Geography*, *9*(3), 319–342. doi:10.1080/14649360801990538

*New Jersey Adoption Resource Clearing House*. (2010). Retrieved from http://www.njarch.org

Niemi, P. M. (2008). Psykosomatiikka. In S. Kähkönen, I. Karila, & N. Holmberg (Eds.), *Kognitiivinenpsykoterapia. Hämeenlinna: KaristoOy:nkirjapaino.*

Noonan, J. H., & Vavra, M. C. (2007). *A study of offenders and arrestees reported via national incident-based reporting system data*. Retrieved from: http://www.fbi.gov/about-us/cjis/ucr/nibrs/crime-in-schools-and-colleges-pdf

Nooney, J. G. (2005). Religion, stress, and mental health in adolescence: Findings from Add Health. *Review of Religious Research*, *46*(4), 341–354. doi:10.2307/3512165

Norris, E., & Alegria, M. (2005). Mental health care for ethnic minority individuals and communities in the aftermath of disasters and mass violence. *CNS Spectrums*, *10*, 132–140. PMID:15685124

North American Council on Adoptable Children. (2009). *Developing a parent-to-parent support network*. Retrieved July 10, 2014, from: http://www.nacac.org/adoptalk/parent2parentnetwork.pdf

Number, E.B. (2014). Rural America at a Glance: 2013 Edition. *USDA-ERS Economic Brief*, (26).

Obeidat, Z. (1997). Bullying and violence in the Jordanian school. In T. Obsako (Ed.), *Violence at school: Global issues and interventions* (pp. 20–35). Paris, France: UNESCO.

Oetinger, M. A., Flanagan, K. S., & Weaver, I. D. (2014). The decision and rewards of working as a mental health professional in a rural area. *Journal of Rural Mental Health*, *38*(1), 50–60. doi:10.1037/rmh0000011

Office of Disease Prevention and Health Promotion. (2005). *Healthy People 2010. US Department of Health and Human Service*. Retrieved from: http://www.healthypeople.gov/document/HTML/Volume2/15Injury.htm#_Toc490549392

Olde, E., van der Hart, O., Kleber, R., & van Son, M. (2006). Post-traumatic stress disorder following childbirth. *Clinical Psychology Review*, *26*(1), 1–16. doi:10.1016/j.cpr.2005.07.002 PMID:16176853

Olds, D. L. (2008). Preventing child maltreatment and crime with prenatal and infancy support of parents: The nurse-family partnership. *Journal of Scandinavian Studies in Criminology and Crime Prevention*, *9*(1), 2–24. doi:10.1080/14043850802450096 PMID:20885797

Olthof, T., & Goossens, F. A. (2008). Bullying and the need to belong: Early adolescents' bullying-related behavior and the acceptance they desire and receive from particular classmates. *Social Development*, *17*(1), 24–46.

Olweus, D. (1993). *Bullying at school: What we know and what we can do*. Blackwell Publishing.

Onetto, J. E., Flores, M. T., & Garbino, M. L. (1994). Dental trauma in children and adolescents in Valparaiso, Chile. *Dental Traumatology*, *10*(5), 223–227. doi:10.1111/j.1600-9657.1994.tb00074.x PMID:7843064

Openshaw, L. L. (2013). Group Interventions in Rural Schools to Assist with a Community Trauma. *Contemporary Rural Social Work*, *5*, 110–124.

Orellana, M. F. (2009). *Translating childhood: Immigrant youth, language, and culture*. Rutgers University Press.

Osgood, D. W., & Chambers, J. M. (2003). Community correlates of rural youth violence. *Juvenile Justice Bulletin*. Retrieved from: http://www.ncjrs.org/html/ojjdp/193591/contents.html

Osterberg, A. M. (2009). Removing the dead hand on the future: Recognizing citizen children's right against parental deportation. *Lewis and Clark Law Review*, *13*, 751.

Ozer, E. J., Best, S. R., Lipsey, T. L., & Weiss, D. S. (2008, August). Predictors of posttraumatic stress disorder and symptoms in adults: a meta-analysis. In *Annual Meeting of the International Society for Traumatic Stress Studies*. Educational Publishing Foundation. doi:10.1037/1942-9681.S.1.3

Palacios, J., Wrobel, G. M., & Neil, E. (2009). The ecology of adoption. *International advances in adoption research for practice*, 71-94.

Palacios, J., & Brodzinsky, D. (2010). Adoption research: Trends, topics, outcomes. *International Journal of Behavioral Development*, *34*(3), 270–284. doi:10.1177/0165025410362837

Palanisamy, R., & Verville, J. (2015). Factors enabling communication-based collaboration in interprofessional healthcare practice: A case study. *International Journal of e-Collaboration*, *11*(2), 8–27. doi:10.4018/ijec.2015040102

Pargament, K. I. (2007). *Spiritually integrated psychotherapy: Understanding and addressing the sacred*. New York: Guilford.

Pargament, K. I., Smith, B. W., Koenig, H. G., & Perez, L. (1998). Patterns of positive and negative religious coping with major life stressors. *Journal for the Scientific Study of Religion*, *37*(4), 710–724. doi:10.2307/1388152

Park, C. L. (2004). The notion of stress-related growth: Problems and prospects. *Psychological Inquiry*, *15*, 69–76.

Parker, R. D., & Slaby, R. G. (1983). The development of aggression. In E. M. Hetherington & P. H. Mussen (Eds.), Handbook of child psychology: Vol. 4. *Socialization, personality, and social development* (pp. 547–642). New York: Wiley.

Passel, J. S., Cohn, D., & Lopez, M. H. (2011). *Hispanics account for more than half of the nation's growth in past decade*. Washington, DC: Pew Hispanic Center.

Pattillo, M., Western, B., & Weiman, D. (2004). *Imprisoning America: The social effects of mass incarceration*. Russell Sage Foundation.

Patton, M. Q. (1990). *Qualitative evaluation methods* (2nd ed.). Thousand Oaks, CA: Sage.

Paul, L. A., Gray, M. J., Elhai, J. D., Massad, P. M., & Stamm, B. H. (2006). Promotion of evidence-based practices for child traumatic stress in rural populations: Identification of barriers and promising solutions. *Trauma, Violence & Abuse*, *7*(4), 260–273. doi:10.1177/1524838006292521 PMID:17065547

Paulsen, C., & Merighi, J. (2009). Adoption preparedness, cultural engagement, and parental satisfaction in inter-country adoption. *Adoption Quarterly*, *12*(1), 1–18. doi:10.1080/10926750902791540

Pearson, G. S., Hines-Martin, V. P., Evans, L. K., York, J. A., Kane, C. F., & Yearwood, E. L. (2014). Addressing Gaps in Mental Health Needs of Diverse, At-Risk, Underserved, and Disenfranchised Populations: A Call for Nursing Action. *Archives of Psychiatric Nursing*. PMID:25634869

Peek-Asa, C., Wallis, A., Harland, K., Beyer, K., Dickey, P., & Saftlas, A. (2011). Rural disparity in domestic violence prevalence and access to resources. *Journal of Women's Health*, *11*(11), 1743–1749. doi:10.1089/jwh.2011.2891 PMID:21919777

Peguero, A. A. (2009). Victimizing the children of immigrants: Latino and Asian American student victimization. *Youth & Society*, *41*(2), 186–208. doi:10.1177/0044118X09333646

Peltoniemi, T. (2003) Päihdeperheidenlapsetauttamisjärjestelmissä. In K. Utslahti & T. Peltoniemi (Eds.), Pikkuaikuisia- KirjoituskilpailunkertomuksiajatutkimustietoaLasinenLapsuushankkeesta. Jyväskylä: GummerusKirjapainoOy.

Pereda, N., Guilera, G., Forns, M., & Gomez-Benito, J. (2009). The international epidemiology of child sexual abuse: A continuation of Finkelhor (1994). *Child Abuse & Neglect*, *33*(6), 331–342. doi:10.1016/j.chiabu.2008.07.007 PMID:19477003

Perez-Fuentes, G., Olfson, M., Villegas, L., Morcillo, C., Wang, S., & Blanco, C. (2013). Prevalence and correlates of child sexual abuse: A national study. *Comprehensive Psychiatry*, *54*(1), 16–27. doi:10.1016/j.comppsych.2012.05.010 PMID:22854279

Perry, B. (1997). Incubated in terror: Neurodevelopmental factors in the cycle of violence. In D. Osofsky (Ed.), *Children in a Violent Society* (pp. 124–149). New York, NY: The Guilford Press.

Perry, B. (2006). Applying principles of neurodevelopment to clinical work with maltreated and traumatized children: The neurosequential model of therapeutics. In N. B. Webb (Ed.), *Working with Traumatized Youth in Child Welfare* (pp. 27–52). New York, NY: The Guilford Press.

Perry, D. G., Kusel, S. J., & Perry, L. C. (1988). Victims of peer aggression. *Developmental Psychology*, *24*(6), 807–814. doi:10.1037/0012-1649.24.6.807

Petersen, A., Joseph, J., & Feit, M. (Eds.). (2014). *New directions in child abuse and neglect research*. Washington, DC: National Academies Press.

Petersen, G. J., Beekley, C. Z., Speaker, K. M., & Pietrzak, D. (1998). An examination of violence in three rural school districts. *Journal for Rural and Small Schools*, *19*(3), 25–38.

Peterson, C., & Seligman, M. E. P. (2003). Character strengths before and after September 11. *Psychological Science*, *14*(4), 381–384. doi:10.1111/1467-9280.24482 PMID:12807415

Peterson, C., & Seligman, M. E. P. (2004). *Character strengths and virtues: A classification and handbook. Washington, DC: American Psychological Association.* Oxford, UK: University Press.

Peters, V., Sottiaux, M., Appelboom, J., & Kahn, A. (2004). Posttraumatic stress disorder after dog bites in children. *The Journal of Pediatrics*, *144*(1), 121–122. doi:10.1016/j.jpeds.2003.10.024 PMID:14722529

Petra, M., & Kohl, P. (2010). Triple P and the child welfare system: A promising fit. *Children and Youth Services Review*, *32*(4), 611–618. doi:10.1016/j.childyouth.2009.12.008 PMID:20419078

Pew Forum on Religion and Public Life. (2008). *U.S. religious landscape survey*. Washington, DC: Pew Research Center.

Pfefferbaum, B., Nixon, S. J., Tucker, P. M., Tivis, R. D., Moore, V. L., Gurwitch, R. H., & Geis, H. K. et al. (1999). Posttraumatic stress responses in bereaved children after the Oklahoma City bombing. *Journal of the American Academy of Child and Adolescent Psychology*, *38*(11), 1372–1379. doi:10.1097/00004583-199911000-00011 PMID:10560223

Pickert, K., & Shuster, S. (2010). When the adopted can't adapt. *Time International (South Pacific Edition*, *176*(2), 22-27.

Pickett, W., Brison, R. J., Berg, R. L., Zentner, J., Linneman, J., & Marlenga, B. (2005). Pediatric farm injuries involving non-working children injured by a farm work hazard: Five priorities for primary prevention. *Injury Prevention*, *11*(1), 6–11. doi:10.1136/ip.2004.005769 PMID:15691981

Pine, D. S., & Cohen, J. A. (2002). Trauma in children and adolescents: Risk and treatment of psychiatric sequelae. *Biological Psychiatry*, *51*(7), 519–531. doi:10.1016/S0006-3223(01)01352-X PMID:11950454

Plante, T. G. (2007). Integrating spirituality and psychotherapy: Ethical issues and principles to consider. *Journal of Clinical Psychology*, *63*(9), 891–902. doi:10.1002/jclp.20383 PMID:17674403

Plante, T. G. (2008). What do the spiritual and religious traditions offer the practicing psychologist? *Pastoral Psychology*, *56*(4), 429–444. doi:10.1007/s11089-008-0119-0

Policy Research Associates, Inc. (n.d.). Substance Abuse and Mental Health Services Administration GAINS Center. *Fact Sheet: Historical Trauma*.

Post, B. (2006). *The adopted child: Trauma and its impact*. Retrieved from http://www.streetdirectory.com/travel_guide/201812/child_adoptions/the_adopted_child_trauma_and_its_impact.htm

Post, B. (2013). *The adopted child: Trauma and its impact*. Retrieved from http://postinstitute.com/blog/2013/11/06/the-adopted-child-trauma-and-its-impact-bryan-post/

Postmus, J. L., Severson, M., Berry, M., & Yoo, J. A. (2009). Women's experiences of violence and seeking help. *Violence Against Women*, *15*(7), 852–868. doi:10.1177/1077801209334445 PMID:19458091

Prinz, R. (2009). Dissemination of a multilevel evidence based system of parenting interventions with broad application to child welfare populations. *Child Welfare*, *88*(1), 127–132. PMID:19653456

Prothrow-Stith, D., & Quaday, S. (1996). Communities, schools, and violence. In A. M. Hoffman (Ed.), *Schools, violence, and society* (pp. 153–161). Westport, CT: Praeger.

Provence, S. (1977). Developmental assessment. In M. Green & R. Haggerty (Eds.), *Ambulatory pediatrics* (pp. 374–383). Philadelphia: Saunders.

Public Health Agency of Canada. (2010). *Canadian incidence study of reported child abuse and neglect–2008: Major findings*. Ottawa, CA: Public Health Agency of Canada.

Puccia, E. (2015). *Evaluation report of the Maine Children's Trauma Response Initiative.* Substance Abuse and Mental Health Services Administration Grant #5U79SM062112-08 (Unpublished Report). Portland, Maine.

Puccia, E., Redding, T. M., Brown, R. S., Gwynn, P. A., Hirsh, A. B., Hoffmann Frances, R., & Morrison, B. (2012). Using Community Outreach and Evidenced-Based Treatment to Address Domestic Violence Issues. *Social Work in Mental Health, 10*(2), 104–126. doi:10.1080/15332985.2011.601704

Pullmann, M. D., VanHooser, S., Hoffman, C., & Heflinger, C. A. (2010). Barriers to and supports of family participation in a rural system of care for children with serious emotional problems. *Community Mental Health Journal, 46*(3), 211–220. doi:10.1007/s10597-009-9208-5 PMID:19551506

Purvis, K. (2010). *Empowering, Connecting & Correcting Principles: Healing Children Through Trust and Relationships.* [DVD]. Fort Worth, TX: Texas Christian Institute of Child Development.

Purvis, K. (2010). *Facilitating Behavioral Change.* [DVD]. Fort Worth, TX: Texas Christian Institute of Child Development.

Purvis, K. (2010). *The Attachment Dance.* [DVD]. Fort Worth, TX: Texas Christian Institute of Child Development.

Purvis, K., Cross, D., & Sunshine, W. (2007). *The connected child: bring hope and healing to your adoptive family.* New York: McGraw Hill.

Quandt, S. A. (2009). Health of children and women in the farmworker community in eastern United States. In S. A. Quandt & T. A. Arcury (Eds.), *Latino farmworkers in the eastern United States* (pp. 173–200). New York: Springer. doi:10.1007/978-0-387-88347-2_8

Quezada, L., Gonzalez, M. T., & Mecott, G. A. (in press). Explanatory model of resilience in pediatric burn survivors. *Journal of Burn Care & Research; Official Publication of the American Burn Association.* PMID:26056758

Quinn, A. (2007). Reflections on intergenerational trauma: Healing as a critical intervention. *First Peoples Child & Family Review, 3*(4), 72–82.

Quintero, G. A., Lilliot, E., & Willging, C. (2007). Substance abuse treatment provider views of "culture" for behavioral health care in rural settings. *Qualitative Health Research, 17*(9), 1256–1267. doi:10.1177/1049732307307757 PMID:17968042

Raffaelli, M., & Wiley, A. R. (2013). Challenges and strengths of immigrant families in the rural Midwest. *Journal of Family Issues, 34*(3), 347–372. doi:10.1177/0192513X11432422

Randall, J. (2009). Towards a better understanding of the needs of children currently adopted from care: An analysis of placements 2003-2006. *Adoption & Fostering, 33*(1), 44–55. doi:10.1177/030857590903300105

Reed, D. F. & Reed, E. L. (1997). Children of incarcerated parents. *Social Justice/Global Options, 24*, 152-169.

Reed, B. G. (1987). Developing women-sensitive drug dependence treatment services: Why so difficult? *Journal of Psychoactive Drugs, 19*(2), 151–16. doi:10.1080/02791072.1987.10472399 PMID:3612383

Reeler, A. P., & Immerman, R. (1994). A Preliminary Investigation Into Psychological Disorders Among Mozambican Refugees: Prevalence and Clinical Features. *The Central African Journal of Medicine, 40*(11), 309–315. PMID:7859272

Reiss, A., & Roth, J. A. (Eds.). (1993). *Understanding and preventing violence.* Washington, DC: National Academy Press.

Rennison, C. M., & Welchans, S. (2000). *Bureau of Justice statistics special report: Intimate partner violence.* Washington, DC: U.S. Department of Justice.

Resnick, M. D., Bearman, R. W., Blum, K. E., Bauman, K. M., Harris, J., Jones, J., & Udry, J. R. et al. (1997). Protecting adolescents from harm: Findings from the National Longitudinal Study of Adolescent Health.[JAMA]. *Journal of the American Medical Association*, *178*(10), 823–832. doi:10.1001/jama.1997.03550100049038 PMID:9293990

Robben, A. C. G. M. (2004). *Death, Mourning, and Burial: A Cross-Cultural Reader*. Malden, MA: Blackwell Pub.

Robers, S., Kemp, J., Rathbun, A., & Morgan, R. E. (2014). *Indicators of school crime and safety*. Washington, DC: National Center for Education Statistics.

Robison, M., Lindeman, S. L., Clemmons, M. P., Doyle-Buckwalter, K., & Ryan, M. (2009). I deserve a family ll: The evolution of an adolescent's behavior and beliefs about himself and others when treated with therapy in residential care. *Child & Adolescent Social Work Journal*, *26*(4), 291–306. doi:10.1007/s10560-009-0177-x

Rochin, R. I. (1995). *Rural Latinos: Evolving conditions and issues: The changing American countryside: Rural people and places*. Lawrence, KS: The University Press of Kansas.

Rodenburg, R., Benjamin, A., De Roos, C., Meijer, A. M., & Stams, G. J. (2009). Efficacy of EMDR in children: A meta-analysis. *Clinical Psychology Review*, *29*(7), 599–606. doi:10.1016/j.cpr.2009.06.008 PMID:19616353

Rodriguez, M. A., Heileman, M. V., Fielder, E., Ang, A., Nevarez, F., & Mangione, C. M. (2008). Intimate partner violence, depression, and PTSD among pregnant Latina women. *Annals of Family Medicine*, *6*(1), 44–52. doi:10.1370/afm.743 PMID:18195314

Rodriguez, M. D., Rodriguez, J., & Davis, M. (2006). Recruitment of first generation Latinos in a rural community: The essential nature of personal contact. *Family Process*, *45*(1), 87–100. doi:10.1111/j.1545-5300.2006.00082.x PMID:16615255

Rodriguez, N., Steinberg, A. M., & Pynoos, R. S. (1999). *UCLA PTSD Index for DSM-IV*. Los Angeles, CA: University of California at Los Angeles Trauma Psychiatric Service.

Rodriguez, N., van de Kemp, H., & Foy, D. W. (1998). Post traumatic stress disorder in survivors of childhood sexual abuse: A critical review of the empirical research. *Journal of Child Sexual Abuse*, *7*(2), 17–45. doi:10.1300/J070v07n02_02

Romero, M. (2000). State violence and the social and legal construction of Latino criminality: From el bandido to gang member. *Denver University Law Review*, *78*, 1081.

Ronald, J. P., Matthew, R. S., Cheri, J. S., Daniel, J. W., & John, R. L. (2009). Population-based prevention of child maltreatment: The U.S. Triple P system population trial. *Prevention Science*, *10*(1), 1–12. doi:10.1007/s11121-009-0123-3 PMID:19160053

Roscigno, V. J., & Crowley, M. L. (2001). Rurality, institutional disadvantage, and achievement/attainment. *Rural Sociology*, *66*(2), 268–293. doi:10.1111/j.1549-0831.2001.tb00067.x

Rosenberg, M. B. (1989). *Growing up adopted*. New York: Bradbury Press.

Rostosky, S. S., Regnerus, M. D., & Wright, M. L. C. (2003). Coital debut: The role of religiosity and sex attitudes in the add health survey. *Journal of Sex Research*, *40*(4), 358–367. doi:10.1080/00224490209552202 PMID:14735410

Rothwell, J. D. (2010). In the Company of Others, An Introduction to Communication. New York: Oxford University Press.

Rotunda, R. J., & O'Farrell, T. J. (1997). Marital and family therapy of alcohol use disorders: Bridging the gap between research and practice. *Professional Psychology, Research and Practice*, *28*(3), 246–4. doi:10.1037/0735-7028.28.3.246

Roussos, S. T., & Fawcett, S. B. (2000). A Review of Collaborative Partnerships as a Strategy for Improving Community Health. *Annual Review of Public Health*, *21*(1), 369–402. doi:10.1146/annurev.publhealth.21.1.369 PMID:10884958

Ruback, B. R., & Menard, K. S. (2001). Rural-urban differences in sexual victimization and reporting: Analyses using UCR and Crisis Center data. *Criminal Justice and Behavior*, *28*(2), 131–155. doi:10.1177/0093854801028002001

Ruggiero, J. A. (2010). When adoption isn't easy. *Newsweek, 155*(17), 14.

Rushton, A., & Monck, E. (2009). Adopters' experiences of preparation to parent children with serious difficulties. *Adoption & Fostering*, *33*(2), 4–12. doi:10.1177/030857590903300202

Sabol, W., Coulton, C., & Polousky, E. (2004). Measuring child maltreatment risk in communities: A life table approach. *Child Abuse & Neglect*, *28*(9), 967–983. doi:10.1016/j.chiabu.2004.03.014 PMID:15450762

Sack, W. H., Seeley, J. R., & Clarke, G. N. (1997). Does PTSD transcend cultural barriers? A Study from the Khmer Adolescent Refugee Project. *Journal of the American Academy of Child and Adolescent Psychiatry*, *36*(1), 49–54. doi:10.1097/00004583-199701000-00017 PMID:9000781

Saenz, R., & Torres, C. C. (2003). Latinos in rural America. In Challenges for rural America in the twenty-first century (pp. 57-70). Academic Press.

Saenz, R. (1997). Ethnic concentration and Chicano poverty: A comparative approach. *Social Science Research*, *26*(2), 205–228. doi:10.1006/ssre.1997.0595

Saguil, A., & Phelps, K. (2012). The spiritual assessment. *American Family Physician*, *86*(6), 546–550. PMID:23062046

SAMHSA's GAINS Center. (n.d.). *How Being Trauma-Informed Improves Criminal Justice System Responses. Historical Fact Sheet*. Policy Research Associates .

Sampson, R. J., & Raudenbush, S. W. (2004). Seeing disorder: Neighborhood stigma and the social construction of "broken windows". *Social Psychology Quarterly*, *67*(4), 319–342. doi:10.1177/019027250406700401

Sanchez, O., Funes, S. M., & Velasquez, R. J. (in press). The mass incarceration of Latinos and Latinas in the United States: A binational-transborder mental health perspective. *Journal of Transborder Studies: Research and Practice.*

Sanders, M. R. (1999). Triple P-Positive Parenting Program: Towards an empirically validated multilevel parenting and family support strategy for the prevention of behavior and emotional problems in children. *Clinical Child and Family Psychology Review*, *2*(2), 71–90. doi:10.1023/A:1021843613840 PMID:11225933

Sanders, M. R. (2008). Triple P-Positive Parenting Program as a public health approach to strengthening parenting. *Journal of Family Psychology*, *22*(4), 506–517. doi:10.1037/0893-3200.22.3.506 PMID:18729665

Sanders, M. R., Baker, S., & Turner, K. M. (2012). A randomized controlled trial evaluating the efficacy of Triple P Online with parents of children with early-onset conduct problems. *Behaviour Research and Therapy*, *50*(11), 675–684. doi:10.1016/j.brat.2012.07.004 PMID:22982082

Sanders-Phillips, K., Moisan, P. A., Wadlington, S., Morgan, S., & English, K. (1995). Ethnic differences in psychological functioning among Black and Latino sexually abused girls. *Child Abuse & Neglect*, *19*(6), 691–706. doi:10.1016/0145-2134(95)00027-6 PMID:7552838

Saxe, G. N., Stoddard, F. J., & Sheridan, R. L. (1988). PTSD in children with burns: A longitudinal study. *Journal of Burn Care & Research; Official Publication of the American Burn Association*, 19.

Saywitz, K. J., Mannarino, A. P., Berliner, L., & Cohen, J. A. (2000). Treatment of sexually abused children and adolescents. *The American Psychologist*, *55*(9), 1040–1049. doi:10.1037/0003-066X.55.9.1040 PMID:11036707

Schimmenti, A., & Caretti, V. (2014). Linking the overwhelming with the unbearable: Developmental trauma, dissociation, and the disconnected self. *Psychoanalytic Psychology*. doi:10.1037/a0038019

Schladale, J. (2002). *The Trauma Outcome Process Workbook For Taming Violence and Sexual Aggression*. East Providence, RI: Signature Printing.

Schladale, J. (2007). A Collaborative Approach for Family Reconciliation and Reunification With Youth Who Have Caused Sexual Harm. In D. Prescott (Ed.), *Knowledge & Practice: Challenges in the Treatment and Supervision of Sexual Abusers*. Safer Society Press.

Schofield, A., & Bourgeois, D. (2010). Socially responsible medical education: Innovations and challenges in a minority setting. *Medical Education*, *44*(3), 263–271. doi:10.1111/j.1365-2923.2009.03573.x PMID:20444057

Schooler, J., Smalley, D., & Callahan, T. (2009). *Wounded children, Healing homes*. Colorado Springs, CO: NavPress.

Schore, A. N. (1994). *Affect regulation and the origin of the self: The neurobiology of emotional development*. Hillsdale, NJ: Erlbaum.

Schore, A. N. (2003a). *Affect dysregulation and disorders of the self*. New York, NY: Norton.

Schore, A. N. (2003b). *Affect regulation and the repair of the self*. New York, NY: Norton.

Schore, J. R., & Schore, A. N. (2008). Modern Attachment Theory: The Central Role of Affect Regulation in Development and Treatment. *Clinical Social Work Journal*, *36*(1), 9–20. doi:10.1007/s10615-007-0111-7

Schorr, L. B., & Marchand, V. (2007). *Pathway to the Prevention of Child Abuse and Neglect*. Retrieved from http://www.childsworld.ca.gov/res/pdf/Pathway.pdf

Schuhmann, E. M., Foote, R. C., Eyberg, S. M., Boggs, S. R., & Algina, J. (1998). Efficacy of parent-child interaction therapy: Interim report of a randomized trial with short-term maintenance. *Journal of Clinical Child Psychology*, *27*(1), 34–45. doi:10.1207/s15374424jccp2701_4 PMID:9561935

Schulte, B. (2013). Child abuse's long-lasting effects. *Arizona Daily Star*.

Schultz, B. (2008). Inside the gilded cage: The lives of Latino immigrant males in rural Kentucky. *Southeastern Geographer*, *48*(2), 201–218. doi:10.1353/sgo.0.0024

Schultz, L., & Jones, P. (1983). Sexual abuse of children: Issues. *Child Welfare*, *62*, 99–108. PMID:6831979

Schwartz, R. C. (1995). *Internal Family Systems therapy*. New York: Guilford Press.

Schwarz, E. D., & Kowalski, J. M. (1991). Malignant memories: PTSD in children and adults after a school shooting. *Journal of the American Academy of Child and Adolescent Psychiatry*, *30*(6), 936–944. doi:10.1097/00004583-199111000-00011 PMID:1757443

Scott, D. M., & Friedli, D. (2002). Attendance problems and disciplinary procedures in Nebraska schools. *Journal of Drug Education*, *32*(2), 149–165. doi:10.2190/JTR4-6L61-4Q2K-WDEN PMID:12206064

Sedlak, A. J., Mettenburg, J., Basena, M., Petta, I., McPherson, K., Greene, A., & Li, S. (2010). *Fourth National Incidence Study of Child Abuse and Neglect (NIS–4): Report to Congress, Executive Summary*. Washington, DC: U.S. Department of Health and Human Services, Administration for Children and Families.

Self-Brown, S., Rheingold, A. A., Campbell, C., & de Aellano, M. (2008). A media campaign prevention program for child sexual abuse: Community members' perspectives. *Journal of Interpersonal Violence*, *23*(6), 728–743. doi:10.1177/0886260507313946 PMID:18378812

Seligman, M., & Csikszentmihalyi, M. (2000). Positive psychology: An introduction. *The American Psychologist*, *55*(1), 5–14. doi:10.1037/0003-066X.55.1.5 PMID:11392865

Semke, C., & Sheridan, S. (2012). Family-School Connections inRural Educational Settings: A Systematic Review of the Empirical Literature. *School Community Journal, 22*(1), 21–48.

Shapiro, F. (2001). *Eye movement desensitization and reprocessing* (2nd ed.). New York, NY: Guilford Press.

Shaver, P. R., & Mikulincer, M. (2002.) *Adult attachment strategies and regulation of emotion.* Retrieved from http://1st-socrates.berkeley.edu:bobley/images/affective%20science%20readings/Shaver/20100309110651377pdf

Shemesh, E., Keshavarz, R., Leightling, N. K., Weinberg, E., Mousavi, A., Sadow, K., & Yehuda, R. et al. (2003). Pediatric emergency department assessment of psychological trauma and posttraumatic stress. *Psychiatric Services (Washington, D.C.), 54*(9), 1277–1281. doi:10.1176/appi.ps.54.9.1277 PMID:12954946

Shen, Y. (2002). Short-term group play therapy with Chinese earthquake victims: Effects on anxiety, depression, and adjustment. *International Journal of Play Therapy, 11*(1), 43–63. doi:10.1037/h0088856

Sherman, A. (1992). *Falling by the wayside: Children in rural America.* Washington, DC: The Children's Defense Fund.

Sherrill, W. W., Crew, L., Mayo, R., Rogers, B. L., & Haynes, D. F. (2005). Educational and health services innovation to improve care for rural Hispanic communities in the U. S. *Education for Health, 18*, 356-367.

Shetgiri, R., Lin, H., Avila, R. M., & Flores, G. (2012). Parental characteristics associated with bullying perpetration in U. S. children aged 10 to 17 years. *American Journal of Public Health, 102*(12), 2280–2286. doi:10.2105/AJPH.2012.300725 PMID:23078471

Shooter, M. (1997). The impact of death, divorce, and disaster on young people. *Current Opinion in Psychiatry, 10*(4), 268–274. doi:10.1097/00001504-199707000-00003

Siegel, D. J. (1999). *The developing mind.* New York: Guilford Press.

Siegel, D. J., & Hartzell, M. (2004). *Parenting from the inside out.* New York: Tarcher.

Silovsky, J. F., Bard, D., Chaffin, M., Hecht, D., Burris, L., Owora, A., & Lutzker, J. (2011). Prevention of child maltreatment in high-risk rural families: A randomized clinical trial with child welfare outcomes. *Children and Youth Services Review, 33*(8), 1435–1444. doi:10.1016/j.childyouth.2011.04.023

Silva, R. R. (2004). *Posttraumatic stress disorders in children and adolescents: Handbook.* New York: W. W. Norton & Company.

Sinclair, R. (2007). Identity lost and found: Lessons from the sixties scoop. *First Peoples Child & Family Review, 3*(1), 65–82.

Sinha, J. W., Cnaan, R. A., & Gelles, R. J. (2007). Adolescent risk behaviors and religion: Findings from a national study. *Journal of Adolescence, 30*(2), 231–249. doi:10.1016/j.adolescence.2006.02.005 PMID:16677701

Sinkkonen, J., & Kalland, M. (2005). Johdanto: Ihminentarvitseetoistenläheisyyttäjaturvaa. In J. Sinkkonen & M. Kalland (Eds.), *VarhaisetIhmissuhteetjaniidenhäiriintyminen.* Vantaa: Werner SöderströmOsakeyhtiö.

Size, T. (n.d.). *Rural Health Can Lead the Way.* Retrieved from http://www.ruralhealthweb.org/go/left/about-rural-health on 5/20/15

Sloan, R. P., Bagiella, E., & Powell, T. (2001). Without a prayer: Methodological problems, ethical challenges, and misrepresentations in the study of religion, spirituality, and medicine. In T. G. Plante & A. C. Sherman (Eds.), Faith and health: Psychological perspectives, (pp. 339–354). New York: Guilford Press.

Slovak, K., & Singer, M. I. (2001). Gun violence exposure and trauma among rural youth. *Violence and Victims*, *16*, 389–400. PMID:11506448

Slovak, K., & Singer, M. I. (2002). Children and violence: Findings and implications from a rural community. *Child & Adolescent Social Work Journal*, *19*(1), 35–56. doi:10.1023/A:1014003306441

Smith, S. (2010). *Keeping the promise: The critical need for post-adoption services to enable children and families to succeed*. Evan B. Donaldson Adoption Institute. Retrieved from http://adoptioninstitute.org/pubs_cat/adoption-support-and-preservation

Smith, S. (2011). *Expanding resources for children III: Research based best practices in adoption by gays and lesbians*. Evan B. Donaldson Adoption Institute. Retrieved from http://adoptioninstitute.org/pubs_cat/adoption-support-and-preservation

Smith, S. (2012). *New: Untangling the web; the Internet's transformative impact on adoption*. Evan B. Donaldson Adoption Institute. Retrieved from http://adoptioninstitute.org/pubs_

Smith, S. (2012). *The vital role of adoption subsidies: Increasing permanency and improving children's lives*. Evan B. Donaldson Adoption Institute. Retrieved from http://adoptioninstitute.org/pubs_keepingthepromise

Smith, B. W., Pargament, K. I., Brant, C., & Oliver, J. M. (2000). Noah revisited: Religious coping by church members and the impact of the 1993 Midwest flood. *Journal of Community Psychology*, *28*(2), 169–186. doi:10.1002/(SICI)1520-6629(200003)28:2<169::AID-JCOP5>3.0.CO;2-I

Smith, C. (2003). Theorizing religious effects among American adolescents. *Journal for the Scientific Study of Religion*, *42*(1), 17–30. doi:10.1111/1468-5906.t01-1-00158

Smith, C., & Denton, M. (2005). *Soul searching: The religious and spiritual lives of American teenagers*. New York: Oxford University Press. doi:10.1093/019518095X.001.0001

Smith, H. A., & Furuseth, O. J. (2006). *Latinos in the new South: Transformations of place*. Ashgate Publishing Ltd.

Smith, M. V., Kruse, A., Weir, A., & Goldblum, J. (2013). Diaper Need and Its Impact on Child Health. *Pediatrics*, *132*(2), 253–259. doi:10.1542/peds.2013-0597 PMID:23897910

Smith, P. K., Madsen, K. C., & Moody, J. C. (1999). What causes the age decline in reports of being bullied at school: Towards a developmental analysis of risks of being bullied. *Educational Researcher*, *41*(3), 267–285. doi:10.1080/0013188990410303

Snell, C., Bailey, C., Carona, A., & Mebane, D. (2002). School crime policy changes: The impact of recent highly publicized crimes. *American Journal of Criminal Justice*, *26*(2), 269–285. doi:10.1007/BF02887831

Snyder, H. N., & Sickmund, M. (1999). *Juvenile offenders and victims: 1999 national report*. Washington, DC: Office of Juvenile Justice and Delinquency Prevention, U.S. Department of Justice.

Söderholm, A. (2004). Johdanto. In A. Söderholm et al. (Eds.), *Lapsenkaltoinkohtelu. Keuruu: OtavanKirjapainoOy*.

Somasundaram, D. J. (1996). Post-traumatic responses to aerial bombing population. *Social Science & Medicine*, *42*(11), 1465–1471. doi:10.1016/0277-9536(95)00249-9 PMID:8771629

Sonkin, D. J. (1999). *Domestic violence and attachment theory: Clinical application to treatment with perpetrators*. Volcano, CA: Volcano Press.

Sonkin, D. J., & Durphy, M. (1997). *Learning to live without violence: A handbook for men* (Rev. Ed.). Volcano, CA: Volcano Press.

Sorenson, S. B., & Telles, C. A. (1991). Self-reports of spousal violence in a Mexican-American and non-Hispanic White population. *Violence and Victims*, *6*(1), 3–15. PMID:1859804

Spangler, G., Johann, M., Ronai, Z., & Zimmermann, P. (2009). Genetic and environmental influence on attachment disorganization. *Journal of Child Psychology and Psychiatry, and Allied Disciplines*, *50*(8), 952–961. doi:10.1111/j.1469-7610.2008.02054.x PMID:19673052

Spencer, G. A., & Byrant, S. A. (2000). Dating violence: A comparison of rural, suburban, and urban teens. *The Journal of Adolescent Health*, *27*(5), 302–305. doi:10.1016/S1054-139X(00)00125-7 PMID:11044701

Spencer-Oatey, H. (2012). *What is culture? A compilation of quotations*. Retrieved from https://www2.warwick.ac.uk/fac/soc/al/globalpad/openhouse/interculturalskills/global_pad_-_what_is_culture.pdf

Sprang, G., Staton-Tindall, M., Gustman, B., Freer, B., Clark, J. J., Dye, H., & Sprang, K. (2013). The impact of trauma exposure on parenting stress in rural America. *Journal of Child & Adolescent Trauma*, *6*(4), 287–300. doi:10.1080/19361521.2013.836585

Springer, D. W., Courtney, L., & Rubin, A. (2000). Effects of a solution-focused mutual aid group for Hispanic children of incarcerated parents. *Child & Adolescent Social Work Journal*, *17*(6), 431–442. doi:10.1023/A:1026479727159

Sprott, J. B. (2004). The development of early delinquency: Can classroom and school climates make a difference? *Canadian Journal of Criminology and Criminal Justice*, *46*(5), 553–572. doi:10.3138/cjccj.46.5.553

Stark, K. D., & Laurent, J. (2001). Joint Factor Analysis of the Children's Depression Inventory and the Revised Children's Manifest Anxiety Scale. *Journal of Clinical Child Psychology*, *30*(4), 552–567.

Stein, B. D., Jaycox, L. H., Kataoka, S., Rhodes, H. J., & Vestal, K. D. (2003). Prevalence of child and adolescent exposure to community violence. *Clinical Child and Family Psychology Review*, *6*(4), 247–264. doi:10.1023/B:CCFP.0000006292.61072.d2 PMID:14719637

Stephens, R. D. (1994). Gangs, guns and school violence. *USA Today, 122*(25584), 29-32.

Stockdale, M. S., Hangaduambo, S., Duys, D., Larson, K., & Sarvela, P. D. (2002). Rural elementary students', parents', and teachers' perceptions of bullying. *American Journal of Health Behavior*, *26*(4), 266–277. doi:10.5993/AJHB.26.4.3 PMID:12081359

Stodolska, M., Acevedo, J. C., & Shinew, K. J. (2009). Gangs of Chicago: Perceptions of crime and its effect on the recreation behavior of Latino residents in urban communities. *Leisure Sciences*, *31*(5), 466–482. doi:10.1080/01490400903199773

Storer, H. L., Lindhorst, T., & Starr, K. (2013). The domestic violence fatality review: Can it mobilize community-wide change? *Homicide Studies*, *17*(4), 418–435. doi:10.1177/1088767913494202 PMID:25741174

Strasser, R. P. (2010). Community Engagement: A Key to Successful Rural Clinical Education. *Rural and Remote Health*, *10*, 1–7. PMID:20815653

*Strengthening Families and Communities: Promising Practices for Adoption-Competent Mental Health services*. (2003). A white paper. Retrieved from www.caseyfamilyservices.org/pdfs/casey_mhpaper_sum.pdf

Suarez-Orozco, C., Yoshikawa, H., Teranishi, R., & Suarez-Orozco, M. (2011). Growing up in the shadows: The developmental implications of unauthorized status. *Harvard Educational Review*, *81*(3), 438–472. doi:10.17763/haer.81.3.g23x203763783m75

Substance Abuse Training. (2007, October 19). *Tri-Town Head Start*.

Sue, S. (1998). In search of cultural competence in psychotherapy and counseling. *The American Psychologist*, *43*(4), 440–448. doi:10.1037/0003-066X.53.4.440 PMID:9572007

Sugai, G., Sprague, J. R., Horner, R., & Walker, H. M. (2000). Preventing school violence: The use of office discipline referrals to assess and monitor school-wide discipline interventions. *Journal of Emotional and Behavioral Disorders*, *8*(2), 94–101. doi:10.1177/106342660000800205

Summerfield, D. (2005). Cross-cultural perspective on the medicalization of human suffering. In Post-traumatic Stress Disorder – Issues and Controversies, (pp. 233-245). John Wiley & Sons.

Summerfield, D. (1995). Addressing human response to war and atrocity. In *Beyond Trauma* (pp. 17–29). New York: Plenum. doi:10.1007/978-1-4757-9421-2_2

Summerfield, D. (1999). A critique of seven assumptions behind psychological trauma programmes in war-affected areas. *Social Science & Medicine*, *48*(10), 1449–1462. doi:10.1016/S0277-9536(98)00450-X PMID:10369444

Swanson, J. A., Sachs, M., Dahlgren, K. A., & Tinguely, J. J. (1987). Accidental farm injuries in children. *American Journal of Diseases of Children*, *141*, 1276–1279. PMID:3687867

Swisher, R. R., & Waller, M. R. (2008). Confining fatherhood incarceration and paternal involvement among non-resident White, African American, and Latino fathers. *Journal of Family Issues*, *29*(8), 1067–1088. doi:10.1177/0192513X08316273

Szalavitz, M., & Perry, B. (2010). *Born for love*. New York: William Morrow.

Tajima, E. A. (2013). Risk factors for violence against children: Comparing homes with and without wife abuse. *Journal of Interpersonal Violence*, *17*(2), 122–149. doi:10.1177/0886260502017002002

Tapia, M. (2014). Latino street gang emergence in the Midwest: Strategic franchising or natural migration. *Crime and Delinquency*, *60*(4), 592–618. doi:10.1177/0011128712458750

Taylor, J. E., Martin, P. L., Fix, M., & Alarcon, R. (1997). *Poverty amid prosperity: Immigration and the changing face of rural California*. The Urban Institute.

Taylor, Z. E., Larsen-Rife, D., Conger, R. D., Widaman, K. F., & Cutrona, C. E. (2010). Life stress, maternal optimism, and adolescent competence in single mother, African American families. *Journal of Family Psychology*, *24*(4), 468–477. doi:10.1037/a0019870 PMID:20731493

Terr, L. (1992). *Too scared to cry: Psychic trauma in childhood.* New York, NY: Basic Books.

The Housing Assistance Council. (n.d.). *Social, Economic, and Housing Conditions in Rural America*. Retrieved from http://www.ruralhome.org/storage/documents/ts2010/ts-report/ts10_rural_people.pdf

The Sentencing Project. (2003). *Hispanic prisoners in the United States*. Washington, DC: The Sentencing Project.

The Sentencing Project. (2009). *Incarcerated parents and their children: Trends 1991-2007*. Washington, DC: The Sentencing Project.

Thelen, R. (2000). *Advocacy in a coordinated community response: overview and highlights of three programs*. Clearwater, MN: Gender Violence Institute.

Thomas, J. (2014, July-August). Veterans Administration is leader in telemental health. The National Psychologist, 6.

Thomas, N. (1997). *When love is not enough*. Glenwood Springs, CO: Families by Design.

Thomlison, R. J., Thomlison, B., Sowers, K. M., Theriot, M. T., & Dulmus, C. N. (2004). School personnel's observations of bullying and victimization among rural elementary and middle school children. In C. N. Dulmus & K. M. Sowers (Eds.), *Kids and violence: The invisible school experience* (pp. 25–43). Binghamton, NY: Haworth Press.

Thompson, M., Burcham, B., & McLaughlin, K. (2008). Violence in our schools. In T. W. Miller (Ed.), *School violence and primary prevention* (pp. 229–248). New York, NY: Springer Publisher. doi:10.1007/978-0-387-77119-9_12

Thulesius, H., & Hakansson, A. (1999). Screening for Post-traumatic Stress Disorder Symptoms Among Bosnian Refugees. *Journal of Traumatic Stress*, *12*(1), 167–174. doi:10.1023/A:1024758718971 PMID:10027150

Tilghman-Osborne, E. M., Bamaca-Colbert, M., Witherspoon, D., Wadsworth, M. E., & Hecht, M. L. (2015). Longitudinal associations of language brokering and parent-adolescent closeness in immigrant Latino families. *The Journal of Early Adolescence*.

Timmis, C. (2002). The impact of language barriers in the health care of Latinos in the United States: A review of the literature and guidelines for practice. *Journal of Midwifery & Women's Health*, *47*(2), 80–96. doi:10.1016/S1526-9523(02)00218-0 PMID:12019990

Tjaden, P., & Thoennes, N. (2000a). *Extent, nature, and consequences of intimate partner violence: Findings from the National Violence Against Women Survey* (NCJ No. 181867). Retrieved from http://www.ncjrs.org/pdffiles1/nij/181867.pdf

Tjaden, P., & Thoennes, N. (2000b). Prevalence and consequences of male to female and female to male intimate partner violence as measured by the National Violence Against Women Survey. *Violence Against Women*, *6*(2), 124–142. doi:10.1177/10778010022181769

Tong, L., Oates, K., & McDowell, M. (1987). Personality development following sexual abuse. *Child Abuse & Neglect*, *11*(3), 371–383. doi:10.1016/0145-2134(87)90011-1 PMID:3676894

Toon, M. H. (2011). Children with burn injuries-assessment of trauma, neglect, violence and abuse. *Journal of Injury & Violence Research*, *3*(2), 98–110.

Torres, R. M., Popke, E. J., & Hapke, H. M. (2006). The South's silent bargain: Rural restructuring, Latino labor, and the ambiguities of migrant experience. In The New South: Latinos and transformation of place (pp. 37-68). Academic Press.

Torres, S. & Vogel, R. E. (2001). Pre- and post-test differences between Vietnamese and Latino residents involved in a community policing experiment reducing fear of crime and improving attitudes toward the police. *Journal of Police Strategies and Management*, 40-55.

Tortorici, J. (1993). *Abuse of the sacred and the need for spiritual healing in the treatment of MPD.* Paper presented at a Menninger conference on Dissociative States: Multiple Personality and Other Trauma-related Disorders, Topeka, KS.

*Trauma-Informed Approach and Trauma-Specific Interventions*. (n.d.). Retrieved June 18, 2015 from: http://www.samhsa.gov/nctic/trauma-interventions

Trovato, F. (1992). A Durkheimian analysis of youth suicide: Canada, 1971 and 1981. *Suicide & Life-Threatening Behavior*, *22*, 413–427. PMID:1488788

Turner, H. A., Finkelhor, D., & Ormrod, R. (2010). Poly-victimization in a national sample of children and youth. *American Journal of Preventive Medicine*, *38*(3), 323–330. doi:10.1016/j.amepre.2009.11.012 PMID:20171535

Turunen, M.-M. (2004). Lapsenkaltoinkohtelunpsyykkisistäseurauksista. In *Lapsenkaltoinkohtelu. Keuruu: OtavanKirjapainoOy*.

Twemlow, S., & Sacco, F. (1996). Peacekeeping and peacemaking: The conceptual foundations of a plan to reduce violence and improve the quality of life in a midsized community in Jamaica. *Psychiatry*, *59*, 156–175. PMID:8837176

U.S. Department of Education. (1994). *The condition of education in rural schools*. Washington, D.C.: U.S. Government Printing Office.

U.S. Department of Education. (2014). *Leadership by principle: How rural values contribute to success in the classroom*. Washington, DC: U.S. Government Printing Office.

U.S. Department of Health and Human Services, Administration for Children and Families, Administration on Children, Youth and Families, Children's Bureau. (2013). *The adoption and foster care analysis and reporting system (AFCARS) report - no. 20*. Retrieved from www.acf.hhs.gov/sites/default/files/cb/afcarsreport19.pdf

U.S. Department of Health and Human Services. (1999). *Blending perspectives and building common ground: A report to Congress on substance abuse and child protection*. Washington, DC: U.S. Government Printing Office.

U.S. Department of Health and Human Services. (2010). *Adoption Assistance and Child Welfare Act of 1980*. Retrieved from https://www.childwelfare.gov/systemwide/laws_policies/federal/index.cfm?event=federalLegislation.viewLegis&id=22

Ugarte, M. B., Zarate, L., & Farley, M. (2004). Prostitution and trafficking of women and children from Mexico to the United States. *Journal of Trauma Practice*, *2*(3-4), 147–165. doi:10.1300/J189v02n03_08

United States Census. (2010). *Urban and rural classification*. Retrieved from: https://www.census.gov/geo/reference/urban-rural.html

Urbina, M. G. (2012). *Hispanics in the U. S. criminal justice system: The new American demography*. Springfield, IL: Charles C. Thomas Publisher.

US Department of Health and Human Services, Administration for Children, Youth and Families, Children's Bureau. (2011). *Child maltreatment*. Retrieved November 7, 2015, from http://www.acf.hhs.gov/sites/default/files/cb/cm11.pdf#page=28

Valenzuela, A. (1999). Gender roles and settlement activities among children and their families. *The American Behavioral Scientist*, *42*(4), 720–772. doi:10.1177/0002764299042004009

Valois, R. F., Zullig, K. J., Huebner, E. S., & Drane, J. W. (2001). Relationships between life satisfaction and violent behaviors among adolescents. *American Journal of Health Behavior*, *25*(4), 353–366. doi:10.5993/AJHB.25.4.1 PMID:11488546

Van De Mark, X., Russell, L. A., O'Keefe, M., Finkelstein, N., Noether, C. D., & Gampbel, J. C. (2005). Children of mothers with histories of substance abuse, mental illness, and trauma. *Journal of Community Psychology*, *33*(4), 445–459. doi:10.1002/jcop.20062

Van den Dries, L., Juffer, F., van IJzendoorn, M. H., & Bakermans-Kranenburg, M. J. (2009). Fostering security? A meta-analysis of attachment in adopted children. *Children and Youth Services Review*, *31*(3), 410–421. doi:10.1016/j.childyouth.2008.09.008

Van der Kolk, B., & D'Andrea, W. (2010). Towards a developmental trauma disorder diagnosis for childhood interpersonal trauma. In R. A. Lanius, E. Vermetien, & C. Pain (Eds.), *The Impact of Early Life Trauma on Health and Disease: The Hidden Epidemic* (pp. 57–68). Cambridge, UK: Cambridge University Press. doi:10.1017/CBO9780511777042.008

Van der Vegt, E. J. M., Van der Ende, J., Ferdinand, R. F., Verhulst, F. C., & Tiemeier, H. (2009). Early childhood adversities and trajectories of psychiatric problems in adoptees: Evidence for long lasting effects. *Journal of Abnormal Child Psychology*, *37*(2), 239–249. doi:10.1007/s10802-008-9272-2 PMID:18807165

Van Gulden, H., & Bartels-Rabb, L. M. (2002). *Real parents, real children: Parenting the adopted child.* New York, NY: Crossroads Publishing.

Van Ommeren, M., Saxena, S., & Saraceno, B. (2005). Mental and social health during and after acute emergencies: Emerging consensus? *Bulletin of the World Health Organization, 83*(1). PMID:15682252

Velasquez, R. J., & Funes, S. M. (2014). The Mass Incarceration of Latinos in the United States: Looking ahead to the year 2050. In S. W. Bowman (Ed.), *Color behind bars: Racism in the U. S. prison system* (pp. 273–289). Santa Barbara, CA: Praeger.

Veltkamp, L. J., & Lawson, A. (2008). Impact of trauma in school violence on the victim and the perpetrator: A mental health perspective. In T. W. Miller (Ed.), *School violence and primary prevention* (pp. 185–200). New York, NY: Springer Publisher. doi:10.1007/978-0-387-77119-9_9

Vermeiren, R., Schwab-Stone, M., Deboutte, D., Leckman, P. E., & Ruchkin, V. (2003). Violence exposure and substance use in adolescents: Findings from three countries. *Pediatrics, 111*(3), 535–540. doi:10.1542/peds.111.3.535 PMID:12612233

Vigil, J. D. (2003). Urban violence and street gangs. *Annual Review of Anthropology, 32*(1), 225–242. doi:10.1146/annurev.anthro.32.061002.093426

Vogt, D. S., King, D. W., & King, L. A. (2007). Risk pathways for PTSD. In Handbook of PTSD: Science and Practice, (pp. 99-115). Academic Press.

Vossekuil, B., Fein, R., Reddy, M., Borum, R., & Modzeleski, W. (2002). *The final report and findings of the safe school initiative: Implications for the prevention of school attacks in the United States.* Washington, DC: U.S. Department of Education.

Waldoff, R. A. (2008). Arrested contact: The criminal justice system, race, and father engagement. *The Prison Journal, 88*(2), 179–206. doi:10.1177/0032885508319154

Walker, L. E. A. (1993b). *Survivor therapy: Clinical assessment and intervention workbook.* Denver, CO: Endolor Communications.

Walker, L. E. A. (1996). Assessment of abusive spousal relationships. In F. W. Kaslow (Ed.), *Handbook of relational diagnosis and dysfunctional family patterns* (pp. 338–356). New York, NY: John Wiley & Sons, Inc.

Wallace, L., & May, D. C. (2005). The impact of parental attachment and feelings of isolation on adolescent fear of crime at school. *Adolescence, 40*, 457–474. PMID:16268126

Walsh, K., Matthews, B., Rassafiani, M., Farrell, A., & Butler, D. (2012). Understanding teachers' reporting of child sexual abuse: Measurement methods matter. *Children and Youth Services Review, 34*(9), 1937–1946. doi:10.1016/j.childyouth.2012.06.004

Walters, N., Bourgois, P., & Loinaz, H. M. (2004). Masculinity and undocumented labor migration: Injured day laborers in San Francisco. *Social Science & Medicine, 59*(6), 1159–1168. doi:10.1016/j.socscimed.2003.12.013 PMID:15210088

Wang, J., Iannotti, R. J., Luk, J. W., & Nansel, T. R. (2010). Co-occurrence of victimization from five subtypes of bullying: Physical, verbal, social exclusion, spreading rumors, and cyber. *Journal of Pediatric Psychology, 35*(10), 1103–1112. doi:10.1093/jpepsy/jsq048 PMID:20488883

Ward, L. S. (2010). Farmworkers at risk: The costs of family separation. *Journal of Immigrant and Minority Health, 12*(5), 672–677. doi:10.1007/s10903-008-9207-6 PMID:18987973

Warthan, S., Mortimer, K., & Allard, E. (2011). Homies in the new Latino diaspora. *Language & Communication, 31*(3), 191–202. doi:10.1016/j.langcom.2011.02.007

Weerts, D. J., & Sandmann, L. R. (2010). Community Engagement and Boundary-Spanning Roles at Research Universities. *The Journal of Higher Education, 81*(6), 702–727.

Wegar, K. (2000). Adoption, family ideology, and social stigma: Bias in community attitudes, adoption research, and practice. *Family Relations, 49*(4), 363–369. doi:10.1111/j.1741-3729.2000.00363.x

Weisskirch, R. S. (2005). The relationship of language brokering to ethnic identity for Latino early adolescents. *Hispanic Journal of Behavioral Sciences, 27*(3), 286–299. doi:10.1177/0739986305277931

Weist, M. D., Myers, C. P., Danforth, J., McNeil, D. W., Ollendick, T. H., & Hawkins, R. (2000). Expanded school mental health services: Assessing needs related to school level and geography. *Community Mental Health Journal, 36*(3), 259–273. doi:10.1023/A:1001957130982 PMID:10933243

Werth, J. L., Hastings, S. L., & Riding-Malon, R. (2010). Ethical challenges of practicing in rural areas. *Journal of Clinical Psychology: In Session, 66*, 537–548. doi:10.1002/jclp.20681 PMID:20222121

Wethington, H. R., Hahn, R. A., Fuqua-Whitley, D. S., Sipe, T. A., Crosby, A. E., Johnson, R. L., & Chattopadhyay, S. K. et al. (2008). The effectiveness of interventions to reduce psychological harm from traumatic events among children and adolescents: A systematic review. *American Journal of Preventive Medicine, 35*(3), 287–313. doi:10.1016/j.amepre.2008.06.024 PMID:18692745

Whitaker, D. J., Ryan, K. A., Wild, R. C., Self-Brown, S., Lutzker, J. R., Shanley, J. R., … Hodges, A. E. (2012). Initial implementation indicators from a statewide rollout of SafeCare within a child welfare system. *Child Maltreatment, 17*(1), 96-101. doi:55951143072210.1177/1077

Wickrama, K. A. S., Elder, G. H., & Arabaham, W. T. (2007). Rurality and ethnicity in adolescent physical illness: Are children of the growing rural Latino population at excess health risk? *The Journal of Rural Health, 23*(3), 228–237. doi:10.1111/j.1748-0361.2007.00095.x PMID:17565523

Wilcox, P., Campbell, M., Bryan, J. P., & Roberts, S. (2005). The "reality" of middle-school crime: Objective vs. subjective experiences among a sample of Kentucky youth. *Journal of School Violence, 4*(2), 3–27. doi:10.1300/J202v04n02_02

Wilke-Deaton, J. (2005). *Attachment and bonding: Effective strategies that work*. Eau Claire, WI: Pesi HealthCare.

Wilson, K. (2003). Therapeutic landscapes and First Nations people: An exploration of culture, health and place. *Health & Place, 9*(2), 83–93. doi:10.1016/S1353-8292(02)00016-3 PMID:12753791

Wilson, P., Rush, R., Hussey, S., Puckering, C., Sim, F., Allely, C. S., & Gillberg, C. et al. (2012). How evidence-based is an 'evidence-based parenting program'? A PRISMA systematic review and meta-analysis of Triple P. *BMC Medicine, 10*(1), 130. doi:10.1186/1741-7015-10-130 PMID:23121760

Wilson, W. C., & Rosenthal, B. S. (2003). The relationship between exposure to community violence and psychological distress among adolescents: A meta-analysis. *Violence and Victims, 18*(3), 335–352. doi:10.1891/vivi.2003.18.3.335 PMID:12968662

Witherspoon, D., & Ennett, S. (2011). An examination of social disorganization and pluralistic neighborhood theories with rural mothers and their adolescents. *Journal of Youth and Adolescence, 40*(9), 1243–1253. doi:10.1007/s10964-009-9499-4 PMID:20047085

Womble, M., & D'Amico, J. J. (Eds.). (1994). *Perspectives on violence and substance use in rural America*. Oak Brook, IL: North Central Regional Educational Laboratory.

World Association for Children and Parents. (2012). *WACAP named 2012 Evergreen Award Winner*. Retrieved from www.wacap.org

World Health Organization and International Society for Prevention of Child Abuse and Neglect. (2006). *Preventing Child Maltreatment: a guide to taking action and generating evidence*. Geneva: WHO.

World Health Organization. (1992). *The ICD-10 Classification of Mental and Behavioural*. Geneva: Disorders.

Wulczyn, F. (2003). Closing the gap: Are changing exit patterns reducing the time African American children spend in foster care relative to Caucasian children? *Children and Youth Services Review*, *25*(5/6), 431-462. Doi:(03)00030-610.1016/S0190-7409

Wulczyn, F. (2004). Family reunification. *The Future of Children*, *14*(1), 95–110. doi:10.2307/1602756 PMID:15072020

Wulczyn, F. (2009). Epidemiological perspectives on maltreatment prevention. *The Future of Children*, *19*(2), 39–66. doi:10.1353/foc.0.0029 PMID:19719022

Yabko, B. A., Hakoda, A., & Ulloa, E. C. (2008). Depression as a mediator between family factors and peer-bullying victimization in Latino adolescents. *Violence and Victims*, *23*(6), 727–742. doi:10.1891/0886-6708.23.6.727 PMID:19069564

Yehuda, R., & Bierer, L. (2009). The Relevance of Epigenetics to PTSD: Implications for the DSM-V. *Journal of Traumatic Stress*, *22*(5), 427–434. doi:10.1002/jts.20448 PMID:19813242

Young, A. (1995). *The harmony of illusions: inventing Post-traumatic stress disorder*. Princeton, NJ: Princeton University Press.

Young, A. (2004). When Traumatic Memory Was a Problem: On the Historical Antecedents of PTSD. In G. M. Rosen (Ed.), *Post-traumatic Stress Disorder – Issues and Controversies*. West Sussex, UK: John Wiley and Sons.

Young, G., & Johnson, R. (2010). Post-Traumatic Stress Disorder in the DSM-5: Group Difference Commentary. *Psychology Injury and the Law*, *3*(4), 314–319. doi:10.1007/s12207-010-9093-9

Zatz, M. S., & Portillos, E. L. (2000). Voices from the barrio: Chicano/a gangs, families, and communities. *Criminology*, *8*(2), 369–402. doi:10.1111/j.1745-9125.2000.tb00894.x

Zayas, L. H., Aguilar-Gaxiola, S., Yoon, H., & Rey, G. N. (2015). The distress of citizen children with detained and deported parents. *Journal of Child and Family Studies*, 1–11. PMID:26640358

Zeanah, C. H., & Gleason, M. M. (2014). Annual research review: Attachment disorders in early childhood – Clinical presentation, causes, correlates and treatments. *Journal of Child Psychology and Psychiatry, 56*(3). Retrieved from www.researchgate.net/publication/267627731

Zeanah, C. H., Gunnar, M. R., McCall, R. B., Kreppner, J. M., & Fox, N. A. (2011). Sensitive periods. In R. B. McCall, M. H. van IJzendoorn, F. Juffer, C. J. Groark, & V. K. Groza (Eds.), Children without permanent parents: Research, practice, and policy. Academic Press.

Zeanah, C. H., Jr., & Boris, N. W. (2000) Disturbance and Disorders of Attachment in Early Childhood. In C. H. Jr. Zeanah (Ed.), Handbook of Infant Mental Health. New York: The Guilford Press.

Zehr, H. (2002). *The little book of restorative justice*. Intercourse, PA: Good Books.

Zuniga, V., & Hernandez-Leon, R. (2005). *New destinations: Mexican immigration in the United States*. Russell Sage Foundation.

# About the Contributors

**Marion A. Baker** received a BS in Nursing from University of Portland in 1971. She worked in Community Mental Health Centers and at CU Medical Center providing counseling and supervision for the next 20 years. In 1991 she received her Psy.D in counseling psychology with an emphasis in family therapy from University of Northern Colorado. She has previously been a licensed clinical psychologist in Colorado and Alaska. Currently she is licensed in Arizona. Dr. Baker has specialized in work with children and their families with an emphasis in trauma assessment and treatment for the past 25 years. She was adjunct faculty in psychology at University of Alaska, Anchorage and Alaska Pacific University. Currently, Dr. Baker is the lead psychologist at Community Partnership of Enrichment Services (CPES) in Tucson, Arizona. In this position she consults and supervises a team of psychologists and doctoral interns. This team provides comprehensive psychological evaluations for children and adults in Arizona with a specialty in trauma identification and treatment recommendations. She has also been instrumental in developing a trauma treatment program at CPES for children and their parents/guardians. She is also a part of the Trauma Informed Care National Learning Community.

**Brittany Canfield**, MS, MA provides psychological services across the state of Arizona for underserved youth. She is honorary lecturer for the Applied Psychology Online Masters Program within the University of Liverpool and Laureate Online Education partnership. Through her experience of working with traumatized children and adolescents, she strives to advocate for appropriate services for the children and families impacted by trauma.

**Traci Grabb** serves as a Clinical Director for Arizona's Children Association (AzCA) where she is responsible for AzCA's outpatient children's behavioral health program in three Southern Arizona counties. Founded in 1912, AzCA is one of the oldest and largest statewide child welfare and behavioral health non-profit agencies in Arizona providing a wide continuum of services to children and families. Ms. Grabb received a Master's degree in Mental Health Counseling from Argosy University in Phoenix, Arizona. She has experience working in community-based programs with adults, children and their families in the child welfare, juvenile and adult justice systems to include work with sex offenders and victims of domestic abuse. Ms. Grabb's interests focus on work with vulnerable children and families, as well as the professional growth of staff in promoting and strengthening the social-emotional well-being of individuals and families impacted by trauma and abuse.

* * *

**Tosin Alabi** is a clinical psychology doctoral student at Fielding Graduate University.

**Apryl A. Alexander** received her B.S. from Virginia Tech and M.S. from Radford University. She received her doctorate in Clinical Psychology with a concentration in forensic psychology and child and family therapy from the Florida Institute of Technology in 2012 following the completion of a pre-doctoral internship in forensic psychology at Patton State Hospital. Dr. Alexander also completed a post-doctoral fellowship in forensic psychology at Minnesota State Operated Forensic Services (MSOFS). She is currently appointed as an Assistant Clinical Professor at Auburn University, where her duties include providing clinical and research supervision to undergraduates and graduate students at the Accountability Based Sex Offender Program (ABSOP) at Mt. Meigs, a juvenile residential treatment facility in Montgomery, Alabama. Her research and clinical interests are broadly focused in the areas of violence, victimization, and forensic psychology and assessment.

**Samar Adi** is a Licensed Associate Marriage and Family Therapist who has worked with both youth and adults in home-based and office outpatient settings. She has worked in rural communities in Cochise and Pima counties.

**Sandra Barnes** is a clinical psychology doctoral candidate at Fielding Graduate University in Santa Barbara, California.

**James Dumesnil**, since completing graduate school in Applied Developmental Psychology over two decades ago, has worked successfully with birth families, foster care, adoption preservation, and crisis intervention for adoptive, birth and foster families. He served a term as President of the California Mental Health Counselor's Association and also as President of the National Association of Forensic Counselor's of California. He served on the board of directors of the Center for Attachment Therapy, Training and Education for Northern CA for over a decade. He has published research in the areas of Restorative Justice and Juvenile Justice Reform, Token Economies & Behavioral Management Interventions, the Facilitation of Group and Family Therapy dynamics. and parenting and therapy interventions for children w/ complex post-traumatic stress disorder.

**Rebecca Hoffmann Frances** is the Director of Clinical Innovation at Maine Behavioral Healthcare in Portland Maine and an Assistant Clinical Professor of Psychiatry at Tufts University School of Medicine. In her position, Ms. Hoffmann Frances manages two large federally funded projects that focus on providing care and treatment for children and families that have been exposed to violence and other types of trauma. One of these projects is part of the Department of Justice Defending Childhood Initiative, and is one of only eight sites funded nationally. This project focuses on prevention of childhood exposure to violence as well as implementation of evidence based treatment for children under five. The other project, through the Substance Abuse and Mental Health Services Administration, is a statewide effort in Maine to raise the level of awareness of the effects of violence and trauma on children and implement the evidence-based trauma-focused cognitive behavioral therapy in every county in the state. In addition, Rebecca has been overseeing the implementation of trauma-focused cognitive behavioral therapy and child parent psychotherapy in greater Portland for almost ten years and has published on the topic of successful community-wide TF-CBT implementation. In addition she oversees and advises innovation activities within her agency to ensure successful implementation and change management. She is a licensed marriage and family therapist with extensive knowledge of trauma and its effects on children and families as well as implementation science and change management.

**Megan Harrelson** received her undergraduate degree from Wake Forest University in 2014. She is currently a second year in Auburn's Clinical Psychology graduate program where she studies under Drs. Apryl Alexander and Barry Burkhart. Her research focuses on the effects of childhood poly-victimization on adolescent functioning. Specifically, she examines how early childhood trauma influences the emotional, cognitive, and social development of juvenile sex offenders. Her clinical interests focus on implementing trauma-focused cognitive behavioral therapy on children/adolescents with sexual behavior problems.

**Eric Jacobs**, MA, MHP, LMHCA holds a bachelor of arts in psychology with a minor in comparative religion form the University of Washington, as well as a master of arts in clinical mental health counseling from the University of San Diego. His is experienced with in-patient psychiatric care, both with group and individual therapy. His clinical interests include trauma informed care, in-patient psychiatric care, anxiety, and mood disorders. Recent publications include topics such as juvenile firesetters, terrorism, evidenced based therapeutic approaches, cultural considerations within law enforcement, and community outreach. Eric currently lives in Washington state and supervises a crisis prevention and intervention team, as well as working in private practice.

**Ronn Johnson**, Ph.D., ABPP is a licensed and board certified clinical psychologist with experience in academic, clinical, and forensic settings. He is a Diplomat of the American Board of Professional Psychology, and has served as a staff psychologist in VA healthcare systems, community mental health clinics, hospitals, schools, and university counseling centers. He has held academic positions at several universities across the country. He founded several counseling centers that currently serve racially diverse populations. These sites include the Urban Corp of San Diego County, Southern California American Indian Resource Center, and the Elim Korean Counseling Center. He is on the community advisory board for the Chancellor at U.C. San Diego. In addition, he established clinical mental health clinics: Korean Mental Health Services, East African Research & Trauma Help (EARTH), Somali Suicide Assessment Project, and Native American Counseling Services at the Southern California American Indian Resource Center (SCAIR).

**Leah Genieve Kenyon-George** is a Registered Psychologist from Calgary, Alberta, Canada with a Masters in Counselling/ Psychotherapy and a Masters of Arts in Clinical Psychology. She is currently pursuing a PhD in Clinical Psychology at Fielding Graduate University. Leah has worked in community, healthcare, outpatient clinic, and residential treatment settings. She has experience working as a therapist and consulting psychologist for a treatment program in a rural setting and is passionate about work in rural communities.

**Karla (Ahrns) Klas**, BSN, RN, CCRP, manages the University of Michigan Trauma Burn Center's nationally acclaimed community and family-centered injury prevention programs. A celebrated educator, speaker, and author, Karla received a Bachelor of Science in Nursing and minor in Psychology degree from Purdue University. Her 23-year background in research, education, critical care nursing, and prevention has produced numerous medical journal articles, textbook chapters, and grant awards.

She is a National Fire Academy graduate and holds multiple specialty certifications. Karla serves on multiple committees devoted to safety and injury reduction: ABA Burn Prevention, YFIRES National Youth Firesetting Database, MI Arson Prevention, MI Fire Inspectors Society, U-M Injury Center, etc. Her work has received numerous accolades, including the Michigan Fire Inspectors Society Public Educator of the Year Award and the ABA Burn Prevention Award. Karla speaks throughout the nation on burn/trauma injuries, safety, prevention, and youth firesetting. In her spare time, she volunteers in burn survivor support programs, mentors at-risk youth, and writes children's books.

**Alejandra Murillo** is an M.A. candidate in the clinical mental health specialization at the University of San Diego.

**Sonja L. Salcido** also known as Soni Cido Sonja is a Minnesota native of 38 years and became a new resident to Benson, Arizona in 1997. Although her family of 10 children kept her busy homeschooling and cooking, she made time to pursue many other things to include publishing a 1990's newsletter featuring homeschooling, homesteading, homemaking, and Christian hospitality which circulated the U.S., Canada, London, and New Zealand. She owned a perennial flower business in Minnesota, and has worked as a Cosmetologist, an American Airlines International Travel Specialist, holds an Associate of Art and Business Degree from the University of Phoenix, is an Apprentice Graduate of the Christian Writer's Guild, has been published in several homeschooling magazines and Indian Life Magazine out of Manitoba, Canada. She has contributed to various creative venues such as, Helium.com, Indy film, book events, political campaigns, and anti-bully forums. A favorite Facebook administrator to many popular pages and groups, she also has two books in the works to include the biography of William "Billy" Fourr, 1800's Pioneer, and a Middle Grade book, "Rudy's Rescue" which addresses dog rescue, childhood issues such as bullying, and growing up in a diverse world. You can find her online at "Blazing Cochise County" (Facebook), "Mess Hall Dining from the Mess Hall Chefs", sonicido.com, sonicido@gmail.com or onlysonicido.blogspot.com.

**Roberto J. Velasquez** has a bachelor's degree in psychology from the University of California, Riverside, a master's degree in counseling and consulting psychology from Harvard University, and a doctorate in counseling psychology from Arizona State University. He is currently completing a master's degree in criminal justice at New Mexico State University. He has authored over 80 articles and books on minority mental health and was primary editor for "The Handbook of Chicana and Chicano Psychology and Mental Health" (2004).

**Michelle F. Wright** is a postdoctoral research fellow at Masaryk University in the Czech Republic. Her major research interests include the contextual influences, particularly cultural and familial, on adolescents' social behaviors, and their pursuit and achievement of peer status. For the past several years, she has studied victimization and aggression through electronic technologies among children, adolescents, and young adults.

# Index

## T



## U



## V



## W

Printed in the United States
By Bookmasters